걸프 사태

# 유엔안전보장이사회 동향 5

걸프 사태

# 유엔안전보장이사회 동향 5

# | 머리말

  걸프 전쟁은 미국의 주도하에 34개국 연합군 병력이 수행한 전쟁으로, 1990년 8월 이라크의 쿠웨이트 침공 및 합병에 반대하며 발발했다. 미국은 초기부터 파병 외교에 나섰고, 1990년 9월 서울 등에 고위 관리를 파견하며 한국의 동참을 요청했다. 88올림픽 이후 동구권 국교 수립과 유엔 가입 추진 등 적극적인 외교 활동을 펼치는 당시 한국에 있어 이는 미국과 국제 사회의 지지를 얻기 위해서라도 피할 수 없는 일이었다. 결국 정부는 91년 1월부터 약 3개월에 걸쳐 국군의료지원단과 공군수송단을 사우디아라비아 및 아랍 에미리트 연합 등에 파병하였고, 군·민간 의료 활동, 병력 수송 임무를 수행했다. 동시에 당시 걸프 지역 8개국에 살던 5천여 명의 교민에게 방독면 등 물자를 제공하고, 특별기 파견 등으로 비상시 대피할 수 있도록 지원했다. 비록 전쟁 부담금과 유가 상승 등 어려움도 있었지만, 걸프전 파병과 군사 외교를 통해 한국은 유엔 가입에 박차를 가할 수 있었고 미국 등 선진 우방국, 아랍권 국가 등과 밀접한 외교 관계를 유지하며 여러 국익을 창출할 수 있었다.

  본 총서는 외교부에서 작성하여 30여 년간 유지한 걸프 사태 관련 자료를 담고 있다. 미국을 비롯한 여러 국가와의 군사 외교 과정, 일일 보고 자료와 기타 정부의 대응 및 조치, 재외동포 철수와 보호, 의료지원단과 수송단 파견 및 지원 과정, 유엔을 포함해 세계 각국에서 수집한 관련 동향 자료, 주변국 지원과 전후복구사업 참여 등 총 48권으로 구성되었다. 전체 분량은 약 2만 4천여 쪽에 이른다.

2024년 3월

한국학술정보(주)

# | 일러두기

· 본 총서에 실린 자료는 2022년 4월과 2023년 4월에 각각 공개한 외교문서 4,827권, 76만
여 쪽 가운데 일부를 발췌한 것이다.

· 각 권의 제목과 순서는 공개된 원본을 최대한 반영하였으나, 주제에 따라 일부는 적절히
변경하였다.

· 원본 자료는 A4 판형에 맞게 축소하거나 원본 비율을 유지한 채 A4 페이지 안에 삽입
하였다. 또한 현재 시점에선 공개되지 않아 '공란'이란 표기만 있는 페이지 역시 그대로
실었다.

· 외교부가 공개한 문서 각 권의 첫 페이지에는 '정리 보존 문서 목록'이란 이름으로 기록물
종류, 일자, 명칭, 간단한 내용 등의 정보가 수록되어 있으며, 이를 기준으로 0001번부터
번호가 매겨져 있다. 이는 삭제하지 않고 총서에 그대로 수록하였다.

· 보고서 내용에 관한 더 자세한 정보가 필요하다면, 외교부가 온라인상에 제공하는 『대한
민국 외교사료요약집』 1991년과 1992년 자료를 참조할 수 있다.

# | 차례

# 정 리 보 존 문 서 목 록

| 기록물종류 | 일반공문서철 | 등록번호 | 2020010027 | 등록일자 | 2020-01-07 |
|---|---|---|---|---|---|
| 분류번호 | 731.33 | 국가코드 | XF | 보존기간 | 30년 |
| 명 칭 | 걸프사태 후 유엔안전보장이사회 동향, 1991. 전3권 | | | | |
| 생 산 과 | 국제연합1과/중동1과 | 생산년도 | 1991~1991 | 담당그룹 | |
| 권 차 명 | V.3 10-12월 | | | | |
| 내용목차 | * 이라크의 안보리 휴전 결의 이행 관련 내용 포함 | | | | |

0001

주 국 련 대 표 부

주국련20313- 740                         1991. 10. 11.

수신 장관

참조 국제기구국장, 중동아프리카국장

제목 걸프사태(안보리)

   표제관련 안보리문서를 별첨과 같이 송부합니다.


   첨 부 : 상기자료. 끝.


주 국 련 대 사

57003

0002

## Security Council

Distr.
GENERAL

S/22871/Rev.1
2 October 1991

ORIGINAL: ENGLISH

<u>Plan for future ongoing monitoring and verification of
Iraq's compliance with relevant parts of section C of
Security Council resolution 687 (1991)</u>

<u>Report of the Secretary-General</u>

## I. GENERAL

### A. <u>Introduction</u>

1.    The present report is submitted in pursuance of Security Council
resolution 687 (1991).  In paragraph 10 of section C of that resolution, the
Security Council requested the Secretary-General, in consultation with the
Special Commission, to develop and submit for approval a plan for the ongoing
monitoring and verification of Iraq's compliance with its obligations under
that paragraph.  The Plan is contained in section II of the present report.

2.    As outlined in my report to the Security Council of 17 May 1991
(S/22614), the provisions of section C of resolution 687 (1991) lend
themselves to a three-stage implementation procedure:  gathering and
assessment of information; disposal of weapons and facilities and all other
items specified in paragraphs 8 and 12 of resolution 687 (1991); and ongoing
monitoring and verification of Iraq's compliance.  The first two stages are
currently being implemented and will continue until their objectives are fully
achieved.

3.    The Plan submitted in the present report addresses the third stage, i.e.
ongoing monitoring and verification of Iraq's compliance with its
unconditional obligation not to use, retain, possess, develop, construct or
otherwise acquire any weapons or related items prohibited under paragraphs 8
and 9 of resolution 687 (1991).  Thus, monitoring and verification will need
to cover not only military but also civilian sites, facilities, material and
other items that could be used or activities that could be involved in
contravention of Iraq's obligations under resolution 687 (1991).  The Plan
incorporates the additional obligations of Iraq under Security Council
resolution 707 (1991) and the corresponding monitoring and verification
activities.

91-32425  2644f (E)

/...

0003

4.    The Plan should enter into force directly upon its approval by the Security Council, which means that the early stages of its implementation and the later stages of the disposal of existing prohibited weapons, facilities and related items would take place simultaneously.  This would, at an early stage, prevent Iraq from developing new capabilities regarding the relevant weapons categories, thus already closing a potential loophole during the first stages of the implementation of section C of resolution 687 (1991).  Carefully managed use of available resources would make it possible to carry out the dual tasks in parallel, to great effect.  With the gradual completion of the disposal of Iraq's present weapons capabilities, resources can gradually be transferred and streamlined without therefore, at any stage, compromising the efficiency of the verification of Iraq's compliance with its obligations under resolutions 687 (1991) and 707 (1991).  In paragraph 14 of its resolution 687 (1991) the Security Council noted that the actions to be taken by Iraq in paragraphs 8, 9, 10, 11, 12 and 13 of that resolution "represent steps towards the goal of establishing in the Middle East a zone free from weapons of mass destruction and all missiles for their delivery and the objective of a global ban on chemical weapons".  The implementation of the Plan, developed pursuant to paragraph 10 of resolution 687 (1991), will contribute to an environment conducive to achieving the above-mentioned goal and objective.

## B.   Institutional and organizational aspects

5.    Bearing in mind that resolutions 687 (1991) and 707 (1991) were adopted by the Security Council acting under Chapter VII of the Charter of the United Nations, it is assumed that the task of carrying out the monitoring and verification provided for under the Plan should be entrusted to an executive body under the authority of the Security Council.  This is particularly important should any situation arise of non-compliance by Iraq with its obligations under section C of resolution 687 (1991) and under resolution 707 (1991).

6.    The intrinsic interrelationship between paragraphs 8, 9 and 10 of resolution 687 (1991) requires that this body make direct use of the expertise, the information gathered and assessed and the experience gained by the Special Commission established as a subsidiary organ of the Security Council pursuant to paragraph 9 of resolution 687 (1991).

7.    In view of these considerations, it would appear most practical and efficient that a compliance unit be organized under the Special Commission in order to carry out the monitoring and verification tasks provided for under the Plan.  The present arrangements for staffing would continue on a revised scale, with appropriate support from the Department for Disarmament Affairs.  The financing of the Plan would have to be determined by the competent United Nations organs, possibly in the same way as the arrangements agreed upon for the present phase of the Special Commission's work.

/...

0004

8.   The operational requirements will be similar to those now in place for the Special Commission.  These include a staff at the United Nations Headquarters in New York to assist the Executive Chairman of the Special Commission, compile and analyse information, schedule, plan and organize inspections and aerial overflights, prepare other field operations and provide general administrative support.  A staff will be needed in the region to provide logistic, administrative and other support for field operations in Iraq.

### C.   Cooperation with the Security Council Committee established by resolution 661 (1990) concerning the situation between Iraq and Kuwait

9.   Through resolution 661 (1990) and subsequent related resolutions, including resolution 687 (1991), inter alia, its section F, a comprehensive set of sanctions was established to be implemented by all States against Iraq.  The prohibition of the acquisition by Iraq of any weapons and related items specified in paragraphs 8 and 12 of resolution 687 (1991) and of the sale or supply to Iraq by other States of these items is of unlimited duration.  However, it cannot be excluded that the Security Council, at a future date, may wish to review the present sanctions regarding items with dual use, i.e. items that could be used for prohibited as well as non-prohibited purposes.  In order to ensure that such items are not used for prohibited purposes, the Plan submitted in the present report includes specific provisions for the monitoring and verification, from within Iraq, of any eventual import by Iraq of relevant items with dual use.

10.   The efficacy of these provisions would be enhanced if they were complemented by transparency and timely information as regards any future sale or supply by other States to Iraq of relevant items with dual use.  Such a comprehensive approach would call for the development of a mechanism that:

     (a)  Upholds the prohibition on the sale and supply to Iraq by other States of any weapons or related items prohibited under section C of resolution 687 (1991);

     (b)  Provides for timely information about any sale or supply to Iraq by other States of items that could be used not only for permitted purposes but also for purposes prohibited under resolution 687 (1991).

11.   The Plan submitted in the present report contains in its annexes lists of items relevant to the monitoring and verification, from within Iraq, of prohibited items as well as of items with dual use.  These should be taken into account in the development of a mechanism related to the sale or supply of items to Iraq by other countries.

12.   Such a mechanism should be developed with the cooperation of the Special Commission, the Director General of the International Atomic Energy Agency and the Committee established by resolution 661 (1990) at the earliest possible date, and not later than before the lifting of sanctions covering relevant items.

0005          /...

II.  THE PLAN

A.  Scope

13.  In accepting unconditionally Security Council resolution 687 (1991), Iraq has undertaken not to use, retain, possess, develop, construct or otherwise acquire:

(a)  Any chemical or biological weapons or any stocks of agents or any related subsystems or components or any research, development, support or manufacturing facilities;

(b)  Any ballistic missiles with a range greater than 150 kilometres or any related major parts, including launchers, or any repair or production facilities.

14.  In order to ensure Iraq's compliance with these undertakings, the Special Commission, pursuant to resolutions 687 (1991) and 707 (1991), shall, through inspections and through aerial overflights, as well as through the provision of information by Iraq, monitor and verify that activities, sites, facilities, material and other items, both military and civilian, are not used by Iraq in contravention of its obligations under resolutions 687 (1991) and 707 (1991).

15.  To this end, the provisions set forth in the Plan and its annexes, which constitute an integral part of the Plan, shall apply.

B.  General provisions

1.  Information

16.  Iraq shall:

(a)  Provide to the Special Commission, on a regular basis, full, complete, correct and timely information on activities, sites, facilities, material and other items, both military and civilian, that might be used for purposes prohibited under paragraph 10 of resolution 687 (1991);

(b)  Provide to the Special Commission full, complete, correct and timely information on any additional activities, sites, facilities, material or other items that the Commission may designate for provision of information on a regular basis;

(c)  Provide to the Special Commission, fully, completely, and promptly, any additional information or clarification that the Commission may request and respond fully, completely and promptly to any questions or requests from the Special Commission.

Further provisions related to the submission of information are set forth in sections C, D and E and in annexes II, III and IV of the Plan.

/...

0006

## 2. Inspections and aerial overflights

17. The Special Commission shall have the right:

(a) To designate for inspection any site, facility, activity, material or other item in Iraq;

(b) To carry out inspections, at any time and without hindrance, of any site, facility, activity, material or other item in Iraq;

(c) To conduct unannounced inspections and inspections at short notice;

(d) To inspect any number of declared or designated sites or facilities simultaneously or sequentially;

(e) To designate for aerial overflight any area, location, site or facility in Iraq;

(f) To conduct, at any time and without hindrance, both fixed-wing and rotary-wing flights throughout Iraq for all relevant purposes, including inspection, surveillance, aerial overflights (surveys), transportation and logistics without interference of any kind and upon such terms and conditions as may be determined by the Special Commission;

(g) To make full use of its own aircraft with appropriate sensors as necessary and such airfields in Iraq as the Special Commission may determine are most appropriate for its work;

(h) To consider and decide upon requests by Iraq to move or destroy any material, equipment or item relating to its nuclear, chemical or biological weapons or ballistic missile programmes, or material, equipment or any item relating to its other nuclear activities.

18. Iraq shall:

(a) Accept unconditionally the inspection of any site, facility, activity, material or other item declared by Iraq or designated by the Special Commission;

(b) Accept unconditionally aerial overflight of any area, location, site or facility designated by the Special Commission;

(c) Provide immediate and unimpeded access to any site, facility, activity, material or other item to be inspected;

(d) Accept unconditionally and cooperate with the Special Commission in conducting fixed-wing and rotary-wing flights throughout Iraq for all relevant purposes, including inspection, surveillance, aerial overflights (surveys), transportation and logistics upon the terms and conditions determined by the Special Commission;

/...

0007

   (e)  Accept unconditionally the Special Commission's determinations regarding use of the Commission's aircraft with appropriate sensors as necessary and airfields in Iraq for such aircraft;

   (f)  Not obstruct aerial overflights or take concealment measures at any area, location, site or facility designated by the Special Commission for inspection or overflight;

   (g)  Accept unconditionally the inspectors and all other personnel designated by the Special Commission and ensure the complete implementation of the privileges, immunities and facilities of the personnel of the Special Commission and their complete safety and freedom of movement;

   (h)  Cooperate fully with the Special Commission and facilitate its inspections, overflights and other activities under the Plan;

   (i)  Accept unconditionally the rights of the Special Commission under the Plan and not take any action to interfere with, impede, or obstruct the exercise by the Special Commission of its functions and rights under Security Council resolutions 687 (1991), 707 (1991) and the Plan;

   (j)  Designate its Inspection Representative for each inspection to accompany the inspection team in Iraq;

   (k)  Invite and accept unconditionally the decision of the Special Commission on any requests by Iraq to move or destroy any material, equipment or item relating to its nuclear, chemical or biological weapons or ballistic missile programmes, or material, equipment or any item relating to its other nuclear activities.

19.  Further provisions on inspections, aerial overflights, security, privileges and immunities and related provisions are set forth in annex I.


### 3.  National implementation measures

20.  Iraq shall adopt the necessary measures to implement its obligations under section C of resolution 687 (1991), resolution 707 (1991) and the Plan, in particular:

   (a)  To prohibit all natural and legal persons under Iraq's jurisdiction or control from undertaking anywhere any activity that is prohibited for Iraq by resolutions 687 (1991), 707 (1991), by other related Security Council resolutions or by the Plan;

   (b)  To enact penal legislation which, in conformity with international law, shall extend to the activities referred to under subparagraph (a) above undertaken anywhere by any natural or legal persons under Iraq's jurisdiction or control.

0008        /...

21.   Iraq shall inform the Special Commission of legislative and administrative measures taken to implement resolutions 687 (1991), 707 (1991), other relevant Security Council resolutions and the Plan, not later than 30 days after the approval by the Security Council of the Plan and thereafter as determined by the Special Commission.

### 4.  Non-compliance

22.   Should the Special Commission discover any item, including any documentation, that Iraq, under resolution 687 (1991), is obliged to destroy or to yield to the Special Commission for destruction, removal or rendering harmless, the Special Commission shall have the right to take it into custody and shall provide for its disposal, as appropriate.  Iraq shall retain no ownership interest in items to be destroyed, removed or rendered harmless pursuant to resolution 687 (1991) and the Plan.

23.   Should the Special Commission discover any activity taking place in contravention of resolutions 687 (1991), 707 (1991) or of the Plan, it shall have the right to call upon Iraq to halt the activity and to prevent its recurrence.  The Special Commission shall also have the right to take any prohibited item involved, including any documentation, into custody and shall provide for its disposal, as appropriate.

24.   Findings by the Special Commission that indicate that Iraq is not in compliance with its obligations under resolutions 687 (1991) and 707 (1991) or the Plan shall be brought to the attention of the Security Council.

### 5.  Reports

25.   The Special Commission shall, through the Secretary-General, report to the Security Council every six months on the implementation of the Plan and at any other time the Security Council may request.

### 6.  Revisions

26.   The Plan may only be revised by the Security Council.  The Special Commission may, however, after informing the Security Council, update and revise the annexes in the light of information and experience gained in the course of the implementation of resolutions 687 (1991) and 707 (1991) and of the Plan.  The Special Commission shall inform Iraq of any such change.

### 7.  Entry into force and duration

27.   The Plan shall enter into force immediately upon its approval by the Security Council.  The duration of the Plan shall be determined by the Security Council.

0009                     /...

## C. <u>Provisions related to chemical items</u>

28.  Chemicals, equipment and facilities set forth herein and in annex II could be used for purposes related to chemical weapons.  They shall therefore be subject to monitoring and verification in accordance with the following additional provisions in order to ensure that Iraq does not use, develop, produce or otherwise acquire chemical weapons or related items prohibited under resolution 687 (1991).

29.  Chemicals that could be used for the development, production or acquisition of chemical weapons but which also have significant uses for purposes not prohibited by resolution 687 (1991) are set forth in list A in annex II.  These chemicals may be used, developed, produced, stored or acquired solely for purposes not prohibited by resolution 687 (1991), subject to the provisions under paragraphs 30 and 31 below, and annex II.

30.  Iraq shall, not later than 30 days after the adoption of the Plan by the Security Council, and on a regular basis thereafter, provide to the Special Commission information in accordance with annex II regarding:

(a)  The total national quantity of the production, processing or consumption of any chemical specified in list A of annex II and of the import and export of any of these chemicals specifying the supplier or recipient countries involved;

(b)  Any site or facility that is involved in production, processing, consumption, storage, import or export of one tonne or more per year of any chemical specified in list A of annex II or that at any time has been involved in activities with any of these chemicals for chemical weapons purposes;

(c)  Any site or facility that is involved in production or processing of organophosphorus chemicals or is involved in production of organic chemicals by chlorination;

(d)  Any site or facility where production, processing, consumption, storage, import or export of one tonne or more per year of any chemical specified in list A of annex II, or where production or processing of organophosphorus chemicals or where production of organic chemicals by chlorination is planned;

(e)  Any import or any other acquisition of equipment or technologies intended for production and processing of any chemical specified in list A of annex II, of any organophosphorus chemical or for production of organic chemicals by chlorination.

31.  Should Iraq plan any production, processing, consumption, storage, import or export not notified under paragraph 30 (d) above, it may begin such an activity only after providing to the Special Commission a special notification in accordance with annex II.

0010 /...

32.  Chemicals that have little or no use except as chemical warfare agents or for the development, production or acquisition of chemical weapons or which have been used by Iraq as essential precursors for chemical weapons are set forth in list B of annex II.  Iraq shall not retain, use, transfer, develop, produce, store, import or otherwise acquire these chemicals.  Should Iraq require any chemical specified in list B of annex II, it shall submit a request to the Special Commission specifying precisely the chemical and the quantities required, the site or facility where it is to be used and the purpose of its use.  The Special Commission will examine and decide on the request and establish the special arrangements it considers consistent with resolution 687 (1991).

33.  Further provisions related to chemical items are set forth in annex II.

### D.  Provisions related to biological items

34.  Micro-organisms and toxins, equipment and facilities set forth herein and in annex III could be used for purposes related to biological and toxin weapons affecting humans, animals or plants.  They shall therefore be subject to monitoring and verification in accordance with the following additional provisions in order to ensure that Iraq does not use, develop, produce or otherwise acquire biological and toxin weapons or related items prohibited under resolution 687 (1991).

35.  Iraq shall, not later than 30 days after the adoption of the Plan by the Security Council, and on a regular basis thereafter, provide to the Special Commission information in accordance with annex III regarding:

(a)  Any site or facility at which work with toxins or with micro-organisms meeting the criteria for risk groups IV, III or II according to the classification in the 1983 World Health Organization (WHO) Laboratory Biosafety Manual is carried out, or any site or facility at which work with genetic material coding for toxins or genes derived from the aforementioned micro-organisms is carried out;

(b)  Any site or facility having a laboratory (unit) meeting the criteria for a "maximum containment laboratory" or "containment laboratory" as specified in the 1983 WHO Laboratory Biosafety Manual, such as those designated as biosafety level 4 (BL4) or P4, biosafety level 3 (BL3) or P3 or equivalent standards and any site or facility being constructed or modified so as to possess such containment capabilities;

(c)  Any site or facility at which fermentation or other means for the production of micro-organisms or toxins using vessels larger than 10 litres individually or 40 litres in the aggregate is carried out;

(d)  Any site or facility for the bulk storage of toxins or of micro-organisms meeting the criteria for risk groups IV, III or II;

0011        /...

(e)  Any site or facility for the production of vaccines;

(f)  Any research, development, testing or other support or manufacturing facility for equipment and other items specified in paragraph 1 of annex III;

(g)  Any imports, other acquisition or exports of micro-organisms meeting the criteria for risk groups IV, III and II, toxins and vaccines, as well as related equipment and facilities, specifying the supplier or recipient countries involved.

36.  Iraq shall, not later than 30 days after the adoption of the Plan by the Security Council, and on a regular basis thereafter, provide to the Special Commission:

(a)  A list of all documents of a scientific and technical nature published or prepared by any site or facility engaged in work relating to toxins or micro-organisms meeting the criteria for risk groups IV, III and II, including those of a theoretical nature.  Full copies of such documents shall be made available by Iraq to the Special Commission upon request.  Documents of a purely diagnostic nature relating to risk group II micro-organisms are excepted;

(b)  A description of all work on toxins or micro-organisms meeting the criteria for risk groups IV, III or II as well as of all work being conducted on the dissemination of micro-organisms or toxins into the environment or on processes that would lead to such dissemination, specifying the site or facility involved.

37.  Iraq shall provide to the Special Commission in accordance with annex III information on all cases of infectious diseases affecting humans, animals or plants, that deviate, or seem to deviate, from the normal pattern or are caused by any micro-organism meeting the criteria for risk groups IV and III and on all cases of similar occurrences caused by toxins.

38.  Iraq shall not:

(a)  Import items referred to in paragraph 35 (g) above without giving prior notice to the Special Commission in accordance with annex III.  As an exception, the emergency import of vaccines may take place with simultaneous notification to the Special Commission;

(b)  Conduct any activities in the field of micro-organisms and toxins except by civilian personnel not in the employ of any military organization. Such activities shall be conducted openly; no classified or secret programmes or activities shall be permitted.  The sites or facilities engaged in such activities shall not be under the control of, or owned by, any military organization.  Should any military organization need to be involved in such activities for prophylactic or therapeutic purposes, Iraq shall submit a request to the Special Commission specifying precisely the toxins, micro-organisms and the quantities required, the site or facility where they

/...

0012

are to be used and the purpose of their use.  The Special Commission will examine and decide on the request and establish the special arrangements it considers consistent with resolution 687 (1991);

(c)  Conduct activities on diseases other than those indigenous to or immediately expected to break out in its environment;

(d)  Conduct any breeding of vectors of human, animal or plant diseases. Should Iraq need to conduct any such activity, Iraq shall submit a request to the Special Commission specifying precisely its requirements, the vectors to be bred, the site or facility where the activity is to take place and the purpose of the activity.  The Special Commission will examine and decide on the request and establish the special arrangements it considers consistent with resolution 687 (1991);

(e)  Possess at any one time more than one facility having a laboratory (unit) meeting the criteria for a "maximum containment laboratory" as specified in the 1983 WHO Laboratory Biosafety Manual, such as those designated as biosafety level 4 (BL4) or P4 or equivalent standard.  Iraq shall not possess at any one time more than two facilities having a laboratory (unit) meeting the criteria for a "containment laboratory", such as those designated as BL3 or P3 or equivalent standard.  Should Iraq require any additional such facilities, Iraq shall submit a request to the Special Commission specifying the precise requirement.  The Special Commission will examine and decide on the request and establish the special arrangements it considers consistent with resolution 687 (1991).

39.  Further provisions related to biological items are set forth in annex III.

### E.  Provisions related to missiles

40.  Facilities, equipment, other items and technologies set forth herein and in annex IV could be used for the development, construction, modification or acquisition of ballistic missiles with a range greater than 150 kilometres. They shall therefore be subject to monitoring and verification in accordance with the following additional provisions in order to ensure that Iraq does not use, develop, construct or acquire any ballistic missiles with a range greater than 150 kilometres or related items prohibited under resolution 687 (1991).

41.  The prohibition applies to any ballistic missiles or missile delivery systems capable of such a range regardless of payload and to any related major parts, which include missile/rocket stages, re-entry vehicles, solid- or liquid-fuel motors, guidance sets, thrust vector controls, warheads and fusing systems, launchers capable of launching ballistic missiles with a range greater than 150 kilometres and related principal launch equipment, missile transporters and other ground support equipment for such missiles.  The prohibition also applies to modification of any missile or any missile delivery system to a ballistic missile with a range greater than 150 kilometres.  The prohibition also applies to launch technologies such as tube- or gun-type launchers, which enable such ranges to be achieved.

/...

0013

42. Iraq shall not construct, otherwise acquire or operate sites or facilities for the use, development, production, training or other support of ballistic missiles capable of a range greater than 150 kilometres, including sites or facilities for research, development, modification, manufacture, assembly, testing, storage, repair, training, flight simulating and operational use of such missiles, nor acquire related major parts specified in paragraph 41 and the items listed in paragraph 1 of annex IV for such missiles.

43. Iraq shall, not later than 30 days after the adoption of the Plan by the Security Council, and on a regular basis thereafter, provide to the Special Commission the following:

(a) A list of all its missiles designed for use, or capable of being modified for use, in a surface-to-surface role with a range greater than 50 kilometres, specifying their name and type, type of propulsion, number of stages and/or boosters, guidance systems, payload, warhead and re-entry vehicle types, launcher types, airframe and warhead transporter, ground support equipment and the sites or facilities where these missiles, items or equipment are located;

(b) Information on any project and on any site or facility for such missiles, including sites or facilities for production, assembly, repair and maintenance, storage and operational bases, specifying their locations;

(c) Information on any project and on any site or facility for missile research, development, modification or testing, specifying its locations;

(d) Information on the development, production, export, import or other acquisition, training or other services related to the items, equipment and technologies listed in annex IV, specifying sites or facilities where such items, equipment and technologies are located, the purposes and the projects for which they are being used and the supplier or recipient countries involved.

44. Iraq shall notify the Special Commission in accordance with annex IV of the developmental or test launch of any missile, specifying where and when the launch is to take place.

45. Further provisions related to missiles are set forth in annex IV.

0014

/...

<u>Annex I</u>

<u>Detailed provisions related to inspections, aerial
overflights, security, privileges and immunities</u>

1.    In addition to the basic rights and obligations set forth in
paragraphs 17 and 18 of the Plan, the provisions set out in this annex shall
apply.

<u>Scope</u>

2.    The Special Commission shall have the right:

    (a)  To secure any site to be inspected and prevent any material or other
item from being taken to or from the site until the inspection is concluded;

    (b)  To stop and inspect vehicles, ships, aircraft or any other means of
transportation within Iraq, any material or other item in movement and to
restrict and/or stop movement of material or other items;

    (c)  To inspect imports or exports of material and other items upon
arrival or departure;

    (d)  To establish special modes of monitoring and verification, including
prolonged or continuous presence of inspectors, use of instruments and other
arrangements to facilitate monitoring and verification;

    (e)  To secure full and free access at any time to all sites, facilities,
areas, locations, activities, material and other items, including
documentation, all persons and all information which, in its judgement, may be
necessary for its monitoring and verification activities.

<u>Notification</u>

3.    The Special Commission shall, at a time it considers appropriate, notify
Iraq of:

    (a)  The site, facility, activity, material or other item to be inspected;

    (b)  The name of the head of the inspection team (the Chief Inspector)
and the estimated number of personnel who will take part in the inspection;

    (c)  The estimated time of departure and arrival of any flight from, to
or within Iraq, and other appropriate details, by any aircraft used by the
Special Commission.

0015                    /...

4.   Iraq shall, upon receipt of the name of the Chief Inspector for an inspection, immediately inform the Special Commission of the name of the individual who will be the Iraqi Inspection Representative for the inspection.

## Conduct of inspections or aerial overflights

5.   The Special Commission shall have the right:

     (a)  To request, receive, examine, copy and remove any record, data, information or documentation and to verify inventories;

     (b)  To examine, retain, move or photograph, including by videotaping, any activity or item;

     (c)  To conduct interviews with any personnel at a site or facility under inspection, or with any Iraqi official;

     (d)  To install containment, surveillance and other equipment and devices and to construct facilities for inspection, observation, testing, verification or monitoring activities;

     (e)  To take samples of any kind and perform on-site analyses of the samples using its own equipment;

     (f)  To remove and transfer samples outside Iraq for analyses off-site at laboratories of its choice;

     (g)  To mark, tag or otherwise identify any material or other item;

     (h)  To use its own instrumentation to collect data during inspections and aerial overflights, including photographic, video, infrared and radar data.

6.   Iraq shall:

     (a)  Provide clarification or explanation of any ambiguity that might arise during an inspection;

     (b)  Perform, upon request by the Special Commission, analyses of samples in the presence of inspectors, including on-site;

     (c)  Perform, upon request by the Special Commission, any additional task.

0016  /...

## Travel, transport and communications

7.    The Special Commission shall have the right:

(a)    To unrestricted freedom of entry into and exit from Iraq, without delay or hindrance, for all its personnel, property, supplies, equipment, spare parts, means of transport, material and other items.    No visa shall be required of such personnel travelling on United Nations laissez-passer or certificate and possessing an inspection assignment document; Iraq shall ensure prompt issuance of visas of entry and exit for such personnel as may not possess a United Nations laissez-passer or certificate;

(b)    To unrestricted freedom of movement within Iraq, without advance notice, delay or hindrance, for all its personnel, property, supplies, equipment, spare parts, means of transport, material and other items;

(c)    To fly the United Nations flag on its premises and means of transport;

(d)    To use its own means of transport, including fixed- and rotary-wing aircraft, throughout Iraq for all relevant purposes, including inspection, surveillance, aerial overflights (surveys), transportation and logistics;

(e)    To use airfields in Iraq for the purposes determined by the Special Commission including landing, take-off, basing, maintenance, refuelling and other support;

(f)    To communicate from any place within Iraq, and without censorship or other hindrance, by radio, satellite or other forms of communication, and to connect with the United Nations by its radio and satellite network, as well as by telefax, telephone, telegraph and other means;

(g)    To use codes and receive papers, correspondence and other items by courier or sealed bags;

(h)    To unrestricted freedom to remove from Iraq, without delay or hindrance, any material or other item, including any documentation, acquired during inspection or other monitoring and verification activities.

8.    Iraq shall:

(a)    Permit, without delay or hindrance, the Special Commission's personnel, property, supplies, equipment, spare parts, means of transport, material and other items to move within Iraq, without advance notice, as well as to enter or leave Iraq, promptly issuing entry and exit visas if required on national passports and accepting United Nations laissez-passers or United Nations certificates as valid travel documents without requiring visas;

(b)    Accept United Nations registration of means of transport on land, sea and in the air and United Nations licensing of the operators thereof;

/...

0017

(c) Provide priority clearance, as well as the basing and all necessary facilities as determined by the Special Commission for any fixed- or rotary-wing aircraft used by the Commission;

(d) Provide, upon the request of the Special Commission, the means of transport, maps or other information needed;

(e) Take every necessary measure to ensure that the inspection team arrives at the site or facility to be inspected by the time notified by the Special Commission;

(f) Provide, upon the request of the Special Commission, appropriate means of communication;

(g) Provide, upon request of the Special Commission, appropriate escort and/or support personnel;

(h) Provide, upon request of the Special Commission, medical, logistical and/or technical support;

(i) Not interfere with or censor any communication to or from the Special Commission or its personnel;

(j) Permit, without delay or hindrance, the Special Commission to remove from Iraq any material or other item, including any documentation, acquired by the Commission during inspection or other monitoring and verification activities.

### Security, privileges and immunities

9.    The Special Commission shall have the right to make its own arrangements to ensure the safety and security of its personnel and property and to take custody of any material or other item, including documentation.

10.   Iraq shall ensure the safety and security of the personnel and property of the Special Commission and shall provide the arrangements to this end when so requested by the Special Commission.

11.   In addition and without prejudice to the foregoing provisions, the Special Commission and any agency of the United Nations system participating in the carrying out of the Plan, its property, funds, assets and personnel shall enjoy the facilities, privileges and immunities provided for in the applicable convention or agreement, namely the Convention on the Privileges and Immunities of the United Nations, the Agreement on the Privileges and Immunities of the International Atomic Energy Agency (IAEA) and the Convention on the Privileges and Immunities of the Specialized Agencies.

0018 /...

12.   Iraq shall extend to:

     (a)   The officers and other members of the Special Commission the privileges and immunities, exemptions and facilities that are enjoyed by diplomatic envoys in accordance with international law;

     (b)   The officials of the United Nations, of IAEA and any of the specialized agencies of the United Nations, performing functions in connection with the implementation of the Plan, the privileges and immunities applicable to them under articles V and VII of the Convention on the Privileges and Immunities of the United Nations; or articles VI and IX of the Agreement on the Privileges and Immunities of the International Atomic Energy Agency; or articles VI and VIII of the Convention on the Privileges and Immunities of the Specialized Agencies;

     (c)   The technical experts and other specialists performing functions in connection with the implementation of the Plan the privileges and immunities accorded to experts performing missions for the United Nations, for IAEA or for the specialized agencies of the United Nations under article VI of the Convention on the Privileges and Immunities of the United Nations, article VII of the Agreement on the Privileges and Immunities of the International Atomic Energy Agency, and the relevant annexes to the Convention on the Privileges and Immunities of the Specialized Agencies, respectively.

### Other provisions

13.   Iraq shall designate the Iraqi authority responsible for liaison with the Special Commission and shall inform the Special Commission of the name or names of the liaison officers within that authority who shall have the full power and shall take the necessary measures to secure for the Special Commission the effective implementation of the Commission's rights laid down in the Plan.

14.   The official points of contact between Iraq and the Special Commission during the course of an inspection shall be the Chief Inspector designated by the Special Commission and the Inspection Representative designated by Iraq.

15.   Iraq shall provide, at no cost to the Special Commission, in agreement with the Special Commission, all such premises as may be necessary for the accommodation and fulfilment of the functions of the Special Commission in Iraq.  All such premises shall be inviolable and subject to the exclusive control and authority of the Special Commission.

16.   All information provided by, and communications from, Iraq to the Special Commission under the Plan shall include the corresponding text in English.

17.   For the purposes of the performance of the functions of the Special Commission in implementation of the Plan, the rights, facilities, privileges and immunities conferred in the Plan where necessary supplement and elaborate

0019        /...

upon the rights, facilities, privileges and immunities provided for in the exchange of notes between the Secretary-General of the United Nations and the Minister for Foreign Affairs of Iraq, which entered into force on 14 May 1991, regarding the status, privileges and immunities of the Special Commission as originally established pursuant to paragraph 9 of Security Council resolution 687 (1991).

0020 /...

## Annex II

## Provisions related to chemical items

1.    The following list contains chemicals that could be used for the development, production or acquisition of chemical weapons, but which also have significant uses for purposes not prohibited by resolution 687 (1991):

|  | List A | Chemical Abstracts Service (CAS) registry No. |
|---|---|---|
| 1. | Chemicals, except for those chemicals specified in list B of this annex, containing a phosphorus atom to which is bonded one methyl, ethyl or propyl (normal or iso) group but not further carbon atoms | |
| 2. | Dialkyl (Me, Et, n-Pr or i-Pr) N,N-dialkyl (Me, Et, n-Pr or i-Pr)-phosphoramidates | |
| 3. | Arsenic trichloride | (7784-34-1) |
| 4. | 2,2-Diphenyl-2-hydroxyacetic acid | (76-93-7) |
| 5. | Quinuclidin-3-ol | (1619-34-7) |
| 6. | N,N-Dialkyl (Me, Et, n-Pr or i-Pr) aminoethyl-2-chloride and corresponding protonated salts | |
| 7. | N,N-Dialkyl (Me, Et, n-Pr or i-Pr) aminoethane-2-ol and corresponding protonated salts | |
| 8. | N,N-Dialkyl (Me, Et, n-Pr or i-Pr) aminoethane-2-thiol and corresponding protonated salts | |
| 9. | Amiton:  O,O-Diethyl S-(2-(diethylamino)ethyl) phosphorothiolate and corresponding alkylated and protonated salts | (78-53-5) |
| 10. | PFIB:  1,1,3,3,3-pentafluoro-2-(trifluoromethyl)-1-propene | (382-21-8) |
| 11. | Phosgene | (75-44-5) |

0021
/...

| List A | Chemical Abstracts Service (CAS) registry No. |
|---|---|
| 12. Cyanogen chloride | (506-77-4) |
| 13. Hydrogen cyanide | (74-90-8) |
| 14. Trichloronitromethane (chloropicrin) | (76-06-2) |
| 15. Phosphorus oxychloride | (10025-87-3) |
| 16. Phosphorus trichloride | (7719-12-2) |
| 17. Phosphorus pentachloride | (10026-13-8) |
| 18. Trimethyl phosphite | (121-45-9) |
| 19. Triethyl phosphite | (122-52-1) |
| 20. Dimethyl phosphite | (868-85-9) |
| 21. Diethyl phosphite | (762-04-9) |
| 22. Sulphur monochloride | (10025-67-9) |
| 23. Sulphur dichloride | (10545-99-0) |
| 24. Thionyl chloride | (7719-09-7) |
| 25. Cyclohexanol | (108-93-0) |
| 26. Hydrogen fluoride | (7664-39-3) |
| 27. Ortho-chlorobenzylidenemalononitrile (CS) | (2698-41-1) |
| 28. Potassium fluoride | (7789-23-3) |
| 29. Ammonium bifluoride | (1341-49-7) |
| 30. Sodium bifluoride | (1333-83-1) |
| 31. Sodium fluoride | (7681-49-4) |
| 32. Sodium sulphide | (1313-82-2) |
| 33. Chloroethanol | (107-07-3) |
| 34. Dimethylamine | (124-40-3) |

0022     /...

|  |  | Chemical Abstracts Service (CAS) registry No. |
|---|---|---|
| **List A** | | |
| 35. | Dimethylamine hydrochloride | (506-59-2) |
| 36. | Potassium cyanide | (151-50-8) |
| 37. | Sodium cyanide. | (143-33-9) |
| 38. | Tri-ethanolamine | (102-71-6) |
| 39. | Di-isopropylamine | (108-18-9) |

2.    The following list contains chemicals that have little or no use except as chemical warfare agents or for the development, production or acquisition of chemical weapons, or which have been used by Iraq as essential precursors for chemical weapons:

|  |  | Chemical Abstracts Service (CAS) registry No. |
|---|---|---|
| **List B** | | |
| 1. | O-Alkyl ($\leq C_{10}$, incl. cycloalkyl) alkyl (Me, Et, n-Pr or i-Pr)-phosphonofluoridates e.g. Sarin:  O-isopropyl methylphosphono- fluoridate | (107-44-8) |
|  | Soman:  O-pinacolyl methylphosphono- fluoride | (96-64-0) |
| 2. | O-Alkyl ($\leq C_{10}$, incl. cycloalkyl) N,N-dialkyl (Me, Et, n-Pr or i-Pr) phosphoramidocyanidates e.g. Tabun:  O-ethyl N,N-dimethylphosphora- midocyanidate | (77-81-6) |
| 3. | O-Alkyl (H or $\leq C_{10}$, incl. cycloalkyl) S-2-dialkyl (Me, Et, n-Pr or i-Pr)-aminoethyl alkyl (Me, Et, n-Pr or i-Pr) phosphonothiolates and corresponding alkylated and protonated salts e.g. VX:  O-ethyl S-2-diisopropylaminoethyl methylphosphonothiolate | (50782-69-9) |

0023

/...

|  | List B | Chemical Abstracts Service (CAS) registry No. |
|---|---|---|
| 4. | Sulphur mustards: | |
|  | 2-Chloroethylchloromethylsulphide | (2625-76-5) |
|  | bis(2-chloroethyl)sulphide: | |
|  | Mustard gas (H) | (505-60-2) |
|  | bis(2-chloroethylthio)methane | (63869-13-6) |
|  | 1,2-bis(2-chloroethylthio)ethane: | |
|  | Sesquimustard (Q) | (3563-36-8) |
|  | 1,3-bis(2-chloroethylthio)-n-propane | (63905-10-2) |
|  | 1,4-bis(2-chloroethylthio)-n-butane | |
|  | 1,5-bis(2-chloroethylthio)-n-pentane | |
|  | bis(2-chloroethylthiomethyl)ether | |
|  | bis(2-chloroethylthioethyl)ether: | |
|  | O-Mustard (T) | (63918-89-8) |
| 5. | Lewisites: | |
|  | Lewisite 1: 2-chlorovinyldichlorarsine | (541-25-3) |
|  | Lewisite 2: bis(2-chlorovinyl) chloroarsine | (40334-69-8) |
|  | Lewisite 3: tris(2-chlorovinyl)arsine | (40334-70-1) |
| 6. | Nitrogen mustards: | |
|  | HN1: bis(2-chloroethyl)ethylamine | (538-07-8) |
|  | HN2: bis(2-chloroethyl)methylamine | (51-75-2) |
|  | HN3: tris(2-chloroethyl)amine | (555-77-1) |
| 7. | 3-Quinuclidinyl benzilate (BZ) | (6581-06-2) |
| 8. | Saxitoxin | (35523-89-8) |
| 9. | Ricin | |
| 10. | Alkyl (Me, Et, n-Pr or i-Pr) phosphonyldihalides | |
|  | e.g. methylphosphonyldifluoride | (676-99-3) |
|  | methylphosphonyldichloride | (676-67-1) |
| 11. | Dimethylmethylphosphonate | (756-79-6) |
| 12. | O-Alkyl (H or $\leq C_{10}$, incl. cycloalkyl) O-2-dialkyl (Me, Et, n-Pr or i-Pr)- aminoethyl alkyl (Me, Et, n-Pr or i-Pr) phosphonites and corresponding alkylated salts and protonated salts | |
|  | e.g. QL: O-ethyl O-2-diisopropylaminoethyl methylphosphonite | (57856-11-8) |

|  | Chemical Abstracts Service (CAS) registry No. |
|---|---|

<u>List B</u>

13. O-Alkyl ($\leq C_{10}$, incl. cycloalkyl) alkyl (Me, Et, n-Pr or i-Pr)-phosphonochloridates

    e.g. Chloro Sarin:  O-isopropyl methylphosphonochloridate    (1445-76-7)

          Chloro Soman:  O-pinacolyl methylphos-phonochloridate    (7040-57-5)

14. N,N-Dialkyl (Me, Et, n-Pr or i-Pr) phosphoramidic dihalides

15. Bis(2-hydroxyethyl)sulphide (thiodiglycol)    (111-48-8)

16. 3,3-Dimethylbutan-2-ol (pinacolyl alcohol)    (464-07-3)

3.    The initial information under paragraph 30 of the Plan to be provided not later than 30 days after the adoption of the Plan by the Security Council shall cover the period from 1 January 1988.  Subsequent information shall be provided each 15 January and 15 July and shall cover the six-month period prior to the provision of the information.  The advance notifications under paragraph 30 (d) of the Plan shall cover the subsequent six months.  The special notifications under paragraph 31 of the Plan shall be provided not later than 30 days in advance.

4.    Whenever the information that Iraq is required to provide under section C of the Plan and this annex is equal to nil, Iraq shall provide nil returns.

5.    The information on chemicals to be provided under section C of the Plan shall for each chemical include:

(a)    The chemical name, common or trade name used by the site or the facility, structural formula and Chemical Abstracts Service registry number (if assigned);

(b)    The purposes for which the chemical is produced, processed, consumed, stored, imported or exported;

(c)    The total amount produced, processed, consumed, stored, imported or exported.

6.    The information on sites or facilities to be provided under section C of the Plan shall for each site or facility include:

(a)    The name of the site or facility and of the owner, company or enterprise operating the site or facility;

(b)    The location of the site or facility;

0025     /...

(c)  A general description of all types of activities at the site or facility;

(d)  The sources and amounts of the financing of the site or facility, and of its activities.

7.  The location of a site or facility shall be specified by means of the address and a site diagram.  Each diagram shall be drawn to scale and shall indicate the boundaries of the site or facility, all road and rail entrances and exits and all structures on the site or facility, indicating their purpose.  If the site or facility is located within a larger complex, the diagram shall specify the exact location of the site or facility within the complex.  On each diagram, the geographic coordinates of a point within the site or facility shall be specified to the nearest second.

8.  In addition to information specified in paragraph 6 of this annex, the following information shall be provided for each site or facility that is or will be involved in production, processing, consumption, storage, import or export of chemicals specified in list A of this annex:

(a)  A detailed description of activities related to these chemicals including, as applicable, material-flow and process-flow diagrams, chemical reactions and end-use;

(b)  A list of equipment used in activities related to these chemicals;

(c)  The production capacity for these chemicals.

9.  In addition to information specified in paragraph 6 of this annex, the following information shall be provided for each site or facility that is or will be involved in production or processing of organophosphorus chemicals or in production of organic chemicals by chlorination:

(a)  A detailed description of activities related to the relevant chemicals, and the end-uses for which the chemicals are produced or processed;

(b)  A detailed description of the processes used in the production or processing of organophosphorus chemicals or in the production of organic chemicals by chlorination, including material-flow and process-flow diagrams, chemical reactions and list of equipment involved.

10.  The information on each import to be provided under section C of the Plan shall include:

(a)  Specification of each item and the quantity imported and the purpose of its use in Iraq;

(b)  Country from which the item is imported and the specific exporter;

(c)  Point or port and time of entry of the item into Iraq;

0026    /...

(d)  Site or facility where it is to be used;

(e)  Name of the specific importing organization in Iraq.

0027

/...

Annex III

Provisions related to biological items

1.    The following list contains equipment and other items relevant to the acquisition of biological and toxin weapons or biological and toxin weapons capability:

(a)   Detection or assay systems specific for risk groups IV, III and II micro-organisms and toxins;

(b)   Biohazard containment equipment;

(c)   Equipment for the micro-encapsulation of living micro-organisms;

(d)   Complex media for the growth of risk groups IV, III and II micro-organisms;

(e)   Bio-reactors and fermentation vessels;

(f)   Recombinant deoxyribonucleic acid (DNA), equipment and reagents for its isolation, characterization or production and equipment and reagents for the construction of synthetic genes;

(g)   Equipment for the release into the environment of biological material;

(h)   Equipment for studying the aerobiological characteristics of micro-organisms or toxins;

(i)   Equipment for breeding of vectors of human, animal or plant diseases.

2.    The initial information under paragraphs 35 and 36 of the Plan to be provided not later than 30 days after the adoption of the Plan by the Security Council shall cover the period from 1 January 1986.  Subsequent information shall be provided each 15 January and 15 July and shall cover the six-month period prior to the provision of the information.  Notifications under paragraph 38 (a) of the Plan shall be provided not later than 60 days in advance.

3.    Whenever the information that Iraq is required to provide under section D and this annex is equal to nil, Iraq shall provide nil returns.

4.    The information on each site or facility to be provided under section D of the Plan shall include the following:

(a)   The name of the site or facility and of the owner, company, or enterprise operating the facility;

0028    /...

(b)  The location of the site or facility (including the address, geographic coordinates to the nearest second, the specific buildings and any structure numbers, location of the facility within any larger complex);

(c)  The sources and amounts of financing of the site or facility and of its activities;

(d)  The main purpose of the site or facility;

(e)  The level of protection, including, as applicable, the number and size of maximum containment or containment laboratories (units);

(f)  Scope and description of activities, including, as applicable, a list of types and quantities of micro-organisms, toxins or vaccines and equipment and other items specified in paragraph 1 of this annex;

(g)  A list of micro-organisms and toxins, equipment and vaccines imported or uniquely isolated for the use of the site or facility, or exported, indicating the supplier or recipient countries involved.

5.    The information on imports to be provided under paragraphs 35 (g) and 38 (a) of the Plan shall cover:

(a)  Toxins and micro-organisms meeting the criteria for risk groups IV, III, and II according to the classification in the 1983 WHO <u>Laboratory Biosafety Manual</u> and genetic material coding for toxins or genes derived from the aforementioned micro-organisms;

(b)  Equipment and facilities for the production, utilization or storage of micro-organisms meeting the criteria for risk groups IV and III according to the classification in the 1983 WHO <u>Laboratory Biosafety Manual</u>, genetic material coding for toxins or genes derived from the aforementioned micro-organisms, as well as of toxins or vaccines;

(c)  Complex media for the growth of micro-organisms meeting the criteria for risk groups IV and III in quantities greater than 100 kilograms;

(d)  Equipment for micro-encapsulation of living micro-organisms;

(e)  Personnel or material for training or technical support services related to the design, development, use, manufacture or support of items· specified in paragraph 35 (a) of the Plan and paragraphs 1 and 5 (a) of this annex;

and shall for each import into Iraq specify:

(a)  Types and quantities of micro-organisms, toxins or vaccines;

(b)  Quantities of any equipment or other items specified in paragraph 1 of this annex;

0029                      /...

   (c)  Country from which the micro-organisms, toxins, vaccines or items are imported and the specific exporter;

   (d)  Point or port and time of entry into Iraq;

   (e)  Site or facility where it is to be used and purpose of its use.

   (f)  Name of the specific importing organization in Iraq.

6.   The information under paragraph 37 of the Plan shall be provided within seven days of the occurrence and the standardized form contained in section III of the annex on confidence-building measures in document BWC/CONF.III/23/II shall be utilized as appropriate.

7.   Iraq shall, not later than each 15 April, provide to the Special Commission the copies of the declarations, information and data that Iraq has sent to the United Nations Department for Disarmament Affairs pursuant to the agreements on confidence-building measures, including the exchange of information and data, reached at the Third Review Conference of the Parties to the Convention on the Prohibition of the Development, Production and Stockpiling of Bacteriological (Biological) and Toxin Weapons and on Their Destruction (document BWC/CONF.III/23/II and its annex on confidence-building measures).

0030

/...

## Annex IV

## Provisions related to missiles

1.    The following list contains equipment, other items and technologies relevant to the development and manufacture of missiles that could be used in the development and manufacture of ballistic missiles capable of a range greater than 150 kilometres:

   (a)   Subsystems usable in missile systems that could be used in the development and manufacture of ballistic missiles capable of a range greater than 150 kilometres:

   (i)    Individual rocket stages;

   (ii)   Re-entry vehicles, and specially designed equipment therefor;

   (iii)  Solid- or liquid-fuel rocket engines;

   (iv)   Guidance sets;

   (v)    Thrust vector controls;

   (vi)   Warhead safing, arming, fuzing and firing mechanisms;

   (b)   Propulsion components and equipment that could be used in the development and manufacture of ballistic missiles capable of a range greater than 150 kilometres:

   (i)    Rocket-motor cases and production equipment therefor;

   (ii)   Staging mechanisms and production equipment therefor;

   (iii)  Liquid-fuel control systems and components therefor, specially designed to operate in vibrating environments of more than 12g/rms between 20/Hz and 2,000/Hz;

   (iv)   Propellants and constituent chemicals for propellants;

   (v)    Production technology or production equipment for the production, handling, mixing, curing, casting, pressing, machining and acceptance testing of the liquid- or solid-fuel missile propellants and propellent constituents;

   (c)   Guidance and control equipment that could be used in the development and manufacture of ballistic missiles capable of a range greater than 150 kilometres:

0031

/...

  (i)   Gyroscopes, accelerometers and inertial equipment and software
        therefor;

 (ii)   Flight control systems usable in missile systems;

(iii)   Avionics equipment specially designed or modified for use in
        unmanned air vehicles or rocket systems and software and components
        therefor usable in missile systems;

  (d)   Equipment and technical data for the production of structural
composites usable in missiles and components, accessories and software
therefor that could be used in the development and manufacture of ballistic
missiles capable of a range greater than 150 kilometres;

  (e)   Pyrolytic deposition and densification equipment and technology that
could be used in the development and manufacture of ballistic missiles capable
of a range greater than 150 kilometres;

  (f)   Launch and ground support equipment and facilities usable for
missile systems that could be used in the development and manufacture of
ballistic missiles capable of a range greater than 150 kilometres;

  (g)   Analog computers, digital computers or digital differential
analysers usable in air vehicles, rocket systems or missile systems that could
be used in the development and manufacture of ballistic missiles capable of a
range greater than 150 kilometres;

  (h)   Test facilities and equipment usable for missile systems, to include
vibration test equipment using digital control techniques, wind tunnels and
test benches for solid- or liquid-fuel rockets that could be used in the
development and manufacture of ballistic missiles capable of a range greater
than 150 kilometres;

  (i)   Specially designed software or components for missile design,
production or operation that could be used in the development and manufacture
of ballistic missiles capable of a range greater than 150 kilometres;

  (j)   Materials and devices for reduced observables in missile systems
that could be used in the development and manufacture of ballistic missiles
capable of a range greater than 150 kilometres;

  (k)   Material and devices for protecting missile systems against nuclear
effects that could be used in the development and manufacture of ballistic
missiles capable of a range greater than 150 kilometres.

2.    The initial information under paragraph 43 of the Plan to be provided not
later than 30 days after the adoption of the Plan by the Security Council
shall cover the period from 1 January 1988.  Subsequent information shall be
provided each 15 January and 15 July and shall cover the six-month period

/...

0032

prior to the provision of the information.  Notifications under paragraph 44 of the Plan shall be provided not later than 14 days prior to the date of launch.

3.    Whenever the information which Iraq is required to provide under section E of the Plan and this annex is equal to nil, Iraq shall provide nil returns.

4.    The information on sites or facilities to be provided under section E of the Plan shall for each site or facility include:

     (a)  The name of the site or facility and of the owner, company or enterprise operating the site or facility;

     (b)  The location of the site or facility;

     (c)  The sources and amounts of the financing of the site or facility, and of its activities;

     (d)  A general description of all types of activities at the site or facility;

     (e)  List of equipment, other items and technologies specified in paragraph 1 of this annex used or present at the site or facility and their quantities;

     (f)  A detailed description of activities related to the equipment, other items and technologies specified in paragraph 1 of this annex.

5.    The location of a site or facility shall be specified by means of the address and site diagram.  Each diagram shall be drawn to scale and shall indicate the boundaries of the site or facility, all road and rail entrances and exits and all structures on the site or facility, indicating their purpose.  If the site or facility is located within a larger complex, the diagram shall specify the exact location of the site or facility within the complex.  On each diagram, the geographic coordinates of a point within the site or facility shall be specified to the nearest second.

6.    The information on each import to be provided under section E of the Plan shall include:

     (a)  Specification of each item and the quantity imported and the purpose of its use in Iraq;

     (b)  Country from which the item is imported and the specific exporter;

     (c)  Point or port and time of entry of the item in Iraq;

0033                    /...

(d)  Project and site or facility where it is to be used;

(e)  Name of the specific importing organization in Iraq.

-----

0034

# Security Council

Distr.
GENERAL

S/23106
2 October 1991

ORIGINAL:  ENGLISH

REPORT OF THE SECRETARY-GENERAL ON THE UNITED NATIONS
IRAQ-KUWAIT OBSERVATION MISSION

(for the period 9 April to 2 October 1991)

## Introduction

1.    By paragraph 5 of its resolution 687 (1991) of 3 April 1991, the Security Council established a demilitarized zone along the Iraq-Kuwait border and decided to set up an observer unit with the following tasks:  to monitor the Khawr 'Abd Allah waterway and the demilitarized zone; to deter violations of the boundary through its presence in and surveillance of the demilitarized zone; and to observe any hostile or potentially hostile action mounted from the territory of one State into the other.  By its resolution 689 (1991) of 9 April 1991, the Security Council approved my report on the implementation of the above provisions (S/22454 and Add.1-3); noted that the decision to set up the observer unit had been taken in paragraph 5 of resolution 687 (1991) and could only be terminated by the Council's decision; and decided to review the question of termination or continuation as well as the modalities of the United Nations Iraq-Kuwait Observation Mission (UNIKOM) every six months.

2.    The purpose of the present report is to provide the Security Council, prior to its review, with an overview of the first six months of UNIKOM activities.  It also updates my reports of 9 May (S/22580), 12 June (S/22692) and 3 September 1991 (S/23000), which covered the greater part of the reporting period in some detail.

## Setting up of UNIKOM in the field

3.    The setting up of UNIKOM in the field began with the arrival of the Chief Military Observer, Major-General Günther G. Greindl, and his advance party in the mission area on 13 April.  The advance party comprising military observers temporarily assigned from the United Nations Truce Supervision Organization (UNTSO) and civilian staff.  Over the following three weeks, UNIKOM conducted a thorough reconnaissance of its assigned zone, developed a deployment plan, organized its transport, set up a communications network, developed its lines of supply and provided training and familiarization for the incoming

91-32366  2645g (E)

0035

/...

personnel.  UNIKOM deployment was completed on 6 May.  UNIKOM then monitored the withdrawal of the armed forces that were still deployed in its assigned zone.  *That withdrawal having been completed, the demilitarized zone (DMZ) established by the Security Council came into effect at 2000 hours Greenwich mean time (GMT) on 9 May 1991.*

## Organization

4.   At the beginning of October 1991, UNIKOM comprised the following personnel:

### Military observers

| | | | |
|---|---|---|---|
| Argentina | 7 | Nigeria | 7 |
| Austria | 7 | Norway | 8 |
| Bangladesh | 7 | Pakistan | 9 |
| Canada | 1 | Poland | 7 |
| China | 20 | Romania | 7 |
| Denmark | 7 | Senegal | 7 |
| Fiji | 8 | Singapore | 7 |
| Finland | 7 | Sweden | 8 |
| France | 20 | Thailand | 7 |
| Ghana | 8 | Turkey | 7 |
| Greece | 7 | Union of Soviet | |
| Hungary | 7 | Socialist Republics | 20 |
| India | 8 | United Kingdom of | |
| Indonesia | 7 | Great Britain and | |
| Ireland | 8 | Northern Ireland | 16 |
| Italy | 6 | United States of America | 19 |
| Kenya | 8 | Uruguay | 8 |
| Malaysia | 8 | Venezuela | 7 |
| | | Total | 295 |

### Administrative and logistic support

| | |
|---|---|
| Engineers (Canada) | 292 |
| Logistics (Sweden) | 30 |
| Movement control/post (Denmark) | 19 |
| Helicopters (Chile) | 50 |
| Medical (Norway) | 50 |
| Total | 441 |

/...

0036

UNIKOM includes also 177 civilian staff, of whom 106 are United Nations staff and 71 are locally recruited. Two small fixed-wing aircraft contributed by the Government of Switzerland are operated by civilians. In addition, UNIKOM had the use of chartered aircraft for the movement of troops and equipment and for communications between Baghdad and Kuwait. The Government of Sweden provided free airlift at the beginning of the mission.

5.    The plan for UNIKOM, which was formulated in the first days of April, took into account the uncertainties existing at the time and the risks that might arise. For this reason, three infantry companies (Fiji, Ghana, Nepal) from the United Nations Interim Force in Lebanon (UNIFIL) and two infantry companies (Austria and Denmark) from the United Nations Peace-keeping Force in Cyprus (UNFICYP) were temporarily assigned to UNIKOM to provide security. Fortunately the risks perceived in early April did not materialize, and by the end of June the infantry companies returned to their parent missions, as did a logistic company (Sweden) that had also been temporarily detached from UNIFIL.

6.    Logistic support for the Mission was difficult at first because the war had resulted in the destruction or severe disruption of the infrastructure in the area. UNIKOM, therefore, relied on substantial support provided by the United States Army and by the forces of other Member States cooperating with Kuwait. The Governments of Iraq and Kuwait also gave support to UNIKOM. The situation has since improved and UNIKOM now has its full complement of transport and communications equipment, much of which came from the United Nations Iran-Iraq Military Observer Group (UNIIMOG). For most of the period, and especially during the summer, living conditions in the DMZ were austere and very demanding, the military personnel being accommodated under canvas. The provision of air-conditioned prefabricated trailers in September has improved conditions greatly. The Mission was launched from and is being supplied through Kuwait, which has the international airport nearest to the DMZ.

7.    A serious hazard from the beginning was the large number of mines and unexploded ordnance left over from the war. UNIKOM engineers cleared some 1,100 kilometres of patrol track and the sites for observation posts, camps and helicopter pads and disposed of some 7,000 mines and pieces of unexploded ordnance. The engineers also carried out construction work on the various camp facilities and on the future headquarters at Umm Qasr. There will be a continuing requirement for explosive ordnance demolition and the maintenance of patrol tracks and facilities in the DMZ. In addition, the Iraq-Kuwait Boundary Demarcation Commission, established under paragraph 3 of resolution 687 (1991), will require significant engineer support. Provision of this has already begun through the clearing of sites and the placing of preliminary survey markers. So far, 121 out of a projected 165 markers have been placed.

8.    As I informed the Security Council in my letter of 6 August 1991 (S/22916), a number of adjustments are being made to the logistic support elements. For the reasons mentioned above, 85 engineers will be retained in UNIKOM but their number will be further reduced when the work in support of the Boundary Demarcation Commission has been completed (see S/22916).

0037                    /...

Further, the Swedish logistic unit, which was made available for six months only, will be withdrawn. Its tasks and that of the movement control staff will be consolidated in one unit of 45 all ranks, which will be provided by Denmark. Finally, the size of the medical unit will be reduced from 50 to 20. These adjustments will be carried out in the next weeks.

9.    With the agreement of the Security Council, I have postponed the reduction in the number of military observers that I had intended to effect (S/22977 and S/22978). I shall keep this matter under review and revert to the Council when appropriate.

10.    UNIKOM headquarters was initially located south of Kuwait City in a hotel annex made available by the Government of Kuwait. In June, the headquarters moved temporarily to the logistic base at Doha. Work continues at the future headquarters at Umm Qasr to make it habitable.

11.    Major-General Greindl and his senior staff have maintained close contact and held regular meetings with the authorities at Baghdad and Kuwait City. In addition, the UNIKOM liaison staff were in daily contact with their Iraqi and Kuwaiti counterparts. UNIKOM maintains liaison offices at Baghdad and Kuwait City. Local liaison with the Iraqi authorities is also effected through an Iraqi liaison office at Umm Qasr.

## Demilitarized zone

12.    The DMZ is about 200 kilometres long, to which must be added the Khawr 'Abd Allah waterway, with a length of about 40 kilometres. For the most part, the DMZ is barren and almost uninhabited, except for the towns of Umm Qasr and Safwan. There are airfields at Safwan and Umm Qasr and a port at Umm Qasr. A number of roads cross the DMZ, most of them in the eastern part, but the terrain makes cross-country travel easy, and there are numerous tracks, especially in the central and southern sectors. There are few features in the terrain and it is easy to mistake one's location by a wide margin. It is also easy to mistake the location of the border, which remains to be marked.

13.    When UNIKOM arrived in the area, a large number of displaced persons were in the Safwan area. Most of these were moved prior to the establishment of the DMZ, and only a small number remain at the Abdali camp on Kuwaiti territory south of Safwan.

## Deployment and concept of operations

14.    For operational purposes, UNIKOM has divided the DMZ into three sectors. Each sector has a headquarters and six observation posts/patrol bases. UNIKOM enjoys full freedom of movement throughout the DMZ. The deployment of UNIKOM is shown on the attached map.

/...

15.   UNIKOM's concept of operations, which has been further refined during recent months, places emphasis on mobile patrols in order to observe the length and breadth of the DMZ.  The fixed observation posts serve as patrol bases from which the military observers patrol their assigned sectors and visit temporary observation points established in areas of particular activity or where roads and tracks enter the DMZ.  In addition to the patrols, all other movements, supply runs for example, are also used for observation; investigation teams are frequently dispatched.  Observation on the ground is supplemented by air patrols, using helicopters and the two fixed-wing aircraft.  Again, all other flights are also used for observation.

## Violations and complaints

16.   Since the DMZ came into effect on 9 May, UNIKOM has observed three types of violations:  minor incursions on the ground by small groups of soldiers, often just one or two; overflights by military aircraft; and the carrying by policemen of weapons other than sidearms.  The largest number of ground incursions, 65, occurred in the month immediately after the establishment of the DMZ.  UNIKOM then put up signs on the main roads and tracks to mark entry into the DMZ; after that, the number of ground incursions dropped significantly.  The overflights were by military aircraft of a type used by the forces of Member States cooperating with Kuwait and, since early September, also of a type used by Kuwait.

17.   In order to reduce the risk of incidents and as envisaged from the outset (S/22454, para. 6), UNIKOM obtained the agreement of the Governments of Iraq and Kuwait that their police operating in the DMZ would carry only sidearms. Both sides have expressed misgivings about this limitation, pointing out that smugglers and other elements with whom the police have to contend are generally armed with rifles and light machine-guns.  UNIKOM has observed a number of violations by both sides, including cases in which policemen have kept rifles out of sight in their posts and vehicles.

18.   The following table summarizes the violations observed by UNIKOM:

| | Iraq | | | | Kuwait/allied forces | | | |
|---|---|---|---|---|---|---|---|---|
| | Ground | Air | Police weapons | Total | Ground | Air | Police weapons | Total |
| 10 May-9 June | 8 | – | – | 8 | 57 | 29 | – | 86 |
| 10 June-9 July | 4 | – | – | 4 | 29 | 28 | – | 57 |
| 10 July-9 August | 1 | – | 6 | 7 | 9 | 9 | 6 | 24 |
| 10 August-9 September | 5 | – | 4 | 9 | 13 | 13 | 1 | 27 |
| 10 September-2 October | – | – | 1 | 1 | 6 | 7 | 3 | 16 |
| Total | 18 | – | 11 | 29 | 114 | 86 | 10 | 210 |

/...

0039

All violations were raised in writing with the party concerned, with a view to preventing a recurrence.

19.  During the reporting period, UNIKOM received 28 written complaints from Iraq and 10 from Kuwait.  It investigated those complaints and was able in 13 cases to establish the facts through its own observation.  The results of the investigations were conveyed to the party concerned.

### Other matters

20.  One of the purposes of UNIKOM is to deter violations of the boundary between Iraq and Kuwait through its presence in, and surveillance of, the DMZ.  Pending demarcation of the boundary, UNIKOM has not taken a position concerning its precise location.  UNIKOM uses a British map, which it has given to both sides for reference.  They have agreed to work with it as a practical arrangement to facilitate UNIKOM's task and without prejudice to their positions concerning the boundary.

21.  In order to avoid friction and incidents, UNIKOM has established the principle that the Iraqi and Kuwaiti authorities, including police, should stay a reasonable distance of 1,000 metres from the boundary line shown on UNIKOM maps.  It is not intended that this should lead to the creation of a no-man's land.  The authorities retain the right to carry out their functions throughout their respective parts of the DMZ, except that they are expected to consult UNIKOM in advance if those functions should require them to approach closer than 1,000 metres to the boundary line shown on UNIKOM's map.  Such consultation enables UNIKOM to take measures to avoid incidents.

22.  Two main problems have arisen in this regard.  First, the removal from storage at Umm Qasr of 11 "HY-2G" missiles and later 4 further missiles of the same type.  I informed the Security Council of this matter on 5 July.  UNIKOM took it up with the Iraqi authorities, who have since returned 4 of the missiles to the storage at Umm Qasr but not the other 11.

23.  Secondly, Iraq has deployed 4 border police centres and 10 border police posts in the DMZ.  Five of the posts are on the Kuwaiti side of the boundary line shown on the UNIKOM map; two are closer to it than 1,000 metres, on the Iraqi side.  Lengthy and intensive efforts have been made at United Nations Headquarters as well as in the field to persuade Iraq to move the seven posts further back.  However, the Iraqi authorities have maintained that they had been in place before 2 August 1990 and that they would not be pulled back because of the political implications.  The Iraqi authorities have assured UNIKOM that Iraq will comply with the reasonable distance principle, once the boundary is demarcated.  UNIKOM has recently observed harbour and local police at Umm Qasr, and the Iraqi authorities have indicated that they intend to deploy more policemen in the DMZ.  They have undertaken to consult UNIKOM in advance of such deployment.

/...

24. For its part, Kuwait has established five police posts and one police observation point in the DMZ. The Kuwaiti authorities have been in touch with UNIKOM about the locations of these posts and of additional posts which they plan to set up. They have also reiterated their willingness to comply with the reasonable distance principle if the Iraqi authorities do so as well.

25. In accordance with the plan approved by the Security Council in its resolution 689 (1991), UNIKOM requires that it be informed in advance of the movement of ships through the Khawr 'Abd Allah waterway (see S/22454, para. 6). In September, UNIKOM observed movements by an Iraqi pilot ship and a maintenance ship between Umm Qasr and the Khawr 'Abd Allah waterway. UNIKOM had not been informed of these movements and raised them with the Iraqi authorities, who have since complied with the UNIKOM notification requirement.

26. In the course of August, tension rose as a result of incursions from Iraq into Kuwaiti territory by persons collecting weapons, ammunition and other battlefield items. These persons, and others similarly engaged in the Iraqi part of the DMZ, were dressed in civilian clothes and used civilian vehicles. The question has been raised whether they are in fact military personnel but UNIKOM has not been able to establish that this is so. It has, however, been informed by the Iraqi authorities that they offer rewards to persons who retrieve weapons and ammunition from the battlefield. It has also had indications that there is an unofficial market for such items in Iraq. In addition to its own observations, UNIKOM has been informed by the Kuwaiti authorities of such incursions and of arrests they have made. One such incident investigated by UNIKOM occurred on 28 August, when the Kuwaiti Coast Guard took 12 small vessels and detained 45 Iraqis off the Kuwaiti island of Bubiyan. I reported on these matters on 3 September (S/23000, paras. 12-14). Subsequently such incursions subsided. However, on 30 September and 1 October, UNIKOM observed in its southern sector Iraqis collecting mines on the Kuwaiti side of the line shown on the UNIKOM map, at a minefield that straddles that line.

27. In the Iraqi part of the DMZ the collection of military equipment and ammunition has continued. Recently, mines and unexploded ordnance have also been lifted. It is evident that there are persons engaged in this dangerous activity who are not trained for it; there have been numerous casualties and to UNIKOM's knowledge at least 16 persons have died during the last 10 days. Many of the casualties were brought to UNIKOM posts, from where they were evacuated by helicopter and treated by UNIKOM's medical staff. UNIKOM raised this matter with the Iraqi authorities on humanitarian grounds. On 2 October 1991, the Iraqi authorities informed UNIKOM that they had issued strict instructions to the police to stop civilians from collecting mines in the DMZ. It is hoped therefore that the problems described in this and the preceding paragraph will not recur.

28. I have reported previously about the so-called "sheep market", an illegal market where alcohol and arms are traded as well as livestock (S/23000, para. 11). That market has recently moved to a location astride the boundary line in the southern sector. On 15 September, UNIKOM received a complaint

/...

0041

from the Kuwaiti liaison staff with the request that it investigate an
incident in which 80 armed men from the market had allegedly attacked a
Kuwaiti police post with rifles and rocket-propelled grenades and had taken
two policemen hostage.  The UNIKOM team investigating the incident found no
evidence of damage to the police cabins or vehicles, and established that the
two missing policemen had been on an errand in Kuwait City.  At the sheep
market, the traders stated that they had approached the police post to borrow
water but the policemen had opened fire, killing one.  The UNIKOM team found
that man's body some 20 metres from the police post and at the sheep market
was shown a water truck with numerous bullet holes.

## Financial aspects

29.  Should the Security Council continue the mandate of UNIKOM beyond
8 October 1991, the cost of maintaining the Mission for a period of six months
would be approximately $40 million, based on the continuance of its existing
strength and responsibilities.  The resources needed for maintaining UNIKOM
beyond 8 October 1991 will be sought from the General Assembly at its
forty-sixth session.  In the event that the mandate is extended beyond six
months, the Secretary-General will report to the Advisory Committee on
Administrative and Budgetary Questions and to the General Assembly during its
forty-seventh session on the additional resources needed.

## Observations

30.  During the last six months, UNIKOM deployed in its area of operation and
carried out its tasks pursuant to the mandate entrusted to it by the Security
Council in paragraph 5 of its resolution 687 (1991) and in accordance with the
implementation plan approved by the Council in its resolution 689 (1991).  The
DMZ established by the Security Council has been generally respected and the
area has been calm.  UNIKOM has thus served the purpose for which it was
created and, in the light of all the circumstances, I recommend that the
Security Council maintain it in the area for a further six-month period.

31.  As indicated by the table in paragraph 18 above, there have been rather
few violations due to ground incursions by military personnel into the DMZ and
their frequency has been falling.  The main source of friction during the
period under review has been the movement of persons from Iraq to Kuwait
across a border which remains to be demarcated.  Given Kuwait's recent
experience, these unauthorized border crossings have understandably given
cause for concern to the Kuwaiti authorities, who have frequently raised them
with UNIKOM.

32.  Some of these border crossings are by bedouins and reflect a longstanding
practice which has been countenanced by both sides in the past.  Others are
attributable to the suppliers and customers of the illegal sheep market, which
itself changes location from time to time in the border area.  These movements
are of some concern to UNIKOM because of the violent incidents to which they

/...

0042

sometimes give rise and because those associated with the sheep market are armed with, and trade in, weapons of a higher calibre than those which the police of either side are permitted to carry in the DMZ. This is essentially a law and order problem, which UNIKOM has drawn to the attention of both Governments.

33. A third category of border crossings is caused by persons from Iraq who have penetrated deep into Kuwait in search of weapons, ammunition and other battlefield items. As far as UNIKOM has been able to ascertain, these persons are civilians attracted by the prices which such items fetch, from official or unofficial purchasers, in Iraq. Again, UNIKOM has raised this matter with the Iraqi authorities both because of the tension to which it can give rise and, on humanitarian grounds, because of the carnage suffered by the persons who engage in this very dangerous practice (see para. 27 above).

34. UNIKOM's responsibilities vis-à-vis unauthorized border crossings in these various categories have been misunderstood in some quarters. When UNIKOM first deployed it encountered the widely held expectation in the area that it would assume overall responsibility in the DMZ and police it. In the same vein, it was often referred to as the "United Nations forces". To some extent, these expectations have persisted. It is therefore worth repeating that UNIKOM has been constituted as an observation mission and does not have the authority, under the terms of resolution 689 (1991), to assume law enforcement functions. Nor does it have the capacity to do so; the military observers are unarmed and the armed infantry elements have been withdrawn.

35. The continued presence of Iraqi police posts on the Kuwaiti side of the line shown on UNIKOM's map remains a matter of concern. I have instructed the Chief Military Observer of UNIKOM to persevere in his efforts to have these police posts pulled back behind the line.

36. UNIKOM has functioned well, with the cooperation of the parties. Its concept of operations has proven adequate to the task and Major-General Greindl is confident that UNIKOM would detect any significant military movement in or close to the DMZ. With additional experience, the UNIKOM operations will be further refined. There is, however, one aspect of its modalities that seems to require early improvement. This relates to its observation capability, particularly when the weather conditions limit visibility and make air surveillance difficult. Such difficulties cannot be overcome by increasing the number of military observers; UNIKOM is very adequately staffed. Electronic instruments, especially radar, would seem to provide the only means of ensuring continuous observation throughout the DMZ. General Greindl has made a recommendation to this effect, which is now being studied, taking into account financial as well as operational considerations.

37. Finally, I wish to express my appreciation to the Governments that have contributed personnel to UNIKOM and have provided support in other practical forms. I also wish to pay tribute to Major-General Greindl, to his military and civilian staff, to the military observers and to the soldiers of the support units for the skill and dedication with which they have carried out their tasks in difficult conditions.

/...

0043

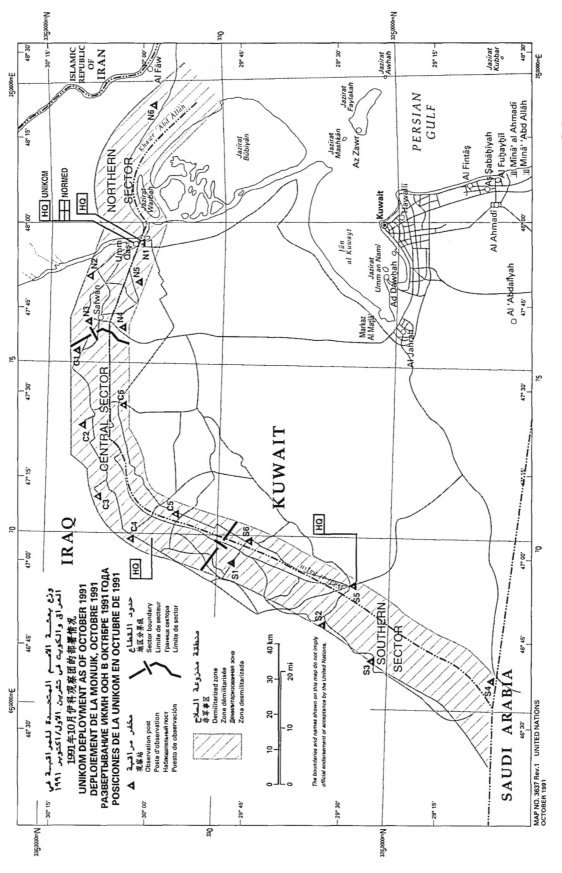

## Security Council

Distr.
GENERAL

S/23107
2 October 1991

ORIGINAL: ENGLISH

### NOTE BY THE PRESIDENT OF THE SECURITY COUNCIL

After the consultations held on 2 October 1991, the President of the Security Council made the following statement to the media on behalf of the members in connection with the item entitled "The situation between Iraq and Kuwait":

"The members of the Security Council held informal consultations on 2 October 1991 pursuant to paragraph 21 of resolution 687 (1991).

"After hearing all the opinions expressed in the course of the consultations, the President of the Council concluded that there was no agreement that the necessary conditions existed for a modification of the regime established in paragraph 20 of resolution 687 (1991), as referred to in paragraph 21 of that resolution."

-----

91-32412  2565c (E)

0045

## Security Council

Distr.
GENERAL

S/23106/Add.1
4 October 1991

ORIGINAL:  ENGLISH

REPORT OF THE SECRETARY-GENERAL ON THE UNITED NATIONS
IRAQ-KUWAIT OBSERVATION MISSION

<u>Addendum</u>

1.    In paragraph 27 of my report of 2 October 1991 (S/23106) on the United Nations Iraq-Kuwait Observation Mission (UNIKOM), I informed the Security Council that on that day the Iraqi authorities had issued strict instructions to their police to stop civilians from collecting mines in the demilitarized zone (DMZ).  However, the Chief Military Observer has since reported that on 2 October 1991 at least 60 Iraqi civilians, with 8 trucks and 40 pick-up vehicles, were observed by UNIKOM collecting mines at a location 15 kilometres south of observation post S-3.  Most of the activity was on the Kuwaiti side of the border, both inside and outside the DMZ.  Iraqi police, when contacted by UNIKOM observers, said that they had no orders to stop the collection of mines.

2.    On 3 October 1991, no mine collecting activity was observed by UNIKOM. On 4 October, however, the Mission observed a resumption of such activity. Some 50 Iraqi civilians, with 13 trucks and 9 pick-up vehicles, were again observed collecting mines 15 kilometres south of observation post S-3.  Once more, they were in the Iraqi and Kuwaiti parts of the DMZ, as well as in Kuwaiti territory outside it.  Also, three trucks loaded with mines and four pick-up vehicles with some 30 civilians were observed travelling south at the edge of the DMZ in Kuwait territory, approximately 16 kilometres north-east of observation post S-4.

3.    On 3 October 1991 the Chief Military Observer again raised the matter with the Iraqi authorities at Baghdad.  He urged them to take immediate action to stop any civilian from crossing the border into Kuwait and, in general, to prevent civilians from undertaking this dangerous practice.  The Iraqi authorities expressed astonishment that it was still continuing and assured the Chief Military Observer that strict instructions had been given to the police authorities to prevent mine collecting by civilians.  They said that they would take urgent measures to rectify the situation.  They also requested UNIKOM to provide them with all dates and locations when Iraqi civilians had

91-32626   2647g (E)

/...

0046

been observed collecting mines in the DMZ.  This information was delivered in writing today, 4 October 1991.

4.    I have instructed the Chief Military Observer to continue to follow this matter closely and I shall keep the Security Council informed, as necessary.

-----

0047

**UNITED NATIONS**

## Security Council

Distr.
GENERAL

S/23110
4 October 1991
ENGLISH
ORIGINAL: ARABIC

**S**

LETTER DATED 2 OCTOBER 1991 FROM THE PERMANENT REPRESENTATIVE OF
IRAQ TO THE UNITED NATIONS ADDRESSED TO THE SECRETARY-GENERAL

On instructions from my Government, I have the honour to transmit to you
herewith a letter dated 2 October 1991 from Mr. Ahmad Hussein, Minister for
Foreign Affairs of Iraq, concerning the conduct and demeanor of Mr. David Kay,
Chief of the sixth nuclear inspection team, and in which the Minister requests
that his letter should be circulated as a document of the Security Council.

(Signed)  Abdul Amir A. AL-ANBARI
Ambassador
Permanent Representative

91-32611  2941b (E)  /...

0048

### Annex

### Letter dated 2 October 1991 from the Minister for Foreign
### Affairs of Iraq addressed to the Secretary-General

I have the honour to apprise you of the behaviour and of the systematically biased demeanour of the Chief of the sixth nuclear inspection team, Mr. David Kay, namely behaviour and demeanour which corroborate our previous statements to the effect that this person is serving the purposes of a United States policy hostile to Iraq, purposes which have no connection with the tasks defined by the United Nations. The recent published reports concerning his direct contacts, from Baghdad, with his superiors in the United States Administration, which are at variance with the apparent nature of his mission to act on behalf of the United Nations, have confirmed this fact.

The true state of affairs was also confirmed by the statements made on 30 September 1991 to a number of correspondents at United Nations Headquarters in New York by Mr. Rolf Ekéus, Executive Chairman of the Special Commission, when he said that Washington had received from David Kay important information relating to Iraqi documents before it was received by the United Nations.

Mr. Ekéus said that he and the members of the Special Commission were dissatisfied with this mode of action, the inspection teams being answerable only to the International Atomic Energy Agency and to the Special Commission itself. He added that Washington was better informed of some intelligence information than was the United Nations. What is highly alarming is that Washington is leaking information received from David Kay to the press.

I

The Chief Inspector insisted on seizing information relating to the personal and family lives of employees of establishments belonging to the Ministry of Industry and Mining and to the Iraqi Atomic Energy Commission. He also insisted on taking scientific and technical reports and the names of those who had collaborated in their preparation as well as administrative reports that had no relation to the appraisal of the nuclear programme.

The seizure of such information is a flagrant violation of a basic human right. What arouses our deepest concern is the fact that this measure was taken in the name of the United Nations and under its aegis, while no one can have any doubt that it is an act which serves the purposes of the United States intelligence community, for which the Chief Inspector works, with the objective of launching a campaign of intimidation against these employees and the members of their families and placing their lives in jeopardy. The Chief of the sixth inspection team went so far as to seek to have the nuclear physics textbooks studied at institutes and colleges regarded as being in violation of the relevant Security Council resolution. This is a serious matter that cannot be ignored or passed over in silence; he is thereby seeking to deprive Iraqi students of another basic human right, namely the right to learn.

/...

0049

Our concern is further aroused by the claim of the Chief Inspector and the members of the sixth inspection team on 23 and 24 September 1991 that documents were seized of which we know nothing.  The team carried out an inspection of the buildings and confiscated documents before the employees concerned arrived, without their knowledge and without them seeing.  This is unacceptable, and we have no explanation for the incident other than that the Chief Inspector and those of the team members who had private links with foreign intelligence circles were seeking particularly on 24 September 1991, to insinuate spurious documents that had nothing to do with us in order to provide a rationale for the false accusations given currency by the governments whose purposes they serve, namely purposes that have no connection whatever with the resolutions of the Security Council.

We reaffirm our position, as communicated by our Permanent Representative in his letter of 26 September 1991 to the President of the Security Council, that we do not and shall not acknowledge any documents other than those the numbers of which were given by the Chief of the Iraqi team in his letter of 23 September 1991 addressed to the Chief of the sixth international inspection team and those with respect to which an inventory was drawn up on 30 September 1991.

## II

During the time the sixth nuclear inspection team under the leadership of Mr. David Kay was in Iraq, the Chief Inspector and some of the team members behaved in a provocative manner that was contrary to the most elementary norms that prevail in all countries.  They performed actions that are incompatible with prevailing customs and values in Iraqi society, and we should like to cite some of them here:

1.   On 23 and 24 September 1991, members of the team forced open doors, broke them down and broke locks.  The team began its visit two hours before the start of the official workday and before the employees occupying the two buildings visited by the team had yet arrived.

2.   On 23 September, some members of the team climbed over the fence before the team convoy arrived with its Iraqi escorts.

3.   Some members of the team opened handbags and briefcases that were the private property of the staff and tampered with their contents, such as family photographs and medication.

4.   Some members of the team thrust their hands into the pockets of the laboratory coats of female members of the laboratory staff.  Such disgraceful behaviour is tantamount to scheming to steal personal items.

5.   Some of them opened envelopes containing private letters, read the letters and tried to copy them.

0050                    /...

6.    They also copied letters sent by a research worker to an international periodical published in a European country requesting it to publish papers he had written.

7.    They photographed the registration plates of private vehicles belonging to the staff.

8.    On the pretext of washing himself one member of the team undressed in the middle of the parking lot in full sight of residents and families living in the apartments opposite.  Such conduct constitutes a provocation to the sentiments of the local people and displays contempt for the values and morals of Iraqi society.

9.    They endeavoured, by all possible means, to obtain personal information on all those employed in the Iraqi nuclear programme and in the industrial establishments that supplied it.

The Iraqi officials accompanying the team and the staffs at the sites the team visited exercised the greatest degree of self-control and behaved judiciously despite such provocative modes of behaviour.

In placing these facts before you, we are hopeful that you, the Security Council and the Executive Chairman of the Special Commission will bring this provocative and offensive behaviour to a halt and that you will issue unequivocal instructions to inspection teams visiting Iraq that they must adhere to the tasks designated by the relevant Security Council resolutions and act in accordance with the proper legal interpretation of those resolutions.  We further stress the matter that we raised at the time of the visit of Mr. Ekéus and Mr. Blix to Baghdad on 1 July 1991, namely that the selection of inspectors from countries that have particular, biased attitudes against Iraq is a major source of problems.  We do not understand the reasons that prompted the Special Commission to include 27 Americans among the 44 members of the sixth inspection team, at a time when no one can be unaware that the United States is persisting in its pursuit of a hostile and biased policy against Iraq, a policy that has no connection with the resolutions of the Security Council.

I request you to have this letter circulated as a document of the Security Council.

(Signed)  Ahmad HUSSEIN
Minister for Foreign Affairs
of the Republic of Iraq

-----

0051

# UNITED NATIONS

## Security Council

S

Distr.
GENERAL

S/23112
4 October 1991

ORIGINAL:  ENGLISH

### NOTE BY THE SECRETARY-GENERAL

The Secretary-General has the honour to transmit to the members of the Security Council the attached communication which he has received from the Director-General of the International Atomic Energy Agency (IAEA).

91-32637  2671h (E)

0052                    /...

<u>Annex</u>

<u>Letter dated 30 September 1991 from the Director-General
of the International Atomic Energy Agency addressed to
the Secretary-General</u>

    Please find attached the report of the fifth IAEA inspection in Iraq
under Security Council resolution 687 (1991).  You may deem it appropriate to
transmit the report to the members of the Security Council.  I remain of
course available with the Chief Inspector, Mr. Leslie Thorne for any
consultations you or the Council may wish to have.

                                        (<u>Signed</u>)  Hans BLIX

0053    /...

Enclosure

# REPORT ON THE FIFTH IAEA ON-SITE INPECTION
# IN IRAQ UNDER
# SECURITY COUNCIL RESOLUTION 687 (1991)

## 14 - 20 September 1991

**INTERNATIONAL ATOMIC ENERGY AGENCY**

/...

0054

1991-09-25

## REPORT ON THE FIFTH IAEA ON-SITE INSPECTION IN IRAQ
## UNDER SECURITY COUNCIL RESOLUTION 687 (1991)

### 14 - 20 September 1991

## SALIENT POINTS

The Inspection achieved the primary objective of ensuring that an inspection team was in Iraq during the period between major inspections to carry out follow-up work. This included:

- A check of all seals on nuclear material and hot cells. Two seals had been cut and one was missing. No explanation has been found, but no sinister purpose is obvious.

- An attempt to verify the inventory of nuclear material under seal. Confusion in the operators' labelling and bookwork requires more extensive work during future inspections.

- An inspection and NDA measurement of the fuel at the IRT 5000 reactor. 30% of the fuel was measured by random sampling, but 13 assemblies were inaccessible.

- Transport of the clandestinely produced plutonium.

- The taking and shipment of 115 samples.

- The shipment of a 93% enriched metal fuel plate.

- A preliminary investigation of the heavy water situation, which, however, produced no new information.

- An investigation into the extent of the chemical enrichment program, which is considered inconclusive.

- An examination of the mass spectrographs which have been been recovered.

/...

0055

## INTRODUCTION

1.  The fifth inspection in Iraq under the terms of Security Council Resolution 687 took place from 14 to 20 September 1991. The team consisted of nine inspectors, with supporting staff consisting of two health physicists, a doctor and a medical auxiliary, a photographer and a communications specialist - i.e. fifteen people overall. Nine nationalities were represented among the inspectors and thirteen overall. Eight of the nine inspectors were from the staff of the IAEA. The ninth inspector was a chemical enrichment expert from an IAEA Member State.

2.  The objectives of the inspection were limited to the carrying out of routine activities necessary as a follow-up to previous inspections. There was no intention to initiate new investigative activities, which were to be left to later, larger teams. In summary the objectives were to verify the seals which had earlier been placed on material and equipment and to verify (by the non-destructive analysis of random samples) that the material present was as declared. Additional tasks were to remove the bulk of the plutonium from the country; to take a rather large number of samples for destructive analysis, to complement previous samples; to establish the heavy water inventory; and to enquire further into the extent of Iraq's chemical enrichment program.

### Hot Cells and Related Equipment

3.  The hot cells and associated manipulators examined during the first inspection had been placed under seal during the third inspection to prevent any possibility of their further use. All such seals were checked. Out of twenty-four seals, twenty-one were found to be in good condition. Two seals were found to have been cut, but were still in place, and one seal was missing.

    The Iraqi counterparts could offer no explanation other than to suggest that thieves had been attempting to recover scrap. This is highly implausible, but there seemed to be no plausible sinister explanation. Surrounding rubble from the bombing appeared to be undisturbed, and seals which had been applied to the two neighbouring cells were still intact. The sealing blocks at the back of the cells had been removed before the first inspection and were still lying damaged in the rubble.

4.  Paper seals which had been applied to the doors of cells with reprocessing equipment in building 89 were intact. Metal seals which had been applied to the manipulators were removed for verification. The equipment in these cells is still intact, and paper sealing is not an adequate long-term protection. The removal or destruction of this equipment is necessary.

## Inventory of Nuclear Material

5.    As a result of the third and fourth inspections, several hundred tons of nuclear material had been collected into storage locations at Tuwaitha. In many cases, collection had been carried out in a hurry, without adequate paperwork. Some containers, which had been buried in the desert, were in poor condition. One of the objectives of this inspection was to go through this material and the associated records and establish a reliable inventory. The task proved even more difficult than expected and was not satisfactorily completed by the time of the team's departure. A larger team working full-time solely on this task for at least a week is required. The National Inspector for Iraq admitted that the figures he was using were from before burial took place and did not allow for any failure to recover the material totally. Random sampling therefore is not based on a known population and has no firm statistical basis. The first requirement is to establish with confidence what material is present. Until this is done, attempts to track the history of the material have no sound basis.

6.    To understand the problem, one must realize that many hundreds of drums in several warehouses and dumps are involved. Also, some of the material is in a variety of inadequate containers - such as polythene bags - without proper labelling. Even when one has a sound container in an apparently well identified stratum, one cannot be sure what material is in it. For example, one sound drum apparently containing uranium trioxide was found - on being opened - to contain no less than six different types of material ranging from ore to metal turnings. Drums labelled "uranium oxide" appeared to be full of sand. It is possible that the declared contents are beneath the sand and that, as the Iraqis claim, the sand is the result of desert burial - but this has to be established. The National Inspector was made aware of the serious concerns of the team and of the impossibility of the team's accepting the Iraqi accounts in their present state.

## Samples

7.    Destructive analysis of material sampled in previous inspections had shown in some cases a highly significant difference in results between the laboratories in the USA and the Safeguards Analytical Laboratory (SAL). A sampling and analysis expert included in the team for this mission repeated some of the sampling in order to ensure that the sampling procedures were carried out correctly. His presence proved invaluable and it is strongly recommended that a similar expert be included in future teams. A total of 115 samples were taken.

8.    In addition to routine sampling, the expert packaged and prepared for transport the plutonium which had been clandestinely produced from diverted uranium and later declared to inspectors. A small quantity of highly diluted material remains together with 33 sealed ampoules of plutonium-238 and six of plutonium-239. These are labelled and in the form in which they were originally shipped from the Amersham (UK) supplier. In all, 4.868 grams of plutonium have now been taken out of the country, leaving only 0.274 gram of plutonium.

0057...

**Fuel Measurements**

9.      Previous Inspections had raised several Important questions about the history of the fuel associated with the IRT 5000 reactor. These questions related both to the Irradiated fuel still In the core, the reactor pool and the spent fuel store and to the unirradiated fuel in the store known as location A. A major objective of this inspection was to attempt to measure by non-destructive means the activity of this fuel and, from an analysis of the measurements, to determine the history of the Irradiated fuel. Knowing Its history would be Important In determining whether clandestine Irradiation had taken place and in estimating the extent of possible plutonium production. Non-destructive analysis of the fresh fuel would establish whether any removal of material may have taken place.

10.     As a result of Intensive work in very difficult conditions, It was possible to measure 15 assemblies of 93 % enrichment and two natural uranium assemblies ( approximately 30% of the Irradiated fuel) and to item-count the IRT 5000 and Tamuz reactor fresh fuel. Measurement of all the Irradiated fuel was not possible, owing to high radiation levels caused by low water levels In the IRT 5000 reactor core and the storage locations. The low water level In the core prevented 13 of the fuel assemblies being lifted to more accessible measuring positions. Twenty-two of the remaining 63 assemblies In the pond and spent fuel store were measured on a random basis. The low water level In storage location B led to radiation levels of 50mSv/hr(5R/hr) at some of the working surfaces. A firm request was made to the Iraqi counterpart to increase the water level and to provide water treatment In a recommended form. On the positive side it must be recorded that the reactor core pond had been cleaned, so that visual examination of the fuel is much easier now than during previous Inspections.

11.     Detailed analysis of the measurements will take time. As a complement to the non-destructive measurements, one plate from the Tamuz fuel was packaged and removed to the IAEA laboratories at Selbersdorf, near Vienna.

12.     During item-counting of the fresh fuel, two of the Soviet-type fuel assemblies were found to have had the top and bottom inert parts cut off. The Iraqi counterpart was asked for an explanation and gave the one which he claimed had been given to the first Inspection team - I.e. that this had been done by mistake in the immediate aftermath of the first attack, when staff were trying to remove the fuel from the reactor site and could not get the fuel Into the container. He volunteered that It was "a stupid thing to do", but cited the extremely excited condition of the personnel following the attack. IAEA records of the safeguards Inspection in November show that the fuel was Intact at that time, which is In line with the claim that the cutting was recent. However, the cuts seem to be rather more clean and precise than the cuts which a panic situation would produce. The evidence Is Inconclusive as between the Iraqi explanation and the hypothesis that the cutting was a preliminary to removal of the highly enriched component of the assembly.

0058                    /...

## Heavy Water

13. Questions were formally put relating to the quantity and location of heavy water. Three tons at least were known to have been supplied to Iraq in 1980. The counterpart replied that the required information had been given to the first inspection team, but there is no record of this. The counterpart stated that the heavy water had been stored at the Tamuz site and had not been used, owing to destruction of the Tamuz 1 reactor in 1981. During the bombing this year, the tank containing the heavy water split and the water escaped. The team were shown the tank in the bombed remains of the reactor; its condition was as described by the Iraqis. On the other hand, there is no way after such a long time of taking meaningful samples of the debris in order to establish whether the heavy water had been removed prior to the bombing. The question of quantity and location must remain open. The existence of any other heavy water was firmly denied.

## Chemical Enrichment

14. Questions about the chemical enrichment program were put to the Iraqis at a formal meeting and were followed by visits to the site of the experimental facilities. The meeting produced no fresh information. The inspection of the site also failed to provide fresh information, the site having been cleared after being bombed. No trace remained of any equipment and, although smears were taken of the floors, evidence of the use of scrubbing machines suggests that these will not produce meaningful results.

15. The chemical enrichment expert who was a member of the team is of the opinion that a far from full disclosure has been made and that other facilities must exist. However, no evidence was presented to the other members of the team to support this belief.

## Mass Spectrometers

16. The team had been assigned the task of checking the situation regarding mass spectrometers. One had been recovered from the rubble and the remains were inspected at Tuwaitha. This machine cannot be re-used. Four other machines were declared to be in existence, but were stated to have been so damaged when being recovered after the bombing that they were unusable. They were stored at the Geological Institute in Baghdad. A visit was paid to this site by the mass spectrometer expert on the team. Two of the machines (THQ machines) were from the Tarmiya site, where they were declared to have been used for product monitoring. Of the other two machines (MAT 26 machines), one had been used for work with gases (probably UF6), and one for work with solids. The wiring had been damaged, but they were otherwise in good condition and - in the opinion of the expert - could be rebuilt and used. The Iraqis expressed a wish to transfer the machines to institutes where they could be put to good use.

0059        /...

**Removal of Fuel**

47.     Regarding the fuel which was to be removed from Iraq, the question was raised of insurance and legal responsibility for that fuel while it was being moved in Iraq. Mr Sami Al-Araji agreed that this was clearly Iraq's responsibility. Iraq would be responsible for safety and legal aspects until the fuel was loaded into the aircraft. He was keen for Iraq to be responsible for as much as possible in order to reduce costs for which Iraq would ultimately be charged. He even offered to transport any material to any other country.

**Site Clearance**

48.     The Iraqis expressed an urgent desire to proceed with site clearance and renovation. They cited the psychological effect upon site staff as a reason. To anyone who has spent an appreciable time at this site, the reason is certainly plausible. The Iraqis were told that, while there would be no objection in principle to the removal of bombed structures, the Agency/Special Commission must be informed in advance so that the work could be authorized and adequately monitored.

**Equipment**

49.     No attempt was made to inspect equipment recovered by the third and fourth inspection teams. This is to be done by a later team with suitable experts. The Iraqis expressed a strong wish to dispose of all recovered equipment as soon as possible, citing problems of security with the present dump sites. On the lines of the response given with regard to site clearance (see previous paragraph), the Iraqis were told that any proposals must be submitted in advance so that due consideration could be given to them.

**Standards**

20.     Questions relating to analytical standards were asked. The Iraqis emphatically denied that they had any foreign analytical standards. They explained that they had tried to obtain some in 1985 or thereabouts but had met with an export embargo. As a result, they had had to generate their own secondary analytical standards.

-----

0060

원 본

# 외 무 부

종 별 :

번 호 : UNW-3334

일 시 : 91 1015 1700

수 신 : 장 관(연일,중동일,기정)

발 신 : 주 유엔 대사

제 목 : 안보리 (이락 석유수출문제)

1. 안보리 대이락 제재위는 금 10.15 안보리결의 706,712 호 이행과 관련 이락 석유수출, 민수필수품목 수입을 위한 절차요강을 채택한바, 동 상세는 당관에서 입수한 동별첨 자료 참조바람.

2. 한편 당관 원참사관이 오지리(제재위 의장국) G.JANDL 서기관으로부터 금일 탐문한 사항은 다음과같음.

가. 오지리대표부는 10.14 상기 절차요강문제 관련 이락측과 접촉하였으나, 이락이 안보리가 부과하는 제반조건하에서 석유수출을 추진할 것인지에 관한 공식적인 최종 입장 표명은 없는 상태임.

나. 다만, 이락측은 본건 절차요강 자체에 대해서는 비교적 적극적인 반응을 보였으며, 시행상의 신축성을 강조함.

다. 현재 터키송유관 사용료 문제와 관련 이락, 터어키간에 이견이 있는바, 양측간에 합의가 이루어진다면 이락은 결국 석유를 수출키로 결정할것으로 보임.

첨부:안보리 제재위 절차요강 및 NYT 지 기사:UNW(F)-650 끝

(대사 노창희-국장)

예고:91.12.31. 까지

국기국     차관     1차보     2차보     중아국     분석관     청와대     안기부

SECURITY COUNCIL COMMITTEE ESTABLISHED
BY RESOLUTION 661 (19▦ CONCERNING
THE SITUATION BETWEEN IRAQ AND KUWAIT

S/AC.25/1991/WP.2/Rev.1
11 Octob▦ 991
ORIGINAL ENGLISH

井 변청

*UNW(TI)-650  11015  1700*
*(연월. 중동일. 기정)*
*총 120h*

Chairman's Draft

Procedures to be employed by the Security Council Committee
established by resolution 661 (1990) concerning the situation
between Iraq and Kuwait in the discharge of its responsibilities
under Security Council resolutions 706 (1991) and 712 (1991)

I. Preparatory steps:

1.  The Committee will select, upon recommendation by the
    Secretariat, three independent experts in international oil
    trade as "overseers" at United Nations headquarters, and
    entrust them with the authority to approve or reject oil sale
    contracts on behalf of the Committee. The overseers will be
    authorized to correspond with applicants as needed. The
    nomination of three persons will ensure a 24-hour availability
    for contract approvals.

2.  Other experts, agents and inspectors (as required below) will
    be appointed by the Secretary-General. The Committee will take
    note of these appointments.

..3. States may, if they so wish, forward to the Committee a list
    of national oil purchasers (private companies, State owned
    companies, State agencies, ministries, etc.) authorized to
    communicate with the overseer. Once the Committee has taken
    note of these lists and passed them on to the overseer, these
    purchasers are entitled to communicate directly with the
    overseer (see II.A.3 below). If States do not submit such a
    list, or if a certain purchaser is not included in the list,
    the communication with the overseer has to go via the
    Permanent Mission in New York.

*12-1*

4. For the purpose of para. II.A.3 below, a standard application form will be elaborated by the Committee and circulated among all States. States and national oil purchasers shall use only these standard application forms.

5. The Secretariat will set up a new fax line (No. ...) to be used exclusively for correspondence with regard to oil transactions. Applicants are requested to send their relevant applications and relating correspondence only via this fax line. Other correspondence with the Committee shall go through the already existing channels.

6. Iraq and Turkey will have to conclude an arrangement on the price and payment modalities for the use of Turkish oil installations. Once this arrangement is concluded, it has to be forwarded to the Committee which will take note of it. UN agents will check the implementation of this arrangement and report periodically to the Committee.

7. Monitoring of delivery to Iraq of foodstuffs, medicines, and materials and supplies for essential civilian needs will be done by independent inspection agents appointed by an appropriate UN programme or orgaization, such as, for example, the Office for Project Services (OPS). Monitoring of the distribution of these goods will be arranged by the Executive Delegate in cooperation with relevant UN programmes and organizations, including appropriate humanitarian NGOs. The Committee will be informed about the relevant arrangements, including those for the purpose of para. III.A.11 below.

8. Upon recommendation by the Secretariat, the Committee will nominate an expert (a staff member of one of the UN programmes or organizations) who will act as an aide to the Committee for the purposes of para. III.A.8 below.

/ 2 - 2

## II. Sales of Iraqi oil and oil products:

### A. sales of Iraqi oil:

1. SOMO signs a contract with the purchaser. The contract has to include the provisions as specified in para. 58 of the SG's report.

2. UN agents at SOMO review the contracts to assure compliance with the provisions of para. 58 of the SG's report and forward by fax copies of the approvable contracts, supporting documents, and their independent reports to the overseer in New York.

3. The national oil purchaser or the Mission of the State of purchase forwards by fax a formal request (standard application form) for approval to the Committee, together with a copy of the contract and all other supporting documents.

4. The overseer reviews the contract and supporting documents to ensure that:
   - they comply with para. 58 of the SG's report, including that a confirmed irrevocable letter of credit is opended providing for payment into the escrow account;
   - the conditions of payment envisaged in the letters of credit are in conformity with existing market practices;
   - they do not appear to contain any attempt of fraud or deception;
   - the transaction's pricing is consistent with world prices and market trends; and
   - the transaction does not exceed the limits imposed by Res. 706 (1991) and 712 (1991).

12-3

5. If the contract and supporting documents are found to be in order, the overseer, on behalf of the Committee, approves the sale (within the shortest period of time possible, at the maximum 24 hours) and informs by fax the approved national oil purchaser or the Mission concerned, as well as SOMO.

6. The overseer sends his notification of sales approval, together with a copy of the contract, supporting documents, and the report of the UN agent at SOMO, by fax to the inspector at Ceyhan who will authorize loading only after these documents are in his posession.

7. Depending on the number of applications, the overseer reports to the Committee, in a structured and standardized manner, at least twice a week on contracts approved by him (including the cumulative quantity and value of oil authorized for export), and informs the SG accordingly.

8. The oil is pumped into storage tanks. Agents at the pipeline check the pumping. Subject to their confirmation, the oil can be loaded on ships and the ships can leave the terminal. The agents will have the authority to prohibit the delivery of the oil if there is any evidence of irregularity.

9. The agents report to the Committee on their assessment of the pumping and loading.

10. The purchaser makes payment into the escrow account.

11. Twice a week, the SG forwards statements of the escrow account, including outlines of anticipated future obligations, to the Committee.

*12 - 4*

### B. Sales of Iraqi oil products:

The regime for the sale of oil products will be broadly similar
to that described above, but the precise arrangements will be
elaborated at a later stage, as and when the need arises.

12 - 5

0066

III. Purchase by Iraq of foodstuffs, medicines, and materials and supplies for essential civilian needs:

A. Purchase by Iraq of foodstuffs, medicines, and materials and supplies for essential civilian needs, to be financed from the escrow account:

1. Iraq sends a categorized list of relevant requirements to the Executive Delegate. (Preferably, a two-months list, quantity- and value-oriented.) If Iraq intends to finance also medicines from the escrow account, these should to be mentioned in general terms on the list, together with their value. The overall value of the list must not exceed that part of the amount authorized by the Committee, in accordance with para. 2 of res. 712 (1991), which is available for humanitarian purchases.

2. The Executive Delegate forwards the list (revised by him, if necessary) to the Committee.

3. The Committee takes action on the list and forwards to the SG and the Executive Delegate the list as approved. (The first list will be taken up at a meeting of the Committee; subject to agreement, later lists might be dealt with under a no-objection procedure.)

4. The SG will make the list known to all States.

5. The Executive Delegate informs Iraq about the clearance.

6. Iraq signs a contract with the exporter, in accordance with normal commercial practice and the relevant SC resolutions.

12-6

7. a) Medicines:

The Mission of the exporter's country informs the Committee of the exporter's wish to be paid from the escrow account. A copy of the relevant contract has to be attached to this communication.

b) Foodstuffs:

The Permanent Mission of the exporter's country notifies the Committee. This notification has to contain the information that the exporter wants to be paid from the escrow account. A copy of the relevant contract has to be attached to this notification.

c) Materials and supplies for essential civilian needs:
The Permanent Mission of the exporter's country requests approval, under the no-objection procedure, by the Committee. This request has to contain the information that the exporter wants to be paid from the escrow account. A copy of the relevant contract has to be attached to this request.

8. An expert (aide to the Committee) checks the contracts, in particular on the price/value relationship, and informs the Chairman. His findings will be attached to the circulation note to Committee Members.

9. a) Medicines:
(i) If the contract is found in order, the Committee informs the Mission concerned and the SG that the contract has been found in order (≈ information that the exporter can expect payment from the escrow account).

/2-7

(ii) If the contract is not found in order, the Committee
informs the Mission concerned and the SG that the contract
has not been found in order (= information that the
exporter cannot expect payment from the escrow account;
but the medical supplies can - of course - be shipped
anyway if the exporter so wishes).

b) Foodstuffs:

(i)  If the contract is found in order, the Committee takes
note of the notification and informs the Permanent Mission
concerned and the SG accordingly and states that the
contract has been found in order (= information that the
exporter can expect payment from the escrow account).

(ii) If the contract is not found in order, the Committee takes
note of the notification and informs the Permanent Mission
concerned and the SG accordingly but states that the
contract has not been found in order (= information that
the exporter cannot expect payment from the escrow
account; but the foodstuffs can, of course, be shipped
anyway if the exporter so wishes).

c) Materials and supplies for essential civilian needs:

(i)  If the contract is found in order, and if the Committee
approves the shipment under the no-objection procedure, it
informs the Permanent Mission concerned and the SG about
the approval and states that the contract has been found
in order (= information that the exporter can expect
payment from the escrow account).

(ii) If the contract is not found in order, and if the
Committee (in spite of this fact) approves the shipment
under the no-objection procedure, it informs the Mission
concerned and the SG about the approval but states that
the contract has not been found in order (= information
that the exporter cannot expect payment from the escrow
account; but the goods can - of course - be shipped
anyway if the exporter so wishes).

(iii) If the Committee cannot approve the shipment (whether or
not the contract is found in order), the goods are - of
course - not allowed to be shipped.

From here on only if the contract has been found in order:

10. The SG may effect part-payment to the exporter, according
to commercial practice.

11. UN agents check the delivery (the quality, quantity,
labelling, etc.) at the unloading port and the entry
points to Iraq and report to the Committee. The agents
will have the authority to inspect the shipment documents
and - if necessary - to open and examine the contents as
needed.

12. The Committee evaluates the reports. If satisfactory, it
approves the final payment and informs the SG.

13. The SG effects final payment.

14. UN agents monitor in-country distribution and report, via
the Executive Delegate, in a consolidated manner to the
Committee.

*12 - 9*

15. The Committee evaluates these reports to ensure that equitable internal distribution is being maintained and takes appropriate action if not.

16. Twice a week, the SG forwards statements of the escrow account, including outlines of anticipated future obligations, to the Committee.

B. Purchase by Iraq of foodstuffs, medicines, and materials and supplies for essential civilian needs, to be financed from the sub-account of the escrow account:

1. According to paragraph 8 of Security Council resolution 712 (1991), imports financed from the sub-account of the escrow account, are, apart from the provision of paragraph 1 c of Security Council resolution 706 (1991), subject only to the provisions and procedures of paragraph 20 of Security Council resolution 687 (1991).

2. Monitoring (paragraph 1 c of Security Council resolution 706 (1991) will be carried out as indicated in Annex II of the SG's report.

3. Twice a week, the SG forwards statements of the sub-account of the escrow account, including outlines of anticipated future obligations, to the Committee.

/ 2 — / ○

# U.N. Says Iraq Was Moving Toward More Potent Bombs

### By WILLIAM J. BROAD

Iraq's efforts to build a hydrogen bomb, described last week by the United Nations, were further along than generally believed and would also have sharply increased the destructiveness of its atomic bombs, according to weapons experts and United Nations documents.

Because hydrogen bombs can be hundreds or thousands of times more powerful than atomic bombs and vastly more destructive, some analysts expressed alarm about the recent disclosures. America's first hydrogen bomb, exploded in 1952, was about 700 times more forceful than the atomic bomb dropped on Hiroshima in August 1945.

Overall, the Iraqi bomb program was more ambitious, advanced and deadly than had previously been suspected, analysts said. A top former intelligence official said its enterprising nature and vast scale showed that the West's intelligence failure had been extensive.

### Longer Work Was Seen

Before the Persian Gulf war, intelligence experts knew of Iraqi efforts to build an atomic bomb but made no mention of a hydrogen bomb program. Even those experts who rated Iraq's progress most highly assumed that it needed at least 2 years to begin production of crude warheads, while most others said it would take 5 to 10 years.

But from the evidence gathered by United Nations inspectors, it is now believed that Iraq could have been making atomic bombs in as little as a year.

Worse, Baghdad was apparently engaged in a broad effort to go down the thermonuclear road, producing not only hydrogen-bomb materials like lithium 6 but also computer software to predict the likelihood of thermonuclear reactions. In addition, it is now known that Iraq had acquired another key ingredient needed to unleash the latent thermonuclear forces of the atom. This is heavy water, or deuterium oxide, which United Nations officials say Iraq imported years ago.

### Fusion Process

Deuterium is a heavy form of hydrogen. When heavy water is mixed with lithium 6, the product is lithium 6 deuteride. This compound is the main component of hydrogen bombs. It undergoes nuclear fusion to give the bombs their fearsome power.

Iraq would have probably needed several years to produce a hydrogen bomb, weapons scientists said. They noted that a prerequisite for any hydrogen bomb is an atomic bomb whose extraordinary heat acts as a trigger.

But the weapons scientists added that Iraq's thermonuclear ambitions were also more immediate. Baghdad, they said, would have used small quantities of hydrogen-bomb fuel to triple or quadruple the explosive force of any atomic bomb.

Such "boosting," as it is known, is fairly easy to do. When lithium 6 is bombarded by subatomic neutrons in a nuclear reactor, a form of heavy hydrogen called tritium

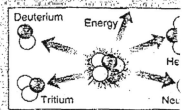

## Seeking a More Destructive Bomb

Evidence shows Iraq worked on thermonuclear reactions used to boost A-bombs and make H-bombs. The key in both cases is fusing deuterium and tritium, which are heavy forms of hydrogen.

Deuterium — Energy — He

Tritium — Neu

### GETTING THE KEY INGREDIENTS

Deuterium is easily obtained from heavy water or deuterium oxide. With more difficulty, lithium 6, a silver-white metal, becomes triti

Reactor turns lithium 6 into tritium; it is mixed with deuterium at A-bomb's core. Resulting neutron bursts speed chain reaction to make bomb more powerful.

**BOOSTED ATOMIC BOMB**

Lithium 6 is mixed with deuterium. Showers of neutrons in exploding H-bombs turns lithium i tritium, which then fuse: with deuterium, releasir huge burst of energy.

**HYDROGEN BOMB**

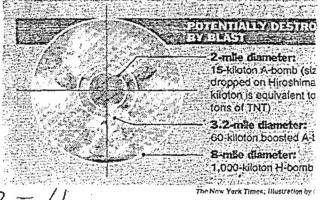

### POTENTIALLY DESTRO BY BLAST

**2-mile diameter:** 15-kiloton A-bomb (siz dropped on Hiroshima kiloton is equivalent to tons of TNT)

**3.2-mile diameter:** 60-kiloton boosted A-t

**8-mile diameter:** 1,000-kiloton H-bomb

The New York Times; Illustration by

*12 — 11*

# U.N. Says Iraq Was on Fast Track To H-Bombs and Bigger A-Bombs

Continued From Page A1

is produced. This is then added to the core of an atomic bomb, along with deuterium from heavy water.

Experts say this deuterium-tritium mixture can sharply improve the efficiency and resulting force of a chain reaction, transforming a crude atomic bomb into a weapon small enough and powerful enough to be suitable for delivery atop a missile.

United Nations officials have already disclosed that Iraq tested a surface-to-surface missile able to carry an atomic bomb as part of its program to develop nuclear weapons.

The explosive power of hydrogen bombs has no theoretical limit. And, weapons experts say, big ones are easier to build than small ones, conjuring up visions of Saddam Hussein with an arsenal of great power.

"It's really astonishing," said Dr. Theodore B. Taylor, a former designer of nuclear arms at the weapons laboratory at Los Alamos, N.M., the birthplace of the atomic and hydrogen bombs. "This shores up the idea that they had a very ambitious and extensive weapons program."

### Scientist Expresses Fear

Leonard S. Spector, an expert on the spread of nuclear arms at the Carnegie Endowment for International Peace in Washington, called the whole episode alarming.

"Iraq clearly anticipated having a very big program that could graduate to hydrogen bombs," he said in an interview. "The Iraqi work wasn't sequential, as has been the case in lots of other places. They were doing everything in parallel."

United Nations officials had previously said that the International Atomic Energy Agency, a specialized agency based in Vienna, was trying to track down hundreds of pounds of heavy water that Iraq imported years ago. As a

sign of hydrogen-bomb work, heavy water is ambiguous since it also has uses in nuclear reactors.

But a week ago today, David Kay, chief of the agency's inspection team in Iraq, told reporters that several of the documents his team had seized indicated that Iraq had already produced several pounds of lithium 6 and that another document referred to a plan to make about 220 pounds a year. Lithium 6 has no significant use other than in bomb manufacturing. This amount of lithium 6, Mr. Kay said, was enough to "raise real concern about weapons production."

### Excess of Lithium 6

Several weapons experts, in interviews, said 220 pounds a year was probably more lithium 6 than was needed for simple boosting and suggested an intention by Baghdad to build hydrogen bombs.

For boosting, 220 pounds of lithium 6 could produce enough tritium for dozens to thousands of atomic bombs depending on the power of the nuclear reactor used as a neutron source to turn it into tritium, Dr. Taylor said.

Experts estimate that the force of this hydrogen bomb would have been equal to somewhere between a million and 10 million tons of high explosives, depending on the bomb's design. The atomic bomb that destroyed Hiroshima had a strength equivalent to 15,000 tons of high explosives.

Lithium, soft and silver-white, is the lightest known metal — more abundant in the earth's crust than lead or tin. In nature, it occurs as a mixture of isotopes, with lithium 6 accounting for roughly 7 percent and lithium 7, roughly 93 percent of the deposits.

Weapons consultants said the design of a boosted atomic bomb or a true hydrogen bomb would have required advanced computer simulations that were apparently under development in Iraq at Al Atheer, 40 miles south of Baghdad.

12-12

주　국　련　대　표　부

91.10.17.

주국련20313-　**775**

수신　장관

참조　국제기구국장 , 중동아프리카국장

제목　걸프사태(안보리)


표제관련 , 안보리문서를 별첨과 같이 송부합니다.


첨　부 : 상기문서. 끝.

1991. 10. 17

주　국　련　대　사

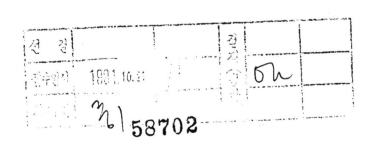

제58702

0074

# UNITED NATIONS

 **Security Council**

Distr.
GENERAL

S/23118
7 October 1991

ORIGINAL: ENGLISH

---

LETTER DATED 7 OCTOBER 1991 FROM THE PRESIDENT OF THE
SECURITY COUNCIL ADDRESSED TO THE SECRETARY-GENERAL

The members of the Security Council have carried out the review, in informal consultations held on 7 October 1991, in accordance with the provisions of resolution 689 (1991), regarding the question of termination or continuation of the United Nations Iraq-Kuwait Observation Mission, as well as of its modalities, in the light of your report (S/23106 and Add.1).

I have the honour to inform you that the members concur with your recommendation, particularly in paragraph 30 of your report.

(Signed)   Chinmaya Rajaninath GHAREKHAN
President of the Security Council

-----

91-32857   2674h (E)

0075

**Security Council**

Distr.
GENERAL

S/23122
8 October 1991

ORIGINAL:  ENGLISH

### NOTE BY THE SECRETARY-GENERAL

The Secretary-General has the honour to transmit to the members of the Security Council the attached communication which he has received from the Director-General of the International Atomic Energy Agency (IAEA).

91-33107  2679h (E)                                                                0076/...

## Annex

### Letter dated 3 October 1991 from the Director-General of the International Atomic Energy Agency addressed to the Secretary-General

Please find attached the first report of the sixth IAEA inspection in Iraq under Security Council resolution 687 (1991).  You may deem it appropriate to transmit the report to the members of the Security Council.  I remain, of course, available with the Chief Inspector, Mr. David Kay, for any consultations you or the Council may wish to have.

(Signed)  Hans BLIX

0077

/...

<u>Enclosure</u>

First report on the sixth IAEA on-site inspection in Iraq
under Security Council resolution 687 (1991)
22-30 September 1991

## Introduction

1.    The following report is based on a field analysis of documents obtained, photographed or seen during inspections of Iraqi establishments visited by the sixth IAEA inspection team. Most of the important documents were obtained, photographed or seen during visits to two establishments, the Nuclear Design Center and Petrochemical Three (PC-3) Headquarters, on 23 and 24 September 1991 respectively.  The Appendix provides a chronology of activities.

2.    The documents obtained or photographed by the team are for the greater part in Arabic, and there has been limited time for scanning. Only a few documents - although some very important ones - have so far been completely translated. Accordingly, a follow-up report will be issued after a thorough analysis of all the documentary material removed from Iraq.

## Summary

3.    The sixth IAEA inspection team obtained conclusive evidence that the Government of Iraq had a program for developing an implosion-type nuclear weapon, and it found documents linking this program - code-named "Petrochemical Three " (PC-3) - to Iraq's Ministry of Industry and Military Industrialization, the Iraqi Atomic Energy Commission (IAEC) and Iraq's Ministry of Defense. Documents were found showing that the nuclear weapons program was supported by broad-based international procurement efforts.  Contrary to Iraq's claims of having only a peaceful nuclear program, the team found documents showing that Iraq had been working on the revision of a nuclear weapons design and one linking the IAEC to work on a surface-to-surface missile project - presumably the intended delivery system for their nuclear weapon.

## PC-3 reports on Al Atheer

4.    On the basis largely of top-secret progress reports found on 23 September 1991, the team concludes that Iraq was engaged in a broad-based effort to design and develop an implosion-type nuclear weapon. The documents, which cover a period up to 31 May 1990, describe nuclear weapons development experiments involving - for example - neutron

0078

/...

neutron initiators, enriched-uranium cores, reflectors, high-explosive lenses and electronic firing sets. One document points to Iraqi success in the machining of nuclear weapons components from natural uranium, but it is not clear from the document whether Iraq had enough highly enriched uranium for an actual explosive device.

5.      One document links the Al Qa Qaa High Explosives and Propellant Facility to the program. Even more importantly, it shows clearly that nuclear weapons design work was conducted at Al Atheer - a facility which Iraq claims to have had no nuclear connection. A top-secret report states that the objective of the Al Atheer facility was to design and produce a nuclear device. Previous teams carrying out inspections under Security Council resolution 687 concluded that the Al Atheer facility was most probably to be used for nuclear weapons component production, high-explosive experiments and device assembly.

6.      The inspection team also found evidence of Iraqi work on sophisticated computer codes used in the development of nuclear weapons, including one- and two-dimensional hydrodynamic and neutronic models which simulate the behaviour of nuclear weapons as they are being fired. Some of these sophisticated codes had been modified by Iraq before being used at Al Atheer. The document states that, as of June 1990, the basic design for Iraq's nuclear explosives device had gone through five modifications.

**Additional evidence of intention to develop nuclear weapons**

7.      The reports on Al Atheer appear to be the most important of those found in four boxes full of classified Iraqi papers.[1] The team also found a document suggesting the parallel development of a missile delivery system for the ongoing nuclear weapons program; in the document, the Ministry of Defense instructed the IAEC to postpone an experiment until after surface-to-surface missile testing.

8.      Other documents contain evidence that since 1981 Iraq intended to produce enriched uranium by methods other than electromagnetic isotope separation. Specifically, the documents showed that Iraq explored gaseous diffusion and centrifuge enrichment techniques as late as 1988 and as early as 1982, respectively. The documents included an IAEC-accredited study in the field of nuclear implosion physics —another clear indication of nuclear weapons development intentions.

---

[1]      It should be recalled, however, that the Government of Iraq seized these boxes from the inspection team on 23 September and has still not returned all of the documents which were in them. Notes by the team on some of these documents indicate that they contained additional information on the Iraqi nuclear weapons program.

0079   /...

**Procurement activities**

9.      On the basis of documents seen during the inspection, the team believes that Iraq conducted substantial nuclear-weapons-related procurement from foreign sources. Catalogues from numerous suppliers were found at the PC-3 Headquarters, many of them translated into Arabic. However, because of the team's hasty exit from this establishment before being detained in a parking lot, much information was lost. Although - as just indicated - the team believes that the procurement in question was in support of the nuclear weapons program, it must be stressed that most items will probably prove to have been innocuous, multi-use items for which export licences were not needed and/or which were dispatched before imposition of the United Nations trade embargo.

10.     From the documents seen it is evident that Iraq drew up lists of approved suppliers whose products would meet the program's technical specifications. On-site inspections of procured equipment and material have already shown that items supplied to the IAEC came from many countries.

11.     The team found evidence that, realizing that large-scale purchasing abroad could attract outside attention, the Iraqi authorities devised cover explanations for purchases. In this connection, a country-wide survey of the types and amounts of the equipment required for the civilian sector was recommended, the idea being that indigenously produced items should be used in the civilian sector, while high-quality imported items bearing the same general descriptions would be used for the clandestine nuclear weapons program.

12.     The team noted that the procurement of machinery had often been coupled with relevant on-the-spot training of Iraqi engineers by the manufacturer. In the case of machinery such as lathes and milling machines, test pieces had sometimes been ordered for the validation of technical specifications and computer numerical control software had sometimes been obtained.

13.     At the PC-3 Headquarters, the team found many volumes of documents related to procurement for the Iraqi nuclear weapons program. A number of cover names used by Iraq in its procurement activities have been identified, and it is expected that this number will grow as further procurement records are translated.

**Administration of the nuclear weapons program**

14.     From the documentation seen by it, the team concluded that the Iraqi nuclear weapons program was under the general control of the Ministry of Industry and Military Industrialization, with specific control assigned to PC-3. The team found numerous classified

0080     /...

communications with the IAEC heading and a sub-heading identifying PC-3, which confirms that some part of the IAEC was involved in the nuclear weapons program. In this connection it should be noted that the IAEC collaborated with the Iraqi Ministry of Defense on defense-related projects. The team has compiled a list of project activities to be followed up in the future.

15.     The PC-3 employee lists show that Dr. Jaffar Dhia Jaffar was a senior administrator for the program. Similar documentation shows that Dr. Jaffar was intimately linked to the uranium enrichment program. The team accordingly believes that Dr. Jaffar had the lead technical and administrative responsibility for the nuclear weapons program as a whole - despite his repeated claims that no such program existed.

## Iraq's obstructing of inspectors

16.     Despite the success of the team in obtaining sensitive, classified documentation on Iraq's nuclear weapons program, one may never discover the true extent of that program. This is due partly to the fact that the Iraqi authorities confiscated documents collected on the first inspection day, despite strong protests by the team's Chief Inspector and the representative of the United Nations Special Commission (UNSCOM). Furthermore, it was obvious after reviewing the material returned to the team that some documents were missing. The team believes that, during the period of nearly seven hours before the return of the documents, the Iraqi authorities reviewed them, withholding the most sensitive ones. Although there might be other explanations, in the light of the continued attempts to conceal the true extent of Iraq's nuclear weapons program and of some very recent correspondence relevant to the programme found at one site, the question remains open whether Iraq has given up its nuclear weapons aspirations.

## Continuing Iraqi non-compliance with Security Council resolutions

17.     On the basis of the above, it is concluded that the documents found by the team clearly demonstrate that the Government of Iraq is in violation of Security Council resolutions 687 and 707. This is underscored by the fact that Iraq detained the inspectors and confiscated documents which had been legitimately collected.

18.     Specifically, the following maybe noted:

-       Iraq had - despite its statements to the contrary - a complex, comprehensive nuclear weapons development program characterized by parallel approaches to fissile material production and by theoretical/experimental design work.

0081      /...

-   Iraq still has substantial facilities which were part of the clandestine program and which have not been declared.

-   Iraq has removed significant documentary material and equipment from identified nuclear program sites · including some documentary material removed shortly before the arrival of the team.

19. Iraq has violated the privileges and immunities to which the inspectors were entitled:

-   It detained the team for five hours on the first inspection day,

-   It confiscated all documents collected by the team during the first inspection visit,

-   It interrupted access to the second inspection site before the team had completed its work.

-   It detained the team for 96 hours in the parking lot next to the second inspection site.

-   it opened official mail addressed to the team's Chief Inspector and to the UNSCOM representative.

20. From the evidence which the team has obtained and from the treatment of the team it is concluded that there was repeated and wilful non-compliance with Security Council resolutions 687 and 707 and violation of the UN/IAEA-specified privileges and immunities agreed to by the Government of Iraq.

0082

/...

# Appendix

## Chronology of Team Activities

The following is a general chronology of the activities of the 6th IAEA nuclear inspection team:

| Date | Time | Activity |
|------|------|----------|
| 91/09/22 | 1000 | Arrive Baghdad from Bahrain |
| 91/09/23 | 0559 | Arrive at first inspection site - the Nuclear Design Center |
| 91/09/23 | 1006 | Four boxes of classified IAEC documents found in basement of Nuclear Design Center |
| 91/09/23 | 1545 | Team attempts to depart first site |
| 91/09/23 | 1600 | First deadline for letting team depart site expires |
| 91/09/23 | 1630 | Iraqi authorities begin to review documents removed by team |
| 91/09/23 | 1825 | Dr. Jaffar arrives and demands a list of all documents |
| 91/09/23 | 1830 | Second deadline given by Chief Inspector to grant release of team expires |
| 91/09/23 | 1900 | Iraqi authorities confiscate documents collected by the team as the inspectors prepare to leave the facility |
| 91/09/24 | 0200 | Iraqi authorities return most, but not all - of the documents collected at the Nuclear Design Center |
| 91/09/24 | 0620 | Arrive at second inspection site, the Headquarters of the Petrochemical Three program |
| 91/09/24 | 1050 | Iraqi authorities demand that all work stop and that the team leave immediately |
| 91/09/24 | 1230 | Dr. Jaffar arrives and demands all documents and film. Stalemate ensues |
| 91/09/27 | 1530 | During continued detainment of the team, a fire is noted on the top floor of one of the two target buildings |
| 91/09/28 | 0546 | Team is released from parking lot and returns to hotel |
| 91/09/28 | 0600-1900 | IAEA-Iraqi inventory and review of documents collected from second inspection site |

0083

| 91/09/29 | 0730 | Depart for final day of inspections |
| 91/09/29 | 0800-0830 | Search of warehouse for documents |
| 91/09/29 | 0930-1300 | Search of the IAEC Training Center |
| 91/09/29 | 1330-1830 | Search of the Reactor Siting and Planning Building |
| 91/09/29 | 1630-1700 | Search of grounds of Meeting House |
| 91/09/30 | 1230 | Depart Iraq for Bahrain |

0084                    /...

Annex to the First Report on the On-site Inspection
in Iraq under Security Council resolution 687 (1991)
22 - 30 September 1991


IMPORTANT NOTICE


This Annex is a translation from Arabic of an Iraqi report found by the 6th
Agency Inspection team on Monday, 23 September 1991 during an Inspection
in an Iraqi Atomic Energy Commission building in dowtown Baghdad.  Its title
is

"Al-Athir [Al-Atheer] Plant Progress Report
for the period 1 January 1990 to 31 May 1990"


0085

/...

((BEGIN TEXT))

1/17

((COVER PAGE))

TOP SECRET - 5 ((SIC))

REPRODUCTION
FORBIDDEN

MINISTRY OF INDUSTRY AND INDUSTRIALIZATION
PETROCHEMICAL PROJECT
3

((END COVER PAGE))

((PAGE 2))

MINISTRY OF INDUSTRY AND INDUSTRIALIZATION
PETROCHEMICAL PROJECT -3-

TITLE: AL-ATHIR PLANT PROGRESS REPORT FOR THE
PERIOD FROM 1 JANUARY 1990 TO 31 MAY 1990

PREPARED BY: HEADQUARTERS, AL-ATHIR PLANT OFFICE

((MOSLEM DATE EQUIVALENT WRITTEN IN LONGHAND))

((END PAGE 2))

((PAGE 3))

THE REPUBLIC OF IRAQ

MINISTRY OF INDUSTRY AND MILITARY INDUSTRIALIZATION
AL-ATHIR PLANT

NUMBER:    172S/697
DATE:      17/11/1410 ((MOSLEM CALENDAR))
DATE:      11 NOVEMBER 1990

TOP SECRET

TO:    DOCTOR NU'MAN SA'D-AL DIN AL-NU 'AIMI
SUBJECT: PROGRESS REPORT

        REFERENCE YOUR LETTER NUMBER M/N 14 DATED 27 MAY
1990.

        WE ENCLOSE HEREWITH A PROGRESS REPORT FOR THE AL-
ATHIR PLANT FOR 1 JANUARY 1990 TO 31 MAY 1990.

        PLEASE NOTE AND TAKE NECESSARY MEASURES. REGARDS.

HIKMAT NU'AIM AL-HILU ((OR JILU?))
ASSISTANT DIRECTOR GENERAL
9 JUNE 1990

COPY TO: DIRECTOR GENERAL. PLEASE NOTE. REGARDS.

((END PAGE 3))

0086/...

2/17

((PAGE 4))

## ACCOMPLISHMENTS OF THE AL-ATHIR PLANT
## FOR THE PERIOD
## 1 JANUARY 1990 TO 31 MAY 1990

((END PAGE 4))

((PAGE 5))

## CONTENTS

((END PAGE 5))

SECRET

0087

/...

S E C R E T

((PAGE 6 TO END))


## AL-ATHIR PLANT PROGRESS REPORT FOR THE PERIOD
## 1 JANUARY 1990 TO 31 MAY 1990


THE GOAL OF THE AL-ATHIR PLANT PROGRAM IS THE DESIGN AND MANUFACTURE OF THE MECHANISM WHICH IS COMPOSED OF THE FOLLOWING PRINCIPAL PARTS:

NUCLEAR INITIATOR (POLONIUM-210 METAL/BERYLLIUM)
CORE (ENRICHED URANIUM METAL)
REFLECTOR (NATURAL URANIUM METAL)
TAMPER (HARDENED IRON)
EXPLOSIVE LENSES (PREPARED BY THE AL-QA' QA' GENERAL ESTABLISHMENT)
ELECTRONIC SYSTEMS (TRIGGERING, CONTROL AND GUIDANCE)

DURING THIS PERIOD A NUMBER OF ACCOMPLISHMENTS WERE ACHIEVED ON BOTH THE THEORETICAL AND PRACTICAL LEVEL. IN LIGHT OF THESE RESULTS, PREPARATIONS ARE UNDERWAY TO UPDATE THE BASIC DESIGN OF THE MECHANISM (FIFTH UPDATE) WHICH INCLUDES VARIOUS OPTIONS AND THE PREFERRED OPTION. THESE RESULTS CAN BE SUMMARIZED AS FOLLOWS:

THEORETICAL CALCULATIONS:

THE THEORETICAL CALCULATIONS ARE AIMED AT COMING UP WITH DESIGNS FOR THE IMPLOSION MECHANISM. IN ORDER TO ACCOMPLISH THIS MISSION THERE MUST BE A CLEAR AND PRECISE UNDERSTANDING OF MULTIPLE ASPECTS OF PHYSICS. THERE ALSO MUST BE A SET OF INTEGRATED CALCULATIONS FOR CONVERTING THE THEORETICAL CONCEPT INTO A PRACTICAL REALITY THROUGH COMPUTATIONS AND DESIGNS WHICH CAN BE APPLIED. THESE INCLUDE THE FOLLOWING:

1. IN THE AREA OF GENERATING THEORETICAL EQUATIONS OF STATE, A GENERAL EQUATION OF STATE WAS DERIVED WHICH USED THE "BARNES" (?) MODEL FOR PRESSURE COMBINED WITH THE THOMAS-FERMI-DIRAC MODEL UNDER HIGH PRESSURE. THIS

S E C R E T

0088

/...

S E C R E T

EQUATION OF STATE WAS COMPARED WITH ANOTHER ANALYTICAL EQUATION AND THE RESULTS SHOWED THAT THE "BARNES" EQUATION OF STATE IS CLOSER TO PRACTICAL RESULTS FOR URANIUM. THERE IS ALSO A CORRELATION BETWEEN THE TWO EQUATIONS IN A HIGH PRESSURE REGIME.

2.      IN THE AREA OF THEORETICAL MODELS, A PLIANT-FLEXIBLE BEHAVIOR AND MODEL FOR STRESSES WERE INSERTED INTO THE COMPUTATION, WHICH SOLVED THE ONE-DIMENSIONAL HYDRODYNAMIC EQUATIONS.

3.      IN THE AREA OF TWO-DIMENSIONAL HYDRODYNAMIC PROGRAMS, PROGRAMS WERE DEVELOPED WHICH SOLVED THE TWO-DIMENSIONAL HYDRODYNAMIC EQUATIONS IN ORDER TO TAKE INTO CONSIDERATION THE DEVELOPMENT OF DISTORTIONS OVER A PERIOD OF TIME. THIS NEW POSSIBILITY OF THE PROGRAM WAS TESTED IN EXPERIMENTS USING FLYING METAL PLATES TO STUDY THE EFFECT OF ELASTICITY AND FLEXIBILITY ON THE WAY IN WHICH DISTORTIONS GROW, AS WELL AS THE EFFECT OF OTHER RELEVANT FACTORS PREPARATORY TO USING THE SAME CONCEPTS IN A STUDY OF SPHERICAL SYSTEMS AND DESIGN OPTIONS. THESE PROGRAMS WERE USED IN AN INITIAL STUDY OF THE STABILITY OF SOME DESIGN OPTIONS PREPARATORY TO STUDY OF THIS SUBJECT IN A MORE DETAILED MANNER. IN THE SAME AREA, A LOCAL PROGRAM WAS COMPLETED WHICH SOLVED THE TWO-DIMENSIONAL HYDRODYNAMIC EQUATIONS AND SOME INITIAL TESTS WERE CONDUCTED ON IT. TESTS ARE NOW BEING CONDUCTED UNDER CONDITIONS IN WHICH THE ((PROGRAM'S)) EFFECTIVENESS IS MORE DIFFICULT TO CONFIRM.

4.      IN THE AREA OF COMBINED HYDRODYNAMIC-NEUTRONIC PROGRAMS AND CALCULATIONS, A PROGRAM WAS DEVELOPED SO THAT IT WOULD BE POSSIBLE TO CALCULATE A NUMBER OF NEUTRONIC GENERATIONS WHICH ARE PRODUCED WHEN LARGE AMOUNTS OF ENERGY ARE LIBERATED FROM THE SYSTEMS WHOSE TOTAL ENERGY HAD PREVIOUSLY BEEN CALCULATED BY USING THE SAME PROGRAMS. TWO COMPUTATIONS WERE ALSO COMPLETED WHICH CARRIED OUT THE COMBINED HYDRODYNAMIC-NEUTRONIC CALCULATIONS. BOTH PROGRAMS USE A HYDRODYNAMIC PROGRAM WHICH HAD BEEN WRITTEN LOCALLY AND WHICH RELIED ON A WELL-KNOWN METHOD IN SOLVING HYDRODYNAMIC EQUATIONS. BY USING THESE INTER-RELATED PROGRAMME,

S E C R E T

0089

/...

5/17

SECRET

VARIOUS CALCULATIONS WERE CARRIED OUT FOR SEVERAL PROPOSED SYSTEMS.

5. IN THE AREA OF THE FLYING PLATES AND THEIR USE IN INCREASING THE PRESSURE WAVE, A STUDY OF THE EVEN SHOCK WAVE WAS CONDUCTED ON THESE PLATES BOTH WITH A LAYER OF EXPLOSIVES AND WITHOUT THIS LAYER. THE RESULT SHOWED GOOD AGREEMENT WITH SOME OF THE PRACTICAL RESULTS WHICH HAD BEEN PUBLISHED FOR AMUMINIUM AND ESPECIALLY IN REGARD TO THE FREE SURFACE VELOCITY AND OBTAINING FISSURES IN THESE FLYING PLATES. THIS WAS PREPARATORY TO CONDUCTING SIMILAR STUDIES ON HOW TO USE THE SPHERICAL FLYING PLATES TO ENLARGE THE PRESSURE WAVE.

6. IN THE AREA OF USING THE LINEAR THEORY OF DISTURBANCE TO STUDY AND CALCULATE THE GROWTH OF DISTORTIONS IN PARTS OF THE MECHANISM OVER A PERIOD OF TIME AS WELL AS THE STABILITY OF THE SPHERICAL SHOCK WAVE, AN INITIAL PROGRAM WAS CONSTRUCTED WHICH SOLVED THE ONE-DIMENSIONAL HYDRODYNAMIC EQUATIONS; THIS PROGRAM WAS COMBINED WITH ANOTHER PROGRAM WHICH USED THE LINEAR DISTURBANCE THEORY EQUATIONS. SOME TESTS WERE PERFORMED ON THIS PROGRAM TO CONFIRM ITS VALIDITY. THESE TESTS INDICATED THE PRESENCE OF SOME DIFFICULTIES AT THE BEGINNING, BUT THESE WERE OVERCOME FOLLOWING CONCENTRATED EFFORTS. WORK IS NOW UNDERWAY TO DEVELOP THIS PROGRAM.

7. IN THE AREA OF MOLECULAR DYNAMICS, A ONE-DIMENSIONAL COMPUTATION WAS DEVELOPED AS AN INITAIL PHASE AND IT IS CURRENTLY BEING APPLIED TO CARRY OUT SOME PRESSURE AND TEMPERATURE CALCULATIONS TO CONFIRM ITS VALIDITY.

8. IN THE AREA OF RESEARCHING THE LITERATURE, A NUMBER ((OF ARTICLES)) OF SPECIFIC IMPORTANCE WERE IDENTIFIED, THEORETICAL UNDERSTANDING OF THE SUBJECT WAS INCREASED THROUGH EXHAUSTIVE STUDY AND A NUMBER OF THE SCIENTIFIC COMPUTATIONS WERE AFFECTED WHICH MOVED THE WORK AHEAD, SUCH AS THE HYDRODYNAMIC PROGRAM, WHICH SOLVED THE ONE-DIMENSIONAL HYDRODYNAMIC EQUATIONS WITH RADIATION TRANSPORT AS WELL AS THE NEUTRONIC PROGRAM

SECRET

0090

/...

6/17

SECRET

WHICH SOLVED THE NEUTRON TRANSPORT EQUATION THROUGH THE MONTE CARLO METHOD. THESE PROGRAMS WERE COMPLETED AND THEY WERE INSERTED INTO THE COMPUTER. CONCENTRATED ATTEMPTS ARE NOW UNDERWAY TO RUN THEM IN PREPARATION TO TESTING THEM AND DEVELOPING THEM IN THE DIRECTION WHICH WOULD HELP MOVE THE THEORETICAL WORK FORWARD AND FACILITATE THE ANSWERING OF A NUMBER OF QUESTIONS.

9.    THE THEORETICAL UNDERSTANDING WAS UTILIZED AND THE COMPUTATION WAS USED WHICH HAD BEEN PREVIOUSLY CONSTRUCTED TO UPDATE THE BASIC REPORT. THIS INCLUDED HYDRODYNAMIC AND COMBINED HYDRODYNAMIC-NEUTRONIC CALCULATIONS WHICH USE THE LATEST THEORETICAL INFORMATION AVAILABLE REGARDING EQUATION OF STATE.

PRODUCTION OF MATERIAL:

1.    PRODUCTION OF POLONIUM-210
      POLONIUM-210 IS CONSIDERED ONE OF THE BASIC COMPONENTS FOR MANUFACTURING THE NUCLEAR INITIATOR. IN ORDER TO PRODUCE IT, A NUMBER OF RESEARCH EXPERIMENTS WERE CONDUCTED AND DEVELOPED IN ORDER TO ESTABLISH A PLAN FOR THE CHEMICAL PROCESSES TO PRODUCE IT THROUGH IRRADIATING BISMUTH IN THE NUCLEAR REACTOR AND THEN EXTRACTING AND PURIFYING THE POLONIUM AND PRECIPITATE IT ELECTRICALLY IN ORDER TO PREPARE THE POLONIUM-210 SOURCES. THROUGHOUT THIS PERIOD A CAMPAIGN WAS CONDUCTED WHICH INCLUDED THE IRRADIATION OF 14.85 KILOGRAMS OF BISMUTH AND OBTAINING SIX MILLIGRAMS OF POLONIUM. SOME OF IT WAS USED TO CONDUCT RESEARCH AND DEVELOPMENT EXPERIMENTS, AND SOME OF IT WAS USED TO PREPARE FIVE SOURCES OF POLONIUM-210 IN QUANTITIES OF BETWEEN 1.25 AND 0.065 MILLIGRAMS BY ELECTROPLATING IT ONTO GOLD IN A NITRIC AND HYDROFLUORIC ACID MEDIUM, IN ORDER TO CARRY OUT THE NUCLEAR INITIATOR TESTS AND MEASUREMENTS.

2.    PRODUCTION OF PLUTONIUM
      THE NEED FOR THE PRODUCTION OF PLUTONIUM CALLS FOR THE PREPARATION OF SOURCES OF ALPHA EMITTERS TO SUPPORT INITIATOR TESTS AND THE NECESSARY MEASUREMENTS. IN ORDER TO PRODUCE PLUTONIUM, THE FOLLOWING WAS CARRIED OUT:

SECRET

0091

/...

SECRET

A.    THE IMPLEMENTATION OF BASIC OPERATIONS PRECEDED THE START OF WORK CAMPAIGNS TO REPROCESS SPENT NUCLEAR FUEL INCLUDING THE PROCESS OF REMOVING HIGHLY RADIOACTIVE WASTE, HOT (WORD ILLEGIBLE) ENGINEERING TESTING OF THE RADIO-CHEMICAL LABORATORY UNIT SYSTEMS WHICH ARE USED TO TREAT THE SPENT NUCLEAR FUEL. IN ADDITION, THE RADIOACTIVE WASTE WHICH ACCUMULATED IN THE RADIO-CHEMICAL LABORATORIES AND WHICH WAS PROCESSED IN THE RADIOACTIVE WASTE PROCESSING STATION WAS REMOVED. THIS WORK IS A PROCEDURE WHICH IS BEING CARRIED OUT FOR THE FIRST TIME.

B.    THE REPROCESSING OF IRAQI NUCLEAR FUEL ELEMENT (EK-07) MANUFACTURED LOCALLY AND IRRADIATED IN THE TAMMUZ 14 ((JULY 14)) REACTOR. THIS RESULTED IN THE SEPARATION OF 510 MILLIGRAMS OF PLUTONIUM, AND WORK IS NOW UNDERWAY TO IMPLEMENT A CAMPAIGN TO PROCESS ANOTHER IRAQI NUCLEAR FUEL ELEMENT IRRADIATED FOR 50 DAYS INSTEAD OF THE 22 DAYS OF IRRADIATION FOR THE FIRST ELEMENT. SO FAR, 750 MILLIGRAMS OF PLUTONIUM HAVE BEEN SEPARATED AS A RESULT OF THE PROCESSING OF 12 FUEL RODS FROM THIS ELEMENT.

THE PROCESSING OF THIS TYPE OF FUEL IS BEING DONE FOR THE FIRST TIME BECAUSE IT IS MANUFACTURED LOCALLY. MOREOVER, THE RAW MATERIAL WHICH GOES INTO ITS MANUFACTURE, URANIUM DIOXIDE, IS DERIVED FROM IRAQI RAW PHOSPHATE. A SPECIAL REPORT WAS SUBMITTED TO THE PROJECT HEADQUARTERS REGARDING THIS ACHIEVEMENT. THE RESULTING PLUTONIUM CONTAINS A LARGE PERCENTAGE OF THE 239 ISOTOPE.

C.    IN ADDITION, 25 MICROGRAMS OF PLUTONIUM-238 WERE PREPARED THROUGH THE IRRADIATION OF 200 MILLIGRAMS OF NEPTUNIUM-237 IN THE TAMMUZ 14 REACTOR. THEN SEPARATION OPERATIONS WERE CONDUCTED USING ANION EXCHANGE RESINS AND THE RECOVERY OF NEPTUNIUM-237 FOR THE PURPOSE OF RE-IRRADIATION. ADDITIONAL QUANTITIES OF PLUTONIUM-238 WERE EXTRACTED FOR THE PURPOSE OF PREPARING OTHER SOURCES OF ALPHA EMITTERS NEEDED FOR NUCLEAR INITIATOR TESTS.

WORK IS CONTINUING ALSO TO CONVERT PLUTONIUM

SECRET

0092

/...

8/17

SECRET

COMPOUNDS RESULTING FROM THE NUCLEAR FUEL REPROCESSING INTO METAL.

3.    PRODUCTION OF NATURAL URANIUM METAL.

NATURAL URANIUM METAL IS USED TO MANUFACTURE PART OF THE REFLECTOR IN THE IMPLOSION MECHANISM. IN ORDER TO PRODUCE IT, A NUMBER OF RESEARCH AND DEVELOPMENT EXPERIMENTS WERE CONDUCTED TO ESTABLISH THE CHEMICAL PROCEDURES FOR PRODUCING URANIUM TETRAFLUORIDE AS AN INTERMEDIATE MATERIAL, AND THEN URANIUM METAL. DURING THIS PERIOD, THE EQUIVALENT OF 2.2 TONS OF URANIUM TETRAOXIDE WERE PURIFIED AND CONVERTED INTO URANIUM DIOXIDE, WHICH WAS USED TO PREPARE THE EQUIVALENT OF 407 KILOGRAMS OF URANIUM TETRAFLUORIDE BY USING LABORATORY PROCEDURES. THIS MATERIAL WAS USED TO PREPARE URANIUM METAL IN THE SHAPE OF CYLINDRICAL BLOCKS. THIS WAS THEN DEVELOPED TO PREPARE THE METAL BY MEANS OF DIRECT CASTING IN THE SHAPE OF DISCS SO THAT THE EQUIVALENT OF 254 KILOGRAMS OF URANIUM METAL WERE PREPARED BY USING LABORATORY PROCEDURES ALSO.

IN THE LIGHT OF THESE RESULTS, BASIC DESIGN REPORTS WERE DRAWN UP FOR SEMI-INDISTRIAL SYSTEMS FOR THE PRODUCTION OF URANIUM TETRAFLUORIDE AND URANIUM METAL. DETAILED DESIGNS WERE SUBMITTED AND SOME OF THE SYSTEMS WERE MANUFACTURED AND INSTALLED. ((WE ARE)) AWAITING COMPLETION OF THE MANUFACTURING PROCESS AND THE INSTALLATION OF OTHER SYSTEMS AT THE AL-AMIL (?) PLANT. IN ADDITION, ALL BASIC DESIGN REPORTS FOR SIMILAR SYSTEMS WERE PREPARED AFTER SOME IMPROVEMENTS WERE MADE ON THEM, ENTAILING THE COMPLETION OF THE DETAILED DESIGNS AND MANUFACTURE OF THE SYSTEMS FOR THE PURPOSE OF PREPARING THEM TO BE INSTALLED IN THE AL-ATHIR PLANT.

IN ADDITION TO THIS, SUPPORT SYSTEMS WERE PREPARED, INCLUDING THE PROCESSING OF CHEMICAL WASTE LEFT OVER FROM THE PRODUCTION OF THESE MATERIALS. MOREOVER, REQUIREMENTS FOR QUALITY CONTROL TO EVALUATE THE MATERIALS WHICH WERE PRODUCED WERE COMPLETED.

4.    PRODUCTION OF ENRICHED URANIUM METAL.

SECRET

0093

/...

SECRET

ENRICHED URANIUM IS USED IN THE MANUFACTURE OF PART OF THE CORE IN THE IMPLOSION MECHANISM. A NUMBER OF RESEARCH AND DEVELOPMENT EXPERIMENTS WERE CONDUCTED TO PURIFY AND RECOVER THE URANIUM. BASIC DESIGN REPORTS FOR THE MANUFACTURE OF URANIUM TETRAFLUORIDE AND ENRICHED URANIUM METAL WERE DRAWN UP IN LIGHT OF THE INITIAL EXPERIMENTS USING NATURAL URANIUM.

A NUMBER OF RESEARCH AND DEVELOPMENT EXPERIMENTS WERE CONDUCTED TO PURIFY URANIUM THROUGH CHEMICAL METHODS AND ESTABLISH A PLAN FOR PROCESSES, AND DETAILED DESIGNS WERE PREPARED. THE SYSTEMS WERE MANUFACTURED SOME OF WHICH ARE NOW BEING INSTALLED; OTHERS ARE AWAITING MANUFACTURE.

5. PRODUCTION OF YELLOW CERIUM SULPHIDE

YELLOW CERIUM SULPHIDE IS CONSIDERED A PREFERRED MATERIAL FOR MANUFACTURING CRUCIBLES FOR THE MELTING AND CASTING OF URANIUM METAL. DUE TO THE DIFFICULTY OF OBTAINING IT IN THE REQUIRED QUANTITIES, A RESEARCH AND DEVELOPMENT PROGRAM HAS BEEN ESTABLISHED TO PRODUCE THIS MATERIAL IN THE LABORATORY THROUGH THE PREPARATION OF INTERMEDIATE MATERIALS.

THROUGHOUT THIS PERIOD 10 KILOGRAMS OF YELLOW CERIUM SULPHIDE WERE PREPARED. IT WILL BE PURIFIED ONCE THE REQUIREMENTS NEEDED FOR MANUFACTURING THE PURIFICATION SYSTEM ARE MET. WORK IS CURRENTLY UNDERWAY TO MANUFACTURE THEM IN LIGHT OF THE DETAILED AND BASIC DESIGNS WHICH HAVE BEEN DRAWN UP.

MATERIALS PROGRAM

THE MATERIALS PROGRAM FORMS THE BACKBONE OF THE WORK OF THE AL-ATHIR PLANT. IT INCLUDES A STUDY OF THE SPECIFICATIONS OF THE MATERIAL BEFORE AND AFTER IT IS SUBJECTED TO PRESSURE AND HEAT EXTREMES. IT ALSO INCLUDES MEASUREMENT AND DESCRIPTION OF THIS MATERIAL. THROUGH THE IMPLEMENTATION OF THESE MISSIONS THE FOLLOWING

SECRET

0094

/...

**S E C R E T**

**ACCOMPLISHMENTS WERE ACHIEVED:**

**1.    DETERMINATION OF THE TECHNOLOGICAL PARAMETERS, DETERMINATION OF THE EQUIPMENT REQUIREMENTS, AND IMPLEMENTATION OF CONTRACTS CONCLUDED WITH A NUMBER OF COMPANIES WITHIN THE MATERIALS PROGRAM.**

**2.    IMPLEMENTATION OF A NUMBER OF ACTIVITIES IN THE FOLLOWING AREAS:**

**A.    MELTING AND CASTING OF URANIUM METAL. THE RESULTS MADE IT POSSIBLE TO MELT AND CAST URANIUM METAL IN THE SHAPE OF RODS EACH WEIGHING 3 KILOGRAMS. THIS WAS DONE THROUGH THE DEVELOPMENT OF LABORATORY MELTING FURNACES CURRENTLY AVAILABLE. IN ADDITION, COATING RESOURCES WERE DEVELOPED WHICH ISOLATE THE METAL FROM THE CRUCIBLE MATERIAL WHICH IS BEING PRODUCED CURRENTLY. THIS IS DONE BY PROVIDING A PLASMA SPRAY SYSTEM WHICH IS CONSIDERED AN ADVANCED SYSTEM IN THIS FIELD.**

**B.    POWDER TECHNOLOGY LINE. A NUMBER OF RESEARCH AND DEVELOPMENT EXPERIMENTS WERE CONDUCTED TO PREPARE THE NECESSARY CERAMIC MATERIAL FOR THE PRODUCTION OF CAPACITORS AND THE PRODUCTION OF RUBBER COVERS FOR USE IN THE FIELD OF "COLD BALANCED PRESSURE" (?) TECHNOLOGY.**

**C.    A NUMBER OF TYPES OF PRESSURE SENSORS WERE PRODUCED FROM MANGANESE (?), PLASTICS AND QUARTZ FOR MEASURING PRESSURE AND VARIABLES.**

**D.    A PROGRAM WAS DRAWN UP FOR THE IMPLEMENTATION OF A NUMBER OF EXPERIMENTS FOR THE STUDY OF CHARACTERISTICS OF MATERIALS WHEN THEY ARE SUBJECTED TO PRESSURE AND TEMPERATURE EXTREMES THROUGH THE USE OF EXPLOSIVE LENSES.**

**3.    QUALITY CONTROL INSPECTION LABORATORIES WERE PREPARED BY PROVIDING SEVERAL PIECES OF EQUIPMENT AND ADVANCED SYSTEMS WHICH ARE USED TO CHARACTERIZE METALS AND CERAMIC MATERIALS FROM PHYSICAL, METALURGICAL AND MECHANICAL ASPECTS. A NUMBER OF PIECES OF EQUIPMENT WERE**

**S E C R E T**

0095

11/17

SECRET

FINISHED AND INSTALLED, THOSE WHICH WERE IMPORTED AND THOSE WHICH WERE TRANSPORTED FROM THE ORIGINAL SITE TO THE AL-ATHIR PLANT. PERSONNEL WERE ALSO TRAINED ON THE OPERATION OF THIS EQUIPMENT IN ORDER TO CONDUCT THE REQUIRED TESTS AND ANALYSES.

THE FOLLOWING IS A SUMMARY OF THE ITEMS OF EQUIPMENT AND SYSTEMS WHICH WERE RECEIVED, TRANSPORTED, INSTALLED, PUT INTO OPERATION DURING THIS PERIOD:

FIRST: SOME EQUIPMENT WAS INSTALLED IN TEMPORARY SITES, THEN DISMANTLED AND TRANSPORTED AND REINSTALLED IN THE WORK SITES; THESE INCLUDE:

- PLASMA SPRAY SYSTEM
- ELECTRONIC SCANNER AND ANALYTIC SENSORS
- PLASMA CHEMICAL ANALYSIS SYSTEM
- SINGLE X-RAY DIFFRACTION SYSTEM

SECOND: INSTALLATION OF SYSTEMS WHICH RECENTLY REACHED THE PLANT SITE DIRECTLY. THESE INCLUDE:

- MECHANICS/CHARACTERISTICS ((TESTING)) SYSTEMS
- NON-DESTRUCTIVE TEST SYSTEMS
- METALLOGRAPHY SYSTEMS
- ELECTRONIC ((SIC)) PIERCING SYSTEM
- MODEL PREPARATION EQUIPMENT

THIRD: TRANSPORTATION OF ITEMS OF EQUIPMENT AND SYSTEMS FROM THE AL-TUWAITHA SITE TO THE PLANT SITE AND THEN INSTALLED AND STARTED UP:

- MELTING AND CASTING FURNACE
- ((ONE WORD ILLEGIBLE)) FURNACE
- OPTICAL COMPARATOR
- POWDER X-RAY DIFFRACTION SYSTEM
- THERMAL ANALYSIS SYSTEMS
- SLIP CASTING SYSTEMS

FOURTH: RECEIPT OF A SET OF EQUIPMENT WHICH IS IN THE

SECRET

0096

/...

I

12/17

**S E C R E T**

**PROCESS OF BEING INSTALLED, AND PREPARATION OF TEMPORARY INSTALLATION SITES FOR OTHER SYSTEMS. THESE INCLUDE:**

- **LARGE COLD ISOSTATIC PRESS**
- **SMALL COLD ISOSTATIC PRESS**
- **SMALL HOT ISOSTATIC PRESS**
- **PULVERISING AND SIFTING SYSTEMS**
- **VAPOR COATING SYSTEMS**
- **DIMENSIONAL MEASURING DEVICE**
- **SET OF SMALL FURNACES**
- **SURFACE ANALYSIS SYSTEMS**

**TESTS:**

**1. DETONATION TESTS**

**BASIC REPORTS FOR DETONATION TESTS WERE DRAWN UP. THESE ARE BEING CONDUCTED AT SITE 100. THE REQUIREMENT NEEDS FOR THESE TESTS ARE BEING PREPARED AND 20 DETONATION TESTS HAVE BEEN CARRIED OUT BY USING EXPLOSIVE LENSES WHICH HAVE BEEN PREPARED AT AL-QA'QA' GENERAL FACILITY. THESE TESTS ARE AIMED AT MEASUREMENT OF THE HOMOGENEITY OF THE WAVE FRONT. SOME ENCOURAGING RESULTS WERE ACHIEVED IN THIS AREA. ALSO, EXPERIMENTS WERE CONDUCTED TO TEST THE INTERNAL INITIATOR MODELS USING EXPLOSIVE LENSES. IN ADDITION TO THAT, AN ELECTRONIC SYSTEM WAS DESIGNED, MANUFACTURED AND CALIBRATED WHICH IS USED TO MEASURE VERY SMALL TIME INTERVALS DURING THESE EXPERIMENTS.**

**2. NEUTRONIC TESTS**

**A LIQUID SCINTILLATION SYSTEM WAS INSTALLED AND CALIBRATED FOR MEASURING WEAK NEUTRONIC YIELD, AND MEASUREMENTS OF THE DEGREE OF URANIUM ENRICHMENT WERE MADE.**

**A SYSTEM WAS INSTALLED AND PUT INTO OPERATION FOR MEASURING NEUTRONS RESULTING FROM THE OXIDATION ((SIC)) OF POLONIUM-210. ALSO THE REQUIREMENTS FOR THE DENSE PLASMA FOCUSING LABORATORY WERE PREPARED. WORK IS CONTINUING WITHIN THE FRAME WORK OF RESEARCH AND DEVELOPMENT WITH**

**S E C R E T**

0097

/...

SECRET

THE GOAL OF USING IT IN THE FUTURE EXTERNAL INITIATOR.

3.     NUCLEAR INITIATOR:

THE NUCLEAR INITIATOR FOR THE MECHANISM CONSISTS OF TWO PRINCIPAL MATERIALS, POLONIUM-210 AND BERYLLIUM, SEPARATED BY A THIN GOLD COATING. WHEN THIS COATING IS RUPTURED AS A RESULT OF THE FIRST EXPLOSION OF THE LENSES AND THE SHOCK WAVE, THE NEUTRONS ARE LIBERATED THROUGH THE INTERACTION OF THE ALPHA PARTICLES EMITTED FROM THE POLONIUM-210 WITH THE NUCLEUS OF THE BERYLLIUM ((ATOMS)). THESE NEUTRONS ARE WHAT CAUSE THE INITIATION OF THE FISSION CHAIN REACTION OF THE NUCLEI OF THE URANIUM-233. AFTER THE DESIGN CALCULATIONS WERE COMPLETED FOR DETERMINING THE NEUTRONS EMITTED FROM THE INITIATOR, SEVERAL DESIGNS FOR THIS INITIATOR WERE DRAWN UP FOR TESTING TO CHOOSE THE IDEAL ONE. IN CONNECTION WITH THESE TESTS, THE A SYSTEM FOR CALIBRATING THE INITIATOR MODEL WITHOUT NUCLEAR COMPONENTS WAS MANUFACTURED AND INSTALLED. TESTS WERE CONDUCTED WITH THE NUCLEAR COMPONENTS AND NEUTRONS WERE OBTAINED.    ALSO, THE INITIAL TESTING SYSTEM WAS MANUFACTURED AND INSTALLED FOR MEASURING THE VELOCITY RANGING BETWEEN 600 AND 1000 METERS PER SECOND. IN ORDER TO OBTAIN THE MAXUMIM VELOCITY, A BASIC REPORT WAS DRAWN UP FOR THE INITIATOR MODEL TESTS ON THE HAMMER SYSTEM FOR WHICH THE CORNERSTONE WAS RECENTLY INSTALLED.

THE FINAL TESTS FOR THE INITIATOR WILL BE CONDUCTED WHEN THE LENSES AND MATERIAL FOR A MOCK CORE OF THE MECHANISM ARE MADE.

4.     PRIMARY FLASH X-RAY SYSTEM (160 KV)

APPARENT CALCULATIONS FOR FIELD EMISSION WERE MADE AND ALSO DESIGNS WERE DRAWN UP FOR THE CATHODE USED IN THE SYSTEM. ALSO THE BASIC REPORT WAS PREPARED FOR THE SUPPLEMENTARY SYSTEM WHICH WAS MANUFACTURED, INSTALLED, PUT INTO OPERATION AND SUCCESSFULLY TESTED.    WORK IS CONTINUING TO COMPLETE THE DESIGN AND MANUFACTURE OF THE 600 KV SUPPLEMENTARY SYSTEM WHICH CANNOT BE OBTAINED COMMERCIALLY.

SECRET          0098

/...

14/17

**S E C R E T**

## FIRING, CONTROL AND GUIDANCE SYSTEMS:

### 1. SYNCHRONIZATION AND TIMING SYSTEMS

AT THE BEGINNING OF 1989 A BASIS DESIGN REPORT FOR THE SYNCHRONIZATION AND TIMING SYSTEM WAS DRAWN UP FOR PROVIDING ENERGY FOR THE DETONATOR CABLES WITHIN SPECIFIC DESIGN OPTIONS. THE DESIGNS WER MADE. THE BRANCHING CABLE DETONATOR SYSTEMS (2, 4, 8, 16, AND 32) WERE IMPLEMENTED AND BUILT IN JULY OF THE SAME YEAR. AT THE BEGINNING OF 1990 AN ADVANCED MINIATURIZED SYSTEM (REDUCED TEN TIMES IN WEIGHT AND SIZE) WAS DEVELOPED FOR 32 CABLES WEIGHING UP TO 5 KILOGRAMS. IT PROVIDES THE ENERGY WITHIN TIME VARIATIONS NOT EXCEEDING 10 NANOSECONDS. AN INTEGRATED SYSTEM FOR FOUR DETONATION CABLES WAS DELIVERED TO THE AL-QA'QA' FACILITY AND ANOTHER IS BEING USED SUCCESSFULLY IN TESTS WHICH ARE BEING CONDUCTED IN THE PLANT. THE ABOVE WORK AMOUNTED TO A SCHOOL FROM WHICH DESIGN CONCEPTS WERE DERIVED FOR TESTING HIGH-SPEED MEASURING DEVICES AND SENSORS, IN ADDITION TO DESIGNS FOR PULSE-POWER DEVICES FOR THE DENSE PLASMA FOCUS SYSTEM AND THE MARX GENERATOR FOR GENERATING SUPER-HIGH VOLTAGE PULSES IN THE FLASH X-RAY SYSTEM. THE ABOVE SYSTEMS ARE WORKING SUCCESSFULLY NOW. NOTE THAT IT IS NOT POSSIBLE TO OBTAIN ANY OF THE ABOVE SYSTEMS COMMERCIALLY.

### 2. PULSE-POWER EQUIPMENT

PULSE-POWER EQUIPMENT WAS DESIGNED AND BUILT FOR DENSE PLASMA FOCUS SYSTEMS, WITH SPECIFICATIONS OF 10 KILOVOLTS, 300 KILOAMPERES, AT A TIME OF 1.8 MICROSECONDS, AND A MARX GENERATOR FOR GENERATING SUPER-HIGH VOLTAGE PULSES IN THE FLASH X-RAY SYSTEM, WITH SPECIFICATIONS OF 160 KILOVOLTS AND A CURRENT OF 1600 AMPERES. THESE SYSTEMS ARE NOW OPERATING SUCCESSFULLY AND THEY ARE BEING DEVELOPED TO BETTER SUIT REQUIREMENTS. NOTE THAT IT IS NOT POSSIBLE TO OBTAIN ANY OF THEM COMMERCIALLY.

### 3. CHARGING POWER EQUIPMENT.

**S E C R E T**

0099

/...

**SECRET**

CHARGING POWER EQUIPMENT WAS DESIGNED AND BUILT TO BE USED IN THE SYSTEM FOR SUPPLYING POWER TO THE DETONATION CABLES. THIS RESULTED IN THE DEVELOPMENT AND DESIGN OF MINIATURIZED POWER EQUIPMENT SYSTEM (1000 TIMES) WEIGHING 500 GRAMS AND MEETING REQUIREMENTS FOR USE. NOTE THAT IT IS NOT POSSIBLE TO OBTAIN THESE SYSTEMS COMMERCIALLY.

4. **JUNCTION SWITCHES**

IN VIEW OF THE HIGHLY SPECIALIZED APPLICATION OF THE HIGH ENERGY PULSE JUNCTION SWITCHES A NUMBER OF JUNCTION SWITCHES WITH A SPARK GAP APPROACHING 200 KILOAMPERES AND VOLTAGE OF 50 KILOVOLTS. THE DEVELOPMENT AND MANUFACTURE OF THIS TYPE OF SWITCH MAKES UP FOR THE USE OF OTHER SWITCHES SUCH AS THE KRYTRON, WHICH CANNOT BE OBTAINED COMMERCIALLY.

5. **CAPACITORS**

CAPACITORS WERE DESIGNED AND BUILT THROUGH THE USE OF TWO TECHNOLOGIES, HIGH-VOLTAGE CHIP SENSORS FOR THE SYNCHRONIZATION AND TIMING SYSTEM, AND THE CERAMIC CAPACITORS WHICH ARE USED IN THE FLASH X-RAY SYSTEMS. CERAMIC CAPACITORS WERE MANUFACTURED. THE SLOW IMPORTED CAPACITORS WERE CONVERTED AND TURNED INTO HIGH-SPEED ((CAPACITORS)) AND INDUCTANCE WAS REDUCED FROM 250 TO 13 NANOHENRYS.

ALSO, 5-NANOHENRY 45-KILOVOLT DISC CAPACITORS WERE MANUFACTURED AND THEY WILL BE USED IN THE MARX GENERATOR TO REACH 600 KILOVOLTS.

6. **MEASUREMENTS**

THE FOLLOWING WERE DESIGNED AND CARRIED OUT:

(1) SYSTEMS FOR MEASURING CURRENT AND PULSE VOLTAGE OF SYSTEMS.

(2) SYSTEMS FOR MEASURING MINUTE SEGMENTS OF TIME FOR

**SECRET**  0100

/...

16/17

SECRET

DETONATION TESTS IN INTERVALS OF BETWEEN NANO- AND MICROSECONDS WITH A HIGH DEGREE OF ACCURACY REACHING SEVERAL PICOSECONDS.

SUPPORT ACTIVITIES:

1. SYSTEMS FOR DERIVING DATA.

A NUMBER IF THESE SYSTEMS WERE CREATED TO SUPPORT TESTS IN VARIOUS PARTS OF THE PLANT. THEY COVERED PROGRAMS TO ANALYZE DATA DERIVED FROM THEORIES FOR NEUTRON INITIATOR TESTS AND THE LOW-NEUTRON BACKGROUND MEASUREMENTS USING AN ANALOG DATA BUS.

2. COMMUNICATIONS SYSTEMS WERE CREATED FOR THE PROJECT SITES TAKING INTO CONSIDERATION THE SPECIAL CHARACTERISTICS OF THE SITES AND GUARANTEEING COMMUNICATIONS SECURITY. THESE NETS WERE DEVELOPED THROUGH LOCAL EXPERTISE AND WITH PROJECT PERSONNEL. THEY INCLUDE SWITCHBOARDS, ((FIBER-))OPTIC AND TELEPHONE CABLES AND DIGITAL COMMUNICATIONS. NOTE THAT SOME OF THE EXPERTISE WHICH IN EMPLOYED IN THE PROJECT IS NOT AVAILABLE IN THE COUNTRY.

3. MECHANICAL DESIGNS:

DESIGNS FOR MECHANICAL SYSTEMS WERE CREATED WHICH ARE REQUIRED BY THE VARIOUS DIVISIONS OF THE PLANT TO SUPPORT THE TESTS AND PRODUCTION OPERATIONS. SOME OF THESE DESIGNS REQUIRE PRECISE OPERATING TECHNOLOGY. THEY INCLUDE:

DESIGNS FOR MODELS OF NEUTRON INITIATORS AND DESIGNS FOR INITIAL TESTING SYSTEMS FOR THE INITIATOR AND THE HAMMER, IN ADDITION TO DESIGNS FOR THE JUNCTION SWITCHES.

4. SUPPORT ACTIVITIES FOR THE PLANT SITE:

ACTIVITIES INCLUDED:

PROVIDING ENGINEERING SUPPORT FOR THE INSTALLATION AND OPERATION OF THE SERVICE SYSTEMS AND THE

SECRET

0101

/...

**S E C R E T**

INSTALLATION OF SOME EQUIPMENT. ((LINE MISSED)) INSTALLATION AND FURNISHING A NUMBER OF TRAILERS.

**TRANSFER TO NEW WORK SITE (AL-ATHIR PLANT)**

IN LIGHT OF THE COMPLETION OF THE FIRST PHASE OF THE AL-ATHIR PLANT FACILITY, MOST OF THE STAFF OF THE PLANT WERE MOVED FROM THEIR DUTY POSTS IN AL-TUWAITHA TO THE NEW PLANT WORK SITE. ALSO THE EQUIPMENT, MACHINERY AND TESTING SYSTEMS WERE MOVED AND WERE INSTALLED AND PUT INTO OPERATION AT THE NEW SITE TO CONTINUE IMPLEMENTATION OF THE ACTIVITIES OF THE PLAN. THE FACILITY OF THIS PHASE WAS OPENED UP BY THE MINISTER OF INDUSTRY AND MILITARY INDUSTRIALIZATION ON 7 MAY 1990. HE LOOKED OVER THE ACCOMPLISHMENTS WHICH HAD BEEN ACHIEVED DURING THE PERIOD. THE WORK IS CONTINUING TO IMPLEMENT THE SECOND PHASE OF THE FACILITY WHICH IT IS HOPED TO BE COMPLETED BY THE END OF THIS YEAR.

((END TEXT))

-----

0102

**Security Council**

Distr.
GENERAL

S/23123
10 October 1991
ENGLISH
ORIGINAL:   ARABIC

LETTER DATED 8 OCTOBER 1991 FROM THE PERMANENT REPRESENTATIVE OF
IRAQ TO THE UNITED NATIONS ADDRESSED TO THE SECRETARY-GENERAL

On instructions from my Government, I have the honour to transmit
herewith a letter dated 8 October 1991 addressed to you by Mr. Ahmad Hussein,
Minister for Foreign Affairs of the Republic of Iraq.

I should be grateful if you would have this letter and its annex
circulated as a document of the Security Council.

(Signed)   Abdul Amir A. AL-ANBARI
Ambassador
Permanent Representative

91-33095   2664f (E)                                                    /...

0103

<u>Annex</u>

<u>Letter dated 8 October 1991 from the Minister for Foreign
Affairs of Iraq addressed to the Secretary-General</u>

I have the honour to inform you of the text of the irregular and
dangerous statements made by the President of a State that occupies a
permanent seat in the Security Council.  On 4 October 1991, the President of
the United States of America stated at a press conference that he wished to
see Saddam Hussein out of power so that the United States could normalize its
relations with the Iraqi people; that was his constant policy.  He said that
getting rid of him would be in the interest of the United States and that the
embargo would continue, United Nations supervision over the marketing of Iraqi
oil would continue, and no imports would be allowed except food and medicine
for the Iraqi people.

These officially documented statements by the President of the United
States of America conflict totally with the letter and spirit of the Charter
of the United Nations.  While the Charter affirms that the Security Council
shall act in accordance with the purposes and principles of the United
Nations, United States President George Bush continues to affirm his policy
publicly in a way that conflicts with those purposes and disregards his
country's obligations as a permanent member of the Security Council not to
intervene in the internal affairs of a sovereign State Member of the United
Nations, threatening the security, safety and independence of Iraq.

Article 2, paragraph 7, of the United Nations Charter provides that
"nothing contained in the present Charter shall authorize the United Nations
to intervene in matters which are essentially within the domestic jurisdiction
of any State", and Article 1, paragraph 2 of the Charter provides for
"friendly relations among nations based on respect for the principle of equal
rights and self-determination of peoples".

It is truly regrettable that silence should prevail in the face of these
dangerous statements by the President of a great Power and permanent member of
the Security Council.  Silence about such policies, which are in open
contradiction to the principles of the United Nations Charter and
international law, will have dire consequences for international peace and
security, which form the core of the duties of the United Nations and the
Security Council.  Moreover, these policies which the President of the United
States of America officially adopts and declares through the media constitute
an extraordinary violation of Security Council resolutions, nay, contempt of
the Council.

We must say that silence concerning this United States behaviour, which
is being passed on through the channels of the international Organization,
constitute a kind of tacit participation in it, unless the States members of
the Council adopt clear positions on it.

/...

0104

Security Council resolution 687 (1991) did not give the right or the competence to any authority or country to intervene in the internal affairs of Iraq. Accordingly, the official position of the United States President clearly disregards not only the above-mentioned resolution but also other relevant resolutions and turns them into an instrument and means for implementing the suspect policy followed by the United States President.

The Government of the Republic of Iraq calls upon you and, through you, the other members of the Security Council to assume their responsibilities under the United Nations Charter and international law by rejecting the United States President's contemptuous disregard of all international covenants, laws and customs and the resolutions of the Security Council.

The President of the United States of America persists in intervening in the internal affairs of Iraq, in implementation of a suspect policy that seeks to subject Iraq and the Iraqi people to United States colonial tutelage, using to that end ways and means that in no way differ from the ways and means of starvation and genocide.

(Signed) Ahmad HUSSEIN
Minister for Foreign Affairs
of the Republic of Iraq

Baghdad, 8 October 1991

-----

0105

# Security Council

PROVISIONAL

S/PV.3012
11 October 1991

ENGLISH

PROVISIONAL VERBATIM RECORD OF THE THREE THOUSAND AND
TWELFTH MEETING

Held at Headquarters, New York,
on Friday, 11 October 1991, at 5.20 p.m.

President:   Mr. GHAREKHAN                (India)

Members:    Austria                   Mr. HOHENFELLNER

| | | |
|---|---|---|
| | Austria | Mr. HOHENFELLNER |
| | Belgium | Mr. NOTERDAEME |
| | China | Mr. LI Daoyu |
| | Côte d'Ivoire | Mrs. KABA |
| | Cuba | Mr. ZAMORA RODRIGUEZ |
| | Ecuador | Mr. AYALA LASSO |
| | France | Mr. MERIMEE |
| | Romania | Mr. FLOREAN |
| | Union of Soviet Socialist Republics | Mr. VORONTSOV |
| | United Kingdom of Great Britain and Northern Ireland | Sir David HANNAY |
| | United States of America | Mr. PICKERING |
| | Yemen | Mr. AL-ASHTAL |
| | Zaire | Mr. BAGBENI ADEITO NZENGEYA |
| | Zimbabwe | Mr. MUMBENGEGWI |

This record contains the original text of speeches delivered in English and interpretations of speeches in the other languages. The final text will be printed in the Official Records of the Security Council.

Corrections should be submitted to original speeches only. They should be sent under the signature of a member of the delegation concerned, within one week, to the Chief, Official Records Editing Section, Department of Conference Services, room DC2-750, 2 United Nations Plaza, and incorporated in a copy of the record.

91-61433   6525V (E)

0106

<u>The meeting was called to order at 5.30 p.m.</u>

ADOPTION OF THE AGENDA

<u>The agenda was adopted.</u>

THE SITUATION BETWEEN IRAQ AND KUWAIT

REPORT OF THE SECRETARY-GENERAL (S/22871/Rev.1)

NOTE BY THE SECRETARY-GENERAL (S/22872/Rev.1 and Corr.1)

The PRESIDENT:  I should like to inform the Council that I have received a letter from the representative of Iraq in which he requests to be invited to participate in the discussion of the item on the Council's agenda. In conformity with the usual practice I propose, with the consent of the Council, to invite that representative to participate in the discussion without the right to vote, in accordance with the relevant provisions of the Charter and rule 37 of the Council's provisional rules of procedure.

There being no objection, it is so decided.

<u>At the invitation of the President, Mr. Al-Anbari (Iraq) took a place at the Council table.</u>

The PRESIDENT:  The Security Council will now begin its consideration of the item on its agenda.

Members of the Council have before them the report of the Secretary-General contained in document S/22871/Rev.1 and the note by the Secretary-General contained in documents S/22872/Rev.1 and Corr.1.

Members of the Council also have before them document S/23134, which contains the text of a draft resolution submitted by Belgium, France, Romania, the Union of Soviet Socialist Republics, the United Kingdom of Great Britain and Northern Ireland and the United States of America.

I call on the representative of Iraq.

0107

Mr. AL-ANBARI (Iraq) (interpretation from Arabic):  First, Sir, allow me to congratulate you on your assumption of the presidency of the Security Council for this month.  I have complete confidence, in view of your vast experience, that you will be able to guide the Council's deliberations with great ability and objectivity.

I also take this opportunity to express my deep appreciation to the Ambassador of France, Mr. Mérimée, for his intensive efforts and the outstanding ability which he demonstrated in his stewardship of the Council during the past month.

The draft resolution seems at first sight to be a detailed procedural draft regarding the implementation of paragraph 10 of resolution 687 (1991) of 3 April 1991 in addition to paragraph 13 of that resolution.  However, this is not the case.  The draft resolution goes far beyond the horizons and objectives of that resolution and, contrary to the provisions of the Charter, aims to put Iraq under the permanent trusteeship of the Special Commission on armaments and to maintain the trade sanctions system indefinitely, contrary to the provisions of that resolution.

The draft resolution also seeks to establish permanent international mechanisms to tighten control on Iraq's future and prevent Iraq from carrying out economic and scientific development, at great cost to Iraq.

The draft resolution introduces very serious principles.  However, the greatest danger is in the plan prepared by the Special Commission on armaments, contained in document S/22871/Rev.1 of 2 October 1991.  The plan omits no detail affecting civil or military life.  All those aspects, together with all Iraqi scientific institutions and educational institutes are placed under tight control and severe restrictions, in an absolutist and arbitrary fashion.

0108

(Mr. Al-Anbari, Iraq)

The plan has been drawn up in great detail with a great deal of complexity. Those details are scattered all over the text, but are intertwined with the threads of all the plan's provisions and those of the so-called four annexes that form an integral part of the plan. Therefore, it is no wonder that many of those concerned with the plan did not fully examine its details and accepted it in good faith as a technical plan to implement paragraph 10 of resolution 687 (1991), adopted six months ago, which has become a fait accompli. They think, therefore, that the plan does not warrant further examination and could not be more serious than resolution 687 (1991) itself.

I should like to cite first paragraph 13 of the plan, which reads:

"In accepting unconditionally Security Council resolution 687 (1991) Iraq has undertaken"

to accept all the items mentioned in that paragraph. It is my duty, in deference to the behests of truth and history, to express the deep regret and disappointment of both the Government and people of Iraq that Iraq accepted resolution 687 (1991) without a guarantee in advance that the Council would lift the economic blockade against Iraq and refrain from adopting one resolution after another against Iraq and its people. Resolution 687 (1991) has become like a mythical tree which goes on sprouting branches that have no relationship with the resolution itself, and indeed are contrary to its provisions.

Iraq accepted resolution 687 (1991) and previous resolutions and implemented their provisions in good faith. Iraq did this, unfortunately, in the erroneous belief that the Council, in return, would look at the economic sanctions and other arbitrary measures adopted by the Council against the

0109

                                                  (<u>Mr, Al-Anbari, Iraq</u>)

people and Government of Iraq.  It is regrettable that Iraq has played its

part but the Council has failed not only to fulfil its mandate but has

tightened its sanctions against Iraq.  In simple language, the Security

Council has not adhered to its own resolutions as it has transformed the

cease-fire resolution 687 (1991) into a document that makes the Iraqi

Government and people hostage of one or two States with veto power in the

Council.

     I must also warn that if this plan is implemented against Iraq, many of

the countries of the developing or the developed worlds which support its

implementation either knowingly or out of ignorance, may well find that they

will be next in line as potential victims of this plan which embodies, in

practical terms, a new type of occupation that, through a system of remote

control, dominates every aspect of life in the target country.

     Paragraph 10 of resolution 687 (1991)

     "Decides that Iraq shall unconditionally undertake not to use,

develop, construct or acquire any of the items specified in paragraphs 8

and 9 above and requests the Secretary-General, in consultation with the

Special Commission, to develop a plan for the future ongoing monitoring

and verification of Iraq's compliance with this paragraph, to be

submitted to the Security Council for approval within one hundred and

twenty days of the passage of this resolution".

0110

(Mr. Al-Anbari, Iraq)

The implementation of the first part of the aforementioned paragraph concerns Iraq.  It was implemented, as Iraq, in a communication dated 18 April 1991 addressed to the Secretary-General from the Minister for Foreign Affairs, has undertaken, unconditionally, not to use, develop, construct, build or acquire any material specified in paragraphs 7 to 12 of resolution 687 (1991).  The latter part of paragraph 10 calls for the formulation of a plan to monitor compliance by Iraq of its obligations under that paragraph and for ongoing verification in future.

The plan contained in the draft resolution, and its implementation, far exceeds that purview and gives the Special Commission and all those authorized by it, unrestricted, permanent and absolute police, political and executive powers.  The plan is made up of 45 paragraphs and four annexes that form an integral part of the Plan.  Strangely enough, while paragraph 26 stipulates that the Plan may be revised only by the Security Council, it gives the Special Commission the power of revising the annexes of the Plan and informing the Council, without prior Council approval.  As the four annexes of the Plan contain detailed provisions that further elaborate the Plan, the Council, by approving the Plan, including paragraph 26, would be giving the Special Commission the authority to amend the Plan itself, which goes beyond the resolution itself.

My question is, does the Council have such authority under the Charter? The first deviation from resolution 687 (1991), especially operative paragraph 10, is what is stated in paragraph 3 of the Plan, which interpreted the future ongoing verification of weapons of mass destruction as inclusive not only of military installations, but also of civil installations and other materials that could be used or the activities that could be undertaken contrary to the obligations of Iraq under resolution 687 (1991).

0111

(Mr. Al-Anbari, Iraq)

Members may notice that that paragraph in expanding the scope of
verification and monitoring to include civilian installations in addition to
military installations also refers to everything that might be used contrary
to the obligations of Iraq.  The expansion of that Plan in such a fashion to
include the military and the civilian both actual and potential leaves the
door wide open in order to abuse the powers granted to the Special Commission
and to all those delegated by the Special Commission.

The Plan calls for establishing an executive body under the authority of
the Security Council, as provided for in paragraph 5, and in paragraph 7,
establishes a compliance unit under the Special Commission to ensure that Iraq
will not import any prohibited material.  This is in addition to the roles of
the IAEA and the Special Commission itself and the Sanctions Committee
established under resolution 661 (1991).  This in fact creates a new
international organ with numerous offshoots in a manner unprecedented in
history.  The Plan, in seeking to tighten further the controls against Iraq,
is not satisfied with one procedural control mechanism.  For instance,
paragraph 10 (b) provides that countries that supply Iraq with multipurpose
materials - both military and civilian - will provide transparent information
under a mechanism to be set up for this purpose.  Yet, paragraph 9 of the Plan
states that the monitoring and verification are required from within Iraq by
the Special Commission and its personnel, who might stay in Iraq for a long
time or even permanently.  Therefore, in all humility, may I suggest that we
confer upon the Head of the Special Commission the title of the political
ruler or the High Commissioner as in the old days of colonial rule.

I have pointed out previously that giving any special commission or any
body absolute powers in interpreting and implementing the provisions of the

0112

(Mr. Al-Anbari, Iraq)

Plan, and even amending the Plan, would create the risk of abuse of power, whether intentionally or inadvertently.  What might strengthen that possibility is the fact that the Plan puts more obligations on Iraq, and gives undefined and open-ended powers to the monitoring mechanism.  For instance, under paragraph 16 (a), the Plan imposes on Iraq the obligation to provide the Commission on a regular basis, with full, complete, correct and timely information on activities, sites, facilities, material and other items that might be used for prohibited purposes.  What are those other items, and how could we determine the purpose of using one material today or in future for a prohibited purpose?  That same paragraph stipulates elsewhere, that Iraq should provide the Special Commission with similar information that I have just mentioned concerning any additional activities, sites, facilities, materials or other items that the Commission may designate.  Paragraph 16 also stipulates that Iraq should fully, completely and promptly respond to any question or request that is made by the Special Commission.  Is there any international organization or body that has such absolute power?  Is it practicable for any country or any party to answer any question or request irrespective of whether or not it is arbitrary or irrelevant or unanswerable? The Plan makes all these obligations, some of which I have referred to, incumbent upon Iraq and gives the Special Commission and all those delegated by the Commission the right to enter Iraq and leave it without Iraq's approval, to use any sites and airports and to send any persons, irrespective of their nationality or identity or intentions, to enter Iraq and to engage in any activities with full diplomatic immunity and absolute freedom to move inside Iraq and to secure their safety and security, as provided for under paragraph 18 of the Plan.

0113

Moreover, in paragraph 20, Iraq shall enact legislation and adopt all
necessary measures to implement its obligations under resolution 687 (1991)
and resolution 707 (1991) and other related resolutions before the passage of
30 days from the date of adoption of the Plan by the Security Council.  This
paragraph of the Plan, while it ignores all the legislative and executive
measures adopted by Iraq to implement the Security Council's resolutions,
comes up with general provisions that Iraq would be required to enforce within
30 days.  It seems that the figure 30 has a very special significance in the
Plan, given the fact that all the information and special statistics Iraq
should provide the Commission with on chemical and biological materials as
well as missiles should be submitted within 30 days.

The fact that the Plan far exceeds the Security Council resolutions and
the provisions of the Charter becomes more evident in the four annexes to the
Plan.  For instance, annex I provides that the Special Commission has the
right to secure any site and to inspect Iraq's exports and imports and any
materials upon their arrival in Iraq or when they leave Iraq.  Is the
inspection of any material exported or imported by Iraq necessary to ensure
compliance by Iraq of its obligations regarding weapons of mass destruction?

Moreover, the Special Commission gives itself, under the Plan, police
powers.  Under paragraph 9 of that annex, the Special Commission would make
its own arrangements to ensure the safety and security of its personnel and
property and to seize any material or other item.

0114

Please note the general terms "any material or other item". We have the right to ask how the Special Commission could make such arrangements? Would the Special Commission come to Iraq on tanks? Does it have military forces to protect it or enable it to secure any site?

The same annex, in paragraph 10, imposes on Iraq the obligation to ensure the safety and security of the personnel and property of the Special Commission, and so on. The proposed Plan is unique in its deliberate complexity and scattering of intertwined provisions in a manner that would make it extremely difficult to implement, while it makes it easy to claim that its provisions are being contravened.

For example, paragraph 6 of annex II calls for the provision of information on sites or facilities, including the name of the site or facility and of the owner, company or enterprise operating the site or facility; the location of the site or facility; a general description of all types of activities at the site or facility; and the sources and amounts of the financing of the site or facility, and of its activities. Paragraph 8 calls for the provision of information in addition to that specified in paragraph 6. Paragraph 9 also calls for more information in addition to that specified in paragraph 6.

The four annexes of the Plan, in addition to the contents of the Plan itself, aim explicitly at denying Iraq the capacity to conduct scientific, biological and chemical research. Indeed, the Plan is so excessive that, in paragraph 38 (c), it prohibits Iraq's conducting activities on diseases other than those indigenous to or immediately expected to break out in Iraq. In paragraph 38 (d), Iraq is prohibited from conducting any breeding of vectors of human, animal or plant diseases. Should Iraq need to conduct any such

0115

(Mr. Al-Anbari, Iraq)

activity, it has to submit a request to the Special Commission specifying all
the information the Commission requires.  The Commission will then accept or
reject the request.

In other words, if Iraq is to abide by its commitment not to produce
biological weapons, then it must desist from conducting medical research on
diseases that are not expected to break out immediately in its environment.
Iraq is also prevented from conducting research on the immunization and
innoculation of children and others against infectious diseases.  Is not the
result of these restrictions the vulnerability of Iraq's people to disease and
gradual extermination?

I may have spoken at length of the Plan, its annexes and details.  But I
do hope that I have been able to show that the Plan gives the Commission and
its personnel absolute powers and imposes on Iraq obligations that gives the
Special Commission absolute authority over the State and people of Iraq.  It
also imposes conditions that would make Iraq powerless to fulfil all the
obligations imposed on it by the Plan.  Furthermore, the Plan is arbitrary in
its interpretation of the tasks outlined in resolution 687 (1991).  While the
provisions of that resolution focus on the weapons of mass destruction and
ballistic missiles with a range greater than 150 kilometres, the Plan goes
further and includes dual and multipurpose materials, scientific activities
and medical activities.  The Plan also introduces a mechanism that would
monitor all Iraq's imports and subject all Iraq's requirements of multipurpose
materials to the prior consent by the Commission established under resolution
661 (1990).  Every member of that Commission has the right of veto regardless
of the legitimacy of the requirements.  Thus, this Plan would make the
economic sanctions against Iraq - which are provisional pending the

0116

(Mr. Al-Anbari, Iraq)

implementation of paragraph 22 of resolution 687 (1991) —  permanent measures

and would make the sanctions committee a permanent organ of the Security

Council.

The main thrust of the Plan is not to destroy Iraq's weapons of mass

destruction but to deprive Iraq of its industrial and scientific

infrastructure and to project an image of Iraq as a State that does not

cooperate with the United Nations or tries to exceed its international

obligations in order to tighten further the economic, scientific and political

siege imposed on Iraq's Government and its people.

If the Plan's aims are illegal and prohibited under the Geneva

Conventions and the instruments of Human Rights and the United Nations

Charter, then they and the draft resolution under consideration lack

international legality and are not consonant with international law or the

United Nations Charter.

The PRESIDENT:  I thank the representative of Iraq for his kind

words addressed to me.

Mr. PICKERING (United States of America):  I hope to be brief, but I

feel I must comment on what we have just heard from the representative of

Iraq.  In contrast to what he has just said, I would like to extend the

compliments of my delegation and my Government to the Special Commission and

to the Director-General of the International Atomic Energy Agency (IAEA), who

prepared excellent monitoring plans for dealing with a very serious and

difficult situation.

We have seen Iraq's performance over the past months.  It has continued

to hide parts of its nuclear-weapons programme, its chemical-warfare

programme, its biological programme and its missile programme.  It has

0117

<u>(Mr. Pickering, United States)</u>

continued to try to block the cooperation that it is committed to give to the Special Commission and to IAEA. We have only to take note of the parking-lot incident and the difficulties which were put in the way of the Special Commission in actually operating the helicopters mandated by the Council.

There is, as we all know now, indisputable evidence that Iraq was seeking to build nuclear weapons and that it misused and abused its peaceful-nuclear facilities. Twice, the Governing Board of IAEA has found that Iraq was in violation of its safeguards agreements under the non-proliferation Treaty. One more such finding, we believe, is now pending on the basis of recent evidence. Several times, including as recently as in resolution 707 (1991), the Council has found Iraq in violation of its obligations under Security Council resolutions. This should all speak clearly for itself as to why this monitoring and verification Plan is required and why it has been so carefully prepared.

The bad news, unfortunately, is that, as we all know, in each of the resolutions relevant to the Iraq and Kuwait situation - between resolutions 661 (1990) and 712 (1991) - we have heard pretty much the same speech from the representative of Iraq. Perhaps the good news is that, at each turn, reluctantly, grudgingly and half-heartedly, Iraq has nevertheless complied with the general tenor of those resolutions as they have been applied by the Council. We hope and expect that Iraq will of course abide by the resolution which we hope the Council will move rapidly now to adopt.

0118

      <u>Sir David HANNAY</u> (United Kingdom of Great Britain and Northern
Ireland):  I, too, feel that, after the statement made by the representative
of Iraq, some points need to be made.  I was struck, I must say, by the
representative of Iraq's analogy, in which he describes resolution 687 (1991)
as a tree.  Having worked in gardens quite a long time myself, I have noticed
that the branches of trees usually belong to the trees.  This draft resolution
belongs to this tree, which is resolution 687 (1991).  It derives directly
from it.

(<u>Sir David Hannay, United Kingdom</u>)

The draft resolution is stringent because of the long chapter of evasions, concealment and trickery that Iraq has employed to avoid revealing what it was required to reveal under resolution 687 (1991) and because of a long history of evasion that has demonstrated beyond any doubt Iraq's determination to preserve and continue the programmes for producing weapons of mass destruction which this Council has interdicted.

The representative of Iraq expressed surprise that there are parts of this continuing compliance programme that relate to dual-use items, civilian items.  But he should hardly be surprised.  After all, Iraq's nuclear-weapons programme was called by the Government of Iraq "Petrochemicals Project Number 3", and Iraq imported parts for a super-gun - which has now, fortunately, been destroyed - that were described as "pipes for petrochemical plant".  So if there is a problem over dual use, there is nobody to blame but themselves.

The representative of Iraq expressed surprise that there should be references to the need to provide for the safety of the Special Commission. That is 10 days after armed Iraqi police detained the Special Commission inspectors for four days, against all of Iraq's international obligations and its agreement with the United Nations.  It is surely hardly surprising that we have to guard against that.

Now, the representative of Iraq suggested that this draft resolution is designed to prevent Iraq from conducting research in the fields of health. Frankly, that is not true.  Paragraph 38 (d) of the report makes it quite clear that projects for breeding vectors of human, animal or plant diseases will be permitted.

0120

<u>(Sir David Hannay, United Kingdom)</u>

Therefore, I think it is a pity that this caricature should have been given to the Council when it is entirely contrary to the truth.

To conclude, the object of the draft resolution, I would say, is quite simply this:  it is to prevent Iraq from breaking in the future the international obligations on weapons of mass destruction it so liberally broke in the past.  One way or another, that objective will be achieved.

The PRESIDENT:  It is my understanding that the Council is ready to proceed to the vote on the draft resolution (S/23134) before it.  Unless I hear any objection, I shall put the draft resolution to the vote now.  There being no objection, it is so decided.

<u>A vote was taken by show of hands.</u>

In favour:   Austria, Belgium, China, Côte d'Ivoire, Cuba, Ecuador, France, India, Romania, Union of Soviet Socialist Republics, United Kingdom of Great Britain and Northern Ireland, United States of America, Yemen, Zaire, Zimbabwe

The PRESIDENT:  There were 15 votes in favour.  The draft resolution has therefore been adopted unanimously as resolution 715 (1991).

I shall now call upon those members of the Council who wish to make statements following the voting.

Mr. MERIMEE (France) (interpretation from French):  In the view of my delegation the resolution we have just adopted is of great importance.  We have approved the plan for future ongoing monitoring and verification, which is the only way to ensure that Iraq will no longer be able to pursue its plans, especially those to acquire nuclear armaments.  The missions of the Special Commission and the International Atomic Energy Agency have furnished ample proof of those plans, and the international community is in duty bound to put an end to them.

0121

(Mr. Mérimée, France)

This matter concerns the heart of the Security Council's responsibilities. My delegation welcomes the unanimity that has prevailed among Council members in this regard. We hope that, faced with this determination on the part of the international community, Iraq will understand that it is in its interests to comply without reservations with the obligations incumbent upon it under the plan and the resolution and cooperate with the Council and with the various bodies under its authority and responsibility.

The PRESIDENT: There are no further speakers inscribed on my list. The Security Council has thus concluded the present stage of its consideration of the item on its agenda. The Security Council will remain seized of the matter.

The meeting rose at 6.05 p.m.

0122

**Security Council**

Distr.
GENERAL

S/23139
14 October 1991
ENGLISH
ORIGINAL:  ARABIC

LETTER DATED 13 OCTOBER 1991 FROM THE PERMANENT REPRESENTATIVE OF
IRAQ TO THE UNITED NATIONS ADDRESSED TO THE SECRETARY-GENERAL

On instructions from my Government, I have the pleasure to enclose
herewith a letter dated 13 October 1991 from Mr. Ahmad Hussein, Minister for
Foreign Affairs of the Republic of Iraq, concerning a violation by Israeli
military aircraft that coincided with a flight of helicopters being used by
United Nations inspectors in the same area as the Israeli violation.

I should be grateful if you would have this letter and its annex
distributed as a document of the Security Council.

(Signed)  Abdul Amir A. AL-ANBARI
Ambassador
Permanent Representative

91-33889   2755j  (E)                                                    /...

0123

Annex

Letter dated 13 October 1991 from the Minister for Foreign
Affairs of Iraq addressed to the Secretary-General

I have the honour to draw your attention to the following two letters addressed to you: the first, dated 6 October 1991, concerns a violation by Israeli military aircraft of Iraqi airspace in western Iraq on 4 October 1991, which coincided with a flight of United Nations helicopters in the same area. The second letter, dated 12 October 1991, concerns a statement made on 9 October 1991 by Marlin Fitzwater, spokesman for the White House in the United States of America, in which he stated that the United States authorities would provide Israel with any information they obtained about Iraq.

I should like here to refer to a matter of considerable importance and sensitivity which will require from you and from the Security Council the necessary serious consideration.

On Friday, 4 October 1991, four Israeli AF-15 fighter-bombers violated Iraqi airspace. This serious violation coincided with a flight of helicopters being used by United Nations inspectors in the same area. The Israeli aircraft were flying in close military formation with the United Nations aircraft, and this could well have caused a tragic accident involving the United Nations aircraft if the Israeli war-planes had attacked targets in the area of Iraqi territory.

The fact that Israeli military aircraft violated the airspace of western Iraq at the same time as United Nations aircraft were flying over the same area was no coincidence: rather, this was deliberate and constituted one of Israel's objectives. Moreover, it is clear that this could cause our anti-aircraft defences to assess the situation wrongly and to target the United Nations aircraft when these defences were in a state of alert, expecting hostile aircraft to violate Iraqi airspace.

The presence of United Nations aircraft over western Iraq at the same time as Israeli war-planes violated that airspace prevented Iraq from taking the necessary anti-aircraft defence measures to repel the Israeli aggression against our airspace.

We are entitled to ask: what would happen if Israeli aircraft reached Baghdad or any other place in Iraq and attacked us, taking advantage of the presence of United Nations aircraft in the airspace over that area?

Such a case, which is extremely probable, would put us in a difficult position, since we would either take action to repel Israeli aggression, thereby exposing United Nations aircraft to danger, or be unable to defend our country, leaving the Israelis to strike any targets they deemed fit. It should be noted in particular that the Israelis have asserted in more than one

0124 /...

official statement that they will continue their violations of Iraqi airspace, claiming that that is one of their duties in maintaining the security of Israel.

We have raised this matter forcefully and in detail with Mr. Rolf Ekéus, Chairman of the Special Commission, during his latest visit to Baghdad from 4 to 6 October 1991.

I urge that you give consideration to this matter, and that either you or the Security Council take the necessary measures to ensure that Israel will not repeat its violations of Iraqi airspace, and give assurances of that. Otherwise, in the event of renewed Israeli aggression against our airspace when United Nations aircraft are present in the same area, we shall not be responsible for the safety of those aircraft and of any United Nations inspectors on board as we respond to aggression by Israeli war-planes in defence of our country and our interests. This is a legitimate right guaranteed under international law and the Charter of the United Nations.

I cannot but express my regret at the failure of the Security Council to respond forcefully to the serious, aggressive conduct manifested by Israel against Iraq, and I can only say that the position taken by the Security Council up to this time confirms once again the pursuit of a policy of double standards and two different yardsticks.

I should be grateful if you would reply to this letter, and I request you to have it distributed as a document of the Security Council.

(Signed)  Ahmad HUSSEIN
Minister for Foreign Affairs of
the Republic of Iraq

-----

0125

# UNITED NATIONS

# Security Council

**S**

Distr.
GENERAL

S/23140
14 October 1991
ENGLISH
ORIGINAL: ARABIC

---

LETTER DATED 13 OCTOBER 1991 FROM THE PERMANENT
REPRESENTATIVE OF IRAQ TO THE UNITED NATIONS
ADDRESSED TO THE SECRETARY-GENERAL

On instructions from my Government, I have the honour to transmit to you herewith a letter dated 12 October 1991 from Mr. Ahmad Hussein, Minister for Foreign Affairs of the Republic of Iraq, concerning the statement made on 9 October 1991 by Marlin Fitzwater, the White House spokesman, to the effect that the United States of America is providing Israel with the intelligence it has obtained on Iraq.

I should be grateful if you would have this letter circulated as a document of the Security Council.

(Signed)  Abdul Amir A. AL-ANBARI
Ambassador
Permanent Representative

91-33895  2673f (E)

/...

0126

<u>Annex</u>

<u>Letter dated 12 October 1991 from the Minister for Foreign
Affairs of Iraq addressed to the Secretary-General</u>

I have the honour to refer to our letter to you of 6 October 1991
concerning the penetration of Iraqi airspace by Israeli war-planes on
4 October and to the reactions subsequently voiced by many countries with
regard to the violation of Iraq's airspace and that of other Arab countries.
In this connection, the statement made on 9 October 1991 by Marlin Fitzwater,
the White House spokesman, in the course of his comments on this action gave
us pause.  He is reported to have said that the United States understands
Israel's concern but that the United States authorities were already providing
"Israel" with intelligence on the alleged Iraqi danger and particularly on
weapons of mass destruction.

This explicit acknowledgement on the part of the spokesman of the United
States White House that the United States Administration is providing Israel
with intelligence on Iraqi military secrets exposes the true state of affairs
that we have long indicated to you in our letters, namely that the United
States is using the Special Commission and the inspection teams as a cover for
its espionage activities against Iraq.  The information obtained by the United
States Administration through the Special Commission and the inspection teams
on Iraq's military secrets goes directly to Israel.

I should like to refer you in particular to our letter to you of
19 August 1991 in which I asked to receive from you an assurance that the
intelligence and photographs gathered by the United States U-2 spy aircraft
would remain in the custody of the United Nations and be used to serve the
purposes of the Special Commission established by Security Council resolution
687 (1991).  I have not, unfortunately, thus far received from you any such
assurance.  It has come to light that the intelligence and photographs
gathered by this American aircraft, which is flown by an American pilot and
takes off from an American base in Saudi Arabia, do not represent an
independent source of information but that the intelligence and photographs go
first to the United States and then to the party identified by Mr. Fitzwater
in his statement.

In another respect, you perhaps recall that in my letter to you of
2 August 1991 I expressed concern at the fact that the Special Commission uses
a majority of United States inspectors in the composition of its teams, while
no one can be unaware that the United States is persisting in its pursuit of a
hostile and biased policy against Iraq.  That letter was written following the
revelation that the Chief of the sixth inspection team, Mr. David Kay, had
transmitted Iraqi documents directly to his superiors in Washington and not to
the Special Commission, thereby confirming Iraq's suspicions that the
Government of the United States was using the Special Commission and the
United Nations as a cover for systematic espionage operations against Iraq.
Then, today, there comes the statement of Mr. Fitzwater to complete a circle

/...

0127

of facts that has demonstrated that the intelligence, photographs and documents gathered by the Special Commission are ultimately going to Israel. This represents a grave threat to Iraq's national security and is incompatible with the role of an Organization among whose priorities is the preservation of the sovereignty and territorial integrity of its Member States.

In light of the facts we have referred to above and in light of the recent military and media escalation against Iraq, among whose manifestations has been the recent Israel violation of Iraq's airspace and that of other Arab States, we urge you to re-examine the procedures and practices of the Special Commission in order to ensure that they do not exceed its mandate as laid down in Security Council resolution 687 (1991).

That you should make such a re-examination is a pressing matter that is enjoined by the need to preserve the credibility of the United Nations and of its role as set forth in the Charter, and in particular with regard to respect for Iraq's sovereignty and territorial integrity, just as it is required by the constraints of preserving the security and stability of the region.

We request you to have this letter circulated as a document of the Security Council.

(Signed)  Ahmad HUSSEIN
Minister for Foreign Affairs

-----

0128

# UNITED NATIONS

## Security Council

Distr.
GENERAL

S/23141
14 October 1991
ENGLISH
ORIGINAL: ARABIC

LETTER DATED 13 OCTOBER 1991 FROM THE PERMANENT
REPRESENTATIVE OF IRAQ TO THE UNITED NATIONS
ADDRESSED TO THE SECRETARY-GENERAL

On instructions from my Government, I am pleased to transmit herewith a letter dated 13 October 1991 from Mr. Ahmad Hussein, Minister for Foreign Affairs of the Republic of Iraq, concerning the protest of the Iraqi Government at Turkey's violation of Iraq's territorial integrity.

I should be grateful if you would have this letter and its annex circulated as a document of the Security Council.

(Signed)  Abdul Amir A. AL-ANBARI
Ambassador
Permanent Representative

<u>Annex</u>

<u>Letter dated 13 October 1991 from the Minister for Foreign
Affairs of Iraq addressed to the Secretary-General</u>

I have the honour to refer to the statement made by the Prime Minister of
Turkey, Mr. Mesut Yilmaz, in Ankara on 11 October 1991 that, on Friday,
11 October 1991, the Turkish Air Force had carried out an aerial operation in
northern Iraq in which eight Turkish warplanes crossed the Iraqi border to the
south of Çukurca in the Hakkâri area.  They penetrated to a distance of
7 kilometres inside Iraqi territory, bombed the Iraqi villages of Banik,
Shilan, Siyar, Sirya and Bighufa in that area and used napalm bombs against
civilians in those villages.  Initial press reports mentioned the wounding of
at least five persons as a result of this savage bombardment.

This flagrant violation of the territory of the Republic of Iraq and its
sovereignty and territorial integrity constitutes a clear breach of the United
Nations Charter, the norms of international law and the Iraq-Turkey border
treaty of 1926.  The continuation of these violations will be extremely
damaging to relations of good-neighbourliness and cooperation between the
Iraqi and the Turkish peoples.

In registering the protest of the Republic of Iraq at this behaviour, I
wish to inform you that the Iraqi Government reserves Iraq's full right to
take such action as it deems appropriate under international law and the
United Nations Charter with regard to the violations committed against its
territory and its national territorial integrity.

In informing you of this blatant violation of the sovereignty and
integrity of Iraqi territory, we request you to intervene and to take
immediate measures to put an end to these violations, which are, first and
foremost, damaging to the credibility of the United Nations and its role in
protecting the independence and territorial sovereignty of Member States.

I request you to have this letter circulated as a document of the
Security Council.

(<u>Signed</u>)  Ahmad HUSSEIN
Minister for Foreign Affairs

-----

0130

# 주 국 련 대 표 부

주국련 20312-    **782**                                1991. 10. 17.

수신 : 장관

참조 : 국제기구국장, 중동아프리카국장

제목 : 걸프사태


　　이락의 안보리 휴전결의 이행 위반 실태에 관한 미측 백서 (white paper)를
별첨과 같이 송부합니다.


첨부 : 상기 백서. 끝.

　　　　　　　　　주 국 련 대


| 59004 | 0131 |

THE REPRESENTATIVE
OF THE
UNITED STATES OF AMERICA
TO THE
UNITED NATIONS

September 25, 1991

Dear Colleague,

I have the honor to enclose a "white paper" on Iraqi performance under United Nations Security Council Resolution 687, the ceasefire resolution.

This paper discusses the requirements set out by UNSCR 687, Iraqi actions, and the position of the United States on what Iraq needs to do to fulfill its obligations under the United Nations ceasefire resolution.

The paper covers in some detail Iraqi actions regarding the implementation of UNSCR 687's provisions concerning weapons of mass destruction. It also discusses Iraqi noncompliance with other United Nations resolutions mandating requirements such as the return of Kuwaiti property, the repression of Iraqi citizens, the repatriation of Kuwaiti detainees, support for terrorism, and the demarcation of the Kuwait/Iraq border.

This "white paper" was drafted before the most recent incidents of Iraqi obstruction of Special Commission investigation teams:  the unwillingness of Iraqi authorities to allow a nuclear weapons team to remove certain documents relevant to the Iraqi nuclear weapons program, their detention of a nuclear weapons inspection team in Baghdad, and Iraqi unwillingness to agree -- at least initially -- to unconditional use of Special Commission aircraft.

I hope you and your colleagues will give careful consideration to this serious study.  We would be pleased to address any questions or receive any comments you might wish to offer.

Sincerely,

Thomas R. Pickering

0132

# IRAQI PERFORMANCE UNDER THE UN CEASEFIRE RESOLUTION

September 20, 1991

0133

## KEY JUDGMENTS

UN Security Council Resolution 687 demands that the government of Iraq agree, unconditionally, to declaration, inspection, and elimination of all of its weapons of mass destruction (WMD) and ballistic missiles. The resolution also demands that Iraq return Kuwaiti property and detainees, cease all support of international terrorist activities, and demands that Iraq and Kuwait respect the inviolability of the international boundary between the two countries as set out in the Agreed Minutes of October 4, 1963. A related resolution, UNSCR 688, demands that Iraq cease repression of its citizens.

The Iraqi government has repeatedly violated the provisions of these Security Council resolutions. The first four months of inspections by the UN Special Commission and IAEA have begun to illuminate Iraq's covert programs for WMD and ballistic missiles. For example, Iraq has:

o  Misrepresented the number and scope of development of its WMD and ballistic missiles, then revealed that information, when compelled by UN inspections and international pressure, calculated to avoid further action by the Security Council. As an example, the chart below shows Iraq's piecemeal approach to declaring its WMD and missile facilities.

| | Declarations of Sites to the UN | | |
| --- | --- | --- | --- |
| | As of Apr 18 | As of Jun 18 | As of Sept 1 |
| Nuclear | 1 | 1 | 29 |
| CW | 8 | 11 | 12 |
| BW | 0 | 0 | 1 |
| Missile | 4 | 9 | 12 |

o  Used deception and concealment to prevent UN inspection teams from locating equipment subject to elimination under Resolution 687;

o  Denied UN inspection teams full and unrestricted access to facilities associated with WMD and ballistic missiles; and

Iraq has not fully complied with the requirements of Resolution 687 to return Kuwaiti property or repatriate Kuwaiti detainees. It has violated its pledge not to support

0134

international terrorism and has deplored the UN process
established to settle the boundary issue. Furthermore, Iraq
continues to repress its citizens in violation of Resolution
687 and 688.

The IAEA Board of Governors voted on July 18, to find Iraq in
violation of its Safeguards Agreement and thus of the
Non-Proliferation Treaty-the first time in the Agency's
existence that such a finding has been made against a member
state.

This pattern of behavior resulted in an August 15 Security
Council resolution (UNSCR 707) condemning Iraq and holding it
in "material breach" of a number of its obligations under
Resolution 687. (Excerpts from the resolution, together with a
list of what still needs to be done by Iraq to comply, are
appended to this document.)

BACKGROUND

On April 3, 1991, the United Nations Security Council
approved Resolution 687, formally ending the Gulf War and
laying the groundwork for restoration of peace and security to
the region. In addition to requirements to respect Kuwait's
border, return stolen Kuwaiti property, repatriate all
detainees, and refrain from support of terrorism, and settle
its boundary with Kuwait, the resolution demanded that the
government of Iraq:

o   Agree, unconditionally, to internationally-supervised
    elimination of all of its weapons of mass destruction
    (WMD) and ballistic missiles, including

        -- any nuclear weapons or nuclear weapons-usable
           material;

        -- all chemical weapons and bulk CW materials;

        -- all biological weapons and bulk agent;

        -- all ballistic missiles with ranges in excess of
           150 kilometers; and

        -- facilities, components, and equipment related to
           each of these areas.

o   Declare the locations, amounts and types of each of the
    above items in its possession and agree to urgent, on-site
    inspections.

0135

Iraq accepted these conditions in return for an end to hostilities. The UN created the Special Commission which, along with the IAEA and World Health Organization, is charged with implementing the Resolution's mandates.

This document reviews Iraq's record of performance under Resolution 687 in the areas of weapons of mass destruction, ballistic missiles, and humanitarian concerns.

## WEAPONS OF MASS DESTRUCTION

### Nuclear Weapons and Nuclear Weapon-Usable Material

Requirement: Resolution 687 mandates that Iraq declare the locations, amounts, and types of all facilities and material associated with its nuclear weapons-related program, accept unconditionally their removal, destruction, or rendering harmless by the IAEA with the assistance and cooperation of the UN Special Commission, and give unimpeded access to the IAEA and UN Special Commission in implementing the Resolution's provisions.

Iraqi Actions: Iraq's original declaration, presented to the UN on April 18, stated that Iraq had no nuclear weapons program, no nuclear weapons-usable material, and that the entire Iraqi nuclear program was devoted to "peaceful purposes." However, the record of the past four months shows that Iraq continually misrepresented and concealed critical aspects of its program, obstructed inspectors, and denied the program's weapons orientation.

### Misrepresentation of Nuclear Program

o    In late June, UN inspectors found evidence of a uranium enrichment program involving electromagnetic isotope separation (EMIS). This discovery, along with previously obtained information on Iraq's nuclear activities, led Iraq to declare both the EMIS program and two other enrichment processes. However, Iraq maintained that these programs were designed to produce power reactor and research reactor fuel.

o    In early July, Iraq admitted to a large-scale EMIS enterprise involving enrichment facilities at Tarmiyah and Ash Sharqat, material production facilities at Al-Qa'im and Mosul, and several other R&D facilities (see map on next page).

0136

o    After the inspection visits, the IAEA/Special Commission inspection teams estimated that, once operational, the complexes could have operated a hundred or more enrichment devices (calutrons) with a capability to produce up to 30 kilograms of weapons-grade uranium annually.

o    In late July, after persistent questions by UN inspection teams, Iraq declared a significant centrifuge enrichment development program.  Iraq revealed a production facility at al-Farat which it said would be able to manufacture 200 or more centrifuges per year.  A subsequent IAEA/Special Commission visit produced evidence that led to an assessment that this plant's capacity could be as high as several <u>thousand</u> centrifuges per year.

o    With each additional declaration of facilities and equipment, Iraq has admitted to possessing more nuclear material, now amounting to large amounts of uranium feedstock, and small amounts of unsafeguarded enriched uranium and plutonium.

o    On August 6 Iraq admitted to producing unsafeguarded plutonium.  Maintaining that it had not earlier reported the extent of its program for fear of it being misunderstood, Iraq admitted that it had violated IAEA safeguards by fabricating and irradiating natural uranium fuel elements in one of its safeguarded Tuwaitha reactors, separating gram quantities of the resulting plutonium, failing to declare any of these activities to the IAEA, and then lying to UN inspectors about the operation's existence.  In spite of this admission, Iraq still maintained that its material production programs were simply peaceful research efforts.

### Pattern of Concealment

o    Iraq stripped large amounts of equipment from buildings at Tuwaitha, Tarmiyah, and al-Hamath and then misrepresented the functions of those buildings to inspectors.  Only when confronted with discrepancies between their declaration and observable features such as electric power, plumbing, and crane capacities -- or when confronted with inconsistencies in its previous statements -- did Iraq admit the true mission of the facilities.

o    Iraq buried EMIS equipment before the first team arrived at Tuwaitha, unearthed it after the team left the area, loaded the equipment onto trucks, and then covertly dispersed it to several undeclared locations.

0137

o   Iraq admitted hiding its clandestine plutonium production
    program at Tuwaitha from IAEA/Special Commission
    inspectors during the first three inspections by placing
    fuel elements on trucks and relocating them prior to
    inspections.

o   Iraq razed nuclear-related structures and regraded areas
    at Mosul and Tuwaitha to hamper inspectors.

o   At Tarmiyah and Mosul Iraq painted over walls and dumped
    thick layers of gravel in areas where relevant material
    samples might have been obtained.

o   At Tarmiyah, Iraq covered EMIS equipment which could not
    be easily relocated with freshly-poured concrete and
    several feet of earth.  In some cases, entire floors or
    ceilings were removed to obscure equipment foundations and
    utility connections, thus disguising the true purpose of
    buildings.

o   Iraq burned documents at both Tuwaitha and Tarmiyah and
    admitted to using explosive charges to destroy EMIS
    components at several remote locations to prevent the
    material or equipment from being viewed by inspectors.

Obstruction of Inspection Teams

o   Iraqi officials repeatedly sought to mislead inspectors
    about the purpose and functions of buildings at Tuwaitha,
    Tarmiyah, and Ash Sharqat.  In the first case, a nuclear
    association was denied; at Tarmiyah the facility was
    portrayed as a chemical processing facility; and at Ash
    Sharqat the building was described as a coating plant.

o   At the Fallujah Transportation Center, inspectors
    requested access to a truck convoy parked inside the
    facility.  While being denied access by Iraqi military
    officers at the front gate, the team photographed the
    convoy leaving the site through another gate.  When
    inspectors tried to intercept the convoy in order to
    inspect the EMIS-related cargo, warning shots were fired
    over their heads by Iraqi security personnel.

o   At Abu Ghurayb, inspectors were denied access to areas
    where EMIS equipment was being stored temporarily.  In
    addition, one inspector was denied medical care when
    requested.

0138

## Insistence on the Peaceful Intent of the Program

o   Contrary to Iraqi claims that EMIS contributed to Iraqi
    energy production,Enrichment of uranium using
    electromagnetic isotope separation requires _far_ _more_
    energy than the enriched uranium product could produce in
    a power reactor.

o   Iraq claims that the EMIS program's target enrichment
    (24%) was, in part, designed to provide fuel for the
    Soviet-supplied IRT-5000 reactor.  Yet the Soviets had
    already supplied fuel for the lifetime of the reactor and
    the size of the EMIS program exceeded any conceiveable
    requirement of the IRT-5000 reactor.

o   Iraq went to great lengths to conceal its uranium
    enrichment and plutonium production programs, as well as
    the material produced by those programs, from the IAEA and
    Special Commission.  By failing to declare nuclear
    material involved in uranium enrichment and plutonium
    reprocessing activities and by failing to provide design
    information on facilities where material was used, Iraq
    did not comply with its obligations under its Safeguards
    Agreement with the IAEA, thereby violating its obligations
    under the Non-Proliferation Treaty.

o   On July 18, Dr. Hans Blix, Director General of the IAEA,
    stated, "The large enrichment program in Iraq was
    clandestine.  It was not placed under safeguards and no
    confidence can arise that it had peaceful purposes."

## Conclusion

Since May, UN and IAEA inspections revealed Iraq has
violated Resolution 687's nuclear provisions in several
fundamental ways.  Iraq has failed to declare fully its
nuclear-related material and equipment, to accept elimination
of all of this equipment, and to provide complete inspector
access. Instead Iraq has:

o   Repeatedly _misrepresented_ its nuclear program -- most
    seriously, failing to declare its nuclear weapons-related
    activities -- and acknowledged particular nuclear
    activities only after identification by inspection or
    intelligence;

o   _Concealed_ proscribed activities and equipment, including
    efforts to remove, hide, destroy, and covertly recover
    equipment; and

o   _Blocked UN inspection teams access_ up to and including
    threats of physical force.

0139

It is now clear that Iraq's nuclear weapons program was multifaceted and well-funded. It involved:

o   thousands of well-educated scientists and engineers;

o   billions of dollars in infrastructure;

o   about 30 research, manufacturing, storage, and production sites nationwide.

o   several methods of manufacturing weapons-grade material, including EMIS, gas centrifuges, plutonium production, as well as research on gaseous diffusion, chemical, and laser isotope separation techniques.

## Chemical Weapons

Requirement:  Resolution 687 mandates that Iraq declare all chemical weapons (CW), agent stocks, and related facilities, provide full and complete access to UN inspectors, and accept the unconditional removal, destruction, or rendering harmless of all CW material, equipment, and facilities.

Iraqi Actions:  The record shows that Iraq misrepresented and concealed the size of its program.

### Misrepresentation

o   Iraq initially declared one production and storage facility, eight storage sites, 11,000 filled chemical munitions, and 1,000 tons of bulk agent and precursor material.  Four months of UN probing elicited four additional declarations which described a much more comprehensive program:

--   46,000 agent-filled chemical munitions, including 2,100 munitions filled with mixed nerve agents;

--   79,000 unfilled munitions;

--   2,700 tons of bulk agent and precursor materials;

--   3 additional chemical weapons storage sites;

--   several dual-use chemical facilities which could augment Iraq's dedicated chemical weapons program.

0140

o   At Samarra the UN Special Commission discovered evidence
    of the capability to produce two undeclared types of nerve
    agents, GB and VX.  To this point, Iraq has revealed
    production of multiple types of chemical weapons,
    including four types of agent(Sulfur Mustard, GA-B-F,
    Mixed Sarin and VX)

---

---

o   <u>Concealment</u>

o   Iraq removed CW-related documents from Samarra in June.
    This removal was noted by the inspection team, which found
    piles of ash from freshly-burnt documents nearby.

o   Inspectors observed areas of the facility which had been
    recently altered by strewing live munitions and rubble in
    front of the entrances to prevent their access.

### <u>Conclusion</u>

Since June, UN inspections have revealed that Iraq has
violated Resolution 687 by failing to: (1) fully declare its CW
weapons agent stocks, and related facilities; (2) to provide
full and complete access to UN inspectors and (3) to accept the
unconditional removal, destruction, or rendering harmless of
all CW material, equipment and facilities.

Iraq's pre-war CW capability, which prior to Operation
Desert Storm included weaponized chemical agents in bombs,
artillery shells, rocket warheads, and ballistic missiles, was
one of the largest in the world.  This, coupled with Iraq's
attempts to misrepresent its capability to the UN, implies
strongly that Saddam Hussein's intent is to circumvent
Resolution 687's chemical weapons provisions and to retain a
chemical weapons inventory.

### <u>Biological Weapons</u>

<u>Requirement</u>:  Resolution 687 mandates that Iraq declare
all biological weapons (BW), agent stocks, and related
facilities, provide full and complete access to UN inspectors,
and accept the unconditional removal, destruction, or rendering
harmless of all BW material, equipment, and facilities.

0141

**Iraqi Actions**:  Iraq maintained it had no biological weapons and had carried out no related activities.  It failed to acknowledge the existence of a biological warfare (BW) program and agent stockpiles and subsequently attempted to misrepresent facilities and programs as legitimate biological research facilities for peaceful or prophylactic purposes.

**Failure to Declare Program**

o    Iraq disclosed a BW research program at the Salman Pak facility only <u>after</u> the arrival of the BW inspection team in early August.

o    Iraq disclosed that it was experimenting with micro-organisms that have potential <u>offensive</u> military applications:

--    Botulism (<u>Clostridium botulinum</u>):  <u>Clostridium botulinum</u> produces a lethal toxin which is 10,000 times more potent than nerve agent per unit mass.

--    Anthrax (<u>Bacillus anthracis</u>):  Once inhaled, spores grow in lungs, releasing a toxin which is fatal in more than 90% of treated cases.

--    <u>Clostridium perfringens</u>:  Attacks wounds in the skin and destroys skin tissue, producing gangrenous infection which can lead to death.

o    When questioned further, Iraq finally acknowledged that it had undertaken ·research which could have had offensive military applications.  Iraq maintains, however, that it has not weaponized BW agents.

o    Iraq claimed that its BW research program, begun in 1986, was terminated in August 1990 and that all materials were destroyed or moved to other locations.  The BW inspection team, however, found clear evidence an existing Iraqi capability to produce what he team's leader characterized as "..vast quantities of biological agents". UN inspectors discovered that Salman Pak had the capacity to produce enough anthrax weekly to contaminate an area of more than 600 square miles.

o    Iraq also turned over to the inspection team a collection of 30 samples of micro-organisms which included "strong candidates" for biological warfare agents, such as brucellosis and tularaemia, that had not been previously declared.

0142

## Concealment and Misrepresentation

o   Iraq claimed that its Salman Pak BW production facility
    was a "food and liquid inspection and analysis facility"
    until confronted with evidence to the contrary by UN
    inspectors.

o   Iraq had recently razed buildings and spread dirt over
    areas that were part of the Salman Pak facility thereby
    preventing inspectors from sampling for traces of
    BW-related materials.

o·  Inspectors found evidence of removal of critical equipment
    from buildings and the removal and destruction of
    documents at several important locations within Salman Pak

o   Unexploded ordnance was recently placed at bunker sites at
    Salman Pak to impede access.  Munitions were directly in
    front of the bunkers and, despite Iraqi explanations, that·
    this resulted from Coalition airstrikes, the material had
    none of the dust and weathering that characterized other
    unexploded ordnance of Desert Storm vintage.

o   Despite the product manufacturer's public assertion to the
    contrary, Iraq continues to claim that Abu Ghurayb -- a
    suspected BW facility -- was a "Baby Milk" factory.  To
    support this assertion, Iraq released a videotape of
    workers at Abu Ghurayb wearing blue smocks with "Baby Milk
    Factory" stenciled in English on the backs.

### Conclusion

Iraq has violated the BW portions of Resolution 687 by
failing (1) to declare biological weapons agent stocks and
related facilities, (2) to provide UN inspectors full and
complete access and·(3) to accept the unconditional
removal, destruction or rendering harmless of all BW
material equipment and facilities.

## Ballistic Missiles

Requirement:  Iraq is required to declare all ballistic
missiles with ranges greater than 150 kilometers, related major
parts, and related repair and production facilities, provide
full and complete access to UN inspectors, and accept the
unconditional removal, destruction, or rendering harmless of
all such equipment and facilities.

0143

**Iraqi Actions**:  Iraq initially declared 52 Scud missiles and Scud variants and 5 sites for production, maintainence, storage, and deployment.  Subsequent inspections revealed that Iraq had misrepresented its inventory of ballistic missiles, components and facilities and attempted to deceive inspectors and conceal missiles and related components from inspection teams.

## Misrepresentation of Equipment Inventories

o   Iraq's original declaration falls hundreds of missiles short of the number that may remain in its inventory. After subtracting those missiles used in the Iran-Iraq War, the Gulf War, in test firings and those which were destroyed by the Special Commission from the 819 which Baghdad admits Moscow gave them, a large number remains unaccounted for.

o   Iraq's original declaration did not include five types of ballistic missiles covered by Resolution 687 -- the al-Fahd, the al-Abbas, and the al-Hijarah, the Tammuz I, and the Badr-2000 (Condor II).  During the initial inspection, 9 undeclared al-Fahds were discovered and destroyed.

o   Iraq initially failed to declare the "Supergun" -- an extremely large artillery-type launcher which has the capability to launch missiles with WMD payloads to ranges of several hundred kilometers. The Commission decided and communicated to Iraq that the "Supergun" therefore fell within the prohibited WMD and that Iraq should have declared it under Resolution 687. In fact, Iraq denied that it possessed such a WMD system.  It was not until mid-July that sites and equipment associated with this system were declared.

o   Iraq understated the extent of its missile production and support infrastructure by failing to declare six missile-related development and production facilities.

o   Iraq declared only 4 decoy missiles despite the existence of a large quantity before the end of Operation Desert Storm.  Subsequently, an inspection team found and destroyed 11 undeclared decoys.

o   Iraq failed to declare large amounts of Scud-related hardware and support equipment which has been discovered and tagged for eventual destruction by UN inspectors.

0144

## Efforts to Deceive Inspectors

o   During inspections of the Nassr facility, Iraq prevented inspectors from photographing suspect areas.

o   At the same time that inspectors were witnessing the destruction of proscribed missiles at the Taji facility, Iraqi officials were concealing additional proscribed missile equipment at a site nearby.

o   Iraq attempted to re-build WMD-related equipment dismantled under SPECOM direction.  Inspectors found four SCUD/Al-Hussein transport trailors previously cut in half at Taji were rewelded together and moved to an undeclared site at Khan al-Mahawil Barracks.

o   In violation of Security Council demands in Resolution 707, Iraq has refused to cooperate with the Special Commission in allowing UN helicopters to operate in Iraq in support of inspections.

## Conclusion

Iraq has violated the ballistic missile provisions in Resolution 687.

Iraq's ballistic missile program is impressive.  Using a nationwide system of research, development, and production facilities, Iraq has developed the indigenous capability to modify, produce, and launch variants of the Scud missile and has made significant progress toward producing its own long-range system.

Iraq's pre-war missile inventory of some 500 was reduced by its attacks on Saudi Arabia, Bahrain and Israel as well as by Coalition airstrikes.  Nonetheless, even after the elimination of 61 missiles by the UN Special Commission, several hundred additional missiles remain somewhere.  These undeclared missiles -- hidden from UN inspections -- will, if allowed to remain, constitute a significant covert missile force.

## Iraqi Noncompliance with Other UN Mandates

## Return of Kuwaiti Property

While publicly claiming that it is prepared to return stolen Kuwaiti property as required by Resolution 687, Iraq has provided only an incomplete list of Kuwaiti property in its possession.  It returned Kuwait's gold only after four months of international pressure.

0145

    Iraq has yet to return other Kuwaiti property, including
contents of its museums, libraries, or billions of dollars of
Kuwaiti military equipment, including Hawk air defense
missiles.  Recently Iraqi units have crossed into Kuwaiti
territory and removed weapons left behind during their retreat
from the Emirate and have also set up observation posts. In
late August,  Kuwaiti Forces detained dozens of Iraqi
personnel engaged in such activities.

Repression of Iraqi Citizens

    Reacting to Iraq's brutal repression of its citizens,
especially the Shi'a in southern Iraq and Kurds in the north,
the Security Council passed Resolution 688, which demands that
Iraq cease repression of its citizens and allow immediate
access by international humanitarian organizations to all those
in need of assistance in Iraq.  While Iraq, under the threat of
military action by Coalition forces, pulled its military forces
back from some of the Kurdish areas in the north, its police,
intelligence operatives, and military forces have continued to
pose a threat to civilians.

    Iraq signed a memorandum of understanding with the UN
Secretary General's Executive Delegate, Prince Sadruddin Aga
Khan, on April 19 covering UN relief efforts throughout the
country.  It promised cooperation and guaranteed the UN access
to all regions where relief is needed.  Despite this, Sadruddin
was initially denied access to the Southern marsh region during
his July fact-finding mission and UN personnel assigned to
establish a feeding center in Hammar were expelled immediately
after his departure.· Sadruddin's formal protest to Saddam
Hussein was answered with a letter noting that Iraq had never
accepted Resolution 688.  Iraqi troops, who had been pulled
back during Sadruddin's visit to the area, were returned to the
marshes immediately after Sadruddin's departure from the region
and the UN still has not been allowed access.

Repatriation of Kuwaiti Detainees

    Iraq agreed to Resolution 687's demand that it release
immediately all Kuwaiti and third-party detainees and provide
the International Committee of the Red Cross (ICRC) with access
to such detainees.  Kuwait has stated that Iraq still holds
about 2,422 Kuwaitis and residents of Kuwait and that Iraq has
returned only 206 adult detainees since the ceasefire in
April.  The ICRC says that Iraq has not cooperated in providing
access to all prisons, camps, and internment areas.

0146

## Support for Terrorism

In spite of Iraq's statement -- as required by Resolution 687 -- that it would not commit or support any act of international terrorism or allow any terrorist organization to operate on Iraqi territory, Iraq still allows terrorist organizations to operate on Iraqi territory.

## Settlement of Kuwait/Iraq Border

Resolution 687 required Iraq to enter into discussions with Kuwait based on the Agreed Minute of October 4, 1963 in order to settle the issue of their boundary demarcation. The Resolution further provides that both countries will respect the border's inviolability.  Although Iraq accepted Resolution 687, at the August meeting of the Boundary Commission, the Iraqi representative to the Commission stated that Iraq rejected the work of the Boundary Commission and its demarcation of the Iraq-Kuwait border.

Excerpts from UN Security Council Resolution 707

Passed unanimously on 15 August 1991

The Security Council...

Condemns Iraq's serious violation of a number of its obligations under ... Resolution 687 ... which constitutes a material breach of the relevant provisions of Resolution 687 ....

Further condemns noncompliance by the government of Iraq with its obligations under its safeguards agreement with the International Atomic Energy Agency ... which constitutes a violation of its commitments as a party to the Treaty on the Non-Proliferation of Nuclear Weapons of 1 July 1968,

Demands that Iraq:

Provide full, final, and complete disclosure ... of all aspects of its programs to develop weapons of mass destruction and ballistic missiles with a range greater than 150 kilometers ... without delay ...

Cease immediately any attempt to conceal, or any movement or destruction of any material or equipment relating to its nuclear, chemical or biological weapons or ballistic missile programs ...

0147

Halt all nuclear activites of any kind, except for use of
isotopes for medical, agricultural, or industrial purposes
until the Security Council determines that Iraq is in full
compliance with this resolution and paragraphs 12 and 13
of resolution 687 .... and the IAEA determines that Iraq
is in full compliance with its safeguards agreement with
that agency.

## What Iraq Must Do
## to Fulfill its Obligations Under
## the UN Ceasefire Resolution

### Nuclear Weapons

o   Completely disclose all aspects of its nuclear weapons
    program; [Declare all its nuclear weapons and nuclear
    weapons usable material and any subsystems, components,
    research, development, or manufacturing facilities related
    to the above;]

o   Turn over to the IAEA and Special Commission for
    destruction, removal, or rendering harmless all proscribed
    nuclear material and equipment [Present to the IAEA for
    destruction, removal, or rendering harmless, with the
    assistance and cooperation of the UN Special Commission,
    all items and material specified above;]

o   Reveal all facilities for weaponization; and

o   Provide all designs and documentation associated with its
    weapons development program.

### Missiles

o   Cease contending all missiles and launchers have been
    destroyed;

o   Give the UN the missiles and launchers it is now hiding;

o   Provide all components, including those indigenously
    manufactured; and

o   Reveal all production and repair facilities for missiles,
    launchers, their components, and propellants.

0148

## Chemical Weapons

o   Turn over to the UN remaining chemical bombs, artillery, shells, and rockets;

o   Reveal all types of chemical weapon agents it manufactured; and

o   Identify all production, weaponization, and storage facilities.

## Biological Weapons

o   Reveal the full extent of its biological weapons program;

c   Turn over to the UN for destruction the biological weapons it is now hiding;

o   Reveal all production, weaponization, and storage facilities.

## Long-Term Monitoring

o   Accept all UN Security Council approved plans for long-term monitoring.

## Other UN Mandates

o   Return all stolen Kuwaiti property.

o   Accept the UN-mandated border demarcation.

o   Cease and desist all incursions across the Kuwaiti border and dismantle any posts which it has established on sovereign Kuwaiti territory.

o   Cease repression of its citizens, particularly the Kurdish and Shi'a populations, and permit full access by international relief organizations.

o   Repatriate all Kuwaiti citizens and other detainees held by Iraq and provide for full access to prisons, internment camps, and other holding areas by the ICRC.

o   Discontinue all support for international terrorist organizations operating on Iraqi territory.

2653R

0149

# 주 국 련 대 표 부

주국련 20312- **783**                                        1991. 10. 17.

수신 : 장관

참조 : 국제기구국장, 중동아프리카국장

제목 : 이락 석유수출 허용 (안보리 결의 712호)


　　　　표제관련 사무국 서한을 별첨과 같이 송부합니다.


첨부 : 상기 서한. 끝.


# 주 국 련 대 사

58700                                                        0150

POSTAL ADDRESS—ADRESSE POSTALE  UNITED NATIONS, N.Y. 10017
CABLE ADDRESS—ADRESSE TELEGRAPHIQUE· UNATIONS NEWYORK

REFERENCE:  SCPC/7/91(6)

The Secretary-General of the United Nations presents his
compliments to the Permanent Representative of the Republic of Korea
to the United Nations and has the honour to transmit herewith, for
the attention of His/Her Excellency's Government, resolution
712 (1991), adopted by the Security Council at its 3008th meeting
held on 19 September 1991, in connection with its consideration of
the item entitled "The situation between Iraq and Kuwait".


24 September 1991


S. B.


Annex enclosed


0151

# UNITED NATIONS

**Security Council**

Distr.
GENERAL

S/RES/712 (1991)
19 September 1991

**S**

RESOLUTION 712 (1991)

Adopted by the Security Council at its 3008th meeting,
on 19 September 1991

The Security Council,

Recalling its previous relevant resolutions and in particular resolutions 661 (1990) of 6 August 1990, 686 (1991) of 2 March 1991, 687 (1991) of 3 April 1991, 688 (1991) of 5 April 1991, 692 (1991) of 20 May 1991, 699 (1991) of 17 June 1991, and 705 (1991) and 706 (1991) of 15 August 1991,

Expressing its appreciation for the report dated 4 September 1991 submitted by the Secretary-General pursuant to paragraph 5 of resolution 706 (1991), 1/

Reaffirming its concern about the nutritional and health situation of the Iraqi civilian population and the risk of a further deterioration of this situation, and underlining the need in this context for fully up-to-date assessments of the situation in all parts of Iraq as a basis for the equitable distribution of humanitarian relief to all segments of the Iraqi civilian population,

Recalling that the activities to be carried out by or on behalf of the Secretary-General to meet the purposes referred to in resolution 706 (1991) and the present resolution enjoy the privileges and immunities of the United Nations,

Acting under Chapter VII of the Charter of the United Nations,

1. Confirms the figure mentioned in paragraph 1 of resolution 706 (1991) as the sum authorized for the purpose of that paragraph, and reaffirms its intention to review this sum on the basis of its ongoing

---

1/   S/23006.

91-30826   3626Z (E)                                                          /...

0152

assessment of the needs and requirements, in accordance with paragraph 1 (d) of resolution 706 (1991);

2.   Invites the Security Council Committee established by resolution 661 (1990) to authorize immediately, pursuant to paragraph 1 (d) of resolution 706 (1991), the release by the Secretary-General from the escrow account of the first one-third portion of the sum referred to in paragraph 1 above, such release to take place as required subject to the availability of funds in the account and, in the case of payments, to finance the purchase of foodstuffs, medicines and materials and supplies for essential civilian needs that have been notified or approved in accordance with existing procedures, subject to compliance with the procedures laid down in the report of the Secretary-General as approved in paragraph 3 below;

3.   Approves the recommendations in the Secretary-General's report as contained in its paragraphs 57 (d) and 58;

4.   Encourages the Secretary-General and the Security Council Committee established by resolution 661 (1990) to cooperate, in close consultation with the Government of Iraq, on a continuing basis to ensure the most effective implementation of the scheme approved in the present resolution;

5.   Decides that petroleum and petroleum products subject to resolution 706 (1991) shall while under Iraqi title be immune from legal proceedings and not be subject to any form of attachment, garnishment or execution, and that all States shall take any steps that may be necessary under their respective domestic legal systems to assure this protection, and to ensure that the proceeds of sale are not diverted from the purposes laid down in resolution 706 (1991);

6.   Reaffirms that the escrow account to be established by the United Nations and administered by the Secretary-General to meet the purposes of resolution 706 (1991) and the present resolution, like the Compensation Fund established by resolution 692 (1991), enjoys the privileges and immunities of the United Nations;

7.   Reaffirms that the inspectors and other experts on mission for the United Nations, appointed for the purpose of the present resolution, enjoy privileges and immunities in accordance with the Convention on the Privileges and Immunities of the United Nations, and demands that Iraq allow them full freedom of movement and all necessary facilities;

8.   Confirms that funds contributed from other sources may if desired, in accordance with paragraph 1 (c) of resolution 706 (1991), be deposited into the escrow account as a sub-account and be immediately available to meet Iraq's humanitarian needs as referred to in paragraph 20 of resolution 687 (1991) without any of the obligatory deductions and administrative costs specified in paragraphs 2 and 3 of resolution 706 (1991);

/...

0153

9.   Urges that any provision to Iraq of foodstuffs, medicines or other items of a humanitarian character, in addition to those purchased with the funds referred to in paragraph 1 of the present resolution, be undertaken through arrangements that assure their equitable distribution to meet humanitarian needs;

10.   Requests the Secretary-General to take the actions necessary to implement the above decisions, and authorizes him to enter into any arrangements or agreements necessary to accomplish this;

11.   Calls upon States to cooperate fully in the implementation of resolution 706 (1991) and the present resolution, in particular with respect to any measures regarding the import of petroleum and petroleum products and the export of foodstuffs, medicines and materials and supplies for essential civilian needs as referred to in paragraph 20 of resolution 687 (1991), and also with respect to the privileges and immunities of the United Nations and its personnel implementing the present resolution, and to ensure that there are no diversions from the purposes laid down in these resolutions;

12.   Decides to remain seized of the matter.

-----

0154

# UNITED NATIONS

## Security Council

Distr.
GENERAL

S/23149
16 October 1991

ORIGINAL: ENGLISH

DECISION TAKEN BY THE SECURITY COUNCIL COMMITTEE ESTABLISHED BY
RESOLUTION 661 (1990) CONCERNING THE SITUATION BETWEEN IRAQ
AND KUWAIT AT ITS 51ST MEETING, HELD ON 15 OCTOBER 1991

<u>Procedures to be employed by the Security Council Committee established by
resolution 661 (1990) concerning the situation between Iraq and Kuwait in the
discharge of its responsibilities under Security Council resolutions
706 (1991) and 712 (1991)</u>

I.   <u>Preparatory steps</u>:

1.   The Committee will select, upon recommendation by the Secretariat, three
     independent experts in international oil trade as "overseers" at United
     Nations Headquarters, and entrust them with the authority to approve or
     reject oil sale contracts on behalf of the Committee.  The overseers will
     be authorized to correspond with applicants as needed.  The nomination of
     three persons will ensure a 24-hour availability for contract approvals.

2.   Other experts, agents and inspectors (as required below) will be
     appointed by the Secretary-General.  The Committee will take note of
     these appointments.

3.   States may, if they so wish, forward to the Committee a list of national
     oil purchasers (private companies, State-owned companies, State agencies,
     ministries, etc.) authorized to communicate with the overseer.  Once the
     Committee has taken note of these lists and passed them on to the
     overseer, these purchasers are entitled to communicate directly with the
     overseer (see sect. II, part A, para. 3 below).  If States do not submit
     such a list, or if a certain purchaser is not included in the list, the
     communication with the overseer must go via the Permanent Mission in
     New York.

4.   For the purpose of section II, part A, paragraph 3 below, a Standard
     Application Form will be elaborated by the Committee and circulated among
     all States.  States and national oil purchasers shall use only these
     Standard Application Forms.

91-34269  2760j (E)                                                  /...

0155

5.   The Secretariat will set up a new fax line to be used exclusively for
     correspondence with regard to oil transactions.  Applicants are requested
     to send their relevant applications and relating correspondence only via
     this fax line.  Other correspondence with the Committee shall go through
     the already existing channels.

6.   Iraq and Turkey will have to conclude an arrangement on the price and
     payment modalities for the use of Turkish oil installations.  Once this
     arrangement is concluded, it must be forwarded to the Committee which
     will take note of it.  United Nations agents will check the
     implementation of this arrangement and report periodically to the .
     Committee.

7.   Monitoring of delivery to Iraq of foodstuffs, medicines, and materials
     and supplies for essential civilian needs will be done by independent
     inspection agents appointed by an appropriate United Nations programme or
     organization, such as, for example, the Office for Project Services
     (OPS).  Monitoring of the distribution of these goods will be arranged by
     the Executive Delegate in cooperation with relevant United Nations
     programmes and organizations, including appropriate humanitarian
     non-governmental organizations (NGOs).  The Committee will be informed
     about the relevant arrangements, including those for the purpose of
     section III, part A, paragraph 11 below.

8.   Upon recommendation by the Secretariat, the Committee will nominate an
     expert (a staff member of one of the United Nations programmes or
     organizations) who will act as an aide to the Committee for the purposes
     of section III, part A, paragraph 8 below.

II.  Sales of Iraqi oil and oil products:

     A.   Sales of Iraqi oil:

1.   The Iraqi State Organization for the Marketing of Oil (SOMO) signs a
     contract with the purchaser.  The contract must include the provisions as
     specified in paragraph 58 of the report by the Secretary-General pursuant
     to paragraph 5 of Security Council resolution 706 (1991) (S/23006).

2.   United Nations agents at SOMO review the contracts to assure compliance
     with the provisions of paragraph 58 of the Secretary-General's report and
     forward by fax copies of the approvable contracts, supporting documents,
     and their independent reports to the overseer in New York.

3.   The national oil purchaser or the Permanent Mission of the State of
     purchase forwards by fax a formal request (Standard Application Form) for
     approval to the Committee, together with a copy of the contract and all
     other supporting documents.

/...

0156

4.   The overseer reviews the contract and supporting documents to ensure that:

   -   they comply with paragraph 58 of the Secretary-General's report, including that a confirmed irrevocable letter of credit is opened providing for payment into the escrow account;

   -   the conditions of payment envisaged in the letters of credit are in conformity with existing market practices;

   -   they do not appear to contain any attempt at fraud or deception;

   -   the transaction's pricing is consistent with world prices and market trends; and

   -   the transaction does not exceed the limits imposed by Security Council resolutions 706 (1991) and 712 (1991).

5.   If the contract and supporting documents are found to be in order, the overseer, on behalf of the Committee, approves the sale (within the shortest period of time possible, at the maximum 24 hours) and informs by fax the national oil purchaser or the Permanent Mission concerned, as well as SOMO.

6.   The overseer sends his notification of sales approval, together with a copy of the contract, supporting documents, and the report of the United Nations agent at SOMO, by fax to the inspector at Ceyhan who will authorize loading only after these documents are in his possession.

7.   Depending on the number of applications, the overseer reports to the Committee, in a structured and standardized manner, at least twice a week on contracts approved by him (including the cumulative quantity and value of oil authorized for export), and informs the Secretary-General accordingly.

8.   The oil is pumped into storage tanks.  Agents at the pipeline check the pumping.  Subject to their confirmation, the oil can be loaded on ships and the ships can leave the terminal.  The agents will have the authority to prohibit the delivery of the oil if there is any evidence of irregularity.

9.   The agents report to the Committee on their assessment of the pumping and loading.

10.   The purchaser makes payment into the escrow account.

11.   Twice a week, the Secretary-General forwards statements of the escrow account, including outlines of anticipated future obligations, to the Committee.

/...

0157

B.    Sales of Iraqi oil products:

The regime for the sale of oil products will be broadly similar to that described above, but the precise arrangements will be elaborated at a later stage, as and when the need arises.

III. Purchase by Iraq of foodstuffs, medicines, and materials and supplies for essential civilian needs:

A.    Purchase by Iraq of foodstuffs, medicines, and materials and supplies for essential civilian needs, to be financed from the escrow account:

1.    Iraq sends a categorized list of relevant requirements to the Executive Delegate.  (Preferably, a two-months list, quantity- and value-oriented.) If Iraq intends also to finance medicines from the escrow account, these too should be mentioned in general terms on the list, together with their value.  The overall value of the list must not exceed that part of the amount authorized by the Committee, in accordance with paragraph 2 of Security Council resolution 712 (1991), which is available for humanitarian purchases.

2.    The Executive Delegate forwards the list, revised by him if necessary, to the Committee.

3.    The Committee takes action on the list and forwards to the Secretary-General and the Executive Delegate the list as approved.  (The first list will be taken up at a meeting of the Committee; subject to agreement, later lists might be dealt with under a "no-objection" procedure.)

4.    The Secretary-General will make the list known to all States.

5.    The Executive Delegate informs Iraq about the clearance.

6.    Iraq signs a contract with the exporter, in accordance with normal commercial practice and the relevant Security Council resolutions.

7.    (a)  Medicines:

The Permanent Mission of the exporter's country informs the Committee of the exporter's wish to be paid from the escrow account.  A copy of the relevant contract must be attached to this communication.

(b)  Foodstuffs:

The Permanent Mission of the exporter's country notifies the Committee. This notification must contain the information that the exporter wants to be paid from the escrow account.  A copy of the relevant contract must be attached to this notification.

/...

0158

(c)  **Materials and supplies for essential civilian needs**:

The Permanent Mission of the exporter's country requests approval, under the "no-objection" procedure, by the Committee.  This request must contain the information that the exporter wishes to be paid from the escrow account.  A copy of the relevant contract must be attached to this request.

8.  An expert (aide to the Committee) checks the contracts, in particular on the price/value relationship, and informs the Chairman.  His findings will be attached to the circulation note to Committee members.

9.  (a)  **Medicines**:

(i)  If the contract is found in order, the Committee informs the Permanent Mission concerned and the Secretary-General that the contract has been found in order, i.e. the exporter can expect payment from the escrow account.

(ii)  If the contract is not found in order, the Committee informs the Permanent Mission concerned and the Secretary-General that the contract has not been found in order, i.e. the exporter cannot expect payment from the escrow account.  However, medical supplies can be shipped anyway if the exporter so wishes.

(b)  **Foodstuffs**:

(i)  If the contract is found in order, the Committee takes note of the notification and informs the Permanent Mission concerned and the Secretary-General accordingly and states that the contract has been found in order, i.e. the exporter can expect payment from the escrow account.

(ii)  If the contract is not found in order, the Committee takes note of the notification and informs the Permanent Mission concerned and the Secretary-General accordingly but states that the contract has not been found in order, i.e. the exporter cannot expect payment from the escrow account.  However, foodstuffs can be shipped anyway if the exporter so wishes.

(c)  **Materials and supplies for essential civilian needs**:

(i)  If the contract is found in order, and if the Committee approves the shipment under the "no-objection" procedure, it informs the Permanent Mission concerned and the Secretary-General of the approval and states that the contract has been found in order, i.e. the exporter can expect payment from the escrow account.

/...

0159

(ii) If the contract is not found in order, and if the Committee nevertheless approves the shipment under the "no-objection" procedure, it informs the Permanent Mission concerned and the Secretary-General of the approval but states that the contract has not been found in order, i.e. the exporter cannot expect payment from the escrow account. However, the goods can be shipped anyway if the exporter so wishes.

(iii) If the Committee cannot approve the shipment, whether or not the contract is found in order, the goods are not allowed to be shipped.

From here on only if the contract has been found in order:

10. The Secretary-General may effect part-payment to the exporter, according to commercial practice.

11. United Nations agents check the delivery (the quality, quantity, labelling, etc.) at the unloading port and the entry points to Iraq and report to the Committee. The agents will have the authority to inspect the shipment documents and, if necessary, to open and examine the contents as needed.

12. The Committee evaluates the reports. If satisfactory, it approves the final payment and informs the Secretary-General.

13. The Secretary-General effects final payment.

14. United Nations agents monitor in-country distribution and report, via the Executive Delegate, in a consolidated manner to the Committee.

15. The Committee evaluates these reports to ensure that equitable internal distribution is being maintained and takes appropriate action if not.

16. Twice a week, the Secretary-General forwards statements of the escrow account, including outlines of anticipated future obligations, to the Committee.

B. Purchase by Iraq of foodstuffs, medicines, and materials and supplies for essential civilian needs, to be financed from the sub-account of the escrow account:

1. According to paragraph 8 of Security Council resolution 712 (1991), imports financed from the sub-account of the escrow account, are, apart from the provision of paragraph 1 (c) of Security Council resolution 706 (1991), subject only to the provisions and procedures of paragraph 20 of Security Council resolution 687 (1991).

/...

0160

2.   Monitoring (paragraph 1 (c) of Security Council resolution 706 (1991))
     will be carried out as indicated in annex II of the Secretary-General's
     report.

3.   Twice a week, the Secretary-General forwards statements of the
     sub-account of the escrow account, including outlines of anticipated
     future obligations, to the Committee.

-----

0161

# 이라크, 미확인 재원으로 다량의 식량구입

( 91.10.22. 워싱턴 포스트 )

1. 이라크는 9.19. UN 안보리결의 712호 (향후 인도적 수요를 위해 6개월간
   16억불 상당의 원유수출 허용)의 실시없이도, 수백만톤의 식량수입 승인을
   UN안보리 제재위에 신청, 허가를 득하였음.

2. 한 서방 외교관에 의하면 이라크는 이외에도 최근 수개월내 2백만톤의
   식량을 수입한바, UN측도 그대금 출처에 대해서는 의아해하는 실정으로
   아마도 사담 후세인 정권이 은닉해둔 재원을 사용하고 있는것으로 추정.

3. 이라크는 현재 상기 안보리결의안 712호를 결코 수락할수 없다는 입장이며
   해외에 동결중인 3억4천만불 상당의 자산도 국제적 문제 해결을 위해
   사용하는 것을 거부해 왔음.

4. 현재 이라크는 요르단으로 육운을 통해 석유를 수출하고 있으나 이는
   이제까지 수입한 식량에 비하면 극히 적은 부분임.

5. 이에 대해 이라크는 동대금이 민간분야에서 지불하는 것으로서, 결코
   비밀재원이 있는것이 아니라고 주장하고 있으나, 서방측은 이는 매우
   큰 액수이며 아마도 이라크 정부가 풍부한 경화재원을 갖고 있음을
   암시하는 것이며 이는 아마도 보유 금괴일 것이라고 말함.

6. UN은 또한 현재까지 이라크내의 식량사정이 점차 악화되고는 있으나
   아직까지 기아상태는 아닌것이 신기하다고 언급하였음.

7. 마지막으로 UN은 이라크가 UN결의안 712호의 이행을 위해 터어키 통과
   소유관 사용 문제를 교섭중이나, 그타결을 지연시키고 있으며 타결시에도
   원유를 수출할 것인지는 불확실한바, 이는 모종의 정치적 계획이거나
   아니면 이라크가 여타의 재원을 갖고 있음을 암시하는 것이라고 밝혔음.

0162

발 : USV(F) - 4461
신 : 중    군 (동동일, 이남, 이아, 천단)발신 : 우어덱서
목 : 이락 식량수입동계                              ( 1 매)

# U.N. Wonders How Iraq Imports Food, Keeps Oil

## Conjecture Includes Sale of Gold Reserves

### By Trevor Rowe
#### Special to The Washington Post

UNITED NATIONS, Oct. 21— U.N. officials say they are puzzled that Iraq has not found it necessary to sell oil or seek to use previously frozen funds to purchase food and medical supplies many predicted would be in "critical" need.

Instead, a senior U.N. official said, Iraq has requested and been given approval by the Security Council's sanctions committee to import "several million tons of food" without indicating where Baghdad got the funds to pay for it.

"We don't know how Iraq financed the import of food until now. Maybe he [President Saddam Hussein] has hidden assets," the U.N. official said. The United Nations did grant permission to import the food, the official added, but it does not know how much already has been delivered to Iraq.

Food and medical supplies are exempt under U.N. economic sanctions against Iraq, and Baghdad is not required to indicate how it intends to pay for those imports.

A Western diplomat said Iraq is believed to have imported up to 2 million tons of food in recent months. All of the food was part of new orders and unrelated to shipments contracted before the Persian Gulf War, he said, adding, "Where did they get the money?"

U.N. officials, including Secretary General Javier Perez de Cuellar, repeatedly have warned of serious food shortages and near-famine conditions in Iraq.

In response to this and warnings from humanitarian groups, the U.N. Security Council on Sept. 19 authorized Iraq to sell up to $1.6 billion in oil to buy medical supplies and food. About $900 million of this amount is slated for food, and the rest is to pay for U.N. administration expenses and for a fund to compensate those who suffered as a result of Iraq's invasion of Kuwait.

However, Iraq has not sold its oil and argues that a U.N. mechanism set up to monitor oil sales and food distribution violates its sovereignty. "Iraqis will eat the earth rather than accept this, you can quote me," an Iraqi diplomat said.

U.N. sources said Iraq also has refused so far to make use of an estimated $340 million that had been frozen in the Bank for International Settlements.

The official said a number of countries and relief organizations have provided humanitarian aid to Iraq and helped to offset its food needs. He also said that overland shipments of oil products to Jordan were another source of money. But he said this accounted for only a small portion of the food imported so far.

The Iraqi denied his government had any "secret" source of money. He said the food imports were paid by the country's private sector. But a Western diplomat said, "This is far too big. It has to be government money, and it suggests they have plenty of hard currency around."

When asked where Iraq would get the money, the diplomat said, "Presumably their gold holdings, since they never told us the amount of their reserves."

The U.N. official said press reports and those sent by U.N. relief officials indicate that while "the food situation keeps slowly deteriorating," there are "no reports" of famine. "Market prices are soaring and rations are low, and we're surprised Iraq is not using its authorization to export oil."

Further delaying any possible petroleum exports is the fact that Iraq has yet to reach an agreement with Turkey on the use of Ankara's oil pipeline. But it is still unclear, even if that agreement is reached, that Baghdad will proceed to sell oil.

"Either this is a political ploy, or Iraq has other resources," said the U.N. official.

Oct. 22, 1991
WP
END

0163

# 이라크서 거부

【바그다드=AP聯】이라크는 제한된양의 원유수출만을 허용한 유엔의 「大이라크 조치들이 잣차 석유시장을 위험에 빠뜨릴것이라고 비난, 이를 거부했다고 오사마 알히티 이라크·석유장관이 24일 말했다.

히티장관은 이날 『이들 두 유엔결의안을 적용하는 것은 매우 복잡하며 어떤 경우에도 원유수출이나 석유시장의 이익에 도움이 되지 못할것』이라고 주장했다.

유엔결의 제706호와

712호는 이라크가 향후 6개월간 최고 16억달러어치의 원유를 수출, 그대금을 부족한 식량및 의약품 구매지원으로 사용토록 허용하는것을 그내용으로 하고있다.

## 이라크 核부품 실험

【유엔본부=AP聯】이라크는 핵무기 개발계획이 상당한 진전을 보여 이미 原爆 관련 부품의 폭발실험까지 마쳤다고 유엔 핵전문가가 24일 전했다.

10.26. 조선.

# 외 무 부

종 별 :

번 호 : UNW-3538          일 시 : 91 1025 2230

수 신 : 장 관(연일, 중동일,미일,기정)

발 신 : 주유엔대사

제 목 : 걸프사태

표제사태관련 금 10.25 자 NYT 지 기사를 별첨송부함.

첨부: UNW(F)-733 끝

(대사 노창희-국장)

---

국기국    1차보    미주국    중아국    외정실    분석관    청와대    안기부

PAGE 1                                                    91.10.26    12:47 WG

외신 1과 통제관

0165

UN(P)-759  11025  2250
중 2014

# IRAQI MINISTER REJECTS U.N. PLAN

## Final Decision Not Yet Made on Exports to Cover Costs of Food and Medicine

### By PATRICK E. TYLER
#### Special to The New York Times

BAGHDAD, Iraq, Oct. 24 — Iraq's Oil Minister said today that he had recommended that his Government reject a United Nations Security Council plan to allow the sale of $1.6 billion in Iraqi crude oil to finance the purchase of food and medicine.

The Oil Minister, Osama A. R. al-Hiti, charged in an interview that the terms laid down by the council's sanctions committee are "impractical" and "damaging" to Iraq's oil industry. He also said that the measures were an attempt by the United Nations to take away Iraq's control over its principal resource as a way to undermine President Saddam Hussein.

The sanctions committee developed the plan to allow limited oil sales to finance purchases of food and medicine while insuring that Iraq pays war reparations to Kuwait and cooperates with the destruction of its arsenal.

Mr. Hiti will not make the final decision on whether Iraq accepts the U.N. procedures, but he said there is no timetable for the Hussein Government to make the decision.

### Pipeline Complications

Mr. Hiti said Iraq had made no recent attempt to determine whether its export pipeline through Turkey could be activated, although he added that Iraq is aware of reports that the pipeline could require months of cleaning after having sat idle since August 1990. He said his ministry was assured by Turkey that there were no obstacles to immediate resumption of pumping.

The United Nations procedures call for Iraq to pump crude oil to the Mediterranean terminal at Ceyhan, where United Nations personnel must approve contracts and every step of the sale and loading of oil. All proceeds would be paid into a U.N.-controlled fund to pay for closely monitored food shipments. Thirty percent will go toward reparations to Kuwait.

"The problems we will face without using this resolution are much easier than the problems we will face after using it," Mr. Hiti said. "It is like a spider web. Once you get into it, there is no end, and you will never be free from this."

Mr. Hiti said the U.N. procedures would prevent Iraq from concluding barter deals and pre-financing arrangements that were established with

lead to high pipeline costs with no assurance that further sales would be authorized.

### Political Objections

Iraq's objections to the arrangements were as much political as technical, he said. "They are trying to change our Government, and it's not going to happen," he said."

Like other members of Mr. Hussein's Cabinet, Mr. Hiti expressed a strong determination to weather the tough conditions Iraq is suffering as a result of the restrictions imposed after the Persian Gulf war.

He said that after United Nations sanctions were lifted Iraq planned to nearly double its prewar production to 6 million barrels a day by 1995, a step that could require the Organization of Petroleum Exporting Countries to relinquish some quotas and markets to Iraq.

"I have put it forward to other OPEC members that Iraq reserves the right to ask for an extra quota to make up for those OPEC members who have gained from our situation," he said.

He asserted that with the lifting of sanctions, Iraq could return to exporting 1.25 million barrels per day "within a few days" and could reach its prewar export level by late 1992.

In a separate interview, Iraq's minister of industry, Amir H. al-Saadi, said that with the onset of cool weather in Iraq and with 70 percent of the country's power-consuming industries idle, his ministry would be able to provide ample electricity for some time.

But if United Nations sanctions continue into next spring with the return of searing daytime temperatures, he said

3D

0166

# Gulf Nations said to Be Committed

## to U.S. Alliance

By YOUSSEF M. IBRAHIM
Special to The New York Times

RIYADH, Saudi Arabia, Oct. 22 — Saudi Arabia and its allies on the Arabian Peninsula have emerged from the year-long Persian Gulf crisis persuaded that their security in the foreseeable future depends on closer military ties to the United States and a significant expansion in the size and armaments of their own military forces, senior Arab officials say.

These officials acknowledged that the elements of a broad security pact that will institutionalize these convictions are still being discussed with the United States, France and Britain, but they disputed reports in the United States that the Saudi Government has been dragging its feet in wrapping up an accord.

More than a dozen officials who discussed these plans here and in Bahrain said that the Saudis were firmly committed to a major component of the plan, a program to more than double the size of their armed forces to about 200,000 over the next five to seven years. One official said the intention was to "raise the threshold under which Saudi Arabia will call for help," as it did after the Iraqi invasion of Kuwait in August 1990.

More modest military buildups are planned for the other members of the Saudi-led Gulf Cooperation Council — a regional alliance that includes Kuwait, Oman, the United Arab Emirates, Bahrain and Qatar. The smaller countries will also make storage places available to position heavy American and perhaps European war materiel.

The officials said that the so-called "forward element" of the United States Central Command, now based in Tampa, Fla., will be stationed either in Oman or in the United Arab Emirates. Earlier reports had suggested that Bahrain, where there is now a small American naval service installation, was the primary candidate for this function.

### Sensitivity on Foreign Troops

Foreign and Saudi officials said the United States had shown understanding for Saudi Arabia's wish not to have any large number of foreign troops on its soil, given the sensitivity of this issue among large segments of the Saudi population.

"The Saudis don't want any foreign troops stationed here, be they Arabs or non-Arabs," said a senior Gulf diplomat who has participated in negotiations on what he described as a "long-term security plan" for the Gulf region.

But the Saudi Government has denied recent reports that the Saudis had refused to accept additional American forces here to prepare for further military action against Iraq, should that be deemed necessary.

"Everything that is needed to undertake such action is in place," a senior envoy here said.

stone of their security, and indeed the security of all G.C.C. members."

Some United States officials in Washington have been described in recent press reports published as disturbed by the pace of negotiations with the Saudis and suggested that a dispute had arisen over the storage here of American military hardware. These reports also suggested that the United States has resisted Saudi requests for the purchase of weapons for an expanded Saudi Army.

But officials here, including Western as well as Arab diplomats, said these accounts were the product of what one senior envoy described as "narrowly focused" Pentagon views that failed to take into account wider considerations. Several of those interviewed insisted that the United States and Saudi Ara-

---

## Stronger local defenses and firm ties to the West.

---

bia, which are the principal parties in the talks, were agreed on the broad outlines of the security plan.

The official said that the still-evolving plan consists of three elements. One is that the six Gulf Cooperation Council countries will strengthen their defenses. This will be supplemented by agreements on the prepositioning of equipment and military cooperation between the six Gulf countries and the United States, France and possibly Britain. Finally the accords will be supplemented with a security agreement between the Gulf alliance and Egypt and Syria, which might be called upon to contribute "a symbolic" military presence in Kuwait.

Kuwait has already announced an agreement to station American troops and equipment there. The United Arab Emirates and Oman are formulating similar agreements. But the program to strengthen Gulf defenses will focus on Saudi Arabia, by far the largest country in the alliance.

A participant in strategy talks this summer between senior Saudi and United States military officials said it was decided "that they need the sort of defense that was established here by the Desert Shield operation which involved some 200,000 troops that can convincingly deter or stop an attacker, at least until help arrives."

One senior Arab official said that Saudi Arabia always assumed that it did not have the kind of enemies against whom it might have to marshal large numbers of troops. That, he said, is why it has always concentrated on having a strong air force but not a

The official said this Saudi thinking has now fundamentally changed. He said that while "Saudi Arabia agreed with the United States assessment" that it needed a force equivalent to the Desert Shield force within Saudi Arabia, such a force had to be Saudi and under total Saudi control.

### 'Confluence of Events'

The reason, he stressed, is that the "confluence of events" that resulted in the sending of American troops to Saudi Arabia may not be repeated.

"I am not sure," he said, "what would have happened, for instance, if Dukakis were the President of the United States. Would he have sent American forces here? Could we gamble on that?"

The officials, virtually all of whom spoke on condition that they not be identified, said that while the Saudi Air Force acquitted itself well in the Gulf war, the performance of the 38,000-man Saudi Army pointed to the need for a vast expansion in its size.

It was concluded that a military reserve system should be established, and that the Saudi National Guard, a 25,000-man force now largely charged with functions related to internal security, should be doubled or tripled. Similarly, the Saudi navy of 10,000 will have to expand to more effectively patrol both the Persian Gulf and the Red Sea. Altogether the officials agreed that the Saudi forces should be increased over the next five to seven years to about 200,000, from the present total of about 90,000.

### System of Recruitment

Saudi officials said they did not expect major difficulties in increasing their military recruitment, which has been based on quotas assigned to the country's various Bedouin tribes. Officials said that the system tended to exclude the country's rapidly growing urban population, and that tapping this group would yield the needed recruits.

Bigger problems were seen in raising the money to pay for the expansion. The senior diplomat estimated that the Saudis spent $65 billion during the Gulf crisis, and that they need time to find way to generate new funds as they have, by all accounts, nearly exhausted their once fabulous reserves which had reached a high of $80 billion in the late seventies.

"For the United States," a diplomat here explained, "the war was brief, inexpensive, perhaps even profitable. It has unified the American people and restored the prestige of the United States military. Here, the war was very expensive, deeply divisive particularly

주 국 련 대 표 부

주국련20313-  **848**

수신  장관

참조  국제기구국장, <u>중동아프리카국장</u>

제목  걸프사태(안보리)

표제관련 안보리문서를 별첨과 같이 송부합니다.


첨 부 : 상기문서. 끝.


주 국 련 대 사

0168

# UNITED NATIONS

 **Security Council**

Distr.
GENERAL

S/23168
25 October 1991
ENGLISH
ORIGINAL: ARABIC

LETTER DATED 25 OCTOBER 1991 FROM THE PERMANENT
REPRESENTATIVE OF IRAQ TO THE UNITED NATIONS
ADDRESSED TO THE SECRETARY-GENERAL

On instructions from my Government, I transmit herewith a quotation from the official minutes of the talks that took place on 5 October 1991 in Baghdad between Mr. Tariq Aziz, Deputy Prime Minister, and Mr. Ekéus, Chairman of the Special Commission. The minutes were drafted in original Arabic and English and represent accurately and fully what the Deputy Prime Minister said to Mr. Ekéus concerning Iraqi research in the scientific and technological fields.

I should be grateful if you would have this letter and its annex circulated as a document of the Security Council.

(Signed) Abdul Amir A. AL-ANBARI
Ambassador
Permanent Representative

91-35552   2604c (E)                                                    /...

0169

### Annex

#### Quotation from the official minutes of the talks that took place in Baghdad on 5 October 1991 between Mr. Tariq Aziz, Deputy Prime Minister, and Mr. Ekéus, Chairman of the Special Commission

The Deputy Prime Minister spoke as follows:

"Twenty-three years have elapsed since the commencement of our experience in power, and we know the dangers arising from transforming an Arab State and bringing it to the nuclear-weapon-manufacturing stage. We know that this is not permitted for Arabs.

"Yes, we have had much research done in the area of science and technology, but knowledge is one thing and going beyond knowledge to the stage of weapon-building is another thing. They are accusing Iraq of spending billions of dollars on research and know-how. Following the great rise in oil prices in the mid-1970s, Iraq became a rich State and directed its wealth and its financial surplus to research and the construction of an advanced scientific and technological base that would contribute to the building of our country and raise the standard of living for our people. We did [that] instead of spending our money on buying palaces, yachts and other luxuries, as [President] Bush's friends do. We spent our surplus money on building an industrial base and advanced infrastructures for the future, not on building up a nuclear industry. Accordingly, the construction of this advanced base has borne fruit in the restoration of the bridges, refineries, electric power plants and communications centres destroyed by the aggression."

-----

0170

# Security Council

Distr.
GENERAL

S/23165
25 October 1991

ORIGINAL:   ENGLISH

## NOTE BY THE SECRETARY-GENERAL

The Secretary-General has the honour to transmit to the Security Council a report submitted by the Executive Chairman of the Special Commission established by the Secretary-General pursuant to paragraph 9 (b) (i) of Security Council resolution 687 (1991).

<u>Enclosure</u>

<u>Letter dated 24 October 1991 from the Executive Chairman of
the Special Commission established by the Secretary-General
pursuant to paragraph 9 (b) (i) of Security Council
resolution 687 (1991) addressed to the Secretary-General</u>

I have the honour to refer to the session of the Special Commission
established by the Secretary-General pursuant to paragraph 9 (b) (i) of
Security Council resolution 687 (1991), which was held at United Nations
Headquarters from 21 to 23 October 1991.  In the course of its work, the
Special Commission had before it a report submitted by me as Executive
Chairman on the activities undertaken by the Special Commission in the initial
five months of operational activities under section C of Security Council
resolution 687 (1991).  The Commission agreed that my report should be
transmitted to you with the request that it be circulated as a document of the
Security Council.

(<u>Signed</u>)  Rolf EKEUS
Executive Chairman
Office of the Special Commission

0172

/...

Annex

Report by the Executive Chairman of the Special
Commission established by the Secretary-General
pursuant to paragraph 9 (b) (i) of Security
Council resolution 687 (1991)

## A.  SCOPE OF THE REPORT

1.    Six months have elapsed since the adoption by the Security Council on
3 April 1991 of its resolution 687 (1991).  Pursuant to section C of that
resolution the Special Commission (UNSCOM) was established to perform the
functions assigned to it in that section.  These relate to the elimination of
Iraq's weapons of mass destruction and the means of their production as well
as to ensuring that the acquisition of such weapons is not resumed in the
future.  Pursuant to his executive responsibilities, the present report is
presented by the Executive Chairman to give an account of the initial five
months of operational activities.

2.    This is the first comprehensive account of the work undertaken to
implement section C of Security Council resolution 687 (1991) and subsequent
related resolutions.  Consequently, it touches upon the establishment,
composition, organization, mandate and financing of the Special Commission, as
well as its operational activities in the chemical, biological and ballistic
missile fields and its responsibilities in the nuclear field.  Where
necessary, separate appendices deal with these various aspects.  The report
highlights significant issues.  It also gives the Executive Chairman's
assessment of the results achieved, the difficulties encountered and what
remains to be done to secure full implementation of the requirements of the
Security Council resolutions.

## B.  SERVICING OF THE SPECIAL COMMISSION

3.    Immediately upon the establishment of the Special Commission as a
subsidiary organ of the Security Council, steps were taken to set up a small,
full-time secretariat to assist the Executive Chairman in the exercise of his
functions.  The secretariat is stationed principally at United Nations
Headquarters in New York, with a field office in Bahrain and a support office
at Baghdad.  The Bahrain office serves as the staging area for the assembly,
briefing and report writing of inspection teams, while the Baghdad office
provides the required logistical support in the field.  The secretariat has
been assisted in its work by members of the Commission.  Other staff have been
provided by Governments, the United Nations Secretariat, in particular the
Department for Disarmament Affairs, and the World Health Organization (WHO).
Inspection teams have consisted of personnel made available by Governments,
members of the Commission, the United Nations Secretariat, WHO and, in the
nuclear field, by inspectors and staff of the International Atomic Energy
Agency (IAEA).  In composing the teams, selection was principally based upon

/...

0173

the technical qualifications and expertise of the inspectors with due regard
to drawing the members of inspection teams from as many Member States as
possible within the range of available capabilities and experience. Nationals
of 34 countries have so far served on inspection teams. In briefing team
personnel on their assignments, attention is drawn to their responsibilities
as experts on mission for the United Nations acting under a mandate from the
Security Council. Further information on the Special Commission and the
functions of the secretariat is contained in appendix I to the present report.

4.    The Executive Chairman wishes to place on record his profound
appreciation to the Secretary-General, to Governments and to the agencies
concerned for the assistance made available as well as to the able staff
placed at his disposal for the dedicated service they have rendered, sometimes
in very trying and dangerous circumstances, to carry out the mandate of the
Security Council.

## C.   STATUS, PRIVILEGES AND IMMUNITIES

5.    After extensive and sometimes difficult negotiations, an agreement was
concluded with the Government of Iraq concerning the status, privileges and
immunities of the Special Commission, the IAEA and United Nations specialized
agencies involved in implementation of Security Council resolution
687 (1991). The provisions in the agreement with Iraq are recapitulated,
elaborated upon and reinforced in the Special Commission's plan a/ for future
ongoing monitoring and verification of Iraq's compliance with relevant parts
of section C of Security Council resolution 687 (1991) which was approved by
the Council in its resolution 715 (1991) of 11 October 1991. An agreement has
also been concluded with the Government of Bahrain in respect of the field
office at Manama.

## D.   PROGRESS MADE

6.    The implementation of section C of Security Council resolution 687 (1991)
involves what can most conveniently be described as a three-stage process.
First, there is the inspection and survey phase, designed to gather the
information necessary to make an informed assessment of Iraq's capabilities
and facilities in the nuclear, chemical, biological and ballistic missile
fields. The second phase is concerned with the disposal of weapons of mass
destruction, facilities and other items related thereto through destruction,
removal or rendering harmless, as appropriate, as provided for in resolution
687 (1991). Third is the long-term monitoring phase, to ensure ongoing
verification of Iraq's compliance with its obligations under section C of
resolution 687 (1991). These phases may run concurrently, but they provide a
convenient basis for assessing what has been achieved so far.

7.    At present, it can be said with some confidence that through rigorous and
intensive inspections by the Special Commission in the chemical, biological
and ballistic missile fields and by IAEA and the Special Commission in the

0174    /...

nuclear field, it has been possible to compile, in the course of the first phase, sufficient information to have a general picture of Iraq's capabilities and facilities in all the areas concerned. However, some important lacunae remain; filling them will be pursued energetically.

8.   By the end of October 1991, 20 inspection missions will have been fielded. For a list of the missions, see appendix II to the present report. Thirteen of these missions related to chemical, biological and ballistic missile areas. The other seven missions were nuclear inspection missions undertaken by IAEA with the assistance and cooperation of the Special Commission. Such assistance and cooperation included the provision of persons with expertise in the fields of nuclear weapons, various nuclear energy related technologies as well as special materials. It also included broad logistical support, such as explosive ordnance disposal, information, communications, medical, interpretation and photographic support and financing. Furthermore, the Commission has the responsibility, in the absence of declarations by Iraq, for designating locations for nuclear inspections as well as for all other inspections. Such designations are based on assessments made within the Special Commission, or on information received from interested Member States.

9.   In the nuclear field, the IAEA-led inspections have disclosed three clandestine uranium enrichment programmes or activities: chemical, centrifuge and electromagnetic isotope separation as well as laboratory-scale plutonium separation. The sixth nuclear inspection finally obtained conclusive evidence of a nuclear weapons development programme, aimed at an implosion-type nuclear weapon linked to a surface-to-surface missile project. Given the information obtained about the advanced nature of Iraqi efforts to develop an implosion system, it appears that it is the availability of adequate amounts of fissile material that would have been the major factor in determining how soon Iraq could have produced a nuclear device. For example, if Iraq would have started with natural uranium using its electromagnetic isotope separation (EMIS) technology, that time could have been as little as 12 to 18 months. Further information will be found in appendix III to the present report.

10.   Subject to confirmation by the completion of the verification phase in the near future, it seems probable that a full assessment of Iraq's chemical weapons capabilities will be achieved. So far Iraq has acknowledged possession of 46,000 pieces of filled munitions. Iraq's facilities include the substantial chemical weapons production complex of the Al Muthanna State Establishment and three planned precursor production plants in the Al Fallujah area. In addition to the central storage of filled chemical munitions, warfare agents and precursor chemicals in bulk at Al Muthanna, filled chemical munitions, often damaged and leaking, are stored at various sites throughout the country. The process of moving these munitions to storage at Al Muthanna prior to destruction has been initiated. Al Muthanna has been designated as the central destruction site for Iraq's chemical weapons. Destruction of filled munitions and bulk agents at Al Muthanna will begin early in 1992 and is expected to continue into 1993. To date, 11,829 unfilled chemical munitions have been destroyed by Iraqi personnel under the supervision of

0175        /...

Special Commission inspectors.  Further information will be found in appendix IV to the present report.

11.  In the area of biological weapons capabilities, the inspection activities initially focused on the major research and development site at Salman Pak but over 10 additional sites have now been inspected.  Conclusive evidence that Iraq was engaged in an advanced military biological research programme has been collected.  No evidence of actual weaponization has been found, but the inspections have provided a sound data base for future monitoring of biological capabilities in Iraq.  Details are given in appendix IV.

12.  In the field of ballistic missiles - those with a range greater than 150 kilometres - the Special Commission inspection teams have supervised the destruction of 62 ballistic missiles, 18 fixed Scud missile launch pads, 10 launchers, 11 decoy missiles, 32 ballistic missile warheads, 127 missile storage support vehicles, a substantial amount of rocket fuel, an assembled 350 millimetre supergun, components for 350 and 1,000 millimetre superguns and 1 tonne of supergun propellant.  In addition, inspectors have confirmed the destruction by coalition bombing of several missile repair and production facilities.  However, important questions remain unresolved; in particular, a satisfactory accounting for all the relevant missiles obtained or constructed by Iraq, and a full disclosure of plans and progress in future ballistic missile development.  Further work is required to obtain a full accounting of Iraq's missile capabilities before the Special Commission can certify that all subject items have been identified.  Details will be found in appendix V to the present report.

13.  Continuing work on concepts and details of compliance monitoring, in conjunction with IAEA, has resulted in the development of plans for long-term monitoring in the chemical, biological and ballistic missile areas and, separately, on nuclear monitoring.  Although these two plans were initially drawn up separately, the drafts have as far as possible been harmonized by the Special Commission and IAEA.  A notable factor in the preparation of the plans has been the cooperation from and the inputs submitted by various Governments.  Monitoring and verification under the Special Commission's plan will need to cover not only military but also civilian sites, facilities, material and other items that could be used or activities that could be involved in contravention of Iraq's obligations under Security Council resolution 687 (1991).  In order to ensure Iraq's compliance with these undertakings, the Special Commission, pursuant to resolutions 687 (1991) and 707 (1991) will, through inspections and aerial overflights, as well as the provision of information by Iraq, monitor and verify these activities, sites, facilities, material and other items.

14.  In sum, the activities of the Special Commission and IAEA have been highly effective in the period under review, particularly taking into account that five months ago the Commission was without staff, resources and plans of operation and was required to build up from the very beginning the infrastructure required for its functioning.  Account must also be taken of the magnitude of the task with which the Special Commission and IAEA have been

0176

/...

faced, given the scope and variety of Iraq's efforts to conduct research and, in certain areas, to produce weapons of mass destruction. These efforts, particularly in the nuclear field, have consumed a significant portion of Iraq's expenditure of billions of dollars derived from its oil revenues, as indicated to the Executive Chairman in his meeting with the Deputy Prime Minister of Iraq, Mr. Tariq Aziz, at Baghdad, on 5 October 1991, when the Deputy Prime Minister, while denying acquisition of nuclear weapons, admitted research in this field.

15. The accomplishments of the Special Commission and the inspection teams, which are described briefly in paragraphs 9-13 above, are thus remarkable. The activities undertaken have resulted in a situation, of significance for the future, where:

(a) Regarding chemical weapons and biological weapons capabilities, a comprehensive data base will shortly be at hand;

(b) In the ballistic missile field, it would also seem that a comprehensive understanding should be within reach, even if further inspections and analysis are required to be able to state with full confidence that a complete disclosure of remaining ballistic missiles has been made by Iraq;

(c) In view of the lack of full cooperation by Iraq and its persistent concealment efforts, a complete disclosure of the nuclear weapons programme of Iraq has yet to be made. The sixth nuclear inspection produced important and definitive evidence that much remains to be done;

(d) The Plans for compliance monitoring prepared by the Special Commission (S/22871/Rev.1) and by IAEA (S/22872/Rev.1) have been submitted to the Security Council. They were formally approved by unanimity on 11 October 1991 in Security Council resolution 715 (1991).

E. ATTITUDE OF IRAQ

16. The inspections undertaken have had to be energetic, rigorous and intensive because of the failure of Iraq, particularly in the nuclear field, to adopt the candid and open approach to the disclosure of its capabilities which is called for in section C of resolution 687 (1991). While cooperation from Iraq has generally been forthcoming at the field level - most notably in the chemical and to a degree in the biological areas - in relation to activities and resources declared by Iraq, a totally different attitude of non-cooperation, concealment and sometimes false information has emerged in relation to non-declared activities, resources and sites that have been designated by the Special Commission on the basis of its own assessments or of data supplied to it by States.

17. This has resulted in a number of serious incidents, including those of 23, 25 and 28 June 1991, when a nuclear inspection team was denied access to

/...

0177

certain facilities and, on the latter occasion, shots were fired by the Iraqi military to deter the team from photographing trucks transporting materials previously removed from Iraqi nuclear programme sites.  These incidents were reported to the Security Council (S/22739 and S/22743), and resulted in the Council dispatching, at the end of June 1991, a high level mission (see S/22746), composed of the Executive Chairman of the Special Commission, the Director General of IAEA and the United Nations Under-Secretary-General for Disarmament Affairs to meet with the highest levels of the Iraqi Government. This mission received various assurances of full cooperation from the Government, which were confirmed to the Secretary-General (S/22762), but, as the mission reported to the Security Council (S/22761, annex, para. 17), "in spite of their unambiguous character, the general assurances given and the specific measures promised can only be evaluated in the light of present and future implementation by the Iraqi authorities".

18.   The misgivings thus expressed by the mission have been amply confirmed by the subsequent conduct of the Iraqi authorities, culminating in the detention of a further nuclear inspection team in a parking lot at Baghdad for four days at the end of September 1991.  This serious and material violation by Iraq of its obligations under the relevant Security Council resolutions and its agreement on the status, privileges and immunities of the Special Commission and IAEA does not stand alone.  Despite express provisions in the agreement, Iraq refused for almost three months to permit the Special Commission to introduce its own helicopter air-support system into Iraq, a matter that had to be reported to and was the subject of representations by the Security Council (S/23064 and S/23070) and which had to be taken up by the Executive Chairman on a special visit to Iraq early in October 1991.  That air-support system is now finally operational in Iraq although certain practical details need to be worked out regarding the most direct flight patterns for particular flights.

19.   The elements of misinformation, concealment, lack of cooperation and violation of the privileges and immunities of the Special Commission and IAEA have not created any trust in Iraq's intentions.  They have had a negative impact on relations with Iraq and have engendered an atmosphere of profound scepticism, particularly in the nuclear area; this atmosphere has to some degree contaminated the other three areas.  It has had for Iraq an effect directly contrary to its professed desire for an early lifting of the sanctions imposed in the relevant Security Council resolutions.  It has led to the adoption of Security Council resolution 707 (1991) of 15 August 1991 and it constituted an element that had to be taken most seriously into account in the preparation by the Special Commission and by IAEA of their plans for securing Iraq's future compliance with the provisions of section C of resolution 687 (1991).  A change in the attitude of Iraq to one of candour, transparency and cooperation at all levels is probably the one single element that could contribute most substantially to a timely and satisfactory implementation of the mandate of the Special Commission and of IAEA.  Only then will it be possible to present a finding by them that Iraq is in substantial compliance with its obligations under section C of resolution 687 (1991).

0178   /...

## F.  ISSUES FOR THE IMMEDIATE FUTURE

20.  The progress made, despite obstacles placed in the way by Iraq, in completing the first stage of activities under section C of resolution 687 (1991), gives increasing urgency to a number of issues, particularly the destruction, removal or rendering harmless of items proscribed by the resolution; the organization and initiation of compliance monitoring; the compilation and provision of information on suppliers of Iraq in the nuclear, chemical, biological and ballistic missile fields; and some critical administrative issues.

### 1.  The issue of destruction

21.  The Special Commission established at an early stage a Destruction Advisory Panel to advise on the particularly difficult and hazardous area of chemical weapons destruction.  The Panel met on 24-28 June 1991, 5-9 August 1991 and 10-14 September 1991, and has submitted three substantive reports.  A small fact-finding mission also visited Baghdad on 11-14 August 1991 for detailed technical discussions with the competent Iraqi authorities on the role of Iraq in the destruction of their chemical weapons munitions, agents, precursors and intermediates.  Final decisions on the technologies to be used to destroy Iraqi chemical warfare agents and the extent of Iraqi involvement in the destruction process now require urgent consideration.  The decisions made will have to take account of the need to ensure public safety, to enforce acceptable emission standards and to be as far as possible rapid and cost-effective.  A second fact-finding mission to Iraq is under preparation in this connection.

22.  Another urgent issue relates to the destruction of equipment and support facilities in prohibited weapons programmes.  Decisions will have to be taken on a number of dual-use items that have been used or were acquired in order to be used in the prohibited areas.  A balance must be found between the requirements of resolution 687 (1991) to destroy, remove or render harmless all such items, on the one hand, and requests from Iraq, on the other, that such items be used for civilian and peaceful purposes.  Team leaders have been issued with provisional guidelines in this regard, but these will have to be refined in the light of experience, also taking due note of any changes in Iraq's attitude to cooperation with the Special Commission and IAEA.

### 2.  Compliance monitoring

23.  Following approval by the Security Council of the compliance monitoring plans drawn up by the Special Commission and by IAEA, it is now urgently necessary that the organization, detailed procedures and resources required to implement these plans should be developed and emplaced.  Included in this implementation programme is the need for a comprehensive data base that will draw together information from various sources.  A start has been made on developing this data base and this will be pressed forward with vigour.

0179                    /...

### 3. Information on suppliers to Iraq

24. Another issue of importance is the release from the Special Commission and IAEA of information pertaining to foreign procurement to the Iraqi weapons programmes. Such information, previously acquired sporadically, is now systematically being collected. It indicates a pattern of broad and successful Iraqi procurement efforts in many countries. While many suppliers obviously have carried out perfectly legitimate exports of general purpose or dual-use items, which have thereafter been transferred to weapons programmes, there are also indications of circumvention of national or multinational export controls and non-proliferation regimes. Until information is more complete and a full analysis of the material has been performed, the Special Commission and IAEA have agreed to release specific information only to Governments requesting information on Iraqi procurement efforts in their countries. However, once a comprehensive data base has been obtained and fully analysed, relevant information will be made available to the Sanctions Committee in connection with compliance monitoring. Furthermore, the broader objective of preventing the spread of weapons of mass destruction will require an active and open release policy.

### 4. Administrative issues

25. Two problems of an administrative nature have faced the Commission from its inception, solutions to which are of crucial importance both for the completion of the current phases and for the implementation of the long-term monitoring plans: these are the staffing and financing of the Special Commission.

26. To date the small staff has been made up of highly qualified experts on loan from Governments and on assignment from other United Nations offices. In the case of experts on loan from Governments, many of them hold positions of high responsibility in their home countries and a pressure is increasingly being felt that they return to their normal work places. In the case of United Nations staff, the same pressure exists from releasing departments for staff on assignment to the Commission. Additionally, because of the press of other responsibilities on the limited human resources of the United Nations Secretariat, there has been and continues to be understandable reluctance to release the personnel identified for staffing the field offices in Bahrain and Baghdad, which, as a result, are still not yet staffed to their full agreed levels. Ways must be found to staff fully the Commission on a more long-term basis at the high level of expertise necessary for it to accomplish its demanding tasks, particularly under the regime for ongoing monitoring and verification.

27. The issue of the financing of the Commission's activities has been complex and controversial. It has been the position of the Secretary-General that, to ensure dependability, the financing of the Special Commission should be secured through the assessment of Member States, and a budget was proposed on this basis for submission to the General Assembly through the Advisory

0180 /...

Committee on Administrative and Budgetary Questions. Approval of a budget through these regular mechanisms has been considered necessary for the establishment of posts other than on a short-term basis for the personnel of the Commission and for long-term obligations of financial resources.

28. However, this course of action was not supported by all Member States and by its resolution 699 (1991) of 17 June 1991, the Security Council called for the maximum assistance, in cash and in kind, from all States to ensure that activities under section C of resolution 687 (1991) were undertaken effectively and expeditiously. The Council also decided that the Government of Iraq should be liable for the full costs of carrying out the tasks authorized by section C, the Secretary-General being requested to submit a report on the most effective means for the fulfilment of Iraq's obligations in this respect. On the basis of that report (S/22792), which expressed the view that the most obvious way of obtaining the necessary financial resources from Iraq would be to authorize the sale of some Iraqi petroleum and petroleum products, the Council, by its resolution 706 (1991), gave such authorization subject to international controls and restrictions, part of the proceeds to be made available for meeting the costs of the Special Commission and IAEA. So far no sales have taken place and thus no proceeds made available.

29. Until these proceeds are forthcoming, the Special Commission's activities are being financed, on an interim basis, from the Working Capital Fund and, as of 1 October 1991, from trust fund sources containing the voluntary contributions from Member States for activities under Security Council resolution 687 (1991), which at this time total $5.5 million.

30. These resources have been supplemented by contributions in kind from Member States, including personnel, land and air transportation, high altitude aerial surveys, communications, chemical and biological protective and detection equipment, medical supplies and ambulances. For further information on the contributions received see appendix VI to the present report. The Executive Chairman is most grateful for all the assistance thus rendered to the Special Commission by Member States. Without it, the progress made in discharging its mandate would have been impossible.

31. However, the Special Commission remains without a formally approved budget, without a guaranteed assurance of the availability of adequate financial resources and without posts for personnel except on a short-term basis. The United Nations Controller has ensured that adequate financing has been available and thus activities of the Commission have not so far been constrained to any serious extent. However, the continuing uncertainty has caused difficulties in long-term planning and staffing. From the present time up to 31 March 1992, it is anticipated that the Special Commission will require funds in the neighbourhood of $79 million. The uncertainties that exist need urgent resolution if the Special Commission is to have the financial and budgetary stability required to implement its responsibilities for the destruction, removal or rendering harmless of Iraq's weapons of mass destruction and to prevent any reacquisition of the same through an effective and timely regime of compliance monitoring as defined in the respective plans of the Special Commission and IAEA.

0181            /...

## G.  CONCLUDING OBSERVATIONS

32.  The success of the Special Commission in carrying out its unique task under section C of resolution 687 (1991) has depended on three factors of crucial importance:

(a)  The full political support of the Security Council.  The Special Commission is a subsidiary organ of the Council, responsible to it through the Secretary-General.  The Council has been kept fully informed of the Commission's activities.  Executive summaries of the Special Commission's inspections in the chemical, biological and ballistic missile fields have regularly been made available to the Secretary-General by the Executive Chairman and by the former to the Security Council.  Reports by IAEA on its inspections have been circulated in Security Council documents (S/22788, S/22837, S/22986 and Corr.1, S/23112 and S/23122).  The Council has also been kept informed of the particular problems and difficulties that have been encountered, and the Council has reacted vigorously and affirmatively.  The statement of 27 June (S/22746) whereby the high-level mission was dispatched to Iraq, and Security Council resolutions 707 (1991) and 715 (1991) were adopted unanimously.  Finally, the strong position taken by the Council vis-à-vis Iraq during the sixth nuclear inspection when team members were detained by the Iraqi authorities (see para. 18 above) further underlined the Council's full support for the activities of the Special Commission and IAEA;

(b)  The support of Governments.  The detachment from important positions in various countries of highly qualified experts to serve in the Office of the Special Commission and on inspection missions has been of decisive importance for the implementation of a unique programme of elimination of weapons of mass destruction.  Of almost equal importance has been the provision of fixed-wing and rotary-wing air support, vehicles, specialized equipment and materials, logistics and information;

(c)  The support of the Secretary-General and of other units of the United Nations Secretariat.  The contributions of the Secretariat in experienced personnel, operations, logistics and administration, in particular from the Department for Disarmament Affairs, the Field Operations Division, the Department of Administration and Management, the Department of Conference Services and the Department of Public Information have been characterized by resourcefulness, flexibility and dedication in coping with a new and challenging task.  They go a long way to demonstrate the capabilities and potentials of the Secretariat, if financial resources are available, to manage new activities rapidly and efficiently.

33.  For the successful continuation of the Special Commission's long-term activities in Iraq, it is imperative that the strong support of the Security Council and the commitment of individual Governments and of the Secretary-General and other units of the United Nations Secretariat be maintained.

0182                    /...

### Notes

a/   S/22871/Rev.1.   See, in particular, paras. 17 and 18 and annex I of the plan.

0183                    /...

## Appendices to the report

0184 /...

Appendix I

Establishment, organization and mandate of the
Special Commission

A. Establishment

1.   By its resolution 687 (1991) of 3 April 1991, the Security Council,
acting under Chapter VII of the Charter of the United Nations, established the
terms and conditions for a formal cease-fire between Iraq and Kuwait and the
Member States cooperating with Kuwait in accordance with Security Council
resolution 678 (1990).   Section C of resolution 687 (1991) is concerned with
the elimination of Iraq's weapons of mass destruction and the means of their
production and with measures to ensure that production is not resumed.   For
these purposes paragraph 9 of section C called for a report by the
Secretary-General on the forming of a Special Commission to perform certain
tasks assigned to it in the resolution (see paras. 5-10 below).   The
Secretary-General submitted his report (S/22508) to the Security Council on
18 April 1991, and it was approved by the Council on 19 April 1991 (S/22509).
The Secretary-General's report provided for the appointment by him of the
Special Commission, headed by an Executive Chairman with a Deputy Executive
Chairman to assist the Chairman.

B. Composition

2.   The Executive Chairman, the Deputy Executive Chairman and the members of
the Special Commission appointed by the Secretary-General are as follows:
(a) Executive Chairman:  Mr. Rolf Ekéus (Sweden); (b) Deputy Executive
Chairman:  Mr. Robert L. Gallucci (United States); and (c) members:
Mr. Paal Aas (Norway); Mr. Ken Adachi (Japan); Mr. B. N. C. Agu (Nigeria);
Mr. Andrzej Badek (Poland); Mr. Bryan C. Barrass (United Kingdom);
Mr. Peter von Butler (Germany); Mr. Armando Caputo (Italy);
Mr. Ronald Cleminson (Canada); Mr. John Gee (Australia); Mr. Helmut Hönig
(Austria); Mr. B. A. Kuvshinnikov (Union of Soviet Socialist Republics);
Mr. A. J. J. Ooms (Netherlands); Ms. Marjatta M. Rautio (Finland);
Mr. Michel Saint Mleux (France); Mr. Roberto Sanchez (Venezuela);
Mr. B. Simandjuntak (Indonesia); Mr. Miroslav Splino (Czechoslovakia);
Mr. Emile Vanden Bemden (Belgium); and Mr. Yuan Renfeng (China).

C. Organization

3.   The report of the Secretary-General (S/22508) provided that, under the
Executive Chairman and the Deputy Executive Chairman, the planning and
operational direction of the functions of the Commission should be carried out
by a number of groups:  biological and chemical weapons; ballistic missiles;
nuclear weapons capabilities; future compliance; and operations support.
Taking this into account, the Special Commission organized its work as

/...

0185

indicated below.  It associated, where appropriate, experts in the fields concerned with members of the Commission on certain groups and on the destruction advisory panel which was set up by the chemical and biological weapons group.

    (a)  Nuclear/IAEA Group:  Mr. B. A. Kuvshinnikov (USSR) (Coordinator); Mr. B. N. C. Agu (Nigeria); Mr. M. Saint·Mleux (France); Mr. E. Vanden Bemden (Belgium); and Mr. Yuan Renfeng (China);

    (b)  Chemical/Biological Weapons Group:  Mr. J. Gee (Australia) (Coordinator); Mr. P. Aas (Norway); Mr. K. Adachi (Japan); Mr. B. C. Barrass (United Kingdom); Mr. H. Hönig (Austria); Mr. A. J. J. Ooms (Netherlands); Mr. R. Sanchez (Venezuela); Mr. J. Santesson (WHO); and Mr. M. Splino (Czechoslovakia);

    (c)  Destruction Advisory Panel:  Mr. R. G. Manley (United Kingdom) (Chairman); Mr. K. Flamm (United States); Mr. A. Leblanc (France); Mr. G. Leonov, (USSR); Mr. J. McAndless (Canada); Mr. R. Mikulak (United States); and Mr. J. Santesson (WHO);

    (d)  Ballistic Missiles Group:  Mr. A. Caputo (Italy); and Mr. B. Simandjuntak (Indonesia);

    (e)  Future Compliance Monitoring Group:  Mr. P. von Butler (Germany) (Coordinator); Mr. A. Badek (Poland); Mr. R. Cleminson (Canada); Ms. M. M. Rautio (Finland).

4.    Responsibilities for operations support have been vested in the Office of the Executive Chairman of the Special Commission (see para. 3 of the report) at United Nations Headquarters and in the Field Office in Bahrain and the Support Office at Baghdad.  The secretariat of these offices, under the direction of the Executive Chairman, carries out the day-to-day verification activities; compiles and analyses information; schedules, plans and organizes inspections and aerial overflights; prepares other field operations; provides general administrative support; ensures liaison with IAEA and the relevant Departments of the United Nations Secretariat; answers inquiries from Governments, the press and the public; and performs such other functions as may be required by the Executive Chairman.  In addition to staff seconded by Governments, the total number of regular United Nations staff who will be servicing the Commission when all posts are filled will be 66: 13 Professionals and 53 General Service.

## D.  Mandate

5.    The mandate of the Special Commission is established by the Security Council in paragraphs 9 (b) and 10 of section C of its resolution 687 (1991). By its resolution 699 (1991) of 17 June 1991, the Council confirmed that a 45-day period mentioned in paragraph 9 (b) did not place a time-limit on the activities to be carried out under section C of its resolution 687 (1991).

0186  /...

The mandate of the Commission and its rights were confirmed and clarified by the Council in its resolution 707 (1991) of 15 August 1991. On 11 October 1991, the Council, by its resolution 715 (1991), approved the Special Commission's plan for future ongoing monitoring and verification of Iraq's compliance with relevant parts of section C of Security Council resolution 687 (1991) (S/22871/Rev.1), which provides for the continuation of the Special Commission and for a compliance unit under it to be organized to carry out the monitoring and verification tasks provided for under the plan. At the present time, the plan is not yet operational and thus the mandate of the Commission in the period under review is governed by the pertinent provisions of resolutions 687 (1991), 699 (1991) and 707 (1991).

6.    The mandate of the Commission in the period under review has been essentially:

      (a)  To carry out immediate on-site inspection of Iraq's biological, chemical and ballistic missile capabilities, based on Iraq's declarations and the designation of any additional locations by the Special Commission itself;

      (b)  To receive from Iraq, possession for destruction, removal or rendering harmless, taking into account the requirements of public safety, of all items specified under paragraph 8 (a) of resolution 687 (1991), including items at the additional locations designated by the Special Commission under paragraph 9 (b) (i) of the resolution and to supervise the destruction by Iraq of all its missile capabilities, including launchers, as specified under paragraph 8 (b);

      (c)  To provide the assistance and cooperation to the Director General of IAEA required in paragraphs 12 and 13 of resolution 687 (1991);

      (d)  To consult the Secretary-General in developing a plan for the future ongoing monitoring and verification of Iraq's compliance with paragraph 10 of resolution 687 (1991).

7.    Paragraph 8 of resolution 687 (1991), which is directly relevant to the Commission's mandate, provides that Iraq:

      "shall unconditionally accept the destruction, removal or rendering harmless, under international supervision, of:

      "(a)  All chemical and biological weapons and all stocks of agents and all related subsystems and components and all research, development, support and manufacturing facilities;

      "(b)  All ballistic missiles with a range greater than 150 kilometres and related major parts, and repair and production facilities."

8.    Under paragraphs 12 and 13 of resolution 687 (1991), IAEA is vested with responsibilities in the nuclear area substantially similar to those of the Special Commission in the chemical and biological weapons and ballistic

/...

0187

missile areas. These responsibilities are to be carried out with the assistance and cooperation of the Special Commission. The Commission also has the responsibility to designate locations for nuclear inspections.

9.    Under Security Council resolution 707 (1991), it is, _inter alia_, confirmed that Iraq must notify and obtain prior consent from the Special Commission before any movement or destruction of any material or equipment relating to Iraq's nuclear, chemical or biological weapons or ballistic missile programmes or material or equipment relating to other Iraqi nuclear activities.

10.   For the future, by its resolution 715 (1991), the Security Council has entrusted the Special Commission with implementation of the Commission's plan for ongoing monitoring and verification. By the same resolution, the Council, _inter alia_, requires the Commission to extend, by mutual agreement, its assistance and cooperation to the Director General of IAEA in his implementation of the Agency's plan for ongoing monitoring and verification. The Council further decided by that resolution that the Commission should continue to have the responsibility for designating additional locations for inspection and overflights and should perform such other functions, in cooperation in the nuclear field with the Director General of IAEA, as might be necessary to coordinate activities under the two plans, including making use of commonly available services and information to the fullest extent possible in order to achieve maximum efficiency and optimum use of resources.

0188    /...

## Appendix II

### List of missions fielded to 31 October 1991

| Team | Inspection | Dates |
|------|-----------|-------|
| IAEA 1/UNSCOM 1 | Nuclear | 14-22 May |
| UNSCOM 2 | Chemical | 9-15 June |
| UNSCOM 3 | Ballistic missile | 30 June-7 July |
| IAEA 2/UNSCOM 4 | Nuclear | 22 June-3 July |
| IAEA 3/UNSCOM 5 | Nuclear | 6-19 July |
| IAEA 4/UNSCOM 6 | Nuclear | 27 July-10 August |
| UNSCOM 7 | Biological | 2-8 August |
| UNSCOM 8 | Ballistic missile a/ | 8-15 August |
| UNSCOM 9 | Chemical | 15-22 August |
| UNSCOM 10 | Ballistic missile | 18-20 July |
| UNSCOM 11 | Chemical | 31 August-9 September |
| UNSCOM 12 | Chemical | 31 August-5 September |
| UNSCOM 13 | Ballistic missile | 6-13 September |
| IAEA 5/UNSCOM 14 | Nuclear | 14-20 September |
| UNSCOM 15 | Biological | 20 September-3 October |
| IAEA 6/UNSCOM 16 | Nuclear | 21-30 September |
| UNSCOM 17 | Chemical | 6 October-9 November |
| UNSCOM 18 | Ballistic missile a/ | 1-14 October |

/...

0189

| Team | Inspection | Dates |
|------|------------|-------|
| IAEA 7/UNSCOM 19 | Nuclear | 11-22 October |
| UNSCOM 20 | Chemical | 22 October-<br>2 November |

---

a/   UNSCOM 8 and UNSCOM 18 also surveyed and rendered harmless the 350 millimetre and 1,000 millimetre long-range guns and components.

0190                    /...

## Appendix III

## Nuclear issues

### (Compiled with the assistance of the International Atomic Energy Agency)

#### A. Declarations

1.    On 6 April 1991, Iraq, by action of its National Assembly, agreed to Security Council resolution 687 (1991).  Pursuant to this resolution, Iraq declared on 18 April 1991 that it had none of the nuclear-related items referred to in the resolution, so "monitoring shall remain confined to the materials currently declared and used with the knowledge of, under the supervision of and subject to the safeguards of the International Atomic Energy Agency".

2.    On 27 April, in response to a letter from IAEA, Iraq declared various forms of safeguarded enriched uranium and various nuclear-related equipment, laboratories and facilities at Al Tuwaitha and Al Qaim.

3.    As a result of findings during subsequent inspections, Iraq declared on 7 July 1991 a large number of activities and facilities characterized as being part of its peaceful nuclear programme.  Key among these were three methods for enriching uranium:  electromagnetic, centrifuge and chemical exchange.

4.    Since then, Iraqi admissions of additional nuclear-related activities and facilities have continued - and inspection work has continued.  Very recently, indisputable evidence of an extensive Iraqi nuclear weapons development programme has been obtained.

#### B. Key findings

5.    The key findings of the first two nuclear inspection teams, during whose inspections (IAEA 1/UNSCOM 1 and IAEA 2/UNSCOM 4) the various forms and quantities of IAEA-safeguarded enriched uranium were located, identified and taken into IAEA custody, were as follows (S/22788):

    (a)  Much equipment and almost all documentation had been removed by the Iraqi authorities from the Al Tuwaitha Nuclear Research Centre;

    (b)  The Iraqi authorities had destroyed evidence of some of Iraq's activities or obscured it by grading, concrete pouring and other methods;

    (c)  2.26 grams of undeclared plutonium had been separated from a safeguards-exempted reactor fuel element;

    (d)  A hitherto undeclared electromagnetic isotope separation programme had existed for enriching uranium.

/...

0191

6.    In the opinion of the inspecting teams, no more than three kilograms of highly enriched uranium could have been produced at Al Tuwaitha, although a high-capacity production programme was planned for the near future.

7.    The key findings of the third nuclear inspection team (IAEA 3/UNSCOM 5) during whose inspection Dr. J. Jaffar, Deputy Chairman of the Iraqi Atomic Energy Commission, denied the existence of a nuclear weapons programme, were as follows (S/22837):

    (a)    Through procurement abroad and/or the mining and processing of indigenous uranium ores, Iraq had built up a large inventory of natural uranium;

    (b)    On the basis of data provided by Iraq, 15 kilograms of highly enriched uranium could have been produced each year when the electromagnetic isotope separation (EMIS) facility at Tarmiya became fully operational;

    (c)    An identical facility at Ash Sharqat was 85 per cent complete when it was destroyed during the war;

    (d)    On the basis of Iraqi disclosures, equivalent efforts had not been devoted to the centrifuge and chemical exchange methods.

8.    The key findings of the fourth nuclear inspection team (IAEA 4/UNSCOM 6) were as follows (S/22986 and Corr.1):

    (a)    On the basis of an Iraqi declaration, under a clandestine programme carried out in violation of its safeguards agreement with IAEA, three grams of plutonium had been separated from irradiated reactor fuel;

    (b)    Sufficient natural uranium was available to produce annually 15 kilograms of highly enriched uranium using electromagnetic isotope separators;

    (c)    On the basis of information provided by the Iraqi authorities, centrifuge production was planned to begin in 1991:  a 100-machine cascade would have been operating in 1993 and a 500-machine cascade in 1996;

    (d)    In the opinion of the inspectors, the centrifuge production facility could have built several thousands of centrifuges a year;

    (e)    Despite Iraqi denials of the existence of a weaponization programme, evidence of activities such as specialized high-explosive testing and items such as exploding bridge wire detonators indicated that a weaponization programme had existed.

9.    The key findings of the fifth nuclear inspection team (IAEA 5/UNSCOM 14) were as follows (S/23112):

    (a)    According to an Iraqi statement, 2.2 tons of heavy water which had been imported had been lost because of bomb damage to the storage tank (inspectors were shown the damaged tank);

0192

/...

(b)   The chemical exchange enrichment facilities shown to the team had been thoroughly cleaned, leaving no evidence of the extent of the programme.

10.   Preliminary key findings of the sixth nuclear inspection team (IAEA 6/UNSCOM 16) were as follows (S/23122):

(a)   Conclusive documentary evidence was found at two facilities that Iraq had had a programme for developing an implosion-type nuclear weapon;

(b)   Other documents linked the nuclear weapons development programme to a surface-to-surface missile project;

(c)   An extensive weaponization programme had been carried out at Al Tuwaitha and Al Atheer, including work with internal neutron initiators and plans for external initiators, high-explosive components, exploding bridge wire detonators and firing sets for multiple detonator systems;

(d)   Some documents indicated the existence of a project to produce a sizeable amount of lithium-6, an isotope contained in natural lithium.  The lithium-6 project was part of the overall Iraqi nuclear weapon development programme.  Lithium-6 is a key component of thermonuclear weapons and is also the source material to produce tritium, an isotope of hydrogen.  Tritium is employed in nuclear weaponry as a "booster" in nuclear weapons and as a component in certain types of neutron initiators;

(e)   The development of internal neutron initiators based on plutonium-238 was being contemplated, which provided a rationale for the Iraqi interest in separating plutonium in quantities inadequate for an explosive device;

(f)   One- and two-dimensional hydrodynamic codes based on well-known hydrodynamic models had been developed by Iraq and were used in conjunction with Iraqi-developed neutronic codes;

(g)   Gaseous diffusion existed as an enrichment method, in addition to the activities declared on 7 July 1991;

(h)   Substantial nuclear weapons-related procurement from foreign sources had been conducted;

(i)   The Iraqi authorities had devised cover explanations for external purchases, including a country-wide survey of related equipment needed in the civilian sector;

(j)   Employee lists indicated that Dr. Jaffar had had the lead technical and administrative responsibility for the nuclear weapons development programme;

(k)   Substantial facilities that had been used in the clandestine programme had not been declared.

0193   /...

## C.  Incidents and problems

11.  In addition to the continuing problem of piecemeal revelation of aspects of the nuclear programme, the following incidents stand out:

     (a)  The concealment of evidence of the EMIS programme went to the extreme of pouring concrete over tell-tale structures and covering the concrete with rubble;

     (b)  A similar concealment procedure was adopted in the case of chemical facilities where the feed material for the different enrichment processes had been prepared;

     (c)  Access to designated sites where EMIS equipment was stored was repeatedly denied;

     (d)  When one of the inspection teams was about to come upon a large quantity of EMIS equipment that the Iraqi authorities were attempting to remove, warning shots were fired in order to impede the team;

     (e)  Documents collected by inspectors in the course of the sixth nuclear inspection were forcibly confiscated by the Iraqi authorities and some of them were not returned;

     (f)  The sixth nuclear inspection team was detained for 92 hours during the week of 23 September.

## D.  Inventory of nuclear materials

12.  Apart from the safeguarded inventories declared by Iraq on 27 April 1991 and the initial estimates made by the inspection teams of the potential capability of Iraq's EMIS facilities, no evidence was found of an inventory of highly enriched uranium - and certainly none of a quantity sufficient for making an explosive device.

13.  Only a few grams of plutonium are known to have been separated.

## E.  Plan for the destruction, removal and rendering harmless of nuclear-related items

14.  The plan, developed by IAEA, addressed nuclear weapons-usable material separately from other items.  Nuclear weapons-usable material cannot be destroyed or rendered harmless in Iraq.  Consequently, the plan stipulated that IAEA will take custody of the material and remove it.

15.  Other items will be removed, destroyed or rendered harmless as appropriate.

0194   /...

### F. Plans for future compliance monitoring

16. The IAEA plan (S/22872/Rev.1) for nuclear monitoring has been closely coordinated with the Special Commission's plan (S/22871/Rev.1) for all other monitoring called for in Security Council resolutions 687 (1991) and 707 (1991). The IAEA's plan takes into account the safeguards agreement concluded with Iraq pursuant to the Treaty on the Non-Proliferation of Nuclear Weapons. It assumes that activities for which the Special Commission is responsible, including site designation and aerial surveillance, will continue in support of IAEA inspections.

17. The plan calls _inter alia_ for:

    (a) Unconditional Iraqi acceptance of all inspection rights cited in the plan;

    (b) The right to carry out inspections in Iraq anywhere and at any time, with or without advance notice;

    (c) The right to install continuous containment and surveillance equipment, including unique identifiers for material or items;

    (d) A complete inventory of items and activities in the nuclear field that might be relevant in the development of nuclear weapons and/or in the acquisition of nuclear weapons-usable material;

    (e) The advance provision of information on nuclear facility construction and imports of nuclear items that might be relevant to the production of nuclear weapons or nuclear weapons-usable material;

    (f) The barring of other States from supplying Iraq with proliferation-sensitive equipment and technology.

18. The extent to which Iraq may engage in any nuclear activity is conditioned by the provisions of section C of Security Council resolution 687 (1991) and of paragraph 3 (vi) of resolution 707 (1991), the latter requiring Iraq to halt all nuclear activities of any kind, except for use of isotopes for medical, agricultural or industrial purposes until the Security Council determines that Iraq is in full compliance with resolution 707 (1991) and paragraphs 12 and 13 of resolution 687 (1991), and IAEA determines that Iraq is in full compliance with its safeguards agreement with IAEA.

0195    /...

## Appendix IV

## Chemical and biological weapons

1.    The first chemical weapons inspection (UNSCOM 2) was a survey of the Al Muthanna State Establishment declared by Iraq as its sole chemical weapons research, development, production and filling facility; some chemical weapons munitions and bulk agents were also stored at this site.  Since it had been heavily attacked during the hostilities, it was expected that the site would be in a very hazardous condition, not only because of the presence on site of unexploded ordnance but also to damaged and leaking chemical weapons munitions and bulk chemical weapons agent stores.  One important task of the survey team, therefore, was to assess the hazards as well as to make a preliminary assessment of the site and of the Iraqi declaration as a necessary preliminary to a subsequent full, detailed and safe inspection of the site; safety considerations were considered to be a priority during this survey because of their unknown nature, magnitude and extent.

2.    Other tasks of this survey team were to include, inter alia, a general description of the Al Muthanna State Establishment; a detailed description of specific areas (identifying any that would require particular attention during the subsequent full inspection); identification of any particular problems likely to be encountered during the subsequent full inspection; any indicators of undeclared activities relevant to Security Council resolution 687 (1991); any factors relevant to the use of the site for the destruction of chemical weapons; and a brief description of the Iraqi chemical weapons munitions present.

3.    The following were the principal outcomes of the inspection:

(a)  None of the information gathered was significantly at variance with the Iraqi declarations;

(b)  No evidence was found at this site for non-chemical weapons activities relevant to Security Council resolution 687 (1991);

(c)  The site was in a highly dangerous condition, which would present problems for the subsequent full inspection, currently being carried out by UNSCOM 17 (see para. 22 below);

(d)  The site would provide a suitable location for the centralized destruction of Iraq's chemical weapons agents and munitions, but the technical details regarding the destruction of these items, particularly the involvement of Iraqi personnel, remain to be fully defined.

4.   The second chemical weapons inspection (UNSCOM 9) consisted of one day at each of three chemical production sites in the Al Fallujah area, two days inspecting the pilot plants at Al Muthanna and one day inspecting the declared storage site at Tammuz (Al Taqqadum) Air Base at Habbaniyah.  Discussions with

/...

0196

Iraqi officials during the inspection clarified previous ambiguities about the Al Muthanna State Establishment, also known as the State Enterprise for Pesticide Production (SEPP). These discussions confirmed that the Al Muthanna Establishment comprises the large production complex at Al Muthanna, the three intended precursor production sites at Al Fallujah and the munitions stores at Al Muhammediyat.

5. The inspections of the Al Fallujah sites in general confirmed the Iraqi declarations. Al Fallujah 1 had never been completed and had therefore not been used for the production of chemical weapons-related items. Al Fallujah 2 commenced production of significant quantities of chlorine in mid-1990. Plans for the large scale production of other materials such as $PCl_3$, $POCl_3$, $SOCl_2$ and other precursors were not realized. Al Fallujah 3 had never been used for the production of chemical weapons agent precursors; instead it had been used for the formulation of pesticides, the active ingredients being imported. Some commercially available chemicals weapons precursor chemicals were found stored at this site. All three sites were extensively damaged by bombing during the hostilities.

6. The Iraqi authorities stated that chemical weapons agents were neither produced nor stored at any of these sites. The team found no evidence which contradicted this statement.

7. The inspections of the pilot plants at Al Muthanna revealed that one had been destroyed by bombing but two were still in a relatively undamaged condition. These two pilot plants were inspected in detail and it was concluded that they could, as proposed by Iraq, be adapted for use as a pilot-scale facility to develop a method for the destruction of the Iraqi nerve agents based on caustic hydrolysis. The team recommended that Iraq should be given permission to carry out the necessary modifications and the relevant process development.

8. In the course of the inspection of Tammuz (Al Taqqadum) Air Base at Habbaniyah, 200 aerial bombs were counted and recorded. Analysis of air samples from two of these bombs, selected at random, confirmed that they contained mustard agent. These findings were consistent with the Iraqi declaration that 200 mustard-filled aerial bombs were stored at this site.

9. The third chemical weapons inspection (UNSCOM 11) visited declared sites at Dujayl, Al Bakr Air Base and the auxiliary Al Matasim Aerodrome, the Proving Ground at Al Fallujah and undeclared sites designated by the Special Commission at Al Fallujah General Headquarters and Al Taji.

10. In the depot at Al Fallujah General Headquarters, which had not been declared as containing any chemical weapons items, chemical protective equipment and related material was found. A variety of grenades containing the riot control agent CS were found but no other chemical filled munitions were found.

0197

/...

11. The team examined the 30 chemical-filled ballistic missile warheads declared by Iraq and found by UNSCOM 8 in the Dujayl area, albeit some 30 kilometres from the location notified to the Special Commission (see appendix V, para. 6). Iraq had informed the Special Commission that 14 of the warheads were of the so-called binary type, filled only with a mixture of isopropanol and cyclohexanol, the organophosphorus component (DF) required to produce the nerve agent being added only immediately prior to use. The resulting agent would have been a mixture of the nerve agents GB and GF. Fifty-six plastic containers filled with DF were also found; these bore evidence of extensive leakage. Iraq stated that the other 16 warheads were filled with a mixture of nerve agents GB and GF. Analysis of samples taken from the binary warheads, one of the nerve agent filled warheads and DF container, by laboratories outside Iraq confirmed the Iraqi declarations. Iraq was instructed by the team to transport the warheads to Al Muthanna for disposal.

12. At Al Bakr Air Base 25 type 250 gauge aerial bombs and 135 type 500 aerial bombs filled with mustard agent had been declared by Iraq. These were found at Al Matasim Aerodrome, an airfield auxiliary to the Al Bakr Air Base, situated about 30 kilometres to the north of the Base, they had evidently developed internal pressure since four had already burst spontaneously and mustard agent vapour was detected at the site, necessitating the use of full individual protective equipment when working close to the bombs or downwind of them. Samples were taken from four of the bombs, which were then resealed. Iraq was instructed to transport the bombs to Al Muthanna subject to strict safety precautions and after venting the excess pressure. No other chemical items were found at this site.

13. The site of Al Taji is a large military installation which had been declared in connection with ballistic missiles but not for chemical weapons. Approximately 6,000 empty aluminium containers intended for filling with nerve agent and insertion into 122 millimetre rocket warheads were found. No other chemical items were found at Al Taji.

14. At the Al Fallujah Proving Ground, Iraq had declared the storage of 6,394 mustard-filled 155 millimetre artillery shells. These were seen by the inspection team essentially in accordance with the declaration. They were stored in the open and appeared to be in good condition. Analysis of samples taken from four of the shells confirmed the presence of mustard agent. No evidence was found of any other activities or material relevant to Security Council resolution 687 (1991).

15. In discussions with Iraqi officials towards the end of the inspection contradictory statements were made regarding the marking of chemical munitions. Iraqi officials also failed to respond satisfactorily to requests for information on Iraq's past chemical weapons programme, particularly as regards foreign suppliers of munitions, equipment and precursor chemicals.

0198 /...

16.  The two primary tasks of the fourth chemical weapons inspection
(UNSCOM 12) were to direct the destruction, by Iraqi personnel, of all
unfilled chemical weapons munitions currently at Al Muthanna and to
reconnoitre, select and show to Iraqi officials the locations at Al Muthanna
where bulk agents, chemical munitions and intermediate, precursor and other
chemical weapons-related chemicals would be collected and the locations where
future destruction operations would be carried out.  These objectives were
successfully achieved, although not without incident.

17.  The destruction operations were successful.  A total of 8,157 unfilled
chemical weapons munitions, consisting of six different varieties of bombs,
155 millimetre artillery shells and 122 millimetre rocket warheads were
destroyed either by crushing with a bulldozer or cutting with an oxyacetylene
torch.  Subsequently, parts of chemical munitions and 3,672 122 millimetre
rocket warheads were destroyed.  Dies used for making bombs remain to be
destroyed.

18.  During this destructive work, a supposedly unfilled 122 millimetre rocket
warhead burst and a nearby Iraqi worker was exposed to nerve agent.  Owing to
the prompt action of a member of the inspection team (Lieutenant Colonel
T. Van Erp, Netherlands) the casualty was very quickly taken to the site
hospital where he received appropriate and timely treatment from Iraqi medical
personnel.  He recovered over a period of a few days.  There were no other
casualties but the incident illustrates that Al Muthanna is still an extremely
hazardous site and that the recovery and destruction of Iraq's chemical
weapons munitions (and agents) will be a protracted and dangerous undertaking.

19.  A separate incident occurred in the case of the 30 chemical-filled
ballistic warheads removed to Al Muthanna from Dujayl in two separate
shipments.  In the first shipment, 14 warheads stated by the Iraqis to be
filled with the mixture of alcohols, and considered relatively harmless, were
moved.  Ten were opened, found to contain the alcohols and were drained
preparatory to destruction.  At this point the senior Iraqi official present
said that the remaining four were filled with the nerve agent sarin.
Apparently these warheads had been moved during the night prior to dispatch to
Al Muthanna and the sarin-filled warheads had been confused with
alcohol-filled ones.  All 20 remaining warheads are now being treated as
sarin-filled until proved otherwise.  This was potentially a very serious
incident, as the warheads were upwind of a number of Iraqi workers and UNSCOM
inspectors.

20.  Iraq has declared 6,120 sarin-filled 122 millimetre rocket warheads and
their attendant motors.  They are stored in the open but have not been counted
nor have their contents been verified.  They present a significant hazard both
from the point of leakage of sarin and instability of the rocket propellant.
In order to improve safety the Iraqis were directed to move the warheads to
the designated storage area; the rocket motors were to be separated and moved
to another storage area separate from the warheads.  They will remain in these
locations until both warheads and motors have been separately counted and
verified.

0199/...

21.  A suitable storage location at Al Muthanna for chemical weapons agents and munitions was identified and the Iraqi officials briefed and given detailed maps of the area.  Four possible destruction sites were identified.

22.  The fifth chemical weapons inspection (UNSCOM 17) began on 6 October and is expected to continue until 9 November.  The large team - over 50 persons - is conducting a detailed and full survey of Al Muthanna in preparation for the destruction phase.

23.  The sixth chemical weapons inspection team (UNSCOM 20) entered Iraq on 22 October and will inspect several sites, including some that are widely separated.  It will need to make use of the United Nations helicopters in order to complete its tasks in the time allocated.

24.  Cooperation by the Iraqis with all the inspection teams has been variable but, in general, it has been good.

25.  The first biological weapon inspection (UNSCOM 7) carried out a full, detailed inspection of the site at Salman Pak.  There were also detailed technical discussions with Iraqi officials.

26.  Although Iraq had previously denied possession of biological weapons and any related items, Iraqi officials admitted on the team's arrival in Iraq to having carried out to a programme of biological research for military purposes which, it was made clear, could have been used for both defensive and offensive purposes.  The micro-organisms involved were Clostridium botulinum, Clostridium perfringens and Bacillus anthracis.  Iraqi officials informed the team that the research programme had commenced in mid-1986 and had been terminated in August 1990, at which point, it was claimed, all stocks had been destroyed.  At a subsequent stage in the inspection, however, the team was given bacterial seed stocks which indicated that Iraq had also possessed the following micro-organisms which are considered as biological warfare agents - Brucellus abortus, Brucella melitensis, Francisella tularensis and various strains of Clostridium botulinum.  In addition, three simulants of biological warfare agents were provided by Iraq; these were Bacillus subtilis, Bacillus cereus and Bacillus megaterium.  No biological weapons or evidence of weaponization was found.

27.  The second biological inspection (UNSCOM 15) visited 10 different declared and undeclared sites.  Four of these were inspected without advance notice.  These 10 sites included a pharmaceutical plant, a blood bank, vaccine production facilities and research and development laboratories with fermentation capabilities and specially designed facilities to enable work with hazardous disease-causing organisms of humans and animals to be carried out.

28.  No biological weapons or facilities for filling weapons were found.  However, the inspection team unanimously agreed that the Iraqi biological weapon programme, which consisted of a research component at Salman Pak, logically would have included a plan for a development and production component.

0200    /...

## Appendix V

## Ballistic missiles and long-range guns

1.    Five ballistic missile teams have conducted inspections in Iraq to make an inventory, identify for destruction, and monitor the destruction of all declared ballistic missiles with a range greater than 150 kilometres, related parts and components and all research, development, support and manufacturing capabilities.   Ballistic missile inspection planning centred on the inspection and destruction of the declared items, the production facilities, and the fixed launch structures in the Western Zone of Iraq.

2.    Destruction of ballistic missiles began with the first inspection team's activities in July 1991 before a comprehensive destruction policy had been established.   The first team (UNSCOM 3) carried out the initial inventory and supervision of the destruction of all declared missiles, launchers and support equipment, visiting seven different sites and facilities.   Missile systems and components destruction was primarily a straightforward task of crushing by bulldozers readily carried out by the Iraqis.   Three of the sites were former production and repair facilities that had been destroyed by coalition bombing.

3.    The second ballistic missile inspection (UNSCOM 10) was conducted in mid-July on short notice to investigate information suggesting additional undeclared missiles and support equipment.   This team found undeclared decoy missiles and additional support equipment in the vicinity of a site previously inspected by the first ballistic missile team.   These were also destroyed.

4.    Subsequent inspections of production and repair facilities encountered less enthusiastic cooperation and outright disagreement on destruction of some equipment and structures.   In July, the Iraqis finally acknowledged possession of a long-range "supergun" and components to build additional and larger calibre weapons.   This type of gun was capable of delivering prohibited munitions beyond 150 kilometres.

5.    The third ballistic missile team (UNSCOM 8) in August conducted inspections focusing on declared and undeclared suspected ballistic missile production facilities.   In addition, a survey of the declared supergun, propellant and unassembled parts at three different sites was undertaken.   A significant number of documents and blueprints related to the construction and development of this system was provided to the inspection team.   The information obtained and photographs taken were collected for study and use in a planned later inspection/destruction activity.

6.    Production, repair and test equipment and machinery associated with the Scud, Al Hussein and Badr 2000 missiles were inspected and identified for destruction at five declared and seven undeclared sites.   All sites suffered damage during the coalition bombing, some extensively, with structures and equipment being completely destroyed or damaged with others virtually intact. Identification for destruction of specific missile tooling and test equipment

0201                                   /...

was readily accepted by the Iraqis. Machinery and equipment identified for destruction which also had non-missile application (dual use) or use in missile systems not prohibited by Security Council resolution 687 (1991) generated vigorous controversy and opposition. This equipment was sealed and guidance was requested from the Special Commission. An inventory was made of all other equipment to enable the Special Commission to decide on its destruction, removal or rendering harmless in consonance with the policies being developed by the Commission in these respects. After return of the inspection to New York, the destruction of certain equipment was called for in a letter to the Iraqi Government based on the inspection report and the provisional guidelines on destruction, removal or rendering harmless initiated by the Special Commission (see para. 21 of the report).

7.    At one undeclared site, the team discovered an additional 187 Scud fuel, oxidizer and starter storage tanks. The team also found 30 Scud warhead canisters containing chemical filled warheads on the same vicinity (see appendix IV, para. 11). Although the warheads had been declared to the Special Commission, they were not at the location specified in the declaration. Upon completion of this inspection Iraq provided the team with a declaration of additional Scud fuel and oxidizer storage tanks.

8.    The fourth ballistic missile team (UNSCOM 13) planned to inspect in September declared fixed launch sites in the Western Zone as well as other undeclared possible missile support facilities using United Nations helicopters in accordance with the provisions of Security Council resolutions 687 (1991) and 707 (1991). Upon arrival in Iraq the team was advised that inspection of the Western Zone using United Nations helicopters would not be permitted. In the expectation that Iraq's approval would be forthcoming before the end of its inspection period, the team was directed by the Executive Chairman of the Special Commission to undertake inspection of the Western Zone only with the use of United Nations helicopters. In the interim the team inspected the destruction of Scud fuel and oxidizer storage tanks located during the third inspection. The oxidizer tanks were leaking toxic level emissions prompting the team to abandon this site until air quality at the site was acceptable. Two inspections at undeclared sites were conducted. Although no missile activity was noted at one facility, at the other site the team found four previously destroyed missile transport vehicles from Al Taji which had been spot welded together and moved to that location. An additional undeclared Scud missile storage support/carrier was observed. All items were destroyed and verified. In the absence of Iraqi agreement to use by the Special Commission of United Nations helicopters, the team's mission was terminated at this stage, and it did not undertake the planned inspection of the Western Zone.

9.    Immediately following the resolution of the helicopter issue in the first week of October, the fifth ballistic missile team (UNSCOM 18) successfully conducted inspections of the fixed launch sites in the Western Zone. Although Iraq declared 25 out of a total of 28 as destroyed, additional destruction was prescribed and carried out. A number of partially constructed fixed launch sites were inspected at undeclared sites and destruction procedures agreed

0202   /...

upon; destruction has still to be verified.  The team also returned to the supergun and supervised the destruction of the gun in the Jabal Hamryn mountains north of Baghdad as well as the propellant for the supergun located south of Baghdad.  The destruction of the other supergun components at Iskanderiyah has commenced but is not yet completed and will have to be verified later.  Several undeclared sites were inspected and found to contain no observable ballistic missile activity.

10.  The geographical areas to be covered and the numbers and extent of military and other installations are large.  The Special Commission has yet to be convinced that it has obtained a comprehensive assessment of Iraq's ballistic missile capabilities.  Future ballistic missile inspection activities will monitor the destruction of outstanding items identified and inspect various sites to complete the information missing on the ballistic missile programme, both the Scud related systems and the system believed to be associated with the nuclear weapon development.

0203

/...

Appendix VI

Voluntary contributions to the Special Commission

1.    Voluntary contributions in cash and in kind, as listed below, have been received to date:

| Type | Government | Amount (United States dollars) | Remarks |
|---|---|---|---|
| In cash | Japan | 2 500 000 | From a trust fund |
| | United States | 2 000 000 | |
| | Kuwait | 1 000 000 | |
| In kind: | | | |
| (a)  Outright grant | Norway | | 15 vehicles<br>5 satellite global positioning system units<br>2 ambulances |
| | United States | | 7 vehicles<br>4 trucks<br>2 ambulances |
| (b)  Loaned for the duration of the operation | Finland | | 2 gas chromatographs |
| | New Zealand | | Medical equipment |
| | Sweden | | Decontamination equipment, chemical weapons protective equipment |
| | United Kingdom | | Laboratory equipment, including a gas chromatograph mass spectrometer and an infrared spectrophotometer |

0204

/...

| Type | Government | Amount (United States dollars) | Remarks |
|------|-----------|-------------------------------|---------|
| | | | 2 biological weapons agent detection kits |
| | | | 6 chemical weapons agent vapour monitors |
| (c) Loaned and returned | Belgium | | Medical equipment |
| | Canada | | Global positioning system |
| | France | | Medical equipment |
| | Germany | | Explosive ordnance equipment |
| | Netherlands | | Chemical weapons analysis equipment |
| | United Kingdom | | Vehicles |

## Personnel

2.    In addition to personnel seconded by the United Nations, the IAEA and WHO, the following Governments have provided personnel services for inspection-related activities:  Australia, Austria, Belgium, Canada, Czechoslovakia, Finland, France, Germany, Greece, Hungary, India, Indonesia, Italy, Japan, Netherlands, Norway, New Zealand, Romania, Sweden, Switzerland, Thailand, United Kingdom of Great Britain and Northern Ireland, United States of America, and Union of Soviet Socialist Republics.

3.    New Zealand has provided a medical team.

## Air support

4.    The Commission has been provided with high altitude reconnaissance flights over Iraq.  The flights are undertaken on a regular basis by an aircraft with crew and support personnel made available to the Commission by the United States.  Flights are directed by the Special Commission.  They are notified to Iraq 72 hours in advance and acknowledged by Iraq within 48 hours.

0205                    /...

5.    The German Government has provided the Commission with two C-160
transport planes, based in Bahrain, and three rotary-wing aircraft, including
crews and support personnel, based at the Al-Rashid airfield at Baghdad since
1 October 1991.

-----

## Security Council

Distr.
GENERAL

S/23149
16 October 1991

ORIGINAL: ENGLISH

DECISION TAKEN BY THE SECURITY COUNCIL COMMITTEE ESTABLISHED BY
RESOLUTION 661 (1990) CONCERNING THE SITUATION BETWEEN IRAQ
AND KUWAIT AT ITS 51ST MEETING, HELD ON 15 OCTOBER 1991

<u>Procedures to be employed by the Security Council Committee established by
resolution 661 (1990) concerning the situation between Iraq and Kuwait in the
discharge of its responsibilities under Security Council resolutions
706 (1991) and 712 (1991)</u>

I.   <u>Preparatory steps</u>:

1.   The Committee will select, upon recommendation by the Secretariat, three
     independent experts in international oil trade as "overseers" at United
     Nations Headquarters, and entrust them with the authority to approve or
     reject oil sale contracts on behalf of the Committee.  The overseers will
     be authorized to correspond with applicants as needed.  The nomination of
     three persons will ensure a 24-hour availability for contract approvals.

2.   Other experts, agents and inspectors (as required below) will be
     appointed by the Secretary-General.  The Committee will take note of
     these appointments.

3.   States may, if they so wish, forward to the Committee a list of national
     oil purchasers (private companies, State-owned companies, State agencies,
     ministries, etc.) authorized to communicate with the overseer.  Once the
     Committee has taken note of these lists and passed them on to the
     overseer, these purchasers are entitled to communicate directly with the
     overseer (see sect. II, part A, para. 3 below).  If States do not submit
     such a list, or if a certain purchaser is not included in the list, the
     communication with the overseer must go via the Permanent Mission in
     New York.

4.   For the purpose of section II, part A, paragraph 3 below, a Standard
     Application Form will be elaborated by the Committee and circulated among
     all States.  States and national oil purchasers shall use only these
     Standard Application Forms.

91-34269   2760j (E)                                                      /...

0207

5.    The Secretariat will set up a new fax line to be used exclusively for
      correspondence with regard to oil transactions.  Applicants are requested
      to send their relevant applications and relating correspondence only via
      this fax line.  Other correspondence with the Committee shall go through
      the already existing channels.

6.    Iraq and Turkey will have to conclude an arrangement on the price and
      payment modalities for the use of Turkish oil installations.  Once this
      arrangement is concluded, it must be forwarded to the Committee which
      will take note of it.  United Nations agents will check the
      implementation of this arrangement and report periodically to the .
      Committee.

7.    Monitoring of delivery to Iraq of foodstuffs, medicines, and materials
      and supplies for essential civilian needs will be done by independent
      inspection agents appointed by an appropriate United Nations programme or
      organization, such as, for example, the Office for Project Services
      (OPS).  Monitoring of the distribution of these goods will be arranged by
      the Executive Delegate in cooperation with relevant United Nations
      programmes and organizations, including appropriate humanitarian
      non-governmental organizations (NGOs).  The Committee will be informed
      about the relevant arrangements, including those for the purpose of
      section III, part A, paragraph 11 below.

8.    Upon recommendation by the Secretariat, the Committee will nominate an
      expert (a staff member of one of the United Nations programmes or
      organizations) who will act as an aide to the Committee for the purposes
      of section III, part A, paragraph 8 below.

II.   Sales of Iraqi oil and oil products:

      A.    Sales of Iraqi oil:

1.    The Iraqi State Organization for the Marketing of Oil (SOMO) signs a
      contract with the purchaser.  The contract must include the provisions as
      specified in paragraph 58 of the report by the Secretary-General pursuant
      to paragraph 5 of Security Council resolution 706 (1991) (S/23006).

2.    United Nations agents at SOMO review the contracts to assure compliance
      with the provisions of paragraph 58 of the Secretary-General's report and
      forward by fax copies of the approvable contracts, supporting documents,
      and their independent reports to the overseer in New York.

3.    The national oil purchaser or the Permanent Mission of the State of
      purchase forwards by fax a formal request (Standard Application Form) for
      approval to the Committee, together with a copy of the contract and all
      other supporting documents.

/...

0208

4.   The overseer reviews the contract and supporting documents to ensure that:

     -   they comply with paragraph 58 of the Secretary-General's report,
         including that a confirmed irrevocable letter of credit is opened
         providing for payment into the escrow account;

     -   the conditions of payment envisaged in the letters of credit are in
         conformity with existing market practices;

     -   they do not appear to contain any attempt at fraud or deception;

     -   the transaction's pricing is consistent with world prices and market
         trends; and

     -   the transaction does not exceed the limits imposed by Security
         Council resolutions 706 (1991) and 712 (1991).

5.   If the contract and supporting documents are found to be in order, the
     overseer, on behalf of the Committee, approves the sale (within the
     shortest period of time possible, at the maximum 24 hours) and informs by
     fax the national oil purchaser or the Permanent Mission concerned, as
     well as SOMO.

6.   The overseer sends his notification of sales approval, together with a
     copy of the contract, supporting documents, and the report of the United
     Nations agent at SOMO, by fax to the inspector at Ceyhan who will
     authorize loading only after these documents are in his possession.

7.   Depending on the number of applications, the overseer reports to the
     Committee, in a structured and standardized manner, at least twice a week
     on contracts approved by him (including the cumulative quantity and value
     of oil authorized for export), and informs the Secretary-General
     accordingly.

8.   The oil is pumped into storage tanks.  Agents at the pipeline check the
     pumping.  Subject to their confirmation, the oil can be loaded on ships
     and the ships can leave the terminal.  The agents will have the authority
     to prohibit the delivery of the oil if there is any evidence of
     irregularity.

9.   The agents report to the Committee on their assessment of the pumping and
     loading.

10.  The purchaser makes payment into the escrow account.

11.  Twice a week, the Secretary-General forwards statements of the escrow
     account, including outlines of anticipated future obligations, to the
     Committee.

/...

0209

B.   Sales of Iraqi oil products:

The regime for the sale of oil products will be broadly similar to that
described above, but the precise arrangements will be elaborated at a
later stage, as and when the need arises.

III. Purchase by Iraq of foodstuffs, medicines, and materials and supplies for
     essential civilian needs:

   A.   Purchase by Iraq of foodstuffs, medicines, and materials and
        supplies for essential civilian needs, to be financed from the
        escrow account:

1.   Iraq sends a categorized list of relevant requirements to the Executive
     Delegate. (Preferably, a two-months list, quantity- and value-oriented.)
     If Iraq intends also to finance medicines from the escrow account, these
     too should be mentioned in general terms on the list, together with their
     value.  The overall value of the list must not exceed that part of the
     amount authorized by the Committee, in accordance with paragraph 2 of
     Security Council resolution 712 (1991), which is available for
     humanitarian purchases.

2.   The Executive Delegate forwards the list, revised by him if necessary, to
     the Committee.

3.   The Committee takes action on the list and forwards to the
     Secretary-General and the Executive Delegate the list as approved.  (The
     first list will be taken up at a meeting of the Committee; subject to
     agreement, later lists might be dealt with under a "no-objection"
     procedure.)

4.   The Secretary-General will make the list known to all States.

5.   The Executive Delegate informs Iraq about the clearance.

6.   Iraq signs a contract with the exporter, in accordance with normal
     commercial practice and the relevant Security Council resolutions.

7.   (a)  Medicines:

     The Permanent Mission of the exporter's country informs the Committee of
     the exporter's wish to be paid from the escrow account.  A copy of the
     relevant contract must be attached to this communication.

     (b)  Foodstuffs:

     The Permanent Mission of the exporter's country notifies the Committee.
     This notification must contain the information that the exporter wants to
     be paid from the escrow account.  A copy of the relevant contract must be
     attached to this notification.

/...

0210

(c) <u>Materials and supplies for essential civilian needs</u>:

The Permanent Mission of the exporter's country requests approval, under the "no-objection" procedure, by the Committee. This request must contain the information that the exporter wishes to be paid from the escrow account. A copy of the relevant contract must be attached to this request.

8. An expert (aide to the Committee) checks the contracts, in particular on the price/value relationship, and informs the Chairman. His findings will be attached to the circulation note to Committee members.

9. (a) <u>Medicines</u>:

(i) If the contract is found in order, the Committee informs the Permanent Mission concerned and the Secretary-General that the contract has been found in order, i.e. the exporter can expect payment from the escrow account.

(ii) If the contract is not found in order, the Committee informs the Permanent Mission concerned and the Secretary-General that the contract has not been found in order, i.e. the exporter cannot expect payment from the escrow account. However, medical supplies can be shipped anyway if the exporter so wishes.

(b) <u>Foodstuffs</u>:

(i) If the contract is found in order, the Committee takes note of the notification and informs the Permanent Mission concerned and the Secretary-General accordingly and states that the contract has been found in order, i.e. the exporter can expect payment from the escrow account.

(ii) If the contract is not found in order, the Committee takes note of the notification and informs the Permanent Mission concerned and the Secretary-General accordingly but states that the contract has not been found in order, i.e. the exporter cannot expect payment from the escrow account. However, foodstuffs can be shipped anyway if the exporter so wishes.

(c) <u>Materials and supplies for essential civilian needs</u>:

(i) If the contract is found in order, and if the Committee approves the shipment under the "no-objection" procedure, it informs the Permanent Mission concerned and the Secretary-General of the approval and states that the contract has been found in order, i.e. the exporter can expect payment from the escrow account.

/...

0211

(ii)   If the contract is not found in order, and if the Committee nevertheless approves the shipment under the "no-objection" procedure, it informs the Permanent Mission concerned and the Secretary-General of the approval but states that the contract has not been found in order, i.e. the exporter cannot expect payment from the escrow account.  However, the goods can be shipped anyway if the exporter so wishes.

(iii)  If the Committee cannot approve the shipment, whether or not the contract is found in order, the goods are not allowed to be shipped.

From here on only if the contract has been found in order:

10.  The Secretary-General may effect part-payment to the exporter, according to commercial practice.

11.  United Nations agents check the delivery (the quality, quantity, labelling, etc.) at the unloading port and the entry points to Iraq and report to the Committee.  The agents will have the authority to inspect the shipment documents and, if necessary, to open and examine the contents as needed.

12.  The Committee evaluates the reports.  If satisfactory, it approves the final payment and informs the Secretary-General.

13.  The Secretary-General effects final payment.

14.  United Nations agents monitor in-country distribution and report, via the Executive Delegate, in a consolidated manner to the Committee.

15.  The Committee evaluates these reports to ensure that equitable internal distribution is being maintained and takes appropriate action if not.

16.  Twice a week, the Secretary-General forwards statements of the escrow account, including outlines of anticipated future obligations, to the Committee.

B.   Purchase by Iraq of foodstuffs, medicines, and materials and supplies for essential civilian needs, to be financed from the sub-account of the escrow account:

1.   According to paragraph 8 of Security Council resolution 712 (1991), imports financed from the sub-account of the escrow account, are, apart from the provision of paragraph 1 (c) of Security Council resolution 706 (1991), subject only to the provisions and procedures of paragraph 20 of Security Council resolution 687 (1991).

/...

0212

2.    Monitoring (paragraph 1 (c) of Security Council resolution 706 (1991))
      will be carried out as indicated in annex II of the Secretary-General's
      report.

3.    Twice a week, the Secretary-General forwards statements of the
      sub-account of the escrow account, including outlines of anticipated
      future obligations, to the Committee.

-----

0213

**UNITED NATIONS**

# Security Council

Distr.
GENERAL

S/23183
31 October 1991
ENGLISH
ORIGINAL: ARABIC

**S**

LETTER DATED 29 OCTOBER 1991 FROM THE PERMANENT
REPRESENTATIVE OF IRAQ TO THE UNITED NATIONS
ADDRESSED TO THE SECRETARY-GENERAL

On instructions from my Government, I am pleased to transmit herewith a letter dated 29 October 1991 from Mr. Ahmad Hussein, Minister for Foreign Affairs of the Republic of Iraq, informing you that the Turkish side is continuing to violate the territorial integrity and sovereignty of the Republic of Iraq.

I should be grateful if you would have this letter and its annex circulated as an official document of the Security Council.

(Signed)  Abdul Amir A. AL-ANBARI
Permanent Representative

91-36246  2737g (E)

/...

0214

<u>Annex</u>

<u>Letter dated 29 October 1991 from the Minister for Foreign
Affairs of Iraq addressed to the Secretary-General</u>

Further to our two letters dated 16 October 1991, I have the honour to inform you that the Turkish side is continuing to violate the territorial integrity and overeignty of the Republic of Iraq, targeting the defenceless and innocent in the northern region and their homes.  The details are as follows:

1.   At 1545 hours on 25 October 1991, Turkish aircraft bombarded the villages of Qunahish and Girgasha in the Amadiyah district.  At 1630 hours on the same day, Turkish aircraft bombarded the villages of Shildizah, Balandah, Ziwah, Qunahish, Girgasha, Belegah and Dayri in the Amadiyah district in Dohuk governerate, which resulted in the death and wounding of a number of Iraqi citizens and the destruction of some houses.

2.   The Chief of General Staff of the Turkish Army claimed that the Turkish combat planes and helicopters had launched raids on the camps and positions of elements of the Turkish Kurdish Workers' Party in northern Iraq, who, according to his allegation, had established bases for carrying out operations against frontier guard posts and army patrols, taking advantage of the conditions prevailing in the northern region.  He added that the Turkish Army operations would continue against what he called "elements of the Workers' Party" and their positions in Iraq as long as it was necessary.

In informing you that the Turkish side's continued repetition of its violations of the territorial integrity and sovereignty of Iraq and its endangering of the security and safety of Iraqi citizens on pretexts that are legally inadmissible constitutes a blatant violation of the United Nations Charter and norms of international law and endangers peace and security in the region, I request you to intervene immediately to take effective measures to put an end to the repeated violations of the Turkish side in a manner that makes clear to the international community the unfoundedness of the belief that the United Nations applies a double standard in dealing with the issues of its Member States, inasmuch as the fundamental goal of the United Nations is to achieve peace, to maintain peace and to protect the territorial sovereignty of all Member States.

I request you to have this letter circulated as a document of the Security Council.

(Signed)  Ahmad HUSSEIN
Minister for Foreign Affairs

-----

0215

# 외    무    부

종    별 :

번    호 : UNW-3662                                일    시 : 91 1104 1900

수    신 : 장 관(중동일,연일,기정)

발    신 : 주 유엔 대사

제    목 : 걸프사태(터키의 북이락 공습)

    이락은 터어키측이 지난 10.25 터어키 쿠르드 노동자당세력 토벌을 구실로 이락
북부지역을 공습, 이락민사상자 및 가옥파괴가 발생하였다고 주장하면서
유엔사무총장이 터어키에 의한 계속적인 이락주권 유린사태의 저지를 위해 효과적인
조치를 취해 줄것을 요청하는 10.29 자 사무총장앞 A.HUSSEIN 외상명의 서한을
안보리문서로 배포하였음.( S.23183)

    첨부:11.3. 자 NYT 기사(이락구호문제):UNW(F)-768 끝

    (대사 노창희-국장)

---

| 중아국 | 차관 | 1차보 | 국기국 | 외정실 | 분석관 | 청와대 | 안기부 |
|--------|------|-------|--------|--------|--------|--------|--------|

PAGE 1                                                        91.11.05    09:53 WG

외신 1과  통제관

0216

# IRAQ IS BLOCKING AID DISTRIBUTION

## Food and Medicine Must Go Through Official System, Relief Groups Are Told

**By PATRICK E. TYLER**
Special to The New York Times

BAGHDAD, Iraq, Nov. 2 — The Iraqi Government is blocking attempts by international relief organizations to distribute food and medicine directly to hundreds of thousands of Iraqis suffering from poor health and malnutrition in the aftermath of war and trade embargo, relief officials and Iraqi authorities say.

Iraq's Minister of Health, Abdul Salam M. Saaid, said in an interview he would not allow food distribution by relief agencies except through the Government's distribution and rationing system. He accused the relief agencies of food distribution "gimmicks" that he said were "designed to keep quiet the good people in the United States who don't like to see others suffer."

The minister indicated that if the people of Europe and the United States saw a vast and direct food distribution effort under way in Iraq, it would quiet their consciences and "shut up" their opposition to continuing United Nations sanctions. These, he said, are the ultimate cause of suffering in Iraq.

Mr. Saaid's remarks, made in an interview this week, reflect how much the struggle to provide emergency care to Iraq's 18 million people has become politicized in the wake of the Persian Gulf war. The United States and its allies are seeking to maintain tight economic sanctions until the Government of President Saddam Hussein fully complies with all of the terms of the cease-fire resolution that ended formal hostilities last winter.

### Food Stays in Warehouses

As a consequence of the Iraqi Government's policy against third-party food distribution, food worth about $4 million, including infant formula and high-protein food packages specially prepared for children under 5, has been sitting in warhouses in Baghdad and Jordan for weeks, relief officials said.

Most of the food belongs to the United Nations Children's Fund, which in August proposed the idea of setting up special nutrition centers across the country to help about 340,000 Iraqi children who are believed to be most vulnerable to dying of malnutrition or infectious disease. The Government rationing system provides only one-quarter of what is generally acknowledged to be an infant's requirement of powdered infant formula.

Douglas Broderick, the representative here of Catholic Relief Services, the private American group, said the Iraqi authorities in recent weeks had shut down a food distribution program that was using churches and mosques in Mosul and Baghdad to serve 60,000 people.

Then, Mr. Broderick said, Health Ministry officials in southern Iraq blocked the direct distribution of 250 tons of food that he had brought into the country to help feed 23,000 families in the Amarra area north of Basra. Mr. Broderick said the food has been sitting in a warehouse for several weeks.

### 'Very Well Focused Effort'

In Amarra, he said, "there are 3,000 pregnant women and this was a very well focused program in a population that is at risk." Iraqi authorities have suggested that the food be turned over to Iraqi Government groups, but so far Mr. Broderick has declined.

Only in Kurdistan, where the Baghdad Government has lost its authority over territory and local government, are United Nations agencies giving food aid directly to the people, officials said.

Mr. Saaid has told relief agency officials that Iraq fears rioting and demeaning scenes of people grasping for food at distribution centers if agencies are allowed to set up their own distribution centers.

"Are we a nation of beggars?" the minister asked.

"The system is there," he said. "Just open the tap for us."

He asked that the United States release some of the $1.4 billion in Iraqi funds still frozen in American banks for the purchase of food and medicine.

### 'Political Game' Cited

A critical battleground in the war of oratory that continues between Baghdad and Washington is the effect of economic sanctions on public health in Iraq. A number of studies have tried to document increased mortality among children under 5 years of age from disease, malnutrition and the destructive effects of inflation, which has left most Iraqi families unable to afford adequate supplies of food.

Mr. Saaid said his ministry was reluctant to release figures on child mortality "because health has become part of a political game designed to undermine a political stand."

But Mr. Saaid's Under Secretary, Dr. Shawki Murqus, disclosed during the interview that projections last May by a Harvard University study team about the war's devastating impact on public health had not been borne out by official Government figures.

The Harvard team's report said increases in infectious disease compounded by poor nutrition could cause 170,000 deaths among children beyond the normal mortality rate. But Dr. Murqus said that the total deaths of children under 5 in Iraq since August 1990 was 19,863. This figure, he said, includes normal mortality as well as excess deaths caused by disease and malnutrition.

The figure is far lower than any projection developed by outside experts. It does not reflect thousands of deaths that occurred. "outside" the public health system during the flight of two million Kurds last winter to the Turkish and Iranian borders and during a rebellion in southern Iraq among Shiite Muslims.

# UNITED NATIONS

## Security Council

**S**

Distr.
GENERAL

S/23193
4 November 1991
ENGLISH
ORIGINAL: ARABIC

---

LETTER DATED 1 NOVEMBER 1991 FROM THE PERMANENT REPRESENTATIVE
OF IRAQ TO THE UNITED NATIONS ADDRESSED TO THE SECRETARY-GENERAL

On instructions from my Government and further to our previous letters concerning violations of Iraqi airspace and territory by Turkish land and air forces, I have the honour to inform you that on 26 October 1991 a group made up of commandos, police and village guards belonging to units of the First Special Forces Brigade and 23rd Police Brigade penetrated the Iraqi areas indicated below, some of which were bombed by Turkish aircraft on the same day: Hossi, Rashmah, Haura, Hal, Hosh, Razkiyah, Jabal Nirah, Sabtu and Miranush. The group in question returned to Turkish territory on 27 October 1991.

In informing you of these violations, we request you, in conformity with the provisions of international law and of the Charter of the United Nations, to take the necessary steps to put an end to the violations and to prevent future repetitions of them.

I should be grateful if you would have this letter circulated as a document of the Security Council.

(Signed) Abdul Amir A. AL-ANBARI
Ambassador
Permanent Representative

-----

91-36883   2839d (E)

0218

# 외 무 부

종  별 :

번  호 : UNW-3678

일  시 : 91 1105 1830

수  신 : 장 관(중동일,연일,기정)

발  신 : 주 유엔대사

제  목 : 걸프사태

연: UNW-3662

1. 이락은 연호에 이어 터어키 군.경찰이 10.26 이락북부지역에 침부(공습병행)하였다가 다음날 터어키로 돌아갔다고 주장하는 내용의 안보리문서를 배포하였음.9 S/23193)

2. 한편, 금11.5. 자 NYT 지 보도에 의하면, 지난 4월 유엔과 이락간에 체결된 유엔의 이락내 구호지원 활동(유엔경비대 500 여명 배치포함)에 관한 협정이 금년말종료되는것과 관련 SADRUDDIN AGA KHAN 대표가 동협정 갱신 추진 및 이락의 석유수출 개시 촉구를 위해 11월중순 이락방문을 희망하고 있다고 함.(상기 협정갱신이 이루어지지 않는경우 대이락 군사조치를 위한 안보리 결의안이 추진될 가능성도 있다는일부 외교소식봉 언급인용)

3.유엔측 발표에 의하면 안보리결의 598호에 의거 이란-이락전후 양국 복구문제와 관련 A.FARAH 전사무차장이 11.5. 부터 이란을 3주간 방문예정이라고 하며 이락방문은 아직 예정되어 있지 않다고 함.

첨부: NYT 기사: UNW(F)-775 끝

(대사 노창회-국장)

---

중아국      장관      1차보      국기국      외정실      분석관      청와대      안기부

PAGE 1

91.11.06    10:51 WH

외신 1과  롱제관

0219

## REMARKS MADE BY THE SECRETARY-GENERAL UPON ENTERING THE SECRETARIAT BUILDING

5 November        UNW(H)-775  11/05 830
                        총 2 04

Q:   There are stories that Prince Sadruddin Aga Khan may go to Baghdad sometime in the near future to try to renegotiate the agreements...

SG:   I have asked him to consider going there in order to make a new assessment of the situation.

Q:. What are your views of Iraq's apparent attitude that the sanctions have to be lifted and they do not want to go ahead with the oil sale because that would just decrease public pressure for lifting of the sanctions ?

SG:   As you know, Iraq is a member country of this Organization and it is not for the Secretary-General to start arguing with the Iraqi Government.  It is for them to present their position and for the Security Council to decide; it is not for me to decide at all.

\*  \*\*\*\*  \*

#UNW-3618
전약

2-1

0220

# U.N. Official Hoping to Visit Iraq To Seek Accord on Security Force

## By PAUL LEWIS
### Special to The New York Times

UNITED NATIONS, Nov. 4. — A senior United Nations official hopes to visit Baghdad around the middle of this month to try to renew the agreement that allows a 500-member security force to remain in the country and permits the distribution of food and medicine in Iraq by humanitarian agencies.

The official, Prince Sadruddin Aga Khan, will also seek to persuade the Iraqi Government to start selling oil under a Security Council plan to pay for normal imports of food and other humanitarian supplies.

So far Iraq has refused to accept the Security Council's offer to allow limited oil sales, saying the strict conditions imposed are an insult to the country's sovereignty.

### Protection for Minorities

The agreement signed in April to allow distribution of food and medicine and keep the United Nations security force in place to protect the Shiite and Kurdish minorities expires Dec. 31. So far, Iraq has not said whether it will extend the agreement, and has not issued a firm invitation to Prince Sadruddin.

Last week Britain, France and the United States, the three Western permanent members of the Security Council, urged Prince Sadruddin to visit Baghdad promptly to discuss the agreements.

If he returns empty-handed, Western diplomats say, it will be clear that Baghdad wants a new confrontation with the Security Council. In effect, Iraq would be presenting the Council with a choice between relaxing trade sanctions or accepting an increase in human suffering in Iraq.

### Threat of Military Action

How the Council would respond to such a challenge remains unclear, but some diplomats are talking of a new resolution that would order President Saddam Hussein to extend the agreement with the United Nations to protect needy segments of the Iraqi population or face the threat of renewed military action.

In Baghdad, some senior officials, such as Health Minister Abdel Salam Said, have said openly that the Government wants to get rid of the relief agencies next year because their activ-ities blunt public pressure on governments to relax sanctions. But senior Foreign Ministry officials say Iraq only wants the Security Council to set a target date for ending such United Nations operations and easing sanctions.

The ability of the United Nations to continue relief operations in Iraq is also closely linked to Baghdad's decision on whether to sell the $1.6 billion in oil that the Security Council will allow. Money to pay for the security force next year is scarce, and humanitarian agencies are reluctant to continue pouring resources into an oil-rich nation when far poorer countries also need their help.

### Monitoring of Distribution

But if Iraq agrees to start selling oil to buy food and medicine, Prince Sadruddin has proposed giving the United Nations guards and other personnel there the job of monitoring its distribution, as the Security Council demands. This means their expenses would be paid by Iraq from the oil sale proceeds, some of which would also be earmarked for reparations to Kuwait.

Part of the reason why Iraq has dismissed the Security Council's offer to let it sell oil for food may be that the Government is able to import quite substantial quantities without exporting oil.

As of last Oct. 18, the Security Council committee overseeing sanctions had authorized 4.2 million tons of food exports to Iraq, more than 80 percent of the 5 million tons of food it normally buys abroad each year.

United Nations officials say they do not known how much food has been imported so far, but from spot checks carried out inside Iraq, they say that considerable amounts are now entering the country. This conclusion is supported by studies of Iraq's domestic food markets where prices have stabilized in recent weeks.

How Iraq is paying for these food imports remains a mystery. But Western diplomats say Baghdad clearly has access to a secret supply of convertible currency that has escaped the effort to impound its foreign assets.

Nevertheless, food prices in Iraq remain extremely high at a time when the Government has refused to increase salaries except for the military and security services.

#UNW-3678
천무

2—2

.0221

# UNITED NATIONS

**S**

## Security Council

Distr.
GENERAL

S/23198
5 November 1991
ENGLISH
ORIGINAL:  ARABIC

LETTER DATED 4 NOVEMBER 1991 FROM THE PERMANENT
REPRESENTATIVE OF IRAQ TO THE UNITED NATIONS
ADDRESSED TO THE SECRETARY-GENERAL

On instructions from my Government, I wish to inform you of the following:

United States warplanes and fighters continue to violate Iraqi airspace. Up to the present, I have notified you daily of the details of these violations, but it appears that the United Nations is not capable of putting an end to the United States of America's continuous violation of the provisions of the United Nations Charter and the violation of the sovereignty of a Member State.

These violations have assumed a "grave" character aimed at disseminating terror and alarm in the minds of Iraqi civilians, particularly children and women, since these aircraft break the sound barrier at very low altitudes over the towns and villages of Iraq, causing, in addition to terror and alarm, large-scale material damage to civilian houses and public buildings and the wounding of innocent people as a result of the smashing of glass and windows and the shaking of buildings.

For some time, United States warplanes taking off from airfields inside Turkish territory, have been violating Iraqi airspace in the governorates of Dohuk, Irbil and Ninawa.  During the past two months, they have been violating the airspace over Mosul almost daily at various altitudes.  At 0942 hours on Wednesday, 30 October 1991, two United States F-16s flew very low at an altitude of 200 metres and broke the sound barrier over the city of Mosul, which caused breakage of glass in windows and the shaking of some buildings and stores and aroused terror among the children, in addition to the unfounded alarm that this violation aroused in civilian citizens.  Other aircraft carried out 12 sorties over Mosul, Dohuk and Zakho, which continued until 0230 hours in the afternoon of the same day.

United States warplanes have continued to violate Iraqi airspace.  At 0916, 0839, 0851, 0991, 0955, 1100 and 1135 hours on Friday, 1 November 1991, United States warplanes violated the airspace over the city of Mosul and its

91-37052  2620c (E)                                                    /...

0222

suburbs and broke the sound barrier from time to time in an attempt to alarm
the citizens on their day of rest and leisure.  Great damage was done also to
buildings and property, in particular the Nineveh Oberoi Hotel, which suffered
great damage as a result of the low flights and the breaking of the sound
barrier by the United States aircraft, inasmuch as the damage included the
breakage of the building's windows and the smashing of a number of false
ceilings, doors and electrical equipment.  Initial estimates of the losses at
this hotel are 80,000 dinars, in addition to other unlisted losses.

The disgraceful actions by the forces of the United States of America,
which claims to be civilized and advanced and to protect human rights and
defend the freedom of the individual, has created states of alarm,
consternation and psychological unrest in children, the effects of which are
immeasurable on the material scale.  They also present a challenge to all
religious values and customs because they present a challenge to the feelings
of Muslims as they are performing their Friday prayers on the holy day which
they reserve for worship.  These violations have also created a state of
sudden disruptions of traffic, leading to collisions.

The Iraqi Government, as it strongly condemns these crimes, calls on the
international community, through the United Nations, to undertake to put a
halt to them, in accordance with the prescriptions of the United Nations
Charter and the rules of international law.

I should be grateful if you would have this letter circulated as a
document of the Security Council.

(Signed) Abdul Amir A. AL-ANBARI
Ambassador
Permanent Representative

-----

0223

# 주 국 련 대 표 부

주국련 20313-
**889**
수신 : 장관

참조 : 국제기구국장, 중동아프리카국장

제목 : 대이락 제재조치 시행 (안보리)

1991. 11. 7.

표제관련 이락대표부 서한 (A. Hussein 외무장관 회람 서한) 및 유엔 사무국
서한 (이락 석유수입 절차 요강)을 별첨과 같이 송부합니다.


첨부 : 상기문서. 끝.


# 주 국 련 대 사

| 선 건 | | | 결재(국장) | | |
|---|---|---|---|---|---|
| 접수일시 1991.11. | 63621 | | On | | |
| 회부 | | | | | |

0224

REFERENCE: SCPC/7/91(6-1)

The Secretariat of the United Nations presents its compliments to the Permanent Mission of the Republic of Korea to the United Nations and has the honour to refer to the note by the Secretary-General dated 30 October 1991 (SCPC/7/91(6)) by which he transmitted Security Council document S/23149, which contains the text of the procedures to be employed by the Security Council Committee established by resolution 661 (1990) concerning the situation between Iraq and Kuwait in the discharge of its responsibilities under Security Council resolutions 706 (1991) and 712 (1991), together with copies in English and French of the Standard Application Form approved by the Committee for use in requesting the Committee's approval of contracts for the sale of Iraqi petroleum.  In this connection, the Secretariat has the honour to request that the French language version of the Standard Application Form be replaced by the copy enclosed herewith.

1 November 1991

S. B.

Annex enclosed

0225

# UNITED NATIONS ☉ NATIONS UNIES

POSTAL ADDRESS—ADRESSE POSTALE  UNITED NATIONS, N Y  10017
CABLE ADDRESS—ADRESSE TELEGRAPHIQUE  UNATIONS NEWYORK

## COMITE DU CONSEIL DE SECURITE CREE PAR LA RESOLUTION 661 (1990) CONCERNANT LA SITUATION ENTRE L'IRAQ ET LE KOWEIT

REFERENCE

### CONTRAT DE VENTE DE PETROLE IRAQUIEN: DEMANDE TYPE D'APPROBATION

Le contrat d'achat de pétrole ci-joint conclu avec l'Organisation étatique de commercialisation de pétrole (SOMO) de l'Iraq est soumis pour approbation conformément au paragraphe 1 a) de la résolution 706 (1991) du Conseil de sécurité, au rapport du Secrétaire général établi en application du paragraphe 5 de ladite résolution (S/23006) et approuvé par le paragraphe 3 de la résolution 712 (1991) du Conseil de sécurité, et à la décision adoptée à sa 51e séance, le 15 octobre 1991 (S/23149), par le Comité du Conseil de sécurité créé par la résolution 661 (1990) concernant la situation entre l'Iraq et le Koweit.

### Renseignements concernant l'acheteur

Nom de l'acheteur :

Lieu d'immatriculation :

Adresse :

Contact :

Téléphone :          Téléfax:          Télex:

0226

## Résumé des conditions du contrat

Quantité de pétrole brut :

Qualité du pétrole brut :

Méthode de fixation des prix et/ou prix par baril US :

Dates du chargement à Ceyhan :

Nom du navire et destination (si disponible) :

Méthode de paiement (lettre de crédit irrévocable, banques d'émission et de confirmation, etc.) :

Veuillez trouver ci-joint copie du contrat, de la lettre de crédit irrévocable et de toutes les pièces justificatives.

Signature

Nom du signataire

Titre

0227

**UNITED NATIONS**

S

# Security Council

Distr.
GENERAL

S/23183
31 October 1991
ENGLISH
ORIGINAL: ARABIC

LETTER DATED 29 OCTOBER 1991 FROM THE PERMANENT
REPRESENTATIVE OF IRAQ TO THE UNITED NATIONS
ADDRESSED TO THE SECRETARY-GENERAL

On instructions from my Government, I am pleased to transmit herewith a letter dated 29 October 1991 from Mr. Ahmad Hussein, Minister for Foreign Affairs of the Republic of Iraq, informing you that the Turkish side is continuing to violate the territorial integrity and sovereignty of the Republic of Iraq.

I should be grateful if you would have this letter and its annex circulated as an official document of the Security Council.

(Signed)  Abdul Amir A. AL-ANBARI
Permanent Representative

91-36246  2737g (E)                                                    /...

0228

<u>Annex</u>

<u>Letter dated 29 October 1991 from the Minister for Foreign
Affairs of Iraq addressed to the Secretary-General</u>

Further to our two letters dated 16 October 1991, I have the honour to
inform you that the Turkish side is continuing to violate the territorial
integrity and overeignty of the Republic of Iraq, targeting the defenceless
and innocent in the northern region and their homes.  The details are as
follows:

1.    At 1545 hours on 25 October 1991, Turkish aircraft bombarded the villages
of Qunahish and Girgasha in the Amadiyah district.  At 1630 hours on the same
day, Turkish aircraft bombarded the villages of Shildizah, Balandah, Ziwah,
Qunahish, Girgasha, Belegah and Dayri in the Amadiyah district in Dohuk
governerate, which resulted in the death and wounding of a number of Iraqi
citizens and the destruction of some houses.

2.    The Chief of General Staff of the Turkish Army claimed that the Turkish
combat planes and helicopters had launched raids on the camps and positions of
elements of the Turkish Kurdish Workers' Party in northern Iraq, who,
according to his allegation, had established bases for carrying out operations
against frontier guard posts and army patrols, taking advantage of the
conditions prevailing in the northern region.  He added that the Turkish Army
operations would continue against what he called "elements of the Workers'
Party" and their positions in Iraq as long as it was necessary.

In informing you that the Turkish side's continued repetition of its
violations of the territorial integrity and sovereignty of Iraq and its
endangering of the security and safety of Iraqi citizens on pretexts that are
legally inadmissible constitutes a blatant violation of the United Nations
Charter and norms of international law and endangers peace and security in the
region, I request you to intervene immediately to take effective measures to
put an end to the repeated violations of the Turkish side in a manner that
makes clear to the international community the unfoundedness of the belief
that the United Nations applies a double standard in dealing with the issues
of its Member States, inasmuch as the fundamental goal of the United Nations
is to achieve peace, to maintain peace and to protect the territorial
sovereignty of all Member States.

I request you to have this letter circulated as a document of the
Security Council.

(<u>Signed</u>)  Ahmad HUSSEIN
Minister for Foreign Affairs

-----

0229

**UNITED NATIONS**

# Security Council

S

Distr.
GENERAL

S/23193
4 November 1991
ENGLISH
ORIGINAL: ARABIC

---

LETTER DATED 1 NOVEMBER 1991 FROM THE PERMANENT REPRESENTATIVE
OF IRAQ TO THE UNITED NATIONS ADDRESSED TO THE SECRETARY-GENERAL

On instructions from my Government and further to our previous letters concerning violations of Iraqi airspace and territory by Turkish land and air forces, I have the honour to inform you that on 26 October 1991 a group made up of commandos, police and village guards belonging to units of the First Special Forces Brigade and 23rd Police Brigade penetrated the Iraqi areas indicated below, some of which were bombed by Turkish aircraft on the same day:  Hossi, Rashmah, Haura, Hal, Hosh, Razkiyah, Jabal Nirah, Sabtu and Miranush.  The group in question returned to Turkish territory on 27 October 1991.

In informing you of these violations, we request you, in conformity with the provisions of international law and of the Charter of the United Nations, to take the necessary steps to put an end to the violations and to prevent future repetitions of them.

I should be grateful if you would have this letter circulated as a document of the Security Council.

(Signed)  Abdul Amir A. AL-ANBARI
Ambassador
Permanent Representative

-----

91-36883  2839d (E)

0230

# UNITED NATIONS

## Security Council

Distr.
GENERAL

S/23198
5 November 1991
ENGLISH
ORIGINAL: ARABIC

LETTER DATED 4 NOVEMBER 1991 FROM THE PERMANENT
REPRESENTATIVE OF IRAQ TO THE UNITED NATIONS
ADDRESSED TO THE SECRETARY-GENERAL

On instructions from my Government, I wish to inform you of the following:

United States warplanes and fighters continue to violate Iraqi airspace. Up to the present, I have notified you daily of the details of these violations, but it appears that the United Nations is not capable of putting an end to the United States of America's continuous violation of the provisions of the United Nations Charter and the violation of the sovereignty of a Member State.

These violations have assumed a "grave" character aimed at disseminating terror and alarm in the minds of Iraqi civilians, particularly children and women, since these aircraft break the sound barrier at very low altitudes over the towns and villages of Iraq, causing, in addition to terror and alarm, large-scale material damage to civilian houses and public buildings and the wounding of innocent people as a result of the smashing of glass and windows and the shaking of buildings.

For some time, United States warplanes taking off from airfields inside Turkish territory, have been violating Iraqi airspace in the governorates of Dohuk, Irbil and Ninawa. During the past two months, they have been violating the airspace over Mosul almost daily at various altitudes. At 0942 hours on Wednesday, 30 October 1991, two United States F-16s flew very low at an altitude of 200 metres and broke the sound barrier over the city of Mosul, which caused breakage of glass in windows and the shaking of some buildings and stores and aroused terror among the children, in addition to the unfounded alarm that this violation aroused in civilian citizens. Other aircraft carried out 12 sorties over Mosul, Dohuk and Zakho, which continued until 0230 hours in the afternoon of the same day.

United States warplanes have continued to violate Iraqi airspace. At 0916, 0839, 0851, 0991, 0955, 1100 and 1135 hours on Friday, 1 November 1991, United States warplanes violated the airspace over the city of Mosul and its

91-37052  2620c (E)

/...

0231

suburbs and broke the sound barrier from time to time in an attempt to alarm the citizens on their day of rest and leisure. Great damage was done also to buildings and property, in particular the Nineveh Oberoi Hotel, which suffered great damage as a result of the low flights and the breaking of the sound barrier by the United States aircraft, inasmuch as the damage included the breakage of the building's windows and the smashing of a number of false ceilings, doors and electrical equipment. Initial estimates of the losses at this hotel are 80,000 dinars, in addition to other unlisted losses.

The disgraceful actions by the forces of the United States of America, which claims to be civilized and advanced and to protect human rights and defend the freedom of the individual, has created states of alarm, consternation and psychological unrest in children, the effects of which are immeasurable on the material scale. They also present a challenge to all religious values and customs because they present a challenge to the feelings of Muslims as they are performing their Friday prayers on the holy day which they reserve for worship. These violations have also created a state of sudden disruptions of traffic, leading to collisions.

The Iraqi Government, as it strongly condemns these crimes, calls on the international community, through the United Nations, to undertake to put a halt to them, in accordance with the prescriptions of the United Nations Charter and the rules of international law.

I should be grateful if you would have this letter circulated as a document of the Security Council.

(Signed) Abdul Amir A. AL-ANBARI
Ambassador
Permanent Representative

-----

0232

# UNITED NATIONS ⊕ NATIO UNIES

POSTAL ADDRESS—ADRESSE POSTALE  UNITED NATIONS, N.Y. 10017
CABLE ADDRESS—ADRESSE TELEGRAPHIQUE  UNATIONS NEWYORK

REFERENCE: SCPC/7/91(6)

The Secretary-General of the United Nations presents his
compliments to the Permanent Representative of the Republic of Korea
to the United Nations and, at the request of the Security Council
Committee established by resolution 661 (1990) concerning the
situation between Iraq and Kuwait, has the honour to transmit
herewith Security Council document S/23149, which contains the text
of the procedures to be employed by the Committee in the discharge
of its responsibilities under Security Council resolutions
706 (1991) and 712 (1991).  These procedures were adopted by the
Committee at its 51st meeting, held on 15 October 1991.  In
accordance with the request of the Committee, the Secretary-General
wishes to draw attention, in particular, to section I, paragraphs 3,
4 and 5 of the procedures set out in document S/23149.

Enclosed also are copies of the Standard Application Form which
has been approved by the Committee for use in requesting the
Committee's approval of contracts for the sale of Iraqi petroleum.
It is the wish of the Committee that in order to facilitate the
expeditious consideration of applications, applicants should use
this Standard Application Form only and should transmit the
completed application form and any related documentation or
correspondence via the United Nations fax line which is being
reserved exclusively for such correspondence, that is, 212-963-8833.

30 October 1991

S. B.

Annexes enclosed

0233

**UNITED NATIONS**

**Security Council**

S

Distr.
GENERAL

S/23149
16 October 1991

ORIGINAL:  ENGLISH

DECISION TAKEN BY THE SECURITY COUNCIL COMMITTEE ESTABLISHED BY
RESOLUTION 661 (1990) CONCERNING THE SITUATION BETWEEN IRAQ
AND KUWAIT AT ITS 51ST MEETING, HELD ON 15 OCTOBER 1991

**Procedures to be employed by the Security Council Committee established by resolution 661 (1990) concerning the situation between Iraq and Kuwait in the discharge of its responsibilities under Security Council resolutions 706 (1991) and 712 (1991)**

I.    **Preparatory steps:**

1.    The Committee will select, upon recommendation by the Secretariat, three independent experts in international oil trade as "overseers" at United Nations Headquarters, and entrust them with the authority to approve or reject oil sale contracts on behalf of the Committee.  The overseers will be authorized to correspond with applicants as needed.  The nomination of three persons will ensure a 24-hour availability for contract approvals.

2.    Other experts, agents and inspectors (as required below) will be appointed by the Secretary-General.  The Committee will take note of these appointments.

3.    States may, if they so wish, forward to the Committee a list of national oil purchasers (private companies, State-owned companies, State agencies, ministries, etc.) authorized to communicate with the overseer.  Once the Committee has taken note of these lists and passed them on to the overseer, these purchasers are entitled to communicate directly with the overseer (see sect. II, part A, para. 3 below).  If States do not submit such a list, or if a certain purchaser is not included in the list, the communication with the overseer must go via the Permanent Mission in New York.

4.    For the purpose of section II, part A, paragraph 3 below, a Standard Application Form will be elaborated by the Committee and circulated among all States.  States and national oil purchasers shall use only these Standard Application Forms.

91-34269  2760j (E)                                                      /...

0234

5. The Secretariat will set up a new fax line to be used exclusively for correspondence with regard to oil transactions. Applicants are requested to send their relevant applications and relating correspondence only via this fax line. Other correspondence with the Committee shall go through the already existing channels.

6. Iraq and Turkey will have to conclude an arrangement on the price and payment modalities for the use of Turkish oil installations. Once this arrangement is concluded, it must be forwarded to the Committee which will take note of it. United Nations agents will check the implementation of this arrangement and report periodically to the . Committee.

7. Monitoring of delivery to Iraq of foodstuffs, medicines, and materials and supplies for essential civilian needs will be done by independent inspection agents appointed by an appropriate United Nations programme or organization, such as, for example, the Office for Project Services (OPS). Monitoring of the distribution of these goods will be arranged by the Executive Delegate in cooperation with relevant United Nations programmes and organizations, including appropriate humanitarian non-governmental organizations (NGOs). The Committee will be informed about the relevant arrangements, including those for the purpose of section III, part A, paragraph 11 below.

8. Upon recommendation by the Secretariat, the Committee will nominate an expert (a staff member of one of the United Nations programmes or organizations) who will act as an aide to the Committee for the purposes of section III, part A, paragraph 8 below.

II. Sales of Iraqi oil and oil products:

A. Sales of Iraqi oil:

1. The Iraqi State Organization for the Marketing of Oil (SOMO) signs a contract with the purchaser. The contract must include the provisions as specified in paragraph 58 of the report by the Secretary-General pursuant to paragraph 5 of Security Council resolution 706 (1991) (S/23006).

2. United Nations agents at SOMO review the contracts to assure compliance with the provisions of paragraph 58 of the Secretary-General's report and forward by fax copies of the approvable contracts, supporting documents, and their independent reports to the overseer in New York.

3. The national oil purchaser or the Permanent Mission of the State of purchase forwards by fax a formal request (Standard Application Form) for approval to the Committee, together with a copy of the contract and all other supporting documents.

/...

0235

4.  The overseer reviews the contract and supporting documents to ensure that:

    -   they comply with paragraph 58 of the Secretary-General's report, including that a confirmed irrevocable letter of credit is opened providing for payment into the escrow account;

    -   the conditions of payment envisaged in the letters of credit are in conformity with existing market practices;

    -   they do not appear to contain any attempt at fraud or deception;

    -   the transaction's pricing is consistent with world prices and market trends; and

    -   the transaction does not exceed the limits imposed by Security Council resolutions 706 (1991) and 712 (1991).

5.  If the contract and supporting documents are found to be in order, the overseer, on behalf of the Committee, approves the sale (within the shortest period of time possible, at the maximum 24 hours) and informs by fax the national oil purchaser or the Permanent Mission concerned, as well as SOMO.

6.  The overseer sends his notification of sales approval, together with a copy of the contract, supporting documents, and the report of the United Nations agent at SOMO, by fax to the inspector at Ceyhan who will authorize loading only after these documents are in his possession.

7.  Depending on the number of applications, the overseer reports to the Committee, in a structured and standardized manner, at least twice a week on contracts approved by him (including the cumulative quantity and value of oil authorized for export), and informs the Secretary-General accordingly.

8.  The oil is pumped into storage tanks.  Agents at the pipeline check the pumping.  Subject to their confirmation, the oil can be loaded on ships and the ships can leave the terminal.  The agents will have the authority to prohibit the delivery of the oil if there is any evidence of irregularity.

9.  The agents report to the Committee on their assessment of the pumping and loading.

10. The purchaser makes payment into the escrow account.

11. Twice a week, the Secretary-General forwards statements of the escrow account, including outlines of anticipated future obligations, to the Committee.

/...

0236

B.   Sales of Iraqi oil products:

The regime for the sale of oil products will be broadly similar to that described above, but the precise arrangements will be elaborated at a later stage, as and when the need arises.

III.   Purchase by Iraq of foodstuffs, medicines, and materials and supplies for essential civilian needs:

A.   Purchase by Iraq of foodstuffs, medicines, and materials and supplies for essential civilian needs, to be financed from the escrow account:

1.   Iraq sends a categorized list of relevant requirements to the Executive Delegate.  (Preferably, a two-months list, quantity- and value-oriented.) If Iraq intends also to finance medicines from the escrow account, these too should be mentioned in general terms on the list, together with their value.  The overall value of the list must not exceed that part of the amount authorized by the Committee, in accordance with paragraph 2 of Security Council resolution 712 (1991), which is available for humanitarian purchases.

2.   The Executive Delegate forwards the list, revised by him if necessary, to the Committee.

3.   The Committee takes action on the list and forwards to the Secretary-General and the Executive Delegate the list as approved.  (The first list will be taken up at a meeting of the Committee; subject to agreement, later lists might be dealt with under a "no-objection" procedure.)

4.   The Secretary-General will make the list known to all States.

5.   The Executive Delegate informs Iraq about the clearance.

6.   Iraq signs a contract with the exporter, in accordance with normal commercial practice and the relevant Security Council resolutions.

7.   (a)  Medicines:

The Permanent Mission of the exporter's country informs the Committee of the exporter's wish to be paid from the escrow account.  A copy of the relevant contract must be attached to this communication.

(b)  Foodstuffs:

The Permanent Mission of the exporter's country notifies the Committee. This notification must contain the information that the exporter wants to be paid from the escrow account.  A copy of the relevant contract must be attached to this notification.

/...

0237

(c)  **Materials and supplies for essential civilian needs**:

The Permanent Mission of the exporter's country requests approval, under the "no-objection" procedure, by the Committee.  This request must contain the information that the exporter wishes to be paid from the escrow account.  A copy of the relevant contract must be attached to this request.

8.  An expert (aide to the Committee) checks the contracts, in particular on the price/value relationship, and informs the Chairman.  His findings will be attached to the circulation note to Committee members.

9.  (a)  **Medicines**:

(i)  If the contract is found in order, the Committee informs the Permanent Mission concerned and the Secretary-General that the contract has been found in order, i.e. the exporter can expect payment from the escrow account.

(ii)  If the contract is not found in order, the Committee informs the Permanent Mission concerned and the Secretary-General that the contract has not been found in order, i.e. the exporter cannot expect payment from the escrow account.  However, medical supplies can be shipped anyway if the exporter so wishes.

(b)  **Foodstuffs**:

(i)  If the contract is found in order, the Committee takes note of the notification and informs the Permanent Mission concerned and the Secretary-General accordingly and states that the contract has been found in order, i.e. the exporter can expect payment from the escrow account.

(ii)  If the contract is not found in order, the Committee takes note of the notification and informs the Permanent Mission concerned and the Secretary-General accordingly but states that the contract has not been found in order, i.e. the exporter cannot expect payment from the escrow account.  However, foodstuffs can be shipped anyway if the exporter so wishes.

(c)  **Materials and supplies for essential civilian needs**:

(i)  If the contract is found in order, and if the Committee approves the shipment under the "no-objection" procedure, it informs the Permanent Mission concerned and the Secretary-General of the approval and states that the contract has been found in order, i.e. the exporter can expect payment from the escrow account.

/...

0238

(ii)  If the contract is not found in order, and if the Committee nevertheless approves the shipment under the "no-objection" procedure, it informs the Permanent Mission concerned and the Secretary-General of the approval but states that the contract has not been found in order, i.e. the exporter cannot expect payment from the escrow account.  However, the goods can be shipped anyway if the exporter so wishes.

(iii)  If the Committee cannot approve the shipment, whether or not the contract is found in order, the goods are not allowed to be shipped.

From here on only if the contract has been found in order:

10.  The Secretary-General may effect part-payment to the exporter, according to commercial practice.

11.  United Nations agents check the delivery (the quality, quantity, labelling, etc.) at the unloading port and the entry points to Iraq and report to the Committee.  The agents will have the authority to inspect the shipment documents and, if necessary, to open and examine the contents as needed.

12.  The Committee evaluates the reports.  If satisfactory, it approves the final payment and informs the Secretary-General.

13.  The Secretary-General effects final payment.

14.  United Nations agents monitor in-country distribution and report, via the Executive Delegate, in a consolidated manner to the Committee.

15.  The Committee evaluates these reports to ensure that equitable internal distribution is being maintained and takes appropriate action if not.

16.  Twice a week, the Secretary-General forwards statements of the escrow account, including outlines of anticipated future obligations, to the Committee.

B.  Purchase by Iraq of foodstuffs, medicines, and materials and supplies for essential civilian needs, to be financed from the sub-account of the escrow account:

1.  According to paragraph 8 of Security Council resolution 712 (1991), imports financed from the sub-account of the escrow account, are, apart from the provision of paragraph 1 (c) of Security Council resolution 706 (1991), subject only to the provisions and procedures of paragraph 20 of Security Council resolution 687 (1991).

/...

0239

2.    Monitoring (paragraph 1 (c) of Security Council resolution 706 (1991))
      will be carried out as indicated in annex II of the Secretary-General's
      report.

3.    Twice a week, the Secretary-General forwards statements of the
      sub-account of the escrow account, including outlines of anticipated
      future obligations, to the Committee.

-----

0240

# UNITED NATIONS  NATIONS UNIES

POSTAL ADDRESS—ADRESSE POSTALE  UNITED NATIONS, N.Y. 10017
CABLE ADDRESS—ADRESSE TELEGRAPHIQUE  UNATIONS NEWYORK

## SECURITY COUNCIL COMMITTEE ESTABLISHED BY RESOLUTION 661 (1990) CONCERNING THE SITUATION BETWEEN IRAQ AND KUWAIT

REFERENCE.

### STANDARD APPLICATION FORM TO REQUEST APPROVAL OF CONTRACTS FOR SALE OF IRAQI PETROLEUM

The attached contract with the Iraqi State Organization for the Marketing of Oil (SOMO) for the purchase of petroleum is submitted for approval in accordance with paragraph 1(a) of Security Council resolution 706 (1991), the report of the Secretary-General pursuant to paragraph 5 of that resolution (S/23006) as approved by paragraph 3 of Security Council resolution 712 (1991), and the decision of the Security Council Committee established by resolution 661 (1990) concerning the situation between Iraq and Kuwait, taken at its 51st meeting held on 15 October 1991 (S/23149).

### Information about the purchaser

Name of purchasing entity:

Place of registration:

Address:

Contact person:

Telephone:                    Telefax:                    Telex:

0241

/...

## Summary of contract terms

Quantity of crude petroleum:

Quality of crude petroleum:

Pricing formula and/or price per U.S. barrel:

Date(s) of loading at Ceyhan:

Name of vessel and destination (if available):

Payment method (e.g. irrevocable letter of credit, issuing and confirming banks, etc.):

Please find attached a copy of the contract, irrevocable letter of credit and all supporting documents.

Signature

Name of signatory

Title

0242

POSTAL ADDRESS—ADRESSE POSTALE UNITED NATIONS, N.Y. 10017
CABLE ADDRESS—ADRESSE TELEGRAPHIQUE UNATIONS NEWYORK

**COMITE DU CONSEIL DE SECURITE CREE PAR LA RESOLUTION 661 (1990) CONCERNANT LA SITUATION ENTRE L'IRAQ ET LE KOWEIT**

REFERENCE.

## CONTRAT DE VENTE DE PETROLE IRAQUIEN: DEMANDE TYPE D'APPROBATION

Le contrat d'achat de pétrole ci-joint conclu avec l'Organisation étatique de commercialisation de pétrole (SOMO) de l'Iraq est soumis pour approbation conformément au paragraphe 1 a) de la résolution 706 (1991) du Conseil de sécurité, au rapport du Secrétaire général établi en application du paragraphe 5 de ladite résolution (S/23006) et approuvé par le paragraphe 3 de la résolution 712 (1991) du Conseil de sécurité, et à la décision adoptée à sa 51e séance, le 15 octobre 1991 (S/23149), par le Comité du Conseil de sécurité créé par la résolution 661 (1990) concernant la situation entre l'Iraq et le Koweit.

### Renseignements concernant l'acheteur

Nom de l'acheteur :

Lieu d'immatriculation :

Adresse :

Contact :

Téléphone :             Téléfax:              Télex:

0243

## <u>Résumé des conditions du contrat</u>

Quantité de pétrole brut :

Qualité du pétrole brut :

Méthode de fixation des prix et/ou prix par baril US :

Dates du chargement à Ceyhan :

Méthode de paiement (type de lettre de crédit, banque
d'émission, etc.) :

     Veuillez trouver ci-joint copie du contrat et de toutes
les pièces justificatives.

                          Signature

                          Nom du signataire

                          Titre

0244

THE PERMANENT MISSION OF IRAQ
TO THE UNITED NATIONS
NEW YORK. N. Y. 10021

المَمثليّة العِراقيّة الدائمة لدَى الأمَم المتحدة
نيويورك

The Permanent Mission of the Republic of Iraq to
the United Nations presents its compliments to the Permanent
Mission of Korea       to the United Nations, and has the
honour to enclose herewith the text of a letter from H.E. Mr.
Ahmed Hussein, Minister of Foreign Affairs of the Republic of
Iraq dated October 24, 1991 together with its unofficial
translation into English, addressed to H.E. the Foreign
Minister of Korea       on the occation of the United Nations
Day

The Permanent Mission of the Republic of Iraq to the
United Nations would be grateful , if the enclosed letter was
forwarded to its highest destination.

The Permanent Mission of the Republic of Iraq to the
United Nations avails itself of this opportunity to renew to
the Permanent Mission of Korea       to the United Nations the
assurances of its highest consideration.

New York, October 24, 1991

Permanent Mission
of Republic of Korea
to the United Nations
New York.

0245

وزارة الخارجية

مكتب الوزير

صاحب السيادة

يوافق اليوم الذكرى ( ٤٦ ) لتأسيس الامم المتحدة عندما اصبح ميثاق المنظمة العالمية نافذاً في ٢٤/تشرين اول ١٩٤٥ ، وكان العراق من الدول المؤسسة للامم المتحدة التي شاركت في مؤتمر سان فرنسيسكو ووقعت على الميثاق في ٢٦/حزيران /١٩٤٥ .

أن العراق اذ يستذكر مبادىء الامم المتحدة. يؤكد في الوقت نفسه على ضرورة التطبيق العادل لاحكام الميثاق وقرارات الامم المتحدة دون تمييز بحيث لا ينتهي امر المنظمة الى وضع تسيطر فيه دولة واحدة او قلة من الدول على مقدراتها وتوجيهها من موقع القوة واستخدام الضغوط المختلفة للتاثير على قراراتها .

أن الوضع التمييزي الذي اعطاه الميثاق للقوى الكبرى المنتصرة في الحرب العالمية الثانية من خلال عضويتها الدائمة في مجلس الامن ومنحها حق النقض لقرارات المجلس قد اسيء استخدامه وخرج عن غاياته في تحمل مسؤولية حفظ السلام والامن الدوليين . ففي ظل ظروف الحرب الباردة ، وعلى سبيل المثال ، استخدمت الولايات المتحدة الاميركية حق النقض عشرات المرات لعرقلة اصدار قرارات من مجلس الامن تكفل حق تقرير المصير للشعب الفلسطيني وحتى القرارات التي صدرت عن مجلس الامن حول قضايا فلسطين والشرق الاوسط واحتلال الاراضي العربية الاخرى والتي تزيد عن ١٧٠ قراراً أو التي صدرت عن الجمعية العامة حول المواضيع والتي اقر قسم منها حق تقرير المصير للشعب الفلسطيني وبلغت اكثر من ٤٠٠ قرار وقفت الولايات المتحدة موقفاً معارضاً لها ولم تحترمها ،مما يؤكد ان الولايات المتحدة تعتمد ازدواجية التعامل مع قرارات مجلس الامن والجمعية العامة وتكيل بمكيالين بما يتناسب ومصالحها واهدافها السياسية .

0246

( ٢ )

وفي ضوء التطورات السريعة التي يشهدها العالم حالياً تحول مجلس الامن الى اداة طيعة بيد الدول الكبرى دائمة العضوية وبالاخص الولايات المتحدة الاميركية ،لاصدار قرارات تخدم المصالح والاهداف السياسية لهذه الدول التي عمدت على استخدام الامم المتحدة. كغطاء لاضفاء ما يسمّى بالشرعية الدولية على تلك القرارات .

واذا كانت الدول النامية هي ضحية الصراع الذي شهده المجتمع الدولي في ظل ظروف الحرب الباردة، فانها اليوم ايضاً ضحية ما يسمى بالنظام الدولي الجديد. وقد برزت اتجاهات في مواقف دول حركة عدم الانحياز والدول النامية توءكد هذه الحقائق من خلال كلمات روءساء وفودها امام الجمعية العامة للامم المتحدة. في دورتها الحالية . وكانت الدورة العاشرة لموءتمر وزراء خارجية عدم الانحياز التي عقدت في أكــرا في الاسبوع الاول من ايلول الماضي قد اكدت هذه الحقائق في تقريرها الذي سيرفع الى القمة العاشرة للحركة المقرر عقده فـي جاكارتا في عام ١٩٩٢ . حيث اكدت الحركة ان بروز عالم احادى القطب يتسم بعناصر جديدة. قد يفضى الى اوضاع تحول دون ايلاء الاهتمام الواجب لاحتياجات ومصالح البلدان غير المنحازة وسائر البلدان النامية. واكدت على ضرورة التعجيل بتنفيذ جميع قرارات الامم المتحدة وخصوصاً قرارات مجلس الامن دون تمييـز . وأكدت الحركة ايضاً على ضرورة اصلاح الامم المتحدة بحيث تضفي الديمقراطية والشفافية على عملية اتخـــاذ القرارات في الامم المتحدة. وفي مجلس الامن بصفة خاصة واعادة النظـر في العدد الحالي لاعضاء مجلس الامن بما يجعله يعبر عن الزيادة التـي طرأت على عدد اعضاء الامم المتحدة ويكفل تمثيلا اكثر انصافاً وتوازناً لاعضاء الامم المتحدة .

اضافة الى ذلك فان التقرير السنوي للامين العام الذي قدمـــه للجمعية العامة في دورتها الحالية قد اشار الى ان الاجراءات التــي

0247

( ٣ )

اتخذت في اللجوء الى القوة لم تتم بدقة وفقاً للفصل السابع من الميثاق حيث اجاز مجلس الامن استعمال القوة من قبل دول أو مجموعة من الدول بدلاً من الامم المتحدة نفسها .

كما أكد التقرير على ضرورة التزام مجلس الامن باحكام التناسب في استعمال القوة وكذلك بتطبيق القوانين الانسانية في النزاعات المسلحة وأهمية الاخذ بعين الاعتبار الاثار الانسانية التي تترتب على سكان الدول التي تطبق ضدها العقوبات الاقتصادية .

أن العراق يؤكد مجدداً تحذيراته السابقة عن أن ملامح ما يسمى بالنظام الدولي الجديد والتي ظهرت حتى الان لاتؤكد سوى ممارسات مفضوحة في التدخل بالشوءون الداخلية للدول الاخرى وتجاهل كبير لحقوق الدول النامية وسياسات انتقائية في السماح لدول معينة بالتسلح كيفما تشاء بما في ذلك التسلح النووي واسلحة الدمار الشامل الاخرى مقابل فرض حظر شامل على دول اخرى . ان تهاون المجتمع الدولي مع هذه الممارسات والسياسات ستجعل من مبادىء واحكام ميثاق الامم المتحدة حبرا على ورق .

ان الامم المتحدة في هذه المرحلة امام امتحان كبير في صيانة الاهداف الاساسية التي كانت وراء اقامتها وبالاخص الحفاظ على الامن والسلم الدوليين واحترام مبدأ المساواة في السيادة بين جميع الدول وعدم التدخل في الشوءون الداخلية وضمان حياة حرة كريمة لشعوب العالم اجمع .

لقد تعرض العراق باسم تطبيق الشرعية الدولية الى دمار شامل استهدف مرافق الحياة كافة بما في ذلك البنى التحتية الاقتصادية والمراكز السكانية المدنية ،وقادت الولايات المتحدة الاميركية عدواناً جوياً استمر ( ٤٣ ) يوماً شمل جميع مدن العراق وقراه وقد دمرت محطات توليد ونقل الطاقة الكهربائية ومصافي النفط والجسور ونواظم الري

0248

( ٤ )

ومراكز تصفية المياه والمصانع المدنية وتمريف المياه الصحية والمستشفيات والمدارس والمساجد والكنائـــس ومعامل حليب الاطفال ومخازن الحبوب وملاجــــئ المدنيين ،حيث لقي ٣١٩ مواطنا غالبيتهم من النساء والاطفال والشيوخ مصرعهم في ابشع عدوان على ملجاء العامرية المعد للمدنيين ،واسقطت الطائرات الحربية ما يقارب ١٠٠ الف طن من المتفجرات على مدن وقــرى العراق ،فهل كان مـــــن اهداف الامم المتحدة ان يدمر بلد باكمله تحت ذريعة تطبيق الشرعية الدولية ؟ وهل من مبادئ الشرعية الدوليـــة دفن آلاف الجنود العراقيين في خنادقهم وهم أحياء ؟ وهـل مــــــن مبادئ حقوق الانسان ان يستمر الحصار اللا انساني ضد شعب العراق رغم اداء العراق لالتزاماته بموجب قرارات مجلس الامن؟ ان ما تعرض له العراق من عدوان وظلم وتعسف وما يتعرض له شعب العراق من حصار جائر يتنافى كليا مــــع مبادئ واهداف ميثاق الامم المتحدة • ورغم ان بعثات الامم المتحـــــدة. التي زارت العراق وقدمت تقارير الى مجلس الامن بعد دراســـــات ميدانيــة ،وبعثات اخرى دولية غير حكومية قامت بنفس المهام ، قـــــد اكدت جميعها فداحة الكارثة الانسانية التي يعانيها الشعب العراقي وبالاخص الاطفال والنساء ، فان الولايات المتحدة الاميركية وحلفائهــــا ممن يرفع شعارات الحرية والديمقراطية وحقوق الانسان يصرون علـــــى استمرار هذا الحصار ومنع وصول المواد الغذائية والدوائية والمدنية الاساسية للشعب العراقي لتحقيق اهداف سياسية مشبوهة تتناقض تناقضـــا تاما مع احكام ميثاق الامم المتحدة وقواعد القانون الدولي وتطلــــع شعوب العالم نحو الاستقلال والحرية والعيش الكريم •

وعلى عكس ما دعت اليه تلك البعثات في تلبية الاحتياجـــــــات الانسانية وتخفيف معاناة الشعب العراقي سعت الولايات المتحدة الاميركية الى اصدار قرارين جائرين وشاذين من مجلس الامن هما القراران ٧٠٦و٧١٢لفرض قيود اقتصادية جائرة على العراق لا سابقة لها في تاريخ العلاقــــات

0249

MINISTRY FOR FOREIGN AFFAIRS

MINISTER'S OFFICE

وزارة الخارجية

مكتب الوزير

( ٥ )

الدوليـــة ولا تجـــد لهـا أي أسـاس او ســند في احكام ميثاق الامــــم المتحدة .

ولم يعد سرّاً   ان هذه السياسات الاميركية التي تخالف قواعـد القانون الدولي والاعراف الدولية التي تنص على احترام سيادة الـــدول وعدم التدخل في شـؤونها الداخـلية تهدف الى تحقيق اغراض سياسيــــة في تغيير نظام الحكم في العراق واخضاع الشعب العراقي للارادة الادارة الاميركيــــة ، وهذا ما اعلنـــه رئيس الولايـات المتحدة الاميركيـــــة في مؤتمره الصحفي في ١٩٩١/١٠/٤ وقد بينت في رسالتي   الى رئيــــس مجلس الامن بتاريخ ١٩٩١/١٠/٨ مخاطر هذه التصريحات ومخالفتها الصريحـة لاحكام الميثاق وبالاخص الفقرة (٢) من المادة الاولى والفقرة (٧) مــن المادة الثانية ، وبيّنت انه من المؤسف ان يسود الصمت تجاه مثـل هذه التصريحات الخطيرة من رئيس دولـة كبرى وعضو في مجلس الامـــــن وان السكوت عن مثل هذه السياسات المناقضــــة لمبادىء ميثــاق الامم المتحدة والقانون الدولي ستكون له عواقب وخيمة على الامـــن والسلم الدوليين وعلى هيئة الامم المتحدة نفسها .

واذا كان الهدف هو جعـل العراق اول ضحايا ما يسمى بالنظام الدولي الجديد فانه لن يكون الضحية الوحيدة ، وستكون دول العالم الثالث والــدول الصغيرة عامة ضحية لسياسة الهيمنة الاميركية الاستعمارية التي تعمل على فرض هذا النظام ، واذا لم يدرك المجتمع الدولي مخاطر هذه السياسة ويضــــــع حدّاً لها فان النضال الطويل الذي خاضته شعوب العالم من اجل الاستقـــلال والسيادة والحياة الحرة الكريمة   سيضيع هدراً .

وتقبلوا فائق التقدير والاحترام

احمد حسين

وزير خارجية الجمهورية العراقية

بغداد في ٢٣/١٠/١٩٩١

0250

Your Excellency,

Today marks the 46th anniversary of the foundation of the United Nations. It was on this day, the 24th of October 1945, that the UN Charter came into effect, and Iraq was amongst the founding member-states which had attended the San Francisco Conference and signed the Charter on 26 June, 1945.

Recalling the principles of the United Nations, Iraq reiterates the necessity of the fair and unbiased implementation of the provisions of the Charter and the resolutions of the United Nations, so that the UN would not end up in a situation in which a single member-state or a group of member-states dominate the organization, control its affairs and determine its policies from a position of power and through the exertion of all sorts of pressure to influence its decisions.

The special discriminatory status given by the Charter to the Big Powers, the victors of the Second World War, granting them permanent membership with the right of Veto in the Security Council, has been abused and has failed to achieve its goal of ensuring the reponsibility of preserving international peace and security. During the cold war, for instance, the United States of America used its right of Veto dozens of times to prevent the Security Council from adopting such resolutions as would have ensured the right of self-determination to the Palestinian people. The Security Council has adopted more than 170 resolutions on this issues of Palestine, the Middle East and the occupations of land by force, while the General Assembly has passed more than 400 such resolutions, recognizing in some of them the right of the Palestinian people to self-determination. The United States objected to, and treated with disrespect, all these resolutions, thus emphasizing the double-standard criteria it adopts in dealing with the resolutions of the Security Council and the General Assembly, in a manner compatible only with US interests and political objectives.

In view of the rapid developments currently witnessed in the world, the Security Council has become an easy tool in the hands of the big powers, the permanent members of the Security Council, especially the United States of America, to issue resolutions serving the interests and political objectives of these countries which have used the United Nations as a cover of international legitimacy for those resolutions.

If the developing countries were victims of the conflict witnessed by the international community under the cold war, they are today victims of the so-called New World Order. Directions have emerged in the attitudes of the member states of the Non-aligned Movement and the developing countries emphasizing these facts in the speeches delivered by

1 - 4

0251

the heads of their delegations to the General Assembly of the United Nations during the current session. The Tenth Ministerial Meeting of the Non-aligned Movement which was convened in Accra during the first week of last September, stressed these facts in its final report which will be put before the Tenth Summit Conference of the Non-aligned Movement to be held in Jakarta in 1992. The Non-aligned Movement has underscored the fact that a world of unipolarity is emerging with new elements which may lead to situations in which no adequate importance is given to the needs and interests of the non-aligned countries and indeed of the developing world in general. The Movement stressed the necessity of expediting the unbiased implementation of all UN resolutions and especially the resolutions of the Security Council. The Movement also stressed the necessity of reforming the United Nations in a manner that would allow democracy and transparency to prevail over the adoptions of resolutions in the United Nations and in the Security Council in particular. The existing number of the members of the Security Council should also be reviewed to accommodate the increase in the membership of the United Nations and thus ensure a fairer and more balanced representation of the UN membership.

Furthermore, the annual report presented by the Secretary General of the United Nations during the current session of the General Assembly points out that the measures taken to use force were not carried out strictly in accordance with Chapter VII of the UN Charter, for the Security Council authorized the use of force on a national and coalition basis rather than by the United Nations itself. The Secretary General also stressed in his report the necessity that the rule of proportionality in the employment of armed forces is observed, and that the rules of humanitarian law applicable to armed conflicts are complied with. The Secretary General stressed the importance that the human effect of economic sanctions on the population of the state subject to such sanctions need to be carefully borne in mind.

Iraq wishes to reiterate the warnings it has voiced on past occasions that the features so far observed in the so-called New World Order highlight nothing other than flagrant practices of interference in the internal affairs of other countries, a gross disregard of the rights of the developing countries, as well as the perpetration of selective policies allowing certain states to acquire all sorts of weapons, including nuclear and other weapons of mass destruction, while imposing a total embargo on other states. International indifference to these practices and policies will turn the principles and provisions of the UN Charter pointless.

The United Nations is currently facing a major test in the maintenance of the basic principles upon which it was founded, particularly the principles of preserving international peace and security, respecting the equal sovereignty of all states, non-interference in the internal affairs of others, and guaranteeing a life of freedom and dignity for all peoples.

0252

2－4

Iraq has been subjected, in the name of international legitimacy, to full-scale destruction targeting all facilities of life including its economic infrastructure and its civilian residential centres. The United States of America led a non-stop air aggression for forty-three days, sparing none of its cities and villages. The aggression destroyed Iraq's electric power generation and transmission plants, oil refineries, bridges and irrigation facilities, water purification centres, sewage treatment plants, civilian factories, hospitals, schools, mosques and churches, baby-milk factories, grain silos and even civilian shelters. The Amiriya civilian shelter witnessed a most heinous crime in which 319 civilians, mostly women, children and elderly, were killed. War planes dropped nearly a hundred thousand tons of explosives onto the cities and villages of Iraq. Was it amongst the objectives of the United Nations that a country be entirely destroyed under the pretext of implementing international legitimacy ? Is it amongst the principles of international legitimacy that thousands of Iraqi soldiers be buried alive in their trenches ? Is it compatible with the principles of human rights that an inhuman blockade be continuously imposed against the people of Iraq despite Iraq's compliance with its obligations in accordance with the resolutions of the Security Council ? The aggression, injustice and bullyism to which Iraq has been subjected and the inhuman blockade imposed upon its people are totally alien to the principles and objectives of the UN Charter. Despite the fact that the UN and other non-governmental international missions to Iraq have all conducted field studies of the situation and prepared reports, some submitted to the Security Council, emphasizing the enormity of the human calamity suffered by the people of Iraq, especially the women and children, the United States and its allies who continue to raise the slogans of liberty, democracy and human rights, insist on the continuation of the blockade and the prevention of food, medicine and other basic civilian needs from being reached to the Iraqi people, in order to achieve suspect political objectives totally contrary to the provisions of the UN Charter, the rules of international law and the aspirations of the peoples of the world to independence, freedom and a life in dignity.

Contrary to the proposals made by these missions to meet the humanitarian needs of the Iraqi people and alleviate their suffering, the United States of America saw to it that two more oppressive and aberrant resolutions are adopted by the Security Council, namely resolutions 706 and 712, to impose such unjust economic restraints upon Iraq,, as has neither been precedented in the history of international relations nor have any basis of support in the provisions of the UN Charter.

It is no longer a secret that the goal of these American policies, contrary as they are to the rules of international law and international norms which stipulate respect for the sovereignty of states and non-intervention in their internal affairs, is to achieve political purposes by

ㅋ_4

0253

changing the system of government in Iraq and sujecting the people of Iraq to the will of the American Administration. The President of the United States himself has made this objective clear in a press conference on 4 October 1991. In my letter of 8 October 1991 to the President of the Security Council, I underscored both the dangers involved in such statements and their flagrant breach of the provisions of the UN Charter, particularly Paragraph (2) of Article (1) and Paragraph (7) of Article (2). I also pointed out that it was regrettable to see silence prevail towards such grave statements made by the President of a superpower and a permanent member of the Security Council, and that silence over such policies which are contradictory to the principles of the UN Charter and international law, shall bring grave consequences to world peace and security and to the United Nations Organization itself.

If the objective is to make Iraq the first victim of the so-called New World Order, Iraq will not be the only such victim. The countries of the Third world and smaller states in general will fall victim to the American imperialist policy of hegemony through which the United states seeks to impose this New World Order. Unless the international community realises the dangers posed by this policy and puts an end to it, then the long struggle fought by the peoples of the world for independence, sovereignty and a life of freedom and dignity will have been in vain.

Accept, Excellency, the assurances of my highest consideration.

Ahmed Hussein,
Minister of Foreign Affairs,
The Republic of Iraq,

BAGHDAD
24 October, 1991

4 - 4

0254

# 외 무 부

종 별 :

번 호 : UNW-3824                       일  시 : 91 1112 2230

수 신 : 장 관(중동일,연일,기정)

발 신 : 주 유엔대사

제 목 : 걸프사태(안보리)

　　1. 쿠웨이트는 지난 10.10 이락어선 7척의 쿠웨이트 영해침범, 10.18 이락인 3명 쿠웨 이트월경(탄약류수거목적) 사례를 들면서 여사한 반복적인 쿠웨이트 침범사태의 책임은 이락당국에 있으며, 이락측이 안보리의 제반관련 결의 준수의사가 없음을 보여주는 것이라고 주장하는 요지의 안보리문서를 배포하였음. (S/23210)

　　2. 금 11.12.자 NYT 지는 유엔 이락화학무기 사찰반에 참여하고 있는 오지리 전문가를 인용, 동 사찰활동을 하는 과정에서 화학탄두가 장착된 다량의 유탄발사, 포탄, 폭탄류가 발견되었다고 보도함.

　　(이락측은 화학무기류 보유량을 4만개로 유엔측에 통보한바 있으나, 유엔사찰결과 10 만개에 이르는 것으로 밝혀짐.)

　　첨부: NYT 기사: UNW(F)-825 끝

　　(대사 노창희-국장)

| 중아국 | 장관 | 차관 | 1차보 | 국기국 | 외정실 | 분석관 | 정와대 | 안기부 |
|---|---|---|---|---|---|---|---|---|

UNW(F)-825   11/12 2230.

총 104

# Iraqi Weapons Had Chemical Warheads

**By JOHN TAGLIABUE**
Special to The New York Times

VIENNA, Nov. 11 — Austrian experts who recently returned from Iraq have said they found large numbers of Iraqi weapons outfitted with chemical warheads that could have been used in the Persian Gulf war.

They also said some of the weapons included Soviet-built Scud missiles. But they said that primitive ballistic technology and warheads that were unevenly filled with deadly liquid chemicals made it unlikely they could have been fired accurately, if at all.

The officials said they found large depots of rifle grenades, artillery shells and bombs with chemical warheads containing sarin, a deadly liquid substance that when distributed as an aerosol spray destroys the nervous system by stopping lung and heart muscles, and mustard gas, another poison gas more likely to incapacitate than to kill, which works similarly on contact with the skin.

The three officials, experts on chemical warfare protection from Austria's federal defense force who were part of a United Nations inspection team, said their last three-week tour, which ended Nov. 5, took them to storage sites reported by Iraq to the United Nations, one at Mosul north of Baghdad, a second west of the Iraqi capital, and a third in the south of Iraq near Basra.

Iraq has reported 40,000 chemical bombs and shells, but inspection has raised the figure to about 100,000, United Nations officials say. Roughly half have already been destroyed.

In an interview, the Austrians said most of the rifle grenades and 122-millimeter artillery shells they examined were outfitted with chemical warheads, often plastic containers with the deadly liquid chemical surrounding a so-called burster tube, a cylinder of TNT or other explosive that detonates on impact, sending the chemical content into the air.

The experts could not say how many Scuds were found in all. But they described Soviet technicians who examined the missiles as startled by the primitive workmanship. They said some experts believed that the missiles would have been destroyed by heat on re-entry into the atmosphere, had they been fired, while others believed that partly filled chemical warheads would probably have caused the kind of destabilization that occurs in half-filled oil tankers at sea, rendering the missiles useless.

There appeared to be no indication that the long-range missiles had ever been tested, the officials said. They said other weapons provided no clues as to why they were not deployed in the war.

The function of the United Nations inspection teams, usually about 25 experts from several countries, including the United States, is to take samples for testing and report the numbers, content and condition of the weapons and the plausibility of removing or destroying them. The Soviet Union and Canada have offered the use of mobile incinerators to destroy the weapons, United Nations officials said, but the technology is slow and costly.

United Nations experts returned to Iraq today to discuss with the Baghdad authorities the destruction of Iraq's chemical and nuclear weapons, Reuters reported. A nuclear team will return 78 rods of enriched uranium to its source, the Soviet Union.

# UNW-3 824

첨부

1-1

0256

# 외 무 부

종 별 :

번 호 : UNW-3879　　　　　　　　　　일 시 : 91 1114 1830

수 신 : 장 관(중동일,연일,기정)

발 신 : 주 유엔대사

제 목 : 걸프사태(안보리)

1. 이란-이락 사태해결에 관한 87년 안보리결의 598호 (7항)에의거 이란-이락전 당시이란의 피해 상황조사를 위해 금월초 A.FARAH 전유엔사무차장이 이란을 방문한 바, 이락은 동방문에 관한 입장을 밝히는 하기 요지의 A.HUSSEIN 외상의 케야르 유엔사무총장앞 서한을 안보리문서로 배포하였음. ( S/23213)

가. 이란이 이락의 걸프전으로 인한 곤경을 틈타 파괴분자들을 이락에 침투시킴으로써 양국간 휴전을 위반하였으며 수천명의 이락 전쟁포로 미송환 상태

나. 휴전 잠정이행을 제외하고 상기 안보리 결의 이행이 중단된 상황에서, 동결의의 특정조항 적용은 결의를 자기에게 유리하게 조각내려는 이란의 기도에 이용당하는 결과 초래

2. 한편 이락은 지난 10.26-11.2.간 쿠웨이트 항공기 이락 영공침범, 양국간 비무장지대( DMZ)에서 이락군 납치, 해상위협사례가 발생하였다고 주장하면서 쿠웨이트측 위반방지 및 억류 이락인 석방을 위한 조치를 취해줄것을 사무총장에게 요청하여옴( S/23209) 끝

(대사 노창희-국장)

| 중아국 | 장관 | 차관 | 1차보 | 국기국 | 외정실 | 분석관 | 정와대 | 안기부 |
|---|---|---|---|---|---|---|---|---|

PAGE 1　　　　　　　　　　　　　　　　　　91.11.15　　10:00 WH

# 외 무 부

종  별 :

번  호 : UNW-4071

일  시 : 91 1126 1930

수  신 : 장 관(연일,중동일,기정)

발  신 : 주 유엔대사

제  목 : 걸프사태(유엔 이락구호 지원활동)

*Sadruddin Aga Khan代표*

1. 표제관련 유엔측은 유엔-이락간 양해각서(MOU)가 금년말에서 92.6.30 까지 연장되었다고 밝힌 바, SADRUDDIN AGA KHAN 대표의 이에 관한 언론발표문을 별첨 송부함.

2. 한편 이락 화학무기 폐기방안 추진현황에 관한 유엔 특위측 발표문도 아울러 송부함.

첨부: UNW(F)-911 끝

(대사 노창희-국장)

---

국기국      장관      1차보      중아국      외정실      분석관      청와대      안기부

PAGE 1

91.11.27    10:24 WH

외신 1과  통제관

0258

INTRODUCTION TO A PRESS CONFERENCE GIVEN BY PRINCE SADRUDDIN AGA KHAN ON TUESDAY 26 NOVEMBER AT 11:15 A.M. IN GENEVA:

I am pleased to report that agreement has been reached with the Government of Iraq for the reaffirmation of the principles enshrined in the Memorandum of Understanding and its extension until 30 June 1992. I welcome this decision and trust that this arrangement will be continued as required thereafter. Certain clarifications have been introduced in the interest of the effective implementation of the programme's objectives and in view of modified circumstances, with the return of the majority of those displaced from neighbouring countries.

The deployment of the United Nations Guards Contingent in Iraq has provided invaluable support to the humanitarian operation and has constituted an essential element of stability in a difficult situation. I therefore considered it of crucial importance that this innovative and enterprising undertaking be maintained in the interest of the humanitarian programme and the population which it is designed to assist.

I am happy to inform you that agreement has also been reached with the Government of Iraq for the continued assignment of the United Nations Guards Contingent.

In the light of recent events in the north, where the peace is once again disturbed with people finding themselves compelled to leave their homes, I wish to call for maximum restraint, so that negotiations towards a political solution that have been under way for some time can move forward without further armed conflict. Those who have been displaced should be permitted to return to their homes at the earliest opportunity.

Turning to the question of petroleum production and export, as well as the financing of essential civilian needs, may I briefly recall the genesis of the current efforts to assure such funding. The mission I led in July to assess the population's humanitarian requirements reported to the Secretary-General that a suitable mechanism should be found whereby these civilian needs, above all of the most vulnerable groups, should be met with no discrimination and funded from Iraq's own resources to the satisfaction of the international community. Following the presentation of my report to the Sanctions Committee, the Security Council eventually proceeded with the adoption of Resolutions 706 and 712, which provided for petroleum sales to the amount of 1.6 billion US dollars to fund the required imports.

In his report to the Council under Resolution 706, the Secretary-General had suggested raising the figure specified to match the amount recommended in my report. Since Resolution 712 was approved on 19 September 1991, and although both Resolutions were adopted under "Chapter VII" provisions of the Charter, no export of oil as foreseen by those Resolutions has yet taken place. In these circumstances, I must stress that all concerned have to find realistic means for the resumption of exports of Iraqi petroleum. #UNW-4071    3-1

- 2 -

If this impasse persists and adversely affects the implementation of the MOU - for lack of funding - the ultimate losers will be the Iraqi people. In the political sphere, one of the parties to the recent conflict will continue to be blamed. Although in the final analysis such arguments are irrelevant to the humanitarian mandate, the Government of Iraq may be held responsible for failing to take advantage of the window of opportunity - narrow and constraining as it may be - afforded by the arrangements for oil exports and imports of essential needs foreseen under the two Resolutions.

Let me emphasise that my concern as Executive Delegate - to see that this crucial programme is implemented fully and effectively - is purely humanitarian. Political rhetoric is not my concern. Nor does it matter where the funding comes from. But the needs of the Iraqi population - especially during the hard winter months - must be adequately addressed. An essential prequisite is that the relief assistance be equitably distributed to all those in need.

3-2

Special Commission Advances Plans for the Destruction

of Iraq's Chemical Weapons

26 November 1991

A United Nations team of four chemical weapons experts recently returned from a week of detailed technical discussions with their Iraqi counterparts to refine plans for the destruction of Iraq's chemical weapons capability, which is expected to get under way early next year. A final decision on who will ultimately be given responsibility for destroying the large toxic arsenal has not yet been made.

The team leader, Professor Bryan Barrass (UK), reported that a good understanding was achieved with the Iraqis on technical issues concerning both mustard gas and nerve agents, and described the talks as "generally constructive and very useful." The discussions took place from 11 to 15 November in Baghdad as well as at Iraq's major chemical weapons facility known as the Muthanna State Establishment near Samarra.

The UN team reviewed an Iraqi proposal for a mustard agent incinerator and concluded that modifications would be required. They now await from the Iraqis revised design drawings as well as a description of related operating procedures.

Similarly, the two sides agreed on a pilot programme to test a process for eliminating nerve agents by caustic hydrolysis. The UN experts discussed modifications to the pilot plant at Muthanna suggested by Iraq, which could eventually lead to a full-scale facility at that site. Those modifications were accepted, paving the way for agreement on procedures for getting a UN-approved pilot programme under way.

The United Nations is considering other possible approaches to the destruction of the mustard and nerve agents, including ones with less significant Iraqi involvement. A final decision will be made after all factors, particularly safety, have been fully assessed.

The UN team selected separate sites at Muthanna for the destruction operations for mustard and nerve agents, and instructed the Iraqis to clear them of all residual hazards, such as unexploded ordnance.

The mission was the second to deal specifically with the forthcoming destruction of chemical weapons, and was organized by the United Nations Special Commission responsible for the elimination of Iraq's weapons of mass destruction.

fg5-19

ㄱ—ㄱ

# 외 무 부

종 별 :

번 호 : UNW-4158　　　　　　　　　　일 시 : 91 1202 2300

수 신 : 장 관(연일,중동일,기정)

발 신 : 주 유엔 대사

제 목 : 걸프사태(안보리)

　　이락은 자국이 현재 보유중인 쿠웨이트 군장비의 반환문제와 관련 91.11월 미,불란서가 이락이 동반환 의무를 이행하지 않고 있다고 이락측에 문제를 제기하여 왔다고 밝히면서, 이를 부인하는 안보리문서를 배포하였음.( R.FORAN 사무차장보와 협조강조)( S/23252)

　　첨부:상기12.1 자 NYT 기사: UNW(F)-951 끝

　　(대사 노창희-국장)

---

국기국　　　장관　　　1차보　　　중아국　　　외정실　　　분석관　　　청와대　　　안기부

PAGE 1　　　　　　　　　　　　　　　　　　　　　　　91.12.03　　13:43 WI

　　　　　　　　　　　　　　　　　　　　　　　　　외신 1과 통제관

　　　　　　　　　　　　　　　　　　　　　　　　　0262

# Iraq: A Clear and Continuing Danger

### By PATRICK E. TYLER

UNW(FT)-951 1/2-2 23:00
총 1/4

##### WASHINGTON

**N**INE months after the remarkably well-executed Desert Storm operation, and six months after it became clear that the allies had imposed on themselves an incomplete victory, a new debate is rising in Washington. As an unforeseen consequence of President Bush's decision last spring to leave Iraq's future to the Iraqis, rather than press then and there for the removal of Saddam Hussein, Iraq has become a time bomb both for the Bush Administration and for the 18 million people living in increasingly desperate conditions under Mr. Hussein's rule.

The problem is made worse for Mr. Bush by the fact that this time bomb is likely to be ticking all through next year's election campaign. If the President needed any evidence, it came in a bipartisan letter signed by 17 senators last week putting the President on notice that "it is increasingly clear that Saddam hopes to use the looming humanitarian crisis in his campaign to end the international sanctions against his outlaw regime."

The President's response to the senators' call for swift but unspecified action was to repeat that his Administration is dedicated to the overthrow of Mr. Hussein, a still formidable task and one for which Mr. Bush still lacks a concrete plan.

When he asked his National Security Council aides to give him some military options, the council consulted the Pentagon, where the initial reaction was: There is no military option that guarantees the overthrow of Mr. Hussein short of a major deployment back to the Persian Gulf, with allied support and international backing for a full-scale assault on Baghdad. In other words, Desert Storm II.

But Washington is buzzing with other ideas, most of them involving Iraq's minority of 3.5 million Kurds, whose divided leadership is lurching toward a decision on whether it would be willing to launch a civil war against Mr. Hussein if it was granted a measure of allied backing.

But such help has pointedly not been offered so far; the reluctance of the Pentagon and the State Department to back a civil war militarily stems from a strong belief that the Kurds — as they showed during their brief uprising last March — would need a great deal of allied support if they were to be effective against the Iraqi Army. Such backing would be all the more problematical since Turkey, which faces a Kurdish rebellion of its own, would certainly oppose arming Kurds or providing rear area bases for a Kurdish-based civil war against Baghdad.

Some Iraqi opposition figures suggest smaller steps. They want Washington to ground Iraq's helicopter fleet and then provide inducements for the Iraqi military to defect in large numbers into Kurdistan, where a provisional army and government could be built to march back to Baghdad and throw out Mr. Hussein. One inducement could simply be food, since regular army units in northern Iraq, unlike Mr. Hussein's Republican Guard, are poorly fed and outfitted.

Another idea, this one from Saudi Arabia, would be for that country and the United States to jointly provide covert financing for small anti-armor missiles with which the Kurds could defend themselves against Soviet helicopter gunships and tanks. One problem, of course, is that any missile that could shoot down an Iraqi helicopter could also shoot down a Turkish warplane.

Gen. Colin L. Powell, Mr. Bush's chief military adviser, has consistently voiced the deepest reservations about the quagmire a Kurdish adventure could turn into, and he has tried to keep the White House focused on what he sees as the fundamental problem: Mr. Hussein's power lies in Baghdad and to remove him would require sending American military force in large numbers. And even if that were done, who would pay for it?

Though the Kurdish option has been thoroughly discussed and repeatedly rejected by Mr. Bush's principal national security aides, the deteriorating conditions of hunger, deprivation and terror in Iraq are only expected to intensify during the 1992 Presidential campaign. Heading into the first postwar winter, there can be little doubt that Mr. Hussein is upping the stakes in his struggle against the American-led coalition.

## A Scent of Jonestown?

In Baghdad, where this reporter spent 10 weeks in several visits over the last year, the defiant and anti-American rhetoric that Mr. Hussein reintroduced this fall has engendered a political scent of Jonestown, where defiance became its own end. The late Jim Jones, like Mr. Hussein, boasted that his people would commit any sacrifice — in the Jonestown case, revolutionary suicide — to demonstrate that their faith in their leader was truly righteous and absolute.

Mr. Hussein's record shows that he can be expected to continue fighting with breathtaking tenacity for his own survival. If his last weapon is the sacrifice of millions of Iraqis to the horrors of starvation and disease until the Western alliance is shocked into saying "Enough!" and relaxing sanctions, then Mr. Hussein will not hesitate to reach for this weapon, many analysts believe.

In large measure, he has already done so.

During a round of interviews in Baghdad last month with Mr. Hussein's cabinet ministers, each sounded the theme of defiance. Iraqis would eat dates and grass rather than "surrender" to the allies' dictates, Trade Minister Mohammed Mehdi Saleh and Oil Minister Osama A. R. al-Hiti

said. With chilling determination, the Health minister, Abdul Salam M. Saaid, explained that he was cutting off programs in which international relief agencies were distributing food directly to Iraqis because this was giving too much comfort to the consciences of the "good people of Europe and the United States." In other words, the minister wanted more pain, not less; in doing so, he showed that the Iraqi leadership is unwilling to play by Western rules of politics and war.

To date, the somewhat cynical consensus in the State Department has held that the American people would be relatively indifferent to Iraqi suffering as long as Mr. Hussein was clearly to blame for it. This consensus, however, appears to be breaking up as the election season draws nearer. The prospect of television images of starvation in Iraq while Mr. Hussein's resilience in Baghdad allows the Democrats to tag Mr. Bush with a major foreign policy failure has some Republican strategists. For some, the possibility of mass starvation in Iraq presents a haunting reminiscence of Pol Pot's purges in Cambodia.

Sensing the debate, the Kurds have already approached Democratic Presidential candidates seeking to find advocates for their cause.

In the end, Mr. Hussein's postwar strategy, geared as it is to insuring his survival at all costs, may present the Bush Administration with a frightful questions: How long can the United States stand by and watch millions of Iraqis slowly starve because Mr. Hussein's Government refuses to submit itself to the intrusive United Nations regime for selling oil to pay reparations? Can a leader such as Mr. Hussein, defeated on battlefield but not conquered or forced to surrender, be allowed to re-emerge and threaten neighbors with whatever instruments of vengeance he can lay his hands on?

If either question is answered in the negative, toppling Mr. Hussein once and for all becomes a matter of methodology and Mr. Bush may be impelled toward choices that, up to now, have seemed too unattractive to consider.

#UNW-4158
첨부

1-1

0263

# 외 무 부

종 별 :

번 호 : UNW-4193　　　　　　　　　　일 시 : 91 1204 1800

수 신 : 장 관(연일,중동일,기정)

발 신 : 주 유엔대사

제 목 : 걸프사태(안보리)

　　1.안보리의 이달 대이락 제재조치 정기심사와 관련 쿠웨이트는 이락의 안보리 결의불이행 사례를 아래요지로 안보리에 통보하여옴.( S/23261 )

　　가.쿠웨이트 국민및 제3국인 송환

　　0.즉각송환거부, 국제 적십자위원회(ICRC)에 대한 면접및 수색관련 불협조

　　나.이락.쿠웨이트간 국경획정

　　0.동 위원회( BDC) 활동에비협조적(회의, 측량조사 활동 참가거부)

　　다.재산반환

　　0.개인.기업재산 미반환, 기반환 재산훼손사례

　　라.쿠웨이트 영토침범

　　0.쿠웨이트 영토내 경찰초소 5개소 유지, 이락측의 침범사례 계속발생

　　2.특히 쿠웨이트측은 상기 쿠웨이트 영토내 상기이락 경찰초소 5개소 유지를 항의하는 다음요지의 안보리문서를 배포하였음.( S/23260 )

　　가.이락은 동 초소들이 90.8.2. 쿠웨이트 침공전에 설치되었으며, 양국간 국경획 정위 작업결과를 기다려야 한다는 입장이나, 이는 유엔 이락.쿠웨이트 옵서버단( UNIKOM)의 양국간 비무장지대내 안전거리 유지원칙에 어긋남.

　　나.동 초소들의 즉각적인 철거필요.끝

　　(대사 노창희-국장)

| 국기국 | 장관 | 1차보 | 중아국 | 외정실 | 분석관 | 청와대 | 안기부 |
|---|---|---|---|---|---|---|---|

PAGE 1　　　　　　　　　　　　　　　　　　　　　　　91.12.05　　09:54 WH

　　　　　　　　　　　　　　　　　　　　　　　　　　외신 1과 롱제관

　　　　　　　　　　　　　　　　　　　　　　　　　　0264

UNITED
NATIONS

S

Security Council

Distr.
GENERAL

S/23264
3 December 1991
ENGLISH
ORIGINAL: ARABIC

LETTER DATED 3 DECEMBER 1991 FROM THE PERMANENT
REPRESENTATIVE OF IRAQ TO THE UNITED NATIONS
ADDRESSED TO THE SECRETARY-GENERAL

On instructions from my Government, I wish to state the following:

In the morning of 18 November 1991, the head of the Iraqi Interests Section in Washington was summoned by Mr. David Mack of the United States Department of State, in the presence of the official responsible for the Iraq Desk in the United States Department of State. The head of the Iraqi Interests Section was handed an official paper containing points for discussion, including the allegation that the Government of Iraq had not fulfilled its obligations with regard to Kuwaiti and Saudi Arabian prisoners and missing persons.

We express our astonishment at the American behaviour in question. It is as though Washington were responsible for following up the implementation of Security Council resolutions, particularly with regard to the repatriation of Kuwaiti and Saudi Arabian prisoners and the search for Kuwaiti and Saudi Arabian missing persons, not the United Nations or the Secretary-General and the International Committee of the Red Cross (ICRC). We wish on this occasion to refer to some facts that are documented with ICRC as a rebuttal of those American allegations and also so that you may take cognizance of them. They are as follows:

1. Since the halt of military operations on 28 February 1991, Iraq has been following the subject of civilians and missing persons and has fulfilled its obligations. Iraq has also cooperated with ICRC on the subject of the repatriation of prisoners and detainees of Kuwaiti and other nationalities. Iraq has provided the necessary facilities to enable the ICRC delegation in Baghdad to collect data on missing persons, and that explicitly includes the right to contact directly all possible sources of information.

2. Since its acceptance of Security Council resolution 687 (1991), Iraq has implemented paragraphs 30 and 31 thereof in respect of Kuwaiti prisoners and detainees. Lists of the names of the above were submitted to the ICRC delegation in Baghdad, with a view to their repatriation to Kuwait.

3.    The Kuwaitis who were accepted by the Kuwaiti authorities were in fact repatriated, as were third-country nationals.  They numbered in toto 6,493, both soldiers and civilians.

4.    To say that Iraq has not complied with its obligations with regard to settlement of the question of Kuwaiti missing persons is inaccurate and contrary to the truth.  In this regard, we would state the following:

Through ongoing coordination and cooperation between the competent Iraqi authorities and the ICRC delegation in Baghdad, 3,905 Kuwaitis were registered in Iraq.  This number represents 625 families, who were all given an opportunity to present themselves at the delegation's headquarters in Baghdad and to register their names of their own free will and without intervention from the Iraqi authorities.  From the beginning, the ICRC delegation has applied to the Kuwaiti authorities for consent to their repatriation to Kuwait, but those authorities consented to the repatriation of only 400 Kuwaitis out of the total.  The others are still in Iraq awaiting the consent of the Kuwaiti authorities to their repatriation.

5.    On 11 November 1991, Iraq officially notified ICRC of its approval of the minutes of the Geneva meetings of 16 and 17 October 1991, in which the Iraqi delegation and the delegations of the allied States participated, under the auspices of ICRC, and at which, the following was agreed on:

(a)  The printing and publication in a local newspaper of the names of the Kuwaiti missing persons alleged by Kuwait to be in Iraq, for the purpose of searching for them and obtaining information about their fate;

(b)  The furnishing of lists of the locations of jails and places of detention to the ICRC delegation for investigation of the whereabouts of Kuwaiti missing persons;

(c)  Visits to detention centres and jails are to be made in coordination with the competent Iraqi authorities and the Ministry of Foreign Affairs;

(d)  The principle of reciprocity is to be followed in verifying that the above-mentioned measures have been taken in Saudi Arabia and Kuwait, inasmuch as Iraq has lists containing large numbers of names of Iraqi missing persons. Some of these have been submitted, and many other lists will be submitted subsequently through ICRC.

6.    The purpose of the tendentious propaganda campaign being launched at this very time by the Kuwaiti regime and others with regard to the situation of Kuwaitis in Iraq is well known.  It is an attempt to perpetuate the unjust economic embargo and boycott imposed on the Iraqi people.

We have already stated, and we repeat now, that the Kuwaitis currently in Iraq have freedom of residence and movement, are scattered throughout Iraq's governorates and live there in a normal fashion and that the ICRC delegation in Baghdad knows this full well.  All that is needed is the Kuwaiti authorities' consent to the repatriation to Kuwait of those still in Iraq.

/...

0266

I should be grateful if you would have this letter circulated as a document of the Security Council.

(<u>Signed</u>)   Abdul Amir A. AL-ANBARI
Ambassador
Permanent Representative

-----

0267

# UNITED NATIONS

 **Security Council**

S

Distr.
GENERAL

S/23269
4 December 1991
ENGLISH
ORIGINAL: ARABIC

**LETTER DATED 4 DECEMBER 1991 FROM THE PERMANENT REPRESENTATIVE OF IRAQ TO THE UNITED NATIONS ADDRESSED TO THE SECRETARY-GENERAL**

On instructions from my Government, I have the honour to inform you of the following:

On the night of 1/2 November 1991, an Iraqi Scania tanker truck driven by Aqil Kazim Sa'd, accompanied by his assistant, Ibrahim Hamid Salman, both members of the Iraqi frontier police force, was delivering water to the Iraqi frontier posts located close to the Iraq-Saudi Arabia borders, when it lost its way, inadvertently entered Saudi territory in the area between the Saudi border posts at Al-Hashrah and Mukur al-Ni'am and was seized by the Saudi frontier authorities. At 0800 hours on 2 November 1991, the truck in question was seen in front of the Saudi Mukur al-Ni'am border post, and it is still being detained by the Saudis, together with its driver, and his assistant.

My Government, which holds the Saudi side responsible for the safety of the two Iraqi nationals indicated above, asks for your humanitarian intervention and requests you to take whatever steps you deem appropriate to induce the Saudi authorities to release them together with their vehicle and to repatriate them to Iraq.

I should be grateful if you would have this letter circulated as a document of the Security Council.

(Signed) Abdul Amir A. AL-ANBARI
Ambassador
Permanent Representative

-----

91-47509  2868j (E)

0268

관리
번호 91-1605

외 무 부

종 별 :

번 호 : UNW-4233

일 시 : 91 1206 2300

수 신 : 장관(연일,중동이,기정)

발 신 : 주 유엔 대사

제 목 : 안보리(걸프사태)

    1. 안보리는 금 12.6 비공식 협의를갖고 대이락 제재조치 정기 심사관련 토의에 들어간바 당관에서 탐문한바에 의하면 비동맹권 이사국(CAUCUS 7 개국)들이아래문제를 제기하여 왔다고함.

    가.AHTISAARI 보고서(S/22366) 상의 민수용, 인도적 목적 수입품의경우 사전동의 불요

    나. 동 보고서에 명시되지 않은 여타 수입품에 대해 이의를제기하는 경우, 상세설명 필요

    다. 사무총장은 이락이 이행하지 못한 의무사항에 대해 보고(동사항에 대해사무총장은 이행에 필요한 조치제의)

    2. 금일 협의시 이사국들간 이견으로 의장이 이사국들과 개별협의를 진행하기로 된바, 관련동향 추보위계임

    3. 한편 이락은 12.3. 자 안보리문서(S/23264) 를 통해 쿠웨이트, 사우디의전쟁포로및실종자 문제에 관한 미국의 개별 항의에 관해 이문제를 미측이 제기하는 것이 적절치 못함을 지적하면서 대이락 제재조치를 정당화하려는 기도의 일환이라고 주장하였음. 또한 이락은 사우디가 억류중인 급수수송차량 1 대및 승무원(지난 11 월초 길을 잃어 사우디지역으로 들어갔다고 주장)송환을 요구하는 안보리문서를 배포함.(S/23269)

    첨부:비동맹권 제의 및 WSJ 기사:UNW(F)-980 끝

    (대사 노창희-국장)

    예고:91.12.31. 까지

| 국기국 | 장관 | 차관 | 1차보 | 2차보 | 중아국 | 외정실 | 분석관 | 청와대 |
|-------|------|------|-------|-------|--------|--------|--------|--------|
| 안기부 | | | | | | | | |

#별첨

Non-Paper                    UNW(F1)-980 11206 2300
                             (연일. 중동일. 기정)  총2매

                                                    6 December 1991

1.    In order to facilitate the utilization of paragraph 20 of
      Resolution 687, it is necessary to lift the requirement for
      prior approval by the 661 Committee on a "no objection" basis
      for those civilian and humanitarian imports to Iraq as
      identified in Mr. Ahtisaari's report (S/22366).  The simple
      notificaton procedure should be applied to these specific
      items.

2.    With regard to other imports not specified in Mr. Ahtisaari's
      report, all objections from members of the Committee
      established under Resolution 661 should be accompanied by
      detailed explanations.

3.    The Security Council should request the Secretary-General to
      report on the remaining obligations and conditions which have
      not yet been met by Iraq as stipulated in paragraph 22 of
      Resolution 687.  If it is determined that some of them have
      not been fully met, the Secretary-General would be requested
      to propose steps that need to be taken towards their
      fulfilment within a specific time frame.

                              2-1

                                                    0270

# Sanctions and Saddam

While the Bush administration focuses its energies on brokering peace between Israel and the Arabs, the real action in the Middle East occurs elsewhere. The steady and joyful release of the Western hostages is surely a direct outgrowth of the overpowering U.S. and allied victory in the Gulf War. It had become obvious to the Syrians and their affiliated Lebanon-based fanatics that little was likely to be gained by using medieval dungeons to torture citizens of a world capable of using F-117s and Tomahawks. Mr. Bush, as is his nature, isn't seeking very much credit for these wonderful returns to civilized life, but it should be noted.

Then there is Iraq itself. This week the U.N. Security Council revisits the famous sanctions against Iraq, and will no doubt continue them. That isn't going to help blockaded Kurds or hungry Shias trapped in Iraq's southern marshlands. It is, however, likely to inflame further the debate over the U.S.'s responsibility for conditions in postwar Iraq.

The Security Council is looking into the implementation of Resolutions 706 and 712, the two international laws passed to permit Iraq to sell oil and use the revenues to feed its people under U.N. supervision. Saddam continues to ignore the deal these resolutions offer. His only oil sales are, reportedly, secret and illegal ones. Iraqi citizens don't get the food. As for the $582 million the U.S. has spent separately to soften conditions in postwar Iraq, the informed guess is that much has ended up in the black market or feeding the Ba'ath clique.

Meanwhile, polemicists are re-assigning the blame. On PBS's "Frontline" recently, Andrew and Leslie Cockburn documented the agony of hospital patients suffering from a lack of drugs—"because" of the U.S.-led embargo. At a November hearing before the House Select Committee on Hunger, a Harvard-affiliated research group, the International Study Team on the Gulf Crisis, bored in further. They reported that the mortality rate of children under five has increased by 380% since August 1990, that some 118,000 children are "either moder-ately or severely malnourished and therefore at increased risk of dying," and that most of Iraq's 10 million citizens are directly exposed to water-borne diseases such as typhus. This state of affairs, they argue, continues despite an Iraqi government whose public distribution of food "is equitable and efficient."

As we've noted here before, the war and its end game is a legitimate issue. The bombing of Iraq's power grid and civil infrastructure made little sense if the intention was to leave the awful Ba'ath Party in control of the country. But these recent complainants about conditions inside Iraq appear to have little interest in the direct role played by Saddam and the Ba'athists.

In the words of the State Department's Jackie Wolcott, who also testified before the House committee, Saddam "is now using innocent Iraqis as human shields, just as last fall, he used Americans and other foreigners."

At no time has any U.N. embargo—including the early Resolution 661 of August 1990—included medicines. As recently as this week, eyewitnesses reported to the State Department that Ba'ath troops guard the dispensaries of Baghdad hospitals. Much of what food there is in Iraq remains in the hands of Ba'ath rulers; Elliot Richardson told colleagues upon his return from an Iraq trip that Tariq Aziz himself enjoys Johnnie Walker Red with his dinner.

Saddam's gamble on this is a clear one: Win world pity, blame the U.S. and get the sanctions lifted. It might work. The British government, for instance, unfroze Iraqi assets worth $125 million in exchange for Baghdad's release of British citizen Ian Richter.

Iraqi dissidents and exiles, who we'd say are in the best position to know, argue that the proper step here is to tighten sanctions. We would go one further. Policy toward Iraq will be prone to such muddled disputes as who's to blame for starving babies so long as the U.N. and Washington fail to accept the possibility that the war against Saddam really isn't over.

2 - 2

0271

주 국 련 대 표 부

주국련 ~0312 - **1004**　　　　　　　　　1991. 12. 6.

수신 : 장관

참조 : 국제기구국장 , 중동아프리카국장

제목 : 걸프사태(안보리)


표제관련 안보리 문서를 별첨과 같이 송부합니다 .


첨 부 : 상기 문서 . 끝 .

주 국 련 대 사

| 선 결 | | | 결 재 (공 란) | | |
|---|---|---|---|---|---|
| 접수일시 | 1991. 12. 9 | | | | |
| 처리과 | 국1 69410 | | 02 | | |

0272

UNITED
NATIONS

**S**

# Security Council

Distr.
GENERAL

S/23212
12 November 1991
ENGLISH
ORIGINAL: ARABIC

---

LETTER DATED 12 NOVEMBER 1991 FROM THE PERMANENT
REPRESENTATIVE OF IRAQ TO THE UNITED NATIONS
ADDRESSED TO THE SECRETARY-GENERAL

On instructions from my Government, I have the honour to transmit to you herewith a letter dated 12 November 1991 from Mr. Ahmad Hussein, Minister for Foreign Affairs of the Republic of Iraq.  It concerns the articles published by the British weekly newspaper <u>The Independent on Sunday</u> on a report prepared by the United Kingdom Atomic Energy Agency in April 1991 on the use by coalition forces during the Gulf war of anti-tank shells fabricated from depleted uranium, a material that contains chemical toxins and radioactive materials that portend a wide-scale human and environmental disaster.

I should be grateful if you would have this letter and its annex circulated as a document of the Security Council.

(<u>Signed</u>)  Abdul Amir A. AL-ANBARI
Ambassador
Permanent Representative

91-38339  2811j (E)                                                    /...

0273

<u>Annex</u>

<u>Letter dated 12 November 1991 from the Minister for Foreign
Affairs of Iraq addressed to the Secretary-General</u>


   I have the honour to enclose with this letter copies of the articles
published by the British weekly newspaper <u>The Independent on Sunday</u> in its
issue for Sunday, 10 November 1991, in which is brought to light important
information contained in a report prepared by the United Kingdom Atomic Energy
Agency (AEA) in April 1991 on the use by coalition forces during the Gulf war
of anti-tank shells fabricated from depleted uranium, which contains chemical
toxins and radioactive materials that portend a wide-scale human and
environmental disaster.

   Based on the AEA report, the newspaper states that tens of thousands of
armour-piercing rounds manufactured from depleted uranium (U-238) were fired
at Iraqi vehicles from American and British aircraft and tanks and that the
chemically toxic and radioactive waste that was emitted by the shells and is
still being emitted by their remnants poses a long-term threat to the lives of
thousands of people.

   Referring to the report, the newspaper states that United States tanks
fired 5,000 depleted uranium rounds against Iraqi vehicles and that United
States aircraft fired tens of thousands of such rounds.  The tank ammunition
alone would contain more than 50,000 pounds of depleted uranium - enough
radioactive material, according to International Commission on Radiological
Protection risk estimates, to cause 500,000 deaths.  The newspaper says
nothing of estimates of the numbers of people whose lives are threatened by
the radiation produced by the tens of thousands of such rounds fired by United
States aircraft on the cities, villages and townships of Iraq during 42 days
of intensive raids, but it must surely be double that number.

   This momentous revelation constitutes a new increment in the United
States crimes being exposed day after day - the most recent but not the last
of which was that of the live burial of thousands of Iraqi soldiers - and it
provides additional proof of the violation by the United States of
international law, the Charter of the United Nations, The Hague and Geneva
Conventions, the Charter of the Nürnberg Tribunal and the laws of armed
conflict.  It is one of the ironies of fate that the United States should be
making use of international law, the Charter of the United Nations and the
resolutions of the Security Council as a cloak for the perpetration of its
crimes against the people of Iraq and the peoples and environment of the
region.

   We call upon you to dispatch a team of United Nations experts to study
the proportions of this human and environmental disaster and to identify ways
to remedy it.  Through you, we further call upon all States, political,
humanitarian and environmental organizations and international public opinion

0274

/...

to raise their voices in condemnation of this crime and in an appeal for the immediate lifting of the despotic economic embargo imposed on the people of Iraq so that that people may make use of its resources in order to contain the immediate and long-term effects of the United States crimes committed against it.

(Signed) Ahmad HUSSEIN
Minister for Foreign Affairs
of the Republic of Iraq

Baghdad, 12 November 1991

/...

0275

**Annex**

## 10 NOVEMBER 1991   THE INDEPENDENT ON SUNDAY

### No action taken after secret report warning of health threat to Kuwaitis and clean-up teams from West

# Radioactive waste left in Gulf by allies

By Nick Cohen

0276

/...

THE ALLIED armies left at least 40 tons of depleted uranium on the Gulf war battlefield, a secret report by the United Kingdom Atomic Energy Authority has warned. The chemically toxic and radioactive waste threatens the long-term health of thousands of Kuwaitis, as well as Western clean-up teams. It could also pass into the food chain and water supply.

The uranium was in tens of thousands of armour-piercing rounds fired at Iraqi vehicles from American aircraft and British and US tanks during the conflict.

An AEA appraisal of the threat, which has been seen by *The Independent* on Sunday, calculates that there is easily enough uranium in Kuwait and southern Iraq to cause "500,000 potential deaths".

The authority says that this is a purely theoretical calculation, which is "obviously not realistic". However, it adds that the sheer volume of depleted uranium does "indicate a significant problem".

The report was prepared in April by decommissioning and decontamination specialists working for AEA Technology, the commercial arm of the atomic authority, at the Winfrith Establishment, Dorset. The authority offered then to send "a small and dedicated team" to the Gulf "in total confidentiality". It wanted to identify the size of the problem and devise a clean-up plan. The worst concentrations of depleted

uranium could then be removed and potential health hazards minimised. But, after six months, no action has been taken by the British government or by Royal Ordnance, the privatised Ministry of Defence munitions supplier responsible for clearing the British sector of the Gulf war battlefield.

"Discussions are continuing with various parties," a senior AEA official said last week. "They have not gone as quickly as

we would have hoped." The authority has so far failed to get the go-ahead despite warning that expert assistance was needed because depleted uranium "requires sensitive equipment and well-trained operators as it is difficult to locate".

An appeal to political self-interest has also failed. The report said: "A further concern is a political one of leaving significant quantities of uranium around Kuwait. The problem will not go away and should be tackled before it becomes a political problem created by the environmental lobby. It is in both the Kuwaiti and the UK interest that this is not left to rear its head in years to come."

The report was sent to Royal Ordnance and unspecified British government departments. The Ministry of Defence and Foreign Office denied any knowledge of its contents. A spokesman for Royal Ordnance, which has about 250 sappers clearing mines in the

desert, was unable at the time the company was contacted to say whether the company had received the report, as was a spokesman for the Kuwaiti Ministry of Defence.

The AEA would not say whether the Kuwaitis had been told. At the time the report was produced no decision had been made on whether to inform the Kuwaitis, who have passed responsibility for clearing the battlefield to contractors from the allied powers. The issue of whether the Kuwaiti government needed to know was described earlier this year as "delicate".

Delays in acting on the report are understood to be the result of problems in co-ordinating the response between the various clean-up teams in the different allied sectors and the fact that much of the waste lies in Iraqi territory.

The Atomic Energy Authority believes some of the waste could still be properly and safely cleared if a decision can be made soon.

The AEA said in April the best estimates were that US tanks fired 5,000 depleted uranium rounds, US aircraft many tens of thousands of rounds, and British tanks "a small number". The tank ammunition alone would contain more than 50,000lb of depleted uranium — enough radioactive material, on International Committee of Radiological Protection risk estimates, to cause "500,000

potential deaths" if it were inhaled, the report says.

This figure bears no relation to real hazards because for half a million to die, the uranium shells would have to be pulverised into dust and 500,000 people would have to line up in the desert and inhale equal quantities.

The AEA says that the real danger comes from uranium dust produced when depleted uranium shells have hit and burned out Iraqi armoured vehicles. If airborne particles are inhaled they can lead to "unacceptable body burdens".

The depleted uranium will be "spread around the battlefield and target vehicles in varying sizes from dust particles to full-size penetrators", the report says. "It would be unwise for people to stay close to large quantities of DU for long periods and this would obviously be of concern to the local population if they collect this heavy metal and keep it.

"There will be specific areas in which many rounds will have been fired where localised contamination of vehicles and the soil may exceed permissible limits and these could be hazardous to both clean-up teams and the local population. Furthermore if DU gets in the food chain or water this will create potential health problems."

*Further reports, page 2*

/...

0277

The DU will be spread around the battlefield and target vehicles in varying and quantities from dust particles to full size penetrators and shot. It would be unwise for people to stay close to large quantities of DU for long periods and this would obviously be of concern to the local population if they collect this heavy metal and keep it. There will be specific areas in which many rounds will have been fired where localised contamination of vehicles and the soil may exceed permissible limits and these could be hazardous to both clean up teams and the local population.

Hazards of war: extracts from the confidential report by the UK Atomic Energy Authority

7. A further concern is a political one of leaving significant quantities of uranium around Kuwait. The problem will not go away and should be tackled before it becomes a political problem created by the environmental lobby. It is in both the Kuwait and the UK interest that this is not left to rear its head in the years to come.

# Gulf teams not told of risk from uranium

### By Nick Cohen and Tom Wilkie

SOLDIERS, mine-clearing experts and reconstruction workers in Kuwait have not received the Atomic Energy Authority report on the health risks posed by depleted uranium ammunition left lying on the Gulf war battlefield by British and American forces.

The amount of uranium used in the Gulf war theatre made it very likely that there would be contaminated areas with large amounts of uranium dust, the authority said in April. Given the conditions in Kuwait, internationally-recognised uranium dosage limits "could easily be exceeded if special arrangements are not made," it predicted.

Gulf in June said they had never received any instructions from the Royal Ordnance project managers on what to do if they encountered depleted uranium.

Even if safety guidelines have been issued subsequently, the Atomic Energy Authority report points out that untrained workers in a contaminated area may not recognise depleted uranium when they meet it.

The authority's six-month-old proposal, still to be accepted, warned that qualified operators

poisonous, like all heavy metals, and its effect was similar to that of lead, he said.

If there is uranium dust around, it is easily kicked up into the air and then people can breathe it into their lungs. The maximum permissible body burden depends on the chemical form of the uranium: some compounds of uranium are cleared from the body within a matter of days; others may reside within the body for years. For the long-residing compounds, the maximum permissible body burden is 600 becquerels — 16 billionths of a Curie — equivalent to 16 billionths of a gram of radium. The

/...

0278

No action has been taken on the report and last week the Ministry of Defence, which had a squadron of Royal Engineers working on battlefield mine clearance and the removal of military equipment in Kuwait for four months this summer with Royal Ordnance, said it was "not aware" of the calls for experts to be brought in to identify and minimise health and environmental risks.

Royal Ordnance, the privatised munitions company which is under contract to the Kuwait government to clear mines and cluster-bombs from the beaches and deserts south of Kuwait City, said that it did know that there were potential dangers. The staff it had hired were under instructions to take proper precautions and wear gloves and protective clothing when they came across depleted uranium.

But former Royal Ordnance employees who returned from the and sensitive equipment were needed as the uranium would be "difficult to locate".

The largest Western contractor in the Gulf — Bechtel, a US engineering and management consultancy company, which has 1,000 employees and 9,000 subcontractors on reconstruction work in Kuwait — was unable to say if it had received any warnings about depleted uranium.

Many — perhaps most — of the uranium rounds in the desert will be in large fragments and not particularly menacing. Risks arise where they have been broken up after smashing into Iraqi armour.

Dr Roger Berry, director of health and safety at British Nuclear Fuels, said that it was the chemical toxicity of uranium rather than its mild radioactivity which posed a threat.

"The big problem is dust," Dr Berry said, "and the main route [into the body] is inhalation." Uranium is a heavy metal and is more permissive limits would allow the equivalent of 160 billionths of a gram of radium.

The body has natural mechanisms for purging such heavy metals, transferring the uranium to the kidneys and then excreting it through the urine. But too much uranium taken up at once will cause kidney failure.

Dr Berry emphasised that he had no direct knowledge of the amounts or type of uranium that might be present as a result of the use of tank-busting shells in the Gulf war, but said the main worry would be dust produced after the shells impacted.

"If it's all retained inside the tanks then there would be no environmental pollution problem." But, Dr Berry said, depending on the chemical composition of the uranium inside the tanks, he would expect that personnel dismantling them would have to be protected by respirators, or at least commercial dust masks.

/...

0279

# 'Arrow' that can stop a tank

**By Christopher Bellamy**
**Defence Correspondent**

AN ENGLISH archer at Agincourt would have had no problem understanding the principles behind a depleted uranium anti-tank round. To penetrate armour, you want a small, hard, dense, sharp head, driven by the power of a much larger device — a longbow, or a tank gun.

Depleted uranium — U-238 — is extremely hard and dense, even more so than the tungsten alloy which is also used for solid armour-piercing shot. Because of this property, it is also used for protection, in the armour of the US M1A1 tank.

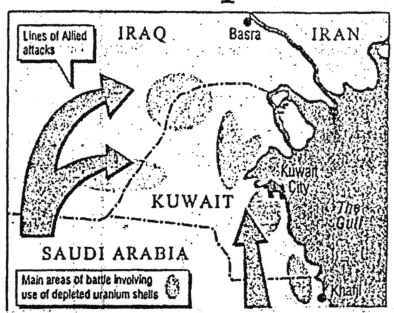

Lines of Allied attacks

IRAQ · Basra · IRAN

KUWAIT
Kuwait City
The Gulf

SAUDI ARABIA

Khafji

Main areas of battle involving use of depleted uranium shells

The core of a DU round is the penetrator — an armour-piercing arrow, much like those shot at Agincourt in 1415. It even has fins or flights at the back to stabilise it.

The penetrator is wrapped in a "sabot" (from the French for clog) which fills the bore of the gun and imparts enormous energy. But after it leaves the barrel, the sabot is kicked off and the thin, hard core carries on. Even if the gun is rifled, the spiralling grooves will only impart spin to the sabot. So the fins are still needed to keep the penetrator stabilised after it has left its cradle. The full name is Armour-Piercing, Fin Stabilised, Discarding Sabot (APFSDS). The smaller DU rounds fired from the A-10 aircraft do not have fins, and are therefore APDS.

When it hits the target, the penetrator punches a hole right through the armour. There were cases in which DU rounds were fired at tanks dug in behind sand berms, and went right through both the berm and the tank. What exactly happens depends on where the round strikes. It may crash into the engine compartment, or fly through the turret, knocking out the gun elevating gear, for example, or it may fragment, killing the crew.

However, DU rounds do behave differently from tungsten. Depleted uranium dust catches fire in air, an effect called "pyrophoretic". As the round bores through the armour and heats up, it gives off dust which, when it catches alight in the crew

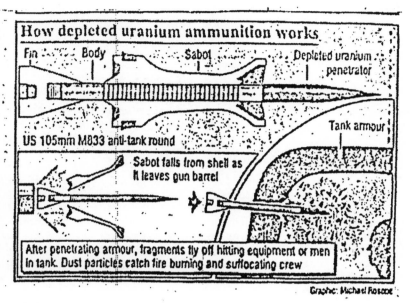

**How depleted uranium ammunition works**

Fin · Body · Sabot · Depleted uranium penetrator

US 105mm M833 anti-tank round

Sabot falls from shell as it leaves gun barrel

Tank armour

After penetrating armour, fragments fly off hitting equipment or men in tank. Dust particles catch fire burning and suffocating crew

Graphic: Michael Roscoe

compartment, can severely burn or kill the occupants. Vehicles hit by DU rounds will be contaminated with DU dust. Incidentally, this helped the Americans confirm that US Marine vehicles destroyed on the southern Kuwaiti border had been hit by "friendly fire", as the Iraqis had no DU ammunition. Rounds which fail to find their mark will just bury themselves in the sand, intact.

US A-10 aircraft never fire DU rounds from their 30mm rapid-firing cannon in peacetime, but it is the standard war ammunition. Many of the 750 rounds on board each A-10 would have been DU. And these would not only have been used during the ground war, from 24 to 28 February, but also throughout the air war against Iraq, which began on 17 January.

British and US tanks also used DU. The British fired fewer than 100 DU rounds; they preferred the High Explosive Squash Head (HESH) round which is of more general use. Exploding against the outside of a tank, HESH blasts a scab off the inside armour of the vehicle, with horrific results for the crew.

But the Americans undoubtedly fired many DU tank rounds. The US Marines fired DU rounds from the 105mm guns of their M-60 tanks and the US Army fired it from the 120mm guns of their M1A1s. A Pentagon spokesman said last week that it was impossible to say how much ammunition had been fired during the 100-hour ground battle, let alone what type. "You're not going to get an accurate count. There really wouldn't be any reason. There's quite enough to do without trying to count the number of bullets fired."

-----

0281

# Security Council

Distr.
GENERAL

S/23220
15 November 1991
ENGLISH
ORIGINAL: ARABIC

---

**LETTER DATED 14 NOVEMBER 1991 FROM THE PERMANENT REPRESENTATIVE
OF IRAQ TO THE UNITED NATIONS ADDRESSED TO THE SECRETARY-GENERAL**

Since the cease-fire entered into force on 3 April 1991, the United
States has been assiduous in daily contravening the provisions of the
cease-fire laid down in Security Council resolution 687 (1991) through the
continued violation of Iraqi airspace by its fighter aircraft. The total
number of such violations since that date and up to the time of the writing of
this letter amounts to more than 1,500 sorties, the particulars of which have
been notified to you one by one. They were accompanied by many instances of
provocation and breaking of the sound barrier, which terrorized civilian
citizens, particularly children, and caused many miscarriages in pregnant
women, as well as large-scale damage to property and public buildings.

Here I wish to state that the number of violations committed by United
States fighter aircraft in Iraqi airspace during the period from 4 to
11 November 1991 totalled 227 sorties for the purpose of surveillance and
provocation, as follows:

| Date | Particulars |
|---|---|
| 4-5 November 1991 | - 19 sorties flown by nine two-aircraft formations and one single aircraft at speeds of 700-850 km/h and at altitudes of 1,000-6,500 m, centred on Amadiyah, Dohuk, Mosul, Tall Afar, Irbil and Dukan. |
| | - At 1130 hours, two F-111s overflew Firnas airfield at a speed of 800 km/h and at an altitude of only 50 m. |
| | - At 1330 hours, two F-16s overflew Firnas airfield at a speed of 800 km/h and at an altitude of 300 m. |
| | - At 1340 hours, two F-1s overflew Firnas airfield at a speed of 850 km/h and at an altitude of 50 m. |

91-38896  2780g (E)

/...

0282

| Date | Particulars |
|---|---|

<u>Date</u> — <u>Particulars</u>

**5-6 November 1991**

- 21 sorties flown by one four-aircraft formation, eight two-aircraft formations and one single aircraft at speeds of 600-900 km/h and at altitudes of 1,500-6,000 m, centred on Zakho, Dohuk, Irbil, Mosul, Tall Afar and Amadiyah.

- At 1118 hours, two F-111s overflew Faruq airfield at a speed of 500 km/h and at an altitude of 300 m.

- At 1130 hours, two Mirage 2000s and two Tornadoes overflew Faruq airfield at a speed of 800 km/h and at altitudes of 100-300 m.

- At 1140 hours, two F-111s overflew Faruq airfield twice, the first time at a speed of 500 km/h and at an altitude of 100 m and the second at a speed of 1,000 km/h and at an altitude of 150 m.

**6-7 November 1991**

- 43 sorties flown by 21 aircraft formations and one single aircraft at speeds of 600-900 km/h and at altitudes of 1,000-6,000 km. The flights centred on Mosul, Irbil, Dohuk, Tall Afar and Amadiyah.

- From 0625 to 0745 hours, three formations, each consisting of two F-16s, overflew Faruq airfield at speeds of 600-700 km/h and at altitudes of 15-100 m.

- From 0800 to 2035 hours, five formations, each consisting of two aircraft of various types, overflew Firnas airfield at a speed of 500-800 km/h and at altitudes from 20 m to 3,000 m. One of the formations dropped two illuminating shells while turning on its afterburners.

**7-8 November 1991**

- 38 sorties flown by 18 two-aircraft formations and one single aircraft at speeds of 600-950 km/h and at altitudes of 500-6,500 m. The flights centred on Mosul, Irbil, Dohuk, Rawanduz, Sinjar and Tall Afar.

- At 0710, 0930 and 1030 hours successively, three formations, each consisting of two F-16s, overflew Faruq airfield at a speed of 600 km/h and at altitudes from 100-200 m.

/...

0283

Date                                                      Particulars

                 - At 0915 hours, two Mirage 2000s overflew Faruq
airfield at a speed of 500 km/h and at an
altitude of 200 m.

                 - At 1345 and 1500 hours, two formations, each
consisting of two F-1s, overflew Faruq airfield
at a speed of 600 km/h and at altitudes of
50-200 m.

                 - At 1645 hours, an F-111 overflew Faruq airfield
at a speed of 600 km/h and at an altitude of 50 m.

8-9 November 1991     - 34 sorties flown by 12 two-aircraft formations,
two four-aircraft formations and one single
aircraft at speeds of 660-900 km/h and at
altitudes of 1,500-18,000 m.  The flights centred
on Zakho, Dohuk, Irbil, Mosul, Tall Afar, Dukan,
Ayn Zalah and Amadiyah.

                 - At 0810, 0915, 1015 and 1040 hours, formations of
F-16s and Tornadoes overflew Faruq airfield at
various speeds and at very low altitudes.

10-11 November 1991   - 18 sorties flown by nine two-aircraft formations
at speeds of 750-900 km/h and at altitudes of
1,500-5,500 m.  The flights centred on Mosul,
Irbil, Zakho, Tall Afar, Dohuk and Ayn Zalah.

                 - At 0720 hours, two F-111s overflew Firnas
airfield at a speed of 650 km/h and at an
altitude of 10 m.

                 - At 1110 hours, two F-1s overflew Faruq airfield
at a speed of 600 km/h and at an altitude of
200 m.

      As we inform you of these United States violations, which endanger
international peace and security by their continuing infringement of the
sovereignty of a State Member of the Organization, we are entitled to ask
about the nature of the measures taken by the United Nations under the Charter
to put a halt to these violations, which are contrary to all international
instruments and customs and whose continuation constitutes a clear and
unambiguous violation of the purposes and principles of the United Nations, in
particular Article 2 (4) of the Charter of the Organization, which expresses
the essence of collective security through the stipulation that all Members
shall refrain in their international relations from the threat or use of force
against the territorial integrity or political independence of any State, or
in any other manner inconsistent with the purposes of the United Nations.

/...

0284

Silence over these actions carried out by the United States of America under cover of international legitimacy can only lead to loss of credibility by the United Nations with regard to the protection of the independence and sovereignty of Member States.  Disregarding them is contrary to the provisions of Article 6 of the Charter, which permits the General Assembly, upon the recommendation of the Security Council, to expel any Member of the United Nations which has persistently violated the principles of the Charter.

In placing these facts before the Secretary-General of the United Nations, the members of the Security Council and all the States, peoples and organizations of the world, we hope that the world will comprehend the extent of the excesses perpetrated by the United States in the use of unjustified force in contradiction to Security Council resolutions and in contempt for the feelings of Iraqi citizens, disturbing their tranquillity, safety and security.

I should be grateful if you would have this letter circulated as a document of the Security Council.

(Signed)  Abdul Amir A. AL-ANBARI
Ambassador
Permanent Representative

-----

0285

# UNITED NATIONS

## Security Council

**S**

Distr.
GENERAL

S/23228
20 November 1991
ENGLISH
ORIGINAL: ARABIC

LETTER DATED 18 NOVEMBER 1991 FROM THE PERMANENT
REPRESENTATIVE OF IRAQ TO THE UNITED NATIONS
ADDRESSED TO THE SECRETARY-GENERAL

On instructions from my Government, I should like to inform you that the relevant Iraqi authorities have obtained information from Lloyd's Maritime Information Services to the effect that the Kuwaiti regime has seized Iraqi ships still in Kuwaiti ports and have handed them over to Kuwaiti owners so that they can operate them in their own interests. The names of the ships are as follows:

| | | |
|---|---|---|
| 1. | Al-Qadisiyah | 155 000 tons |
| 2. | Hattin | 155 000 tons |
| 3. | Al-Mutanabbi | 132 000 tons |
| 4. | Tariq bin Ziyad | 118 000 tons |

Another ship, Al-Faw, of 79,000 tons, is still moored at a Kuwaiti port.

The Iraqi Government, in communicating this information, affirms the wish that you should take the necessary measures for the return of the five ships in question as soon as possible.

I should be grateful if you would have this letter circulated as a document of the Security Council.

(Signed) Abdul Amir A. AL-ANBARI
Ambassador
Permanent Representative

-----

91-39535  2748f  (E)

0286

# UNITED NATIONS

 **Security Council**

S

Distr.
GENERAL

S/23252
27 November 1991
ENGLISH
ORIGINAL:  ARABIC

---

**LETTER DATED 27 NOVEMBER 1991 FROM THE PERMANENT REPRESENTATIVE
OF IRAQ TO THE UNITED NATIONS ADDRESSED TO THE SECRETARY-GENERAL**

On instructions from my Government, I wish to state the following:

In the morning of 18 November 1991, the Head of the Iraqi Interests
Section in Washington was summoned by Mr. David Mack of the United States
Department of State, in the presence of the official responsible for the Iraq
Desk in the United States Department of State.  The Head of the Iraqi
Interests Section was handed an unofficial paper containing points for
discussion, including the allegation that the Government of Iraq had failed to
comply with regard to the return of Kuwaiti military equipment transported to
Iraq.  The United States Department of State also gave the Iraqi Interests
Section a list of that military equipment (copy annexed hereto), and the
United States official claimed that Iraq had not fulfilled its obligations to
hand over that equipment.

The Ambassador of France raised the same issue with us on
22 November 1991.

We express our astonishment at the American behaviour in question.  It is
as though Washington were responsible for following up the implementation of
Security Council resolutions, particularly with regard to the return of
Kuwaiti assets, not the United Nations or the Secretary-General and his
representative, Mr. Foran.  We wish on this occasion to refer to some facts
that are documented with the United Nations and Mr. J. Richard Foran as a
rebuttal of those American allegations and also so that you may take
cognizance of them.  They are as follows:

I.    Iraq has expressed its full readiness to cooperate with Mr. Foran,
Assistant Secretary-General of the United Nations and coordinator for the
return of the assets transported from Kuwait, including military equipment,
and also to cooperate with the United Nations team currently in Baghdad.
Iraq, for its part, has prepared and made available all kinds of facilities
for implementation and is continuing to furnish such cooperation with ongoing
efforts.  One example is the field visits to military camps and airbases for
inspection of the military assets and equipment and aircraft made ready for

91-46274  2898e (E)                                                    /...

0287

handing over.  Another is Mr. Foran's visit to the region from 3 to
7 November 1991 and his field inspection of the aircraft that the Iraqi side
has stated its readiness to hand over.

II.  We have sent Assistant Secretary-General Foran a number of telegrams
expressing the readiness of the Iraqi side to hand over the military
equipment, including some of the items contained in the list that the United
States official handed to the Head of the Iraqi Interests Section (such as
Chieftain and Centurion tanks and Vickers tanks), as follows:

1.    M109 self-propelled guns

      AMX F3 self-propelled guns

      BTT/CVA gun support vehicle (within the AMX F3 system)

      A-4 aircraft

      Mirage F-1 aircraft (destroyed, as the United Nations representative in
      Baghdad was informed by Iraq at the time)

      Hawk MK 64 aircraft (five fit for handing over, two damaged, three
      destroyed - our telegram No. 3626 of 20 November 1991 to our New York
      Mission)

2.    On 12 July 1991, Iraq sent a letter by fax No. 10/687/A/92851 to
      Mr. Foran stating the readiness of the Iraqi side to hand over the items
      prepared and Iraq's readiness to follow the same procedures as in the
      hand-over of the aircraft.

3.    On 15 July 1991, Iraq sent letter No. 1164 by fax to Mr. Foran,
      confirming the readiness of the Iraqi side to hand over the military
      equipment on the basis of the talks conducted by the United Nations
      representative in Baghdad on 1 July 1991.

III.  The United Nations representative in Baghdad, at his meeting with the
Iraqi side at the Iraqi Ministry of Foreign Affairs on 16 May 1991, confirmed
the position with regard to the aircraft removed from Kuwait and ready for
handing over by Iraq after repairs by the Iraqi side.  That has also been
confirmed earlier by the Permanent Representative of Iraq to the United
Nations in New York in March 1991 by a letter addressed to you on this subject.

      From all of the above,             that Iraq has cooperated with the
Assistant Secretary-General and coordinator in the return of the
above-mentioned equipment.  An effort is currently under way, in coordination
with the United Nations representative in Baghdad, to carry out arrangements
for the return of that equipment as it is made ready, and Iraq is fulfilling
its obligations in this regard.

/...

0288

With regard to the military equipment transported from Kuwait, the Iraqi side is prepared to hand over the portion that is ready, lists of which were handed over at the appropriate time.  We await the reply of the Kuwaiti side, through the United Nations coordinator, Mr. Foran, or his representative currently in Baghdad for agreement on the manner, time and place of the hand-over, which will be followed by the preparation of other, new lists of assets ready for handing over.

I should be grateful if you would have this letter circulated as an official document of the Security Council.

(<u>Signed</u>)   Abdul Amir A. AL-ANBARI<br>Ambassador<br>Permanent Representative

0289  /...

<u>Annex</u>

Chieftain tanks

Centurion and Vickers tanks

BMP-11 infantry fighting vehicles

Fahd type armoured personnel carriers

M-113 armoured personnel carriers

M 109 self-propelled guns

AMX F3 self-propelled guns

BTT/CVA gun support vehicles

FROG SSM missile systems

A-4 aircraft

Mirage F-1 aircraft

Hawk MK G-1 aircraft

Puma or Super Puma helicopters

I-Hawk surface-to-air missile systems

SA-S SAM systems

Skyguard SAM systems

35 mm AAA Oerlikon guns

Skyguard fire-control radar

AIM-9-11 air-to-air missiles

LASS radar

KASS IBM computer system

Mark 84 bombs

Mark 82 bombs

/...

0290

Mark 20 bombs

ZUNI 20 missiles

The response of the Head of the Iraqi Interests Section was that Iraq is faithful to the obligations which it assumed under United Nations resolutions and is bound by them.

-----

0291

# UNITED NATIONS

**S**

## Security Council

Distr.
GENERAL

S/23260
2 December 1991

ORIGINAL: ENGLISH

LETTER DATED 2 DECEMBER 1991 FROM THE PERMANENT REPRESENTATIVE
OF KUWAIT TO THE UNITED NATIONS ADDRESSED TO THE PRESIDENT OF
THE SECURITY COUNCIL

On instructions from my Government, I should like to place on record publicly our strong protest against the continued presence of five Iraqi police posts inside Kuwaiti territory. Kuwait has earlier communicated this protest to Major-General Gunther Greindl, Commander of the United Nations Iraq-Kuwait Observation Mission (UNIKOM). In this connection, I should like to state the following:

1. Iraq claims that the posts had been in place before 2 August 1990. In fact, these five posts were established just before the Iraqi invasion of Kuwait, ostensibly to monitor the Kuwaiti side in preparation for Iraq's aggression on 2 August 1990.

2. In spite of Kuwait's protestations through UNIKOM, Iraq refuses to pull back these posts, allegedly "because of the political implications". This stance clearly places Iraq in violation of the territorial sovereignty of Kuwait.

3. The rationale behind Iraq's intransigence is that the location of these police posts would be settled by the Iraq-Kuwait Boundary Demarcation Commission. Without prejudice to the outcome of the Demarcation Commission's work, it is an established fact that the Iraqi posts are within Kuwaiti territory. The continued presence of these posts is an attempt by the Iraqi regime to present the Demarcation Commission with a _fait accompli_.

4. The continued presence of the Iraqi posts runs counter to the reasonable-distance principle of 1,000 metres from the boundary line shown on UNIKOM maps. This principle was set by UNIKOM to avoid frictions and incidents in the demilitarized zone (DMZ). Iraq's refusal to abide by this principle is a clear violation of its commitment to facilitate the work of UNIKOM.

5. To claim that Iraqi police are under orders to avoid any clashes is but an attempt by the Iraqi regime to convey a position of cooperation and flexibility while it maintains its presence on Kuwaiti territory.

91-46806 2810g (E)

0292 /...

While lodging this protest, I am also instructed by my Government to demand the immediate dismantling of the five Iraqi police posts.

I should appreciate it if you would bring this letter to the immediate attention of the members of the Security Council and to arrange for its circulation as an official document of the Council.

(Signed)  Mohammad A. ABULHASAN
Ambassador
Permanent Representative

-----

0293

# UNITED NATIONS

**Security Council**

S

Distr.
GENERAL

S/23261
3 December 1991

ORIGINAL: ENGLISH

LETTER DATED 2 DECEMBER 1991 FROM THE PERMANENT REPRESENTATIVE
OF KUWAIT TO THE UNITED NATIONS ADDRESSED TO THE PRESIDENT OF
THE SECURITY COUNCIL

With the Security Council currently reviewing the compliance by Iraq with its relevant resolutions, I am instructed by my Government to convey the following.

1. In connection with the repatriation of all Kuwaiti and third-country nationals, Iraq continues to defy the terms of Security Council resolutions 686 (1991) of 2 March 1991 and 687 (1991) of 3 April 1991. Not only is Iraq refusing <u>immediate</u> release and repatriation of these nationals, but it is also denying the International Committee of the Red Cross access to such persons "<u>wherever located or detained</u>" and not "facilitating the search by the International Committee of the Red Cross for those Kuwaiti and third-country nationals still unaccounted for".

2. In connection with the Boundary Demarcation Commission, Iraq's position is far from being cooperative or constructive. To illustrate, Iraq's representative in the Demarcation Commission placed on record at the meeting held at Geneva on 16 August 1991 "Iraq's objection to the whole operation from its initiation because it does not achieve justice and equity to Iraq's territorial rights". Moreover, Iraq has refused to participate in the meeting of the technical committee of the Demarcation Commission held in Sweden on 19 and 20 August 1991. Iraq has further declined to participate in the work of the survey team of the Demarcation Commission visiting the DMZ area from 2 to 6 November 1991.

3. Notwithstanding the provision of paragraph 2 (d) of resolution 686 (1991) that Iraq <u>immediately</u> begin to return <u>all</u> Kuwaiti property seized by Iraq, the return to be completed in the shortest possible period, Iraq has refused to return property seized from individuals and corporations. Furthermore, property returned so far has not all been intact. For example, property of the National Council for Culture, Art and Letters was found incomplete, and that of Kuwait News Agency is in large part seriously damaged.

91-46859  2856j (E)                                                0294      /...

4.    Iraq is under obligation to cease hostile or provocative actions against Member States.  Moreover, while it claims to be cooperating with the United Nations Iraq-Kuwait Observation Mission, Iraq continues to maintain five police posts on Kuwaiti territory.  Iraq's violation of the territorial sovereignty of Kuwait is further demonstrated by repeated Iraqi infiltrations into Kuwaiti territory.

Needless to say, the above-mentioned facts indicate that the "policies and practices of the Government of Iraq" are not in implementation of relevant Security Council resolutions.  Clearly, what is required of Iraq is implementation in full of all relevant Security Council resolutions.

I should appreciate it if you would bring this letter to the immediate attention of the members of the Security Council, and arrange for its distribution as a document of the Security Council.

(Signed)   Mohammad A. ABULHASAN
Ambassador
Permanent Representative

-----

0295

**Security Council**

Distr.
GENERAL

S/23266
4 December 1991

ORIGINAL: ENGLISH

LETTER DATED 2 DECEMBER 1991 FROM THE PERMANENT REPRESENTATIVE
OF THE SUDAN TO THE UNITED NATIONS ADDRESSED TO THE PRESIDENT
OF THE SECURITY COUNCIL

On instructions from my Government, I have the honour to transmit herewith a letter addressed to the President of the Security Council from the Executive Committee of Shabab Alwatan Organization in the Sudan in relation to Security Council resolution 687 (1991) dated 3 April 1991.

I should be grateful if you would have the text of this letter circulated as a document of the Security Council.

(Signed)  Joseph LAGU
Permanent Representative

91-47251  3061b (E)                                                      /...

<u>Annex</u>

[Original: Arabic]

We address you today on behalf of the youth of the Sudan, inasmuch as you have the role of protector of international security, peace and justice.

You all know the adversities which the people, including children, women and old people, of Iraq are suffering as a result of the economic embargo, namely:

-  A state of slow starvation for lack of food;

-  The death of children owing to lack of food and medicine;

-  Terrible deterioration in humanitarian and environmental conditions in this fraternal State.

As you know, paragraph 20 of resolution 687 (1991) of 3 April 1991 states that the embargo shall not apply to basic foodstuffs and materials needed to meet humanitarian needs.

We draw your attention to the fact that the Government of Iraq has committed itself to the implementation of all the Council's resolutions.

Accordingly, we ask you to transmit the request of the youth of the people of the Sudan for the lifting of the economic embargo against the fraternal people of Iraq and the non-imposition of any conditions that infringe on the sovereignty of this people and its fundamental rights provided for in international covenants.

In conclusion, the world today looks to your credibility and your adherence to the standards of justice, and the violation of these standards will lead to complications in the future of this international Organization.

The Executive Leadership of the Youth
of the Nation Organization

-----

0297

| 관리<br>번호 | 91-16-9 |
| --- | --- |

외　무　부

원　본

종　별 :

번　호 : UNW-4278　　　　　　　일　시 : 91 1210 2230

수　신 : 장관(연일,중동일,기정)

발　신 : 주 유엔 대사

제　목 : 안보리(걸프사태)

연:UNW-4233

　　1. 당관에서 관련 대표들에 탐문한바에 의하면, 안보리의장(소련)은 연호 비동맹권(CAUCUS 7 개국)제안 관련이사국들과 개별협의를 계속중이나, 특기할 진전이 없어 전체비공식협의 일정이 아직 잡히지 않고있다고함.

　　2. 미.영은 연호 제안중 가 항(통보방식으로 전환)에 반대, 나 항(이의제기시 상세설명필요) 은 이미 시행되고 있다고 보고있으며, 다. 항 (사무총장 보고서)은 사실기술식인(FACTUAL) 보고서라면 무방하다는 입장인반면, 중국은 비동맹권 제안에 동조하고 있다고함.

　　3. 관련사항 추보위계임.

　　첨부:WP 기사:UNW(F)-1000 끝

　　(대사 노창희-국장)

　　예고:91.12.31. 까지

| 국기국<br>안기부 | 장관 | 차관 | 1차보 | 2차보 | 중아국 | 외정실 | 분석관 | 청와대 |
| --- | --- | --- | --- | --- | --- | --- | --- | --- |

PAGE 1　　　　　　　　　　　　　　　　　　91.12.11　　13:36

외신 2과  통제관 BD

0298

*UNW (Ħ)-1000  11210  2230*
*(연일 중동일 기정)  총204*

# Iraq, Despite U.N. Sanctions, Is Able to Buy Food, Rebuild

## *Embargo-Busting, Hidden Reserves Are Cited*

By Caryle Murphy
Washington Post Foreign Service

BAGHDAD, Iraq—Despite almost 16 months of U.N. sanctions, Iraq's government appears to have access to funds that it is using to buy food and to finance some reconstruction projects, according to diplomats and U.N. officials here.

The sources of this income are a mystery, but they may include gold reserves held before Iraq's August 1990 invasion of Kuwait; cash stolen from Kuwait; and limited sanctions-busting sales of Iraqi products, according to these officials and a recent staff report by the U.S. Senate Foreign Relations Committee.

In addition, exiled Iraqi opposition sources have said they believe that President Saddam Hussein has access to secret bank accounts overlooked when Western governments froze Iraq's foreign assets in August 1990.

Whether Baghdad's financial resources are enough to allow it to withstand sanctions for a long period is not known, and this uncertainty is a major complication for those attempting to project the political future of Saddam and his government, according to a senior diplomat here.

"There are no statistics, everything is secret," he said. "So you can't predict the situation. Certainly, you can see that the [economic] trend is negative. But at same time, they are restoring lots of things. This means that nobody knows for sure what their real financial and technical capabilities are."

Some observers here suspect that access to secret revenue may help explain why Iraq refused to sell $1.6 billion worth of oil to buy food and medicine under the strict conditions set up by U.N. Security Council resolutions in September.

Iraqi officials have called the U.N. terms insulting violations of Iraq's sovereignty, and portrayed their refusal to sell oil as a matter of principle and national pride. But the knowledge that they have a secret cushion of funds to import at least some food during the period U.N. sanctions have been in force may also have been a factor in their decision, a U.N. official said.

The government needs food imports to sustain its rationing system, which gives every Iraqi family about 10 days' worth of ba-

BY CLARICE BORIO—THE WASHINGTON POST

sic foodstuffs monthly at highly subsidized prices.

Food and medicine have not been banned by sanctions. But Iraq has always said it had no money to buy them since all its known assets abroad—about $4 billion—were frozen. The first major unfreezing of those funds came only two weeks ago when Britain released $125 million after Iraq freed a British businessmen from prison here. Shortly before, however, about a dozen European commercial banks released tens of millions of dollars despite strong U.S. protests.

Iraqi officials have said that food imports, which keep shops around the country well-stocked but at highly inflated prices, are done by Iraqi businessmen using their own money. The government encouraged this private sector trade after sanctions were imposed by lifting its tight controls on foreign currency transactions, customs fees and licenses—offering private businessmen an opportunity to cash in.

Diplomats here say they believe much of Iraq's foreign trade—both illegal sanctions-busting and legal food transactions—is controlled by relatives and close associates of Saddam.

"We don't know from where and how much, but food is coming in," one U.N. official in Baghdad said recently. In his view, Iraq may be able to purchase food "for the next six to eight months. But that's the maximum, because the assets they have are finite."

Other indications that Iraq has some fi-

2—1

nancial resources include the continuing repair of facilities such as hospitals, rural health centers, bridges, and communications sites that were damaged by the U.S.-led allied bombing campaign in the war and by rebels in the uprisings that followed.

The Justice Ministry, gutted by an allied bomb, is under reconstruction here, and workers are clearing rubble from the Ministry of Military Industrialization, the Conference Palace and a suspension bridge over the Tigris River.

Some materials for reconstruction were already in Iraq before sanctions were imposed because the government had some major development projects underway, an Arab diplomat said. But it is clear other materials and equipment banned under sanctions are coming in.

For example, four truckloads of lumber were recently seen by this reporter on the highway to Baghdad from Amman. The contents were marked "Made in Indonesia," and stamped "Jordan Aqaba," a port that can be reached only through a U.N. naval blockade.

Sources said the plywood may have been consigned to a Jordanian company, which resold it to an Iraqi firm. Use of Jordanian intermediaries has been a common practice since sanctions were imposed, according to diplomatic and Iraqi sources in Baghdad and Amman.

There are indications Iraq may be financing such purchases by illegal exports. Truckloads of Iraqi dates have been seen on their way to Amman. In a recent report, Senate Foreign Relations Committee staffer Peter Galbraith, citing Iraqi opposition sources, wrote that "Jordan reportedly permits the transit through its territory of Iraqi urea, sulphur, refined oil products, and infrastructure including trucks and earthmoving equipment."

Iraqi opposition sources speak of possible exchanges of Iraqi oil for Jordanian credits and hidden foreign bank accounts that one exiled opposition figure, London-based Jawad Hashim, has estimated in a memo sent to the U.S. and British governments last July could be worth $31.3 billion. Diplomatic sources say, however, that they have seen no clear evidence of a credit arrangement with Jordan or secret accounts abroad.

Meanwhile, sanctions-busting trade also appears to be taking place in northern Iraq, from border areas under the control of Kurdish guerrillas, according to Galbraith and U.N. sources. Turkish truckers bringing food and other goods into Zakhu and other northern Iraqi towns load up with Iraqi diesel fuel and gasoline, which they resell at a profit in Turkey. Sometimes hundreds of such trucks, outfitted with extra fuel tanks, cross the Iraqi-Turkish border each day, the U.N. sources said.

In his report, Galbraith described seeing large amounts of bulldozers, construction cranes and earthmoving equipment being readied for clandestine export to Iran during a recent trip to Iraqi areas controlled by Kurdish guerrillas.

It is not clear who is profiting from this trade, Galbraith said in his report, but it may be both the Kurds and Saddam's government, since "much, if not most, of the trade seems to involve infrastructure and other goods from the government-controlled part of Iraq being shipped through Kurdish-controlled lands . . . to Iran."

2-2

0300

# 외  무  부

종  별 :

번  호 : UNW-4305                                        일  시 : 91 1211 2210

수  신 : 장 관(중동일,연일,기정)

발  신 : 주 유엔 대사

제  목 : 걸프사태

　　1.금 12.11 NYT 지는 부시행정부가 이락군부 구테타발생에 대비한 미국의 군사적
대안을 검토중이며, 최근 이락 지도부 내부의 심각한 갈등에 관한 정보보고가
있었다고 보도하였음.

　　2.한편 동지는 별도기사에서 이락 핵무기 개발계획에 제품이 사용된 13 여개 회사
(미 DUPONT 사, 다수 독일사) 명단을 IAEA 측이곧 유엔사무총장에게 통보예정이라고
보도함. (동 명단여부는 사무총장이 결정예정)

　　첨부: NYT 기사: UNW(F)-1015 끝

　　(대사 노창희-국장)

---

중아국　　1차보　　　국기국　　　외정실　　　분석관　　　안기부

PAGE 1                                                      91.12.12    14:02 WG

　　　　　　　　　　　　　　　　　　　　　　　　　　외신 1과  통제관

　　　　　　　　　　　　　　　　　　　　　　　　　　　　0301

# U.S. WEIGHS PLANS FOR FOES OF IRAQI

## Seeing 'Strains' in Leadership in Baghdad, White House Considers Responses

UNW(FI)-1015   11/21  22/0
총 20너

**By PATRICK E. TYLER**
Special to The New York Times

WASHINGTON, Dec. 10 — The Bush Administration is reviewing military options on how the United States would respond to a coup in Iraq by senior members of the Iraqi armed forces, Administration officials said today.

The Administration has received recent intelligence reports of "serious strains" in the Iraqi leadership and wants to insure that President Bush is not caught without a plan of action, as he was during a coup attempt in Panama in October 1989, a move that preceded the invasion by United States forces two months later.

The military options, prepared by the Joint Chiefs of Staff over the last three weeks, would prepare the United States for a situation in which key officers in Iraq's armed forces might request support from Washington in an attempt to seize power from President Saddam Hussein.

The options are to be reviewed on Thursday at a high-level meeting of the so-called deputies committee of key Cabinet departments, which is headed by Adm. Jonathan T. Howe, the deputy national security adviser.

### Timing of Military Plans

The planning comes as Mr. Bush's re-election bid is about to be begin, and it seems likely to prompt critics to suggest that Mr. Bush is contemplating a foreign venture to divert attention from his domestic political troubles, or to insulate his re-election campaign from charges that the otherwise successful American military effort in the Persian Gulf war last winter failed to dislodge Mr. Hussein from power.

Some Democrats and Republicans have been urging the President to take stronger steps to remove Mr. Hussein and to avert a new humanitarian crisis in Iraq, where United Nations sanctions have led to widespread malnutrition among the poor, a condition that Mr. Hussein appears to be exploiting.

The military options were provided by Gen. Colin L. Powell, Chairman of the Joint Chiefs of Staff and the President's top military adviser. They were reviewed by Defense Secretary Dick Cheney before being sent to the White House late last week.

One potential dispute that emerged from the military review of coup "scenarios" posed by the White House centers on the issue of whether United States ground forces would be needed to back a successful coup attempt against Baghdad's current leadership.

### White House Preference

The White House wants a military solution based only on air forces and naval forces, officials said, while General Powell is said to believe strongly that the removal of Mr. Hussein cannot be guaranteed under any coup scenario without committing American ground troops, a decision that would present a politically debilitating and risky condition for the White House.

A classified discussion paper from General Powell is said to point out the difficulties of confronting the four Republican Guard divisions that ring Baghdad. While United States air forces might be sufficient to assist an Iraqi military coup by destroying and tying down loyalist forces, air power alone could not deal with every contingency or guarantee a final victory over Mr. Hussein, as one official described the military argument.

The military review did not appear to be prompted by intelligence information indicating that Mr. Hussein's top officers were actually plotting against him.

"We have had intelligence information very recently that indicated some serious strains" within Mr. Hussein's inner circle, an Administration official said.

### 'Armed Conflict'

One intelligence report, received after Mr. Hussein changed defense ministers last month, described an incident of "armed conflict" between rival security forces of the new Iraqi Defense Minister, Ali Hassan al-Majid, a cousin of Mr. Hussein, and the relative he replaced, Hussein Kamel Hassan, who is Mr. Hussein's son-in-law.

The "conflict" resulted in "injuries and some deaths and was carried out in a revenge fashion" by Mr. Hassan's forces, the official said. The official added that other intelligence reporting indicated a general disaffection with Mr. Hussein among Iraq's traditional Sunni Muslim elite, which dominate the merchant class, the army and the upper ranks of the ruling Arab Baath Socialist Party.

By undertaking this review, however, the Administration may be hoping to foster the planning of a coup by keeping Mr. Hussein's regime under tight economic sanctions and by taking intrusive steps to remove or destroy all vestiges of Iraq's nuclear, chemical and biological weapons programs, as well as laboratories and factories taking part in ballistic missile work.

The military review was conducted in response to two specific scenarios posed by the National Security Council staff, officials said. Under one scenario, Iraqi military commanders began a coup attempt that bogged down and then asked for American assistance. Under a second scenario, Iraqi military leaders signaled to Washington they were ready to depose Mr. Hussein if the United States would provide support, particularly air support, since the Iraqi Air Force remains grounded as part of the allied cease-fire conditions imposed last winter.

To be successful in the removal of Mr. Hussein, General Powell is said to have forcefully argued, United States ground troops would be necessary and warned that the consequences of failure would undermine the long term gains United States foreign policy achieved with the gulf war victory.

# UNW-4305 첨부
2-1

0302

# U.N. LINKS DU PONT TO IRAQ ARMS PLAN

## Secret Nuclear Program Used Oil From Chemical Giant —German Firms Cited

**By PAUL LEWIS**
*Special to The New York Times*

UNITED NATIONS, Dec. 10 — The big American chemical producer, E. I. du Pont de Nemours & Company, and the Pennsylvania subsidiary of a German engineering company are among companies whose products were used in Iraq's covert nuclear weapons program, United Nations inspectors who have examined the equipment say.

A list of some 13 companies, most of them German, is being prepared by the International Atomic Energy Agency, the United Nations body charged with tracking down and destroying the secret Iraqi program. It will be sent to Secretary General Javier Pérez de Cuéllar later this week along with the report of the eighth and most recent nuclear inspection team to visit Iraq.

Officials in Vienna say Hans Blix, the director of the atomic energy agency, is leaving it up to the Secretary General to decide whether the list of involved companies should be published. This appears to represent a change of policy by the agency. Until now it has given to governments that have asked for them the names of their national companies whose nuclear equipment has been found in Iraq and has said that it is up to the government in question to decide whether to release the names.

The agency does not accuse the companies on its list of deliberately and knowingly helping Iraq in its bid to become a nuclear power or even of supplying their products directly.

### Most Goods Very Specialized

But experts say that much of the equipment is highly specialized and would have required government licenses before it could be exported legally. As a result, agency officials say they believe the manufacturers must at least have suspected what it might be used for.

"The list shows Saddam Hussein was able to import highly sensitive machinery, which means we should look at our export control laws again," said Garry Milhollin, director of the Wisconsin Project on Nuclear Arms Control in Washington. "The United Nations should stop protecting companies and tell the world exactly what it knows about foreign involvement in Iraq's nuclear weapons project."

While the list of involved companies is still being prepared by experts in Vienna, the Du Pont company is currently the only fully American company on it, officials say. The giant chemical producer is listed as having manufactured vacuum pump oil found at an unnamed Iraqi nuclear installation.

Experts say this is a special low density oil that would have been used in the vacuum pumps employed in Iraq's attempt to make nuclear explosives by the centrifuge enrichment method.

Clint Archer, a spokesman for Du Pont at the corporation's headquarters in Wilmington, Del., said the oil was probably manufactured at the company's Conoco petroleum refining subsidiary in Houston, but he said he could provide no further details.

### Subject to Destruction

United Nations officials say many companies on the list manufactured equipment that was used in Iraq's bid to enrich uranium up to weapons grade levels by the centrifuge method. This equipment is all liable for destruction under the terms of the Security Council's terms for the Persian Gulf war cease-fire, unless Iraq can show it has a justified civilian use for it.

After the cease-fire, atomic energy agency inspectors found a secret plant near Baghdad capable of manufacturing up to 1,000 centrifuge machines annually. The plant had escaped damage during the air war because the allies had not known it existed.

Leybold Vacuum Products Inc. of Export, Pa., the American subsidiary of Leybold A.G., the engineering company based in Cologne, Germany, provided Iraq with special electron beam welding machines that would have been used in the assembly of these centrifuge enrichment machines.

Dr. Milhollin, who has analyzed American nuclear-related exports to Iraq, said the Commerce Department granted an export license for this sale in December 1987. The license specified that the electron beam welders were for "general military applications such as jet engine repair, rocket cases, etc."

### Company Plans Statement

Michael Adams, a spokesman for company president, James Callahan, said the German parent company would issue a statement Wednesday.

The Cologne state prosecutor is currently investigating charges that two former Leybold executives smuggled blueprints for an uranium enrichment centrifuge into Switzerland in September 1983 and that these blueprints subsequently found their way to Pakistan, which is suspected of running a clandestine nuclear weapons program.

A German engineering company, Dr. Reutlinger & Sohn, supplied horizontal balancing machines that are used to balance very precisely the rotors which spin at high speeds inside the centrifuges. H. H. Metalform of Drensteinfurt manufactured Iraq's slow-turning machines that produced the thin-walled hollow cylinders used as centrifuge rotors.

A Swiss company, Acomel, manufactured the centrifuge drive converters which regulate the speed at which the centrifuges spin. Another German firm, Neue Magdeburgerwerkzeugmaschinenfabrik G.m.b.H., supplied computer controlled metal lathes. And another Swiss company, Vacuum Apparat Technik, was one of the producers of specialized valves used in the enrichment centrifuges.

2-2

# 외 무 부

원 본

종 별 :

번 호 : UNW-4324

일 시 : 91 1212 2130

수 신 : 장 관(연일,중동일,기정)

발 신 : 주 유엔 대사

제 목 : 안보리(걸프사태)

1.표제사태관련 안보리 이락제재위는 그간 대이락 무기공급금지 위반사례가 신고접수 된 것이 없음을 안보리에 통보하였음. ( S/23279)

2. 유엔이락 특정무기특위 ( UNSCOM)화학,생물무기 합동조사반 사찰결과를 별첨참조 바람.

첨부:안보리문서 및 UNSCOM 사찰결과(12.11):UNW(F)-1019 끝

(대사 노창희-국장)

S/23279

---

국기국     1차보     중아국     외정실     분석관     청와대     안기부

PAGE 1

91.12.13     11:36 WG

외신 1과 통제관

0304

UNW(FR-1019  11/12  213=
흥 304

The first combined chemical and biological weapons inspection team to
Iraq has reported the discovery of chemical bomb-making equipment at a sugar
factory in Mosul, 350 kilometres north of Baghdad.

The United Nations inspectors found equipment from a bomb casing workshop
which, according to a June directive by the Special Commission on Iraqi
Disarmament, should have been moved to the Muthanna State Establishment for
destruction early next year.  The items found were clearly intended for the
manufacture of aerial bombs for the delivery of chemical warfare agents.

In a press release today, the Special Commission said that the 18-member
United Nations expert team had inspected 16 sites throughout Iraq, locking for
evidence of undeclared chemical and biological weapons activity.  The mission
was unique, it said, in that all designations were undeclared sites, and
concentrated on possible chemical or biological weapons storage sites, such as
airfield bunkers and ammunition depots.  All inspections were carried out
without advance notice to the Iraqi side.  The mission used United Nations
helicopters as a fast means of transport and for conducting aerial
reconnaissance.

The team further reported the discovery at an ammunition storage facility
west of Karbala of three undeclared SCUD transporter carriers, which had
apparently been discarded and overlooked.  The Iraqis were directed to move
these carriers to Taji for future destruction.

On a number of occasions, the Special Commission says, the inspection
team was hindered when carrying out the inspection.  However, following the
registering of an official protest by the Chief Inspector, the Iraqi
authorities concerned were cooperative for the remainder of the inspection.

#UNW-4324
첨부

3-1

0305

S/23279
English
Page 2

<u>Annex</u>

<u>Report of the Security Council Committee established by resolution
661 (1990) concerning the situation between Iraq and Kuwait
pursuant to paragraph 6, subparagraph (f) of the guidelines to
facilitate full international implementation of paragraphs 24, 25
and 27 of Security Council resolution 687 (1991)</u>

1.   The present report is submitted by the Security Council Committee
established by resolution 661 (1990) of 6 August 1990 concerning the situation
between Iraq and Kuwait in accordance with paragraph 6, subparagraph (f) of
the guidelines, 1/ for facilitating full international implementation of
paragraphs 24, 25 and 27 of Security Council resolution 687 (1991) of
3 April 1991 approved by Council resolution 700 (1991) of 17 June 1991.

2.   The first report of the Committee was submitted on 13 September 1991. 2/
Under paragraph 6, subparagraph (f) of the guidelines, the Committee is
required to report at 90-day intervals to the Security Council on the
implementation of the arms and related sanctions against Iraq contained in the
relevant resolutions of the Security Council.

3.   By paragraph 12 of the guidelines, all States are requested to report to
the Committee any information that may have come to their attention relating
to possible violations of the arms and related sanctions against Iraq
committed by other States or foreign nationals.  During the period under
review, no information, as requested by paragraph 12 of the guidelines, has
been received by the Committee.

4.   In accordance with paragraphs 13 and 15 of the guidelines, all States and
international organizations ought to consult the Committee on the question of
whether certain items fall within the provisions of paragraph 24 of
resolution 687 (1991), as well as in cases relating to dual-use or
multiple-use items, i.e. items meant for civilian use but with potential for
diversion or conversion to military use.  During the period under review, no
States or international organizations have consulted the Committee on these
questions.

5.   By paragraph 14 of the guidelines, international organizations are
requested to provide the Committee with any relevant information that may come
to their attention.  In that connection, the Committee received a letter from
the Chairman of the Security Council Committee established by resolution
421 (1977) concerning the question of South Africa which the Committee
considered and took note of at its 52nd meeting held on 18 October 1991.

6.   In a note dated 2 October 1991, 3/ the President of the Security Council
published the text of the statement made to the media, on behalf of the
members of the Council.  He stated that the members of the Council had held
informal consultations on 2 October 1991 pursuant to paragraph 21 of
resolution 687 (1991).  After hearing all the opinions expressed in the course

3-2

/...

0306

S/23279
English
Page 3

of the consultations, the President of the Council concluded that there was no
agreement that the necessary conditions existed for a modification of the
regime established by paragraph 20 of resolution 687 (1991), as referred to in
paragraph 21 of that resolution.

7.    Since the submission of the previous report of the Committee on
13 September 1991, 2/ no allegations of violations, particularly in connection
with paragraph 24 of resolution 687 (1991), have been reported to the
Committee, apart from the letter mentioned in paragraph 5 above.

8.    The Committee will continue its efforts to fulfil the mandate entrusted
to it.  The Committee recommends that the Secretary-General should send an
early reminder to those States that have not yet replied in accordance with
paragraph 4 of Security Council resolution 700 (1991) on measures they have
instituted for meeting the obligations set out in paragraph 24 of Security
Council resolution 687 (1991). 4/

## Notes

1/    S/22660, annex.

2/    S/23036.

3/    S/23107.

4/    The States that have replied so far pursuant to paragraph 4 of
Security Council resolution 700 (1991) are listed in the reports of the
Secretary-General contained in documents S/22884, Add.1 and Add.2.

3-3

0307

**UNITED NATIONS**

 **Security Council**

Distr.
GENERAL

S/23283
12 December 1991

ORIGINAL:  ENGLISH

NOTE BY THE SECRETARY-GENERAL

The Secretary-General has the honour to transmit to the members of the Security Council the attached communication which he has received from the Director-General of the International Atomic Energy Agency (IAEA).

91-48842  2711c (E)

/...

0308

## Annex

### Letter dated 11 December 1991 from the Director-General of the International Atomic Energy Agency addressed to the Secretary-General

Please find attached the report of the eighth IAEA inspection in Iraq under Security Council resolution 687 (1991).  You may deem it appropriate to transmit the report to the members of the Security Council.  I remain, of course, available with the Chief Inspector, Mr. Demetrius Perricos, for any consultations you or the Council may wish to have.

(Signed)  Hans BLIX

0309     /...

Enclosure

REPORT ON THE EIGHTH IAEA ON-SITE INSPECTION IN IRAQ
UNDER SECURITY COUNCIL RESOLUTION 687 (1991)

11 - 18 November 1991

**SALIENT POINTS**

- The in-field activities related to information on the procurement of equipment essential to the Iraqi nuclear programme continued despite persistent efforts by Iraq to conceal such information. Manufacturers of a number of specific equipment items were identified.

- The Iraqi authorities provided additional answers to questions about weaponization which had been put by the seventh IAEA inspection team and which related mainly to the results of initiator design work and tests, to work on flash X-ray systems, to the theoretical calculations and design options studied, and to the energy released. The answers were vague and general, especially as regards questions deriving from the secret PC-3 progress reports obtained during the sixth IAEA inspection.

- The Iraqi authorities repeated that they had never produced any quantities of 93%-enriched uranium and had never obtained any, other than those known to the Agency, and expressed their concern about the IAEA's findings. The matter is still under investigation.

- Systematic destruction of the EMIS double-pole magnets started, using thermal cutting equipment and with the co-operation of the Iraqi authorities. Basic equipment related to the EMIS and the centrifuge programme was destroyed or rendered harmless. Two high-speed streak video camera systems were removed from Iraq; they are now in storage on the premises of the IAEA.

/...

0310

All fresh highly enriched uranium of Soviet origin was shipped out of Iraq in two consignments, on 15 and 17 November, with the full co-operation of the Iraqi authorities. The airlifting operation was arranged through a contract between the USSR Ministry of Atomic Power and Industry and the IAEA. Only 400 g of 93%-enriched fresh uranium, in the form of 23 fuel plates, and the irradiated fuel elements of French and Soviet origin remain in Iraq.

The verification of nuclear material in the Tuwaitha area was completed, and only 16.7 tons of uranium in waste solutions stored in the Mosul area remain to be properly verified. During evaluation of the nuclear material balance, a number of discrepancies were identified; explanations and clarifications to be provided by the Iraqi authorities were requested in writing.

Monitoring activities initiated during the seventh inspection mission continued during the eighth. It is the opinion of the eighth inspection team that inspection efforts in Iraq should gradually shift to monitoring, with occasional identification and characterization activities performed when new information becomes available. For the time being, certain activities related to the destruction of equipment and removal of the irradiated highly enriched uranium (HEU) fuel (including the 400 g of 93% enriched fresh uranium) should continue in parallel with monitoring inspections and follow-up activities.

0311

/...

## INTRODUCTION

1. This report summarizes the findings of the eighth inspection carried out by the IAEA under Security Council resolution 687 (1991) with the assistance and co-operation of the Special Commission of the United Nations. The inspection took place from 11 to 18 November 1991 and was headed by Mr. Demetrius Perricos of the IAEA as Chief Inspector. The team consisted of 12 inspectors and 7 supporting staff; it comprised 16 nationalities.

   The objectives of the inspection were broadly

   - to continue field activities related to the foreign procurement by Iraq of equipment essential to its nuclear programme.

   - to further investigate and assess the extent of the Iraqi weaponization studies.

   - to continue the destruction or rendering harmless of enrichment- and reprocessing-related equipment.

   - to prepare and supervise the removal from Iraq of the fresh HEU fuel of Soviet origin.

   - to finalize the verification of nuclear material in the Al Tuwaitha area and perform nuclear material accountancy follow-up activities.

   These broad objectives were assigned to two groups within the overall team, with a group leader responsible for co-ordinating the work of each group.

2. The inspection activities related to foreign procurement by Iraq which were initiated in a systematic manner during the seventh inspection mission continued. The inspection revealed new data on procurement and provided additional understanding of the Iraqi procurement strategy, which was based on the use of different State establishments as buyers and contractors, on direct procurement from manufacturers and on indirect procurement through foreign intermediaries. A number of manufacturers of equipment directly related to the programme were identified, but this does not necessarily mean that the manufacturers were also the suppliers.

/...

0312

3.      In the area of weaponization, investigation and questioning continued.  The Iraqi authorities provided some additional information regarding the design of the initiator and completed the answers to the questions put to them by the seventh team on 12 October 1991. The answers were vague and general, especially as regards questions deriving from the secret Iraqi progress reports obtained during the sixth inspection. Additional facilities were inspected at the Al Atheer site, some of them in depth for the first time.  They provided additional evidence that Iraq was investing very substantial resources in a complete programme of weapons development studies.

4.      Regarding the destruction of equipment directly related to Iraq's enrichment and reprocessing programmes, activities initiated during the seventh inspection were expanded, the emphasis being on equipment that had been used for the manufacturing of centrifuges or had been procured especially for the centrifuge programme. Destruction of the large double-pole magnets from the EMIS programme began.

5.      In compliance with Security Council resolution 687, the fresh HEU fuel of Soviet origin, comprising 68 fuel assemblies of 80% enrichment and 10 of 36% enrichment, was removed from Iraq in two consignments. The Iraqi authorities co-operated fully during preparation of the shipment, the transfer from Tuwaitha to Habanniya airport and loading onto the plane.  Confirmation has been received from the USSR Ministry of Atomic Power and Industry that all the fresh fuel arrived in the USSR and it is available for inspection in accordance with the terms of the contract with the IAEA.

6.      The verification of nuclear material was completed.   With the exception of approximately 16 tons of uranium in waste solutions stored in the Mosul area, the material has been brought together at locations in and around the Tuwaitha site and is now under Agency seals.  During verification, a number of discrepancies were identified, related mainly to the balancing of nuclear material processed using Brazilian $UO_2$ as feed.

7.      Table I summarizes the chronology of 1991 events related to IAEA activities under Security Council resolution 687 (1991).  With the completion of the eighth inspection, all known facilities and sites involved in enrichment and weaponization in Iraq have been inspected.  However, owing to the unresolved inconsistencies and ambiguities in statements made by the Iraqi authorities, no assurance can be given that the full

/...

0313

extent of the Iraqi programme has been revealed. It is the opinion of the eighth team that inspection efforts in Iraq should gradually shift to monitoring, with occasional identification and characterization activities performed when new information becomes available. For the time being, certain activities related to the destruction of equipment and removal of the irradiated HEU fuel (including the 400 g of 93%-enriched fresh uranium) should continue with monitoring inspections and follow-up activities.

A full record of the correspondence between the Chief Inspector and the Iraqi counterpart while the eighth IAEA inspection team was in Iraq is given in Annex 1.

0314                    /...

## TABLE 1

### CHRONOLOGY OF EVENTS
### 1991

| | |
|---|---|
| APRIL 03 1991 | UNSC RESOLUTION 687 |
| APRIL 06 1991 | IRAQ FORMALLY ACCEPTS CONDITIONS OF UNSC 687 |
| APRIL 18 1991 | IRAQ SUBMITS FIRST DECLARATION; DENIES HAVING NUCLEAR-WEAPONS-USABLE MATERIAL |
| APRIL 27 1991 | IRAQ SUBMITS SECOND DECLARATION; FIRST ADMISSION TO HAVING SOME NUCLEAR MATERIAL AND FACILITIES IN ADDITION TO THOSE KNOWN TO THE AGENCY |
| MAY 14-22 1991 | FIRST INSPECTION UNDER UNSC 687; FIRST IAEA TEAM INSPECTS DECLARED IRAQI FACILITIES AND THE TARMIYA SITE |
| JUNE 17 1991 | UNSC RESOLUTION 699, APPROVING IAEA PLAN FOR THE DESTRUCTION, REMOVAL OR RENDERING HARMLESS OF THE ITEMS SPECIFIED IN PARA. 12 OF UNSC 687 |
| JUNE 22-JULY 03 1991 | SECOND IAEA INSPECTION OF IRAQI FACILITIES; ACCESS DENIED AT VARIOUS SITES, IN ONE CASE USING WARNING SHOTS |
| JULY 04 1991 | HIGH-LEVEL UN MISSION REPORTS THAT IRAQI RESPONSE TO REQUEST FOR ACCESS BY INSPECTION TEAM ON JUNE 28 WAS LESS THAN WHAT WAS CALLED FOR BY THE SECURITY COUNCIL |
| JULY 07-18 1991 | THIRD IAEA INSPECTION OF IRAQI FACILITIES |
| JULY 07 1991 | IRAQ SUBMITS THIRD DECLARATION ON ITS NUCLEAR PROGRAMME IN LETTER TO SECURITY COUNCIL, MAINTAINING THAT IRAQ HAD COMPLIED WITH NPT AND IAEA SAFEGUARDS AGREEEMENT; DISCLOSED THREE METHODS OF ENRICHMENT: CENTRIFUGE, CHEMICAL AND ELECTROMAGNETIC |
| JULY 14 1991 | IRAQ SUBMITS ADDITIONAL CLARIFICATION ON ITS THIRD DECLARATION AND PROVIDES LIST OF MANUFACTURING FACILITIES RELATED TO ITS NUCLEAR PROGRAMME |
| JULY 25 1991 | DEADLINE FOR IRAQI DECLARATION OF ALL REMAINING NUCLEAR SITES |
| JULY 28 1991 | IRAQ SUMBITS ADDITIONAL LIST OF NUCLEAR MATERIAL |

/...

0315

| JULY 27 - AUGUST 10 1991 | FOURTH IAEA INSPECTION OF IRAQI FACILITIES, INCLUDING THE AL FURAT SITE INTENDED FOR PRODUCTION OF CENTRIFUGES, AND THE AL JESIRA PLANT, INTENDED FOR PRODUCTION OF FEED MATERIAL |
|---|---|
| AUGUST 15 1991 | UNSC RESOLUTION 707 WHICH OBLIGES IRAQ, INTER ALIA, TO "HALT ALL NUCLEAR ACTIVITIES OF ANY KIND, EXCEPT FOR USE OF ISOTOPES FOR MEDICAL, AGRICULTURAL OR INDIVIDUAL PURPOSES" UNTIL THE SPECIAL COMMISSION DETERMINES THAT IRAQ IS IN FULL COMPLIANCE WITH UNSC 707 AND PARAS. 12 AND 13 OF UNSC 687 AND THE IAEA DETERMINES THAT IRAQ IS IN FULL COMPLIANCE WITH ITS SAFEGUARDS AGREEMENT WITH THE AGENCY |
| SEPTEMBER 14 - 20    1991 | FIFTH IAEA INSPECTION OF IRAQI FACILITIES MAIN EMPHASIS ON VERIFICATION OF NUCLEAR MATERIAL AND REMOVAL OF THE PRODUCED PLUTONIUM AND INVESTIGATION OF THE CHEMICAL ENRICHMENT PROCESS |
| SEPTEMBER 22-30 1991 | SIXTH IAEA INSPECTION OF IRAQI FACILITIES CONTAINING DOCUMENTATION ON THE IRAQI NUCLEAR PROGRAM AND NUCLEAR WEAPONS DEVELOPMENT |
| SEPTEMBER 24-28 1991 | SIXTH IAEA INSPECTION TEAM DETAINED BY IRAQI AUTHORITIES IN PARKING LOT OF PETROCHEMICAL 3 HEADQUARTERS, BAGHDAD |
| OCTOBER 11 1991 | UNSC RESOLUTION 715, APPROVING IAEA PLAN FOR ON-GOING MONITORING OF IRAQ'S COMPLIANCE WITH RESOLUTIONS 687 AND 707 |
| OCTOBER 11-21 1991 | SEVENTH IAEA INSPECTION OF IRAQI FACILITIES START OF DESTRUCTION OF ENRICHMENT AND REPROCESSING RELATED EQUIPMENT |
| OCTOBER 14 1991 | IRAQ ACKNOWLEDGES THAT RESEARCH AND STUDIES HAD BEEN UNDER WAY IN THE AREA OF NUCLEAR WEAPONIZATION |
| OCTOBER 21 1991 | IRAQ ADMITS THAT THE AL ATHEER SITE WAS BUILT TO SERVE THE WEAPONIZATION PROGRAMME IN ADDITION TO ITS USE AS A MATERIALS PRODUCTION SITE. |
| NOVEMBER 11-18 1991 | EIGHTH IAEA INSPECTION OF IRAQI FACILITIES<br>- ACTIVITIES FOR DESTRUCTION OF EQUIPMENT RELATED TO CENTRIFUGE AND CHEMICAL ENRICHMENT<br>- INITIATION OF SYSTEMATIC DESTRUCTION OF LARGE DOUBLE-POLE MAGNETS RELATED TO EMIS<br>- IN-FIELD ACTIVITIES RELATED TO PROCUREMENT OF EQUIPMENT |
| NOVEMBER 15 + 17 1991 | SHIPMENT FROM IRAQ OF FRESH HEU OF SOVIET ORIGIN |

/...

0316

**FOREIGN SUPPLIES TO THE IRAQI NUCLEAR PROGRAMME**

8.　　The Iraqi Atomic Energy Commission had, in support of its uranium enrichment and planned weaponization efforts, established a large, secure and highly successful procurement network. The procurement strategy included:

- The use of other Iraqi State establishments as buyers and contractors;

- The placing of orders for equipment (especially manufactured components) directly with foreign manufacturers and indirectly through foreign intermediaries (multiple pieces of some equipment were obtained both directly and indirectly); and

- The utilization of indigenous capabilities to complete the manufacture of some items.

The Iraqi authorities have gone - and are still going to great lengths to prevent the discovery of procurement data. Most procurement-related information has been removed and presumably destroyed.

The large amount of information regarding the Petrochemical-3 (PC-3) project collected during the sixth inspection is still in the process of being translated and evaluated. So far, it appears to include only limited procurement data. Manufacturer name tags have been removed from individual pieces of equipment, and forms of identification such as serial numbers have been filed away. This process is continuing: procurement data on a particular piece of equipment discovered during the seventh inspection were painted over during the interval between the seventh and eighth inspections.

9.　　The Iraqi authorities now freely acknowledge a political decision calling for efforts to prevent disclosure of the procurement network. They recognize that their efforts have not been entirely successful and that the inspection teams have collected enough information to be able eventually to put the pieces together. Their stated motivation is to protect the relationships with their various suppliers.

/...

0317

10. The casting and rough machining of large iron components for the EMIS programme was done at foundries outside Iraq. The acquisition of these pieces provides a good example of the Iraqi procurement strategy. A large west European foundry received an order from the Iraqi State Electric Establishment for six pieces as shown in Figure 1 (drawing was provided to the IAEA Action Team by the foundry's management). The pieces were produced at the foundry and shipped directly to Iraq. At about the same time, the foundry received an order from a European company for 28 large iron pieces; six of them had specifications identical to those of the pieces produced for the Iraqi State Electric Establishment; twelve of them were halves - along the horizontal axis - of the pieces depicted in Figure 1. These pieces were, in the team's opinion, pre-machined cores for the 1200 mm double-pole magnets installed or destined for installation at Tarmiya. Final machining was done at Al Radwan (Aqba bin Nafi State Establishment) to specifications depicted in Figure 2 (solid core) and Figure 3 ("sandwich" core); the drawings in Figures 2 and 3 were obtained in Iraq. The remaining ten pieces were various parts of the horizontal and vertical return irons for the 1200 mm system. The foundry shipped the components to a seaport in Germany, where they were redirected to their final destination.

11. The foundry's management has indicated that they would have received a larger order from what has turned out to be an intermediary company if they could have met the required production schedule. This, together with the numbers of pieces seen in Iraq, suggests that one or more additional contracts must have been placed with other foundries. The investigation of this matter is continuing.

12. Iraqi officials have described the EMIS component machining work done at the Al Radwan facility as having been carried out under conditions of great secrecy: people simply showed up with components/specifications and removed everything when the work had been completed; they had no idea of what the equipment was for or the identity of the customer. Managers of various Iraqi firms involved in manufacturing aspect of the EMIS programme tell a similar story.

13. A large number of the centrifuge components described in the report of the seventh inspection team, were also obtained from foreign sources. Examples of all major components (rotor tubes, end caps, pin bearings, etc.) removed from Iraq by the third and seventh inspection teams have been and are currently being examined in order to identify the manufacturers. This investigation is vital for follow-up activities to determine the completeness of Iraqi declarations, particularly those relating to carbon fiber rotors.

0318          /...

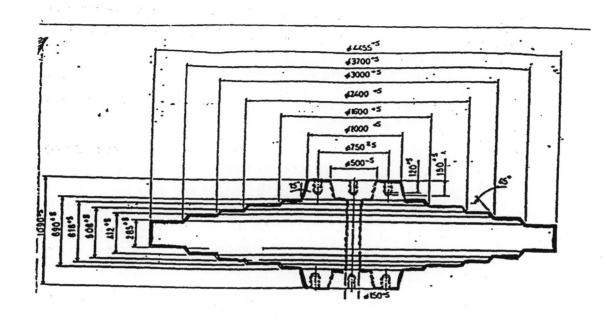

**FIGURE 1:** CROSS SECTION OF PRE-MACHINED CORE FOR 1200 MM DOUBLE POLE MAGNETS

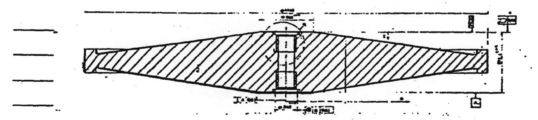

**FIGURE 2:** CROSS SECTION OF CORE FOR 1200 MM DOUBLE POLE MAGNET MACHINED TO FINAL DIMENSIONS

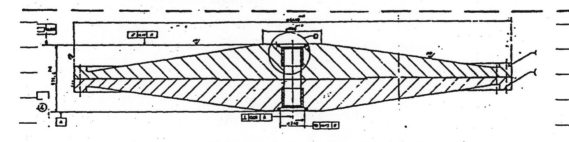

**FIGURE 3:** CROSS SECTION OF CORE FOR "SANDWICHED" 1200 MM DOUBLE POLE MAGNET MACHINED TO FINAL DIMENSIONS

/...

0319

14.  The manufacturers of most equipment used or intended for use in Iraqi efforts to establish a centrifuge production and operation capability have been firmly identified. A summary of some of the more important equipment follows:

-   A flow forming machine with application-specific mandrel, expanding mandrel and rollers was manufactured by <u>H & H Metallform Maschinenbau und Vertriebs GmbH</u>.

-   An electron beam welder with a special fixture for holding the rotor tube during welding was manufactured by <u>Leybold Heraeus AG</u>.

-   Three large CNC machines, two with application-specific fixtures, were manufactured by <u>Neue Magdeburger Werkzeugmaschinenfabrik GmbH</u>.

-   A large oxidation furnace with special temperature control features was manufactured by <u>Degussa</u>.

-   High frequency converters capable of operating a large number of centrifuges were produced by <u>Acomel GmbH & Co KG</u>.

-   Horizontal and vertical balancing machines were manufactured by <u>Dr. Reutlinger & Söhne KG</u>.

-   Hand operated, pneumatic and electrically controlled bellows valves were manufactured by <u>NUPRO</u>, <u>VAT AG</u> and <u>Balzer AG</u> respectively.

-   Quantities of Krytox, a nuclear grade fluorinated vacuum pump oil were manufactured by <u>Dupont</u>.

Identification of a manufacturer does not necessarily mean identification of the supplier. As pointed out earlier, orders were often placed with manufacturers through intermediaries; this appears to have been the case with at least one of the Magdeburger CNC machines - and a shipping invoice discovered by the inspection team inside the packing crate for a large oxidation furnace appears to provide the name of an intermediary for that procurement.

15.  Much of the equipment listed above is multi-purpose in the sense of being useful in a number of manufacturing processes. However, the application-specific fixtures remove most doubt as to the intended uses. Some of the companies may not have been aware that Iraq was the final customer, but the intermediaries certainly were -

/...

0320

and they must have known (or could reasonably have inferred) the intended uses. The large iron pieces destined for the EMIS programme are a different matter: the foundry(ies) may have known that Iraq was the customer, but the iron pieces prior to final machining provided no clue as to their intended use.

Additional procurement-related data are in the possession of the IAEA. This information is being treated as confidential at present since premature disclosure could compromise the ongoing investigation.

16. The manufacturers of large quantities of general-purpose and infrastructure equipment located at Al Tuwaitha, Tarmiya, Ash Sharqat and Al Atheer have been identified. Concerning this equipment, the plan is that follow-up will be limited to instances where the manufacturer appears also to have provided specific services to one or more of these facilities. Most of the equipment at Al Atheer is consistent with the Iraqi declaration that Al Atheer was intended to be a material sciences research centre. Among the exceptions is a large cold isostatic press manufactured by Asea Brown Boveri (which could be used for shaping explosive charges) and very high temperature furnaces (e.g. vacuum-induction furnaces) manufactured by Arthur Pfeiffer Vakuum Technik GmbH. A large number of smear samples from Al Atheer equipment were taken in order to further evaluate the Iraqi declaration that this facility was never used for weapons-related research.

17. The eighth inspection team removed two streak video cameras and related equipment from Iraq. These cameras, manufactured by Hamamatsu, have sufficient speed and resolution for weaponization work. At the time of their removal, they were being used by the Technical University of Baghdad. According to Iraqi authorities, their use was limited to graduate student studies of internal combustion engines; they were never employed in Iraq's weaponization programme. Statements regarding the planned use of the cameras made to the manufacturers at the time of procurement are consistent with declarations made to the inspection team. Smear samples from the cameras may provide further evidence regarding their use.

## ACTIVITIES RELATED TO THE WEAPONIZATION PROGRAMME

18. On 12 November 1991, the Iraqi authorities provided answers to weaponization questions which had been put by the seventh inspection team on 21 October 1991 -

/...

0321

the last day of its mission - and which related mainly to design studies (including initiator design studies, tamper interface, core and energy release calculations, detonators, hydrodynamic tests, flash X-ray systems and lithium enrichment studies. The answers provided were vague and general, especially as regards questions deriving from the secret PC-3 progress reports obtained during the sixth IAEA inspection.

19.  The inspection team requested further information about research or studies on a gun-type weapon design and specific values used in calculations of the design explosion energy and received the following answer:

> "The researched literature indicates that the "Gun" type need more material although the design idea is simpler and the calculation requirements are less. Therefore, the study of this literature led us (Iraq) to concentrate on understanding the implosion type mechanics.

> The literature quoted a yield of 20 KT as an approximate figure for the energy released from the implosion device used in Nagasaki. In the calculation models the yield depends on several parameters including the pressure applied on the outer surface, its pulse width, and the device dimensions. Theoretically different yields starting from 1 KT could result depending on these parameters. Since predetermined values for these parameters were not available, a study was performed to determine its effect using one dimensional integrated code and not two dimensional."

20.  The inspection team requested information (descriptions and an indication of precise locations) of the mainframe computers which had been used or intended for use at Al Tuwaitha and elsewhere in Iraq in pursuit of the PC-3 programme's objectives (and meeting the Tarmiya and Ash Sharqat requirements).  The Iraqi answer was as follows:

> "The Computer Office at Tarmiya was initially designed to accommodate the option of a large computer (mainframe). Due to the special circumstances in operating individual separators, it was discovered through experience that the best condition would be to connect the separators to small dedicated computers. After achieving the steady operating conditions for the separators, the small computers would have been connected through a network located in the above-mentioned office. This approach was adopted at Tarmiya. It also applies to the design of the Computer Office at Ash-Sharqat, although computers were never introduced at this site.

> At the Al Tuwaitha site, the large computer was an IBM-370; in addition there were a number of personal computers (PCs) including IBM PS/2. The approach adopted at Al Tuwaitha was to use the computer capability available in the country when needed in addition to the above-mentioned computers.".

This answer is not complete and not compatible with a statement in the PC-3 progress report for the period 1 July - 16 November 1989 which indicates that a mainframe NEC

/...

0322

750 computer was used to run a program obtained from the literature which solves hydrodynamic equations in one-dimensional space and in the presence of a shock wave.

21.  In reply to the team's question about the scope of the lithium enrichment programme, the Iraqi authorities stated that the studies had not been directed towards a specific objective and that the $Li^6$ separation activities belonged to the area of general scientific research, with no specific production rate envisaged. The Iraqi reports on this topic were classified secret. Their explanation for the secret classification was that "the outside world would not have understood why they were working on lithium and they were afraid that they would have been severely criticized for undertaking this programme".

22.  The inspection team indicated to the Iraqi authorities that it had documentary evidence of several attempts by Iraq to obtain a uranium standard (NBS U930) enriched to 93% in U235. Although these attempts were acknowledged, the fifth and seventh inspection teams had been told that they had not been successful. The inspection team questioned the intended purpose of such a standard, given the lower declared enrichments achieved in the Iraqi enrichment programme, and requested further explanations in view of the persistent appearance of uranium with 93% enrichment in environmental samples collected at and near Al Tuwaitha. The Iraqi authorities stated - as they had on 14 October 1991 - that they had never produced or obtained any quantities (even small ones) of 93%-enriched uranium other than the Tamuz-2 reactor fuel. They indicated their "surprise and worry that such material appeared in the collected samples from the sites" and expressed their willingness to discuss and follow up this matter. The Iraqi side expressed the fear that the sample data are a result of deliberate sabotage by a disgruntled citizen or foreign enemy. This is highly unlikely given the history of sample collection and analysis. The inspection team took additional samples for further analysis. This matter is still under investigation.

Activities at the Al Atheer site

23.  In a letter of 14 October 1991 to the seventh IAEA inspection team, the Al Atheer site was declared to be a national centre for research in material science and materials production which provided a missing link in Iraqi industry and technology. The declaration disclosed, however, that the design requirements for the buildings met the needs of a weapons programme, if a decision to launch such a programme were to

/...

0323

be taken in the future. The individual identified as the leader of the nuclear weapons investigation programme was also on the Al Atheer Site Advisory Committee.

24. The task of the eighth inspection team at this site was to complete the site examination by visiting buildings which have not been inspected by earlier teams, to identify and photograph process equipment and analytical instruments, and to interview the staff in the light of earlier discussions and new declarations.

25. Among the buildings visited by the team (see Figure 4) were the Polymer Laboratories (Building 84), the Materials Characterization Building (Building 85), the Internal Explosion Test Laboratory (Building 18) and the associated control building (Buildings 19), the laboratories stated to belong to the Hatteen Establishment (Building 21), the manufacturing workshop (Building 41), the maintenance workshop (Building 40) and warehouses (Buildings 53, 54 and 56), and the High Explosives Test Firing Bunker (Building 33, designated by Iraq as Site 100).

26. The Iraqi management declared that Building 18 was an explosive chamber to be used for the study of the fragmentation of mortar shells up to 155 mm. This explanation does not make sense. Although no final judgement can be made at present about the intended use of this building, in the opinion of the eighth team this multi-million dollar facility was certainly not meant for the fragmentation testing of mortar shells. Further investigations are needed in order to determine the intended use of Buildings 18 and 19, which appear to have been related.

27. The Polymer Laboratories (Building 84) were a large complex about 50% complete. The stated purpose of the building was polymer and plastic development for petrochemical projects. Since construction was in a very early stage, it is not possible to confirm or deny the statement.

28. The warehouses (Buildings 53, 54 and 56) had extensive ventilation and cooling - to prevent chemical hazards due to high temperatures during the summer - and fire detection/suppression (Halon) systems.

29. The Iraqi management have declared that the Carbide Building (Building 55) is for the production of tungsten carbide (100 t/a). The Al Atheer staff indicated that the main customer was to be the Bader plant, as they were planning to produce carbide tools and dyes for industry. Since a lot of the necessary equipment has not been delivered because of the embargo, they are currently considering alternative uses, such as the production of ceramic materials. IAEA inspection teams have pointed out some insufficiencies with regard to hydrogen safety for such a plant, but explanations are

/...

0324

**FIGURE 4**

AL-ATHEER

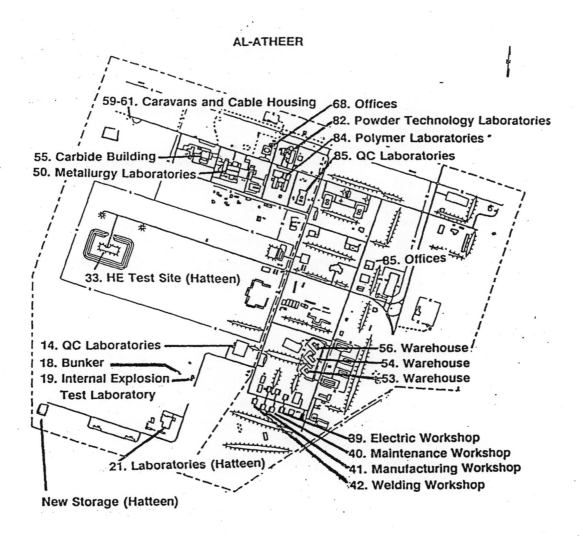

59-61. Caravans and Cable Housing
68. Offices
82. Powder Technology Laboratories
84. Polymer Laboratories
55. Carbide Building
85. QC Laboratories
50. Metallurgy Laboratories
85. Offices
33. HE Test Site (Hatteen)
14. QC Laboratories
18. Bunker
19. Internal Explosion Test Laboratory
56. Warehouse
54. Warehouse
53. Warehouse
39. Electric Workshop
40. Maintenance Workshop
41. Manufacturing Workshop
42. Welding Workshop
21. Laboratories (Hatteen)
New Storage (Hatteen)

/...

still expected. The Al Atheer staff claimed that the tungsten carbide production was not linked to the PC-3 project, but there is documentary evidence that the two were linked.

30. The Iraqi side now refer to the IAEA Building 33 firing bunker as Site 100. They describe this as a Hatteen facility but Site 100 is mentioned several times in the PC-3 progress reports. Plans for Al Atheer development to make it suitable for weaponization studies must have included Site 100. The Iraqi side has persistently denied that any improvement or repair work has been done at this site since it was bombed even though the inspection team has unequivocal evidence to the contrary. The damage to the bunker is repairable.

31. According to the PC-3 progress report covering the period 1 January - 31 May 1990, the Al Atheer site was opened in May 1990. The inspection teams have taken samples to determine whether equipment and facilities were used for weaponization-related research; the sample analysis results are not yet available. Equipment such as isostatic presses and high-temperature furnaces have been identified and placed under IAEA seal. Action is being taken the determine - with the help of the manufacturers - the delivery dates and the number of equipment items and accessories supplied to Iraq. This information and the analytical results will be used in determining whether the site ever started operations.

## DESTRUCTION OF EQUIPMENT/COMPONENTS

32. Activities, begun during the seventh inspection, to destroy or render harmless equipment/components associated with the Iraqi uranium enrichment programme continued during the eighth inspection. The Iraqi authorities, anxious to salvage what they can, made a number of suggestions as to how specific equipment could be rendered useless for enrichment applications and still be available for other uses (with appropriate monitoring). In some cases, the suggestions were accepted for further evaluation; in other cases, they were not and an immediate decision to destroy was taken. The centrifuge-related equipment destroyed during the eighth inspection included:

- Three large high-frequency converters stored at the Ash Shakyli warehouse;
- A vertical balancing machine and the bed for the horizontal balancing machine;
- The jig for a MIG (Metal Inert Gas) welder specially designed for welding aluminium centrifuge casings;

/...

0326

- A mandrel, the expanding mandrel and roller bearings used in the flow forming manufacture of maraging steel rotor tubes (the holding collar of the mandrel was removed from Iraq for further evaluation of the extent of use);

- An electron beam welder fixture designed to hold maraging steel rotors while the end caps are being welded on;

- A rotating spindle and mandrel for the CNC machine used to cut maraging steel rotor tubes to length, and the special collet and whirling head from the CNC machine used to manufacture molecular pumps.

33. The destruction of the application-specific fixtures associated with the centrifuge manufacturing equipment has rendered this equipment useless for centrifuge applications. However, uncertainty remains regarding the completeness of Iraqi declarations as to the number of machine-tools of various types existing in Iraq. Follow-up investigations with equipment manufacturers and suppliers may help. The remaining equipment has not been released for use; it is under Agency seal pending a final decision.

34. At the conclusion of the seventh inspection, the destruction of EMIS components stored at Al Nafad was complete except for the large iron cores of the double-pole magnets and a number of machined parts of the vertical return iron. Several attempts to destroy these pieces were unsuccessful. The solution found was high-temperature cutting fueled by large amounts of oxygen. Destruction of the magnet cores by three 1-1.5 meter long cuts through each has started; will require several weeks since this is a slow process. By the end of the inspection, eight cores had been destroyed. The Iraqi side, which co-operated fully, will continue this work and it is expected that all components will have been destroyed by the time the next IAEA team arrives.

35. Equipment that had been used in Iraqi chemical separation work was destroyed. The mixer-settlers in Building 9 at Al Tuwaitha, which had been used in reprocessing research, were destroyed by filling the mixer and settler chambers with Araldite. This was a difficult task because of the high level of radioactive contamination. A number of hot cells were rendered harmless, at least for the time being, by the cutting and removal of manipulators. The manipulator parts are under seal in a central location.

/...

0327

## NUCLEAR MATERIAL VERIFICATION ACTIVITIES

### Location C, Buildings 1 and 2 (Nuclear Material Storage)

36.   The decision was taken to verify the nuclear material on the basis of a random sampling plan with a 90% confidence level and a goal quantity corresponding to 1 ton of uranium. The verification activities were completed during the eighth inspection and are summarized in Table 2. Only 16.7 tons of uranium contained in waste and stored in a petrol tank in the Mosul area remain to be properly verified. During compilation of the nuclear material balance, a number of discrepancies were identified; the Iraqi authorities were requested, in writing, to provide explanation and clarification in due course. Details of the verification and the discrepancies are given in Annex 2.

### REMOVAL OF NUCLEAR MATERIAL FROM IRAQ

37.   Representatives of the USSR Ministry of Atomic Power and Industry and staff of the IAEA, with the help of the Iraqi counterparts, made all the preparations necessary for the shipments, packing all Soviet-made fuel assemblies into the original drums and sealing them. The 23 plates of a Tamuz-2 fuel assembly were placed in a drum, which was sealed pending future removal. To comply with IAEA nuclear safety requirements, the material to be removed from Iraq was taken to Habanniya in two convoys of special trucks and flown out in two shipments. The first consignment consisted of six drums, each containing seven fuel assemblies (80% enrichment); the second consisted of five drums, one containing ten fuel assemblies (36% enrichment). Two Soviet AN-12 cargo planes arrived at Habanniya airport on 15 and 17 November. The drums were placed in special Soviet-constructed overpacks designed to fulfill the more stringent requirements formulated in the latest IAEA transport regulation. At present, the only remaining nuclear material stored at Location A are 23 MTR plates (400 g uranium, 372 g U235).

/...

0328

## TABLE 2

## Summary of Inspection Results

| MATERIAL TYPE | ORIGIN Processing Site | PRESENTED TO TEAM NO. | DECLARED INVENTORY | | | VERIFIED INVENTORY VERIFICATION | | | | LEFT UNDER SEAL Y/N |
|---|---|---|---|---|---|---|---|---|---|---|
| | | | No. of Items | COMPOUND Weight (kg) | ELEMENT Weight (kg) | I | NDA | B | D | |
| Yellow Cake | Niger | 1,3,8 | 858 | 276844 | 199934 | 858 | 329 | 122 | 41 | Y |
| Yellow Cake | Portugal | 1,3 | 916 | 286435 | 213016 | 915 | 322 | 127 | 48 | Y |
| | Al-Qaim | 3 | 12 | 3000 | 2200 | 12 | 12 | 12 | 5 | Y |
| $UO_2$ Pellets | P | 4 | | | 14 | 1 | 1 | 1 | 1 | Y |
| $U_3O_8$ Powders | r | 1,3 | | | | 10 | 6 | 3 | 3 | Y |
| $UO_2$ Powders | v | 1 | 47 | | 1162 | 22 | 18 | 7 | 3 | Y |
| $UO_2$ Powders | i | 1 | | | | 1 | 1 | 1 | 1 | Y |
| Mx U Oxides | o | 1 | | | | 6 | 6 | 3 | 2 | Y |
| $UO_4$ Slurry | Safe-guards | 4 | | | | 8 | 8 | 8 | 2 | Y |
| $UO_4$ Filters | | 4 | 37 | 100 | | 37 | | | 1 | Y |
| $UO_2$ Powders | Brazil | 3,4 | 227 | 22578 | | 227 | 48 | 227 | 10 | Y |
| U Metal | Brazil/Al.T.Bld #10 | 4 | 22 | 1000 | 1000 | 22 | 7 | 22 | 3 | Y |
| Liquid Waste | Brazil/Al.T.Bld #15 | 4 | 4 | 1000 | 6 | 4 | | | 1 | Y |
| $UF_6$ | Brazil/Al.T.Bld #15 | 3 | 1 | 0.465 | | 1 | | | 1 | Y |
| $UF_4$ Powders | Brazil/Al.T. Bld #15 | 1,3,4 | 5 | 379 | | 3 | 3 | 3 | 6 | Y |
| $UO_2$ Powders | Brazil/Al.T. Bld #15 | 1,3,4 | | | | 1 | | 1 | 2 | Y |
| Mixed U Pdrs | | | | | | 1 | | 1 | 6 | Y |
| $UCl_4$ | Brzl./Al.T.Bld #85 | 3,4 | 43 | 1520 | | 43 | 41 | 43 | 10 | Y |

I = item counting,   B = weighing,   D = sample analysis,   NDA = non-destructive analysis

/...

## TABLE 2

## Summary of Inspection Results

| | MATERIAL TYPE | ORIGIN Processing Site | PRESENTED TO TEAM NO. | DECLARED INVENTORY — No. of Items | COMPOUND Weight (kg) | ELEMENT Weight (kg) | VERIFICATION I | NDA | B | D | LEFT UNDER SEAL Y/N |
|---|---|---|---|---|---|---|---|---|---|---|---|
| N A T / U | ADU Powders | Brazil/Al.T. Bld #85 | 3 | 31 | 1850 | | 11 | 11 | 11 | 12 | Y |
| | ADU Scrap | | | | | | 4 | 4 | 4 | 5 | |
| | UO3 Powders | | | | | | 2 | | 2 | 2 | |
| | U3O8 Powders | | | | | | 1 | | 1 | 1 | |
| EU | Liquid Recovered | Brazil/Al.T. Bld #85 | 3 | 2 | | 1.015 | 2 | | 2 | 29 | Y |
| DU | | | | | | 11.55 | | | | | |
| NU | | | | | | 0.78 | | | | | |
| N A T U R A L | ADU Powders | Al-Qaim/Al-Jesira | 4 | 3 | 220 | | 3 | 3 | 3 | 4 | Y |
| | UO2 Powders | | 3 | 2 | 2255 | 1533 | 2 | 1 | 2 | 4 | Y |
| | U3O8 Powders | | 4 | 9 | 100 | 84 | 9 | 9 | 9 | 3 | Y |
| | UCl4 | | 3 | 8 | 1207 | 780 | 4 | 4 | 4 | 1 | Y |
| D R A N I U M | UO2 Powders | | 3 | 44 | 2050 | 1640 | 8 | 8 | 8 | 3 | Y |
| | UO2 Powders | | | | | | 8 | 8 | 8 | 10 | Y |
| | Mx U Oxides | | | | | | 2 | 2 | 2 | 1 | Y |
| | UO3 Powders | | 3 | 409 | 96967 | 84446 | 19 | 19 | 19 | 2 | Y |
| | | | | | | | 409 | 307 | 97 | 46 | Y |
| | Scrap | Al-Tuwaitha | 3 | 1 | | | 1 | | 1 | 1 | Y |

I = item counting, B = weighing, D = sample and analysis, NDA = non-destructive analysis

/...

0330

**OTHER ACTIVITIES**

<u>Inspection at Tarmiya</u>

38.     An inspection of the Tarmiya EMIS site took place in order to:

-       Take verification samples from the uranyl nitrate solutions stored in tanks in Building 62 (at the time of the third inspection, these solutions were in plastic containers buried in a field adjacent to the Tarmiya site; the solutions have been moved back to the storage tanks at the request of the inspection team);

-       Assess the condition of and take samples from the mixer-settlers in Building 57;

-       Place an identifying seal on the Delta precision measuring device installed in Building 271; and

-       Monitor the clean-up of Tarmiya buildings and identify any new uses.

39.     Samples were taken from the most highly enriched uranyl nitrate solution (5-10% U235) and most depleted (~.1% U235). The container with the 5-10% solution was sealed. The mixer-settlers in Building 57 had been moved to Al Tuwaitha; the reasons given for the move are vague and this matter should be followed-up. The Delta measuring device has been dismantled and placed in crates, which are now being stored in the room where the device had been installed; the Iraqi side indicated that this was done because of the poor environment and that the device would not be removed without prior consultation with an inspection team.

40.     The overall level of activity at the Tarmiya site appears to be modest. There has been little change since the third inspection, in July. Building 245 is now being used for the manufacture and repair of transformers.

/...

0331

## Inspection at the Badr State Establishment

41.  The Badr State Establishment was one of the partners (with Daura) in the development of the Al Furat centrifuge manufacturing and testing facility. Besides the organizational connection, ten of the 13 CNC machines known to have been associated with the development of Iraq's centrifuge manufacturing capability are stored here (Building 24). These machines had been inspected previously and identifying seals had been placed on each machine during the seventh inspection. The purpose of the 14 November visit was to check the seals and search for additional supplier information.

42.  A seal on one of the machines was found to have a broken wire; the Iraqi side could offer no explanation. The seal was replaced. The remaining seals were intact. The manufacturers of the machine components were noted, but most of the components are of general use. One exception may be the main spindle drive. Information on the manufacturer of the main spindle drive had been stripped from the drive housing of every machine but one. This information was recorded.

## Inspection at the Aqba bin Nafi State Establishment

43.  The Aqba bin Nafi State Establishment consists of general mechanical and engineering workshops at three locations - Al Ameen at Badr, Al Radwan near Khandri and Al Amir at Al Fallujah. The headquarters of the Establishment is at Al Ameen, within the boundaries of the Badr plant.

44.  Prior to the Gulf War, the Al Ameen portion of the Aqba bin Nafi State Establishment had three primary functions:

- The assembling of CNC machine tools;
- The maintenance of T-72 tanks and the construction of parts for their repair; and
- The manufacture of parts for hydroelectric power stations.

/...

0332

The assembling of CNC machine tools was carried out under licence from a west European company. About 5-6% of the parts were manufactured at Al Ameen and the rest were imported. The control panels were manufactured at the Salladine Establishment, which was inspected by the seventh team.

45. The Establishment is still assembling CNC machines. The Iraqi management indicated that the contracts for tank maintenance and repair and the manufacture of hydroelectric power station parts have been cancelled. Work for the Iraqi Atomic Energy Commission was apparently done only at the Al Radwan and Al Amir facilities. The Director of the Establishment described the conduct of the work in much the same terms as the Director of the Salladine Establishment - i.e. people showed up with plans and materials, they did not identify themselves, and they removed the plans and product when the work had been done.

46. The facilities appear consistent with Iraqi statements. Modest damage was sustained during the war, but most of it seems to have been repaired. The facilities include large, modern cleaning and welding shops. The welding shop is dominated by a huge electron beam welder with a chamber approximately 10 meters on a side. All equipment looked as though it had been in place for quite some time.

## Sampling at Al Tuwaitha buildings

47. The seventh inspection team had received a request from the Iraqi side for permission to demolish a number of Al Tuwaitha buildings that had been severely damaged during the war - Buildings 9, 15, 55, 60, 64, 72, 73 and 74 and the Annex to Building 15. Permission was given by the IAEA after consultation with the Special Commission. The inspection team visited each of these buildings, to which access is limited because of severe damage, in order to collect additional samples (24 samples, a combination of smears and environmental samples, were taken). A number of other samples, unrelated to the demolition request, were taken at Location C and in Building 86.

/...

Short-notice inspection

**The "Al-Amil" Liquid Nitrogen Plant**

48.     Information collected during the sixth inspection revealed the existence of a plant named "project 7307", built in 1988-89, to provide liquid nitrogen for the EMIS diffusion pumps at Tarmiya. This plant, also called "Al Amil", was the subject of a short-notice inspection on 17 November 1991 following designation by the Special Commisssion. The team was accompanied by the plant manager during the inspection.

49.     The Al Amil facility, located about six kilometers west of Tarmiya is a small, single-purpose and apparently well-run facility for - as indicated - the production of liquid nitrogen.    With the destruction of Tarmiya and the cessation of the Iraqi EMIS programme, other customers for the liquid nitrogen were found and production continued unabated.    There are plans to expand the capacity of this facility. Substantial amounts of used equipment have been brought to this location from one or more other sites and are being stored pending installation. The Al Amil facility was constructed with the help of a foreign firm.

**The Karkh water treatment plant**

50.     The Karkh water treatment plant borders on the Al Amil liquid nitrogen facility and was covered by the same short-notice inspection designation. The Karkh plant was built to expand and improve the water supply to Baghdad. It was essentially complete at the time of the Gulf War, when the remaining contractor personnel left Iraq. A number of foreign firms were involved, the general contractor being Continental Construction Limited (India). The plant manager described the construction work as a 1.5 billion dollar project resulting in the largest water purification plant in the Middle East and one of the largest in the world. The capacity is about 2 million gallons of water/day.

0334                                                         /...

51.  The Karkh water treatment plant is well constructed and laid out, with a number of indications of a well-run facility (e.g. attention to industrial safety practices). All major buildings were inspected. None of the buildings showed any sign of functional change or of recent modification to utilities or ventilation systems. Nothing that might indicate a connection with the Iraqi nuclear programme was observed. There are some temporary structures at the site which, according to Iraqi statements, belong to the various contractors. They were inspected and the contents found to be consistent with the stated purpose. The plant manager indicated that the buildings and their contents would be disposed of upon return of the contractors.

### Inspection at Al Qa Qaa

52.  The six bunkers containing 255 tons of HMX high explosive were visited. The seals on the bunkers were checked and verified by seal replacement.

0335       /...

**ANNEX 1**

**LIST OF REQUESTS SUBMITTED AND DECLARATIONS RECEIVED
DURING THE 8TH IAEA INSPECTION**

8-1.   Mr. Al Hajjaj to Mr. Perricos on 911112 - response to the letter of 911021 providing information on the weaponization studies, hydrodynamic calculations made, Li-6 laboratory experiments, exploding wire laboratory studies, energy sources, initial tests of initiators, and studies on flash X-ray systems.

8-2.   Mr. Al Hajjaj to Mr. Perricos on 911112 - response to the letter of 911021 providing information about equipment ordered for Powder technology laboratory, Ceramic slip casting laboratory, Sample preparation laboratory, and Casting building at Al Atheer. The letter includes some technical specifications of the equipment.

8-3.   Mr. Al Hajjaj to Mr. Perricos on 911112 - response to the letter of 911021 providing information about the tests performed by PC-3 at Hatteen HE Test bunker site in Al Atheer during the period of March - May 1990.

8-4.   Mr. Al Hajjaj to Mr. Perricos on 911112 - response to the letter of 911021 providing information about the design and completion of the Ash Sharqat site.

8-5.   Mr. Perricos to Mr. Al Hajjaj on 911112 - acknowledging the receipt of U-233 and neptunium samples.

8-6.   Mr. Zifferero to Ambassador Alkital on 911113 - regarding the levelling of certain buildings at Al Tuwaitha.

8-7.   Mr. Perricos to Mr. Al Hajjaj on 911114 - requesting information about the location and quantities of bismuth used for the $Po^{210}$ production, list of graphite machining equipment moved to the Al Rabie Plant, removal of the streak video system, the location of EMIS ion sources and collectors of building 80, the return of microfiches taken from the 6th IAEA inspection team by the Iraqi authorities, detailed schedule for the levelling of damaged buildings, and a site visit to such buildings, declaration on the Abu Sukhayr mine ore processed. In addition, a request for proposals regarding the destruction, and rendering harmless of equipment related to the centrifuge programme, research and development work on the use of cerium sulphide, research and study on the gun type design, hydrodynamic calculations, details of $Po^{210}$ initiator design, and clarifications regarding the appearance of 93 % U-235 in environmental samples taken at Al Tuwaitha.

8-8.   Mr. Perricos to Mr. Al Hajjaj on 911115 - documenting that the IAEA has shipped the first consignment of fresh highly enriched uranium from Iraq.

8-9.   Mr. Perricos to Mr. Al Hajjaj on 911116 - requesting information on mainframe and other computing power used in the nuclear programme, additional tritium sources located, uranium metal production, and referring to an Al Atheer programme progress report movement of people and equipment from Al Tuwaitha to Al Atheer.

0336        /...

8-10.   Mr. Perricos to Mr. Al Hajjaj on 911116 - acknowledging the receipt of the holding piece of a destroyed mandrel from the centrifuge flow forming machine.

8-11.   Mr. Perricos to Mr. Al Hajjaj on 911117 - documenting that the IAEA has shipped the second consignment of fresh highly enriched uranium from Iraq.

8-12.   Mr. Al Hajjaj to Mr. Perricos on 911117 - as a response to para 3 of the letter 911114 (item 8-7 above) providing information of the use of the streak cameras.

8-13.   Mr. Al Hajjaj to Mr. Perricos on 911117 as a response to the letter 911116 (item 8-9 above) providing information on the mainframe and other computers at Al Tarmiya, Ash Sharkat and Al Tuwaitha, tritium sources, and tests and manufacturing of uranium metal at Al Tuwaitha.

8-14.   Mr. Al Hajjaj to Mr. Perricos on 911117 - as a response to the letter of 911114 (item 8-7 above) providing information on Bismuth in Iraq, tools for graphite machining moved to Al Rabie Laboratory, EMIS ion sources from Al Tuwaitha, returning microfiches taken from the 6th IAEA team, timetable for the building removals at Al Tuwaitha, processed uranium ore from Abu Sukhayr mine, research conducted with cerium sulphide, gun type weapons, polonium used for initiators, and that they have never produced or obtained any quantities of 93% enriched uranium.

8-15.   Mr. Perricos to Mr. Al Hajjaj on 911118 - acknowledging the receipt of 156 pcs of microfiches taken from the 6th IAEA inspection team, a segment sample of a ring from the center of a double pole (EMIS), and 3 pcs of vacuum valves.

8-16.   Mr. Perricos to Mr. Al Hajjaj on 911118 - requesting additional information on the receipt of yellow cake from Portugal, differences found in pellets, $UO_4$ slurry and filters, $UO_3$ of Al Mosul, ADU of Al Mosul, $UO_4$ samples from Al Qaim, scrap, $UO_2$ from Brazil, $UF_4$, ADU and $UCl_4$ made from material of Brazilian origin, uranium penetrators, and retained waste at Al Mosul.

8-17.   Mr. Perricos to Mr. Al Hajjaj on 911118 - requesting comments on the organization and functions of group IV of PC-3, which have been summarized using data from reports provided by Iraq.

8-18.   Mr. Perricos to Mr. Al Hajjaj on 911118 - acknowledging the receipt of Hamamatsu streak video system components to the IAEA custody.

8-19.   Mr. Perricos to Mr. Al Hajjaj on 911118 - requesting the destruction and rendering harmless of the EMIS related equipment, reminding the need to check water levels in storage tanks at location B, covering of the $Po^{210}$ glove-boxes at Al Tuwaitha, and acknowledging the receipt of beryllium.

8-20.   Mr. Al Hajjaj to Mr. Perricos on 911125 - referring to the discussions on the liquid uranium waste and informing that the containers are ready for shipment from the Al Mosul facility.

8-21.   Mr. Al Hajjaj to Mr. Perricos on 911114 - informing about the reconstruction of buildings 10, 67, 82 and 90.

## ANNEX 2

## NUCLEAR AND OTHER MATERIAL VERIFICATION ACTIVITIES

Location C, Buildings 1 and 2 (Nuclear Material Storage)

### Yellow cake inventory

a) Originating from Niger (199.9 tonnes uranium content in 858 drums). Part of this material (99.7 tonnes uranium content, 428 drums) had been stored at Tikrit and was moved to Location C, where the eighth team verified it.

b) Originating from Portugal (213 tonnes uranium content in 916 drums). Weighing showed that there was no difference between the shipper's weight-list and the IAEA weighing, with the exception of about 40 kg in one damaged drum. However, 100 drums have been painted and the identification numbers erased, so that there is no way of comparing the weights with the shipper's list. No adequate explanation has been given by Iraq concerning this issue.

c) Originating from Iraq - Al Qaim (2.2 tonnes uranium content in 12 drums). On 7 July 1991, the Iraqi side declared that a total of 164 tonnes of yellow cake was produced at Al Qaim, out of which 161 tonnes were processed in Al Jesira and the remaining 3 tonnes were stored at Tikrit. During the eighth inspection, these 3 tonnes of yellow cake (2.2 tonnes uranium content) in 12 drums were brought to Al Tuwaitha, verified and stored at Location C.

### Nuclear material previously placed under Agency safeguards

a) 1 box containing 14 kg of uranium as $UO_2$ pellets (excluding 8.5 kg kept at the New Storage - Building 50 at Al Tuwaitha).

b) 37 filters containing $UO_4$ powder with a declared weight of 100 kg uranium content.

c) Uranium oxides. A total of 1,162 kg of uranium in various oxide forms in 46 containers.

0338

/...

The following discrepancies have been found regarding the material previously under safeguards:

a) The total uranium content in the UO$_2$ pellets presented by the Iraqi side is 33.9 kg (including 8.5 kg stored at the New Storage), which does not correspond to the 22.5 kg reported by the Iraqi side during the November 1990 IAEA safeguards inspection.

b) The weight of the 8 drums containing UO$_4$ slurry amounts to 1180kg. Additionally, 100 kg of uranium contained as UO$_4$ in 37 filters were declared and presented to the fourth team. During the eighth inspection, the Iraqi side declared orally that this material belonged to the inventory previously under safeguards. If that is the case, this amount is greater than what was previously under safeguards.

A written explanation of these discrepancies was requested on 18 November 1991.

### UO$_2$ of Brazilian origin

A total of 27 tonnes of UO$_2$ was declared by the Iraq side in the 7 July 1991 declaration, and 22 578 kg (declared value) of UO$_2$ were presented in 227 containers as part of this material. The remaining 4422 kg were declared as having been processed in Al Tuwaitha Buildings 10, 15 and 85. The verification details are presented in Figure I.

### Material processed in Building 10 - Al Tuwaitha

One tonne (approximately) of uranium metal in 22 containers is stored at Location C. It was processed by the reduction of UF$_4$ with magnesium. Part of this material (19.7 kg in one box containing uranium metal pieces cast and/or machined to various shapes) is stored in the New Storage. Additionally, the Iraqi side declared that 3.5 kg of uranium metal had been used in the production of armour-piercing shells.

### Material processed in Building 15 - Al Tuwaitha

One cylinder contained 465 g of UF$_6$ produced by fluorination of UO$_2$. The Iraqi authorities also admitted to having tested the dry method for the fluorination of UO$_2$ using Freon gas, but no material produced this way was presented.

0339 /...

0340

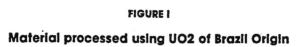

FIGURE I

**Material processed using UO2 of Brazil Origin**

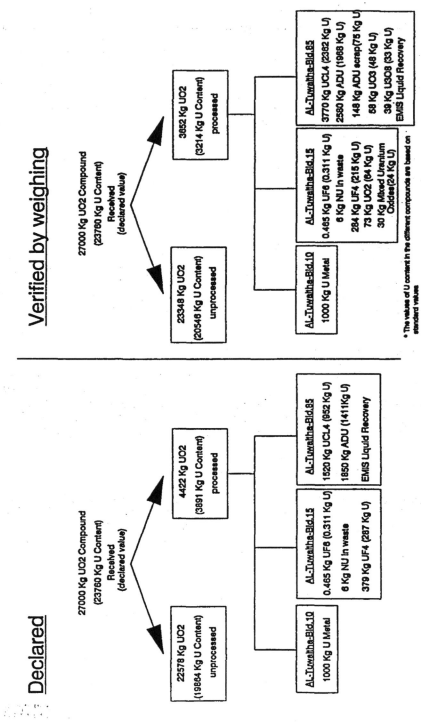

/...

379 kg of $UF_4$ originally contained in 5 drums had been repackaged in three drums. Additionally, 73 kg of $UO_2$ and 30 kg of mixed uranium oxides were found inside the $UF_4$ containers.

Four containers with an aqueous solution of uranium slurry with a total uranium content of 6 kg were presented.

**Material processed in Building 85 - Al Tuwaitha**

1520 (compound weight) of $UCl_4$ were presented in 43 containers.

1850 kg of ammonium diuranate (ADU) contained in 31 drums were presented. The drums were emptied and the material placed in 11 drums and four containers with ADU scraps. Furthermore, two containers with 58 kg of $UO_3$ and one container with 39 kg of $U_3O_8$ were found inside the drums with ADU.

Material from the EMIS enrichment programme, in the form of liquid solutions and small sample bottles with powders containing natural, depleted and enriched uranium was presented in two drums.

The following discrepancies were found in the verification of the material of Brazilian origin:

a)  The Iraqi side declared 22 578 kg of $UO_2$ remaining out of the 27 000 kg received from Brazil. After weighing of all the drums, the correct amount was found to be 23 348 kg.

b)  The drums with $UF_4$ were found to contain the following material:

> $UF_4$ :- 284 kg
> $UO_2$ :- 73 kg
> Mixed uranium oxides :- 30 kg

The declared contents were 379 kg of $UF_4$ (compound weight). The Iraqi side stated that the mixed uranium oxides were rejects from early development work.

c)  All drums containing $UCl_4$ were weighed and, instead of the declared amount of 1520 kg, it was found that the amount contained was in excess of 3700 kg.

0341 /...

d)   The Iraqi side declared 1850 kg of ADU.  All drums were emptied and the following material found:

        ADU        :- 2,580 kg
        ADU scrap  :- 148 kg
        $UO_3$ scrap :- 58 kg
        $U_3O_8$   :- 39 kg

A written explanation of the discrepancies has been requested.

Figure I shows schematically the material processed at Al Tuwaitha using $UO_2$ of Brazilian origin. It compares the Iraqi declarations of material with the results obtained by weighing all the containers in which the produced material was presented.

On the basis of standard concentration values, it has been found that 5795.3kg uranium content were presented by the Iraqi side and that the uranium in the processed $UO_2$ amounted to 3214 kg.

A written explanation of this discrepancy has been requested.

Processed material originating from Al Qaim

This material, produced by the processing of 161 tonnes of yellow cake from Al Qaim, includes:

-   2250 kg of $UO_4$ in nine drums sent from Al Jesira to Tikrit and then moved to Location C during the eighth inspection.

-   96 095 kg of $UO_2$ presented to the third inspection team in 409 drums.

-   220 kg of ADU presented to the fourth team in three drums.

-   2050 kg of $UO_3$ declared on 7 July 1991 and presented in 44 drums. All the drums have been emptied and the $UO_3$ placed in eight drums. In addition to the $UO_3$, 200 kg of mixed uranium oxides in 19 containers were found. Also, 58 kg of $UO_4$ were found inside two $UO_3$ containers.

-   1207 kg of $UCl_4$ in eight containers were declared on 7 July 1991.

-   100 kg of $U_3O_8$ were presented in four containers.

-   Two drums containing $UO_4$ samples were presented.

0342

/...

The following discrepancies were found with regard to the material of Al Qaim origin:

a)      The amount of $UO_2$ declared on 7 July, 1991 was 96095 kg (in 409 drums). However, in a list presented by the Iraqi authorities later, the amount was 96967kg (in 409 drums).

b)      The amount of ADU declared was 220 kg. However, the amount weighed was 317 kg.

c)      The amount of $UO_3$ declared was 2050 kg. All containers were emptied and the following material found:

> $UO_3$ :- 2020 kg
> Mixed uranium oxides :- 200 kg
> $UO_4$ :- 58 kg

d)      Two drums containing 88 kg of $UO_4$ in sample bottles were presented to the third team but not included in any declaration.

Figure II shows schematically the flow of material into and out of Al Jesira. It compares the Iraqi declaration of material produced at Al Jesira with results obtained by weighing the material.

It was impossible to verify the material (16.73 tonnes of uranium) contained in the uranium waste tank but, on the basis of the value given by the Iraqi authorities, it was estimated that 105.735 tonnes of uranium were produced - not the declared amount of 104.65 tonnes.

The explanation given by the Iraqi authorities is that they overestimated the amount of uranium waste. In order to clarify the situation, they have proposed emptying the uranium waste tank and carrying out an accurate measurement of the uranium quantities.

One drum containing 53 kg of scrap presented to the third team was not included in any declaration.  A written explanation about the origin of this material has been requested.

These verifications - summarized in Table 2 of the report - complete the activities required in order to verify the material brought to Location C. However, the results of destructive analysis, careful evaluation of all the data obtained during the different inspections and the discrepancies described above may call for some additional verification activities.

All the material at Location C has been left under seal.  Figures III and IV show the arrangement of the nuclear material at Location C (Buildings 1 and 2).

0343      /...

**FIGURE II**

**Flow Material In and out of AL JESIRA**

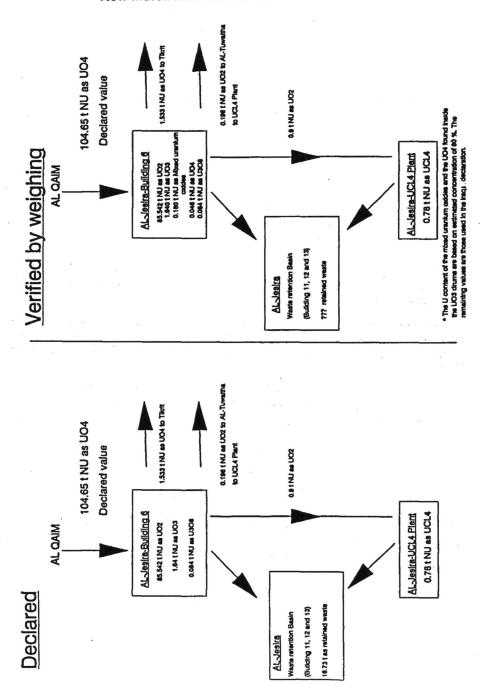

## FIGURE III

## Building 1 of Location C

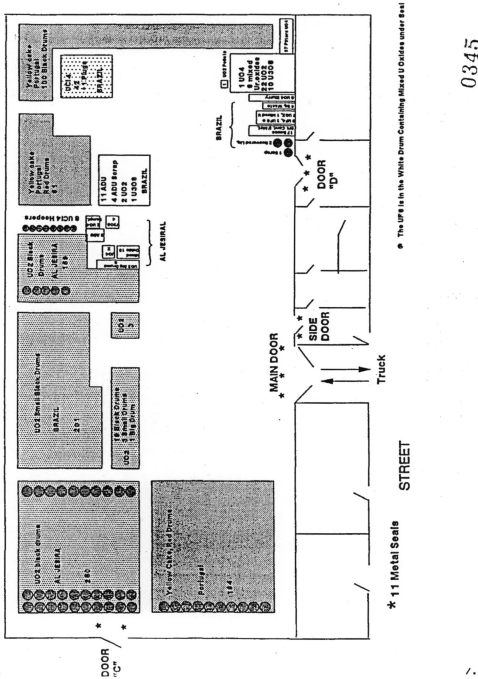

0346

## FIGURE IV

## Building 2 of Location C

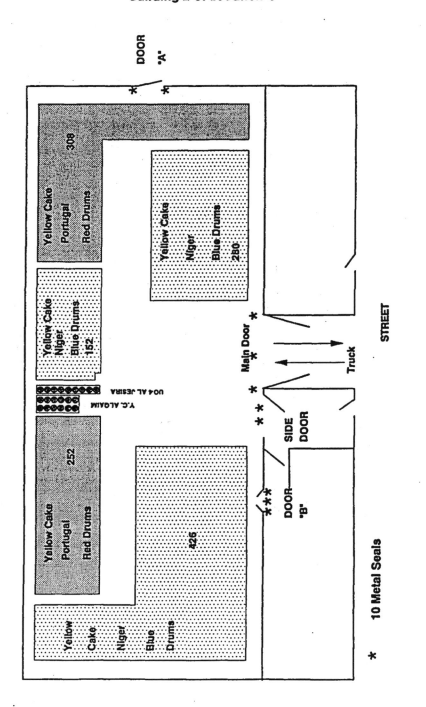

/...

### Location C, Building 3 (Isotope Storage)

There are 115 radioisotopic sources stored at this location. As least nine of them are neutron sources and seven tritium sources.

During the eighth inspection, all sources were sealed, but detailed identification of them was left for a future inspection, when samples from the tritium sources should be taken. The Iraqi counterpart has been asked to provide additional information about the acquisition and utilization of the tritium sources.

### Location C, Building 4

The Iraqi authorities declared that this building had been used for storing natural uranium and had been emptied after the bombing of Al Tuwaitha. Soil samples and smears were taken.

### Verification activities at the IRT-5000 reactor

Verification of the nuclear material and beryllium blocks present at the IRT-5000 reactor was completed during the eighth inspection. There were 13 fuel elements in the spent fuel pond; they had previously been inaccessible for NDA verification. During this inspection, they were item-counted and four of them were randomly selected and measured by non-destructive assay techniques. The 17 beryllium blocks present at the reactor were also verified.

### Verification activities at Location B

All the irradiated fuel and the beryllium blocks present at Location B were verified by seal checking.

/...

0347

## Activities at the New Storage (Building 50 at Al Tuwaitha)

All remaining plutonium, $U^{233}$ (63 mg) and $Np^{237}$ (<0.2 g) was removed and sent to (SAL) the IAEA's Safeguards Analytical Laboratory. Nine seals were replaced.

## Armour-piercing uranium penetrator programme

The Iraqi authorities have declared that 3.5 kg. of uranium metal had been used in producing ten bullets for an armour-piercing projectile programme being conducted at Hatteen. They presented three bullets and stated that three had been used for testing.

-----

0348

외 무 부

종   별 :

번   호 : UNW-4472                           일   시 : 91 1223 1830

수   신 : 장 관(연일,중동일,기정)

발   신 : 주 유엔 대사

제   목 : 안보리(걸프사태)

연:UNW-4233,4278,4305

1. 안보리는 12.20 비공식협의에서 대 이락 제재조치 정기심사 문제를 토의한바,
다음요지의 안보리의장 언론발표문을 채택하였음.(S/23305)

가. 현제재조치 변경을위한 조건이 존재한다는데 대해 이사국간 합의가 없었음.

나. 안보리 대이락 제재위는 AHTISAARI 보고서(S/22409) 에 명시된 인도적
민수품목들을 검토하여 "NO-OBJECTION " 절차에서 단순통보 절차로 전환이 가능한
품목명세표 작성(안보리의 동의필요)

다."NO-OBJECTION" 절차 해당품목에 대해서는 동 이의 제기국은 분명한 이유설명

라. 이락억류 쿠웨이트인 (약 2,000 명), ICRC 의 접근권 보장, 군사장비를 포함한
쿠웨이트 재산반환 문제를 포함하여 사무총장은 이락의 안보리결의 이행현황 전반에
관해 다음 정기심사전 안보리에 보고

마. 이락의 구호품목 수입이 가능하도록 안보리가 유류판매의 길을 열어 주었으나
(안보리결의 706,712 호), 이락이 이를 활용치 않고 있음.

2. IAEA 의 제 8 차 핵사찰 결과(91.11.11-18) 보고서및 핵관련 폐기업무 제1 차
보고서 (91.6.17-12.17)가 안보리문서로 배포된바, 동보고서 주요부분 별첨
송부함.(S/23283,23295)

3. 12.11 자 NYT 지의 미행부 대이락 군사적 대안검토 보도(UNW-4305) 와 관련한
이락 A.HUSSEIN 외무장관의 사무총장앞 대미비난 서한이 안보리문서로 배포(S/23297)
되었으며, 쿠웨이트는 DMZ 내 이락경찰 초소 5 개소 및 이달초 이락병력(12
명)침부사례를 항의하는 안보리문서를 배포하였음.(S/23303-04)

4. 또한 연호 유엔 이락배상위(UNCC) 집행이사회 제 3 차 회기결과가 안보리문서로
배포되었음.(S/23292)

---

국기국       장관       차관       1차보      중아국      외정실      분석관      청와대      안기부

첨부:안보리의장 언론발표문(S/23305) 및 IAEA 보고서(발췌):UNW(F)-1071.끝.
(대사 노창희-국장)
예고:91.12.31. 까지

UNITED NATIONS

UNW(FR)-1071   11223  1830
(연월. 종동일. 기간)  총604

S

## Security Council

Distr.
GENERAL

S/23305
20 December 1991

ORIGINAL: ENGLISH

### NOTE BY THE PRESIDENT OF THE SECURITY COUNCIL

After the consultations held on 20 December 1991, the President of the Security Council made the following statement to the media on behalf of the members in connection with the item entitled "The situation between Iraq and Kuwait":

"The members of the Security Council held informal consultations on 6 December 1991 pursuant to paragraph 28 of resolution 687 (1991), paragraph 6 of resolution 700 (1991) and paragraph 21 of resolution 687 (1991). After hearing all the opinions expressed in the course of the consultations, the President of the Council concluded that there was no agreement that the necessary conditions existed for a modification of the regimes established in paragraphs 22, 23, 24 and 25, as referred to in paragraph 28 of resolution 687 (1991), in paragraph 6 of resolution 700 (1991), and in paragraph 20, as referred to in paragraph 21 of resolution 687 (1991).

"However, with a view to alleviating the humanitarian conditions for the civilian population in Iraq and in order to facilitate the utilization of paragraph 20 of resolution 687 (1991), the 661 Committee is requested to study immediately those materials and supplies for essential civilian and humanitarian needs as identified in the Ahtisaari report (S/22409) with the purpose of drawing up a list of items which may, with the approval of the Security Council, be transferred from the 'no-objection' procedure to a simple notification procedure. Members of the Council may submit proposals of items for this purpose.

"With regard to imports of items subject to prior approval under the 'no-objection' procedure by the Security Council Committee established by resolution 661 (1990) (i.e. items other than food and medicine), any member of the Committee putting forward an objection to such an import will offer a specific explanation at a meeting of the Committee.

"The members of the Council are aware of reports received concerning the approximately 2,000 Kuwaitis believed to be still detained in Iraq, access by the ICRC to all detainees and places of detention, the return

91-41832  2715c (E)                                                /...

6-1

of Kuwaiti property, and particularly the return of Kuwaiti military equipment and their bearing upon the present state of Iraqi compliance with resolution 687 (1991).

"In light of the above, the Security Council will request the Secretary-General to prepare a factual report on Iraq's compliance with all the obligations placed upon it by resolution 687 (1991) and subsequent relevant resolutions. This report will be made available to the Security Council in good time before the Council undertakes its next review under paragraph 21 of resolution 687 (1991).

"In the course of consultations it was noted that resolutions 706 (1991) and 712 (1991) gave to Iraq the possibility for oil sales to finance the purchase of foodstuffs, medicines and materials and supplies for essential civilian needs for the purpose of providing humanitarian relief. However, this possibility has not yet been used."

-----

6-2

0352

Enclosure

First semi-annual report (covering the period 17 June - 17 December 1991)
on the implementation by the IAEA of the plan for the destruction,
removal or rendering harmless of items listed in paragraph 12
of UN Security Council resolution 687 (1991)

## Introduction

· Security Council resolution 699 of 17 June 1991 approved the plan submitted by the IAEA through the Secretary-General for the destruction, removal or rendering harmless of all items listed in paragraph 12 of Security Council resolution 687. Resolution 699 at the same time called for a report to be submitted every six months on progress in implementing the plan. This is the first such report.

At the time the plan was drawn up, the first on-site inspection under the terms of resolution 687 had just started. The objectives of that inspection were based on the declarations made by the Government of Iraq on 18 and 27 April 1991. The plan took into account the material and facilities known to exist at the time, but stressed that inspections would have to determine whether items additional to those declared by Iraq existed. As subsequent inspections have shown, the Iraqi nuclear program was far more extensive than what was indicated by the declarations of 18 and 27 April 1991 - and the full extent of the program may not even now be known. This report therefore covers not only the items known at the time of submission of the IAEA plan but also items revealed subsequently.

Throughout this period, Iraq's persistent practice of only limited acknowledgement of activities exposed through inspections, its concealment of evidence in such critical areas as uranium enrichment and nuclear weapons development, its denial of unrestricted access to certain sites, its detaining of the Agency's team on one occasion and its confiscating of documents from inspectors have made it rather difficult for the Agency to discharge its duties.

6-3

/...

0353

## Summary

The present situation regarding destruction, removal or rendering harmless can be summarized as follows:-

Directly usable material (High Enriched Uranium)

68 fuel assemblies 80% enriched     - removed

10 fuel assemblies 36% enriched     - removed

(Remaining - 372 grams of U235 in 93%-enriched uranium contained in MTR-type fuel plates)

Plutonium

6 grams     - removed

Natural uranium

Approximately 400 tons     - stored under IAEA seal

EMIS equipment

Magnet poles     - 8 destroyed

Vacuum chambers     - all destroyed

Coils     - all destroyed

Centrifuge equipment

Centrifuges     - destroyed (some specimens removed to IAEA)

Manufacturing equipment     - key components destroyed

Hot Cells     - rendered harmless

-----

6-4

0354

Enclosure

REPORT ON THE EIGHTH IAEA ON-SITE INSPECTION IN IRAQ
UNDER SECURITY COUNCIL RESOLUTION 687 (1991)

11 - 18 November 1991

**SALIENT POINTS**

- The in-field activities related to Information on the procurement of equipment essential to the Iraqi nuclear programme continued despite persistent efforts by Iraq to conceal such information.  Manufacturers of a number of specific equipment items were identified.

- The Iraqi authorities provided additional answers to questions about weaponization which had been put by the seventh IAEA Inspection team and which related mainly to the results of initiator design work and tests, to work on flash X-ray systems, to the theoretical calculations and design options studied, and to the energy released. The answers were vague and general, especially as regards questions deriving from the secret PC-3 progress reports obtained during the sixth IAEA inspection.

- The Iraqi authorities repeated that they had never produced any quantities of 93%-enriched uranium and had never obtained any, other than those known to the Agency, and expressed their concern about the IAEA's findings. The matter is still under investigation.

- Systematic destruction of the EMIS double-pole magnets started, using thermal-cutting equipment and with the co-operation of the Iraqi authorities. Basic equipment related to the EMIS and the centrifuge programme was destroyed or rendered harmless. Two high-speed streak video camera systems were removed from Iraq; they are now in storage on the premises of the IAEA.

/...

All fresh highly enriched uranium of Soviet origin was shipped out of Iraq in two consignments, on 15 and 17 November, with the full co-operation of the Iraqi authorities. The airlifting operation was arranged through a contract between the USSR Ministry of Atomic Power and Industry and the IAEA. Only 400 g of 93%-enriched fresh uranium, in the form of 23 fuel plates, and the irradiated fuel elements of French and Soviet origin remain in Iraq.

The verification of nuclear material in the Tuwaitha area was completed, and only 46.7 tons of uranium in waste solutions stored in the Mosul area remain to be properly verified. During evaluation of the nuclear material balance, a number of discrepancies were identified; explanations and clarifications to be provided by the Iraqi authorities were requested in writing.

Monitoring activities initiated during the seventh inspection mission continued during the eighth. It is the opinion of the eighth inspection team that inspection efforts in Iraq should gradually shift to monitoring, with occasional identification and characterization activities performed when new information becomes available. For the time being, certain activities related to the destruction of equipment and removal of the irradiated highly enriched uranium (HEU) fuel (including the 400 g of 93% enriched fresh uranium) should continue in parallel with monitoring inspections and follow-up activities.

/...

| | | | | | | |
|---|---|---|---|---|---|---|
| **정 리 보 존 문 서 목 록** | | | | | | |
| **기록물종류** | 일반공문서철 | **등록번호** | 2020010146 | **등록일자** | 2020-01-28 | |
| **분류번호** | 731.33 | **국가코드** | IQ | **보존기간** | 30년 | |
| **명 칭** | 유엔안전보장이사회 이라크 대량살상무기 폐기 특별위원회, 1991. 전3권 | | | | | |
| **생 산 과** | 국제연합1과/중동1과 | **생산년도** | 1991~1991 | **담당그룹** | | |
| **권 차 명** | V.1 4-7월 | | | | | |
| **내용목차** | * 4.3 유엔 안보리, 걸프전 휴전에 관한 결의안 채택 (안보리 결의 687호)<br>     - 이라크의 군비통제를 위한 특별 위원회 설치 등 포함<br><br>  4.19 유엔안보리, 이라크 군비통제 특별위원회 설치 승인<br><br>  6.17 이라크 특정 무기 폐기 이행 계획 채택 (안보리 결의 699호)<br>    대이라크 무기류 공급금지 시행안 채택(안보리 결의 700호)<br><br>  6.28 이라크 군의 유엔 핵사찰 요청 불응 관련 안보리 의장 성명 발표<br><br>  7.18 IAEA 이사회, 이라크의 핵 안전협정 불이행 규탄 결의 채택<br><br>* 유엔 핵 조사단의 핵 사찰 실시 포함 | | | | | |

0001

외 무 부

종 별 : 지급

번 호 : UNW-0787

일 시 : 91 0403 2000

수 신 : 장 관(국연,중동일,기정)

발 신 : 주 유엔 대사

제 목 : 걸프사태(안보리)

연: UNW-0762,0774

1. 안보리는 금 4.3.(수) 12:00-16:30 공식회의를 개최하여 연호 미측 휴전결의안 (S/22430)을 표결한바, 찬 12 (중국포함), 반 1 (쿠바), 기권2 (예멘,에쿠아돌)로 채택되었음. (안보리 687 호결의)

2. 상기 회의 주요경과는 다음과같음.

가. 의제채택( S/AGENDA/2981)

나. 쿠웨이트, 이락 토의참가 요청처리: 안보리의사규칙 37조에 의거 양국 토의참가허용

다. 미측안 공동제안국 추가: 원제안국인 미, 영, 불, 루마니아에 벨지움, 자이르추가(총 6개국)

라. 쿠웨이트, 이락 발언

1) 쿠웨이트: 휴전결의안 의의 강조, 이락책임, 쿠웨이트 재건노력 언급

2) 이락: 다국적군의 월권, 이락국민 피해, 휴전결의안상의 문제점 (국경문제 강제, 배상부담, 이락의 배상청구권, 이락 군사력의 일방적 제한, 경제제재 존속), 대미비난.

마. 표결전 발언

1) 예멘: 이락국민 피해, 휴전결의안문제점 (국경문제는 당사국간 합의 및 ICJ 를 통한 해결이 합당, 지역 군사력 균형파괴 우려, 경제제재 해제지연, 다국적군의 철수장 기화우려), 아랍제국간 유대회복

2) 자이르: 휴전결의안 지지

3) 짐바베: 지역전반의 군비제한 필요, 경제제재완화 (인도적 목적), 휴전결의안본문 32항 (테러리즘)해석유보 (민족해방 운동에 불영향)

국기국    1차보    중아국    정문국    청와대    안기부

91.04.04    10:59 WG

외신 1과 통제관

0002

4)쿠바:휴전결의안 문제점 (안보리의 국경문제개입은 유엔헌장 위반이며 660호결의의 양국간협의 원칙에도 상치, 일방적 군사력제한부당, 이락이 쿠웨이트 철수한 이상 경제조치 존속 근거없음. 배상문제는 ICJ 를 통해처리), 안보리관련 결의안 이행에따른 21개국의 경제난 문제언급, 본건 결의안 반대

5)인도:경제제재조치 완화 (인도적목적), 국경조항은 쿠웨이트-이락간 기존합의 (62년)에 근거한 것으로 이해 (당사국간 합의원칙 확인)

6)코트디브와르:휴전결의안 지지

바.표결후 발언

1)미국: 휴전결의안 취지 및 특징설명, 아랍.이스라엘 문제해결 노력

2)프랑스:이락내전 관련 유혈진압 문제제기 (특히, 쿠드족 탄압)

3)중국: 경제제재 조기해제, 외군철수추진, 지역국가간 해결노력

4)쏘련: 그간 확전방지를 위한 자국노력, 국경문제에 관한 당사국간 합의원칙 확인, 아랍-이스라엘 문제 해결 기여 용의

5)에쿠아돌: 휴전결의안중 국경조항 유보 (당사국간합의원칙)

6)영국: 이락의 군사비과다 (개발 재원으로전용가능), 내란유혈진압 규탄

7)오스트리아: 내란 유혈진압과 관련한 불.터어키의 안보리조치 요청지지, 이락에 대한 유엔평화유지군참여 용의, 아랍-이스라엘 및 팔레스타인 문제해결 노력

8)루마니아: 이락의 본건 결의안 조속 수락촉구, 안보리관련 결의안 이행에 따른 21개국 경제난문제언급, 이락의 외채상환 의무

9)벨지움: 이락 내전관련 소수민족 탄압문제제기, 경제제재 완화(인도적 목적)

아.쿠웨이트 및 이락발언

1)쿠웨이트: 이락발언중 이락의 피해, 이락의 청구권, 국경문제 언급 반박

2)이락: 이락의 소수민족 융화노력 언급, 인접국의개입비난, 난민귀환 문제협조용의

3.금일 채택된 상기 휴전결의안은 연호 기존 미측안을 비동맹이사국들의 의견을 일부 반영하여 약간의 수정을가한것임.(수정조항:전문:E,X, 본문:6,19,20,21항)

4.연호 이락내전 유혈진압 사태와관련한 불,터어키의 안보리 조치요청 문제에 대해서는 현재 이사국들간 개별협의가 진행중인 것으로 알려짐.

5.금일 표결에서 에쿠아돌이 기권한것과 관련, 동국 대표부 관계관에게 그 경위를 문의한바, 동관계관은 국경문제는 당사자간에 타결되어야한다는 원칙을 지지하며

PAGE 2

0003

동국으로서는 페루와의 국경문제에 미칠수있는 영향을 고려해야할 입장에 있다고말함.

　　첨부:상기 휴전결의: UNW(F)-150

　　끝

　　(대사 노창희-국장)

0004

# 長官報告事項

報告畢

1991. 4. 6.
國際機構條約局
國際聯合課 (17)

題 目 : 걸프戰爭 休戰에 관한 安保理決議 採擇

---

유엔安保理는 91.4.3(水) 걸프戰爭 休戰에 관한 美側이 주도한
決議 687 (1991)호를 採擇한 바, 同 內容 아래 報告합니다.

---

1. 決議案 共同提案國(6개국) : 美, 英, 佛, 루마니아, 벨지움, 자이르

2. 安保理 表決結果 : 찬성 12 : 반대 1(쿠바) : 기권 2(예멘, 에쿠아돌)
   * 中國도 贊成 表決함.

3. 表決後 主要國 發言槪要

   ○ 美 國 : 休戰 決議案 趣旨 및 特徵說明, 아랍-이스라엘 問題解決에
             努力 豫定

   ○ 中 國 : 經濟制裁 早期解除, 外軍 撤收, 地域國家間 問題解決 强調

   ○ 蘇 聯 : 걸프戰 확전 防止를 위한 自國 努力 說明, 國境問題에
             관한 當事國間 合意原則 强調

| 공 | 담 당 | 과 장 | 국 장 | 차 관 보 | 차 관 | 장 관 |
|---|---|---|---|---|---|---|
| 람 | (서명) | (서명) | (서명) | | | |

0005

o 에쿠아돌 : 決議案 內容中 國境條項때문에 棄權(當事國間 合意原則 强調)

　　－ 에쿠아돌-페루간의 國境問題에 미치는 影響이 棄權事由

　　　　※ 에쿠아돌의 기권라면, 등 배경들을 　~~(handwritten)~~ 에서

## 4. 쿠웨이트 및 이락 發言 槪要

* 쿠웨이트.이락은 紛爭當事國으로서 安保理議事規則(37조)에 따라 投票權
　없이 討議에만 參加

o 이　　　락 : 이락의 少數民族 融和努力 言及, 隣接國의 介入非難,
　　　　　　　　難民歸還 問題 協調要請

o 쿠웨이트 : 이락의 被害 및 請求權, 國境問題에 관한 이락의 言及
　　　　　　　內容 反駁

## 5. 休戰決議 後續措置

　　　조정 기구 ~~(handwritten)~~
가. ~~企劃團~~ (Coordinating Group) 設置

　　o 構　成 : 事務總長(주재), 事務次長 7명, 事務次長補 2명으로 構成
　　o 任　務 : 安保理決議 687호에 따라 事務局內에 同 決議 履行業務 總括

나. 유엔 옵서버단 配置 計劃 準備

　　o 名　　稱 : UNIKOM (United Nations Iraq-Kuwait Observation
　　　　　　　　　Mission)
　　o 準備現況 : M. Goulding 特別政治擔當 事務次長이 準備中
　　　　　　　　　4.5-4.6.中 安保理에 計劃 提出 豫定

* 其他 參考事項

　　o 이락 內戰 流血鎭壓 事態와 關聯한 불란서, 터키의 安保理 措置 要請
　　　問題에 대하여는 現在 理事國間 個別 協議 進行中

添 附 : 安保理決議 687호 主要內容. 끝.

0006

# 안보리결의 687 (1991)호 주요내용

* 뉴욕시간 1991.4.3(수) 채택

o 1963.10.4. 이락.쿠웨이트간에 체결한 조약(Agreed Minutes Between the State of Kuwait and the Republic of Iraq Regarding the Restoration of Friendly Relations, Recognition and Related Matters) 상의 양국국경선 상호 존중 및 보장

o 유엔사무총장은 동 결의채택후 3일이내 이락.쿠웨이트 국경지대에 양측간 휴전감시를 임무로하는 유엔 감시단 파견계획 수립, 안보리에 제출

o 이락이 "생물.화학무기의 개발, 생산, 저장 금지에 관한 조약(1972.4.10)" 비준토록 촉구

o 이락은 국제 감시하에 모든 생물, 화학무기 및 관련시설을 파괴 또는 철거하고 사정거리 150Km 이상의 미사일 및 관련부품, 시설물을 파괴 또는 제기토록 결정

o 상기 사항의 실효적 이행확보를 위하여 유엔사무총장은
   - 이락의 생물.화학무기.시설감시를 임무로 하는 특별위원회의 설립등에 관한 계획 수립

o 유엔사무총장은 향후 이락의 생물.화학무기의 사용, 생산, 획득방지를 위하여 동 결의안 채택후 120일이내에 이락감시 방안을 작성, 안보리에 제출

o 이락은 일체의 핵무기 또는 핵무기관련 물자 또는 시설의 개발 및 획득 불가

o IAEA 사무처장은 유엔사무총장 및 특별위원회의 지원하에 이락이 현재 보유하고 있는 핵관련 장비 및 시설의 사찰 즉시 실시, 제반 위험 방지조치 실시

0007

ㅇ 유엔사무총장은 쿠웨이트 자산의 반환을 위하여 취해진 조치에 관하여
  안보리에 보고

ㅇ 이락이 90.8.2. 이후 외채에 관하여 발효한 모든 사항은 무효이며 외채
  상환의무 이행 요구

ㅇ 손해배상을 위한 기금과 기금운영을 위한 위원회 설치 및 본 결의채택후
  30일이내에 유엔사무총장은 손해배상 청구와 관련, 이락의 석유 수출능력
  및 경제상황등을 감안한 동 기금에의 기여비율등을 포함한 세부내용 작성,
  안보리에 보고

ㅇ 이락에 대한 식품, 의약품등 반입 허용 및 대이락 금수조치의 단계적 완화

ㅇ 대이락 무기류, 군수품 및 관련기술의 금수 지속 및 실효적 이행 확보

ㅇ 이락이 자국내 쿠웨이트 및 제3국 국민들의 귀환 및 실종자 확인을 위해
  국제적십자 위원회(ICRC)에 최대한 협조토록 결정

ㅇ 이락, 국제테러 행위 지원 불가

ㅇ 이락이 상기 제조항 수락시 종전 발효

0008

**Security Council**

Distr.
GENERAL

S/RES/687 (1991)*
8 April 1991

RESOLUTION 687 (1991)

Adopted by the Security Council at its 2981st meeting,
on 3 April 1991

The Security Council,

Recalling its resolutions 660 (1990) of 2 August 1990, 661 (1990) of
6 August 1990, 662 (1990) of 9 August 1990, 664 (1990) of 18 August 1990,
665 (1990) of 25 August 1990, 666 (1990) of 13 September 1990, 667 (1990) of
16 September 1990, 669 (1990) of 24 September 1990, 670 (1990) of
25 September 1990, 674 (1990) of 29 October 1990, 677 (1990) of 28 November 1990,
678 (1990) of 29 November 1990 and 686 (1991) of 2 March 1991,

Welcoming the restoration to Kuwait of its sovereignty, independence and
territorial integrity and the return of its legitimate Government,

Affirming the commitment of all Member States to the sovereignty, territorial
integrity and political independence of Kuwait and Iraq, and noting the intention
expressed by the Member States cooperating with Kuwait under paragraph 2 of
resolution 678 (1990) to bring their military presence in Iraq to an end as soon as
possible consistent with paragraph 8 of resolution 686 (1991),

Reaffirming the need to be assured of Iraq's peaceful intentions in the light
of its unlawful invasion and occupation of Kuwait,

Taking note of the letter sent by the Minister for Foreign Affairs of Iraq on
27 February 1991 1/ and those sent pursuant to resolution 686 (1991), 2/

------------

\*    Reissued for technical reasons.

1/   S/22275, annex.

2/   S/22273, S/22276, S/22320, S/22321 and S/22330.

   <u>Noting</u> that Iraq and Kuwait, as independent sovereign States, signed at
Baghdad on 4 October 1963 "Agreed Minutes Between the State of Kuwait and the
Republic of Iraq Regarding the Restoration of Friendly Relations, Recognition and
Related Matters", thereby recognizing formally the boundary between Iraq and Kuwait
and the allocation of islands, which were registered with the United Nations in
accordance with Article 102 of the Charter of the United Nations and in which Iraq
recognized the independence and complete sovereignty of the State of Kuwait within
its borders as specified and accepted in the letter of the Prime Minister of Iraq
dated 21 July 1932, and as accepted by the Ruler of Kuwait in his letter dated
10 August 1932,

   <u>Conscious</u> of the need for demarcation of the said boundary,

   <u>Conscious also</u> of the statements by Iraq threatening to use weapons in
violation of its obligations under the Geneva Protocol for the Prohibition of the
Use in War of Asphyxiating, Poisonous or Other Gases, and of Bacteriological
Methods of Warfare, signed at Geneva on 17 June 1925, <u>3/</u> and of its prior use of
chemical weapons and affirming that grave consequences would follow any further use
by Iraq of such weapons,

   <u>Recalling</u> that Iraq has subscribed to the Declaration adopted by all States
participating in the Conference of States Parties to the 1925 Geneva Protocol and
Other Interested States, held in Paris from 7 to 11 January 1989, establishing the
objective of universal elimination of chemical and biological weapons,

   <u>Recalling also</u> that Iraq has signed the Convention on the Prohibition of the
Development, Production and Stockpiling of Bacteriological (Biological) and Toxin
Weapons and on Their Destruction, of 10 April 1972, <u>4/</u>

   <u>Noting</u> the importance of Iraq ratifying this Convention,

   <u>Noting</u> moreover the importance of all States adhering to this Convention and
encouraging its forthcoming Review Conference to reinforce the authority,
efficiency and universal scope of the convention,

   <u>Stressing the importance</u> of an early conclusion by the Conference on
Disarmament of its work on a Convention on the Universal Prohibition of Chemical
Weapons and of universal adherence thereto,

   <u>Aware</u> of the use by Iraq of ballistic missiles in unprovoked attacks and
therefore of the need to take specific measures in regard to such missiles located
in Iraq,

_____

   3/    League of Nations, <u>Treaty Series</u>, vol. XCIV (1929), No. 2138.

   4/    General Assembly resolution 2826 (XXVI), annex.

                                                                          /...

                                                          0010

Concerned by the reports in the hands of Member States that Iraq has attempted to acquire materials for a nuclear-weapons programme contrary to its obligations under the Treaty on the Non-Proliferation of Nuclear Weapons of 1 July 1968, 5/

Recalling the objective of the establishment of a nuclear-weapons-free zone in the region of the Middle East,

Conscious of the threat that all weapons of mass destruction pose to peace and security in the area and of the need to work towards the establishment in the Middle East of a zone free of such weapons,

Conscious also of the objective of achieving balanced and comprehensive control of armaments in the region,

Conscious further of the importance of achieving the objectives noted above using all available means, including a dialogue among the States of the region,

Noting that resolution 686 (1991) marked the lifting of the measures imposed by resolution 661 (1990) in so far as they applied to Kuwait,

Noting that despite the progress being made in fulfilling the obligations of resolution 686 (1991), many Kuwaiti and third country nationals are still not accounted for and property remains unreturned,

Recalling the International Convention against the Taking of Hostages, 6/ opened for signature at New York on 18 December 1979, which categorizes all acts of taking hostages as manifestations of international terrorism,

Deploring threats made by Iraq during the recent conflict to make use of terrorism against targets outside Iraq and the taking of hostages by Iraq,

Taking note with grave concern of the reports of the Secretary-General of 20 March 1991 7/ and 28 March 1991, 8/ and conscious of the necessity to meet urgently the humanitarian needs in Kuwait and Iraq,

Bearing in mind its objective of restoring international peace and security in the area as set out in recent resolutions of the Security Council,

Conscious of the need to take the following measures acting under Chapter VII of the Charter,

_____

5/    General Assembly resolution 2373 (XXII).

6/    General Assembly resolution 34/146.

7/    S/22366.

8/    S/22409.

/...

0011

1.    Affirms all thirteen resolutions noted above, except as expressly changed below to achieve the goals of this resolution, including a formal cease-fire;

A

2.    Demands that Iraq and Kuwait respect the inviolability of the international boundary and the allocation of islands set out in the "Agreed Minutes Between the State of Kuwait and the Republic of Iraq Regarding the Restoration of Friendly Relations, Recognition and Related Matters", signed by them in the exercise of their sovereignty at Baghdad on 4 October 1963 and registered with the United Nations and published by the United Nations in document 7063, United Nations, Treaty Series, 1964;

3.    Calls upon the Secretary-General to lend his assistance to make arrangements with Iraq and Kuwait to demarcate the boundary between Iraq and Kuwait, drawing on appropriate material, including the map transmitted by Security Council document S/22412 and to report back to the Security Council within one month;

4.    Decides to guarantee the inviolability of the above-mentioned international boundary and to take as appropriate all necessary measures to that end in accordance with the Charter of the United Nations;

B

5.    Requests the Secretary-General, after consulting with Iraq and Kuwait, to submit within three days to the Security Council for its approval a plan for the immediate deployment of a United Nations observer unit to monitor the Khor Abdullah and a demilitarized zone, which is hereby established, extending ten kilometres into Iraq and five kilometres into Kuwait from the boundary referred to in the "Agreed Minutes Between the State of Kuwait and the Republic of Iraq Regarding the Restoration of Friendly Relations, Recognition and Related Matters" of 4 October 1963; to deter violations of the boundary through its presence in and surveillance of the demilitarized zone; to observe any hostile or potentially hostile action mounted from the territory of one State to the other; and for the Secretary-General to report regularly to the Security Council on the operations of the unit, and immediately if there are serious violations of the zone or potential threats to peace;

6.    Notes that as soon as the Secretary-General notifies the Security Council of the completion of the deployment of the United Nations observer unit, the conditions will be established for the Member States cooperating with Kuwait in accordance with resolution 678 (1990) to bring their military presence in Iraq to an end consistent with resolution 686 (1991);

C

7.    Invites Iraq to reaffirm unconditionally its obligations under the Geneva Protocol for the Prohibition of the Use in War of Asphyxiating, Poisonous or Other Gases, and of Bacteriological Methods of Warfare, signed at Geneva on 17 June 1925,

/...

0012

and to ratify the Convention on the Prohibition of the Development, Production and Stockpiling of Bacteriological (Biological) and Toxin Weapons and on Their Destruction, of 10 April 1972;

8.  <u>Decides</u> that Iraq <u>shall unconditionally accept the destruction</u>, removal, or rendering harmless, under international supervision, of:

(a)  All chemical and biological weapons and all stocks of agents and all related subsystems and components and all research, development, support and manufacturing facilities;

(b)  All ballistic missiles with a range greater than 150 kilometres and related major parts, and repair and production facilities;

9.  <u>Decides</u>, for the implementation of paragraph 8 above, the following:

(a)  Iraq shall submit to the Secretary-General, within fifteen days of the adoption of the present resolution, a declaration of the locations, amounts and types of all items specified in paragraph 8 and agree to urgent, on-site inspection as specified below;

(b)  The Secretary-General, in consultation with the appropriate Governments and, where appropriate, with the Director-General of the World Health Organization, within forty-five days of the passage of the present resolution, shall develop, and submit to the Council for approval, a plan calling for the completion of the following acts within forty-five days of such approval:

(i)  The forming of a Special Commission, which shall carry out immediate on-site inspection of Iraq's biological, chemical and missile capabilities, based on Iraq's declarations and the designation of any additional locations by the Special Commission itself;

(ii)  The yielding by Iraq of possession to the Special Commission for destruction, removal or rendering harmless, taking into account the requirements of public safety, of all items specified under paragraph 8 (a) above, including items at the additional locations designated by the Special Commission under paragraph 9 (b) (i) above and the destruction by Iraq, under the supervision of the Special Commission, of all its missile capabilities, including launchers, as specified under paragraph 8 (b) above;

(iii)  The provision by the Special Commission of the assistance and cooperation to the Director-General of the International Atomic Energy Agency required in paragraphs 12 and 13 below;

10.  <u>Decides</u> that Iraq shall unconditionally undertake <u>not to use, develop, construct or acquire any of the items specified in paragraphs 8 and 9 above and requests the Secretary-General, in consultation with the Special Commission, to develop a plan for the future ongoing monitoring and verification of Iraq's compliance with this paragraph, to be submitted to the Security Council for approval within one hundred and twenty days of the passage of this resolution;</u>

/...

0013

11.   Invites Iraq to reaffirm unconditionally its obligations under the Treaty on the Non-Proliferation of Nuclear Weapons of 1 July 1968;

12.   Decides that Iraq shall unconditionally agree not to acquire or develop nuclear weapons or nuclear-weapons-usable material or any subsystems or components or any research, development, support or manufacturing facilities related to the above; to submit to the Secretary-General and the Director-General of the International Atomic Energy Agency within fifteen days of the adoption of the present resolution a declaration of the locations, amounts, and types of all items specified above; to place all of its nuclear-weapons-usable materials under the exclusive control, for custody and removal, of the International Atomic Energy Agency, with the assistance and cooperation of the Special Commission as provided for in the plan of the Secretary-General discussed in paragraph 9 (b) above; to accept, in accordance with the arrangements provided for in paragraph 13 below, urgent on-site inspection and the destruction, removal or rendering harmless as appropriate of all items specified above; and to accept the plan discussed in paragraph 13 below for the future ongoing monitoring and verification of its compliance with these undertakings;

13.   Requests the Director-General of the International Atomic Energy Agency, through the Secretary-General, with the assistance and cooperation of the Special Commission as provided for in the plan of the Secretary-General in paragraph 9 (b) above, to carry out immediate on-site inspection of Iraq's nuclear capabilities based on Iraq's declarations and the designation of any additional locations by the Special Commission; to develop a plan for submission to the Security Council within forty-five days calling for the destruction, removal, or rendering harmless as appropriate of all items listed in paragraph 12 above; to carry out the plan within forty-five days following approval by the Security Council; and to develop a plan, taking into account the rights and obligations of Iraq under the Treaty on the Non-Proliferation of Nuclear Weapons of 1 July 1968, for the future ongoing monitoring and verification of Iraq's compliance with paragraph 12 above, including an inventory of all nuclear material in Iraq subject to the Agency's verification and inspections to confirm that Agency safeguards cover all relevant nuclear activities in Iraq, to be submitted to the Security Council for approval within one hundred and twenty days of the passage of the present resolution;

14.   Takes note that the actions to be taken by Iraq in paragraphs 8, 9, 10, 11, 12 and 13 of the present resolution represent steps towards the goal of establishing in the Middle East a zone free from weapons of mass destruction and all missiles for their delivery and the objective of a global ban on chemical weapons;

D

15.   Requests the Secretary-General to report to the Security Council on the steps taken to facilitate the return of all Kuwaiti property seized by Iraq, including a list of any property that Kuwait claims has not been returned or which has not been returned intact;

/...

E

16. _Reaffirms_ that Iraq, without prejudice to the debts and obligations of Iraq arising prior to 2 August 1990, which will be addressed through the normal mechanisms, is liable under international law for any direct loss, damage, including environmental damage and the depletion of natural resources, or injury to foreign Governments, nationals and corporations, as a result of Iraq's unlawful invasion and occupation of Kuwait;

17. _Decides_ that all Iraqi statements made since 2 August 1990 repudiating its foreign debt are null and void, and demands that Iraq adhere scrupulously to all of its obligations concerning servicing and repayment of its foreign debt;

18. _Decides also_ to create a fund to pay compensation for claims that fall within paragraph 16 above and to establish a Commission that will administer the fund;

19. _Directs_ the Secretary-General to develop and present to the Security Council for decision, no later than thirty days following the adoption of the present resolution, recommendations for the fund to meet the requirement for the payment of claims established in accordance with paragraph 18 above and for a programme to implement the decisions in paragraphs 16, 17 and 18 above, including: administration of the fund; mechanisms for determining the appropriate level of Iraq's contribution to the fund based on a percentage of the value of the exports of petroleum and petroleum products from Iraq not to exceed a figure to be suggested to the Council by the Secretary-General, taking into account the requirements of the people of Iraq, Iraq's payment capacity as assessed in conjunction with the international financial institutions taking into consideration external debt service, and the needs of the Iraqi economy; arrangements for ensuring that payments are made to the fund; the process by which funds will be allocated and claims paid; appropriate procedures for evaluating losses, listing claims and verifying their validity and resolving disputed claims in respect of Iraq's liability as specified in paragraph 16 above; and the composition of the Commission designated above;

F

20. _Decides_, effective immediately, that the prohibitions against the sale or supply to Iraq of commodities or products, other than medicine and health supplies, and prohibitions against financial transactions related thereto contained in resolution 661 (1990) shall not apply to foodstuffs notified to the Security Council Committee established by resolution 661 (1990) concerning the situation between Iraq and Kuwait or, with the approval of that Committee, under the simplified and accelerated "no-objection" procedure, to materials and supplies for essential civilian needs as identified in the report of the Secretary-General dated 20 March 1991, 9/ and in any further findings of humanitarian need by the Committee;

---

9/  S/22366.

/...

21. <u>Decides</u> that the Security Council shall review the provisions of paragraph 20 above every sixty days in the light of the policies and practices of the Government of Iraq, including the implementation of all relevant resolutions of the Security Council, for the purpose of determining whether to reduce or lift the prohibitions referred to therein;

22. <u>Decides</u> that upon the approval by the Security Council of the programme called for in paragraph 19 above and upon Council agreement that Iraq has completed all actions contemplated in paragraphs 8, 9, 10, 11, 12 and 13 above, the prohibitions against the import of commodities and products originating in Iraq and the prohibitions against financial transactions related thereto contained in resolution 661 (1990) shall have no further force or effect;

23. <u>Decides</u> that, pending action by the Security Council under paragraph 22 above, the Security Council Committee established by resolution 661 (1990) shall be empowered to approve, when required to assure adequate financial resources on the part of Iraq to carry out the activities under paragraph 20 above, exceptions to the prohibition against the import of commodities and products originating in Iraq;

24. <u>Decides</u> that, in accordance with resolution 661 (1990) and subsequent related resolutions and until a further decision is taken by the Security Council, all States shall continue to prevent the sale or supply, or the promotion or facilitation of such sale or supply, to Iraq by their nationals, or from their territories or using their flag vessels or aircraft, of:

(a) Arms and related <u>matériel</u> of all types, specifically including the sale or transfer through other means of all forms of conventional military equipment, including for paramilitary forces, and spare parts and components and their means of production, for such equipment;

(b) Items specified and defined in paragraphs 8 and 12 above not otherwise covered above;

(c) Technology under licensing or other transfer arrangements used in the production, utilization or stockpiling of items specified in subparagraphs (a) and (b) above;

(d) Personnel or materials for training or technical support services relating to the design, development, manufacture, use, maintenance or support of items specified in subparagraphs (a) and (b) above;

25. <u>Calls upon</u> all States and international organizations to act strictly in accordance with paragraph 24 above, notwithstanding the existence of any contracts, agreements, licences or any other arrangements;

26. <u>Requests</u> the Secretary-General, in consultation with appropriate Governments, to develop within sixty days, for the approval of the Security Council, guidelines to facilitate full international implementation of paragraphs 24 and 25 above and paragraph 27 below, and to make them available to all States and to establish a procedure for updating these guidelines periodically;

/...

0016

27.   Calls upon all States to maintain such national controls and procedures and to take such other actions consistent with the guidelines to be established by the Security Council under paragraph 26 above as may be necessary to ensure compliance with the terms of paragraph 24 above, and calls upon international organizations to take all appropriate steps to assist in ensuring such full compliance;

28.   Agrees to review its decisions in paragraphs 22, 23, 24 and 25 above, except for the items specified and defined in paragraphs 8 and 12 above, on a regular basis and in any case one hundred and twenty days following passage of the present resolution, taking into account Iraq's compliance with the resolution and general progress towards the control of armaments in the region;

29.   Decides that all States, including Iraq, shall take the necessary measures to ensure that no claim shall lie at the instance of the Government of Iraq, or of any person or body in Iraq, or of any person claiming through or for the benefit of any such person or body, in connection with any contract or other transaction where its performance was affected by reason of the measures taken by the Security Council in resolution 661 (1990) and related resolutions;

G

30.   Decides that, in furtherance of its commitment to facilitate the repatriation of all Kuwaiti and third country nationals, Iraq shall extend all necessary cooperation to the International Committee of the Red Cross, providing lists of such persons, facilitating the access of the International Committee of the Red Cross to all such persons wherever located or detained and facilitating the search by the International Committee of the Red Cross for those Kuwaiti and third country nationals still unaccounted for;

31.   Invites the International Committee of the Red Cross to keep the Secretary-General apprised as appropriate of all activities undertaken in connection with facilitating the repatriation or return of all Kuwaiti and third country nationals or their remains present in Iraq on or after 2 August 1990;

H

32.   Requires Iraq to inform the Security Council that it will not commit or support any act of international terrorism or allow any organization directed towards commission of such acts to operate within its territory and to condemn unequivocally and renounce all acts, methods and practices of terrorism;

I

33.   Declares that, upon official notification by Iraq to the Secretary-General and to the Security Council of its acceptance of the provisions above, a formal cease-fire is effective between Iraq and Kuwait and the Member States cooperating with Kuwait in accordance with resolution 678 (1990);

/...

0017

34.  <u>Decides</u> to remain seized of the matter and to take such further steps as may be required for the implementation of the present resolution and to secure peace and security in the area.

-----

0018

# 외 무 부

종 별 :

번 호 : UNW-0937

일 시 : 91 0416 1930

수 신 : 장 관(국연,중동일,기정)

발 신 : 주 유엔 대사

제 목 : 걸프사태(안보리)

연: UNW-0806

1. 휴전결의 후속조치

가. 안보리 휴전결의 (687 호) 이행관련 업무총괄을 위해 유엔사무국내에 설치된 연호 기획단은 그간 수차회의를 갖고 제반후속조치 문제들을 계속 협의하고 있는 것으로 알려짐.

나. 휴전결의 본문 9항에 의거 이락측은 4.18까지 생화학무기, 미사일관련 자료를 유엔사무총장에게 제출토록 되어있는바, 이에대비하여 앞으로 이락 무기파기 관련 업무를 관장할 특별위원회 (SPECIAL COMMISSION)설치를 위해 사무국 (Y.AKASHI 사무차장 주관)과 관련국간에 사전협의가 현재 진행중이라고함.

다. 일본대표부에 의하면 상기 특별위원회는 25명정도의 전문가로 이루어질 것으로 보인다고함. (일본도자국 전문가 추천을 요청받고있음.)안보리상임이사국들이 모두 동 위원회에 참여하게 되며, 의장에는 이집트, 부의장에는 미국이 유력하다고함. 라. 한편 유엔옵서버단 (UNIKOM) 경비문제에 대한 토의가 총회속개회의 (91.4.29-5.3)중있을 것으로 알려짐.

2. 이락 난민구호 활동

가. 4.15자 일본 안보리문서 (S/22499) 에 의하면,동국은 천만불 공여에 추가하여 구호품, 인력지원예정임.또한 동 문서를 통해 일본은 미,영,불등의 구호품 공수활동에 적극적인 지지를 표명함.

나. 스웨덴은 프레스릴리스를 통해 쿠르드족난민구호를 위한 1,630 만불 지원계획을 발표함.(동국의 걸프사태관련 인도적지원총액 : 6870 만불)희랍도 쿠르드족에 대한 구호품공여 계획을 발표하였음. (규모미상)

3. 이란-이락휴전 합의 위반주장

---

국기국    1차보    중아국    정문국    정와대    안기부

PAGE 1

최근 양국은 88.8월 휴전합의 위반 사례를 안보리 문서를 통해 상호 비난해 오고 있는바, 특히 이란은 4.14. 이락군이 자국 GHAR-E-SHIRIN북부지역 (국경에서 3 KM) 을 공격, 점령중이라고 주장함.끝

(대사 노창희-국장)

# 외 무 부

종 별 :

번 호 : UNW-0954    일 시 : 91 0417 2000

수 신 : 장 관(국연,중동일,기정)

발 신 : 주 유엔 대사

제 목 : 걸프사태(안보리)

연: UNW-0937

1. 4.16 이락은 식량을 비롯한 필수품 긴급수입 (4개월분)을 위해 약 10억불 상당의 석유수출을 허가해 줄것을 안보리 제재위원회에 요청하여 온바, 동 위원회 의장 (오지리대사)은 이사국들과의 개별협의를 거쳐 4.19 경 위원회소집 예정인 것으로 알려짐.

2. 유엔 S.KHAN 대표일행은 이락 당국과 쿠르드족, 쉬아교파 난민보호소 ( RECEPTION CENTERS)설치문제를 협의해온바, 금명간 동협의결과가 발표될것으로 관측되고있음. 한편 이락 북부지역에 미, 영, 불 병력이 관할하는 난민수용소 (5-6 개소)를 설치하는 문제에 대한 유엔사무총장 반응은 별첨 총장대변인 발표내용 참조바람.

3. 안보리 휴전결의 (687호) 후속조치 문제와 관련하여 다음사항 참고바람.

가. 무기폐기 관련 특별위원회

동 위원회 (위원:20-25 명)는 5가지분야 (화학무기, 미사일, 핵무기, 검증, 지원업무)로 나누어 분임반 (UNITS)을 두며, 상당수지원인력 (수백명)을 갖게될 것으로알려짐. 위원회 의장국으로 스칸디나비아 국가도 거론되고 있음.

나. 배상기금

동 기금 적립을 위한 이락 석유수출수입 공제분은 10-15 프로 수준이 보도되고있음. (4.17자 NYT 지)

첨부: 사무총장 대변인 발표내용: UNW(F)-172

끝

(대사 노창희-국장)

---

국기국    1차보         정문국    청와대    안기부 중아국

Asked if the intention of the United States, the United Kingdom and France to provide military protection for the Kurds had been discussed, the Secretary-General said that it was an aspect "on which we have to reflect; because we would first of all like to be in touch with the Iraqis to see what their reaction would be to this military presence on their territory." Did a military presence constitute a problem, he was asked? "It depends", the Secretary-General replied. "If it is a military presence under the UN flag, of course I must obtain the consent, so to speak, of the Security Council. If it is up to countries which do not request the UN flag, the situation is completely different."

Did this mean, the Secretary-General was asked further, that a resolution would be needed before action was taken? The Secretary-General replied "not necessarily. But in any case, we are studying the situation with a great deal of attention so that Iraq's sovereignty shall be respected, and we hope that the Iraqis will understand that the objective of the three countries is quite simply humanitarian, as also is that of the UN. The Iraqi government received my team, Sadruddin Aga Khan and Ambassador Suy, and I shall see them in Paris on Saturday when they will inform me of what they heard and then we shall take decisions."

Asked whether he was hostile to a military presence in Iraq, the Secretary-General said "the word 'military' is awkward. If the objective is humanitarian, I do not see a difficulty, I mean a difficulty from the moral point of view. But from the legal point of view, of course it is a problem."

The Secretary-General was then asked what he thought about the possibility of establishing enclaves in Iraqi territory. He replied "the word 'enclave' has never been used. The term that is used is 'reception centre'. The word 'enclave' has, of course, a connotation which affects the sovereignty of Iraq. I still have good hopes that the Iraqis will accept the reception centres. Whether these centres will have a kind of military observation or not, that is another story."

Asked whether the military presence could be established in Iraq before a reply from the Iraqi government, the Secretary-General replied "No, no, no. For me, we have in any case first of all to be in touch with the Iraqis - it is a question of sovereignty."

0022

# UNW-0954 첨부물

# 외 무 부

종 별 :

번 호 : UNW-0989

수 신 : 장 관(국연,중동일,기정)

발 신 : 주 유엔 대사

제 목 : 걸프사태(유엔동향)

일 시 : 91 0419 2100

연: UNW-0954

1. 안보리 제재위원회는 금 4.19 이락의 연호 필수품 긴급수입 및 이를 위한 석유 '수출' (약10억불 상당)허가신청 문제를 토의하였으나, 여러 이사국들이 본건 필수품목, 석유수출물량 및 수출대상국에 관해 추가 해명을 요구함에 따라 동위원회의장 (오지리) 주재 개별협의회를 거쳐 다음주 재 토의 예정임.

2. 이락은 안보리 휴전결의 (687) 에 의거 자국의 폐기대상 무기현황 (화학무기, 미상일,핵)을 4.18유엔 사무총장에게 통보 (핵 관련현황은 IAEA에도 제출) 해온바, 이락측이 동 통보문서 배포를 요청하지 않은관계로 유엔문서로 배포되지는않을 것이라고함. (보도에 의하면, 화학무기, 스커드미사일 보유는 시인하였으나 핵무기 보유는 부인)

3. 안보리는 사무총장이 제출한 이락 무기폐기 업무를 관장할 특별위 설치계획을 NO-OBJECTIONPROCEDURE (일정시점까지 이의제기 이사국이 없는경우 자동승인)에 의거 4.19 오후 승인한바, 당관에서 입수한 동 사무총장 관련 보고서를 별첨송부함.

4. 유엔옵서버단 (UNIKOM) 은 본대 (300 명)대부분이 금주 배치완료 예정이며, 다음주까지는 여타 지원병력들도 배치지역에 도착예정이라고 하는바, 동 옵서버단 구성내용은 별첨참조 바람.

5. 표제관련 구호업무를 총괄하고있는 S.KHAN유엔대표가 4.19 제네바에서 가진 기자회견 요지를 별첨송부함.

첨부:1.특별위 설치계획복서

2. UNIKOM구성내용

3. S.KHAN 대표기자회견 요지:UNW(F)-177

끝 ( 대사 노창희 - 국장 )

April 1991

ORIGINAL:   ENGLISH
PRELIMINARY DRAFT

## Report of the Secretary-General

## Implementation of paragraph 9 (b)(i) of Security Council resolution 687 (1991)

1.     The present report is submitted in pursuance of Security Council resolution 687 (1991) of 3 April 1991. In paragraph 9 (b) (i) of that resolution the Council decided that the Secretary-General should submit to it for approval a plan calling _inter alia_ for the forming of a Special Commission to carry out the tasks ennumerated in paragraphs 9 (b) (i-iii), 10 and 13.

2.     To enable the Special Commission to play its proper part in assessing information and preparing and planning the activities envisaged in Section C of the resolution, including assisting the Director-General of the International Atomic Energy Agency to present a plan within his designated area, there is an urgent need for the Special Commission to be established.  The implementation, within or near the timeframes indicated by the resolution, of all the mandates in section C will in fact depend on the existence of the Commission, and its advice in the early stages would be essential.

3.     Subject to the approval of the Security Council, it is my intention to set up the Special Commission as described below and

w-0989
ꭹ
1991 04 10 15.07

7-1

312 3701954  P.02

0024

- 2 -

to make all necessary arrangements for it to begin implementation of its tasks.

4.    In setting up the structure for the Special Commission I wish to emphasize the need for an efficient and effective executive body.  I propose that it should have an Executive Chairman with a Deputy Executive Chairman to assist the Chairman in carrying out his functions.  Following the appointment of these two individuals the remainder of the Special Commission would be established on an expanding basis as appropriate individuals are found to fill the positions.  Under the Executive Chairman and Deputy Executive Chairman, the planning and operational direction of the functions of the Commission should be carried out by five groups, each under a head of group with appropriate executive experience in the assigned field and each consisting of a small number of experts.  The major areas of responsibility would be:  biological and chemical weapons; ballistic missiles; nuclear weapons capabilities; future compliance and operations support.  Thus the formal membership of the Special Commission would be of the order of 20 to 25 persons.

5.    Although the specific timing of the Special Commission's activities have yet to be determined, under the provisions of Section C of the resolution, most of the Commission's functions are time limited.  With the accomplishment of the tasks entrusted to four of the five groups, the major active phases would be completed and those four groups would cease to exist.  The fifth group would continue in order to implement the activities relating to future compliance.

6.    In carrying out its various tasks the Special Commission would be assisted by a number of technical experts serving as inspectors, disposal teams and field support officers.  These

7-2

- 3 -

experts would be either specially engaged for this purpose or
made available to the Commission by Member States.  Their total
number would have to be determined in relationship to the size of
the task to be carried out.  This can be fully assessed only
after the baseline field inspections have been completed by the
Special Commission, but it is likely that the personnel involved
will number in the several hundreds.

7.     As soon as the baseline field assignments of the Special
Commission and of the International Atomic Energy Agency have
been completed, I intend to work out, in consultation with the
Commission, a detailed plan for the implementation of the various
tasks entrusted to it, and to submit it to the Security Council
for its approval.

8.     Following the acceptance by the Government of Iraq of the
Security Council resolution 687 (1991), expressed in the
penultimate provision of the letters addressed respectively to me
and to the President of the Security Council on 6 April 1991 by
the Minister for Foreign Affairs of the Republic of Iraq, the
execution of the baseline field inspections and the subsequent
implementation plan is predicated on the assumption of full cooperation by the Iraqi authorities.  The Special Commission would
enjoy the relevant privileges and immunities provided for in the
Convention on the Privileges and Immunities of the United
Nations.  Members of the Special Commission, experts attached to
it and other specialists assigned to assist it in the
implementation of Section C of the Security Council resolution
687 (1991), would be regarded as experts on mission within the
meaning of Article VI of the Convention on the Privileges and
Immunities of the United Nations, relevant Annexes to the
Convention on the Privileges and Immunities of the Specialized
Agencies and Article VII of the Agreement on the Privileges and

0026

Immunities of the IAEA, respectively.  Taking into account the
tasks to be performed by the Special Commission, it may be
necessary to conclude special agreements covering the status,
facilities, privileges and immunities of the Commission and its
personnel. The existing agreements mentioned above would equally
apply to tasks to be performed in Iraq by the IAEA and could be
supplemented by special agreements, should the need arise.

9.    While the financial implications relating to the
establishment and functioning of the Special Commission cannot at
this stage be assessed with accuracy, it is anticipated that
certain start up funds will be required.  This sum will defray
the initial costs of establishing the Headquarters of the Special
Commission in New York as well as a field office in the region
and the early deployment of advanced elements of the operation in
the field. This sum will also defray some of the initial costs to
be borne by the IAEA in carrying out the assignments entrusted to
it under Section C of the resolution.  Comprehensive cost
estimates will, of course, be provided to the Security Council as
soon as possible.  It is my intention, however, to proceed in
this regard on the basis of the following principles:  (a) that
Member States whose nationals will serve on the Commission or
assist it in the discharge of its responsibilities should be
responsible for their salaries, while the United Nations will
bear the costs of travel and daily subsistence, and (b) that the
whole exercise will be carried out in the shortest possible time,
with a progressive decrease in the number of technical experts
and of members of the Special Commission as various operations
are completed.

7-4

# COMPOSITION OF THE UNITED NATIONS IRAQ-KUWAIT
## OBSERVATION MISSION (UNIKOM)

19 April 1991

1. Military Observers (300 in all)

> Five Permanent Members of the Security Council
> Pakistan
> Fiji, Ghana, India, Ireland, Kenya, Malaysia,
>      Norway, Uruguay
> Argentina, Austria, Bangladesh, Denmark, Finland,
>      Greece, Hungary, Italy, Nigeria, Pakistan, Poland,
>      Romania, Senegal, Singapore, Sweden, Thailand,
>      Turkey, Venezuela
> Canada

2. Support Units

> Canada: Engineers unit (300 all ranks)
> Chile: Helicopter unit (6 choppers; crew of 50)
> Switzerland: Fixed Wing unit (2 planes; crew of 3)
> Norway: Medical unit (50 all ranks)

3. Logistics units

> Denmark: Movement Control and Postal unit (25 all ranks)
> Sweden: Supply unit (35 all ranks)

4. Infantry Units

> On loan from UNFICYP (Cyprus)--two companies:
>      Austria
>      Denmark
>
> On loan from UNIFIL (Lebanon)--three companies plus:
>      Fiji
>      Ghana
>      Nepal
>      plus Norway/Sweden (composite logistics unit)

ikom-4

7-5

0028

19 April 1991

## PRESS CONFERENCE BY EXECUTIVE DELEGATE TO CO-ORDINATE UNITED NATIONS INTER-AGENCY HUMANITARIAN ASSISTANCE

Prince Sadruddin Aga Khan, Executive Delegate of the Secretary-General to co-ordinate a United Nations inter-agency humanitarian programme for Iraq, Kuwait and the Turkish and Iranian border areas, briefed journalists at the Palais des Nations in Geneva Friday, 19 April, on his recent trip to Iraq. They had brought back an agreement with Baghdad which would enable them to set in motion the Organization's efforts to promote the voluntary return of Iraqi displaced persons as well as humanitarian measures to avert new flows of refugees.

He said he attached great importance to the co-operation of the Iraqi authorities, who seemed to be very open in this regard. Freedom of movement, of access, of communications, the presence of United Nations staff in the area, the input by the Red Cross, the ICRC and other humanitarian agencies - all these provided a large field for them to operate in order to try to stabilize the situation of an extremely vulnerable population. The agreement had been signed and it was now time to translate it into action. Nonetheless, it was clear that many problems remained to be resolved.

He said he would be meeting shortly with the Secretary-General in Paris to discuss such questions as the practical aspects of implementing the humanitarian assistance programme and fund-raising.

Asked who the "Co-ordinator" was, the Prince replied that that was his counterpart in Iraq, a Swede who was a senior member of the United Nations Development Programme (UNDP). Co-ordination had to be done at the field level and the Co-ordinator would report directly to the Executive Delegate at Geneva.

In response to a question concerning how the United Nations intended to guarantee the safety of the Kurds, the Prince replied that "the United Nations is not a police force". However, it would seek to establish a climate of confidence, among other things, by assisting the returning populations, by setting up relay stations, and assuring that there was no discrimination in assistance to the various groups in the country. It was important to set up a United Nations radio communciations system on both sides of the border, he added. Iraq's concern for its territorial integrity and sovereignty were also covered by the agreement. The operations to be undertaken should be completed by the end of the year.

The Prince said he saw no reason why reconciliation was not possible. There was no way for the United Nations to establish in a few days' time the sort of humanitarian relief operations needed. "We are no match for hundreds of helicopters and thousands of troops," he noted, referring to the recent relief efforts undertaken by the United States and other allies.

.../....

7-6

0029

Asked whether the United Nations staff in the region intended to
co-operate with the allies in this respect, he said that inevitably the United
Nations had a presence in the host country, so it was in touch with what was
being done there.  The United Nations also had to have a very clear idea of
what was being done bilaterally in order to avoid duplication of effort.
Inevitably there had to be liaison and contacts between the different groups.
It was still too early to say how many centres would be needed.  The size of a
centre would depend on the needs and size of the population in the region to
be served by it.  These details were being worked out now by his Co-ordinator
in Iraq.

However, "all that would remain an empty shell unless we get the money
up front and unless bilateral sources can muster the millions of dollars
needed for the operation".  The international community had to put its money
where its mouth was, he added.

In reply to questions, the Prince said he had not met with Saddam
Hussein during his visit and furthermore, as he was not a member of the
Revolutionary Council, he did not know why the Iraqi authorities had changed
their minds about letting foreign forces on their territory.  An additional
$400 million had to be added to the amounts already announced for United
Nations humanitarian programmes in the region, since the situation was
constantly evolving there.  Asked if he had any money to start relief work or
just pledges, the Prince said that the United Nations system had not waited
until the signing of the agreement.  Relief activities had already begun, but
the ongoing process had to be continued and strengthened.

The Executive Delegate said he could not state officially what the Iraqi
authorities were going to say or do following the forthcoming meeting between
them and the United States military officials.  The United Nations efforts
were strictly humanitarian.  Concerning the situation in the south, the Blue
Helmets would have to deal with very sensitive groups.  The United Nations had
to do everything possible to ensure that no human rights violations or
settling of accounts occurred.

Eric Suy said he had nothing to add to what the Prince had already said
and made a number of observations concerning conditions in the country.  The
needs of the refugees, whether in the north or the south, where there were
fewer of them, were enormous.

Asked what the Kurds could be offered in order to gain their confidence,
the Prince replied that the terms of reference were clear in the agreement and
that parameters had been elaborated.  He did not want to get involved in the
arrangements covering the cease-fire.  The United Nations concern in the
region was strictly humanitarian, it could not act as a police force there.
Personally, he said, if he was a Kurd he would hope to have the right to live
in peace in his own country, something anybody would want.  There was not just
one category of Kurd - not all of them had been involved in the insurgency, so
each refugee would have to decide for himself the question of going home.

Asked if the United Nations would agree to the handing over of the camps
now being set up by the United States and other allies, he said that such a
move could not be made unilaterally;  there would have to be very serious
discussions about the modalities for such a transfer.  As to whether the
enormous flow of bilateral aid now headed for the region ought to be
multilateral, the Prince said that he worked for a multilateral organization
and that in principle aid should be multilateral.  However, it also had to be
effective.

7-7

0030

# 외 무 부

종 별 :

번 호 : UNW-0994

일 시 : 91 0422 1830

수 신 : 장관(국연,중동일,기정)

발 신 : 주유엔대사

제 목 : 걸프사태(유엔동향)

연: UNW-0989

안보리 휴전결의(687 호) 에 의거 이라크무기 폐기업무를 관장할 연호 특별위설치 계획을 4.19안보리가 승인함에따라, 금 4.22. 유엔사무총장은동 위원회 의장및 부의장을 다음과같이임명, 발표하였음.

1. 의장( EXECUTIVE CHAIRMAN):R.EKEUS 대사(스웨덴)

2. 부의장( DEPUTY E.C.):R.GALLUCI ( 미국)

끝

(대사 노창희-국장)

국기국    중아국    안기부  1차보

91.04.23    10:10 FN

외신 1과 롱제관

0031

외 무 부

종 별 :

번 호 : UNW-1106                      일 시 : 91 0501 2000

수 신 : 장 관(국연,중동일,기정)

발 신 : 주 유엔 대사

제 목 : 걸프사태

연: UNW-1096

1. 안보리 제재위원회는 연호 4.30 회의에 이어 5.3(금) 회의개최 예정인바,
오지리 (의장국)G.JANDL 서기관에 의하면 본건관련 지금까지 이락측이 제기해온 요청
사항은 다음과같음.

　　가. 석유수출 (약 9,500 만불 상당)허가

　　나. 이락 동결자산 (약 1억불상당:미, 영, 스위스, 일은행) 해제

　　다. 제재조치에 앞서 거래가 이루어진 선적품 (민수용)반입허가

2. 안보리 휴전결의에 의거한 유엔의 이락 특정 무기폐기업무 추진동향에 관해서는
별첨 5.1.자 WP지 기사를 참조바람.

3. 유엔이락, 쿠웨이트 옵서버단 (UNIKOM)배치현황에 관한 4.30 자 유엔
발표내용을 별첨송부함.

　　첨부:1. 이락무기 폐기관련 WP 기사

　　2. UNIKOM배치현황: UNW(F)-189

끝

(대사 노창희-국장)

---

국기국　　1차보　　　　　　정문국　　청와대　　안기부 중동일

PAGE 1                                      91.05.02   10:49 WW

외신 1과 통제관

0032

# Destroying Iraq's Chemical Arsenal Expected to Be Lengthy Task for U.N.

By R. Jeffrey Smith
Washington Post Staff Writer

The United Nations faces major obstacles in organizing a speedy destruction of Iraq's arsenal of chemical weapons, including an immediate lack of equipment, funds and personnel, according to the top U.N. officials appointed to carry out the task.

Although the agency is working against a midsummer deadline, the officials said they believe that technical, political and environmental problems could easily delay completion of their work for a year or more.

"It is a bigger and bigger problem, the more you look into it," said Rolf Ekeus, Swedish ambassador, who last Thursday began his first full day as chairman of a special U.N. commission appointed to find, hold and destroy the chemical weapons. "It is a . . . huge amount of weaponized material."

Robert L. Gallucci, a former State Department official, recently appointed the commission's vice chairman, said separately that destruction of the material "is a significant technical and political challenge—there is no question about it." He said the agency was beginning its work with substantial uncertainties about the method and cost of rendering the chemicals harmless.

Gallucci also said the commission did not know where it will get the funds to pay for the work, which might cost as little as several tens of millions of dollars or as much as several hundred million dollars.

The magnitude of the effort was suggested by Iraq's official declaration two weeks ago that it has 355 tons of lethal chemicals in bulk storage and 11,131 poison gas weapons. But U.S. government analysts say they believe Iraq is secretly harboring tons of additional chemical agents that the U.N. commission is also responsible for finding and destroying.

Thousands of the Iraqi weapons have been described by Baghdad as buried beneath the contaminated debris of bombed Iraqi storage sites and production factories, a circumstance that U.N. officials say will force ordnance experts to conduct much of their salvage work in awkward protective suits.

The first U.N.-organized inspections of suspected and confirmed Iraqi chemical weapon plants and storage sites are expected to begin next week, even as U.N. officials continue to interrogate Iraq about its holdings of such weapons, the officials said in telephone interviews from U.N. headquarters in New York.

But the inspections by up to 200 experts are likely to last more than a month, forcing a delay in the startup of weapon destruction under a plan to be submitted to the U.N. secretary general in mid-May, they said.

Once the inspections are completed, the special commission is slated to take possession of the Iraqi weapons, they said. Ekeus said he did not anticipate that U.N. troops will be needed but declined to spell out any alternative.

A panel of experts to be appointed later this week will evaluate several different methods of destroying the weapons. Ekeus said open-pit burning may be the quickest and least costly approach, but "the initial indication is that it will not be possible due to environmental and health consequences."

Other experts said burning some of the weapons probably would release sulfur and nitrogen oxides and various acids harmful to human health. Anyone nearby would be advised to wear a gas mask, said Gordon Burck, a senior policy analyst and chemical weapons expert at LAI Corp. in Alexandria.

Another approach would involve commandeering one of the Iraqi chemical weapons production plants and "turning it around to break down the deadly liquids," said Ekeus, who previously was chairman of the U.N. negotiations on a global ban of chemical weapons. But "I don't think that any [plants] survived the bombing," he said.

Officials said i.e. "U.N. instead probably would choose between building a central furnace to incinerate the weapons more safely, and using a number or smaller, portable destruction facilities borrowed from the United States, the Soviet Union or Canada.

The U.S. Army, which has constructed large chemical weapons furnaces in Utah and on a remote Pacific Island, said yesterday that a new mid-sized plant might be constructed and tested within three years for roughly $200 million. "I want to make clear that we're not looking for the responsibility for destroying this stuff," added Army spokesman Joe Padilla in mid-April.

No nation has stepped forward to volunteer territory for construction of such a plant, which independent experts say should be used to destroy chemical arms produced by other Middle Eastern nations under a wider arms control scheme.

Ekeus indicated it would have to be built on Iraqi soil, however. "I doubt highly that we will move the weapons outside of Iraq," he said. Gallucci said the tab for building such a plant might be paid by voluntary contributions from U.N. members or a special fee assessed against all U.N. members, but no plan has yet been developed.

# Iraq Withholding Location of Nuclear Material

By R. Jeffrey Smith
Washington Post Staff Writer

Iraq has told the International Atomic Energy Agency that it relocated some of its nuclear materials during the war to escape allied bombing, but will not disclose the materials' exact whereabouts unless the agency guarantees they will not be destroyed, according to U.S. officials.

The material includes a substantial quantity of highly enriched uranium that Iraq's neighbors and Western governments say eventually could be used to construct at least one nuclear weapon. Baghdad was ordered to surrender the material to the IAEA under a United Nations resolution approved on April 2.

IAEA regulations require that Iraq's declared nuclear materials not be moved unless under international supervision. U.S. officials, who spoke on condition they not be identified, said they considered Iraq's movement of the nuclear fuel to be a violation. The IAEA head-quarters in Vienna could not be reached yesterday for comment.

Many experts had expressed concern about the whereabouts of the highly enriched uranium after U.S. military commanders disclosed that wartime air raids had destroyed two research reactors at the Tuwaitha complex near Baghdad, where the uranium was last seen, without causing any detectable radiation release.

The Iraqi letter, received on Monday at the Vienna IAEA headquarters, contained 13 items under a listing of nuclear materials; of these, six were said by the Iraqis to have been moved within the Tuwaitha complex "for reasons of safety" and four were said to have been moved near Tuwaitha.

The remaining three items, including uranium powder and pellets as well as natural uranium fuel bundles and rods, were listed as having been trapped at locations that were "completely destroyed" in the allied bombing campaign. In one of these cases, the bombardment resulted in what Iraq described as "radiation contamination of the region," according to a U.S. translation of the letter.

U.S. officials said, however, that the 10 items listed as unaffected by the bombing included the bulk of Iraq's highly enriched uranium. The Iraqis promised to provide details of the items' location only if IAEA officials guaranteed their safety from further aerial attack, according to the U.S. translation.

A senior U.S. official said Washington's position was that no such assurance is required, even though another bombing raid would "in practical terms" not occur. He expressed concern that Iraq appeared to be trying to safeguard material that it cannot keep.

State Department spokesman Margaret Tutwiler declined to describe the letter's contents yesterday. But she characterized it as providing "substantial further information" about Iraq's nuclear facilities and materials, as demanded by the United Nations.

An earlier Iraqi letter was criticized by U.S., U.N. and IAEA officials because it omitted any mention of the reactor fuel, which IAEA experts last inspected in November.

But the new letter disclosed the existence of several facilities not previously known by the IAEA, a senior U.S. official said. Included were an "engineering services workshop" and a "mechanical production workshop" that U.S. analysts are now anxious for inspectors to see, he said.

The official also said the letter failed to disclose an additional stockpile of nuclear materials believed held by Iraq that was never subject to IAEA inspection. He said U.S. analysts believe the materials are being hidden by Iraq and will have to be ferreted out in U.N. organized inspections.

# 외 무 부

원  본

종  별 :

번  호 : UNW-1303

일  시 : 91 0520 2010

수  신 : 장 관(국연,중동일,기정)

발  신 : 주 유엔 대사

제  목 : 걸프사태(유엔동향)

1. 금 5.20 사무총장 대변인은 유엔과 이락 양측은 이락 난민구호 관련 유엔경비대(SECURITY GUARDS)배치에 금명간 공식합의할 것이라고 밝혔음.

2. 한편 안보리 휴전결의 (687호)에 의거 사무총장은 이락군비봉제 이행안 (S/22614)을 4.17 자로 안보리에 제출한바, 상세별첨 참조바람. 이락군비봉제위 (SPECIAL COMMISSION) 는 1차로 핵관련 조사반 (반장: D.PERRICOS IAEA검사관)을 이락에 파견한데 이어, 이달중 2차로 화학무기 관련 조사반을 파견예정인 것으로 알려짐.

첨부:1. 사무총장 기자문답내용

2. 사무총장이락군비봉제 이행안

3. IAEA 핵관련이락군비봉제 계획: UNW(F)-219

끝

(대사 노창희-국장)

---

국기국    1차보    중아국    정문국    안기부

PAGE 1                                                    91.05.21    09:43 WG
외신 1과  통제관
0035

---

UNW(F)-219   10520 2010
(국연. 중동익. 기련)

총 10대

Remarks made by the Secretary-General upon entering the Secretariat building on 20 May 1991 at approximately 10 a.m.

Q:     What is the latest on Mr. Bernander's talks in Baghdad?

SG:    Everything is ready for signature. I hope that the agreement or understanding will be signed in the next few hours.

Q:     How big is the UN security force in Iraq?

SG:    So far, it is just a token of 10 men, but the idea is to have up to 400 or 500 men.

Q:     When will they begin arriving?

SG:    I think in about two weeks. Of course, the arrival has to be phased but I hope in about two weeks we will have our full force.

Q:     Is Mr. Bernander in Baghdad for the signature?

SG:    He is in Baghdad.

Q:     This has the full understanding of the Security Council?

SG:    The Security Council is aware of the idea, but now I am going to inform the Security Council of the implementation of the idea.

Q:     Right now, with so few UN guards in Dahuk, is it reasonable to expect the Kurds to start coming back?

SG:    I think they have been well received by the population, but since they are only 10 they are not a deterrent or a guaranteee. Once they see the whole army of guards perhaps they will feel a little more reassured.

Q:     Also, can you tell us about the shipments of food to Iraq, I understand 17 million dollars worth of food is going to Baghdad, could you tell me a little about this?

SG:    We are of course very glad that the international community has reacted so quickly and I think that my people there, Sadruddin Aga Khan from Geneva and Mr. Bernt Bernander will try to to have this food distributed as soon as possible.

****

#UNW-1303
천부묵

10—1

0036

# UNITED NATIONS

## Security Council

Distr.
GENERAL

S/22614
17 May 1991

ORIGINAL: ENGLISH

### Plan for the implementation of relevant parts of section C of Security Council resolution 687 (1991)

### Report of the Secretary-General

### Introduction

1.  The present report is submitted in pursuance of Security Council resolution 687 (1991) of 3 April 1991. In paragraph 9 (b) of that resolution, the Council decided that the Secretary-General, within 45 days of the adoption of the resolution, should develop and submit to it for approval a plan calling for the completion of the tasks enumerated in paragraphs 9 (b) (i to iii) and 10.

2.  For the purpose of developing this plan, consultations were held with appropriate Governments, as called for in paragraphs 9 (b) and 13 of the resolution, and, where appropriate, with the Director General of the International Atomic Energy Agency (IAEA) and the Director-General of the World Health Organization (WHO). Furthermore, in order to assess the information submitted by the Government of Iraq and to assist me in developing the plan for the implementation of the tasks enumerated in section C of the resolution, I set up a Special Commission as described in my report of 18 April 1991 to the Security Council (S/22508), which the Council accepted on 19 April.

3.  I appointed 21 experts as members of the Special Commission. I have requested Ambassador Rolf Ekeus (Sweden) to serve as its Executive Chairman and Dr. Robert Gallucci (United States of America) to serve as its Deputy Executive Chairman. The other members of the Special Commission are as follows: Dr. Paal Aas (Norway), Lieutenant General (ret.) Ken Adachi (Japan), Professor B. N. C. Agu (Nigeria), Lieutenant-Colonel Andrzej Badek (Poland), Professor Bryan C. Barrass (United Kingdom of Great Britain and Northern Ireland), Mr. Peter von Butler (Germany), Colonel Armando Caputo (Italy), Mr. Ronald Cleminson (Canada), Dr. John Gee (Australia), Professor Helmut Hönig (Austria), Mr. B. A. Kuvshinnikov (Union of Soviet Socialist Republics), Dr. A. J. J. Ooms (Netherlands), Dr. Marjatta Rautio (Finland),

91-16170  2993a (E)

/...

10-2

0037

S/22614
English
Page 2

Mr. Michel Saint Mleux (France), Mr. Roberto Sanchez (Venezuela), Lieutenant Colonel B. Simandjuntak (Indonesia), Dr. Miroslav Splino (Czechoslovakia), Mr. Emile Vanden Bemden (Belgium), Dr. Yuan Renfeng (China).

4.    In order to enable the Special Commission as well as IAEA to discharge their responsibilities properly, a number of technical arrangements are being made to facilitate their work.  They include the establishment of a field operations office and a support office.  After consultations with the Governments concerned, the Field Operations Office is being set up in Bahrain.  The Office will become fully operational by the end of May 1991. The Support Office is being established at Baghdad, Iraq.

## I.   THE PLAN

5.    The provisions of section C of resolution 687 (1991) lend themselves to a three-stage implementation procedure:  gathering and assessment of information; disposal of weapons and facilities and all other items specified in paragraphs 8 and 12 of resolution 687 (1991); and monitoring and verification of Iraq's compliance in the future.

### A.   Gathering and assessment of information

6.    The first stage of the plan is of crucial importance for the success of the entire operation.  It requires input from both the Iraqi Government and the Special Commission.  Pursuant to paragraphs 9 (a) and 12, Iraq is responsible for the submission, within fifteen days of the adoption of the resolution, of information on the locations, amounts and types of all items specified in paragraphs 8 and 12, which are to be destroyed, removed or rendered harmless.  The Special Commission, pursuant to paragraphs 9 (b) (i) and 13, is responsible for designating any additional locations of these items in Iraq.  In carrying out the immediate on-site inspections envisaged in paragraphs 9 (b) (i) and 13 of the resolution, the Special Commission and IAEA respectively must retain the right to choose the timing and locations of the inspection.

7.    On 18 and 28 April and 4 May 1991, the Government of Iraq forwarded to the Secretary-General information relating to its chemical and biological weapons and ballistic missiles.  On 18 April, the Government of Iraq also forwarded to the Director General of IAEA information of relevance to the responsibilities entrusted to the Agency as stated in paragraphs 12 and 13 of resolution 687 (1991).  Further information was communicated to the Agency on 27 April.  In communications both to the Secretary-General and the Director General, the Government of Iraq also conveyed its acceptance of on-site inspections as called for in paragraphs 9 (a) and 12.  There has also been a continued exchange of communications between the Special Commission and the Government of Iraq with a view to obtaining additional information and clarifications.

/...

0038

S/22614
English
Page 3

8.    Based on the information received so far from the Iraqi authorities, as
well as taking into account additional locations designated by the Special
Commission, the process of on-site inspections by the Special Commission and
IAEA has been initiated.  In the course of the inspections, the Special
Commission will check the information that has been gathered earlier against
the actual situation in the field (i.e. establishing a database); assess the
magnitude of the task of disposal of weapons and facilities that it will
perform in the second stage of the plan; and determine, with the advice of
WHO, the requirements and modalities for carrying it out.  The Special
Commission is also rendering assistance and cooperation to the Director
General of IAEA in connection with on-site inspections for which the Agency is
responsible.

9.    The on-site inspections to be carried out by both the Special Commission
and IAEA cover a large number of sites with different numbers of facilities at
each site.  For the purpose of ensuring safe access to sites subject to the
measures specified in paragraphs 9 (b), 12 and 13 of resolution 687 (1991),
teams of explosive ordnance disposal (EOD) experts, construction engineers and
security personnel have been engaged to assist the Special Commission and IAEA
in the process of carrying out the on-site inspections.  The safety of all
such personnel is a major consideration.  Detailed arrangements covering these
and related aspects and governing the precise modalities for carrying out the
inspections are embodied in an agreement between the United Nations and the
Government of Iraq.  The volume of work as well as the physical state of the
various objects, installations and facilities subject to inspection, and the
paramount concern regarding the safety of the inspection teams and the local
population, make it difficult to establish, at the present stage, the exact
time frame within which the first stage can be concluded.  Early assessments
of the tasks involved make it possible, nevertheless, to outline the general
framework of the second stage of the plan, which is described below.

## B.    Disposal of weapons and facilities

10.    The main purpose of the second stage of the plan, as specified in
paragraphs 8, 9 and 13 of resolution 687 (1991), is to dispose of weapons,
facilities and all other items specified in paragraphs 8 and 12 of the
resolution.  Owing to the highly different nature of the weapons, material and
facilities involved, separate procedures are envisaged for their actual
disposal, with different teams of experts carrying them out.

11.    Regarding chemical weapons and biological weapons-related items and
facilities, technical modalities are being worked out with a view to ensuring
the complete and safe yielding of possession by Iraq of all items referred to
in paragraph 8 (a) of the resolution, for their subsequent destruction,
removal or rendering them harmless.  Regarding ballistic missiles, procedures

10-4

/...

0039

S/22614
English
Page 4

for the identification and securing of all items referred to in
paragraph 8 (b) of the resolution are being developed with a view to ensuring
the supervision of their complete destruction by Iraq.  The Special Commission
will further assist and cooperate with IAEA in carrying out inspections and in
the destruction, removal or rendering harmless of all items referred to in
paragraph 12 of the resolution.

12.  As far as the disposal process itself is concerned, Iraq will destroy,
under the supervision of the Special Commission, all its missile capabilities,
including launchers, as specified under paragraph 8 (b) of
resolution 687 (1991).  The Special Commission and IAEA respectively, with
appropriate Iraqi assistance, will dispose of all other items specified under
paragraphs 8 (a) and 12 of the same resolution, including missile warheads
fitted with chemical warfare agents.  It should be noted that under the
resolution the Special Commission has the authority to conduct activities
related to inspection, yielding and disposal of the items specified in
paragraph 8 (a) of the resolution and the inspection and disposal of the items
specified in paragraph 8 (b) of the resolution after the expiration of the
45-day period that follows the approval of this plan, if such activities have
not been completed.

### 1. Ballistic missiles

13.  The disposal of ballistic missiles and related items and facilities
raises a relatively smaller number of problems as compared to other types of
weapons and facilities.  In principle, their disposal should not pose any
danger to public safety as it involves a largely mechanical operation.
Consequently, the disposal of missiles and related major parts including
launchers will be carried out in situ and, if possible, it will be done
concomitantly with the initial on-site inspection process.  Those items not
disposed of immediately will be secured, sealed and appropriately documented
for later disposal.  Furthermore, items such as warheads and fuel might be
moved to a special destruction location or facility and disposed of there.

14.  As regards repair and production facilities, many of them appear no
longer operational as a result of the hostilities.  The Special Commission
will ascertain the extent to which these facilities are permanently affected,
with a view to determining what other steps, if any, are necessary to comply
with paragraph 9 (b) (ii) of the resolution.

15.  In order to carry out the responsibilities regarding this category of
weapons and related facilities, the Special Commission will require
individuals with expertise in such fields as launching and guidance systems,
propellants and warheads.  Teams of experts will be needed to conduct both the
on-site inspections and the supervision of the disposal process.  The number
of teams and their exact composition is currently under study.

10-5

/...

0040

S/22614
English
Page 5

## 2. Chemical weapons

16. As regards chemical weapons, in view of the practical problems inherent in their destruction, including possible safety and environmental hazards, the Special Commission, in consultation with WHO, has focused its attention on determining the best methods for their disposal. Taking into account the paramount importance of maintaining acceptable safety standards for the disposal teams and for the local population, the Special Commission will identify and evaluate safe destruction techniques that could be made operable within stringent time-frames.

17. Given the danger chemical weapons represent, their disposal will be initiated only after thorough on-site inspection and assessment of the conditions of stocks and facilities. In this connection, the Special Commission has requested the inspection teams to mark munitions and relevant facilities, to the extent possible, with tamper-indicating devices. In addition, the Special Commission foresees monitoring, between the time of the inspections and the disposal process, by inspectors at relevant locations.

18. The disposal methods will involve neutralization and/or incineration. Movement of chemical weapons and agents will be minimized. In this connection the Special Commission is investigating the use of transportable or mobile destruction equipment. The Special Commission may also consider the possibility of the construction of a destruction facility which would have greater capacity than that offered by transportable or mobile equipment. In this and other options the question of costs will need to be kept under review.

19. As regards research, development, support and manufacturing facilities in connection with chemical weapons, information available to the Special Commission at present suggests that a number of them may have been destroyed as a result of the hostilities. Upon establishing firm data the Special Commission will determine its requirements, both in terms of equipment and human resources, for complying with provisions of paragraph 9 (b) of resolution 687 (1991).

## 3. Biological weapons

20. In the area of biological weapons, it is noted that, in accordance with paragraph 7 of Security Council resolution 687 (1991), Iraq has become a party to the Convention on the Prohibition of the Development, Production and Stockpiling of Bacteriological (Biological) and Toxin Weapons and on Their Destruction. 1/ The Government of Iraq deposited, on 8 April, its instrument of ratification in Moscow.

21. However, as required by the Security Council in its resolution 687 (1991), the Special Commission is seeking to determine whether Iraq possesses any biological weapons-related items that should be disposed of pursuant to the resolution and whether there remains in Iraq a capability to produce such weapons that would also be subject to disposal. In this context,

...

10-6

S/22614
English
Page 6

the Special Commission has brought to the attention of the Government of Iraq
the report of the Ad Hoc Meeting of Scientific and Technical Experts from
States Parties to the Biological Weapons Convention held at Geneva from
31 March to 15 April 1987 and contained in document BWC/CONF.II/EX/2 of
21 April 1987 and has requested the information called for in section II of
that report.

22.  Biological warfare agents can be destroyed through either standard
laboratory equipment or special mobile units.

### 4.  Nuclear weapons-related items

23.  In the area of nuclear-weapons-usable material and related items and
facilities, the Special Commission will assist IAEA in the removal of
weapons-usable material from Iraq and in the disposal of all other relevant
items and facilities covered by resolution 687 (1991), by removal or
destruction as appropriate.

24.  An inspection team, composed of experts from IAEA and the Special
Commission, is currently in Iraq to carry out a first inspection based on
declarations by the Government of Iraq and the designation by the Special
Commission of additional locations.  Further inspections will follow prior to
the disposal of weapons-usable-material and other items subject to
paragraph 12 of resolution 687 (1991).

### C.  Monitoring and verification of compliance

25.  The third stage of the plan represents a long-term operation.  Its main
purpose is to ensure ongoing monitoring and verification of Iraq's compliance
with paragraphs 8, 9, 10 and 12 of resolution 687 (1991).  A detailed plan as
called for in paragraph 10 of resolution 687 (1991), will be submitted to the
Security Council for its approval, subsequent to the establishment of a
complete database.  In developing the plan, the Special Commission will also
take into account the provisions for permitted activities in the framework of
the Biological Weapons Convention and by the monitoring/verification methods
under discussion in the context of a future Convention on the Prohibition of
Chemical Weapons.  With the eventual entry into force of such a Convention,
the inspectorate envisaged in it should at an appropriate time take over the
function of monitoring and verification of compliance in the area of chemical
weapons.

26.  The verification will be conducted through full and effective on-site
inspections including those on short notice.  The inspections will cover, as
appropriate, military bases, production facilities and storage, as well as
research facilities and laboratories.  The frequency of on-site inspections
will vary considerably for each category of weapons, facilities and activities
in question.  It will be contingent on previous findings and also on Iraq's
clear and continuous demonstration of compliance with resolution 687 (1991).

10-7

/...

0042

## II.  GENERAL CONCEPT OF OPERATIONS

27.  The Special Commission, under the guidance of its Executive Chairman, will use a small staff at United Nations Headquarters in New York to prepare detailed plans for field operations in Iraq with regard to all items related to chemical and biological weapons and to ballistic missiles, and together with IAEA with regard to items related to nuclear weapons and nuclear-weapons-usable materials.  The plans will describe the composition of teams of experts, drawn from a number of countries, and their movements and activities in Iraq - whether survey, inspection or disposal.  The teams will assemble for briefing at the field office in Bahrain and move by dedicated aircraft to Baghdad or some other point-of-entry in Iraq.  Vehicles or rotary-winged aircraft will be used to move the teams within Iraq to the sites concerned.  Teams will leave the area via Bahrain following debriefing and initial analysis of any samples or data collected in Iraq.

## Notes

1/    General Assembly resolution 2826 (XXVI).

-----

<u>Enclosure</u>

<u>Plan for the destruction, removal and rendering harmless of
the items specified in paragraph 12 of Security Council
resolution 687 (1991)</u>

<u>Introduction</u>

1.     Paragraph 13 of Security Council resolution 687 (1991) <u>inter alia</u>
requests the Director General of IAEA through the Secretary-General, with the
assistance and cooperation of the Special Commission ... to develop a plan for
submission to the Security Council within 45 days calling for the destruction,
removing or rendering harmless of all items listed in paragraph 12 of the
resolution.

2.     In order to implement the actions required of the Agency pursuant to
paragraphs 12 and 13 of the resolution, the Director General of IAEA
established on 15 April 1991 an action team placed under the direction of an
Agency Deputy Director General and composed of a Deputy Director for
Administration and Management and a Deputy Director for Operations.

3.     The Agency established contact with the Special Commission set up by the
Secretary-General following the approval by the Security Council on
19 April 1991 of the Secretary-General's report submitted to it in document
S/22508.  Assistance and cooperation is being rendered by the Special
Commission and certain modalities for this cooperation have been agreed upon.

<u>Immediate on-site inspection</u>

4.     On 18 April 1991, the Government of Iraq submitted to the Director
General of IAEA a declaration required by paragraph 12 of resolution
687 (1991).  Further information was provided on 27 April 1991.

5.     The first on-site inspection, based on the Iraqi declaration to IAEA and
additional designations by the Special Commission, started on 15 May 1991.
The inspection team on this occasion was headed by a Chief Inspector appointed
by IAEA and consisted of 34 persons, including Agency officials and experts as
well as representatives and other personnel of the Special Commission.  The
team's expertise covers all areas of nuclear technology as well as supporting
specialties such as radiation protection, explosive ordnance disposal,
communications and field security.

<u>The plan</u>

<u>Nuclear-weapons-usable material</u>

6.     Nuclear-weapons-usable material or, as it is referred to in Agency
practice, "direct-use material" <u>a</u>/ cannot be destroyed or rendered harmless in

/...

10-9

0044

S/22615
English
Page 4

Iraq. The Agency will have to take exclusive control of this material for custody and removal from Iraq pursuant to paragraph 12. This is considered t be the foremost task to be undertaken. Known amounts of direct-use material, located in the Tuwaltha area and listed in the Iraqi statement of 27 April 1991, are contained in fresh or irradiated fuel assemblies. Part of this material appears to be stored in accessible conditions. The on-site inspection, which is now under way, is verifying declared quantities and conditions of this material. Further direct-use material, according to the Iraqi declaration, consisting of irradiated fuel assemblies for the IRT 5000 nuclear research reactor, is buried under the rubble of the reactor building. In all probability, a complex and costly decommissioning operation will be needed to render this material accessible for removal and disposal.

7.    Following the preliminary on-site verification now under way of the existence of irradiated direct-use material in the damaged reactor building, it is intended to begin the early removal of easily accessible direct-use material, the decommissioning of the building and the removal of the irradiated fuel assemblies, once their accessibility is achieved.

8.    In the event that any additional sites are designated by the Special Commission under paragraphs 9 (b) (ii) and 13 of resolution 687 (1991) further inspections will be carried out.

9.    The Agency will take custody, through the application of Agency verification, containment and surveillance methods, of the direct-use material in Iraq. Agency safeguards will be applied to all direct-use material removed from Iraq.

10.   Negotiations with countries possessing the technology for the transportation and storage of direct-use material to ascertain their willingness to receive this material are under way. Consideration is being given to various options for the long-term disposal or rendering harmless of this material.

Other items subject to paragraph 12 of resolution 687 (1991)

11.   The declaration of Iraq listed only direct-use material and a yellow-cake production unit. Inspection of sites for other items subject to paragraph 12 of resolution 687 (1991) that may be designated by the Special Commission will aim to determine if such items exist and, if so, to remove, destroy or render them harmless.

12.   Identification of research, development, support or manufacturing facilities and materials relevant or connected to reprocessing of irradiated fuel and isotopic enrichment of uranium will be given priority as they are capable of producing additional direct-use material.

/...

/6—/0

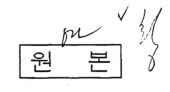

# 외 무 부

종 별 :

번 호 : UNW-1323          일 시 : 91 0522 1800

수 신 : 장 관(국연,중동일,기정)

발 신 : 주 유엔 대사

제 목 : 걸프사태(유엔동향)

안보리 휴전결의 (687호) 에 의거 이락군비 통제를 위한 제 1차 현지조사단 (핵관련 전문가 19개국 총34명)이 5.14-22 이락을 방문한바, 동방문 결과에대한 유엔측 발표내용을 별첨송부함.

    첨부:상기 유엔측발표내용: UNW(F)-222

    끝

    (대사 노창희-국장)

---

국기국    1차보    중아국    정문국    안기부    청와대

# United Nations

## Press Release

UNW(F)-222 /05-22 /80
(국연.중동일 기정) 총 /미

### Department of Public Information • News Coverage Service • New York

IAEA/1161
IK/21
22 May 1991

## EXPERTS COMPLETE FIRST ON-SITE INSPECTION OF IRAQ'S NUCLEAR CAPABILITIES AUTHORIZED BY SECURITY COUNCIL RESOLUTION 687 (1991)

VIENNA, 22 May (IAEA) -- The first team of international experts to visit Iraq under the terms of Security Council cease-fire resolution 687 (1991) of 3 April has just completed its initial work, returning to Vienna.

The International Atomic Energy Agency (IAEA) carried out the first inspection in Iraq from 14 to 22 May with the assistance and cooperation of the Special Commission established under resolution 687. The inspection involved a team of 34 experts, which included nationals from 19 countries.

Security Council resolution 687 (1991) required IAEA to carry out immediate on-site inspection of Iraq's nuclear capabilities based on a declaration by the Government of Iraq and the designation of any additional locations by the Special Commission. Following such initial inspections, the Agency is charged with developing and carrying out a plan for the destruction, removal or rendering harmless of all nuclear-weapons-usable material.

The first inspection covered the main Iraq nuclear research facility at Al Tuwaitha and one additional site in the Baghdad area, which had been designated by the Special Commission. The principal purpose of this inspection was to verify the quantities and conditions of nuclear materials existing at the Al Tuwaitha site as declared by Iraq in its letter of 27 April. At Al Tuwaitha, IAEA took custody from Iraq of nuclear-weapons-usable material and applied Agency verification, containment and surveillance procedures, as required by resolution 687.

During the inspection, the Government of Iraq fully cooperated and complied with all requests of the Agency team. Further inspections will follow, and operations to remove from Iraq all nuclear-weapons-usable materials are being planned.

* **** *

# UNW-1323
첨부물

3141P

0047

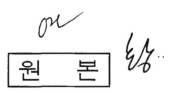

# 외 무 부

원 본

종 별 :

번 호 : UNW-1428                                    일 시 : 91 0530 2100

수 신 : 장 관(국연,중동일,기정)

발 신 : 주 유엔 대사

제 목 : 걸프사태(유엔동향)

　　1. 안보리 휴전결의에 의거 이락군비 통제를 위한 유엔 2차 조사단 (화학무기 전문가 8개 국 35명)이 6.9경부터 이락 방문예정이라고함. 유엔측은 바레인에이락 군비통제를 위한 기지설치를 추진중인 것으로 알려짐.

　　2. 유엔 이락-쿠웨이트 국경획정 위원회는 지난 5.23-24 당지에서 회의를 가진바, 6월 현지조사활동을 마친다음 7월 제네바 유엔사무소에서 본격적인 작업에 들어갈 예정이라고 함. 끝

　　(대사 노창희-국장)

---

국기국 　　1차보 　　중아국 　　외정실 　　안기부

91.05.31    10:40 WG
외신 1과  통제관

0048

# 외 무 부

종 별 :

번 호 : UNW-1470

일 시 : 91 0605 1920

수 신 : 장 관(국연,중동일,기정)

발 신 : 주 유엔대사

제 목 : 걸프사태(안보리)

1.유엔사무총장은 휴전결의(687호 본문 26항)에 의거 이락에 대한 무기류 공급 금지시행계획(안)을 6.2.자로 안보리에 제출한 바, 동주요내용은 다음과 같음.

가.업무관장

1)안보리 661 호 결의에 의거 이미 설치, 운영중인 안보리 이락 제재위원회가 본건 무기류(관련기술 및 인력포함)공급차단 업무도 관장

2)동 업무관련 제재위원회는 이락 군비통제특위, IAEA 와 긴밀히 협조

3)제재위원회는 본건 관련 안보리에 90 일마다 보고

나.국별조치

1)각국( ALL STATES) 은 필요한 국내조치 의무

2)안보리의 본계획 승인후 45일내 각국은 국내조치 내용 사무총장에게 통보

2.안보리의 관련 토의동향은 추보위계임.

첨부:상기계획(안): UNW(F)-246

끝

(대사 노창희-국장)

---

국기국    1차보    중아국    외정실    안기부

UNW(冊)-246  10605  1920
(국연·중동일·기정)                  총 50매

<u>Annex</u>

<u>Draft guidelines to facilitate full international
implementation of paragraphs 24, 25 and 27 of
Security Council resolution 687 (1991)</u>

INTRODUCTION

1.   The present guidelines have been developed in accordance with
paragraph 26 of Security Council resolution 687 (1991), to facilitate full
international implementation of paragraphs 24, 25 and 27 of that resolution.

I.   CATEGORIES OF PROHIBITED ITEMS AND ACTIVITIES

2.   For the purpose of the present guidelines, the items and activities
proscribed are those referred to in paragraph 24, in conjunction with
paragraphs 8 and 12, of resolution 687 (1991) and are the following:

(a)   Arms and related <u>matériel</u> of all types, specifically including the
sale or transfer through other means of:

(i)   All forms of conventional weapons and military equipment, including
for paramilitary forces, and spare parts and components and their
means of production, for such equipment;

(ii)   All chemical and biological weapons and all stocks or agents and all
related subsystems and components;

(iii)   All ballistic missiles with a range greater than 150 kilometres and
related major parts;

(iv)   Nuclear weapons or nuclear-weapons-usable material or any subsystems
or components;

(b)   All research, development, support and manufacturing facilities for
the items as specified and defined in paragraphs 8 (a) and 12 of resolution
687 (1991);

(c)   Repair and production facilities for all ballistic missiles with a
range greater than 150 kilometres and related major parts;

(d)   Technology under licensing or other transfer arrangements used in
the production, utilization or stockpiling of items as specified in
paragraphs 24 (a), 8 and 12 of resolution 687 (1991);

(e)   Personnel or materials for training or technical support services
relating to the design, development, manufacture, use, maintenance or support
of items as specified in paragraphs 24 (a), 8 and 12 of resolution 687 (1991).

/...

∴ UNW-147°
첨부필

5 — 1

0050

## II.  UNITED NATIONS MECHANISM FOR MONITORING THE ARMS
## AND RELATED SANCTIONS

3.    The Committee established by resolution 661 (1990) concerning the
situation between Iraq and Kuwait (hereinafter referred to as "the Committee")
will be the organ of the Security Council responsible for monitoring the
prohibitions against the sale or supply of arms to Iraq and related sanctions
established in paragraph 24 of resolution 687 (1991) (hereinafter referred to
as "arms and related sanctions").  The Committee will carry out its functions
in accordance with the mandate provided in resolutions 661 (1990), 665 (1990)
and 670 (1990) in so far as it relates to the items proscribed under
paragraph 24 of resolution 687 (1991).

4.    The Committee will closely cooperate and coordinate its activities with
any present and future bodies that will, pursuant to paragraphs 10 and 13 of
resolution 687 (1991), be responsible for the monitoring and verification of
Iraq's compliance with the obligations set forth in paragraphs 10 and 12 of
that resolution, in so far as they concern the acquisition of the items
referred to in those paragraphs.  The bodies referred to above will therefore
have access to the Committee and will draw its attention to any problems that
they may encounter in pursuing their mandate.

5.    In discharging its tasks as regards the items referred to in
paragraphs 8 (a) and 12 of resolution 687 (1991), the Committee will work in
close cooperation with the Special Commission established under paragraph 9 of
the resolution and with the International Atomic Energy Agency.  In carrying
out its work, the Committee will also be able to make use of any expertise or
information relevant to its functions available elsewhere within the United
Nations system.

6.    For the purposes of the present guidelines, the functions of the
Committee will be the following:

     (a)  To meet at regular intervals to examine reports submitted by the
Secretary-General on the implementation of the relevant resolutions;

     (b)  To provide guidance to States and to international organizations,
either upon their request or at its own initiative, on matters concerning the
implementation of paragraph 24 of resolution 687 (1991), inter alia, through
the elaboration, as necessary, of relevant criteria;

     (c)  To reach, in connection with subparagraph (b) above, when needed,
agreed interpretations of items falling within the specified categories of
proscribed items and activities;

     (d)  To seek information and maintain contact with States, international
organizations and those non-governmental organizations whose activities and/or
expertise are likely to promote strict implementation of the arms and related
sanctions against Iraq;

/...

5 - 2

0051

S/22660
English
Page 6

(e) To bring to the attention of the States and international organizations concerned information reported to it of alleged violations of the arms and related sanctions against Iraq for appropriate action by those States and international organizations;

(f) To report at 90-day intervals to the Security Council on the implementation of the arms and related sanctions against Iraq contained in the relevant resolutions.

### III. PRINCIPLES OF IMPLEMENTATION

7. The actual implementation of the arms and related sanctions against Iraq will be effected at three levels: by all States, by international organizations and through intergovernmental cooperation. States and international organizations are called upon to act strictly in accordance with the arms and related sanctions, notwithstanding the existence of any contracts, agreements, licences or any other arrangements.

### A. States

8. All States should report to the Secretary-General within 45 days of the approval by the Security Council of the present guidelines on the measures they have instituted for meeting the obligations set out in paragraph 24 of resolution 687 (1991).

9. All States should ensure the institution or maintenance of national controls, procedures and other measures consistent with the present guidelines as may be necessary to ensure compliance with the terms of paragraph 24 of resolution 687 (1991). On that basis, States should ensure that these measures:

(a) Prevent any circumvention of the arms and related sanctions against Iraq, including but not limited to direct circumvention, indirect or clandestine circumvention, and circumvention through subcontracts to companies within the State itself or in other States;

(b) Prohibit the export to Iraq of those dual-purpose or multi-purpose items that States may have reason to believe will be used for military purposes;

(c) Ensure against the provision of any technology, research, personnel or materials for training or technical support services relating to the production, utilization, stockpiling, design, development, manufacture, use, maintenance or support for any of the items as described in paragraph 2 of the present guidelines;

(d) Require that the sale, licensing or other contracts with States or foreign companies contain end-user transfer assurances that ensure no

5-3

/...

0052

transfer, retransfer, transshipment or servicing to Iraq or to individuals or
bodies inside Iraq or to individuals or bodies outside Iraq acting for the
benefit of Iraq or of individuals or bodies inside Iraq of any of the items
described in paragraph 2 of the present guidelines;

(e) Require from exporters and other commercial intermediaries a
declaration that the items for export described in paragraph 2 of the present
guidelines are not destined for Iraq directly or through third-party
arrangements;

(f) Provide for legal powers to inspect documents and goods and to
detain and seize goods where appropriate;

(g) Impose appropriate penalties for non-compliance in their territories
and by their nationals elsewhere, and to notify the Committee of all incidents
of such non-compliance.

10. Nothing in the present guidelines will preclude any State or group of
States from adopting further measures aimed at achieving effective
implementation of the arms and related sanctions against Iraq, in accordance
with the relevant provisions of resolution 687 (1991).

11. States should ensure that the provisions of the national measures
instituted by them are adequately publicized and disseminated within their
territories and among their nationals elsewhere, particularly to arms
technology developers, producers, traders and exporters and to the transport
sector. In implementing the present guidelines, States should pay particular
attention to companies known to have been involved in illegal arms procurement
activities on behalf of Iraq.

12. States are requested to report to the Committee any information that may
come to their attention relating to possible violations of the arms and
related sanctions against Iraq committed by other States or foreign
nationals. In this regard, States are reminded of their duties under
paragraph 7 of resolution 661 (1990) to cooperate fully with the Committee in
the fulfilment of its task, including supplying such information as may be
sought by the Committee.

13. States ought to consult the Committee on the question whether certain
items fall within the provisions of paragraph 24 of resolution 687 (1991), as
well as in cases relating to dual-use or multiple-use items, that is to say,
items meant for civilian use but with potential for diversion or conversion to
military use.

B. International organizations

14. In accordance with paragraphs 25 and 27 of resolution 687 (1991)
international organizations should take all appropriate steps to assist in
ensuring full compliance with the arms and related sanctions against Iraq.

5 - 4                                                              /...

0053

S/22660
English
Page 8

including providing to the Committee any relevant information that may come to
their attention.

15.   International organizations having any dealings with, or activities in,
Iraq should carefully review their programmes to make sure that they do not
facilitate any of the activities prohibited under paragraph 24 of resolution
687 (1991).  Paragraph 13 above shall also apply to international
organizations.

### C.   Intergovernmental cooperation

16.   States are encouraged to cooperate with each other bilaterally or within
the framework of existing regional or other appropriate intergovernmental
organizations or through other appropriate intergovernmental arrangements in
the implementation of the arms and related sanctions against Iraq.  Such
cooperation would be particularly useful in matters, among others, of
verification of the origin and destination of the items specified in
paragraph 24 of resolution 687 (1991), as well as in the exchange of
documentary evidence relating thereto.

### IV.   REVIEW OF THE GUIDELINES

17.   Taking into account Iraq's compliance with resolution 687 (1991), the
general progress towards the control of armaments in the region, information
received from States and international organizations and from the Committee,
the Security Council may wish to review the guidelines at the same time as its
regular reviews of paragraphs 22, 23, 24 and 25 of resolution 687 (1991), as
set out in paragraph 28 of the same resolution, that is to say, with the first
review being undertaken 120 days after the adoption of that resolution.

18.   The Security Council may also wish to consider, in the light of any
comments or reports that the Committee may make to it, what further action may
be necessary to ensure the implementation of the arms and related sanctions
against Iraq.

-----

5-5

0054

# 외 무 부

종 별 :

번 호 : UNW-1527　　　　　　　　　　　일 시 : 91 0611 1830

수 신 : 장 관(국연,중동일,기정)

발 신 : 주 유엔 대사

제 목 : 걸프사태(안보리)

　　1. 대이락 경제제재 완화문제 정기심사 (휴전결의본문 21항)

　　가. 금 6.11 안보리 비공식 협의에서 본건관련 토의가 있었으나, 특기할 진전은 없었다고함.

　　나. 미, 영, 불은 제재완화에 부정적인 입장을 나타냈으며, 소련은 일부완화 문제에 관심을 보인것으로 알려짐. 본건관련 사무총장 보고서 요청문제도 제기되었으며 , 예멘, 쿠바는 공식회의 소집희망을 시사하였다고함.

　　2. 이락 군비통제 문제

　　가. 사무총장의 본건시행안 (UNW-1303) 승인을 위한 안보리 결의안 교섭이 현재 진행 중인바, 동 결의안에는 관련 경비의 이락부담 원칙, 회원국에 대한 기여금등 협조요청이 포함될것이라고함.

　　나. 상기 이락 경비부담원칙과 관련 6.9.자 사무총장앞 서한 (S/22682) 에서 이락측은 유엔주관하의 자국화학무기 폐기경비를 부담할수없다는 입장을 표명함. (유엔 감시하에 자국이 자체적으로 폐기하는 대안제시)

　　3. 이락 남부 쉬아파 주민 공격

　　이락 정부군이 이락남부 쉬아파 주민을 공격하고 있다고 주장하는 이란측 서한이 유엔에 접수된것으로 알려진바 (6.11. 현재 미배포), 이와관련 사무총장 대변인은 이란측 주장이 아직확인되지않고 있다고 금일 논평하였음. 끝

　　(대사 노창희-국장)

---

국기국　　1차보　　중아국　　외정실　　분석관　　정와대　　안기부

외   무   부

원   본

종   별 :

번   호 : UNW-1566                             일   시 : 91 0617 1930

수   신 : 장 관(국연,중동일,기정)

발   신 : 주 유엔 대사

제   목 : 안보리회의(걸프사태)

연: UNW-1470,1527,1550

1. 안보리는 금 6.17 공식회의 (2994 차 회의)를 갖고 연호 이락 특정무기 폐기
이행계획, 대이락 무기류 공급금지 시행안을 표결결과 만장일치로 채택하였음.

가. 이락 특정무기폐기이행계획 (S/22684)( 결의699 호)

나. 대이락 무기류 공급금지 시행안 (S/22698)(결의 700 호)

2. 금일 회의시 표결전및 표결후 각국 발언요지는 다음과 같음.

가. 표결전발언

이락만이 표결전 발언한바, 이락의 휴전결의 이행실적을 설명하고
유엔주관하의자국 화학무기 폐기의 경비를 부담할수 없다는 입장표명
(S/22682,22687,22689 참조)

나. 표결후 발언 (예멘,쿠바)

1) 예멘은 이락군비제한이 중동지역전체 수준의 군비통제로 이어져야 함을 강조하고
(이스라엘군비문제, 군사적 불균형우려), 결의 699 호 본문 4항의 이락경비 부담의
부당성제기 (무기파괴의 강제성, 이락 경제난)

2) 쿠바는 결의 699호 관련 본건무기 폐기추진 일정불명, 이락의 경비부담
능력의문, 회원국의 재정지원확보 불투명, 군비통제의선별시행 (이스라엘 거명)의
문제를 제기 하였으며, 결의 700 호에 관해서는 무기류 공급금지 업무를 안보리의
대이락 경제제제 위원회가 맡는것이 적절치 못하다는 입장을 표명

3. 상기 회의에는 유럽및 아프리카순방에서 금일 귀임한 케야르 유엔 사무총장도
참석하였음.

첨부:1. 안보리결의 699 및 700 호 : UNW(F)-265

끝 ( 대사 - 국장 )

| 국기국 | 1차보 | 중아국 | 외정실 | 분석관 | 청와대 | 안기부 |
|--------|-------|--------|--------|--------|--------|--------|

PAGE 1                                              91.06.18   09:36 WG

외신 1과   통제관

0056

418   걸프 사태 유엔안전보장이사회 동향 5

UNITED
NATIONS

## Security Council

PROVISIONAL

S/22686
10 June 1991

ORIGINAL: ENGLISH

France, Union of Soviet Socialist Republics, United Kingdom of
Great Britain and Northern Ireland and United States of America:
draft resolution

The Security Council,

Recalling its resolution 687 (1991),

Taking note of the report of the Secretary-General of 17 May 1991 (S/22614),
submitted to it in pursuance of paragraph 9 (b) of resolution 687 (1991),

Also taking note of the Secretary-General's note of 17 May 1991 (S/22615),
transmitting to the Council the letter addressed to him under paragraph 13 of the
resolution by the Director-General of the International Atomic Energy Agency (IAEA),

Acting under Chapter VII of the Charter,

1. Approves the plan contained in the report of the Secretary-General;

2. Confirms that the Special Commission and the IAEA have the authority to
conduct activities under section C of resolution 687 (1991), for the purpose of the
destruction, removal or rendering harmless of the items specified in paragraphs 8
and 12 of that resolution, after the 45-day period following the approval of this
plan until such activities have been completed;

3. Requests the Secretary-General to submit to the Security Council progress
reports on the implementation of the plan referred to in paragraph 1 every six
months after the adoption of this resolution;

4. Decides to encourage the maximum assistance, in cash and in kind, from
all Member States to ensure that activities under section C of resolution 687 (1991)
are undertaken effectively and expeditiously; further decides, however, that the
Government of Iraq shall be liable for the full costs of carrying out the tasks
authorized by section C; and requests the Secretary-General to submit to the
Council within 30 days for approval recommendations as to the most effective means
by which Iraq's obligations in this respect may be fulfilled.

3304E

0057

**S**

**Security Council**

PROVISIONAL

S/22698
12 June 1991

ORIGINAL: ENGLISH

<u>Belgium, France, Union of Soviet Socialist Republics,
United Kingdom of Great Britain and Northern Ireland
and United States of America:  draft resolution</u>

The Security Council,

    <u>Recalling</u> its resolutions 661 (1990) of 6 August 1990, 665 (1990) of
25 August 1990, 670 (1990) of 25 September 1990 and 687 (1991) of 3 April 1991,

    <u>Taking note</u> of the Secretary-General's report of 2 June 1991 (S/22660)
submitted pursuant to paragraph 26 of resolution 687 (1991),

    <u>Acting</u> under Chapter VII of the Charter of the United Nations,

    1.    <u>Expresses its appreciation</u> to the Secretary-General for his report of
2 June 1991 (S/22660);

    2.    <u>Approves</u> the Guidelines to Facilitate Full International Implementation
of paragraphs 24, 25 and 27 of Security Council resolution 687 (1991), annexed to
the report of the Secretary-General (S/22660);

    3.    <u>Reiterates</u> its call upon all States and international organizations to
act in a manner consistent with the Guidelines;

    4.    <u>Requests</u> all States, in accordance with paragraph 8 of the Guidelines, to
report to the Secretary-General within 45 days on the measures they have instituted
for meeting the obligations set out in paragraph 24 of resolution 687 (1991);

    5.    <u>Entrusts</u> the Committee established under resolution 661 (1990) concerning
the situation between Iraq and Kuwait with the responsibility, under the
Guidelines, for monitoring the prohibitions against the sale or supply of arms to
Iraq and related sanctions established in paragraph 24 of resolution 687 (1991);

    6.    <u>Decides</u> to remain seized of the matter and to review the Guidelines at
the same time as it reviews paragraphs 22, 23, 24 and 25 of resolution 687 (1991)
as set out in paragraph 28 thereof.

-----

3318E                                        2 - 2

17 June 1991

PRESS BRIEFING BY COORDINATOR OF RETURN OF KUWAITI PROPERTY FROM IRAQ


    J. Richard Foran, Acting Under-Secretary-General for Administration and
Management and Assistant Secretary-General for General Services, told
correspondents at a press briefing last Friday, 14 June, that his mandate
stemmed from an exchange of letters between the Secretary-General and the
Security Council in March.  At that time, following the adoption of Security
Council resolution 686, the Council had indicated to the Secretary-General
that the members of the Council felt the Secretary-General could assist in
developing the modalities for the return of property from Iraq to Kuwait.  The
Secretary-General had then designated Mr. Foran to coordinate the return of
the items in question.

    He reviewed the relevant Council resolutions and said he had been
receiving lists of property from Kuwait which had been forwarded to Iraq for
comment.  He had been to the region in May, accompanied by Hans Glittenberg,
head of administration at the United Nations Office in Vienna; Milad Saliba,
head of general services at the Economic and Social Commission for Western
Asia (ESCWA); and Harbachan Singh, head of transportation at Headquarters.
They had spent a month in the area during which time they had arranged to have
a Kuwaiti 727 airplane transferred to Kuwait Airways from Iraqi Airways.  The
team had also gone to Baghdad and Kuwait to meet with officials concerned with
the properties.

    He said the Kuwaitis had given priority to the categories of gold, coins
and bank-notes; museum pieces; the national library; and civilian aircraft and
airplane spare parts.  On the basis of proposals he had made to both the
Iraqis and the Kuwaitis, they had, as of yesterday, agreed on the general
modalities.  Mr. Glittenberg would return to the region in a week or so to
work out details of the arrangement.  Mr.Foran would follow approximately a
week later to oversee the the return of gold, bank-notes and coins, as well as
aircraft and spare parts.

    In response to a question he said the goods he had referred to were ready
now to be transferred and had been so for a month, but logistics and
transportation had to be worked out.  There would be a monitoring system at
the time of transfer to ensure accurate records of the details.  The transfer
of the gold would take place in Ar'Ar, Saudi Arabia, the area where the
prisoners were being exchanged, about 60 kilometres south of the Iraqi border
and 400 kilometres west of Kuwait.  The arrangements between the Kuwaiti and
Saudi Governments were complicated and based on proposals made by Mr. Foran to
ensure that the transfer took place under United Nations auspices.  Both sides
had agreed on the amount of gold in question -- 3,216 bricks of gold -- and
both wanted to have the gold weighed.  Thus the agreement included a
professionally executed joint weigh-in.

    Responding to a question, he said he did not deal with the value of the
property.  His function was to assist in its return.  The question of value
would come under claims and compensation.

(more)

3193B

0059

Other categories of properties would come from the Kuwaiti Ministries. The Defence Ministry had submitted a list that included military aircraft and other vehicles. He had also received lists from the Oil Ministry which referred to equipment, furnishings and vehicles. Lists from the libraries were also expected.

A correspondent asked what had happened to the "tens of thousands of automobiles and fridgidaires". Mr. Foran said he had not yet received lists of those items.

Was it true that Iraq had offered to return Kuwaiti property at two points in Jordan but that Kuwait had refused to receive the property in those locations? a correspondent asked. Mr. Foran said that was not true. The Kuwaitis had preferred Ar'Ar for the transfer while the Iraqis preferred Amman and Safwan. He had recommended that the transfer of the remaining civilian aircraft and spare parts be carried out by plane. That would require permission from the Sanctions Committee.

A correspondent said there were weekly letters stating that Iraq had not fulfilled its obligations under Council resolutions to return the property. Some of the Council members had agreed with Kuwait on that issue but what Mr. Foran seemed to be saying was that much of it was a question of logistics. Was he proceeding category by category without any opposition from Iraq? she asked. Mr. Foran said the situation in the region was far from normal. The difficulty in Baghdad was primarily one of communications. There had been many understandable delays. In addition, there had been some points of difference as to where the transfer would take place. He thought things had been accomplished in a reasonable amount of time.

In response to another question he said he did not see it as non-compliance to Security Council 687 and other resolutions although the compliance might not be as swift as a number of people would like.

Asked if he had any information on the report that thousands of Kuwaiti art treasures were available in the international art market, Mr. Foran said no. He had examined and had been able to identify items taken from the national museum and from the home of Sheik Nasser Al-Sabah. Those items had been kept separate.

Did that mean that the "looting of Kuwait was an organized effort?" a correspondent asked. Mr. Foran replied that he was not an expert in looting. His contribution was to assist in getting the items back. He had made a point in his discussions with the parties involved to concentrate solely on what had happened between August 1990 and now.

Asked if the looted property in Iraq was being held in one place, he answered no. In reply to other questions he said the museum pieces were being held in the National Museum of Iraq. The National Library was also in the National Museum. Allegedly 124,000 volumes were being held. They had been professionally packed and were ready to be returned. The lists from the university libraries and a number of other libraries had yet to be documented and submitted.

Asked if there were any major areas of discrepancy between the Kuwaitis and the Iraqis on the return of the property, Mr. Foran said that while it was too early to tell, there had been no discrepancy on the gold. There had, however, been a discrepancy on the bank-notes.

0060

* *** *

# Security Council

Distr.
GENERAL

S/RES/699 (1991)
17 June 1991

RESOLUTION 699 (1991)

Adopted by the Security Council at its 2994th meeting,
on 17 June 1991

The Security Council,

Recalling its resolution 687 (1991),

Taking note of the report of the Secretary-General of 17 May 1991
(S/22614), submitted to it in pursuance of paragraph 9 (b) of resolution
687 (1991),

Also taking note of the Secretary-General's note of 17 May 1991
(S/22615), transmitting to the Council the letter addressed to him under
paragraph 13 of the resolution by the Director-General of the International
Atomic Energy Agency (IAEA),

Acting under Chapter VII of the Charter,

1. Approves the plan contained in the report of the Secretary-General;

2. Confirms that the Special Commission and the IAEA have the authority
to conduct activities under section C of resolution 687 (1991), for the
purpose of the destruction, removal or rendering harmless of the items
specified in paragraphs 8 and 12 of that resolution, after the 45-day period
following the approval of this plan until such activities have been completed;

3. Requests the Secretary-General to submit to the Security Council
progress reports on the implementation of the plan referred to in paragraph 1
every six months after the adoption of this resolution;

4. Decides to encourage the maximum assistance, in cash and in kind,
from all Member States to ensure that activities under section C of resolution
687 (1991) are undertaken effectively and expeditiously; further decides,

91-19968  3477Z (E)

/...

0061

however, that the Government of Iraq shall be liable for the full costs of carrying out the tasks authorized by section C; and requests the Secretary-General to submit to the Council within 30 days for approval recommendations as to the most effective means by which Iraq's obligations in this respect may be fulfilled.

-----

0062

## Security Council

Distr.
GENERAL

S/RES/700 (1991)
17 June 1991

RESOLUTION 700 (1991)

<u>Adopted by the Security Council at its 2994th meeting,
on 17 June 1991</u>

<u>The Security Council</u>,

<u>Recalling</u> its resolutions 661 (1990) of 6 August 1990, 665 (1990) of 25 August 1990, 670 (1990) of 25 September 1990 and 687 (1991) of 3 April 1991,

<u>Taking note</u> of the Secretary-General's report of 2 June 1991 (S/22660) submitted pursuant to paragraph 26 of resolution 687 (1991),

<u>Acting</u> under Chapter VII of the Charter of the United Nations,

1.    <u>Expresses its appreciation</u> to the Secretary-General for his report of 2 June 1991 (S/22660);

2.    <u>Approves</u> the Guidelines to Facilitate Full International Implementation of paragraphs 24, 25 and 27 of Security Council resolution 687 (1991), annexed to the report of the Secretary-General (S/22660);

3.    <u>Reiterates</u> its call upon all States and international organizations to act in a manner consistent with the Guidelines;

4.    <u>Requests</u> all States, in accordance with paragraph 8 of the Guidelines, to report to the Secretary-General <u>within 45 days</u> on the measures they have instituted for meeting the obligations set out in paragraph 24 of resolution 687 (1991);

5.    <u>Entrusts</u> the Committee established under resolution 661 (1990) concerning the situation between Iraq and Kuwait with the responsibility, under the Guidelines, for monitoring the prohibitions against the sale or supply of arms to Iraq and related sanctions established in paragraph 24 of resolution 687 (1991);

6.    <u>Decides</u> to remain seized of the matter and to review the Guidelines at the same time as it reviews paragraphs 22, 23, 24 and 25 of resolution 687 (1991) as set out in paragraph 28 thereof.

-----

91-19974   3480Z (E)

0063

# 외 무 부

종 별 :

번 호 : UNW-1566                                              일 시 : 91 0617 1930

수 신 : 장 관(국연,중동일,기정)

발 신 : 주 유엔 대사

제 목 : 안보리회의(걸프사태)

연: UNW-1470,1527,1550

1. 안보리는 금 6.17 공식회의 (2994 차 회의)를 갖고 연호 이락 특정무기 폐기 이행계획, 대이락 무기류 공급금지 시행안을 표결결과 만장일치로 채택하였음.

　　가. 이락 특정무기폐기이행계획 (S/22684)( 결의699 호)

　　나. 대이락 무기류 공급금지 시행안 (S/22698)(결의 700 호)

2. 금일 회의시 표결전및 표결후 각국 발언요지는 다음과 같음.

　　가. 표결전발언

이락만이 표결전 발언한바, 이락의 휴전결의 이행실적을 설명하고 유엔주관하의자국 화학무기 폐기의 경비를 부담할수 없다는 입장표명 (S/22682,22687,22689 참조)

　　나. 표결후 발언 (예멘,쿠바)

1) 예멘은 이락군비제한이 중동지역전체 수준의 군비통제로 이어져야 함을 강조하고 (이스라엘군비문제, 군사적 불균형우려), 결의 699 호 본문 4항의 이락경비 부담의 부당성제기 (무기파괴의 강제성, 이락 경제난)

2) 쿠바는 결의 699호 관련 본건무기 폐기추진 일정불명, 이락의 경비부담 능력의문, 회원국의 재정지원확보 불투명, 군비통제의선별시행 (이스라엘 거명)의 문제를 제기 하였으며, 결의 700 호에 관해서는 무기류 공급금지 업무를 안보리의 대이락 경제제제 위원회가 맡는것이 적절치 못하다는 입장을 표명

3. 상기 회의에는 유럽및 아프리카순방에서 금일 귀임한 케야르 유엔 사무총장도 참석하였음.

첨부:1. 안보리결의 699 및 700 호 : UNW(F)-265

끝( 대사 -국장)

국기국　　1차보　　　중아국　　외정실　　　분석관　　　청와대　　　안기부

**Security Council**

PROVISIONAL

S/22686
10 June 1991

ORIGINAL: ENGLISH

**France, Union of Soviet Socialist Republics, United Kingdom of Great Britain and Northern Ireland and United States of America: draft resolution**

The Security Council,

Recalling its resolution 687 (1991),

Taking note of the report of the Secretary-General of 17 May 1991 (S/22614), submitted to it in pursuance of paragraph 9 (b) of resolution 687 (1991),

Also taking note of the Secretary-General's note of 17 May 1991 (S/22615), transmitting to the Council the letter addressed to him under paragraph 13 of the resolution by the Director-General of the International Atomic Energy Agency (IAEA),

Acting under Chapter VII of the Charter,

1.    Approves the plan contained in the report of the Secretary-General;

2.    Confirms that the Special Commission and the IAEA have the authority to conduct activities under section C of resolution 687 (1991), for the purpose of the destruction, removal or rendering harmless of the items specified in paragraphs 8 and 12 of that resolution, after the 45-day period following the approval of this plan until such activities have been completed;

3.    Requests the Secretary-General to submit to the Security Council progress reports on the implementation of the plan referred to in paragraph 1 every six months after the adoption of this resolution;

4.    Decides to encourage the maximum assistance, in cash and in kind, from all Member States to ensure that activities under section C of resolution 687 (1991) are undertaken effectively and expeditiously; further decides, however, that the Government of Iraq shall be liable for the full costs of carrying out the tasks authorized by section C; and requests the Secretary-General to submit to the Council within 30 days for approval recommendations as to the most effective means by which Iraq's obligations in this respect may be fulfilled.

3304E    #UNW-1566
첨부물          2-1

0065

# Security Council

PROVISIONAL

S/22698
12 June 1991

ORIGINAL: ENGLISH

**Belgium, France, Union of Soviet Socialist Republics,
United Kingdom of Great Britain and Northern Ireland
and United States of America: draft resolution**

The Security Council,

Recalling its resolutions 661 (1990) of 6 August 1990, 665 (1990) of 25 August 1990, 670 (1990) of 25 September 1990 and 687 (1991) of 3 April 1991,

Taking note of the Secretary-General's report of 2 June 1991 (S/22660) submitted pursuant to paragraph 26 of resolution 687 (1991);

Acting under Chapter VII of the Charter of the United Nations,

1. Expresses its appreciation to the Secretary-General for his report of 2 June 1991 (S/22660);

2. Approves the Guidelines to Facilitate Full International Implementation of paragraphs 24, 25 and 27 of Security Council resolution 687 (1991), annexed to the report of the Secretary-General (S/22660);

3. Reiterates its call upon all States and international organizations to act in a manner consistent with the Guidelines;

4. Requests all States, in accordance with paragraph 8 of the Guidelines, to report to the Secretary-General within 45 days on the measures they have instituted for meeting the obligations set out in paragraph 24 of resolution 687 (1991);

5. Entrusts the Committee established under resolution 661 (1990) concerning the situation between Iraq and Kuwait with the responsibility, under the Guidelines, for monitoring the prohibitions against the sale or supply of arms to Iraq and related sanctions established in paragraph 24 of resolution 687 (1991);

6. Decides to remain seized of the matter and to review the Guidelines at the same time as it reviews paragraphs 22, 23, 24 and 25 of resolution 687 (1991) as set out in paragraph 28 thereof.

-----

3318E

2 - 2

0066

| | 분류번호 | 보존기간 |
|---|---|---|
| | | |

# 발 신 전 보

번    호 :   WUN-1731    910619 1431 ED    종별 :

수    신 : 주   유엔   대사. 총영사/

발    신 : 장 관 (국기)

제    목 : IAEA 특별사찰

1. 주 오스트리아 대사 보고에 의하면 IAEA는 유엔안보리 결의 687에 의거 91.
5.14-22간 이라크의 핵시설에 대한 특별사찰(Special Inspection)을 실시하였다 하는
바, 유엔 사무국에 제출된 동 사찰 결과 보고서를 구득 송부바람.

2. 또한 6.15자 뉴욕타임즈 보도에 의하면 이라크가 핵무기 원료 및 생화학
무기의 보유량을 실제보다 줄여서 허위 신고했다는 (최근 망명) 이라크 핵과학자의
증언을 토대로 유엔이 6월말 핵전문가들을 이라크에 보내 정밀사찰을 벌일 예정이라
하는 바, 이와관련 사항에 대해서도 파악 보고 바람.

3. 망명 이라크 학자에 의하면 이라크는 91.4 유엔 안보리에 신고한 45Kg보다
40Kg의 고농축 우라늄을 더 갖고 있으며 핵 개발 연구센터 8개소중 3개소만 걸프전시
파괴되었고 나머지는 지하 비밀장소에 그대로 남아있다고 함을 참고바람.    끝.

(국제기구조약국장  문동석)

일반문서로 재분류(1991. 12. 11)

검토필(1991. 6. 30.)

| | 보 안<br>통 제 | |
|---|---|---|

| 앙<br>고<br>재 | 91<br>년<br>6<br>월<br>19<br>일 | 국<br>제<br>기<br>구<br>과 | 기안자<br>성 명 | 과 장 | 국 장 | 차 관 | 장 관 | | 외신과통제 |
|---|---|---|---|---|---|---|---|---|---|
| | | | 신종영 | | | | | | |

0067

외 무 부

종 별 :

번 호 : UNW-1588

일 시 : 91 0619 1900

수 신 : 장관(국기,국연,중동일,기정)

발 신 : 주 유엔 대사

제 목 : IAEA 사찰(이락)

대:WUN-1731

연:UNW-1303,1323

1. 대호 사찰(91.5.14-22)관련 사항은 연호 참조바람.

2. 원참사관이 유엔 이락군비통제 특위 M.RYAN 담당관에 알아본바에 의하면, 본건사찰 보고서는 IAEA 이사회, 유엔사무총장 및 동 특위에 제출될 예정이나현재 정식 보고서 작성이 완료되지 않았다고함.(IAEA 실무진이 작성중)

3. 또한 동 담당관에 의하면, IAEA 전문가들(20 여명)이 6.22 부터 약 일주일간 이락방문을 추진중이라고함. 동 방문은 특위측에 입수된 새로운 정보(대호 제보와의 관련시사)에 따른 것이라고 하며, 핵사찰 활동일정과 아울러 이락외상과의 면담도 주선중에 있다고함. 이와 별도로 당초예정되었던 7 월 핵사찰 방문실시여부는 현재 미정인것으로 알려짐.끝

(대사 노창희-국장)

예고:91.12.31. 까지

국기국      장관      차관      1차보      중아국      국기국      분석관      정와대      안기부

PAGE 1

# 외 무 부

종 별 :

번 호 : UNW-1630　　　　　　　　　일 시 : 91 0624 2000

수 신 : 장 관(국연,중동일,기정)

발 신 : 주 유엔 대사

제 목 : 걸프사태(이락 화학무기)

1. 안보리 휴전결의에 의거한 <u>이락 군비통제 특위</u> 화학무기의 이락방문 (6.9-14)결과에 관한 금 6.24.자 유엔측 발표내용을 별첨송부함.

2. 동 내용중 이락측과 <u>이락주관하의 화학무기폐기</u> 문제를 일차 토의하였다는 부분은 동폐기추진 방안과 관련 주목됨.

첨부:상기 유엔측발표내용: UNW(F)-278

끝

(대사 노창희-국장)

---

국기국　　1차보　　중아국　　외정실　　안기부　　분석관

# United Nations

## Press Release

### Department of Public Information • News Coverage Service • New York

IK/27
24 June 1991

## SPECIAL COMMISSION CONDUCTS EXPLORATORY INSPECTION AT MUTHANNA STATE ESTABLISHMENT, IRAQ'S CHEMICAL-WEAPON FACILITY, 9-14 JUNE

The following information was made available by the Special Commission established by the Security Council to carry out tasks enumerated in paragraphs 9 (b) (i-iii) of resolution 687 (1991):

The Special Commission carried out an initial exploratory inspection of the Muthanna State Establishment -- also known as the State Enterprise for Pesticide Production -- in Iraq from 9 to 14 June.

The Muthanna State Establishment is a major chemical-weapon-production facility whose existence and location were declared by the Iraqi authorities to the Secretary-General on 18 April, as required under Security Council resolution 687 (1991) of 3 April. It is located in semi-arid country, some 80 kilometres north-west of Baghdad and 50 kilometres south-west of Samarra, and is the facility which has often been referred to in Western media reports in recent years as the Samarra facility.

The Iraqi declaration of 18 April also confirmed the presence at the site of a number of research and development, production, munitions manufacturing, filling and storage facilities, as well as the presence on the site of substantial quantities of bulk chemical warfare agents, chemical weapons precursor chemicals and chemical munitions of various types.

The purpose of the initial exploratory inspection was to obtain a detailed description of the site, including the nature and condition of the facilities, chemical warfare agents, chemical munitions and precursor chemicals on the site and an indication of the hazards present so as to enable a full inspection of the Muthanna State Establishment to be carried out at a later stage. The team was also instructed to make an initial assessment of the suitability of the site for the destruction of Iraq's chemical weapons capabilities, and to report any indication of undeclared activity related to nuclear, chemical, biological or missile capability.

The inspection was carried out by a team of 20 experts from eight different countries and the World Health Organization (WHO), selected by the Executive Chairman of the Special Commission, Ambassador Rolf Ekeus, for that

#UNW-1630 정부목

(more)

purpose. The specialist skills in the team included explosive ordnance
disposal, structural engineering, chemical agent detection, decontamination,
chemical monitoring, biochemistry and microbiology. Support personnel — two
interpreters, a photographer, a recorder, a communicator and two
administrative officers — were supplied by the United Nations. Dr. Peter
Dunn of Australia was appointed Chief Inspector, and Liutenant Colonel Jim
Knapp of Canada his Deputy.

The Muthanna State Establishment is a large complex some 170 square
kilometres in area. The major facilities on the site, however, are
concentrated in an area of approximately 25 square kilometres and this area
was the focus of the inspection team's activities.

In carrying out the inspection, the safety of the inspection personnel
was a prime consideration. Conditions in many areas of the site are hazardous
in the extreme. Most major structures on the site have either been totally
destroyed or severely damaged as a result of the bombing during the
hostilities; few buildings have escaped unscathed. While much unexploded
ordnance has been removed, some still remains on the site. The site also
contains leaking chemical munitions, and the presence of chemical agent was
detected in some areas and structures. There is a clear need to clean up the
site and to commence the destruction process as quickly as possible, bearing
in mind the requirement for public safety and the safety of the personnel
involved.

The team verified the presence on the site of mustard gas and
organophosphorus nerve agents, both as bulk agent and in the form of
munitions. It was informed by the Iraqi authorities that the nerve agents
were of the types GB and GF. The team also clarified with the Iraqi
authorities its understanding of the term "binary sarin", as used in Iraq's
declaration to the Secretary-General. In Iraqi terminology, the term sarin
covers all G-type nerve agents based on esters, both single and mixed, and in
this context binary sarin is therefore a chemical munition containing both GB
and GF.

The team found evidence for the presence on the site of impure tabun
(agent GA), whose use in the Iran-Iraq war had been verified by the United
Nations investigations of 1984, 1986 and 1987. It was informed that
production of GA at the site had ceased in 1986. The team was informed that
the site had been used for the production of herbicides known as Propanil and
Dalapon.

The team was also informed that research had been carried out at the
Muthanna State Establishment on the nerve agents soman (agent GD) and VX, but
that no large-scale production of these agents had been undertaken. It saw
nothing on this occasion which was inconsistent with that statement, but
concluded that two undamaged and sophisticated pilot plants found on the site
would require further investigation.

The team also verified the presence on site of a number of precursor
chemicals, mainly acquired from abroad. Some of these were present in large

(more)

3518P

quantities. It also found that the site contained equipment obtained from a variety of sources.

During the inspection, the Iraqi authorities sought permission to remove certain items of equipment from the site for use in a water purification plant at Fallujah and for the formulation of insecticides. This request was granted by the Executive Chairman, subject to certain strict control arrangements being observed by the Iraqi authorities. The team found no evidence at the site of any undeclared activity related to biological, nuclear or missile capability.

As this was only an initial exploratory inspection, it has not been possible for the Special Commission to come to any conclusion as to the veracity of the overall Iraqi declaration concerning the Muthanna State Establishment. The inspection team found no indication that Iraq was deliberately trying to mislead the Commission; indeed, the attitude of the Iraqi authorities throughout was cooperative.

The team also held initial informal discussions with the Iraqi authorities on the Iraqi offer of 9 June (document S/22682) to carry out the process of destruction. The team found that the site would be suitable for the destruction of Iraq's chemical weapons capabilities.

The next steps will be a full inspection of the site and further discussions with the Iraqi authorities on the destruction process. Evaluation of the information collected during the initial exploratory inspection has commenced, and detailed planning for the full inspection will commence in the very near future. Because of the size of the site and the extent of the facilities, as well as the hazards involved, the full inspection could well be a lengthy process.

Ambassador Ekeus said he wished to place on record his appreciation of the dedication, enthusiasm and superb professionalism with which all members of the inspection team went about their tasks and which were, he said, fully in accord with the highest traditions of the United Nations.

* *** *

3518P

3-3

P.4

# 외 무 부

종 별 :

번 호 : UNW-1655

일 시 : 91 0626 1800

수 신 : 장 관(국연,중동일,국기,기정)

발 신 : 주 유엔 대사

제 목 : 안보리 비공식협의(이락 핵사찰)

1. 이락군비 통제특위 R.EKEUS 의장이 금 6.26 유엔 사무총장에게 통보해온바에 의하면, 유엔핵사찰반이 6.23 및 6.24 바그다드 ABU GHARAIB육군병영의 관련 시설을 조사하려고 시도하였으나, 이락당국이 동 사찰반의 접근을 금지내지 제한하였으며 6.26 동 접근허용에 앞서 이락측이 조사대상 물체를 미리 제거하였다고함.

2. 상기관련 안보리는 금 6.26 오전 비공식협의를 개최한바, 미측 요청으로 금일 오후 공식회의를 갖기로 하였음.

3. 한편 금일 비공식협의중간에 안보리 이사국들은 대사들만이 참석한 가운데 이락의 핵관련 은익정보에 관한 미측 브리핑을 청취하였음.

4. 관련 동향 추보위계임.

첨부: R.EKEUS 특위의장및 BLIX IAEA사무처장의 유엔사무총장앞 서한: UNW(F)-285
끝

(대사 노창희-국장)

---

국기국    1차보    중아국    국기국    외정실    분석관    안기부

# UNITED NATIONS ⚜ NATIONS UNIES

POSTAL ADDRESS — ADRESSE POSTALE  UNITED NATIONS, N.Y. 10017
CABLE ADDRESS—ADRESSE TELEGRAPHIQUE  UNATIONS NEWYORK

REFERENCE

26 June 1991

Your Excellency,

I regret to inform you that, on 23 and 25 June 1991, Iraqi military authorities have denied an International Atomic Energy Agency/Special Commission Nuclear Inspection Team, appointed pursuant to Part C of Security Council resolution 687 (1991), access to facilities at a designated site. The facilities concerned are within the Abu Gharaib Army Barracks, a site in Baghdad designated by the Special Commission under paragraph 9(b)(ii) of Security Council resolution 687 (1991) and notified by it to the Government of Iraq for urgent on-site inspection in accordance with the terms of the resolution.

The inspection team in question arrived in Baghdad on Saturday, 22 June 1991, and that evening the Deputy Executive Chairman of the Special Commission, Mr. Robert Gallucci, and the representative of the Director-General of IAEA and Chief Inspector, Mr. Maurizio Zifferero, met with the Foreign Minister of Iraq to discuss Iraq's previous declaration regarding nuclear facilities and arrangements for the forthcoming inspection. After a detailed discussion, it was agreed that at 7:00 a.m., on Sunday 23 June 1991, a representative of Iraq would be informed of the designation of a site and that the inspection of that site could proceed before 12 noon on the same date, despite the fact that the inspection would be taking place on a religious holiday in Iraq.

The inspection team, accompanied by an Iraqi Liaison Officer, arrived at the site about 12 noon. However, upon arrival, the local military authorities denied all access to the site, on the grounds that they had no written authorization or orders to that effect. After a discussion of about an hour, some access to the site was permitted. It was, however, denied to the locations and facilities which the team indicated it wished to inspect. The right to take photographs was in some instances prohibited and in others limited. The team was, nevertheless, able to observe that, in areas to which access was denied, considerable activity was under way, involving cranes, trucks, forklifts, other equipment and work crews.

/...

His Excellency
Mr. Javier Pérez de Cuéllar
Secretary-General

After leaving the site on 23 June, the team leader and the representative of the Special Commission addressed a formal protest to the Minister for Foreign Affairs regarding the denial of the inspection team's rights under Security Council resolution 687 (1991) and the exchange of notes between the Secretary-General and the Foreign Minister of Iraq regarding the status, privileges and immunities of the inspection teams in Iraq. A copy of that protest is attached.

On the evening of 24 June, Mr. Gallucci and Mr. Zifferero were invited to the Ministry for Foreign Affairs to discuss their protest. At the conclusion of the discussion, assurances were given that the problems had been resolved and that the following day unimpeded access would be given to the site.

On Tuesday, 25 June 1991, the inspection team returned to the site, but was again denied access by the military authorities on the spot to the particular facilities it wished to inspect. In the face of this denial, the Chief Inspector, Mr. Zifferero, decided to suspend further inspection activities for consultations with the IAEA on how to proceed. He was authorized to perform a third inspection at the particular site.

Shortly thereafter, Mr. Zifferero was informed by the Foreign Ministry that full access would be given on the morning of Wednesday, 26 June 1991. On 26 June 1991, access to the site and to the requested facilities was finally granted to the inspection team. However, on this occasion activities which had been observed from a distance during the first visit had ceased and objects that had been seen had been removed.

The Director-General of the IAEA and I have expressed our grave concern to the representatives of Iraq in New York and Vienna. You may wish to inform the President of the Security Council of the foregoing developments.

Accept, Your Excellency, the assurances of my highest consideration.

Rolf Ekéus
Executive Chairman
Office of the Special Commission

3-2

0075

RECEIVED

JUN 2  91

# INTERNATIONAL ATOMIC ENERGY AGENCY

THE DIRECTOR GENERAL

26 June 1991

Dear Secretary General,

I know that the Chairman of the Special Commission is reporting to you on the inspection that the Agency is performing in Iraq with the assistance and cooperation of the Special Commission, and there have been consultations with us about the contents of his report.

I confirm that after the second denial and restrictions of access to the Abu Gharalb Army Barracks, which occurred on Tuesday, 25 June 1991, the Chief inspector, Mr. Zifferero suspended further inspection activities for consultations with us. Shortly thereafter, Mr. Zifferero was informed by the Foreign Ministry that complete and unimpeded access would be given to the Agency inspection Team on the morning of Wednesday, 26 June 1991. He was therefore authorized by me to perform a third inspection with the Team at the particular site.

Today, Wednesday 26 June, the new visit took place in the morning at the Abu Gharalb Army Barracks. There were now no restrictions of access but also no longer any trace of the activities and objects which the inspection Team had observed from a distance during the first visit of the site on Sunday, 23 June 1991.

Mr. M. Zifferero has now been instructed to return to Vienna as soon as possible, leaving the rest of the Team in Iraq to continue inspections. Mr. Zifferero, in his capacity as Chief inspector, is preparing a report of his own on the inspection of the Abu Gharalb Army Barracks and the denial and restrictions of access that his Team encountered at that site. This report will be forwarded to you promptly. Meanwhile I trust you will make the information contained in the report of the Chairman of the Special Commission and in this letter available as appropriate to the members of the Security Council.

Yours sincerely,

Hans Blix

Mr. Javier Pérez de Cuéllar
Secretary General
United Nations
New York, 10017
U.SA

3-3

0076

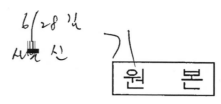
# 외 무 부

종    별 : 지 급

번    호 : UNW-1663                       일    시 : 91 0627 1530

수    신 : 장관(국연,중동일,국기,기정)

발    신 : 주유엔대사

제    목 : 안보리회의(이락 핵사찰)

연: UNW-1655

1. 안보리는 연호 이락군비봉제 특위조사반의 핵사찰 활동과 관련한 이락의 협조의무불이행 문제 토의를 위한 공식회의를 6.26 오후 개최한바, 미.불.벨지움.오지리.영.에쿠아돌.루마니아.이락의 발언만을 청취하고 종료되었음.

2. 상기 회의시 각국 발언요지는 다음과같음.

가. 미국

1) ABU GHARAIB 육군병영에는 핵무기 개발과 관련한 우라늄 농축장비 및 재료를일시 저장한것에 불과하며 이락은 핵무기 개발관련 시설을 여러곳에 은익

2) 핵관련     기만행위외에도     이락은     미사일,화학무기     보유량을 허위신고(은익목적)하였으며, 생물무기도 보유(이락측은 동 보유부인)

3) 휴전결의상의 제반 의무를 위반하고 있는 이락에 대한 경제제재 완화는 불가,유엔군비봉제조사반의 전면 사찰관철 대책필요

나. 불란서(조사반 활동방해 개탄,여사한 사례계속시 이락 협조확보를 위한 안보리 조치불가피), 벨지움(이락의 휴전결의 위반행위,국제사회 주의환기 필요), 오지리 (휴전결의 중대위반, 이락의 의무불이행시 원치않는 결과초래), 영국(휴전결의 위반, 이락당국의 의무이행 재확인 필요), 에쿠아돌(본건이 우발적인 사례이기를 희망),루마니아(본건중대사안, 이락의무 전면이행 강조)

다. 이락

1) 이락은 유엔조사반에 전면협조중

2) 본건은 종교휴일, 봉신상의문제, 군사시설의특수성, 편익주선 필요로 지연이 있었던 것에 불과( NON-ISSUE)

3) 반이락공세의 일환(제재조치 계속구실,이락에 대한 재공격을 위한 여론 형성)

---

국기국    1차보    중아국    국기국    외정실    분석관    안기부

PAGE 1                                          91.06.28    05:35 DN
외신 1과  통제관

3.본건관련   안보리의장은   이락측에   유엔핵사찰관련   협력을   촉구하고 군비통제관련이락의 제반 의무이행 약속 재확인을요청할것으로 알려짐.

첨부: NYT 기사 및 WP 지 사설:UNW(F)-288

끝

(대사 노창희-국장)

0078

# U.S. Shows Photos to Argue Iraq Hides Nuclear Material

### By PAUL LEWIS
Special to The New York Times

UNITED NATIONS, June 26 — The Bush Administration showed reconnaissance photographs to the United Nations Security Council today to back up its assertion that Iraq is trying to conceal equipment used for making nuclear explosives.

At a private briefing this morning, American intelligence officials showed the 15-member Council classified photographs of uranium-enrichment machinery being moved around on trucks or buried to evade detection by United Nations inspectors.

At a Security Council meeting that was hastily called tonight to review the charges, the deputy United States representative went further, saying that Iraq had also underreported its stocks of chemical weapons and ballistic missiles to the United Nations.

The deputy representative, Alexander F. Watson, said that the United States had "strong evidence" that Iraq was trying to conceal factories for manufacturing these weapons. He also cast doubt on Baghdad's claim that it has no biological weapons, although he did not offer any specific proof.

### Confronting Baghdad

The United States contended at the intelligence briefing and the meeting tonight that by concealing nuclear material and weapons, Iraq has been violating the Security Council resolution ending the Persian Gulf war. The resolution called for the removal or destruction of all dangerous nuclear materials, chemical and biological weapons and ballistic missiles in its possession.

Representatives of France, Britain, Belgium, Austria, Ecuador and Romania said tonight that Iraq appeared to be in serious violation of the resolution.

The Security Council's current president, Jean-Jacques Bechio of the Ivory Coast, is to demand on Thursday that Iraq immediately hand over the sensitive nuclear material described by the United States for inspection and possible destruction, diplomats said.

Mr. Bechio also plans to ask Baghdad's representative to the United Nations for high-level assurances that Iraq will cooperate fully with the disarmament process in the future.

United States officials said the photographs that were shown to the Security Council at the briefing this morning could not be released because they would enable experts to assess American reconnaissance capability.

Mr. Watson said Iraq had sought to hide equipment "designed to enrich uranium by electromagnetic isotope separation" — an old-fashioned technology that the United States experimented with when it was building the first atomic bomb toward the end of World War II but later abandoned.

The briefing was arranged for the Council after the United Nations commission charged with destroying Iraq's weapons of mass destruction reported that its inspectors were denied entry to a military base outside Baghdad for 72 hours this week. Iraqi soldiers removed heavy equipment stored at the base while the inspectors were kept out, the commission reported.

Experts sent by the special commission said they tried to conduct a challenge inspection at the Abu Gharaib barracks north of Baghdad on Sunday and again on Tuesday. They said they were denied full access, but that they could see heavy objects being lifted onto trucks with cranes and forklifts.

### Inspectors Finally Admitted

When the experts were finally allowed to fully inspect the barracks today, they found nothing incriminating, the commission said. The commission ordered the inspection after receiving earlier American intelligence reports that suspicious objects had been moved there, including some materials from Iraq's principal nuclear installation at Tuwaitha, southwest of Baghdad.

In the inventory of nuclear material submitted to the Security Council in April, Iraq made no mention of any electromagnetic isotope separation program. The list was limited to equipment that Iraq was already known to have and that had been placed under international safeguards.

At the Council briefing, American intelligence officials showed members satellite photographs of recent developments at the Abu Gharaib barracks, at the Tuwaitha nuclear site, and at a plant near Tarmaiya, north of Baghdad, where the special commission conducted its first challenge inspection earlier this month but found nothing, envoys said.

Diplomats said the photographs showed uncrated machines called calutrons, which are used in electromagnetic isotope separation, being moved onto trucks just before United Nations inspectors arrived at the sites.

The photographs also indicated that Iraq sometimes buried pieces of equipment at these sites, the diplomats said. In digging them up again, the Iraqis carefully filled in holes with fresh earth -so there would be no traces of radioactivity left in the soil, the envoys added.

Although electromagnetic separation is a slow and costly way of producing enriched uranium, officials say that the machinery needed to build a calutron is readily available and could be ordered without arousing suspicion.

Diplomats said the briefing today bore out earlier assertions by a defecting Iraqi scientist that Baghdad had a secret nuclear weapons program in which it was using about 25 calutrons to produce highly enriched uranium.

The scientist, who gave himself up to American forces in northern Iraq, also reported several weeks ago that Baghdad had succeeded in enriching some 90 pounds of uranium to weapons-grade level, providing it enough explosive material for several crude atomic bombs. No trace of this uranium has been found by inspectors.

### State Department's Demands

In Washington, the State Department spokeswoman, Margaret D. Tutwiler, reiterated the charges. "There is ample evidence from multiple sources that Iraq has been conducting a covert nuclear weapons program that has included activities to produce nuclear weapons material," she said.

Miss Tutwiler called on Iraq to "make available for inspection all — repeat, all — equipment and material connected with its nuclear-weapons capabilities, including items clandestinely removed from sites."

The only officials permitted to attend the Security Council briefing this morning were the permanent representatives of its 15 member nations; the United Nations Secretary General, Javier Pérez de Cuéllar, and two other senior United Nations officials.

#UNW-1.663
첨부물

2-1

0079

# *Iraqis in Distress*

THE GULF WAR has left two groups of Iraqi citizens in distress requiring special attention from the United States and its allies. The Kurds of the north have received considerable publicity, policy focus and care. But, less tended, a wide swath of the civilian population, especially children, is in dire straits as a result of difficulties stemming from the war.

The Kurds continue to move nervously back into the cities and villages they had fled in fear of Saddam Hussein's butchery last spring. As they do, the United States and other allies are removing the forces they put in Iraq to protect them. The United Nations is expanding a small police guard force, but even enlarged it will be no match for the intimidating ranks of soldiers and intelligence agents that Iraq will have on hand.

Kurdish leaders are attempting to take up some of the slack by negotiating an autonomy agreement with Baghdad. Another measure of protection for the Kurds may be afforded by the economic sanctions that the allies still wield against Iraq—sanctions also and necessarily being used to compel a still-deceptive Saddam to yield up his weapons of mass destruction. But a responsible close-by military deterrent with a strong American component remains essential. The allied coalition is now preparing to set up a 5,000-man rapid-reaction force in nearby Turkey to give credibility to coalition pledges to protect the Kurds. This is a mission of conscience, and Saddam Hussein should be left in no doubt that the allies will assume it.

Iraqi civilians are carrying the principal burden of the destruction and hardship wrought by Saddam Hussein's war. Bombing raids knocked out most of the power and fuel facilities on which Iraq's rather modern social as well as economic plant relied—without electricity for instance, sewage doesn't get treated and vaccines can't be refrigerated. Meanwhile, with the oil embargo still very much in effect, cash is short to permit Iraqis to buy essential (and unembargoed) foods and medicines. International experts report that the public's health is deteriorating and forecast that upward of 100,000 children could die this summer. Who would then have the heart to walk away on the ground, however truthful, that it was at bottom Saddam Hussein's fault?

There is another way, and it is to let Baghdad resume selling some oil but then to use the existing U.N. sanctions and the increasing number of international and private agency people on the ground in Iraq to make sure that the proceeds go for internationally approved purposes—food and medicine, refugee and disarmament expenses and the like. It would be a technical break in the embargo, which President Bush has pledged to sustain until Saddam Hussein no longer holds power. But it would be a break designed on U.N. terms to serve U.N. goals, to prevent Saddam Hussein from diverting resources to his army and his Sunni followers, to save children's lives.

2-2

# 외 무 부

종 별 :

번 호 : UNW-1682

일 시 : 91 0628 2030

수 신 : 장 관(국연,중동일,국기,기정)

발 신 : 주 유엔 대사

제 목 : 안보리회의(이락 핵사찰)

연: UNW-1655,1663

1. 안보리는 이락군당국의 유엔 핵사찰요청 불응사례가 6.28 재발 (유엔조사반의 FALLUJAH 시부근 군수송시설 접근불허 및 위협사격)함에 따라 금 28일 오전및 오후 비공식협의를 거쳐 야간 공식회의를 갖고 다음요지의 안보리 의장성명을 발표하였음.

가.연호및 금번 유엔 핵사찰 불응사태 개탄 및 이락당국 처사 규탄

나.동사태를 휴전결의 위반으로규정

다.유엔 고위 대표단 이락 파견

1) H.BLIX  IAEA 사무처장, R.EKEUS 특위의장, Y.AKASHI 유엔사무차장으로 대표단을 구성, 6.28이락향발

2)동 대표단은 이락 최고위 당국자들에게 핵사찰을 포함한 유엔 이락군비 통제특위 활동보장요청

3)대표단은 이락 방문결과를 사무총장을 통해 안보리에 보고

라.중동지역에서의 대량파괴무기 제거 (ESTABLISHMENT IN THE MIDDLE EAST OF A ZONE FREE OF WEAPONSOF MASS DESTRUCTION) 추진 필요 재확인

2.금일 회의시 발언국 없었음.

첨부:1.상기 안보리의장 성명

2. R.EKEUS특위의장의 유엔사무총장앞 서한: UNW(F)-294

끝

(대사 노창희-국장)

---

국기국    1차보    중아국    국기국    외정실    분석관    안기부

PAGE 1

2nd REVISED

## DRAFT STATEMENT

The members of the Security Council have learnt with grave concern of an incident which occurred today when the Iraqi military authorities denied a joint IAEA/Special Commission Nuclear Inspection Team immediate and unimpeded access to a site designated for inspection by the Special Commission under paragraphs 9 and 13 of Security Council resolution 687 (1991). In the course of this incident, the Iraqi military did not comply with a request by the Acting Chief Inspector that there should be no movement of transport or equipment pending inspection. The Iraqi military fired small arms into the air when members of the Team were endeavouring to photograph loaded vehicles leaving the site. This incident followed earlier incidents on 23 and 25 June 1991 when the Iraqi military authorities denied the Nuclear Inspection Team access to certain facilities at another designated site.

On 26 June 1991, the Security Council held a meeting to consider the incidents of 23 and 25 June at which time the Permanent Representative of Iraq confirmed that Iraq had accepted Security Council resolution 687 (1991) and was doing its best to implement all the requirements and obligations imposed on it by the resolution. He further asserted that Iraq was co-operating with all United Nations missions, including the Special Commission. The President subsequently conveyed the Council's serious concern regarding the incidents to the Government of Iraq.

#UNW-1682
첨부묵

5-1

0082

The members of the Council strongly deplore the incidents of
23, 25 and 28 June, and in this connection condemn the conduct of
the Iraqi authorities.  All these incidents constitute flagrant
violations of Security Council resolution 687 (1991) and of the
undertakings contained in the exchange of letters between the
Secretary-General of the United Nations and the Foreign Minister
of Iraq governing the status, privileges and immunities of the
Special Commission and of the Inspection Teams mandated under the
Security Council resolution.  Furthermore, these incidents
demonstrate Iraq's failure to abide by its solemn undertakings to
comply with all the provisions of Security Council resolution 687
(1991).

The members of the Security Council have decided to ask the
Secretary-General to send a high-level mission to Baghdad
immediately to meet with the highest levels of the Iraqi
Government to convey the Council's urgent demand for unequivocal
assurances that the Government will take all necessary measures
to ensure that no hindrances are placed in the way of the
discharge of the Special Commission's mandate and that it will
accord full co-operation, including immediate and unimpeded
access, to the inspection teams in compliance with Iraq's
obligations and commitments vis-a-vis the United Nations and the
IAEA.  The members of the  Council have also stressed that the
Government must furnish the high-level mission with unconditional
guarantees for the safety and security of all personnel engaged
in the performance of functions in connection with Security
Council resolution 687 (1991).  The mission, composed of the

5—2

0083

Director-General of the International Atomic Energy Agency
(IAEA), the Executive Chairman of the Special Commission and the
Under-Secretary-General for Disarmament Affairs, will depart New
York this evening, 28 June 1991.

At this time, the members of the Council call upon Iraq to
grant the IAEA/Special Commission Nuclear Inspection Team
currently in Iraq immediate and unimpeded access to the objects
which the Team had endeavoured to inspect on 28 June 1991 and any
other site deemed necessary.

The members of the Security Council request the high-level
mission to report to it at the earliest opportunity, through the
Secretary-General, on the results of its meetings with the
highest levels of the Iraqi Government and, in particular, on
such further undertakings by the Government to ensure compliance
at all levels, including local military and civilian authorities,
with Iraq's obligations under Security Council resolution 687
(1991).

The members of the Council wish to make it clear that the
Council remains seized of this matter and that any recurrence of
non-compliance would have serious consequences.

The members of the Council reiterate their views expressed
in resolution 687 (1991) of the threat that all weapons of mass
destruction pose to peace and security in the Middle East and of
the need to work towards the establishment in the Middle East of
a zone free of such weapons.

0084

<u>Annex</u>

[Original: English]

<u>Letter dated 28 June 1991 from the Executive Chairman of the
Special Commission addressed to the Secretary-General</u>

I write to inform you that on Friday, 28 June 1991, the Iraqi military
authorities denied an International Atomic Energy Agency/United Nations
Special Commission team immediate access to a site designated for inspection
by the Special Commission under paragraph 9 of Security Council resolution
687 (1991). The circumstances are described below.

The inspection team, under its Acting Chief Inspector, Mr. David Kay, and
accompanied by an Iraqi Liaison Officer, proceeded to a military
transportation facility situated east of Fallujah on the morning of 28 June.
On arrival at the site, Mr. Kay presented the formal notification of the site
to be inspected to his escorts. At that time he also requested that there
should be no movement whatsoever of transport or equipment from the site
pending the inspection.

While awaiting for permission to enter, the team observed vehicles within
the compound loaded with the objects which they specifically desired to
inspect under the terms of the Security Council resolution. After some
minutes, drivers were seen moving quickly to the vehicles which then began
leaving the facility through an exit to the south.

A small number of the team members were directed by the team leader
towards that exit to observe and photograph the vehicle movements. At that
time the Iraqi military fired small arms into the air and efforts were made to
seize the cameras. These actions took place despite the fact that all team
members were clearly identifiable as United Nations personnel and that the
vehicle was painted white and carried United Nations markings.

Although the team did not gain access to the site, they were able to take
photographs of the vehicles and their cargoes leaving the site. After the
departure of the vehicles, the team returned to the area of the main gate.
The camp commander appeared and stated that while he would like to allow the
team to enter, he had no orders to do so. The Acting Chief Inspector
responded by stating that he had no option but to report to his superiors that
the team had been denied immediate access to the site, that equipment had been
removed contrary to his request, and that he had been obstructed from carrying
out his duties in accordance with the Security Council resolution. He
particularly and strongly protested the use of firearms.

/...

   I have informally relayed the above information to the President of the
Security Council.

                                          (Signed)  Rolf EKEUS
                                                    Executive Chairman
                                                    Special Commission

                               -----

5—5

# 이라크 核시설 제거
# 美軍事力사용 검토

## 이라크 유엔調査團에 發砲

[유엔본부·바그다드·워싱턴聯合] 이라크는 핵시설로 추정되는 장소를 조사하려는 유엔 조사단의 접근을 28일 또다시 거부, 이를 감시하던 유엔 조사단에 공포를 발사했으며 조지 부시 美대통령은 즉각적으로 이를 걸프전 휴전협정 위반이라고 경고하는 한편, 최고위 안보 보좌관 회의를 소집했다.

美 행정부의 한 고위관리는 이날 부시 대통령의 안보보좌관 회의를 소집한 뒤 이라크가 자국내 핵시설에 대한 유엔 조사단의 사찰을 허용하지 않으면 미국이 이라크의 핵시설을 공격할 가능성이 높다고 말했다.

이 관리는 이라크가 유엔 조사단의 핵사찰을 거부함으로써 국제법을 위반

하고 있다고 말하고 「아직 어떤 결정이 내려지지 않았지만 우리가 뭔가를 해야할 좋은 기회라고 생각한다」면서 미국의 對이라크 군사공격 가능성을 50%이상으로 전망했다.

그러나 사담 후세인 이라크 大統領은 이사태후 라크 핵시설 사찰에 나선 유엔 조사단이 사찰을 원하는 시설을 방문, 사찰

시설들을 다른 새로운 장소로 수송하려던 것으로 調査團의 한 요원이 전했다.

한편 관계 당국에 지시 보기는 한 수송단의 모습을 촬영하려면 유엔 조사단은 이라크군인들은 이날 팔 루크市 동부의 한 이라크 군 수송시설내에서 핵관련 장비를 탈취하려 했다고 조사단의 한 요원이 전했다.

91. 6. 30 <한국> 4면

# 美"이라크에 核사찰 先例남기자"

## 現場접근 제지 대응 武力사용 공식거론
## 외교적방법 병행… 또다른 制裁가능성도

미국이 이라크에 대해 또 한차례의 무력공격 가능성을 거론하기 시작했다.

걸프戰 종결에 따른 유엔결의 제687호에 따라 비재래식 무기조사에 나섰던 유엔검색반이 23, 25일 이틀간 현장접근을 금지당하다가 28일에는 軍보초들에 의해 소총발사를 통한 위협까지 당해 이라크를 결국 무력공격하지 않을수 없을 것이라는 여론이 일기시작한 것이다.

무력사용여부에 관한 공식적인 거론은 두차례 현장접근이 저지당한 26일 국무, 국방, 국가안보 회의의 차관급회의서 처음으로 나왔는데 이 회의에서 무력사용을 건의하기로 결정했는지, 아니면 단순히 무력사용을 검토만 했는지는 즉각 알려지지 않고있다.

부시대통령은 28일「무력을 사용할 것인가」라는 질문에 대해「일단 이문제는 외교노력을 통해 유엔결의에 맡기겠다. 두고보라」는 말만 하고 있으며 베이커국무장관역시「심각한 사태이니 두고보기 바란다」며 뚜렷한 언질을 주지않고있다.

그러나 이라크의 핵문제와 관련하여 이번사태가 가져올 몇가지 결론은 분명해지고 있는듯하다.

첫째는 국제핵사찰의 선례를 세운다는것. 이라크는 국제원자력기구(IAEA)의 핵안전감시협정과는 별개로 걸프전휴전조건의 일환으로 핵·화학및 세균무기의 제조와 관련된 모든 시설과 물질을 파기하기로 약속하고 이를위한 유엔의 감시를 받겠다고 약속했다. 유엔결의 687호에 들어있는 내용이다.

28일의 국무부브리핑에서 이 결의안이 무력사용권을 내포하고있는것이냐는 질문에 대해 터트와일러 대변인은 답변을 보류했지만 일반적 견해는 이결의가 휴전조건으로 가결된것이기때문에 결국 무력사용권이 내포돼 있는것으로 보고있다.

문제의 핵장비이동이 포착됐거나 검색반의 출입이 방해된 곳은 바그다드에서 1백마일 (1백60㎞)지점에 있는 알파루시와 알가리브이다.

걸프전중 슈와르츠코프사령관은 공중포격으로 이라크의 핵능력을 완전히 파괴했다고 말한바 있었다. 이번 핵장비의 내용이 아직 밝혀지지 않고있는 상태여서 사실 이라크가 사찰을 받기를 거부하는 내용들이 핵무기관련 장비인지 아닌지도 확실치 않다.

이라크는 핵시설보유를 부인하고 있는데 이는 북한이 平和的 핵시설만을 갖고있으면서도「우리는 핵무기를 가질 의사도 없고 그럴 능력도 없다」고 주장하는것과 비슷한 맥락이다.

그러나 미국이나 유엔측으로서는 내용을 일단 공개하지 않으면 알수없다는 것이다. 국제협상을 통하는 외교압력 또는 최후의 수단으로 무력을 동원해서라도 미국은 이번 이라크사태를 통해 핵사찰규정의 철저한 이행을 위한 선례를 남기려고 있는것이다.

둘째 미국은 이번 기회에 사담·후세인의 독재에 대한 새로운 제재를 마련하려고 하는 것이다.

국방부 대변인은 27일의 브리핑서 만일의 경우 이라크를 공격할수 있는 미군병력을 발표했었다.

사우디주둔 육군만 5만명이며 공군 해군 해병대 등이 갖고있는 지상 해상 및 공중공격력은 걸프전 직후와 전혀 변함없이 강력하다는 것이다.

이라크에 대한 국제경제 제재조치로 이라크국민생활은 급속도로 악화되고 있는데도 사담·후세인 정부는 건재하고 있다.

미국은 이번 의회를 통해 사담·후세인에 대한 제재방법을 강구하든지 아니면 어떤 타협점을 찾아내서라도 이라크사태를 다소 해결하려 들것으로 보인다.

【워싱턴=鄭逸和특파원】

0088

# 美「이라크核」공격시사

## 유엔은 사찰업무 전면중단

【바그다드·케네벙크포트 (美메인州)=AP·로이터聯合】 유엔핵사찰조사원들이 파이라크 병사들간의 충돌이 발생함에 따라 29일 유엔의 對이라크 핵사찰이 중단됐다.

해서는 밝히지 않았다.

그러나 익명을요구한 한 유엔사절은 도착하게될 유엔사절은 30일까지는 사찰업무가 중단될 것이라고 말했다.

한편 존치 부시美대통령은 29일 유엔핵사찰조사단가한 사건에 업덕「국제조 사단을 괴롭힌것은 누구에게나 용납될 수 없는것」이라고 거듭 강조했다.

부시大통령은 이날 후세인의「기만과 거짓말을 일삼고 있다」고 비난하면서 기존 유엔결의들이 걸프전

A)대표단의 데이비드·케이부단장은 「우리는 이제부터 핵사찰활위한 우리조세인 이라크대통령의 다짐에 의구심을 표시하면서 이라크에 대해 군사적 조치를 취할 가능성을 배제하지 않았다.

국제원자력기구 (IAE A)대표단의 데이비드·케이부단장은 「우리는 이제부터 핵사찰활위한 우리조세인 이라크대통령의 다짐에 의구심을 표시하면서 이라크에 대해 군사적 조치를 취할 가능성을 배제하지 않았다.

심의 하계휴양소 골프장 에서 기자들에게 28일이라크軍이 바그다드저 핵시설이 있는것은 것으로 추정되는 지역을 출발하는

이라크에대한 유엔의 핵사찰은 걸프전의 영구휴전조건들을 규정한 유엔안보리결의 687호에 따르것으로 이결의에는 이라크내모든핵시설뿐만 유엔이 이라크에 파괴하도록 명령한 화학무기및 기타 대량살상무기봉시설들에 대한 사찰이 포함돼있다.

을 종식시킨 휴전결의의틀 이행하기위해「필요한 모든수단」의 사용을 승인하고 있다고 말해 공습이나 미사일공격등 무력사용의 가능성을 배제하지 않았다.

외 무 부

종 별 :

번 호 : UNW-1691                     일 시 : 91 0701 1800

수 신 : 장 관 (국연,중동일,기정)

발 신 : 주 유엔 대사

제 목 : 걸프사태 (안보리)

　　　연: UNW-1682

　　1. 금 7.1. 사무총장 대변인에 의하면 연호 이락 핵사찰 관련 유엔 고위대표단은 6.30. 저녁 이락에 도착, 동국 외상 (6.30), 부수상 (7.1.)과 이미 만났으며 7.1. 저녁 또는 7.2. 아침 이락 수상과 면담 예정이라고함.

　　2. 안보리의 연호 이락 경제제재 조치 첫번째 정기심사가 안보리에서 정식으로 토의되지 않고 이사국간 비공식 협의에서 사실상 종결되어 버린것 (UNW-1527,1617 참조)과 관련 쿠바는 6.29.자 안보리 의장앞 서한을 통해 본건 제재조치 심사는 안보리가 공식 처리할 사항으로서 지난번 처리방식이 앞으로 선례가 되어서는 안된다고 주장하였음. (S/22750) 끝

　　(대사 노창희-국장)

　　첨부: FAX (UNW(F)-297)

---

국기국　　1차보　　　중아국　　　외정실　　　분석관　　　안기부

91.07.02　　10:04 WG

외신 1과 통제관

0090

UNW(F)-297  10701 1800   첨부물 UNW-1691   총 1PH

# Feed Iraqis, Starve Saddam

The suffering of the Iraqi people cries out for compassion. Shortages of food, medicine, clean water and electricity now threaten to cause more death and disease than the Persian Gulf war. Indeed, the worsening plight of Iraq's vulnerable children and powerless adults virtually demands some easing of the economic sanctions. Why make the Iraqi people suffer for the crimes of Saddam Hussein?

But the sanctions remain one of the few levers by which the allied coalition hopes to disarm Iraq's nuclear, chemical and biological capabilities. As Iraq disdainfully evades international inspectors, the allies know they need every bit of pressure they can muster.

There may be a way out of this dilemma: Permit Iraq to resume oil exports, but impound the earnings and apply some of them to humanitarian assistance.

•

Satellite photos and defectors' reports make clear that Iraq continues to violate the terms of the United Nations cease-fire. Iraq supplied misleading accounts of its nuclear arms program and still tries to conceal arms-making equipment and facilities from international inspectors. As if to underscore reports that Washington is weighing military options, President Bush says "all means necessary" may be used to enforce the cease-fire resolution. But bombing during the war did not succeed in eliminating Saddam Hussein's nuclear capacity.

Lifting sanctions without qualification would leave the Iraqi dictator with no reason to obey the U.N. cease-fire resolution. Worse yet, he'd give priority to rebuilding the military machine that keeps him in power. And he would speciously blame his foreign foes for whatever pain his people continued to endure.

A wiser course would be to let Iraq export oil but turn the proceeds over to the United Nations. The Security Council can empower a special committee to disburse the money, allocating 30 percent to a reparations fund for Kuwait.

Part of the balance could be earmarked for genuine humanitarian aid, to be distributed under U.N. auspices by relief agencies. The Iraqi people should be left in no doubt about who is providing the emergency aid. Another portion could be used to defray expenses of the international effort to assure safe havens for Iraqi Kurds. And finally, as some suggest, the remainder could be kept in a special fund to be given Iraq once it is rid of Saddam Hussein.

What makes this feasible is Iraq's dependence on readily monitored petroleum sales. Allied bombing did not destroy Iraq's refineries or its pipelines to Turkey and Saudi Arabia. There are no major obstacles to a swift resumption of exports that can earn Iraq $17 billion a year. And Saddam Hussein has little choice but to accept any terms that the world dictates.

( 출연. 중동일. 기정 )

외 무 부

종 별 :

번 호 : UNW-1724    일 시 : 91 0703 1900

수 신 : 장 관 (국연,중동일,기정)

발 신 : 주 유엔 대사

제 목 : 걸프사태 (유엔동향)

1. 이락 핵사찰

유엔 고위대표단은 이락 방문결과를 7.3. 제네바에서 CUELLAR 사무총장에게 보고 예정이며 사무총장은 동 내용을 안보리 의장에게 제출할것 이라고함.

2. 인도적 문제 관련 유엔대표단 이락방문

S.AGA KAHN 대표는 지난주 이락 남부지역 난민실태 파악을 위한 조사단 파견에 이어, 다음주 이락 주민들의 인도지원 수요를 조사하기 위해 고위대표단을 인솔하고 이락 방문 예정 (특히 HOWR AL-HAMMAV 지역에 관심)

3. 유엔경비대 (UN GUARDS) 이락 배치 현황

현재 156명이 배치되어 있으며 최근 독일은 동경비대 경비중 275만불 지원 결정발표

4. 총회의장 쿠웨이트 방문

DE MARCO 의장은 쿠웨이트 정부 초청으로 7.5-7. 동국을 방문계획 (동 방문후 제네바 방문:ECOSOC 회의 참가, UNHCR 측과의 협의등목적) 끝

(대사 노창희-국장)

첨부: NYT 지 사설(7.3.), WP 지 기사(7.3)FAX(UNW(F)-304)

국기국    1차보    중아국    외정실    청와대    안기부

UNW(FI)-304   10703 1800   첨부물 UNW-1724 홍 2매
                                    (국연. 중동일. 기정)

# The Godfather and the Kurds

Having gassed Kurdish villages and dishonored a 1970 agreement for Kurdish autonomy, Saddam Hussein now makes another offer that he believes his Kurdish subjects cannot refuse. He promises them free elections to a Kurdish parliament, pluralism and a free press. But the fine print exposes these concessions as a sham.

He demands that Iraqi Kurds support his own Baath Party "until martyrdom," denounce the international intervention that saved their lives and oppose all of Baghdad's enemies, including "the Zionist-American imperialist threat."

These are godfather terms, rubbed in by Saddam Hussein's insistence on undivided control of the oil city of Kirkuk, the major Kurdish city in northern Iraq. The two principal Kurdish leaders, Massoud Barzani and Jalal Talabani, have rejected these humiliating conditions. What should strengthen their negotiating power are allied plans, now under discussion in Ankara, for stationing a mobile force of 5,000 American and European troops in southeastern Turkey.

This seems the least the world can do for Iraqi Kurds who fled in terror from Saddam Hussein's tanks and warplanes when it became clear that Desert Storm would not protect them. It took a global outcry to induce President Bush to come to the rescue. Beginning in April, 12,000 allied soldiers entered northern Iraq to create a safe haven for as many as two million Kurdish refugees. Only 3,700 troops remain, and Saddam Hussein is plainly calculating that American impatience will hasten a final withdrawal as soon as the Kurds reach agreement with Baghdad on autonomy.

This contemptuous approach to the Kurds is consistent with Saddam Hussein's refusal to permit allied scrutiny of his nuclear facilities. He is the same leader who calculated that revolutionary Iran would be a pushover, that Iraq could devour Kuwait. A tyrant with no claim to legitimacy, who has brought ruin to his people, Saddam Hussein has yet to utter a syllable that suggests remorse or error.

Sanctions and the possible threat of resumed hostilities may be the only means of staying a vengeful blood bath in Iraq.

•

What Kurds are demanding makes moral and political sense: a new Iraqi constitution, with democratic rights for Shiites as well Kurdish minorities. The Kurds look hopefully to the rest of the world for help, despite past betrayals at the hands of foreign friends.

Pulling allied forces from northern Iraq will remove the shield that now protects the Kurds. Allied agreement to station a mobile force in Turkey seems essential to prevent another panicky exodus. It would also give an immediate boost to Kurdish negotiators in Baghdad and provide a vital guarantee of their future security in the sole language that Saddam Hussein respects.

2-1

# U.N. Team, Declaring Dissatisfaction, Set to Leave Iraq

By Caryle Murphy
Washington Post Foreign Service

BAGHDAD, Iraq, July 2—A top-level U.N. delegation prepared to leave Iraq, possibly Wednesday morning, after having been denied access to the equipment—believed by some U.N. specialists to be for the manufacture of weapons-grade uranium—that was spotted and photographed by U.N. inspectors Friday in trucks on a highway.

International Atomic Energy Agency Director General Hans Blix, head of the delegation, said Iraqi authorities today had shown him only some "nuclear research-oriented" equipment for civilian use that had been inexplicably destroyed by the Iraqis.

[At U.N. headquarters, the Security Council was expected to meet in emergency session in the next few days to discuss Iraq's failure to comply with pro-

visions of the cease-fire ending the Persian Gulf War, the Associated Press reported.]

The U.N. delegation was sent here after Iraqi soldiers fired warning shots as U.N. inspectors photographed the convoy Friday. The delegation is to leave Wednesday morning, apparently without getting the access they had requested to the nuclear enrichment equipment.

In response to U.N. complaints that Iraq is not granting access, a Foreign Ministry spokesman said, "Iraq has given a decisive commitment, at the highest levels, to facilitate the international organization's search of all the [nuclear] instruments, equipment and sites all over Iraq."

"The Security Council asked for a number of assurances," Blix said tonight after returning from his inspection tour at the unidentified military site, "and a number of assurances have been given. But as for the objects that exited from

the al-Fallujah site [on Friday], we don't have a satisfactory explanation of what they were or where they went."

Blix said that what he saw today was related to "nuclear research" and had been destroyed by the Iraqis "as part of an effort they had made to destroy certain types of nuclear research equipment." Asked why they would destroy this equipment, he said he did not know.

U.N. officials who saw the equipment Friday have said they are certain it is for enriching uranium. But Blix said the photographs taken Friday need to be analyzed before the United Nations can be certain.

Meanwhile, another U.N. inspection team today observed the destruction of 12 of Iraq's 61 long-range ballistic missiles, according to the team's chief inspector, U.S. Army Col. Douglas Englund.

That team was taken to al-Taji military base north of Baghdad, Englund said, and watched as the Iraqis used bulldozers to

crush the 12 al-Hussein missiles, an upgraded version of the SCUD. Englund said the Iraqis posed no obstacles to his group. "I would say they are being cooperative and professional," he said.

Under the terms of U.N. Resolution 687 ending the Persian Gulf War, Iraq is required to disclose and destroy not only its nuclear capabilities, but also its ballistic missiles. Iraq told the United Nations that it possessed 61 long-range missiles.

Blix's tour followed discussions today with top Iraqi officials, including Deputy Prime Minister Tariq Aziz, the foreign and defense ministers and the head of Iraq's Atomic Energy Commission.

One U.N. participant called the session "awful," with the Iraqi officials "talking in circles." When shown a photograph of the nuclear equipment taken by the U.N. team Friday, according to one U.N. source, the Iraqis said it was equipment "relevant to the reconstruction of Iraq."

# "이라크서 核장비 목격"

## IAEA국장밝혀 조사단접근 또 거부당해

IAEA국장밝혀 조사단접근 또 거부당해

【바그다드=AP=聯合】이라크의 비밀핵무기프로그램에 대한 증거 수집작업을 벌였던 한스·블릭스 국제원자력기구(IAEA) 사무국장은 이라크내에서 현장사찰활동을 수행하던 3명의 유엔핵조사단이 핵 관련장비를 목격했다고 2일 밝혔다.

유엔안전보장이사회가 파견했던 3명의 유엔핵조사단의 일원인 블릭스 사무국장은 그러나 지난달29일 이라크병사들이 공포를 발사하며 이들 조사단의 접근을 거부했던 사건이 발생한 당시의 장비가 핵 관련장비인지의 여부는 밝히지않았다.

그는 안전보장 이사회의에 앞서 기자들에게 '우리는 80여점의 것을 목격했다'고 말하고 그가 목격한것이 핵관련장비였느냐는 질문에 '그렇다'고 답변했다.

앞서 조지·부시 美대통령가들은 아직도 이라크목표에 대해 군사적공격을 가할 수있도록 유엔의 권한을 부여받고 있다고 경고한바 있다.

한편 이라크는 핵사찰에 판 유엔결의에 협조할것 이라고 유엔관리들이 말했다.

은 이라크가 유엔핵조사단의 접근을 거부하자 사담·후세인 이라크 대통령이 비밀핵무기프로그램을 숨기위해 거짓말을 하고있다고 비난하는 한편 단독적

이란고 거듭 약속했음에도 불구하고 2일 핵폭탄제조에 사용되는 것으로 단정되는 장비와 재료를 적재한 수송대에 대한 유엔조사단의 접근을 또다시 거부했다.•

# 외 무 부

종 별 :

번 호 : UNW-1740          일 시 : 91 0705 1840

수 신 : 장 관 (국연,중동일,국기,기정)

발 신 : 주 유엔 대사

제 목 : 걸프사태 (이락 핵사찰)

   연: UNW-1724

   1. 이락 핵사찰 관련, 연호 유엔 고위대표단의 이락방문 (6.30-7.3.) 결과보고서가 사무총장을 통해 7.5. 안보리에 제출된바, 당관에서 입수한 동보고서 내용을 별첨 송부함. (동 보고서는 서문, 대표단구성, 방문개요, 이락측과의 접촉내용, 관찰사항으로 구성된 바 이중 접촉내용 및 관찰사항 부분을 발췌 송부함)

   2. 상기 보고서에서 고위대표단은 이락측이 사찰활동을 보장하고 관련 조치들을 약속하였으나 이는 실제적 이행을 통해서 만평가가 가능하며 특히 지난 6.28. 유엔조사단이 사찰을시도했던 문제의 장비등에 대한 사찰요청에 관해 이락측 반응이 미흡함을 지적하였음.

   3. 한편 유엔측 발표에 의하면 사무총장은 7.4.제네바에서 주제네바 이락대사를 면담코 S.HUSSEIN이락대통령 앞으로 친전멧시지 ( PERSONALMESSAGE) 를 보냈으며 회신을 금일 접수하였다고 하는바, 동 회신 내용은 상기 이락방문 결과보고서에 첨부됨.

   4.안보리는 상기 보고서를 접수함에 따라 금일 오후 비공식 협의 예정인바 관련동 향은 추보 위계임.끝

   (대사 노창희-국장)

   첨부: FAX (UNW(F)-307)

   1. 보고서 (발췌)

   2. NY,WP 지 사설 및 기사

---

국기국    1차보    중아국    국기국    안기부

**(ii)  Presentation of the demands of the Security Council**

7.      During its meetings, the mission emphasized that it had been sent to Iraq in order to convey the urgent demand of the Security Council for unequivocal assurances that the Government of Iraq will take all the necessary measures to ensure that no hindrances are placed in the way of the discharge by the Special Commission of its mandate under Security Council resolution 687 (1991) and accord, in compliance with Iraq's obligations and commitments vis-à-vis the United Nations and the IAEA, full cooperation, including immediate and unimpeded access, to sites declared or designated under paragraphs 9 and 13 of Security Council resolution 687 (1991), to the inspection teams sent to Iraq by the Special Commission and the IAEA.  The mission further emphasized that it was under instructions from the Council to obtain unconditional guarantees for the safety and security of all personnel engaged in the performance of functions in connection with Security Council resolution 687 (1991).  It was also under instructions to seek detailed information on undertakings and measures by the Government to ensure compliance at all levels, including local military and civilian authorities, with Iraq's obligations under Security Council resolution 687 (1991).

8.      In transmitting the Council's demands, the mission stressed the Council's grave concern over the incident of 28 June, in particular the use of firearms by Iraqi personnel, and drew attention to the fact that the members of the Council had strongly deplored the incidents of 23, 25 and 28 June 1991 and had condemned the conduct of the Iraqi authorities in this connection.  It also underlined that the President's statement recorded the unanimous view of the members of the Council.

9.      The mission drew attention to the fact that the Council remains seized of the matter.  The mission underlined the importance of full compliance by Iraq so as to enable the United Nations to continue to

10-1

0097

carry out resolution 687 (1991) and that any non-compliance by Iraq would
have serious consequences. The mission monitored the view of the
Security Council on the threat that weapons of mass destruction pose to
peace and security in the Middle East and on the need to work towards the
establishment in the Middle East of a zone free of such weapons.

(iii)   <u>Assurances given by the Government of Iraq</u>

10.     The mission received from the Ministers with whom it met the
various assurances indicated below:

(a)   A decision by the President of Iraq, which had
      been conveyed to the Security Council in New York
      by Iraq's Permanent Representative (S/22799),
      to the effect that the President had ordered all
      the Iraqi authorities concerned to extend full
      cooperation to the United Nations representatives
      and to facilitate their tasks in line with the
      obligations undertaken by Iraq.  The President
      had also instructed that all bureaucratic
      problems arising in the cooperation process should be
      overcome and had authorized the Minister for Foreign
      Affairs to issue immediate instructions to all
      authorities and departments, which the United Nations
      representatives desired to visit and inspect, to give
      access without hesitation.

(b)   A further statement by the President of Iraq which,
      <u>inter alia</u>, contained the assurance that Iraq has
      abandoned all activities that may be in contravention
      of Security Council resolution 687 (1991).

(c)   An assurance that Iraq will take all necessary
      measures to ensure that no hindrances are
      placed in the way of the inspection activities of
      the Special Commission and IAEA and that it will
      accord full cooperation to the inspection teams,
      including immediate and unimpeded access, and the
      right to stop and inspect vehicles in movement.

(d)   The information that, in order to implement the
      assurances of cooperation at all levels, orders
      had been issued to all Iraqi military and civilian
      personnel to this effect.

10-2

0098

(e) The information that full authority has been given
to the Minister for Foreign Affairs to issue directives
relating to compliance with Special Commission and
IAEA requests under resolution 687 (1991), and that
a high-level military liaison officer was, as of now,
placed in the Ministry for Foreign Affairs with
authority to grant immediate access to any military
site or installation.

(iv) <u>Access to the objects observed by the nuclear
inspection team</u>

11.    The mission insisted throughout on the call by the members of the
Security Council that Iraq grant the nuclear inspection team, present in
Iraq, immediate and unimpeded access to the objects which the team had
endeavoured to inspect on 23, 25 and 28 June 1991.  The mission
reiterated this call when it was reported to it that materials which the
team was invited to inspect at Fallujah on 1 July and on 2 July 1991 did
not comprise objects which the team had observed on 28 June.

12.    The Iraqi side explained that some equipment and material
belonging to the Atomic Energy Commission of Iraq had been transferred to
the Ministry of Defence for purposes of destruction of items that might
be in contravention of resolution 687 (1991) and of redistribution of
other items which could be used for the civilian reconstruction programme
in Iraq.  It was further stated that some of this equipment and material
had been present at the Fallujah site.  No specification of these items
was given, but the Chairman of the Atomic Energy Commission of Iraq
promised to provide, in the near future, a list of all items that had
been destroyed.  Following these explanations, in the afternoon of 2 July
the inspection team, accompanied by the Director-General of IAEA, was

10-3

0099

taken to a destruction site and was shown certain destroyed equipment. The large pieces of equipment which were thus inspected were related to nuclear research and could not have had relevance for the production of weapons-usable material. No meaningful explanation was given why they had been destroyed.

13.     The mission stated that if Iraq had interpreted resolution 687 (1991) in such a way as not to cover research or other facilities, or equipment for the enrichment of uranium or the separation of plutonium, an additional declaration would be needed to include such items as centrifuges, calutrons, facilities for production of uranium tetrachloride or uranium hexafluoride. The Chairman of the Atomic Energy Commission of Iraq stated categorically that there had not been and there was currently no programme under the Commission for the enrichment of uranium in Iraq. The Deputy Prime Minister added that there was only one nuclear programme in Iraq.

### (v)   Observations by the Government of Iraq

14.     The Iraqi side, while reiterating the Government's acceptance of the Security Council's resolutions, nonetheless, considered the resolutions to be harsh and unjust. In this connection, reference was made in particular to Security Council resolution 600 (1991), concerning the liability of Iraq for the costs incurred under Part C of Security Council resolution 687 (1991) and their offer to undertake destruction of chemical weapons. The mission stated that this offer was under serious consideration in the Special Commission.

*10-4*

0100

15.    The Iraqi side, when referring to the incidents of
23, 25 and 28 June 1991, complained that insufficient notice of
inspection had been given.  Furthermore, insistence on undertaking the
inspections during the Moslem religious holiday of Eid, when the civilian
or military officers concerned could not be easily contacted, was
inappropriate.  Iraq's industrial base had been badly damaged during the
conflict and serious communications and logistical problems existed.  All
these factors had contributed to the incidents.  The mission stated that
appropriate notice would always be given, but that the Special Commission
and the IAEA had the right to inspect mobile objects with short or no
notice.  The inspection teams had no intention to disregard the religious
feelings of the people of Iraq.  However, it was now a common feature of
verification under modern arms control agreements that inspections might
take place at any time when there were reasons for believing that
otherwise the purposes of the inspection might be frustrated.
Furthermore, on 23 June, it was noticed that considerable Iraqi activity
was under way at the inspection site, despite the religious holiday.

16.    The Iraqi side referred to their reservations concerning the
composition of certain inspection teams and expressed the hope that in
the future they would be more widely drawn.  The mission stated that,
in composing the teams, primary emphasis has to be put on technical
competence.  Most teams were composed of personnel of many
nationalities.  A restricting factor exists in the nuclear weapons and
related fields, where the available expertise is largely limited to the
five nuclear weapons States.  It was agreed that the selection of the
members of the inspection teams was within the sole prerogative of the
Special Commission and of the IAEA.

10-5

0101

E.     <u>Findings of the high-level mission</u>

17.     In spite of their unambiguous character, the general assurances given and the specific measures promised can only be evaluated in the light of present and future implementation by the Iraqi authorities. As described in this report, the Iraqi response to the request for access to the objects which the inspection team had endeavoured to inspect on 28 June, falls short of what has been called for by the Security Council.

Geneva, 4 July 1991.

Rolf Ekéus          Hans Blix          Yasushi Akashi

10-6

0102

/Original English7

ANNEX A

PAPER HANDED BY THE SECRETARY GENERAL
TO THE PERMANENT REPRESENTATIVE OF IRAQ
IN GENEVA ON 4 JULY, 1991.

The high level mission was given unambiguous assurances as regards full cooperation and specific measures to ensure compliance by Iraq with its obligations under Security Council Resolution 687.

However, the response by Iraq to the request for access to the objects, which the nuclear inspection team had observed on a long convoy of trucks and had endeavoured to inspect 28 June, was deemed not satisfactory by the Mission. Only a full demonstration of what all these objects were and inspection of them by a nuclear inspection team would be satisfactory.

The high level mission noted information given to it that a decision had been taken by Iraq not to retain any items which might be in contravention with Security Council Resolution 687, nuclear or other, and that equipment of the Atomic Energy Commission of Iraq had been transferred to the army, some for destruction, other for use in the reconstruction work. Explanations were not given on what nuclear items Iraq had considered to be in contravention with Security Council Resolution 687.

Full explanations about nuclear activities and equipment which had been deemed by Iraq to be in contravention of the resolution and inspection of this equipment and facilities related to them - destroyed or not - are imperative.

10-7

/Original: Arabic/

91-21905/2452f                              -2-
edd                                     Annex III

### Letter dated 5 July 1991 (Baghdad time) from President Saddam Hussein addressed to the Secretary-General

We highly appreciate the initiative of the Secretary-General of the United Nations and affirm the guarantees, given to the high-level mission during its visit to Baghdad, whereby prompt and unimpeded access will be ensured to the locations and items designated for inspection in accordance with Security Council resolution 687 (1991), in addition to guaranteeing the security and safety of members of the inspection team. We also affirm that Iraq is committed to the fulfilment of its obligations under the aforesaid resolution.

With respect to the concerns of the mission, it has been arranged that the mission should be provided with a list of the items about which it sought information. This list will be ready on the evening of Sunday, 7 July, or the morning of Monday, 8 July 1991, at which time it may be studied by the inspection team.

-----

10-8

0104

# Iraqi Army Blockading Shiites In Marshes, U.N. Team Says

**By PAUL LEWIS**
Special to The New York Times

UNITED NATIONS, July 3 — Iraq's armed forces are blockading 40,000 to 100,000 dissident Iraqi Shiite Muslims in the marshlands of southern Iraq under appalling conditions and periodically shelling them, a team of United Nations officials say.

Prince Sadruddin Aga Khan, the United Nations relief coordinator for Iraq, plans to visit the marshes next week in an attempt to get the refugees released when he travels to Iraq to assess the country's humanitarian needs and decide whether to recommend some easing of trade sanctions.

Prince Sadruddin will seek first to distribute food, water and medical aid to the refugees and then to establish United Nations-supervised release points through which the refugees can safely leave the marshes and return to their homes, officials say.

In Washington today, a State Department official said, "We welcome the Prince's mission and we urge the Iraqi Government to cooperate fully with his requests."

The Shiite refugees fled to the marshes earlier this summer to escape retribution after a failed uprising against President Saddam Hussein. Last month, Iran complained to the Security Council that the Iraqi Army had surrounded them and was planning to attack.

United Nations officials believe this warning deterred Iraq's forces from a full-scale assault. But a team of United Nations officials who visited the area around Howr al Hammar last week found the refugees and reported that the army had surrounded the marshes with machine gun and artillery posts and appeared to be deliberately imprisoning them there.

The refugees are short of food and being forced to drink dirty marshland water. They lack proper housing and dare not light open fires because the Iraqi Army lobs shells in the direction of the smoke. And temperatures are soaring.

### Plans to Tour Iraq

In assessing Iraq's humanitarian needs 11 months after the Security Council imposed its comprehensive trade ban, Prince Sadruddin will be assisted by a team that includes a former United States Attorney General, Elliot L. Richardson; Jean-Daniel Levi, a former energy adviser to President François Mitterrand of France and now head of the French Space Institute; Sir John Moberli, a former British Ambassador to Iraq, and Thomas Hammerberg, head of the Swedish Save the Children's Fund, who formerly directed the human rights organization Amnesty International.

The team, which plans to tour Iraq, will assess the civilian population's immediate needs. Prince Sadruddin will then report his findings through the Secretary General to the United Nations Security Council.

In particular, he is expected to advise the Council whether it should grant Iraq's request to export nearly $1 billion worth of oil to pay for food and other supplies.

10-9

# Iraq Miscalculates, Again

LAST AUTUMN the Iraqi government gambled that the United States and its allies would never actually use force to push it out of Kuwait. Now it is gambling that the allies will do nothing about its refusal to carry out its commitments under the cease-fire agreement and accept nuclear disarmament.

President Saddam Hussein and his friends, in the aftermath of a devastating military defeat, are now apparently trying to use their defiance of the United Nations to repair their damaged prestige. But they are making another portentous misjudgment. They have chosen to violate the cease-fire on a subject of such great and obvious danger to the world that the allies cannot let it pass.

The Iraqis have some highly enriched uranium, material of which nuclear explosives can be made. How much they might have is a question yet to be answered. In years past they were given a small amount by the French and the Soviets for research—but it's enough for a couple of bombs. They apparently also have equipment that could be used to make more of it. That equipment has been the object of the chase by the U.N.'s inspectors over the past couple of weeks. Twice they have closed in on it, and twice the Iraqi army has prevented them by force from getting a close look, firing over their heads on the second occasion.

A close look is crucial, because it will reveal whether this equipment has been used to produce additional enriched uranium. Under the cease-fire, the inspectors are to seize and remove or destroy all nuclear components as well as the equipment to produce them. Last weekend the U.N. responded to the Iraqi stonewalling by sending a delegation to Baghdad. The talks evidently were unsuccessful, and the delegation has returned to Geneva. But if the exercise accomplished nothing else, it has given the Iraqis a careful warning that the rest of the world is utterly serious about the necessity of enforcing the terms of the cease-fire agreement.

Once again the Iraqis have left the allies, and especially the United States, with no easy choices. No one wants to see the war recommenced. But it would be intolerable to leave the Iraqis in possession of unknown amounts of enriched uranium and the capacity to produce more of it. The Iraqis' interference with the U.N. inspections sharpens an issue that, one way or another, the U.N. must resolve promptly.

# Iraqis Say Sanctions Hurt the Wrong People

## Saddam 'Has Everything' but Others Suffer

By Caryle Murphy
Washington Post Foreign Service

BAGHDAD, Iraq, July 4—Iraqi civilians, complaining that the country's worsening economic crisis is hurting them far more than the government, are expressing bewilderment and annoyance at U.S. insistence on continuing international trade sanctions.

Although they recognize that the U.S. aim is to force the ouster of President Saddam Hussein—a goal many Iraqis support—they say this is not likely and in the meantime they are bearing the brunt of the economic hardship. As a result, many say, they are beginning to think that the Iraqi people, not the government, are the target of U.S. hostility.

Iraqis say that "If the strongest power in the world couldn't [oust Saddam], then how can the poor, oppressed, scared Iraqi people do it?" one diplomat here said. "A lot of

Iraqis believe the war was not against Saddam Hussein and his regime, but against the Iraqi people," the diplomat added. "Really, many people say it. Of course they know he doesn't suffer. President Bush's strategy is the correct one, but at the same time, the situation is very difficult."

This questioning of the efficacy of continued sanctions is in tune with official government statements that accuse Washington of waging economic war against the Iraqi people. It is also the message the government wishes to see carried by the Western press, which is being given unusually open access here in the hope that its reporting of economic hardships will generate sympathy in the West for the lifting or easing of sanctions.

10-10

0106

# 외 무 부

종 별 :

번 호 : UNW-1742

일 시 : 91 0705 1930

수 신 : 장 관 (국연,중동일,국기,기정)

발 신 : 주 유엔 대사

제 목 : 안보리 비공식협의 (이락 핵사찰)

연: UNW-1740

1. 연호 유엔 고위대표단의 이락방문 (6.30-7.3)결과 보고서 토의를 위한 안보리비공식 협의가 7.5.오후 늦게 열린바, R.EKEUS 단장으로 부터 이락방문 결과를 청취한 다음 핵사찰 조사반의 보고등 사태추이를 더관망키로 하고 일단 종결되었음.

2.다음주중 재협의가 있을것으로 보이는 바, 관련동향은 추보 위계임. 끝

(대사 노창희-국장)

---

국기국    1차보    중아국    국기국    안기부

91.07.06    09:40 WI

외신 1과 통제관

0107

# Iraq's Shell Game

## Saddam tries to hide nuclear-war technology—and risks a new showdown

JEAN-PIERRE LAFFONT—SYGMA

**On Ready Alert**

Incirlik: F-16s

TURKEY

Mediterranean: Aircraft carrier Forrestal

SYRIA

JORDAN

Falluja: Iraqis fired shots in the air to prevent U.N. inspection

Abu Ghraib army base: One of a number of possible hiding places of nuclear-processing equipment. U.N. inspection was delayed by Iraq.

Baghdad
IRAQ

IRAN

SAUDI ARABIA

KUWAIT

Saudi Arabia: Strike aircraft still present include F-15Es, F-16s and F-117A Stealth bombers

Persian Gulf: Aircraft carrier Nimitz

**N**ow you see it, now you don't. For almost a week, Saddam Hussein ran a nuclear shell game on United Nations officials assigned to monitor Iraqi compliance with the gulf war cease-fire. First the team said it wanted to inspect the sprawling military complex outside Baghdad called Abu Ghraib. Fresh American intelligence showed it was a secret repository of Iraqi nuclear-weapons technology. The inspectors were kept waiting for three days. Meanwhile, trucks sped from the base, carrying huge objects draped in canvas covers. On Wednesday, June 26, the team was allowed in—and found nothing. Friday, the U.N. team appeared at a base near Falluja, about 30 miles west of Baghdad. U.S. intelligence indicated the crates from Abu Ghraib had been taken there. Once again, heavily laden trucks began leaving the facility. When inspectors drove quickly to the exit to take photographs, Ira-

qi soldiers fired their guns in the air, then tried to seize the inspectors' cameras. Finally the Iraqis said they could come in. The inspectors said they had seen enough.

So had George Bush. The cease-fire agreement was clear: Baghdad must dismantle its nuclear-weapons program and scrap all other weapons of mass destruction. But the evidence of violations, Bush said, was "incontrovertible, inarguable, clear." A second round of military con-

frontation with the Iraqi dictator seemed possible. "We can't, from a U.S. standpoint, permit this brutal bully to go back on what was a solemn agreement and to threaten people that are there under U.N. jurisdiction," he said. "This man has no shame." All 15 members of the U.N. Security Council, including Iraq's lone friends Cuba and Yemen, agreed to demand that Iraq let the inspectors see the material that had been removed, at once, or face

KOL AL ARAB—SIPA

**Back to the brink?** *Saddam displays atomic triggers, May 1990; Bush heads for Kennebunkport last week; U.S. carrier Nimitz in the Mediterranean*

(map). The Navy has two aircraft carriers in the region. But raids could prove difficult. Saddam could multiply the targets by dispersing the nuclear material in a large number of vehicles. That could foil even American smart weapons.

For the moment, the White House leaned toward diplomacy. A united front at the United Nations might convince Saddam that compliance was his only hope of seeing economic sanctions lifted. It would also provide political cover for any subsequent military action. But there was no rush, some officials argued; Saddam couldn't lob a nuclear bomb at a neighbor tomorrow. White House aides predicted Saddam would get at least a few more days to let inspectors in. "Look, we're still wiping our brow, thanking God we're out of there," said one. "The last thing the president wants on July Fourth"—when he will appear at Desert Storm victory parades in the Midwest—"is to have bombs dropping over Baghdad."

Saddam's game of hide-and-seek probably began well before the first shot of the gulf war. An Iraqi electrical engineer who defected to U.S. Marines in Iraq last month told American intelligence that, in contrast to Gen. Norman Schwarzkopf's Jan. 30 boast that U.S. smart bombs and cruise missiles had "destroyed all of [Iraq's] nuclear facilities," the allies had in fact located and bombed only three of seven nuclear weapons-related facilities in Iraq. The defector also revealed that from the facilities that had been destroyed, key nuclear equipment was evacuated before the bombers came. The defector, who claims he worked at one of the secret, undamaged sites, a uranium-enrichment facility buried in a

mountain near Mosul in northern Iraq, said the facility housed an array of devices called calutrons. They enrich uranium to a grade capable of explosive fission, through an electromagnetic isotope-separation technique developed by the U.S. Manhattan Project in the 1940s. The defector says Iraq had produced 88 pounds of weapons-grade nuclear material—enough for two Nagasaki-size bombs. In an inventory submitted to the United Nations last April as part of the initial cease-fire proceedings, Baghdad did not mention either the equipment or the enriched uranium.

**'Massive deception':** The 80 or so trucks that the U.N. inspectors pursued from Abu Ghraib to Falluja could contain that uranium; Bush administration sources believe they almost certainly contained the components of some 20 isotope-separation devices. Based on the defector's report and satellite photos, U.S. intelligence officials also determined that Iraqi technicians buried crates containing sensitive nuclear equipment and parts at the Tuwaitha nuclear complex near Baghdad, which the allies bombed. After the war ended, the Iraqis dug up the equipment and attempted to hide it at Abu Ghraib. After the Iraqis stonewalled inspectors there, U.S. special forces saw the contraband convoy en route to Falluja. Again Washington alerted the inspectors, setting the stage for last Friday's confrontation. "There's a massive deception program going on here," said a U.S. intelligence source. Whether George Bush waits out the diplomatic game, or ultimately resorts to force, it seemed unlikely that an American president who has already been stung by criticism over Saddam's continuing grip on power would acquiesce in an Iraqi nuclear resurgence.

CHARLES LANE *with* MARGARET GARRARD WARNER *and* DOUGLAS WALLER *in Washington and* ANN McDANIEL *in Kennebunkport, Maine*

JAMES COLBURN—PHOTOREPORTERS

"serious consequences." With no political cover, Saddam finally offered the United Nations full access. The White House, unimpressed, hinted it was still considering force pending proof of Saddam's compliance.    Before leaving for a Maine weekend, Bush held a strategy session with senior advisers. The Pentagon has contingency plans for airstrikes. The Air Force still has fighter and fighter-bomber squadrons in Saudi Arabia and Turkey

0109

민오 : USW(Г) - 2683

수신 : 경  관 (중동일, 미일, 미이, 정보신) : 주미덕서

재무 : 이각 핵개발 관련

# U.N. Skeptical of Iraq's Promise to Inspectors

### By FRANK J. PRIAL
Special to The New York Times

UNITED NATIONS, July 5 — President Saddam Hussein assured the United Nations in a letter today that he would comply with all the demands of inspection teams seeking to account for Iraq's nuclear-weapons potential.

But members of the Security Council, meeting to consider the letter and the report of a United Nations delegation that has just returned from Iraq, said they were not convinced of the Iraqi leader's sincerity.

"The proof of the pudding is in the eating," said Ambassador Thomas Richardson, Britain's deputy representative here. He said the Council would need stronger assurances of compliance with the cease-fire resolution that requires Iraq to turn over all weapons of mass destruction, including weapons-grade nuclear material, to the United Nations for removal and destruction.

In Washington, the White House reemphasized President Bush's belief that he has the authority to resume military action if Iraq continues to resist international efforts to seek out equipment thought capable of producing enriched uranium.

#### 'Prompt and Unimpeded Access'

Referring to the resolutions on a cease-fire in the Persian Gulf war, which authorized "every means necessary to preserve the peace and stability" of the gulf region, a White House spokesman, Roman Popadiuk, said: "We have the right and the international groundwork for enforcing those resolutions."

In a letter to Secretary General Javier Pérez de Cuéllar, President Hussein said a list of the devices used to produce enriched uranium would be made available by Sunday or Monday.

"Prompt and unimpeded access will be ensured to the location and items

## The U.S. clings to the threat of military action.

designated for inspection in accordance with Security Council Resolution 687," the letter said.

As he left the Security Council meeting, Ambassador Alexander F. Watson, the deputy United States representative, said, "clearly the Iraqis are not cooperating." Referring to the inspection team that had been denied access to uranium processing equipment, he said: "Why on earth has this particular nuclear team been treated so badly? What has it come across?"

Yuli Vorontsov, the Soviet Ambassador here, said the possibility of a military option, raised by President Bush, had not come up in the consultations.

"We're not discussing that. They never have within the walls of the United Nations suggested the military option. We haven't yet finished our diplomatic efforts. And I think they will succeed."

While Mr. Hussein's letter answered some questions, the Soviet Ambassador said, it did not answer the primary one about the missing nuclear devices. "I think they have to understand how serious this is," he said.

The three-member United Nations team, headed by Rolf Ekeus, director of a special commission on Iraq's weapons of mass destruction, said Iraq's response to a request for access to nuclear equipment "falls short of what has been called for by the Security Council."

Their report noted that Iraq's "general assurances and the specific measures promised" could be evaluated only "in the light of present and future implementation by the Iraqi authorities."

NYT
July 6, '91

2683-1

0110

발신 : 05%(F) -

수신 : 경 권

발신 : 주미대॥

제목 :

보안
동정

(     예)

# Iraq Promises Access to Nuclear Sites;
# U.N. Agrees to Wait and S

**By John M. Goshko**
Washington Post Staff Writer

UNITED NATIONS, July 5—Iraqi President Saddam Hussein promised today to provide the United Nations with a complete list of his country's nuclear equipment and to give U.N. inspectors "prompt and unimpeded access" to nuclear installations from which they have been barred by Iraqi troops.

Saddam gave those assurances in a letter to Secretary General Javier Perez de Cuellar that was received here as the Security Council met to discuss what to do about the failure of a high-level U.N. delegation to gain access to the materiel and weapons sites involved in the dispute.

As a result of Saddam's letter, the council members decided to wait until early next week to see if Iraq will keep its latest promises.

The three-member delegation went to Baghdad after a series of incidents late last month when U.N. inspectors were barred from locating and inspecting weapons of mass destruction that Iraq is supposed to destroy under the terms of the Persian Gulf War cease-fire accord.

President Bush has condemned the Iraqi actions, including an incident on June 28 when soldiers fired over the heads of U.N. inspectors filming the hasty withdrawal of equipment from a military transportation base near Baghdad. In his letter today, Saddam said the United Nations would be given a list of the removed equipment by Sunday night or Monday morning.

Bush has said the United States will not rule out a military strike if Iraq fails to give satisfactory proof that it is complying with its promise to get rid of all nuclear weapons and weapons-related materiel.

The 15-member Security Council also condemned the Iraqi action and sent the three-member delegation to Baghdad with a demand for immediate access to all weapons equipment and areas. But the commission informed the council today that it had been unsuccessful.

Several other council members, including the Soviet Union, have argued that all possible diplomatic means should be exhausted

> ### "Neither the United States nor anyone else has said one word within the walls of the United Nations about a resort to military options."
> —Soviet Ambassador Yuli Vorontsov

before the United Nations threatens further military action against Iraq.

Those advocating a go-slow approach have pointed out that aerial bombing of suspected sites would not clear up the questions about what kind of nuclear capability Iraq retains. Despite Bush's rhetoric, there appears to be little enthusiasm here for an invasion of Iraq by ground forces.

"Neither the United States nor anyone else has said one word within the walls of the United Nations about a resort to military options," Soviet Ambassador Yuli Vorontsov said. "We are talking strictly in terms of diplomatic solutions."

However, Vorontsov added: "This is a very serious matter and the letter we received today is not a satisfactory answer to all the questions in this business. Until these things are cleared up, there is no chance that the Security Council will address such questions as relieving the economic sanctions against Iraq. Iraq must understand that it is in its interest to resolve this."

U.S. and other Western diplomats said one bothersome question was how the United Nations can check the accuracy of the list of equipment Iraq has promised to provide.

The delegation, which spent three days in Baghdad, was led by Rolf Ekeus, who heads

the special U.N. inspection group charged with identifying Iraq's nuclear weapons. It report, given to Perez de Cuellar in Geneva Thursday and the Security Council today said that "the Iraqi response . . . falls short of what had been called for by the Security Council."

The report said that in talks with a variety of senior Iraqi officials, the delegation had been given "unambiguous assurances," similar to those made by Saddam today, that the United Nations would be given access to sites it wants to inspect and would be able see the equipment that was hurriedly trucked away during the June 28 confrontation.

But, the report said, the Iraqis did n match their promises with deeds.

After receiving the report Thursda Perez de Cuellar sent a message to Bag dad that said in part: "Only a full demonstration of what all these objects were and i spection by them by a nuclear inspecti team would be satisfactory."

That message drew the letter from Sa dam that arrived here unexpectedly today

W.P
July 6, '91.

2683 -2

발신 :  USW(I)

수신 :  정   권

제목 :

발신 : 주미대사

(        대)

# Saddam Signals Bold Defiance On Nuclear Issue

## Observers Say Quest for Power Underlies Stand on Inspections

By Caryle Murphy
Washington Post Foreign Service

BAGHDAD, Iraq, July 6—President Saddam Hussein has finally agreed, at least on paper, to permit U.N. inspection of Iraq's nuclear equipment, but diplomats and Iraqis here say his weeks of defiance on this issue appear to reflect the Iraqi leader's revived self-confidence and renewed military ambitions.

Given the secrecy surrounding decision-making here, it is difficult to confirm the reasons for the hard-line position Iraq has taken on this issue up to now. Baghdad's hesitation, highlighted by its refusal to permit U.N. inspection of equipment believed to be used for enriching uranium to weapons-grade quality, has prompted threats of renewed military action from Washington and seems to contradict Iraq's three-month record of compliance with other stipulations of the U.N. resolution that formally ended the Persian Gulf War.

But diplomats and Iraqi officials cite several factors that appear to have influenced Baghdad's position on the nuclear dispute. These include Saddam's restored grip on power—badly shaken by his gulf war defeat and by subsequent, wide-scale internal rebellions—and the high value he places on obtaining nuclear weapons as a way to realize his regional leadership ambitions.

In addition, some diplomats suggest, the Iraqi leadership may believe that any unilateral U.S. military action will not enjoy the same kind of international support that underpinned Operation Desert Storm because of growing disillusionment, especially in the Arab world, with the lack of progress in resolving the Israeli-Palestinian conflict since the end of the war.

"Perhaps Saddam Hussein thinks that it's not easy for the United States to use military means as it did during the gulf crisis, because it cannot muster the support from Europe and Arab countries for military action against Iraq," one diplomat here speculated.

"People would ask," the diplomat added, "'Why do they take military action against Iraq for every single issue, and not against Israel, which is also not complying with United Nations resolutions?' It would become very clear that the United States is only targeting Iraq and its allies."

On Friday, Saddam promised the United Nations that he would permit U.N. inspectors "prompt and unimpeded access" to locations designated for inspection.

A new U.N. nuclear inspection team arrived here today to follow up on Saddam's offer and investigate ways to destroy previously located Iraqi nuclear materials. It will also ask to inspect equipment believed to be for manufacturing weapons-grade uranium.

This is the same equipment to which a senior U.N.

See IRAQ, A22, Col. 1

W.P
July 7, '91

2683-3

0112

# Saddam's Challenge on Inspections Signals Renewed Military Ambitions

**IRAQ, From A21**

delegation was refused access after a team of U.N. nuclear inspectors photographed it on June 28. The filming took place as the equipment was being driven in open trucks down a public highway in an apparent attempt to hide it from the inspectors, U.N. officials have said.

Some U.S. officials have expressed skepticism that Saddam will furnish the equipment for inspection, despite his written promise on Friday to U.N. Secretary General Javier Perez de Cuellar.

During a visit to northern Iraq today, U.S. Rep. Stephen Solarz (D-N.Y.) said that "if Saddam refuses to comply with his obligations, the cease-fire should be considered null and void," Reuter reported. Solarz warned that if Iraq again failed to comply, "we will have no alternative but to resume the use of force."

In contrast to three months ago, when Saddam accepted the terms of the gulf war cease-fire, the Iraqi leader now appears to have significantly regained control of internal events. His security apparatus and armed forces, then in disarray following the war in Kuwait and internal rebellions by Shiite Muslims and Kurds, are back in charge.

Reflecting this renewed self-confidence, Saddam has stepped up his criticism of the United States, though not by name, for its perceived double standard toward Iraq. Even as the U.N. envoys were here seeking access to his nuclear equipment last Monday, the Iraqi leader belittled their efforts in a televised address:

"Notice those talking about justice and international legality," he said. "How are they talking about the Palestinian issue? When we said, 'Let us solve the Palestinian issue according

to international legality,' which they were talking about, they said that the Palestinian issue will have its turn in finding a solution after the withrdrawal from Kuwait.

"Look what's happening now. How they try to deprive those who have principles of their arms. Just

---

*The allies "had a military victory, but politically, Saddam Hussein is in power and everything is like old times. It means the mission was not accomplished."*

— Diplomat in Iraq

---

to keep the Israeli arms free. ... Look how they neglect the right of your brothers, the Palestinian people, who are scattered. ... Where is justice and where is international legality as they said?"

Saddam's sense of security may also have been enhanced by the fact that neither Western countries nor his Arab foes took advantage of the rebellions last March to unseat him.

On the contrary, Washington's inaction during the Iraqi army's brutal suppression of southern Shiites was cited by one Iraqi official as evidence that U.S. officials shared the Iraqi leadership's fears that the rebellion could have resulted in an Iranian-supported Islamic republic in southern Iraq.

"Did you see a man afraid of to-

morrow?" another senior government official asked, referring to one of Saddam's recent public appearances. "They compare him to [Romania's Nicolae] Ceausescu. He packed up and left after three days of demonstrations. Tell me a Third World leader who's gone through what Saddam Hussein has gone through in the last 15 years" and remained in power, he said.

If Iraq was found to possess equipment for the production of nuclear weapons, for Saddam it would represent the crown jewel of his military arsenal, now otherwise severely depleted through the war's allied bombing raids and the U.N.-mandated destruction of Iraq's ballistic missiles and chemical weapons.

A nuclear capability—which no other Arab state is believed to possess—would likely fulfill Saddam's ambition to be the Middle East's pre-eminent Arab challenger of Israel.

Iraq claims it is being unfairly singled out, while Israel goes unchallenged despite its widely reported production of nuclear weapons. Such claims strike a resonant chord in many Arabs. Even Egypt, Washington's closest Arab ally, has insisted that regional disarmament proposals encompass Israel's nuclear arsenal.

One diplomat here said he believes the Bush administration is exaggerating the ability of Iraq to produce a nuclear weapon anytime soon.

This diplomat suggested Washington is using the nuclear issue as a "pretext" to continue sanctions or renew military action in order to remove Saddam from power. The Bush administration wants "to accomplish now what was not solved during the war," he said. "They had a military victory, but politically, Saddam Hussein is in power and everything is like old times. It means the mission was not accomplished."

WP
July 7, '91

2683-4

0113

빈호 : (JSW(F) -

수신 : 장   관

제목 :

발신 : 주미대사

보안
등급

(        매)

---

## Baghdad's Nuclear Cat-and-Mouse Game

# A Rising Sense That Iraq's Hussein Must Go

### By THOMAS L. FRIEDMAN

WASHINGTON

WHILE President Bush is going through the diplomatic motions of trying to get the Iraqis to peacefully surrender their nuclear weapons-making equipment, many Administration officials are beginning to come around to the view that there is no diplomatic solution for their Iraq problem. The only solution, in this view, is the removal of President Saddam Hussein.

Wars do not usually end with the defeated general still in power in his capital, but for a variety of reasons the Bush Administration was prepared to live with the Iraqi leader. But that decision is now under review. Mr. Hussein's relentless efforts to retain his nuclear bomb components are making it increasingly difficult for Washington to justify having left him in power. In fact, many officials now acknowledge, as long as he is there the gulf war will never really be over.

Few in the Administration, though, want to admit that stark conclusion publicly, because to speak the words aloud would require doing something about them, and the fact is that President Bush has been ambivalent about Mr. Hussein's fate since the day the war ended. Mr. Bush inadvertently acknowledged the source of that ambivalence last week when he was asked whether he was disappointed about the lack of democratization in Kuwait. "The war wasn't fought about democracy in Kuwait," Mr. Bush bluntly retorted.

The war was, instead, fought to restore the status quo. And, as every American policymaker knows, before Mr. Hussein invaded Kuwait, he was a pillar of the gulf balance of power and status quo preferred by Washington. His iron fist simultaneously held Iraq together, much to the satisfaction of the American allies Turkey and Saudi Arabia, and it prevented Iranian Islamic fundamentalists from sweeping over the eastern Arab world. It was only when the Iraqi dictator decided to use his iron fist to dominate Kuwait and Saudi Arabia that he became a threat. But as soon as Mr. Hussein was forced back into his shell, Washington felt he had become useful again for maintaining the regional balance and preventing Iraq from disintegrating.

That was why Mr. Bush never supported the Kurdish and Shiite rebellions against Mr. Hussein, or for that matter any democracy movement in Iraq. The President felt that Mr. Hussein and his army were broken and no longer represented any external threat, especially since Mr. Bush contentedly assumed that his intelligence reports were correct and that all of Mr. Hussein's nuclear capabilities had been destroyed. Sooner or later, Mr. Bush argued, sanctions would force Mr. Hussein's generals to bring him down, and then Washington would have the best of all worlds: an iron-fisted Iraqi junta without Saddam Hussein. In the meantime, the foreign policy expert in Mr. Bush said: Ignore him.

But Mr. Hussein and his generals are not following the scripts Washington handed them. The generals have not ousted Mr. Hussein, and he is refusing to play the chastened and defeated foe ready to tacitly preserve a Pax Americana in the gulf. The April 3 gulf war cease-fire resolution enjoined him to turn over for destruction all of his large ballistic missiles and chemical-, biological- and nuclear bomb-making equipment. In order not to make himself an easy target, and to lull the West into forgetting him, he has cleverly cooperated in all these areas — except the nuclear. There, he has played cat and mouse for three months, hiding from United Nations inspectors, right up to last week, secret nuclear bomb-making equipment he managed to preserve, and perhaps enough enriched uranium for two Nagasaki-size bombs.

By refusing to turn over his remaining nuclear equipment he is both resurfacing as a potential strategic threat and noisily taunting Washington, swaggering out of his bunker and firing his pistol into the air. "You see, there are two Saddams," said Fouad Ajami, a Middle East expert at Johns Hopkins University. "The man in power with whom we were ready to live because we thought he was diminished, and keeping him around seemed convenient; and the symbolic Saddam — the man whom George Bush turned into a devil to mobilize the American public in a national crusade against, and whose continuing presence still taunts the victor."

Mr. Bush was ready to ignore the symbolic Saddam Hussein, taunts and all, as long as the real one was a strategic asset, not a threat. But those days may be over. Mr. Bush has begun hinting at a military strike to knock out Mr. Hussein's remaining nuclear equipment, while leaving him in power. But some officials wonder whether he won't just try to build another bomb. The problem is not his capabilities but his intentions. Mr. Hussein's willingness to risk the continuation of economic sanctions in order to preserve his nuclear program suggests that he remains more interested in personal aggrandizement and revenge than in rebuilding his country.

Indeed, Mr. Hussein has a unique personal incentive to continue trying to obtain a nuclear weapon quickly: it would deter the West from coming after him; it could be the vehicle for his revenge, blackmail, or intimidation against Israel or those Arab states who opposed him; it would be of enormous value for his own political resurrection in the Arab world and, symbolically, it would be the ultimate thumb in the eye of George Bush. Moreover, given Mr. Hussein's own grandiose self-delusions, he finds it very hard to take orders from the United Nations, said Laurie Mylroie of the Washington Institute for Near East Policy. Defiance is an essential part of his strategy; to appear to be taking orders from the United Nations is to appear weak, and weakness in his habitat — the snakepit of Iraqi politics — will be exploited.

Mr. Hussein's continued rule in Baghdad is not only becoming a strategic problem for Mr. Bush, but a political one. Certainly one reason that the Syrians have not responded to American efforts to entice them to the conference table with Israel is because President Hafez al-Assad is afraid that Mr. Hussein would depict him as a lackey of the Americans. Moreover, the longer Mr. Hussein is in power, the more incentive his Arab neighbors will have for doing business with him again and reintegrating him into Arab politics. Business is business and there is a lot of reconstruction business to be done in Iraq. Already, one can hear murmurings from Egypt that Iraq has been punished enough.

In the Middle East, "the hand you cannot cut off, you kiss," said Elie Kedourie, the Iraqi-born historian. The Arab leaders, he added, know well the rules of their world, which Mr. Bush too may soon have to confront: "Either you cut a deal with Saddam or you kill him, but there is no third way."

*NYT Jul 7. '91*

2683 -5 (END)

0114

# 외 무 부

종 별 :

번 호 : UNW-1755                                                  일 시 : 91 0708 1930

수 신 : 장 관(국연,중동일,국기,기정)

발 신 : 주 유엔 대사

제 목 : 걸프사태

연: UNW-1740

1. 후세인 이락대통령이 연호 유엔사무총장앞 서한에서 핵관련 품목 명세를 7.7 또는 7.8제출하겠다고 언급한것과 관련, 금 7.8 사무총장 대변인은 이락측으로부터 외상 명의 사무총장 앞서한 (이락의 핵관련 계획, 핵장비 및 물질보유 현황포함)을 7.7. 접수하였으며 현재 동서한 내용을 검토중이라고 언급하였음.

2. 사우디는 이락이 안보리 휴전결의에 규정된 쿠웨이트 및 제 3국인 송환의무를 이행치 않고있다고 주장 (최소한 사우디인 15명 미송환)하는 안보리문서를 7.3 자로 배포 하였음.

첨부: NYT, WSJ 지 기사: UNW(F)-310

끝

(대사 노창희-국장)

---

국기국    1차보    중아국    국기국    외정실    분석관    안기부

By THOMAS L. FRIEDMAN

WASHINGTON

WHILE President Bush is going through the diplomatic motions of trying to get the Iraqis to peacefully surrender their nuclear weapons-making equipment, many Administration officials are beginning to come around to the view that there is no diplomatic solution for their Iraq problem. The only solution, in this view, is the removal of President Saddam Hussein.

Wars do not usually end with the defeated general still in power in his capital, but for a variety of reasons the Bush Administration was prepared to live with the Iraqi leader. But that decision is now under review. Mr. Hussein's relentless efforts to retain his nuclear bomb components are making it increasingly difficult for Washington to justify having left him in power. In fact, many officials now acknowledge, as long as he is there the gulf war will never really be over.

Few in the Administration, though, want to admit that stark conclusion publicly, because to speak the words aloud would require doing something about them, and the fact is that President Bush has been ambivalent about Mr. Hussein's fate since the day the war ended. Mr. Bush inadvertently acknowledged the source of that ambivalence last week when he was asked whether he was disappointed about the lack of democratization in Kuwait. "The war wasn't fought about democracy in Kuwait," Mr. Bush bluntly retorted.

The war was, instead, fought to restore the status quo. And, as every American policymaker knows, before Mr. Hussein invaded Kuwait he was a pillar of the gulf balance of power and status quo preferred by Washington. His iron fist simultaneously held Iraq together, much to the satisfaction of the American allies Turkey and Saudi Arabia, and it prevented Iranian Islamic fundamentalists from sweeping over the eastern Arab world. It was only when the Iraqi dictator decided to use his iron fist to dominate Kuwait and Saudi Arabia that he became a threat. But as soon as Mr. Hussein was forced back into his shell, Washington felt he had become useful again for maintaining the regional balance and preventing Iraq from disintegrating.

That was why Mr. Bush never supported the Kurdish and Shiite rebellions against Mr. Hussein, or for that matter any democracy movement in Iraq. The President felt that Mr. Hussein and his army were broken and no longer represented any external threat, especially since Mr. Bush contentedly assumed that his intelligence reports were correct and that all of Mr. Hussein's nuclear capabilities had been destroyed. Sooner or later, Mr. Bush argued, sanctions would force Mr. Hussein's generals to bring him down, and then Washington would have the best of all worlds: an iron-fisted Iraqi junta without Saddam Hussein. In the meantime, the foreign policy expert in Mr. Bush said: Ignore him.

But Mr. Hussein and his generals are not following the scripts Washington handed them. The generals have not ousted Mr. Hussein, and he is refusing to play the chastened and defeated foe ready to tacitly preserve a Pax Americana in the gulf. The April 3 gulf war cease-fire resolution enjoined him to turn over for destruction all of his large ballistic missiles and chemical, biological and nuclear bomb-making equipment. In order not to make himself an easy target, and to lull the West into forgetting him, he has cleverly cooperated in all these areas — except the nuclear. There, he has played cat and mouse for three months, hiding from United Nations inspectors, right up to last week, secret nuclear bomb-making equipment he managed to preserve, and perhaps enough enriched uranium for two Nagasaki-size bombs.

P.1

By refusing to turn over his remaining nuclear equipment he is both resurfacing as a potential strategic threat and noisily taunting Washington, swaggering out of his bunker and firing his pistol into the air. "You see, there are two Saddams," said Fouad Ajami, a Middle East expert at Johns Hopkins University. "The man in power with whom we were ready to live because we thought he was diminished, and keeping him around seemed convenient, and the symbolic Saddam — the man

---

## In Washington and in Baghdad, scripts differ on what role Hussein should play. Will he stabilize the region, or intimidate it?

---

whom George Bush turned into a devil to mobilize the American public in a national crusade against, and whose continuing presence still taunts the victor."

Mr. Bush was ready to ignore the symbolic Saddam Hussein, taunts and all, as long as the real one was a strategic asset, not a threat. But those days may be over. Mr. Bush has begun hinting at a military strike to knock out Mr. Hussein's remaining nuclear equipment, while leaving him in power. But some officials wonder whether he won't just try to build another bomb. The problem is not his capabilities but his intentions. Mr. Hussein's willingness to risk the continuation of economic sanc-

tions in order to preserve his nuclear program suggests that he remains more interested in personal aggrandizement and revenge than in rebuilding his country.

Indeed, Mr. Hussein has a unique personal incentive to continue trying to obtain a nuclear weapon quickly: It would deter the West from coming after him; it could be the vehicle for his revenge, blackmail, or intimidation against Israel or those Arab states who opposed him; it would be of enormous value for his own political resurrection in the Arab world and, symbolically, it would be the ultimate thumb in the eye of George Bush. Moreover, given Mr. Hussein's own grandiose self-delusions, he finds it very hard to take orders from the United Nations, said Laurie Mylroie of the Washington Institute for Near East Policy. Defiance is an essential part of his strategy; to appear to be taking orders from the United Nations is to appear weak, and weakness in his habitat — the snakepit of Iraqi politics — will be exploited.

Mr. Hussein's continued rule in Baghdad is not only becoming a strategic problem for Mr. Bush, but a political one. Certainly one reason that the Syrians have not responded to American efforts to entice them to the conference table with Israel is because President Hafez al-Assad is afraid that Mr. Hussein would depict him as a lackey of the Americans. Moreover, the longer Mr. Hussein is in power, the more incentive his Arab neighbors will have for doing business with him again and reintegrating him into Arab politics. Business is business and there is a lot of reconstruction business to be done in Iraq. Already, one can hear murmurings from Egypt that Iraq has been punished enough.

In the Middle East, "the hand you cannot cut off, you kiss," said Elie Kedourie, the Iraqi-born historian. The Arab leaders, he added, know well the rules of their world, which Mr. Bush too may soon have to confront: "Either you cut a deal with Saddam or you kill him, but there is no third way."

---

## U.S. Still Weighs Military Raid on Iraq Despite Pledge on Nuclear Inspection

### By Gerald F. Seib

*Staff Reporter of The Wall Street Journal.*

WASHINGTON—The Bush administration continues to seriously consider military action to destroy Iraqi nuclear-weapons equipment, despite a new pledge by Saddam Hussein to allow the United Nations full access to previously hidden nuclear equipment.

Administration aides remain incensed at Iraqi leader Saddam Hussein over his regime's refusal to give a U.N. inspection team access last week to equipment the U.S. believes is used for the enrichment of uranium for use in nuclear bombs. The Iraqi leader on Friday sent the U.N. Secretary-General a letter promising full access to the equipment this week, and a new U.N. inspection team arrived over the weekend in Baghdad to test that offer.

But U.S. officials are openly cynical about the promise of improved behavior by Saddam Hussein. "He says he'll be a good boy now," one senior official said. "And if you believe that I've got some real estate in the desert to offer you."

As a result, the administration continues to actively consider launching a bombing raid to strike at the nuclear equipment the U.S. has been tracking by reconnaissance photos. A decision could be made soon, officials suggest, and action wouldn't be put off just because Mr. Bush plans to begin a period of travel and visits with foreign leaders later this week.

The president and his top national security advisers haven't yet met to make a final determination, officials said. Nor, they said, has the administration made a final decision on the sensitive question of whether to seek another U.N. resolution specifically authorizing action in the event of a new raid.

Officials say there is a "general consensus" within the administration that adequate authority for a new military strike is sought information."

contained in existing U.N. cease-fire resolutions that lay out the steps Iraq must take to eliminate its unconventional weapons programs before economic sanctions against it will be lifted. The resolutions include general language saying the Security Council can take steps to ensure that Iraq obeys the resolutions.

Still, the administration is weighing the possibility of seeking a U.N. resolution specifically approving military action against Iraq's nuclear-weapons program, which the U.S. military once thought was largely eliminated by bombing during the Gulf War. If it could be obtained, a new resolution would eliminate doubts about whether the U.S. is legally entitled to act and solidify international support for a move.

On the other hand, seeking a resolution would be a risky course that could end up undermining any U.S. hopes of acting militarily. Though Britain is prepared to fully support a military strike, some other members of the Security Council seem to have reservations. If a resolution is sought but voted down in the Security Council, the U.S. would find it politically difficult to move.

Tensions over Iraq's nuclear program rose sharply in the past two weeks when Iraq blocked a U.N. team from inspecting nuclear equipment three times. In one incident, Iraqi soldiers fired warning shots to stop U.N. inspectors who were trying to see and photograph equipment that they believe is used for enriching uranium to weapons-grade material. The equipment was being spirited away from an Iraqi military installation by trucks at the time.

In an apparent effort to head off military action or other drastic reprisals from the U.S. and the U.N. team from inspecting Friday sent the U.N. Secretary General a letter promising that a new U.N. mission would receive by today an accounting of, and access to, "the items about which it

# Arab Nations Put Off Talks To Create a Kuwait Force

### By ALAN COWELL
Special to The New York Times

CAIRO, July 7 — An Arab effort to create a force to replace the dwindling American and allied presence in Kuwait appeared to have encountered new difficulties today with the postponement of negotiations on the composition of the Arab military unit.

Egypt, which had seen the force as a means of securing both significant financial help and new regional influence, sought to play down the delay as technical, but Kuwait, which announced the postponement, said no new date had been scheduled. It offered no explanation for the holdup.

The foreign ministers of Egypt, Syria and six Arab countries grouped in the Gulf Cooperation Council had planned to meet in Kuwait on Tuesday to discuss the composition of a force to protect Kuwait in light of the Iraqi invasion and occupation last August and the subsequent Persian Gulf war to retake the country.

Egypt's Foreign Minister, Amr Moussa, told reporters here that the "meeting has been postponed three or four days because some of the ministers were tied up with engagements" and would take place later in the week.

### Brief Unity Has Evaporated

But Western diplomats said the postponement seemed to reflect difficulties of Arab nations with divergent senses of history and destiny to maintain the alliance they were able to forge while facing a common enemy, Iraq, during the war.

At that time, Egypt and Syria sent tens of thousands of soldiers to join the American-led buildup in Saudi Arabia, and Egyptian forces played a symbolic role in the retaking of Kuwait. In March, Egypt, Syria and the six gulf nations — Saudi Arabia, Kuwait, Bahrain, Qatar, Oman and the United Arab Emirates — signed an agreement in Damascus that foresaw the Egyptians and Syrians contributing division-strength forces to the defense of Kuwait in return for financial aid.

Since then, Arab diplomats said, Iran has registered strong opposition to any military presence by non-gulf Arabs in a region that it considers its realm of influence. Few gulf states want to antagonize Iran, which is feared as a potential source of political destabilization.

While some countries in the gulf would prefer the allied troops to remain, Western diplomats here said, Syria and Egypt have insisted that the gulf states maintain their commitment to the Damascus agreement.

In negotiations since then, Syria, Egypt and the six others have discussed stationing a 26,000-member force in Kuwait that would include a token presence of 3,000 troops each from Egypt and Syria. The bulk of the force — 10,000 men — would come from Saudi Arabia, with a further 10,000 from the other gulf nations.

### Fear of Syrian Intentions

"The Kuwaitis sense that all the Egyptians want is the money," said a Western diplomat who declined to be further identified, "and when they look at the Syrians, they remember how Syria intervened in Lebanon and finished up running the show."

As much as anything, some Egyptians believe, the indecision over stationing an Arab force in Kuwait points up a paradox of the gulf war: While President Saddam Hussein of Iraq sought to cast the war against the allies as a pan-Arab conflict, the fighting only sharpened a sense that pan-Arabist slogans had outlived their relevance.

And the notion of Egypt and Syria playing meaningful roles in gulf security sharpened distinctions that Arabs draw among themselves. "Sending Egyptians to guarantee the security of the gulf is like asking the Iranians to guarantee the security of the Suez Canal," a diplomat said.

3-3

C118

# 외 무 부

종 별 :

번 호 : UNW-1768                                        일 시 : 91 0709 1730

수 신 : 장 관 (국연,중동일,국기,기정)

발 신 : 주 유엔 대사

제 목 : 걸프사태 (이락 핵사찰)

연: UNW-1755

1. 연호 이락 외상 명의의 사무총장앞 서한은 이락측이 안보리 문서로 배포를 요청해오지 않음에 따라, 안보리 이사국, 대이락 군비통제 특위에게 배부되고 안보리문서로는 현재 배포되지 않고있음.

2. 상기 이락측 서한관련 금 7.8 언론에 보도된 주요내용은 다음과 같음.

가. 이락 핵개발 계획

1) 이락측은 IAEA 에 밝히지 않은 우라늄 농축계획이 일부 있었음을 시인 (이락은동 농축계획의 평화적 목적, 국가안보상 부분적인 보유유지의 불가피성 주장)

2) 이락은 우라늄 농축을 위한 3가지 방식 (ELECTROMAGNETIC, CENTRIFUGAL AND CHEMICAL SEPARATIONPROCESSES ) 을 병행 추진한 것으로 보이는바, 특히 이락이 독자적으로 전기자석식 분리방식을 개발할수 있었던 것은 개도국들의 핵무기 개발 잠재력과 관련 우려

나. 관련장비 및 물질보유현황

1) 우라늄 농축용 CALUTRON 30 기등 장비보유

2) IAEA 에 공개해온 농축 우라늄 80 파운드외에 일정량 (1-9 파운드) 보유(이락에서 망명한 과학자의 제보로는 90 파운드)

3. 본건관련 현재 안보리의 특기할 움직임은 없으며, 이락 방문중인 유엔 핵사찰반 의 활동결과 보고가 주말경 있을 예정인 바, 관련동향 추보위계임.

첨부: 상기 NYT, WP 지 기사: UNW(F)-312

끝

(대사 노창희-국장)

---

국기국    1차보    중아국    국기국    외정실    안기부

PAGE 1                                        91.07.10    09:10 WI

외신 1과  통제관

0119

*(handwritten annotations)* UNW(F)-312 / 0709 1730 (국연.중동원.국기.기정) 총4매

# IRAQ NOW ADMITS A SECRET PROGRAM TO ENRICH URANIUM

## DOCUMENT GIVEN TO U.N.

### Amount Cited Is Not Enough for Nuclear Weapons, but Officials Are Skeptical

**By PAUL LEWIS**
Special to The New York Times

BAGHDAD, Iraq, July 8 — Facing mounting international pressure and even the possibility of a military attack, Iraq admitted today that it has been running three clandestine programs designed to produce enriched uranium, which could be used as explosive in an atomic bomb.

In a statement issued here and in Vienna, the United Nations commission charged with destroying Iraq's most dangerous weapons said Baghdad today submitted a new list of its nuclear sites and material that contained information it had not given earlier.

In particular, Iraq disclosed details of "an extensive nuclear program" that contained three parallel operations for enriching uranium.

#### Little Material Produced

Iraq has only admitted to having produced about one pound of slightly enriched uranium from these programs. This would mean that the Iraqi program had not produced the material necessary for nuclear weapons.

Officials here insist that the United Nations does not necessarily believe that the list provided today is definitive. As a result, the United Nations inspectors will now examine what Iraq is declaring to see whether there is any reason to believe it is still concealing material.

In particular, there are doubts as to whether Iraq has declared all the enriched uranium it has produced, officials say.

[The Bush Administration said it believes that Iraq has secretly enriched enough uranium into weapons-grade quality to build at least one nuclear device, Administration officials said Monday. Page A11.]

An Iraqi scientist who recently defected to American forces in northern Iraq has been widely reported to have told American intelligence officials that the country had about 90 pounds of undisclosed highly enriched uranium, sufficient for about two crude atomic bombs.

#### Signer of Arms Treaty

As a signer of the treaty to prevent the spread of nuclear weapons, Iraq has declared possession of about 100 pounds of highly enriched uranium and placed this under international safeguards.

Inspectors who visited its nuclear plants shortly after the Persian Gulf war say they have accounted for part of this and that the remainder is probably buried underneath nuclear reactors and other installations bombed by the coalition forces.

Announcing the new Iraqi list, the chief United Nations nuclear inspector, Demitri Perricos, said Baghdad had provided more information as a result of "political pressure" from the United States and other countries after the United Nations said it was hiding suspicious-looking equipment from its inspectors.

President Bush has said the United States, one of the five permanent members of the Security Council, has not ruled out a military strike if Iraq does not get rid of all its weapons of mass destruction. Under the terms of the Council's cease-fire resolution, Iraq must provide details of its chemical, biological, ballistic and nuclear weapons so that the material can be removed or destroyed.

Acting on a tip from American intelligence last month, United Nations inspectors chased a convoy of some 60 trucks carrying equipment to two separate military camps. But on each occasion, the inspectors were refused permission to look at the trucks and on one occasion Iraqi soldiers drove them away by firing warning shots.

This is the first time that Iraq has ever admitted to trying to enrich uranium. And by today's declaration, Iraq in effect admits violation of its obligations under the treaty on the spread of nuclear arms.

By accepting this treaty, Iraq promised never to acquire nuclear weapons and said it would place all its nuclear material under safeguards administered by the International Atomic Energy Agency in Vienna to insure they are not used for military ends. But the equipment disclosed today has never been revealed to the atomic energy agency and is under no international supervision.

Mr. Perricos said Iraq has admitted enriching uranium by an old-fashioned system known as electromagnetic isotopic separation, which the United States used to produce most of the explosive used in the first atomic bomb dropped on Hiroshima in World War II.

He said Iraq has also admitted to working on enrichment using the centrifuge process and to trying to enrich uranium by chemical means as well.

Mr. Perricos also said he has ordered an inspection on Tuesday at the Akashat mine in western Iraq near the Syrian border. This means that United Nations inspectors will descend on the mine in the morning with only a few hours notice and demand to see what is going on inside.

In the past, the inspectors have usually only ordered such inspections after being tipped off by American intelligence that a site might contain evidence about Iraq's nuclear program.

Mr. Perricos disclosed that Iraq has said that some of the new equipment it declared today has been damaged by allied bombing. It has also damaged some itself, he said, while other machinery has apparently been buried.

But Mr. Perricos said that Iraq has promised to hand over everything declared on the list today to the United Nations inspectors. However, he did not say when this would happen.

A high-level United Nations mission arrived here today still without any assurance that Iraq would allow the United Nations to rescue thousands of dissident Shiite Muslims blockaded by the Iraqi Army in southern marshlands under steadily worsening conditions.

Prince Sadruddin Aga Khan, the mission leader, said he would press the Iraqi authorities to allow the United Nations to send relief supplies from its humanitarian aid center in the southern city Basra to the 40,000 to 100,000 Shiite refugees cornered by the army in the huge marshlands nearby.

Prince Sadruddin also wants Iraq to allow the United Nations to set up safe-conduct points through which the refugees can leave the marshes and return to their homes.

The Shiite Muslims fled to the marshlands fearing reprisals earlier this year after an unsuccessful uprising in southern Iraq against President Saddam Hussein.

*(handwritten)* # UNW-176A 첨부물

*(handwritten)* 4—1

*(handwritten)* 0120

# U.S. Doubts Iraq's Accounting of Nuclear Material

**By ELAINE SCIOLINO**
Special to The New York Times

WASHINGTON, July 8 — The Bush Administration believes that Iraq has secretly enriched enough uranium into weapons-grade quality to build at least one nuclear device, Administration officials said today. This is considerably more than the pound of enriched uranium that the Iraqis conceded today that they had made clandestinely.

The uranium, which was enriched through a cumbersome technique known as electromagnetic isotope separation, is in addition to the estimated 100 pounds of highly enriched uranium that is under international safeguards and that has been sealed by United Nations officials for disposal under terms of the cease-fire resolution that passed after the Persian Gulf war. It is believed that a bomb can be made from about 55 pounds. An Iraqi scientist who defected recently said that Baghdad had hidden about 90 pounds of such material.

The Administration disclosure suggests that either the Bush Administration knew about Iraq's secret uranium enrichment program and did not succeed in eradicating it during the 43 days of bombing, or that there was a failure of intelligence because the United States did not believe that Iraq had placed a high priority on such an old-fashioned technology.

What is especially troubling to the Administration is that unlike Iraq's unsuccessful attempts to enrich uranium through the centrifuge system, a much more advanced system dependent on imported equipment, the uranium in this case was enriched by industrial equipment developed inside Iraq. The Iraqi effort indicates that almost any developing country with moderate resources can embark on its own secret nuclear program.

## Imported Material Unnecessary

"Building this technology does not depend on procuring materials abroad," said one Administration official familiar with the process. "If you have the scientists, the electricity, and a metal-working foundry, you can do it indigenously." Even if Iraq's current production capability is destroyed, he added, "what's to stop anyone from doing this again in 1995?"

The Administration disclosure follows an admission by the Iraqi Government today that it has conducted three clandestine programs to produce enriched uranium, which could be used as the explosive in an atomic bomb.

The Iraqi admission, contained in a lengthy document submitted to the United Nations, acknowledges that Iraq has produced about one pound of slightly enriched uranium during testing. One Administration official, who spoke on condition of anonymity, said the Iraqi document "severely underestimates what they've done, in terms of what might have been produced."

The Iraqi document also states that Iraq possesses 30 calutrons, the machines used in the uranium-enrichment technology, although Administration officials say they believe that the figure is higher.

The State Department spokeswoman, Margaret B. Tutwiler, said today that "in the document, Saddam Hussein's Government admits Iraq was engaged in a nuclear weapons program contrary to previous repeated denials of the Iraqi Government." Although she acknowledged that the admission was "a step forward," she added that the United States will judge Iraq by "the actions of the Iraqi Government, not by these words."

The White House spokesman, Marlin Fitzwater, said that the document substantiates charges that Iraq has not complied with the Security Council resolution setting out stringent terms for a cease-fire and "continues to engage in various activities related to the weapons of mass destruction," also

forbidden by the cease-fire resolution. Neither Miss Tutwiler nor Mr. Fitzwater discussed the scope of the secret uranium enrichment program or accused Mr. Hussein of concealing material or equipment.

## Concern Over Secret Program

But one Administration official said the United States is "at least as concerned" about the uranium enriched through the secret program as it is about the weapons-grade material currently under international safeguards. Although the United States believes that Iraq's secret enrichment program was stopped just before or at the beginning of the allied bombing campaign, it does not know the location of the unregulated material.

There is no evidence that Iraq has tried to assemble a nuclear device with the material it has secretly produced, Administration officials said.

"This is a very worrisome development," said Leonard S. Spector, Senior Associate at the Carnegie Endowment for International Peace, of the revelations about the secret projects. "At least the inspected material has been observed and is acknowledged and will be removed. But the unexpected material has not been seen and no one has any idea of where it might be."

# Iraq Gives Information to U.N. On Extensive Nuclear Program

### By John M. Goshko
#### Washington Post Staff Writer

UNITED NATIONS, July 8— Iraqi President Saddam Hussein has disclosed to the United Nations details of an extensive, largely secret nuclear development program that the United States charged today is capable of producing atomic weapons.

The details, including an extensive list of the nuclear material and equipment in Iraq's possession, were sent Sunday night to the U.N. Security Council and the International Atomic Energy Agency (IAEA) in Vienna. U.S. officials and diplomatic sources said the information shows that Iraq has been evading IAEA safeguards and violating its obligations as a signatory to the Nuclear Nonproliferation Treaty by conducting uranium-enrichment programs whose existence it previously has denied.

"Iraq. . . at last admits it has engaged in a nuclear weapons program," White House press secretary Marlin Fitzwater said in Washington.

Both Fitzwater and State Department spokesman Margaret Tutwiler said the Iraqi disclosures underscore the need for continued comprehensive inspections, as well as spot checks, by U.N. and IAEA teams.

However, non-American sources here were more cautious. They said that while the activities that Iraq acknowledges engaging in could produce nuclear weapons, the letter from Iraqi Foreign Minister Ahmed Hussein did not admit to a weapons program but instead contended that Iraq's nuclear program is devoted to peaceful purposes. . . .

Iraq reluctantly provided the information after heavy pressure from the Security Council to explain why a U.N. inspection team was barred late last month from locating and inspecting what the team alleged was nuclear-related equipment. Under the terms of the Persian Gulf cease-fire accord, Baghdad is supposed to destroy such equipment. Friday, Saddam sent a letter to the United Nations promising to cooperate and to provide a list of nuclear equipment in Iraq's possession.

In an incident on June 28, Iraqi soldiers fired over the heads of U.N. inspectors filming the hasty withdrawal of equipment from a military transportation base near Baghdad. The incident prompted President Bush to warn that the United States would not rule out a

See IRAQ, A16, Col. 4

4-3

0122

# Iraq Gives U.N. Details on Nuclear Program

IRAQ, From A1

military strike if Iraq fails to give satisfactory proof that it is complying with its promise to get rid of all nuclear-weapons-related material.

"We have no way of independently verifying either how accurate or how complete the information furnished by Iraq is," Fitzwater said.

"We will judge Saddam Hussein's pledges today by the actions of the Iraqi government, not these words," Tutwiler said of the document. She added that to be "credible," Saddam's "promises must be followed by concrete cooperation" with a 37-member IAEA inspection team that arrived in Baghdad on Sunday. The team is scheduled to report back to the U.N. by the end of the week, and U.S. officials said they will be waiting to see if full inspection of the elusive material was allowed.

A senior U.S. official, who asked not to be identified, said, "We're dealing here with people who only last week claimed that they had no nuclear enrichment program. The only way to find the full extent of what they've been up to is to examine all known and suspected sites fully—a process that will take some time."

"We will have to look at the stuff they declared in the letter to the U.N.," the official added. "Then we'll have to see how closely that squares with our own intelligence information about what they have. The Security Council will have to stay in a watching mode until that is completed, and it's necessary to consider whether further steps are required to make Iraq turn over the equipment called for by the cease-fire agreement."

According to some sources, the Iraqi document says that Iraq already has destroyed some of the equipment on the list to avoid giving the United States a pretext for resuming the bombing that destroyed much of the country's infrastructure during the gulf war.

All of the information is contained in a 29-page document that has not

been made public because it was still being translated from Arabic tonight. However, U.S. and other sources said it was composed of two parts: the first, according to one source, is "a political statement and justification of Iraq's need for a nuclear program," and the second is a detailed list of material and equipment Iraq has in its possession.

The sources said the information made clear that Iraq has been engaged secretly in three parallel methods of producing weapons-grade, enriched uranium. They said the Iraqis were working with electromagnetic, centrifugal and chemical separation processes.

Among the items on the equipment list, the sources said, are 30 calutrons, plus associated generators for electrical power to separate isotopes electromagnetically.

The calutron-enrichment method is regarded as a primitive, outdated process, but it was used by the United States to produce enriched uranium for the atomic bomb detonated over Hiroshima in 1945. The method subsequently was described widely in nonclassified articles on nuclear weapons, leading U.S. analysts to conclude that the Iraqis could have constructed the equipment without significant outside help.

U.N. inspectors involved in the June 28 incident said that some of the crated material they saw being trucked hastily away from the Iraqi military base was of a size and shape that led them to suspect the boxes contained calutrons.

In addition, U.S. officials have been told by an Iraqi engineer who defected that Iraq was conducting nuclear weapons experiments, some involving the use of calutrons. U.S. suspicions about the Iraqi program were fueled further by reconnaissance satellite surveillance and other intelligence data.

Some sources said that the Iraqi list also acknowledges possession of four kilograms, or about 9 pounds, of enriched uranium. However, it was not immediately clear whether that quantity was part of, or in addition

to, 80 pounds of uranium that Iraq declared earlier.

The sources said that in the document, Iraq's foreign minister argues that Iraq's involvement in nuclear development was necessary for peaceful purposes. He reportedly added that national security considerations justified keeping some parts of the program secret.

However, various sources said that argument appears to be rejected by all U.N. delegations who have expressed an opinion. Most were unwilling to go as far as the United States in declaring that Iraq was building nuclear weapons, but they seemed unanimous in agreeing that Iraq had sought to conceal its program and had lied about it in apparent hopes of avoiding detection.

*Staff writer Ann Devroy contributed to this report from Washington.*

4—4

0123

# 외 무 부

종 별 :

번 호 : UNW-1790 일 시 : 91 0710 2120

수 신 : 장 관(국연,중동일,국기,기정)

발 신 : 주 유엔 대사

제 목 : 걸프사태(이락 핵사찰)

1. 안보리는 이락 핵사찰 문제관련 7.15비공식협의예정임.

2. 금 7.10자 이락 핵사찰관련 NYT.WP 지 기사를 별첨송부함.

첨부:상기 기사: UNW(F)-317

끝

(대사 노창희-국장)

| 국기국 | 1차보 | 중아국 | 국기국 | 외정실 | 분석관 | 안기부 |
|---|---|---|---|---|---|---|

PAGE 1

91.07.11 10:13 WG

외신 1과 통제관

0124

UNW(F) - 317  10716  2120
(국연 . 중동일 . 최기 . 기정)  총 2 매

# The Search for Iraq's Uranium

REVERSING itself again, Iraq now says it will cooperate fully with the United Nations inspectors searching for nuclear equipment. To demonstrate this change of heart, Iraq allowed the inspectors into three sites yesterday and conceded to the U.N. in a letter that it had in fact been secretly engaged in enriching uranium. That is a monumentally important disclosure. It is an acknowledgment that the Iraqis were violating their commitments under the Nuclear Nonproliferation Treaty and that their previous vehement denials were untrue. While that will not greatly surprise anyone familiar with the Iraqi government's record, it brings a little more clarity to a dark and complex subject.

The next question is whether the Iraqis succeeded in enriching the uranium to weapons grade—the presumption must be that they did succeed—and how much of it they produced. Only about one pound, they say. The U.S. government suspects that it may be a substantially larger amount, perhaps enough to make one or two bombs. It's a reasonable suspicion; the intelligence services of the United States and its allies earlier failed to discover the illicit nuclear activities that the Iraqis have now admitted. The U.N. inspection teams face the formidable job of determining what they actually have left, and where.

It's going to take time, but the inspectors believe they can come to a reliable answer by careful examination of the Iraqis' enrichment equipment, including all that they destroyed or buried during their previous phase of noncooperation. While this continues, it is going to be essential to keep the economic sanctions on Iraq and to keep reminding it that the possibility of further military strikes will not be lifted until the cease-fire agreement has been completely fulfilled. It unconditionally requires the destruction and removal of all equipment that could conceivably contribute to the fabrication not only of nuclear weapons but of biological and chemical weapons as well.

The sanctions, as good-hearted people in the West have been warning, threaten to create a public health crisis in Iraq. But it has to be said that the public health consequences of mistakenly leaving 50 kilograms of highly enriched uranium in Iraqi hands could prove considerably greater than the present damage to the water system. If present conditions in Iraq are uncomfortable and unhealthy, the Iraqis themselves have the means to ease the sanctions. Full cooperation with the U.N. will do it.

But even after the sanctions are lifted, the United Nations will need to continue the inspections. The rebuilding of the country will move rapidly. But certain facilities are not to be rebuilt—the hidden laboratories and shops where nuclear, biological and chemical weapons are produced. The world is entitled to continuing assurance that Iraq will not violate its arms commitments again.

FUNW-1790
첨부물

2 —1

0125

# Word of Iraqi Nuclear Effort Is a Mixed Blessing for Bush

### By ELAINE SCIOLINO
#### Special to The New York Times

WASHINGTON, July 9 — Iraq's disclosure that it has embarked on a secret program to enrich uranium that could be used to make a nuclear weapon has left the Bush Administration both heartened and dismayed.

President Bush and some other senior officials initially interpreted the admission as a positive indication that Iraq was responding to American threats of renewed military strikes and capitulating to the stringent terms of the United Nations cease-fire that requires the destruction of Iraq's nuclear, chemical and biological weapons and long-range ballistic missiles.

Underlying the public statements apparently is embarrassment that Iraq may have succeeded in hiding an ambitious nuclear program from American intelligence, and the firm belief that Baghdad is still withholding information. The State Department spokeswoman, Margaret D. Tutwiler, said today that the document that Mr. Hussein turned over to the United Nations and the Vienna-based International Atomic Energy Agency on Monday was full of "significant omissions and discrepancies."

There is also a growing sense within the Administration of the limits of renewed military action; fixed sites can be readily destroyed in military strikes, but it is not so easy to target easily moveable military equipment or weapons-grade uranium. Administra-

## Hussein owns up to an arms program; now, what to do about it?

tion officials have begun to conclude, reluctantly, they say, that as long as Mr. Hussein is in power, any weapons-destruction program relies to some extent on his good will.

"We can bomb all we want, but we'll never get all his material and equipment by bombing," said a Pentagon official. "We can use bombing as a technique to punish Saddam or to scare him. But when the dust has settled, you still could have some material left plus the nuclear experts."

Baghdad on Monday submitted the declaration detailing its clandestine nuclear program and material as it came under mounting international pressure after United Nations inspectors discovered that it trying to hide a convoy of suspicious equipment.

The Iraqi document, obtained at the United Nations, openly justified the secret nuclear program, arguing that it was intended for peaceful purposes. Iraq feared "exaggeration, abuse and aggression" if the program were revealed, said Iraq's Foreign Minister, Ahmed Hussein Khudayer, in a letter to Secretary General Javier Pérez de Cuéllar that accompanied a lengthy inventory of Iraq's nuclear program.

Iraq, Mr. Khudayer added, "had sound reasons of national security which induced it not to declare certain components of the program."

The document revealed the existence of sites where clandestine activity designed to produce enriched uranium was taking place, as well as a complicated network of intermediate installations to prepare large amounts of uranium ore for use in those processes.

One unnamed installation was so large that it produced 100 tons of uranium dioxide and had the capacity of producing 185 tons of uranium a year.

Reacting to news of the Iraqi disclosure, President Bush told a group of foreign journalists on Monday: "There is some, quote, good news, unquote, coming out of Baghdad today. I haven't seen it, but wherein Saddam once again states that he will fully cooperate and have inspectors. Well, let's see whether that can work before we have to go further with options."

When specifically asked about military action, Mr. Bush replied, "No, I can't talk about anything other than to just say the options are open."

The current Administration strategy is to continue a stringent sanctions regime against Iraq and to bolster the United Nations team of experts that is combing the Iraqi countryside in search of Iraq's weapons of mass destruction. The idea is to blanket the country with as many intrusive international inspectors as possible, for as long as it takes.

The United States has assigned some of its best non-proliferation experts and analysts to the team, while others are supposed to provide the team with detailed intelligence on the location and scope of Mr. Hussein's arsenal of unconventional weapons.

### 'Tip of the Iceberg'

"In our view what Iraq has revealed is just the tip of the iceberg," said a senior Administration official. "This underlines the need for having an extremely active, intrusive and exhaustive inspection effort until we satisfy ourselves."

Particularly troubling to Administration officials is the belief that Iraq has produced enough weapons-grade uranium, through a cumbersome World War II technology using machines known as calutrons, to build at least one nuclear device. The officials said the equipment used in enriching the uranium was produced indigenously, so that there was no trail of export licenses pointing to Iraq.

Because the sites resembled industrial rather than nuclear installations, there was little reason to suspect clandestine activity. Miss Tutwiler today declined to say whether Iraq had secretly enriched enough uranium to build at least one nuclear device, but said, "The extent of Iraq's program, along with information we have from numerous sources, makes us believe strongly that Iraq has a program to develop nuclear weapons."

### U.N. Team Sees Iraqi Plant
#### Special to The New York Times

BAGHDAD, Iraq, July 9 — United Nations inspectors said today that they had for the first time been shown "crucial elements" of Iraq's clandestine nuclear program during a visit to a plant whose existence was disclosed by Baghdad only on Monday.

But the chief United Nations nuclear inspector, Demitri Perricos, refused to describe what the inspection team had seen or to give the location of the site.

Inspectors also conducted a surprise inspection of a phosphate strip mine and processing plant at Akashat, near the Syrian border. They said Iraq had been extracting small quantities of uranium from the phosphate, apparently in preference to buying it openly on the world market. The inspection on short notice was ordered by the special United Nations commission overseeing the destruction of Iraq's weapons of mass destruction under terms of the cease-fire ending the Persian Gulf war.

Mr. Perricos would not say what inspectors were looking for at the phosphate mine. He noted that the American-led coalition had bombed it in the gulf war, suggesting that they believed that something was under way.

2-2

0126

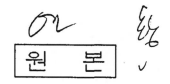

# 외 무 부

종 별 :

번 호 : UNW-1817　　　　　　　　　일　시 : 91 0712 1830

수 신 : 장 관(국연,중동일,기정)

발 신 : 주 유엔 대사

제 목 : 걸프사태(언론보도)

　　1.금 7.12자 NYT 지는 이락이 핵폐기의무를 이행하지 않는 경우 공격할 20 여개의
이락측 지휘통제 목표를 부쉬대통령이 승인했다고 보도한바, 동 기사를 별첨송부함.

　　2.한편 금일자 WP 지는 이락의 인도적 수요를 조사하기 위해 현재 동국을 방문중인
유엔대표단 (단장: SADRUDDIN AGA KHAN 대표)이 대이락 경제제재조치의 일부 완화를
다음주 건의할 가능성이 크다고 보도하였음.

　　첨부:상기기사: UNW(F)-324

　　끝.

　　(대사 노창희-국장)

---

국기국　　1차보　　중아국　　외정실　　안기부

PAGE 1　　　　　　　　　　　　　　　　　91.07.13　　09:28 WG

UNW(F—324   10712  1/000
(국연. 중동원. 기전)                    총 2대

# List of Potential Iraq Targets Gets Presidential Approval

## By ERIC SCHMITT
### Special to The New York Times

WASHINGTON, July 11 — President Bush has approved a list of about 20 Iraqi command-and-control targets that would be attacked if Baghdad refused to comply with international demands that its nuclear technology be destroyed, Pentagon officials said today.

Administration officials have concluded that punitive strikes on Iraqi leaders would inflict more pain on President Saddam Hussein and his high command than strikes aimed at sites where Baghdad is suspected of hiding equipment and materials used to develop nuclear or chemical weapons, a senior Pentagon official said today.

Administration officials quickly added that no air strike is imminent. The United States has several squadrons of fighter and attack planes, including about 20 F-117 Stealth fighters, left in Saudi Arabia.

The announcement of the new target list is another attempt to intimidate the Iraqi Government into full compliance with the United Nations-mandated destruction or removal of its nuclear materials and biological and chemical arsenals. It also reflects a shift in thinking by senior Administration officials, who in recent days have acknowledged the difficulty of striking this material, much of which can be moved easily.

### British Concur

In a 15-minute telephone call today, Mr. Bush and Prime Minister John Major of Britain voiced agreement that President Hussein had violated the United Nations resolution ordering Baghdad to provide details of its nuclear weapons so they can be removed or destroyed, British officials said.

Administration officials said today that some United Nations inspectors had concluded that Iraq possessed enough raw uranium to build 20 to 40 nuclear weapons over 10 years, but only if work proceeded without a hitch. That assessment reflects the "high end" of Iraq's nuclear potential, they said.

[mate goal, but it "doesn't reflect anything like their current capability," an Administration official said.

About 100 pounds of weapons-grade uranium that Iraq has acknowledged to be in its possession is under international safeguards. But Administration officials said this week that they believe Baghdad may have clandestinely produced enough to build at least one nuclear device. It is believed that a bomb can be made from as little as 55 pounds of enriched uranium.

Other experts in the Administration, however, estimate that Iraq has secretly produced only a few pounds of enriched uranium at the most.

### Last Troops Moving Out

As Western officials continue to monitor Iraq's compliance with the resolutions, the United States and its European allies will withdraw the last troops from northern Iraq by Monday, Pentagon officials and European diplomats said.

To protect Iraqi Kurds from possible retribution by Mr. Hussein, the officials said the United States and seven European countries have agreed to leave behind a 2,500-member rapid deployment force in southeastern Turkey.

Ground forces equipped with artillery and attack helicopters from the United States, Britain, France, Belgium, Turkey, Italy, Spain and the Netherlands will be based in Silopi, Turkey, near the Iraqi border, a Pentagon official said.

And dozens of American fighter and attack aircraft, capable of striking targets in northern Iraq, will be stationed at the NATO base at Incirlik, Turkey, and aboard a United States aircraft carrier in the Mediterranean Sea.

N-1817
부록                    2-기

# Iraq Lets Shiite Refugees Quit Swamp

**By PAUL LEWIS**
Special to The New York Times

HAMMAR, Iraq, July 11 — Iraq has withdrawn its forces from the vast southern swampland under United Nations pressure and allowed some of the thousands of Shiite Muslim refugees hiding there to escape, apparently in the hope of persuading the Security Council to relax trade sanctions this month.

This was the news awaiting Prince Sadruddin Aga Khan and a team of United Nations officials and journalists today when they reached this dusty little village of cracked and tumbledown buildings lying on the edge of a sea of dark green rushes.

All along the dike that borders Hor al Hammar, as this part of the marshland is called, pillboxes stand empty and abandoned. There, the United Nations team visiting the area last month saw Iraqi machine-gunners fire sporadic bursts into the rushes.

### A Scene of Tranquillity

The 40 or so miles of raised road that runs across the marshes and paddy fields from Nasiriya was free of army roadblocks, and virtually no military activity was visible.

Instead, the scene was one of tranquillity, with the Marsh Arabs, as the locals are called, wading about in their paddy fields tending rice plants or watching water buffalo graze on the reeds standing knee-deep in mud. In the distance, fishermen cast their nets by hand from elegant wooden canoes.

But last month, the same United Nations team reported a large and active military presence in the area when it warned that the Iraqi Army was deliberately barricading the refugees inside the marshes under appalling conditions with little food or fresh water.

Members of a United Nations team that brought a convoy of relief trucks here today from Basra said that local Iraqis had told them on the way that the army had just withdrawn from the area and that many Shiite Muslims who had taken refuge in the swamps had been able to return home safely in the last few days.

### Number in Hiding Unknown

Those left hiding in the marshes, they said, are mainly people who had played an active role in the abortive Shiite uprising against President Saddam Hussein earlier this year, including members of the armed forces, the

People in Hammar say Shiites are emerging from the marshes now that Iraqi soldiers have departed.

local administration and the governing Baathist Party.

"We appear to have achieved some of what we wanted to achieve already," Prince Sadruddin said after hearing the news.

Exactly how many refugees are hiding in the marshes is unknown. United Nations has estimated the number at between 40,000 and 100,000, though Iran has said there may be as many as half a million.

Many are thought to be living with the Marsh Arabs, who build themselves homesteads of artfully plaited reeds on mud banks far out in the swamps and travel around by canoe.

### A U.N. Presence

The principal mission of Prince Sadruddin's team is to report to the Security Council on Iraq's humanitarian needs nearly a year after the trade embargo went into effect.

This report is likely to influence the Council's reply to Iraq's request to sell $940 million worth of oil to buy food and other humanitarian goods.

But after hearing of the plight of the marsh refugees, Prince Sadruddin also decided to establish a United Nations presence in this area that would simultaneously provide relief aid to refugees and give them confidence to return home.

"We are trying to provide the same care for the Shiites in the south that we're already providing for Kurds in the north," he said.

While Iraq finally granted Prince Sa-

druddin's request today to allow him to bring in food and set up a United Nations humanitarian center here, it did so with evident reluctance and bad grace.

A well-organized mob of local Iraqis led by a turbaned clergyman and a police officer staged a "spontaneous" demonstration as Prince Sadruddin arrived, dancing around his car waving sticks and portraits of President Hussein while chanting anti-American slogans like "Bush, Bush, we won't bow to sanctions."

The Iraqi Government also refused to allow Elliot L. Richardson, a former United States Attorney General who is on the United Nations team, to travel down here, saying that as a "politician" he had no place on a mission Prince Sadruddin described as humanitarian.

### Dragging Out the Talks

Two other members of the team were also denied permission to make the trip for the same reason — Jean-Daniel Levi, a former scientific adviser to President François Mitterrand of France, and Sir John Moberly, a former British Ambassador to Iraq.

Before the United Nations was allowed to come here, Prince Sadruddin had to negotiate for two days in Baghdad, spending four hours in talks with Foreign Minister Ahmed Hussein Khader and another four hours with Deputy Prime Minister Tariq Aziz.

Many United Nations officials suspect that Iraq deliberately dragged out the talks to give the army time to clear out of the area. United Nations officials also say they think that the Iraqi authorities knew that they would have to give way in the end if they are to have any chance of persuading the Security Council to relax the trade embargo and allow them to sell some oil again.

Baghdad also stepped up its pressure on Prince Sadruddin's team to recommend lifting sanctions tonight by organizing a demonstration of about 50 sick people outside the hotel in Baghdad where its members are staying.

2-2

0129

# 외 무 부

종 별 :

번 호 : UNW-1835　　　　　　　　　　　　　일 시 : 91 0715 2040

수 신 : 장 관(국연,중동일,국기,기정)　사본:노창희 대사

발 신 : 주 유엔 대사대리

제 목 : 걸프사태(유엔 동향)

　　1.안보리는 금 7.15 오후늦게 비공식협의를 갖고 H.BLIX IAEA 사무처장등으로 부터 안보리휴전 결의에 의거한 이락핵사찰 현황에 관해 보고를 청취한바, 동협의 관련 주요동향은 다음과같음.

　　가. BLIX 처장은 지난 7.7 이전 이락측이 문제의 우라늄 농축추진 계획을 IAEA 에 통보하지 않은것은 NPT 안전협정 불이행 (NON-COMPLIANCE) 이며, 7.18 IAEA 이사회 특별회의에서 이에관한 공식결론이 나는대로 IAEA 규정 12조 (항)에 의거 안보리및 총회에보고 예정이라고함.

　　나.금일 회의에서는, 이락측이 7.14 새로 제출한 핵시설명세에 대해서 특별한 논의는 없었던 것으로 알려짐.

　　다.다음 협의일자는 잡히지 않았으나 금주중 협의가 열릴것으로 관측되고 있으며, 상임이사국들간 결의안 초안 토의 가능성도 거론되고 있음.

　　2.한편 이락은 7.12자 외상명의 유엔사무총장 및 안보리의장앞 서한에서, 미국이 중동지역에서의 패권장악이라는 미.이스라엘의 목표달성을 위해 이락에 대한 대규모 군사공격을 준비중이라고 주장하고, 안보리가 이락에 대한 여사한 미국의 재공격을 저지 시켜줄것을 요망하였음. (S/22786)

　　3. 금일 유엔측이 공개한 SADRUDDIN AGA KHAN대표의 이락실태조사 보고서 요지는 다음과같음.

　　가.이락 기본수요: 일년기간 68 억불상당 품목수입필요 (식수및 위생 1.8 억불,보건 5억불, 식량 16.2 억불, 농업용품 4 억불, 유류 20억불, 동력발전 22 억불) (초기 4개월분:26.3 억불)

　　나.이락 외환등 보유고 (이락측주장): 외한 1,475만불, 지불준비용 금 일정량

　　다.상기 기본수요품목 수입 경비조달방법 (건의)

---

| 국기국 | 1차보 | 중아국 | 국기국 | 외정실 | 분석관 | 안기부 | 국기국 (에나녹), 청아에 |

1)이락 석유수출 '허가: 일년간 55 억불상당수익발생 가능 (수출용 일 생산 100 만 배럴)

(단, 초기 4개월 관련장비등 10 억불 상당수입필요)

2)이락 해외자산 동결해제

3)본건 석유수출 및 기본수요 품목반입과 관련한 감시체계구축

첨부: NYT 지 관련기사: UNW(F)-330

끝

(대사대리 신기복-국장)

PAGE 2

UNW(肝)- 330  10745 2040
(국연.중동일.국기.기정) 축3며

# Baghdad Hands U.N. a New List
# Of Clandestine Atom Installations

### By PAUL LEWIS
Special to The New York Times

BAGHDAD, Iraq, July 14 — Iraq gave the United Nations a new list of clandestine nuclear installations today, but the chief United Nations nuclear inspector refused to disclose any details of what it contains or to say whether he thinks it is accurate.

"I can't express an opinion," the inspector, Demitri Perricos, said tonight. "It is very early. The list is still being studied."

The new list was submitted after the United States said earlier lists of Iraqi nuclear installations were inadequate. The lists have been submitted to satisfy the Security Council's insistence that all Iraq's nuclear weapons materials must be destroyed or removed under the cease-fire resolution that ended the Persian Gulf war.

Another member of the inspection team said today that the new list appears to include all the undeclared clandestine nuclear plants that American and other intelligence services had described to the team.

#### Suspicions Remain

But this official said the team remains suspicious of the list because it has no way of knowing whether Iraq still has other nuclear installations that no one else knows about.

"Basically we have been lied to by the Iraqis for four months now, so we are going to be very cautious," the official said.

The Security Council is scheduled to meet Monday to consider the new Iraqi list.

Under the Council's cease-fire resolution, Iraq is required to hand over all weapons-grade nuclear material to the United Nations for removal or destruction. It is also required to surrender its chemical and biological weapons and its ballistic missiles.

Iraq appears anxious to satisfy the United States and other Security Council members that it is telling the truth about its nuclear plans because it wants the Council to ease the trade embargo imposed after the invasion of Kuwait by allowing it to sell $1 billion worth of oil to buy food and other goods.

After first declaring that it has no secret nuclear installations at all, Iraq acknowledged July 7 under pressure from the United States that it was in fact trying to enrich uranium by three different methods at eight clandestine sites around the country.

Mr. Perricos said his inspectors had found evidence that Iraq was enriching uranium by an electromagnetic method using calutrons, as well as by the centrifuge method and by chemical means.

The United States said this list was incomplete and gave the special commission charged with destroying Iraq's weapons of mass destruction further information about other suspected nuclear plants that did not appear on the July 7 declaration.

The special commission then asked Iraq to provide details of any nuclear research and development laboratories, special storage sites and nuclear manufacturing plants that it possesses. Last week the United Nations inspectors carried out a challenge inspection of a uranium production unit in the north of Iraq that Baghdad had failed to declare.

Members of the United Nations inspection team here say the special commission had been told that Iraq in fact had undeclared nuclear installations falling into all three categories.

Tonight Mr. Perricos said Iraq declared sites in all these categories on the list submitted today.

#### Allied Troops Quit North Iraq

ZAKHO, Iraq, July 14 (Reuters) — Allied troops streamed out of northern Iraq today, and a United States general tried to soothe Kurdish fears of being left exposed to the wrath of President Saddam Hussein.

Maj. Gen. Jay Garner said an allied strike force to be based in southeastern Turkey would have plenty of notice from United Nations observers and others if the Iraqi leader threatened the Kurds again. Weekly American-Iraqi military coordination meetings are to take place in this Iraqi border town after allied troops complete their pullout on Monday, the general told reporters.

Coalition officials said the strike force would be based at Silopi, just north of the border, with units at Batman, 87 miles to the northwest, and Incirlik in southern Turkey.

# UNW-1835
첨부물

3-1

10

0132

# IRAQI ATOM EFFORT EXPOSES WEAKNESS IN WORLD CONTROLS

## SUCCESS SHOCKS EXPERTS

### Baghdad's Gains Cast Doubt on Feasibility of Halting Nuclear Arms' Spread

**By WILLIAM J. BROAD**

Scientists and weapons experts, surprised that Iraq secretly used a method abandoned by the West half a century ago to enrich uranium, say Iraq's feat is a blow to international efforts to stem the spread of nuclear arms.

In a single stroke, it has overturned decades of assumptions about which procedures and materials need to be safeguarded. Up to now, the control effort has focused on keeping certain techniques secret and limiting export licenses for high-technology equipment that can be used in making bombs.

But Iraq has shown that a low-tech method openly described in scientific literature can be readily used to circumvent the restrictions, making the Iraqi weapons effort far more ingenious and dangerous than believed.

#### Enough for 2 Bombs

The clandestine Iraqi method is reported by a defector to have produced about 90 pounds of highly enriched uranium, enough for two bombs. Experts say the 30 enrichment machines that Iraq has admitted to using could make enough fuel for one warhead a year.

Iraq probably has the skill to perfect an atom bomb, weapons experts say. They stress that it is unlikely that Iraq has already done so, though some suggest it might be able to build one on short notice. Before the Persian Gulf war, many intelligence analysts said Iraq's engineers might start limited production of nuclear warheads in 5 to 10 years, but not much sooner. The estimates were based on how rapidly the Iraqis might build high-technology devices for uranium enrichment.

Concern soared in May when the Iraqi defector reportedly told American officials that Iraq used the antiquated, low-tech method to produce 90 pounds of enriched uranium. The technique uses electromagnetism in machines known as calutrons.

Under international pressure, Iraq told the United Nations last week that it had indeed used the old method, saying it produced a pound of enriched uranium. Experts believe that much more was produced, and in response to continued pressure and skepticism from abroad that it was not being completely forthcoming, Baghdad yesterday submitted to the United Nations a new document on its nuclear operations.

The fact that the Iraqis quietly used the forsaken method at all to produce weapons fuel showed great cleverness, the experts say.

"It's astonishing," said Dr. Glenn T. Seaborg, a Nobel laureate in physics and former chairman of the Atomic Energy Commission, which built most of the nation's nuclear bombs. "It represents quite a technical effort."

Dr. Edward J. Lofgren, a physicist at the Lawrence Berkeley Laboratory in California who helped develop calutrons during World War II, said Iraq's choice of enrichment method, while surprising, made eminent sense.

"The other methods are very efficient but take lots of capital and big plants," he said. "A calutron, on the other hand, in one stage enriches a large amount. It's not energy efficient. But it doesn't take a lot of capital."

Dr. J. Carson Mark, a former official of the Los Alamos National Laboratory in New Mexico who has studied the Iraqi program, said 90 pounds of highly enriched uranium might produce two bombs. He added that it was impossible to know whether the Iraqis had actually made such bombs.

#### Spy Agencies Criticized

"It's conceivable," he said. "The magnitude of their effort is suggestive. If they went through all that enrichment work, it puts weight to the argument that they took further steps. But there's no way of saying, on the basis of logic, whether they have done that."

Dr. Mark also criticized the nation's intelligence agencies for apparently failing to have discovered the clandestine effort at uranium enrichment.

"Why spend all that money on intelligence when it apparently and evidently learns nothing?" he asked.

Paul L. Leventhal, president of the Nuclear Control Institute, a private group in Washington that studies the spread of nuclear technology and has worked closely with Dr. Mark, said it was unlikely that the Iraqis already had a bomb, especially in light of the disarray caused by the gulf war and Iraq's moves to hide nuclear materials around the country.

"But do they have the components there, to put one together in short order?" he asked. "I would say yes."

Mr. Leventhal added that the reemergence of the old enrichment technique would force the development of a whole new set of international safeguards and precautions.

#### 'Genie Back in the Bottle'

"We can't put the genie back in the bottle," he said. "The main thing is to try to improve our intelligence-gathering ability" so that existing calutrons can be tracked down. He added that new sanctions would be needed to inhibit their use for uranium enrichment.

Leonard S. Spector, an expert on the spread of nuclear arms at the Carnegie Endowment for International Peace in Washington, said news of the Iraqi enrichment success had toppled the international program to stem weapons proliferation, which has focused on limiting advanced methods. "It's cataclysmic," he said. "All this was being done in Iraq without anybody knowing it. So who else is doing it? Everybody in the community knew this kind of thing was a possibility. But to be confronted by an example is devastating."

Though slow and costly, experts say, the electromagnetic process has many virtues from the Iraqi point of view. For one thing, it has been declassified for decades. Detailed blueprints of its workings have been published by the Federal Government and academic scientists, in contrast to the secrecy maintained around more advanced methods of uranium enrichment.

Most important, experts say, calutrons are relatively easy to build. They use few exotic materials, in principle allowing them to be largely constructed without Western aid.

#### Appetite for Power

The main drawback is that their bulky electromagnetic coils have a large appetite for electrical power.

But experts note that Iraq, with large oil supplies, can cheaply generate electricity for the process.

Though bulky and cumbersome, the Iraqi calutrons achieved one of the most delicate tasks of science: separation of isotopes. Isotopes are different varieties of the same element that differ only in the number of neutrons in their nuclei. U-235, the material needed for nuclear weapons, has 143 neutrons in its nucleus. U-238 has 146, making it fractionally heavier.

3-2

0133

In natural ore, U-238 accounts for 99.283 percent of uranium, while U-235 accounts for 0.711 percent. The scientific challenge, on which untold billions have been spent, is to separate the extremely rare isotope from the common one. Uranium suitable for atomic weapons is usually enriched to contain at least 80 percent U-235 and more commonly 90 percent or more.

The person who came up with the idea for the calutron and promoted it extensively in the early 1940's was Dr. Ernest O. Lawrence, inventor of the cyclotron particle accelerator and director of a physics laboratory at the University of California at Berkeley. The name calutron derives from California University cyclotron.

Dr. Lawrence's goal was to enrich uranium with the aid of cyclotrons, large circular electromagnets used to accelerate subatomic particles.

The principle was simple: Uranium would be ionized into charged particles and fired into the powerful electromagnetic fields of a cyclotron. The lighter the ion, the tighter its circular path. At the end of the arc, two beams of ions would feed into separate collectors.

### Flying Screwdrivers

The process worked experimentally at Berkeley, producing minuscule amounts of fairly pure U-235. In 1943, the Government embarked on a huge project at Oak Ridge, Tenn., to expand its scale. At its peak, the program employed nearly 25,000 people.

The electromagnetic coils were 15 feet in diameter and weighed thousands of tons. So powerful were the magnetic fields that hammers and screwdrivers flew out of workers' hands if they came too close. The U-235 produced by the calutrons helped power the bomb that destroyed Hiroshima in August 1945.

One discovery of the electromagnetic program was that separation worked more effectively if the uranium fed into calutrons was already partly enriched, to 10 percent U-235. By the end of the war, other enrichment methods were working better than the calutrons, and the costly machines were abandoned for uranium enrichment.

But a few of them were still used at Oak Ridge to separate hundreds of other isotopes, in part for medical use. The separated isotopes included thorium, americium and curium.

Over the years, the technology of electromagnetic separation has advanced. Mr. Leventhal of the Nuclear Control Institute said some 180 patents have been filed on the process over the decades, apparently for isolating tiny amounts of rare isotopes.

Scientists say the electromagnetic method may have been refined and simplified by the Iraqis, making calutrons smaller, more competitive with advanced enrichment methods and far better producers of bomb fuel than they were in World War II.

### Improvements of 50 Years

"Anybody who would be capable of building one of these things now would be capable of improving it over what we did 50 years ago," said Dr. Lofgren, who helped develop it in World War II.

Mr. Leventhal of the Nuclear Control Institute estimated that 30 Iraqi calutrons, if they were fairly modern ones and fed uranium that had already been slightly enriched, could probably produce up to 44 pounds of bomb-grade fuel a year. That, he said, would be enough for about one bomb.

Last week, Iraq said it had been running a total of three clandestine programs to enrich uranium. In addition to the electromagnetic method, it cited a centrifuge process and a chemical one. Several experts suggested that these might have produced slightly enriched uranium to feed the calutrons.

A scientist who advises the Federal Government, who spoke on condition of anonymity, said the Iraqi claim of having 30 calutrons was widely felt to be underestimated. "We think they have many more," he said. "Therefore the production rates are much higher" than private experts have calculated.

Experts on the spread of nuclear weapons say that their field, which for decades has focused on ways to stem the spread of advanced bomb-making methods, will now have to be rethought from the bottom up to focus on calutrons.

"How are we going to find this stuff?" asked Mr. Spector of the Carnegie Endowment. "What's the nonproliferation regime going to look like?

"Maybe there are bits and pieces of this technology that we can control. But if we can't, then you've got the possibility that one of the real underpinnings for the control of nuclear weapons won't be there anymore."

3-3

0134

美등 앞다튼「壓力」의 波長

東 亞 日 報

1991年7月15日 月曜日

# 이라크核「中東새雷管」으로

## 安保理서 중단서지 警告 긴장高潮
## 후세인 제거戰略 간주 査察 비협조

"친애하는 국민이여, 나는 핵무기개발을 선택했습니다." <유엔決議>

외 무 부

종 별 :

번 호 : UNW-1835                    일 시 : 91 0715 2040

수 신 : 장 관(국연,중동일,국기,기정)  사본:노창희 대사

발 신 : 주 유엔 대사대리

제 목 : 걸프사태(유엔 동향)

1. 안보리는 금 7.15 오후늦게 비공식협의를 갖고 H.BLIX IAEA 사무처장등으로 부터 안보리휴전 결의에 의거한 이락핵사찰 현황에 관해 보고를 청취한바, 동협의 관련 주요동향은 다음과같음.

가. BLIX 처장은 지난 7.7 이전 이락측이 문제의 우라늄 농축추진 계획을 IAEA 에 통보하지 않은것은 NPT 안전협정 불이행 (NON-COMPLIANCE) 이며, 7.18 IAEA 이사회 특별회의에서 이에관한 공식결론이 나는대로 IAEA 규정 12조 (항)에 의거 안보리및 총회에보고 예정이라고함.

나. 금일 회의에서는, 이락측이 7.14 새로 제출한 핵시설명세에 대해서 특별한 논의는 없었던 것으로 알려짐.

다. 다음 협의일자는 잡히지 않았으나 금주중 협의가 열릴것으로 관측되고 있으며, 상임이사국들간 결의안 초안 토의 가능성도 거론되고 있음.

2. 한편 이락은 7.12자 외상명의 유엔사무총장 및 안보리의장앞 서한에서, 미국이 중동지역에서의 패권장악이라는 미.이스라엘의 목표달성을 위해 이락에 대한 대규모 군사공격을 준비중이라고 주장하고, 안보리가 이락에 대한 여사한 미국의 재공격을 저지 시켜줄것을 요망하였음. (S/22786)

3. 금일 유엔측이 공개한 SADRUDDIN AGA KHAN대표의 이락실태조사 보고서 요지는 다음과같음.

가. 이락 기본수요: 일년기간 68 억불상당 품목수입필요 (식수및 위생 1.8 억불,보건 5억불, 식량 16.2 억불, 농업용품 4 억불, 유류 20억불, 동력발전 22 억불) (초기 4개월분:26.3 억불)

나. 이락 외환등 보유고 (이락측주장): 외한 1,475만불, 지불준비용 금 일정량

다. 상기 기본수요품목 수입 경비조달방법 (건의)

| 국기국 | 1차보 | 중아국 | 국기국 | 외정실 | 분석관 | 안기부 | 국기3(대사요). |
|--------|-------|--------|--------|--------|--------|--------|----------------|

1)이락 석유수출 허가: 일년간 55 억불상당수익발생 가능 (수출용 일 생산 100 만 배럴)

(단, 초기 4개월 관련장비등 10 억불 상당수입필요)

2)이락 해외자산 동결해제

3)본건 석유수출 및 기본수요 품목반입과 관련한 감시체계구축

첨부: NYT 지 관련기사: UNW(F)-330

끝

(대사대리 신기복-국장)

*UNW(行)- 330   1075  2040*
*(국연·중동일·국기·기전)  총구역*

# Baghdad Hands U.N. a New List Of Clandestine Atom Installations

### By PAUL LEWIS
Special to The New York Times

BAGHDAD, Iraq, July 14 — Iraq gave the United Nations a new list of clandestine nuclear installations today, but the chief United Nations nuclear inspector refused to disclose any details of what it contains or to say whether he thinks it is accurate.

"I can't express an opinion," the inspector, Demitri Perricos, said tonight. "It is very early. The list is still being studied."

The new list was submitted after the United States said earlier lists of Iraqi nuclear installations were inadequate. The lists have been submitted to satisfy the Security Council's insistence that all Iraq's nuclear weapons materials must be destroyed or removed under the cease-fire resolution that ended the Persian Gulf war.

Another member of the inspection team said today that the new list appears to include all the undeclared clandestine nuclear plants that American and other intelligence services had described to the team.

### Suspicions Remain

But this official said the team remains suspicious of the list because it has no way of knowing whether Iraq still has other nuclear installations that no one else knows about.

"Basically we have been lied to by the Iraqis for four months now, so we are going to be very cautious," the official said.

The Security Council is scheduled to meet Monday to consider the new Iraqi list.

Under the Council's cease-fire resolution, Iraq is required to hand over all weapons-grade nuclear material to the United Nations for removal or destruction. It is also required to surrender its chemical and biological weapons and its ballistic missiles.

Iraq appears anxious to satisfy the United States and other Security Council members that it is telling the truth about its nuclear plans because it wants the Council to ease the trade embargo imposed after the invasion of Kuwait by allowing it to sell $1 billion worth of oil to buy food and other goods.

After first declaring that it has no secret nuclear installations at all, Iraq acknowledged July 7 under pressure from the United States that it was in fact trying to enrich uranium by three different methods at eight clandestine sites around the country.

Mr. Perricos said his inspectors had found evidence that Iraq was enriching uranium by an electromagnetic method using calutrons, as well as by the centrifuge method and by chemical means.

The United States said this list was incomplete and gave the special commission charged with destroying Iraq's weapons of mass destruction further information about other suspected nuclear plants that did not appear on the July 7 declaration.

The special commission then asked Iraq to provide details of any nuclear research and development laboratories, special storage sites and nuclear manufacturing plants that it possesses. Last week the United Nations inspectors carried out a challenge inspection of a uranium production unit in the north of Iraq that Baghdad had failed to declare.

Members of the United Nations inspection team here say the special commission had been told that Iraq in fact had undeclared nuclear installations falling into all three categories.

Tonight Mr. Perricos said Iraq declared sites in all these categories on the list submitted today.

### Allied Troops Quit North Iraq

ZAKHO, Iraq, July 14 (Reuters) — Allied troops streamed out of northern Iraq today, and a United States general tried to soothe Kurdish fears of being left exposed to the wrath of President Saddam Hussein.

Maj. Gen. Jay Garner said an allied strike force to be based in southeastern Turkey would have plenty of notice from United Nations observers and others if the Iraqi leader threatened the Kurds again. Weekly American-Iraqi military coordination meetings are to take place in this Iraqi border town after allied troops complete their pullout on Monday, the general told reporters.

Coalition officials said the strike force would be based at Silopi, just north of the border, with units at Batman, 87 miles to the northwest, and Incirlik in southern Turkey.

0138

# IRAQI ATOM EFFORT EXPOSES WEAKNESS IN WORLD CONTROLS

## SUCCESS SHOCKS EXPERTS

### Baghdad's Gains Cast Doubt on Feasibility of Halting Nuclear Arms' Spread

By WILLIAM J. BROAD

Scientists and weapons experts, surprised that Iraq secretly used a method abandoned by the West half a century ago to enrich uranium, say Iraq's feat is a blow to international efforts to stem the spread of nuclear arms.

In a single stroke, it has overturned decades of assumptions about which procedures and materials need to be safeguarded. Up to now, the control effort has focused on keeping certain techniques secret and limiting export licenses for high-technology equipment that can be used in making bombs.

But Iraq has shown that a low-tech method openly described in scientific literature can be readily used to circumvent the restrictions, making the Iraqi weapons effort far more ingenious and dangerous than believed.

#### Enough for 2 Bombs

The clandestine Iraqi method is reported by a defector to have produced about 90 pounds of highly enriched uranium, enough for two bombs. Experts say the 30 enrichment machines that Iraq has admitted to using could make enough fuel for one warhead a year.

Iraq probably has the skill to perfect an atom bomb, weapons experts say. They stress that it is unlikely that Iraq has already done so, though some suggest it might be able to build one on short notice. Before the Persian Gulf war, many intelligence analysts said Iraq's engineers might start limited production of nuclear warheads in 5 to 10 years, but not much sooner. The estimates were based on how rapidly the Iraqis might build high-technology devices for uranium enrichment.

Concern soared in May when the Iraqi defector reportedly told American officials that Iraq used the antiquated, low-tech method to produce 90 pounds of enriched uranium. The technique uses electromagnetism in machines known as calutrons.

Under international pressure, Iraq told the United Nations last week that it had indeed used the old method, saying it produced a pound of enriched uranium. Experts believe that much more was produced, and in response to continued pressure and skepticism from abroad that it was not being completely forthcoming, Baghdad yesterday submitted to the United Nations a new document on its nuclear operations.

The fact that the Iraqis quietly used the forsaken method at all to produce weapons fuel showed great cleverness, the experts say.

"It's astonishing," said Dr. Glenn T. Seaborg, a Nobel laureate in physics and former chairman of the Atomic Energy Commission, which built most of the nation's nuclear bombs. "It represents quite a technical effort."

Dr. Edward J. Lofgren, a physicist at the Lawrence Berkeley Laboratory in California who helped develop calutrons during World War II, said Iraq's choice of enrichment method, while surprising, made eminent sense.

"The other methods are very efficient but take lots of capital and big plants," he said. "A calutron, on the other hand, in one stage enriches a large amount. It's not energy efficient. But it doesn't take a lot of capital."

Dr. J. Carson Mark, a former official of the Los Alamos National Laboratory in New Mexico who has studied the Iraqi program, said 90 pounds of highly enriched uranium might produce two bombs. He added that it was impossible to know whether the Iraqis had actually made such bombs.

#### Spy Agencies Criticized

"It's conceivable," he said. "The magnitude of their effort is suggestive. If they went through all that enrichment work, it puts weight to the argument that they took further steps. But there's no way of saying, on the basis of logic, whether they have done that."

Dr. Mark also criticized the nation's intelligence agencies for apparently failing to have discovered the clandestine effort at uranium enrichment.

"Why spend all that money on intelligence when it apparently and evidently learns nothing?" he asked.

Paul L. Leventhal, president of the Nuclear Control Institute, a private group in Washington that studies the spread of nuclear technology and has worked closely with Dr. Mark, said it was unlikely that the Iraqis already had a bomb, especially in light of the disarray caused by the gulf war and Iraq's moves to hide nuclear materials around the country.

"But do they have the components there, to put one together in short order?" he asked. "I would say yes."

Mr. Leventhal added that the reemergence of the old enrichment technique would force the development of a whole new set of international safeguards and precautions.

#### 'Genie Back in the Bottle'

"We can't put the genie back in the bottle," he said. "The main thing is to try to improve our intelligence-gathering ability" so that existing calutrons can be tracked down. He added that new sanctions would be needed to inhibit their use for uranium enrichment.

Leonard S. Spector, an expert on the spread of nuclear arms at the Carnegie Endowment for International Peace in Washington, said news of the Iraqi enrichment success had toppled the international program to stem weapons proliferation, which has focused on limiting advanced methods. "It's cataclysmic," he said. "All this was being done in Iraq without anybody knowing it. So who else is doing it? Everybody in the community knew this kind of thing was a possibility. But to be confronted by an example is devastating."

Though slow and costly, experts say, the electromagnetic process has many virtues from the Iraqi point of view. For one thing, it has been declassified for decades. Detailed blueprints of its workings have been published by the Federal Government and academic scientists, in contrast to the secrecy maintained around more advanced methods of uranium enrichment.

Most important, experts say, calutrons are relatively easy to build. They use few exotic materials, in principle allowing them to be largely constructed without Western aid.

#### Appetite for Power

The main drawback is that their bulky electromagnetic coils have a large appetite for electrical power.

But experts note that Iraq, with large oil supplies, can cheaply generate electricity for the process.

Though bulky and cumbersome, the Iraqi calutrons achieved one of the most delicate tasks of science: separation of isotopes. Isotopes are different varieties of the same element that differ only in the number of neutrons in their nuclei. U-235, the material needed for nuclear weapons, has 143 neutrons in its nucleus. U-238 has 146, making it fractionally heavier.

3—2

0139

In natural ore, U-238 accounts for 99.283 percent of uranium, while U-235 accounts for 0.711 percent. The scientific challenge, on which untold billions have been spent, is to separate the extremely rare isotope from the common one. Uranium suitable for atomic weapons is usually enriched to contain at least 80 percent U-235 and more commonly 90 percent or more.

The person who came up with the idea for the calutron and promoted it extensively in the early 1940's was Dr. Ernest O. Lawrence, inventor of the cyclotron particle accelerator and director of a physics laboratory at the University of California at Berkeley. The name calutron derives from California University cyclotron.

Dr. Lawrence's goal was to enrich uranium with the aid of cyclotrons, large circular electromagnets used to accelerate subatomic particles.

The principle was simple: Uranium would be ionized into charged particles and fired into the powerful electromagnetic fields of a cyclotron. The lighter the ion, the tighter its circular path. At the end of the arc, two beams of ions would feed into separate collectors.

#### Flying Screwdrivers

The process worked experimentally at Berkeley, producing minuscule amounts of fairly pure U-235. In 1943, the Government embarked on a huge project at Oak Ridge, Tenn., to expand its scale. At its peak, the program employed nearly 25,000 people.

The electromagnetic coils were 15 feet in diameter and weighed thousands of tons. So powerful were the magnetic fields that hammers and screwdrivers flew out of workers' hands if they came too close. The U-235 produced by the calutrons helped power the bomb that destroyed Hiroshima in August 1945.

One discovery of the electromagnetic program was that separation worked more effectively if the uranium fed into calutrons was already partly enriched, to 10 percent U-235. By the end of the war, other enrichment methods were working better than the calutrons, and the costly machines were abandoned for uranium enrichment.

But a few of them were still used at Oak Ridge to separate hundreds of other isotopes, in part for medical use. The separated isotopes included thorium, americium and curium.

Over the years, the technology of electromagnetic separation has advanced. Mr. Leventhal of the Nuclear Control Institute said some 180 patents have been filed on the process over the decades, apparently for isolating tiny amounts of rare isotopes.

Scientists say the electromagnetic method may have been refined and simplified by the Iraqis, making calutrons smaller, more competitive with advanced enrichment methods and far better producers of bomb fuel than they were in World War II.

#### Improvements of 50 Years

"Anybody who would be capable of building one of these things now would be capable of improving it over what we did 50 years ago," said Dr. Lofgren, who helped develop it in World War II.

Mr. Leventhal of the Nuclear Control Institute estimated that 30 Iraqi calutrons, if they were fairly modern ones and fed uranium that had already been slightly enriched, could probably produce up to 44 pounds of bomb-grade fuel a year. That, he said, would be enough for about one bomb.

Last week, Iraq said it had been running a total of three clandestine programs to enrich uranium. In addition to the electromagnetic method, it cited a centrifuge process and a chemical one. Several experts suggested that these might have produced slightly enriched uranium to feed the calutrons.

A scientist who advises the Federal Government, who spoke on condition of anonymity, said the Iraqi claim of having 30 calutrons was widely felt to be underestimated. "We think they have many more," he said. "Therefore the production rates are much higher" than private experts have calculated.

Experts on the spread of nuclear weapons say that their field, which for decades has focused on ways to stem the spread of advanced bomb-making methods, will now have to be rethought from the bottom up to focus on calutrons.

"How are we going to find this stuff?" asked Mr. Spector of the Carnegie Endowment. "What's the nonproliferation regime going to look like?

"Maybe there are bits and pieces of this technology that we can control. But if we can't, then you've got the possibility that one of the real underpinnings for the control of nuclear weapons won't be there anymore."

3-3

0140

# UNITED NATIONS

S

## Security Council

Distr.
GENERAL

S/22788
15 July 1991

ORIGINAL:  ENGLISH

NOTE BY THE SECRETARY-GENERAL

The Secretary-General has the honour to transmit to the members of the Security Council the attached communication which he has received from the Director-General of the International Atomic Energy Agency (IAEA).

91-22864   2499e (E)

/...

0141

Annex

### Letter dated 12 July 1991 from the Director-General of the International Atomic Energy Agency addressed to the Secretary-General

Attached herewith is a consolidated report on the first two IAEA inspections under Security Council resolution 687 (1991). You may deem it appropriate to transmit this report to the Security Council members.

(Signed) Hans BLIX

/...

Enclosure

# CONSOLIDATED REPORT ON THE FIRST TWO IAEA INSPECTIONS UNDER SECURITY COUNCIL RESOLUTION 687 (1991) OF IRAQI NUCLEAR CAPABILITIES

INTERNATIONAL ATOMIC ENERGY AGENCY

11 July 1991

/...

0143

# CONSOLIDATED REPORT ON THE FIRST TWO IAEA INSPECTIONS UNDER SECURITY COUNCIL RESOLUTION 687 (1991) OF IRAQI NUCLEAR CAPABILITIES

1. This report summarizes the principal findings of the first two inspections under Security Council resolution 687 (1991) conducted by the IAEA of Iraqi nuclear capabilities. These inspections were carried out between 15 - 21 May 1991 and 22 June - 3 July 1991 with the assistance and co-operation of the Special Commission of the United Nations. The first inspection was carried out by a team of 34 drawn from 20 Member States and was headed by Mr. D. Perricos of the IAEA as Chief Inspector. The second inspection consisted of a team of 18 personnel from 8 Member States and was headed by Mr. M. Zifferero (22 June - 26 June) and Mr. D. Kay (26 June - 3 July), both from the IAEA.

2. These two initial inspections had three principal inspection objectives:
- first, the verification of the accuracy and completeness of the Iraqi declarations submitted under the requirements of Security Council resolution 687,
- second, to conduct inspections of sites designated by the Special Commission established under resolution 687 where there were ground to believe that undeclared nuclear activities had been conducted or that undeclared equipment might be stored, and
- third, to develop an over-all picture of the nature, direction and capabilities of the Iraqi nuclear programme.

*Verification of the accuracy and completeness of the the Iraqi declarations*

3. The declaration by the Government of Iraq of 27 April 1991 principally concerned facilities, material and activities at Al-Tuwaitha Nuclear Research Centre.[1] Inspection of Al-Tuwaitha found the

[1] Al-Tuwaitha Site Map in Annex I

/...

following:

### a. Facilities

i.   The inspection found that many building where significant activities may have taken place were thoroughly destroyed -- in many cases by military activities during the conflict, but in some significant cases by extensive clearing operations carried out by Iraqi authorities during and after the conflict. In almost all cases documentation and records had disappeared and were not available. Smear tests and samples of intact or only partially damaged equipment and of the surrounding areas were taken and their analysis continues. However, much of the site was damaged or cleared to such an extent that this analysis process is very difficult, and in some cases is incapable of definitive results. The overall impression is of a site where most significant buildings have been thoroughly destroyed or cleared and, with only a few exceptions noted below, provide only limited concern for future verification unless substantial rebuilding takes place.[2] However, it is clear that much of the equipment which once existed at Al-Tuwaitha has been removed to other locations, most of which were not disclosed to the first two inspections.

ii.   Research reactors. (B24 and B13)[3] Both the Tamuz 1 & 2 reactors were heavily damaged. They would be difficult to restore and, in any event, the weapons significance of the facilities is now dependent on the HEU fuel only. In the case of Tamuz 1, there had been no attempt to rebuild the reactor since the 1981 attack, and the heat exchangers and pumps were found in a separate store and had not been used elsewhere. The building housing the IRT-5000 reactor was very heavily damaged, but the pool with reactor fuel and storage racks was still intact, albeit covered with substantial amounts of debris and rubble. The fuel was still inside the core, the pool and the external storage bay. The fuel is highly enriched uranium (80% and 36%) and, therefore, requires future action to remove it as required by resolution 687. After the fuel is removed the remains of the reactor building will be unusable.

iii.   Hot cells. The hot cells in the reactor building (B24) are mechanically badly damaged with the master-slave manipulators

---

[2] Annexes II and III summarize the status as of the first inspection.

[3] Numbers refer to Al-Tuwaitha Site Map in Annex I

/...

destroyed on the outside but with the concrete structure intact. Because of the surrounding debris it was impossible during the first mission to confirm the situation inside the cell and monitoring is required until the status is determined. Hot cells with damaged manipulators, but with their basic structure sound, remain in the Radioisotope Production Laboratory (B15). Additional hot cells remain in the "LAMA" Hot Metallurgy Testing Laboratory and in the radioactive waste treatment station. Future monitoring will be required of all these cells.

iii. **Laboratory and Workshop Building (B23).** The Iraqi authorities declared this building to have been used mainly for laser and optics work. However, due to the total destruction of this building and the removal by Iraq of all accessible equipment it was not possible to verify its use.

iv. **"LAMA" Hot Metallurgy Testing Laboratory (B22).** This building had been heavily bombed and there was no independent evidence of the use that had been made of this building. There had been salvage of some of the equipment from the two hot cells.

v. **Radioactive Waste Treatment Station (B35).** This building was partially damaged, but had two hot cells in good condition and with the machinery inside the station undamaged. The cells were not equipped with manipulators and were equipped for the specialized waste treatment process consistent with the declared use of the building.

vi. **Radiochemistry Laboratories (B9).** All three compartments of the hot cells with 150 mm of lead shielding were intact. The first part was used for dissolution, the second for equipment maintenance and the third for mixer settlers. The equipment had been used for separation of fission products from spent fuel. A separate room had 10 free-standing alpha glove-boxes for actinide separation. The process was on a small scale (2.26 g of plutonium was declared as separated) but has a larger significance in establishing the capability for plutonium separation.

vii. **Radioisotope Production Laboratory (B15).** This building contained two hot cells, one with 900 mm of shielding, the other with 1200 mm barytic shielding. The building was extensively damaged with all services destroyed. There were also originally 23 lead cells which are now scattered as a result of the bombing. the applications for which this building was declared to be used would be allowed under the terms of

/...

0146

resolution 687, but future monitoring would be required to ensure that its use was limited to these purposes.

viii. **The "Italian" Area (B73).** This area was heavily bombed and the fuel fabrication plant and chemical engineering research were almost completely destroyed. The material testing building sustained some damage but the essential equipment survived.

ix. **Materials Testing laboratory (Ceramics and Metals) (B63).** The building was rendered unusable by the bombing, and all of its equipment had been removed. Equipment said by the Iraqis to be from this building was later shown to the first inspection team. This equipment, if indeed from this building, would be consistent with its stated use.

x. **Nuclear Physics Laboratories (B80).** The Iraqi authorities declared that these building had been devoted to plasma physics, ion source physics, magnet development and for future operation of a cyclotron. The building had been heavily damaged during the bombing and had been subjected to an unusually heavy site clearance operation by the Iraqis -- which included even removing the substantial, concrete reinforced floor and -- by the time of the second mission -- regrading the site to a level field. All equipment had been removed from the building before the first mission -- except for two magnets left on the top of the rubble. The building had been serviced by unusually large electrical (7.4 megawatts) and cooling services which appeared to exceed its declared needs.

xi. **Complex Chemistry and Chemical Engineering Research and Development (B85).** The declared purposes of this building were chemical and chemical engineering-related R&D, including a pilot-scale extraction process to recover uranium from ore with a high organic content. The building had been very extensively damaged, first from bombing, then from a vigorous removal operation of the Iraqi authorities. At the time of the first inspection, Iraq had completely removed the two process halls of this building, and by the second inspection very little remained of this complex. The building had an unusually large ventilation system, but the lack of any residual equipment together with the extensive site levelling has made it difficult to determine with certainty the actual uses of this building. Environmental samples were taken and are now being analyzed.

/...

0147

### b. Nuclear Materials

i. With respect to the nuclear material declared by Iraq, the Agency inspection teams had to locate, identify, characterize, verify, "freeze" the material so it could only be moved with Agency approval and assess the accessibility for removal of the nuclear-weapons-usable material. The Iraqi declaration of 27 April 1991 had covered all the nuclear material that had been subject to safeguards.[4] The Iraqi authorities had relocated a substantial amount of the nuclear materials to both areas adjacent to and further removed from Tuwaitha.[5]

ii. Extensive verification efforts were carried out during the first inspection on all declared nuclear material. For the nuclear weapons-usable material this involved the following: The presence of all fresh high enriched uranium was confirmed by measurements (17664 g U/12633 g U-235). The presence of irradiated high enriched uranium was confirmed -- [61 items = 16.8 kg U =52% verified by fuel type identified and non-destructive assay (NDA) carried out] [41 items = 8.3 kg U =26% verified by item counting and NDA] [35 items = 7.0 kg U =22% presence indirectly confirmed by radiation dose mapping]. Presence of recovered plutonium [2.26 g] was confirmed.

iii. For non-nuclear weapons-usable material the measurements involved: The presence of low-enriched uranium was confirmed by measurement [irradiated fuel, 10% enrichment = 69 items = 87.8 kg U] [fresh bulk = 2.6% enrichment = 75 items =1762 kg U]. The presence of depleted and natural uranium was confirmed by measurement [3% of inventory =327 kg uranium was reported to be under rubble]. The presence of yellow cake was confirmed by measurements[752 items = 204 tons of natural uranium]. The presence of previously exempted material was confirmed.

iv. The nuclear material outside of the damaged reactor was brought under Agency custody by means of the extensive applications of Agency seals and a regime was established for frequent inspection until this material can be removed from Iraq. Studies were begun for the

---

[4] Annex IV provides an overview of the nuclear materials and there locations.

[5] Annex V indicates the distribution of this material.

/...

0148

removal from the damaged reactor of the material still there and for applying seals as an interim control measure.

### Inspection of Sites Designated by the Special Commission

4.      Beginning with the first IAEA inspection, short-notice inspections were carried out of sites designated by the Special Commission. These have included sites at Tarmiya (20 May and 24 June), Abu Ghraib 23, 25, and 26 June), Al Hamath ( 24 June), Zaafaruniya (26 June), Al Musayyib (27 June) and Falluja (28 June). At two of these site, the Iraqi authorities denied the right of access for the purposes of inspection and removed materials even after the Chief Inspector had ordered that no material or equipment be moved for the sites under the inspections had been completed. Photographic evidence substantiated a strong case that the material which was moved was related to undeclared uranium enrichment activities.

### Over-all Development of the Iraqi Nuclear Programme

5. At the end of the second inspection, the team concluded that based on the evidence it had found the Iraqis had been pursuing an undeclared uranium enrichment programme using the electromagnetic isotope separation technique (EMIS).[6]

6. The technologies that must be mastered for a successful EMIS programme include high current ion source development, high voltage DC power supply design and manufacture, high current power supply

---

[6] EMIS is accomplished by creating a high current beam(10's to 1000's of milliamps) of low energy (10's of KeV) ions and allowing them to pass through a magnetic field (typically 3000-7000 Gauss. or .3-.7 Tesla). The heavier ions bend in a larger radius than the lighter ions and suitable placed collector pockets capture the different isotopes. EMIS is the process originally used by most of the nuclear weapons states to prepare their first highly enriched uranium for nuclear explosives. Its advantages are a well understood design, with much detail available in the open literature, and the ready availability of much of the hardware. The disadvantages of EMIS are the large energy cost per unit of HEU produced and high labor costs associated with operation. This latter disadvantage can now be reduced, however, with the use of readily available computer control software.

/...

0149

design and manufacture, large vacuum system design and operation, collector design and fabrication, and insulator design and fabrication. In addition specific chemical process technologies are required for operation of a uranium EMIS facility: acid washers to clean the vacuum chambers, combustors to burn the graphite collectors, dissolvers to dissolve the ash, solvent extraction systems to purify the uranium solutions, and chemical reactors to prepare uranium tetrachloride feed material. Mechanical engineering capabilities are required for fabrication of massive steel magnet pole pieces, support fixtures, and equipment transport. By the end of the second inspection the following dedicated facilities for each of these required technologies had been located and inspected by the first two IAEA inspection teams. These facilities included:

   i.      **Buildings Within the Berm at Tuwaitha.** When the first IAEA team visited Tuwaitha it was noted that building 80 had installed power of 7.4 megawatts. This is an inordinately large amount of power for a building of its size and declared function. Building 85 was declared to be a chemical engineering building and therefore should have had equipment in it that would have allowed lab/pilot scale EMIS process chemistry to be demonstrated. These buildings were heavily damaged during the war, as were many other buildings at Tuwaitha. However, these two buildings were singled out for unusually thorough demolition after the first team's visit. The sites where these buildings stood have been graded and cleared to an inexplicable extent. This action, in combination with the extraneous rubble which the first team noted covered the site, suggests an attempt to render difficult the identification of the activities and purposes of these buildings. Environmental samples were taken from nearby objects during this inspection.

   ii.     **The Al Hamath Workshop.** A significant new site was inspected outside the berm just south of the water purification complex in the northwest portion of the Tuwaitha facility. This site was called Al Hamath by the Iraqis. Our Iraqi military representative stated that the site was used for truck maintenance. This declaration was later amended when the Iraqis said that the facility was a machine shop. Neither declared usage of these buildings is credible. The site had two high bay buildings sharing over 1 megawatt of electrical service and a suitably sized water purification and chiller system. Neither building had been damaged during the war, yet both buildings had been stripped of their contents and the concrete floors had sections removed. If the

/...

0150

facilities had been used for either of the declared purposes there would be
no need for either this much power or this much cooling capacity, and
there certainly would be no need to gut the buildings. These high bay
buildings each had multiple utility drops consisting of high capacity, 380
volt, three phase receptacles, and 220 volt single phase receptacles cooling
water facilities spaced along the walls. Each building had large traveling
cranes of the same type installed at Tarmiyah, one of which was labeled,
"Iraqi Atomic Energy Commission". One of the two cranes was very
strongly magnetized. It is the consensus of the team that this site was
used as a magnet test facility. Because there was not a nearby suitable
chemical processing facility, and because the installed power is relatively
low, it is surmised that this facility did not do actual uranium isotope
separation (though environmental samples were taken at this site). It is
surmised that buildings 80 and 85 did do lab/pilot scale uranium isotope
separation with approximately five units for some unknown period of
time. The Al Hamath buildings are believed to have been used for
magnet tests (possibly including coil winding) and for engineering
integration tests of separator systems.

    iii.    Tarmiyah. The Tarmiyah site[7] when inspected by the
first team was noted as being unusual because of the mix of buildings
with unusually large installed electrical power co-allocated with
buildings with large chemical processing capabilities. When the second
team reinvestigated the facilities it was clear that the site was a multi-
billion dollar EMIS facility. Building 33 was stated by the Iraqis to be used
for transformer fabrication. In the technical view of the inspection team
this is simply not credible. A transformer plant required metal forming,
coil winding, and other capabilities that were clearly absent from this
building. The building had two ten ton bridge cranes and two twenty-five
ton bridge cranes, an enormous installed electrical supply (over 100
megawatts), and a supply of purified and chilled water. These features
are consistent with building 33 housing EMIS machines. The interior of
the building was configured as a large bay with two large (5m by 60m)
parallel piers for electromechanical equipment with utility outlets and
space suitable for approximately 100 EMIS units. The EMIS units would
sit approximately three meters above the floor of the central bay, with the
power supplies in the adjacent bay and the vacuum pumps on the floor.
It is surmised that this building was the site for the first stage of
enrichment. The consensus of the team is that this building was never
operational, with initial operation six to eighteen months away.

---

[7]Tarmiyah Site Map in Annex VI

/...

Building 245 is in important ways a smaller version of building 33. The building has approximately 40 megawatts of power, uninterruptable power systems, for control computer power and a large unfinished control room.

It is hypothesized to be the building for the second stage of enrichment. The building could have held 20 EMIS units. The facility utilities were incomplete and it is believed that this facility was twelve to eighteen months from operation.

Building 46 was a process chemistry building that was suitable for high quality batch chemistry work. The building had little process equipment installed and was probably six to twelve months from first operation. This building may have been designed for uranium tetrachloride processing.

Building 57 was stated as being for parts cleaning. The washing facilities in the building were designed for washing heavy objects of the size postulated for the EMIS vacuum chamber. A rail system two meters above the floor was installed for conveniently loading a heavy object into the pressure washers. This building was incomplete with first operation estimated to be in six to twelve months. The team emphasizes that this building was built to conveniently wash parts of a particular configuration and it is the team's opinion that these parts were to be vacuum boxes used in EMIS separators.

Building 225 was stated by the Iraqis to be a heavy metal recovery facility. This is assessed to be a true statement. The building appears to be designed for recovering uranium for recycle into the process. The air handling and filtration equipment in this building was enormous. It is surmised that the extensive filtration was both to conserve valuable enriched material and to prevent isotopic signatures from escaping the plant.

The configuration of buildings 33 and 245 with their unusual electrical and cooling utilities led the team to conclude that Tarmiyah was an EMIS site. The co-located buildings containing all of the necessary ancillary functions completes the case. The only purpose of a multi-billion dollar facility of this type apparent to the team is EMIS of uranium. It is the opinion of the team that Tarmiyah was never operational. Initial startup of the facilities was six to eighteen months away. It has effectively been rendered non-operational and may be adequately monitored by periodic inspections.

/...

0152

iv.     **Zaafarniyah.** The IAEA had reason to believe that the Al Dijila and Al-Rabee sites located in Zaafarniyah were used to fabricate EMIS components. Al Dijila is a Ministry of Industry site with electrical engineering design and fabrication facilities. The manufacturing plants inspected were observed to have the following capabilities: coil winding, chassis assembly, computer aided design, printed circuit board fabrication, and control system design and assembly. Some of the equipment at Tarmiya appeared to originate from this site. It is the team's belief that the required electrical components for an EMIS program could be designed and fabricated at Al Dijila but that this facility is not dedicated to EMIS work.

The Al-Rabeeh metal working shops were excellently equipped for precision work as well as very large metal piece work on steel, stainless steel, and aluminium. There was no evidence that facilities for working with pyrophoric (e.g. uranium) or toxic (e.g. beryllium) are present. Al-Rabeeh clearly has the capacity to fabricate the major EMIS metal components but was not being used for EMIS fabrication at the time of the inspection.

v.     **Possible EMIS Components and Equipment.** As detailed elsewhere in the full inspection report many storage facilities and trucks were inspected by the team. A substantial amount of dual-use equipment suitable for use in EMIS power supplies was noted. None of this equipment is conclusive by itself, but taken as a whole, enough equipment was documented to state that there seemed to be an unusual amount of electrical equipment that would be appropriate for an EMIS program. Equipment that appeared to be real EMIS equipment (coils, magnet pole pieces, and vacuum chambers) was seen and photographed by several team members as the Iraqis attempted to move it from Fallujah.

## Conclusions

There is Iraqi declared evidence of the research and development required for EMIS work (ion source, magnet development, and insulator research at Tuwaitha). There is documented evidence of the ability to manufacture all required components for an EMIS separator. There is evidence that lab or pilot scale EMIS development was done at Tuwaitha. There is further evidence that this research was successful and that a large EMIS process plant was under construction at Tarmiyah. Conclusive evidence that uranium isotope separation was accomplished must await the results from the environmental samples. Uranium unusually depleted in U-235 would be prima facie evidence that EMIS

/...

(large scale laser isotope separation is not credible for Iraq) has been done in Iraq. Accurate assessments of actual production are impossible at this point. It is the opinion of this team that Tarmiyah has never operated and that Tuwaitha had facilities to operate at most five to ten separators. If each separator can produce 1 gram of highly enriched uranium per day (as estimated in a technical-note prepared by the second inspection team) then the maximum amount of HEU produced can be estimated if the initial commissioning dates and operating time can be determined. Our best estimate is that Tuwaitha could have had five machines operating for no more than two years and could not have produced more than three kilograms of highly enriched uranium.

0154 /...

Annex I

The Tuwaitha site map

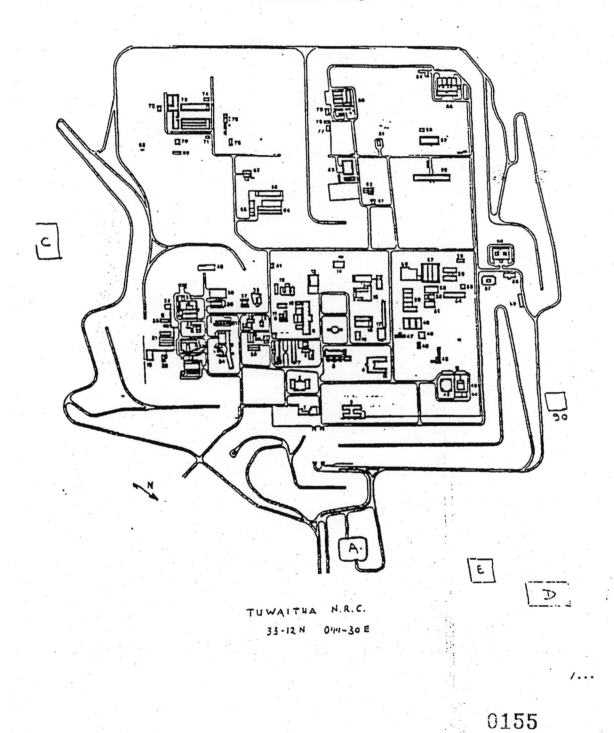

TUWAITHA N.R.C.

33-12 N   0144-30 E

/...

0155

ACTION TEAM CONFIDENTIAL

UNSC 687 ACTION TEAM
FIRST ON-SITE INSPECTION

Annex II

List of buildings at Al-Tuwaitha

| Bldg. No. | Iraqi Declaration 1991-05-15 | Inspector's specification (if different) |
|---|---|---|
| 1 | Personal Control Office | |
| 2 | Restaurant | |
| 3 | Administrative Building | |
| 4 | Biology and Agricultural Labs | |
| 5 | Head Administration | |
| 6 | Administration | |
| 7 | Administration | Training Office |
| 8 | Training Offices | External Relations Department |
| 9 | Chemical Analyses Labs and Radiochemical Labs | |
| 10 | Chemical Analyses Labs | |
| 11 | Telephone Communication | |
| 12 | Engineering Services Workshop | Engineering & Neutron Generator |
| 13 | Research Reactor IRT-5000 | |
| 14 | Sub-Station | |
| 15 | Isotope Production Laboratory | |
| 16 | Mechanical Production Workshop | Workshop for IRT |
| 17 | Mechanical Production Workshop | |
| 18 | Medical Analyses Lab | |
| 19 | Offices and Stores | Open Air Pool |
| 20 | Offices and Stores | |
| 21 | Offices and Stores | |
| 22 | Hot Laboratories LAMA | |
| 23 | Laboratory Workship Building | |
| 24 | Tamuz-2 Zero Power Reactor | |
| 25 | Store | |
| 26 | Chemical Cleaning Workshop | |
| 27 | Caravan | |
| 28 | Caravans | |
| 29 | Chemical Cleaning Workshop | Caravan |

/...

0156

| Bldg. No. | Iraq: Declaration by Iraq (as is) | Inspector's specification (if different) |
|---|---|---|
| 30 | Chemical Cleaning Workshop | |
| 31 | Cooling Tower | Cooling Tower for Tamuz |
| 32 | Cooling Tower | Warehouse |
| 33 | Offices | |
| 34 | Offices and Stores | |
| 35 | Radioactive Waste Treatment Station (RWTS) | |
| 36 | Store | Solid Waste Store |
| 37 | Training Offices | Storage |
| 38 | Training Offices Labs | |
| 39 | Store | Permanent Solid Waste Storage |
| 40 | Solid Waste Storage | Waste Storage for IRT |
| 41 | Control Room for No. 40 | Nuclear Instrument Calibration and Waste Storage |
| 42 | Technical Library and Conference Rooms | |
| 43 | Technical Library and Conference Rooms | |
| 44 | Technical Library and Conference Rooms | |
| 45 | Water Treatment Station | |
| 46 | Biology and Agricultural Labs | |
| 47 | Biology and Agricultural Labs | |
| 48 | Biology and Agricultural Labs | |
| 49 | Biology and Agricultural Labs | |
| 50 | Mechanical Workshops and Stores | (includes also IOZ-) |
| 51 | Mechanical Workshops and Stores | |
| 52 | Mechanical Workshops and Stores | |
| 53 | Mechanical Workshops and Stores | |
| 54 | Mechanical Workshops and Stores | Graphite Workshop |
| 55 | Mechanical Workshops and Stores | |
| 56 | Mechanical Workshops and Stores | |
| 57 | Mechanical Workshops and Stores | |
| 58 | Cafeteria | |
| 59 | Health Physics Building | |
| 60 | Offices | |

/...

0157

| Bldg No. | Iraqi Declaration 1991-05-18 | Inspection specification (if different) |
|---|---|---|
| 61 | Incinerator | |
| 62 | Sewage-Station | |
| 63 | Cold Material Testing Laboratories | |
| 64 | Chemical Waste Treatment (liquids) | Rad Waste Process Building |
| 65 | Chemical Waste Treatment (liquids) | |
| 66 | Chemical Waste Treatment (liquids) | Offices/Training Building |
| 67 | Deionized Water Production Units | |
| 68 | Utilities | Storage |
| 69 | Utilities | Oil Storage |
| 70 | Utilities | Electrolytical/Production of Hydrogen |
| 71 | Utilities | |
| 72 | Utilities | |
| 73 | Workshops | Workshop for Fuel Fabrication Laboratory and Hall for Material Testing |
| 74 | Power Sub-Station | |
| 75 | Caravans | |
| 76 | Power Sub-Station | Canteen |
| 77 | Utilities Workshop | |
| 78 | Utilities Workshop | |
| 79 | Caravans | |
| 80 | Nuclear Physics Laboratories | |
| 81 | Cafeteria | |
| 82 | Electronic Research Laboratories | Electronics Department & Computer Center |
| 83 | Utilities | |
| 84 | Utilities | Chemistry & Chemical Engineering R&D |
| 85 | Chemical Research Laboratories | |
| 86 | Mechanical Design Laboratories | |
| 87 | Medical Centre | |
| 88 | Health Center | |
| 89 | Caravans | |
| 90 | Polymer Chemistry Laboratory | |

bldgrev/bio/oi 08-04

/...

0158

Annex III

Summary of follow-up actions

| | Building | Status of Building | Recommended further Action |
|---|---|---|---|
| 1 | H24 TAMUZ 1,2 | heavily damaged | Future monitoring of recovered equipment from Tamuz 1 (e.g., heat exchangers and pumps) required |
| 2 | B24 Hot Cells | badly damaged (but concrete structure intact) | Monitoring until positive confirmation of status |
| 3 | B23 Laboratories and workshop | totally damaged | Future monitoring of recovered equipment (e.g., lasers and optics work) required |
| 4 | B22 "LAMA" | damaged | - Monitoring of the status of hot cells<br>- Future monitoring of recovered equipment (e.g., some parts of 2 hot cells - one concrete and one lead) required |
| 5 | B35 Radioactive waste treatment | partially damaged but 2 hot cells in good condition | Future monitoring of hot cells |
| 6 | B13 IRT-5000 | heavily damaged | Removal of 80% and 36% enriched fuel |
| 7 | B13 Hot Cells | concrete structure undamaged | - clearance of debris<br>- monitoring until positive confirmation of status and removal of fuel from IRT-5000 |
| 8 | B9 Radiochemistry Laboratories | equipment within B9 largely escaped damage | Future monitoring |

/...

| | Building | Status of Building | Recommended further Action |
|---|---|---|---|
| 9 | B15 Radioisotopes Production Laboratory | damaged but 2 hot cells structure intact | Future monitoring if the building is restored |
| 10 | B73 The "Italian" area | heavily bombed | - Future monitoring of the material testing laboratory<br>- Future monitoring of recovered equipment (e.g., equipment relevant to reprocessing) required |
| 11 | B64, 56, 66, 67 | buildings damaged | Future monitoring |
| 12 | B63, B80, B85 (new R&D area) | heavily damaged | Future monitoring of recovered equipment (e.g., related to material testing, plasma physics and uranium extraction) required |
| 13 | B45 to B58 workshop area | many buildings, one still usable | - Future monitoring<br>- Future monitoring of recovered equipment (e.g., graphite machine shop tools) required |
| 14 | Remaining areas | many buildings are still usable | - Monitoring of any future reuse of buildings<br>- Check of removed equipment |

(0185B)

Annex IV

UNSC687

Summary-description of locations

| S.No. | LOCATION | | STATUS | |
|---|---|---|---|---|
| 1 | IQA- IRT Research Reactor | | 1. | Facility destroyed; however no $H_2O$ leackage for core pool and spent fuel detected yet. |
| | | | 2. | Nuclear Material: |
| | | | (a) | Apparently no damage of fuel since contamination of pool water not above normal level. |
| | | | (b) | In both pools significant amounts of soil and rubble were discovered. |
| | | | (c) | It was not possible to confirm the presence of all fuel items. |
| | | | (d) | Fresh fuel removed, verified at new site. |
| 2 | IQB- Tamuz 2 Research Reactor | (empty = no nuclear material present) | 1. | Facility destroyed. |
| | | | 2. | Nuclear material: all material (fresh and spent fuel) was removed from the facility. (Fresh fuel to Site A, spent fuel to Site B). |
| 3 | IQC- Fuel Fabrication Laboratory | | 1. | Facility destroyed, area contamination. |
| | | | 2. | Nuclear Material: - Fuel assemblies damaged, under rubble - 53 out of 55 fuel rods recovered. - 74% of bulk material recovered, rest suspected under rubble. |
| 4 | IQZ- Storage Facility | (empty = no nuclear material present) | 1. | Facility destroyed. |
| | | | 2. | Nuclear material: all nuclear material removed to a new storage. |
| 5 | New Storage Facility | | | Nuclear Material: |
| | | | (a) | Previously "exempted" material |
| | | | (b) | IQZ- material = DU, NU, LEU (2.5%) |
| | | | (c) | rods, pellets recovered from IQC. |
| 6 | Location A | | | Nuclear Material: |
| | | | (a) | Fresh fuel, HEU; from IQA- |
| | | | (b) | Fresh fuel, HEU; from IQB- |
| 7 | Location B | | | Nuclear Material: Spent fuel from IQB-. |
| 8 | Location C | | | Nuclear Material: |
| | | | (a) | Yellow Cake in drums |
| | | | (b) | Bulk material recovered from IQC. |

ACTION TEAM CONFIDENTIAL

/...

June 13, 1991                    Annex V

### Location, types and quantities of nuclear fuel assemblies

**I. Fresh Fuel Assemblies at Location A Adjacent to Nuclear Site**
- 68 items of IRT-5000, tubular type, total U-235 content 10,973 g (enrichment: 80%) [1]
- 10 items EK-36 type (rod cluster) total U-235 content 1,272 g (enrichment: 36%)
- 1 item Osirak type (French MTR) total U-235 content 388 g (enrichment: 93%)

**II. Spent Fuel Assemblies Stored at Location B Near Nuclear Site**
- 38 items Osirak type (French MTR) total U-235 content 11,050 g (enrichment: 93%)
- 20 items IRT-5000 tubular type initial U-235 content 3,165 g (enrichment: 80%) [2]
- 3 items EK-36 type (rod cluster) initial U-235 content 360 g (enrichment: 36%) [3]
- 69 items EK-10 type (rod cluster) initial U-235 content 8,778 g (enrichment: 10%) [4]

**III. Spent Fuel Assemblies Remaining in the IRT 5000 Core, Pool and Storage Bay [5]**
- 22 items in core, IRT-5000 tubular type, total U-235 content 3,510 g (enrichment: 80%)
- 42 items in adjacent storage bay, IRT-5000 tubular type, total U-235 content 6,832 g (enrichment: 80%)
- 12 items in core pool storage rack, IRT-5000 tubular type, total U-235 content 1,890 g. (enrichment: 80%)

[1] Detailed drawings available. Two items damaged but nuclear material not affected.

[2] Estimated burn-up is 40%.

[3] Burn-up unknown, but probably very low.

[4] Removal of these items still to be decided.

[5] Detailed drawing of fuel assembly available. Estimated average burn-up of 42 items and the 12 items is 40%; burn-up of remaining 22 items in core unknown.

/...

0162

Annex VI

Tarmiya
Possible Nuclear Facility
33-36N 044-23E

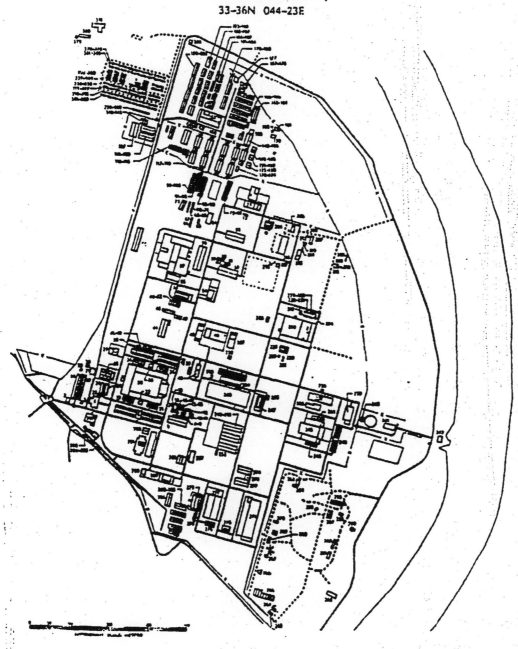

# 외 무 부

종 별 :

번 호 : UNW-1843          일 시 : 91 0716 1830

수 신 : 장 관(국연,중동일,기정) 사본:노창희대사

발 신 : 주 유엔대사대리

제 목 : 걸프사태(유엔동향)

연: UNW-1835

1. 안보리 대이락 제재위원회는 7.22 또는 23회의 소집예정이며, SADRUDDIN AGA KHAN 대표도 연호보고와 관련 동회의에 참석할 것으로 예상됨.

2. 유엔사무총장은 안보리결의 699 호에 의거 이락의 대량파괴 무기 폐기경비 부담 시행안( S/22792)을 7.15 차로 안보리에 제출해온 바, 동시행안에 의하면 동경비재원은 이락 석유수출 수입에서 조달하며, 이를 위한 제반 절차와 관련 적절한 감시체계수립 필요성이 제기되고 있음. 이락측이 제의한 화학무기 자체폐기 방안은 유엔 이락 특정무기폐기특위에서 계속 검토중이며, 본건 이락무기폐기와 관련 상기 결의에의거 유엔측에 접수된 각국 자발 기여금은 현재 총 200만불이라고 함.

3. 한편 유엔측발표에 의하면 이락.쿠웨이트 국경획정위원회는 제네바에서 7월초부터 지난주까지 제2차 회기를 갖고 서쪽지역( WESTERNPORTION) 획정방식, 북쪽지역 SAFWAN부근국경의 대체적인 위치등에 합의하였다고 함.

동 위원회는 8.12 부터 제네바에서 제3차 회기를 가질예정이며, 오는 가을 국경지역 측량을 시작할 것이라고 함.

첨부: NYT 기사및 WP 지 사설.: UNW(F)-332

끝

(대사대리 신기복-국장)

---

국기국    1차보    중아국    국기국    외정실    안기부

UNW(乃-331 / 0716 1873
(국연.중동알 : 과정)  총2대

# Iraq Still Conceals Nuclear Effort, Inspection Team Reports to U.N.

### By FRANK PRIAL
Special to The New York Times

UNITED NATIONS, July 15 — Baghdad continues to defy demands that it disclose the nature and extent of its nuclear program to United Nations inspectors, the leaders of a mission to Iraq told the Security Council tonight.

Hans Blix, Director General of the International Atomic Energy Agency, and Rolf Ekeus, executive chairman of the special commission overseeing the elimination of Baghdad's weapons of mass destruction, told the Security Council that a new list of nuclear sites, provided by the Iraqis on Sunday, added nothing new to a list of sites released on July 7, which was quickly characterized by American intelligence officials as incomplete and misleading.

As part of the cease-fire resolution that ended the Persian Gulf war, Iraq is required to grant the inspectors immediate access to all nuclear sites so that materials and equipment that could be used to manufacture nuclear weapons can be destroyed.

#### 'Iraqis Have Not Complied'

"The Iraqis have not complied with the resolution," said Mr. Blix, who is a member of the mission. Teams from the agency are carrying out the inspections at the request of the Security Council.

In the July 7 list, the Iraqis admitted for the first time that they were pursuing three clandestine programs designed to produce enriched uranium, which could be used to make nuclear weapons.

Thomas R. Pickering, the United States representative to the United Nations, said after the meeting that the list released on Sunday included "more details rather than revelations." He added, "I don't really see how the list has changed the situation."

Although Iraq's Prime Minister, Saadun Hamadi, predicted in Baghdad today that a new American attack on his country was a "probability," further military action was not raised in the Security Council consultations.

#### 'No Discussion' of Attack

Sir David Hannay, the British representative, said that "there was no discussion" of military action, but added, "One way or another, this program of Iraq's will have to be removed."

Speaking to reporters after the Security Council meeting, Mr. Blix said it was not possible to determine how quickly the Iraqis could construct a nuclear weapon. Everything they have done to date, he said, "is at the pilot program level." Of two installations that were designed to move production to "industrial scale," one may have been destroyed during the war and the other has never been started up. It would take 6 to 18 months to start it up and an undetermined length of time to build a weapon after that, Mr. Ekeus said.

According to the inspectors, the two plants represented a $4 billion to $8 billion investment.

"The contention of Iraq that its program is peaceful is simply not plausible," Mr. Blix said. "To make a single gram of enriched uranium by the electromagnetic approach would require five times the energy likely to be retrieved from that gram," he added. "There is no cost justification."

UNW-1843
첨부물

2-1

# The Struggle for Food in Iraq

IN IRAQ the struggle for food is sharpening. While widespread starvation has not yet appeared, events seem to be moving in that direction amid a general paralysis of the economy. It is now up to the United Nations, and particularly the United States, to find a way to avert that disaster without strengthening President Saddam Hussein, his regime or his army. That's not impossible, but it's not going to be easy, and it requires rapid action.

Before its invasion of Kuwait a year ago, Iraq imported most of its food and paid for it with oil. The oil has been embargoed by the United Nations, and except for a small dribble moving by truck to Jordan, the embargo has been highly effective. President Bush says that the sanctions will remain as long as Saddam Hussein stays in power. One possibility is to allow Iraq to export limited amounts of oil, measured to its needs for food. Another is to allow it to use some of the money now frozen in foreign banks. The allies suspect that Iraq may also have other funds hidden abroad. The Iraqis deny it but after the recent discoveries of their nuclear weapons programs following years of similar denials, no one is much inclined to take Iraqi assurances on faith.

Deciding how to let Iraq pay for food imports is the least difficult of the decisions confronting the U.N. The harder part of the job is to ensure that the money goes only for food and genuinely humanitarian purposes—and that it serves the people who need help most urgently. At present the army appears well fed, and the restaurants in the big Baghdad hotels are operating normally. The duress is most visible, as you would expect, among poor people whom the regime can afford to ignore. The price of milk has shot up to many multiples of its prewar price, and there is beginning to be real suffering even in Baghdad. It gets worse in the provinces, particularly in the south, where the Shiites who rose against Saddam Hussein live. Along with the food shortages, malfunction of water and sewer systems has greatly increased the possibility of epidemics.

It's relatively simple to ease the blockade to allow milk and grain, water piping and sewage pumps to pass through. It's harder—but essential—to monitor the distribution of the supplies and ensure that the milk actually goes to the children and that the sewers are repaired first in the areas of greatest need. That means drawing the United Nations and some of its agencies such as UNICEF into a highly demanding process of surveillance inside Iraq, in which it will inevitably be thrown into collisions with the Iraqi administration. It will be an extraordinarily difficult relief operation, but it's essential to get it underway, and fast.

In the great test of wills that has developed between a vengeful government and the allies who won the desert war, it is not permissible that the next victims should be children and the poor. Saddam Hussein appears ready to sacrifice them. But the United Nations has the resources to prevent that, if it uses them forcefully.

2-2

0166

관리
번호 : 91-
      1147

# 외 무 부

종 별 :

번 호 : UNW-1847                    일   시 : 91 0718 1620

수 신 : 장관(국연,중동일,국기,기정),사본:노창희대사

발 신 : 주 유엔 대사대리

제 목 : 걸프사태(이락 핵사찰)

대:WUN-1731

1. 안보리 휴전결의에 의거한 IAEA 조사반의 이락 핵사찰 결과 보고서가 안보리에 7.15 자로 제출된바, 동 보고서(S/22788)에는 1차(5.15-21) 및 2 차(6.22-7.3) 사찰 결과가 포함되어있음.(금파편 송부위계)

2. 이락의 핵개발 계획 공개(7.7)이후진행된 금번 사찰결과는 상기 보고서에는 포함되어 있지 않은바, 7.15 안보리 비공식협의시 H.BLIX IAEA 사무총장은 이락의 핵개발계획이 평화적 목적만을 위한것으로 보기어렵다는 입장을 표명한바있음.

3. 한편 금 7.18 자 NYT 보도에 의하면, IAEA 현지 사찰반은 이락측이 핵무기 제조가 가능한 정도의 양의 농축우라늄을 비밀리에 생산해내지는 못한것으로 보고있다고함.

4. 이락은 7.14 자국이 유엔측에 제출한 핵시설명세는 새로운 사항을 통보하기 위한 것이 아니었으며 ,7.7 제출 내용의 일부분(AN INTEGRAL PART)으로 보아야 한다는 요지의 안보리문서(S/22803)를 7.16 자로 배포하였음.(이는 7.14 자명세에 새로운 것이 없다는 비판과 이락측이 관련정보를 은익하고 있다고 압력을 받고 나서야 마지못해 조금씩 시인하고 있다는 비난을 의식한 것으로 보임.)

5. 금 7.18 A.POSSO 에쿠아돌 공사가 당관 원참사관 접촉시 언급한 바에 의하면, H.BLIX 사무총장은 상기 7.15 안보리협의시 이락핵개발 계획의 평화적 용도에 대한 의문을 설명하는 과정에서 원자력을 평화적으로 이용하는 국가의 모범적인 예로서 아국을 들었다고함.

첨부:상기 NYT 기사및 D.SCHEFFER (카네기 국제평화재단) 기고문:UNW(F)-333

(대사대리 신기복-국장)

예고:91.12.31 개정문에 의거 일반문서로 재분됨

| 국기국 | 장관 | 차관 | 1차보 | 2차보 | 미주국 | 미주국 | 중아국 | 국기국 |
|--------|------|------|--------|--------|--------|--------|--------|--------|
| 외정실 | 분석관 | 청와대 | 안기부 | | | | | |

#별첨

UNW(FR)-333 /0718 /620   총2매
(국연.중동인.추기:기점)

# Iraq Atom Effort Ruined, Inspectors Say

### By PAUL LEWIS
#### Special to The New York Times

BAGHDAD, Iraq, July 17 — Contradicting reports that Iraq had produced enough nuclear material to build at least one atomic bomb, United Nations inspectors have concluded that bombing raids during the Persian Gulf war probably destroyed Iraq's uranium enrichment installations before they produced any weapons-grade material.

The inspectors, part of the team sent here by the Security Council to check on Iraq's nuclear potential, say Iraqi officials have deluged them with information about the enrichment program since Monday. On that day, the International Atomic Energy Agency's Director General, Hans Blix, told the Security Council that Iraq's disclosures about its nuclear installations were still inadequate, even though Iraq had acknowledged that it had a secret enrichment program.

The inspection team's conclusion appeared to support Iraq's claim that it is not hiding nuclear installations. A report in May by an Iraqi defector said Iraq had produced 90 pounds of enriched uranium, enough for two bombs. After this report, Mr. Bush said President Saddam Hussein was lying and indicated that the United States might resume attacks on Iraq if it kept trying to produce nuclear weapons.

[State Department and other officials familiar with intelligence reports on Iraq's nuclear ability said they remained skeptical of the new report. "That doesn't ring right," an official said. "We know they produced some highly enriched material and that material was taken out of some of those facilities."]

### U.N. Council to Get Report

As a result of the inpsectors' conclusion that the enrichment installations were probably knocked out in the allied raids, the United Nations officials say the team is likely to send the Security Council a new and more positive report on the Iraqi disclosures.

Mr. Hussein, in a 45-minute televised address marking the anniversary of his Baath Party's seizure of power in 1968, made no reference to his clandestine nuclear weapons program, to the renewed threat of American bombing.

A positive report by the United Nations inspectors to the Security Council on Iraqi nuclear disclosures could lead some diplomats and officials to argue that the United States should not be quick to fulfill its threat to resume attacks on Iraq if it continues to refuse to disclose the location of its nuclear installations, as required by a Security Council resolution.

But the United Nations team has also asked Iraq for a categorical assurance that it is not concealing other nuclear installations.

Asked tonight whether the United Nations is giving Iraq a last chance to come clean about any other secret nuclear installations, Demitri Perricos, the chief United Nations inspector, said, "Yes, you could say that is what we are doing."

### U.N. Aides Satisfied

The United Nations officials now say they know all they need to about these plants and are reasonably sure that they have not produced any weapons-grade enriched uranium by the time the allies destroyed them. Tonight, Mr. Perricos said he did not believe the press reports that Iraq had enriched nearly 90 pounds of uranium up to weapons-grade level.

The United Nations inspectors discovered that one of the installations bombed by the allies — at Tarmia about 30 miles from Baghdad — was an enrichment plant using electromagnetic technology and was about six months from becoming operational.

It was equipped with some 30 calutron machines used for enriching uranium. The machines, all of which were damaged by the raid, were spotted by the inspectors being removed from the plant on trucks and were subsequently buried at sites around the country.

Iraq has now dug up the remnants and showed them to the inspectors. "They were trying to hide the evidence," an official said.

Iraqi nuclear officials have told the inspectors that Baghdad has tried to keep its enrichment program secret because it was afraid that Israel would bomb the plants otherwise. In 1981 Israeli warplanes destroyed an Iraqi nuclear reactor that the Israelis said was being used to develop an atomic bomb.

2-1

0168

## By David J. Scheffer

WASHINGTON

President Bush's threat, backed by Britain and France, to resume military action against Iraq if it does not fully disclose its nuclear arms program is just the latest misstep in the clumsy dance that the U.S. and the U.N. Security Council have been engaged in since the end of the gulf war. Fortunately, there is now an opportunity to avoid further miscues, but the Council must take the lead.

The U.S., Britain and France wield dubious legal authority to use force, either alone or together, in order to enforce Iraq's obligations. The cease-fire resolution leaves it up to the Security Council, not the White House, "to take such further steps as may be required for the implementation of the present resolution and to secure peace and security in the area."

Yet the Security Council has been slow to act, and the U.S. has moved to fill the vacuum. Lacking clear authorization from the Council, the U.S. and some of its European allies sent troops into northern Iraq in April to create a security zone for the Kurds. Given the human tragedy that was taking place along the Iraqi-Turkish border, the allies had little choice but to intervene.

The Council failed not only to authorize direct military intervention to protect the Kurds; it refused to adopt Britain's proposal to create a safe haven in northern Iraq under U.N. protection.

Now the U.S. and its allies have withdrawn — perhaps too quickly — from northern Iraq. Again lacking Council authorization, they have threatened to re-enter Iraq if Saddam Hussein assaults the Kurds or even moves his army northward into the abandoned security zone.

With all the reactive and uncoordinated policy-making guiding Washington and the Security Council these days, Iraq seems likely to become a Vietnam-like quagmire for both.

Is every Iraqi violation of the April 2 cease-fire resolution going to be resolved with a U.S. bombing run? What if Iraq fails to make good on its reparations by refusing to pump enough oil after the sanctions are lifted? What if Iraq does not pay its foreign debt or balks at destroying its weapons of mass destruction?

Nonetheless, the leaders of the

*David J. Scheffer, an international lawyer, is a senior associate of the Carnegie Endowment for International Peace.*

world's wealthiest democracies, meeting in London this week, called on the U.N. to assume a "central role in strengthening the international order." Council members have given Iraq until July 25 to divulge all information about its nuclear capabilities, or suffer "serious consequences." What might those consequences be?

The Council should adopt a new enforcement resolution with these provisions:

First, the Security Council declares that Iraq has forfeited its protection from interference in its internal affairs under the U.N. Charter.

Second, the Council will deploy as soon as possible a large, well-armed U.N. security force to critical areas of Iraq to protect citizens from the Iraqi Army and to provide security for

## Decisions should be collective, not left to the superpowers.

U.N. humanitarian workers and U.N. arms control inspectors.

Third, disarmament and humanitarian teams will be given full and immediate access to any site in Iraq. There will be no Iraqi right to challenge or impede U.N. personnel, any destruction program of weapons or ballistic missiles, or distribution of aid.

Fourth, sizable percentages of the Iraqi Government's foreign reserves and future oil revenues will be directly administered by the Security Council to alleviate suffering in Iraq. U.N. agencies will distribute imported food and medicine directly to those in need and supervise reconstruction of sewage facilities.

Fifth, the U.N. security force, and any coalition forces it authorizes, may use military means to prevent the Iraqi Army from violating the cease-fire conditions or from endangering its own people. Punitive use of force is available, but only with the prior approval of the Security Council.

The Council also should inform the Iraqi leadership that if they were to hold genuine, free elections (monitored by the U.N.) the Council would re-evaluate the entire security and sanctions regime.

Without this determined collective effort by the Security Council to enforce its own resolutions, then big power thuggery — however just its cause — will prevail.  □

2-2

0169

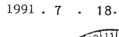

주 국 련 대 표 부

주국련 20313- **574**     1991 . 7 . 18.

수신 장관

참조  국제기구조약국장, 중동아프리카국장

제목  대이락류공급 금지

　　　안보리 결의 700호에 의하면 각국은 표제관련 자국 조치결과를
유엔에 제출토록되어 있는바, 7.18현재 안보리 문서로 배포된 각국
제출내용을 별첨과 같이 송부합니다.


　　　첨 부 : 상기 안보리 문서.  끝.

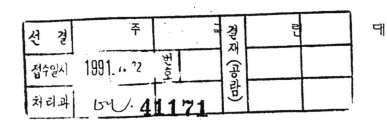

0170

## Security Council

Distr.
GENERAL

S/22783
11 July 1991

ORIGINAL:  ENGLISH

NOTE VERBALE DATED 8 JULY 1991 FROM THE PERMANENT
MISSION OF NORWAY TO THE UNITED NATIONS ADDRESSED
TO THE SECRETARY-GENERAL

The Permanent Representative of Norway to the United Nations presents his compliments to the Secretary-General of the United Nations and with reference to paragraph 4 in resolution 700 (1991) of the Security Council, has the honour to inform the Secretary-General of the following:

Norwegian laws and regulations fully meet the obligations set out in resolution 687 (1991), including paragraph 24, as well as previous mandatory decisions by the Council.  The Guidelines adopted by Security Council resolution 700 (1991) fall within the scope of the Norwegian legislation.

Act No. 4 of 7 June 1947 relating to the implementation of mandatory decisions by the United Nations Security Council empowers the King in Council to adopt regulations in order to implement such decisions.  Regulations adopted concerning the implementation of Security Council resolution 687 (1991) took effect on 8 April 1991.  The relevant section of the regulations reads as follows:

"It is prohibited for any person on Norwegian territory, and for any Norwegian national, enterprise, company, foundation or association, regardless of its whereabouts, to sell, supply or by any other means convey commodities or products of any kind, including weapons and other military equipment as well as technology and services for military purposes, regardless of their country of origin, to Iraq.

The prohibition set out in the first paragraph also applies to the sale, transport or conveyance by other means of commodities or products to any natural or legal person acting on behalf of any business carried on in or operated from Iraq.

The prohibition of transport set out in the first and second paragraphs applies to ships, aircraft and motor vehicles registered in Norway or managed or otherwise at the disposal of any Norwegian national, company or association."

91-22552  2376c (E)

/...

0171

Norway has implemented mandatory decisions by the Security Council by means of prohibition legislation using imprisonment, fines or both as penalties. In addition, objects which have been exported or have been attempted to be exported may be confiscated by court order irrespective of ownership and without the institution of criminal proceedings. If confiscation does not prove possible, the court may order the offender to pay an amount equivalent to the partial or entire value of the objects without instituting criminal proceedings. The same applies to any means of payment or securities employed in contravention of any provisions issued pursuant to the act relating to the implementation of mandatory decisions by the Security Council. The practical control of import of commodities and products is carried out by the customs and police authorities. The final adjudication lies with the courts if the public prosecution authority finds that there is adequate reason to suspect that an offence has been committed under the prohibition legislation.

The Norwegian legislation applies to anyone who wilfully or negligently violates the legislation or is an accessory thereto. Any attempt to commit a felony is also punishable.

In addition to the special regulations which have been adopted in connection with the sanctions against Iraq, Norway has comprehensive legislation concerning export controls on weapons and military equipment as well as technology and services for military purposes. This legislation includes a specific act relating to the control of strategic goods, services and technology, with appurtenant regulations. This act also contains penalty clauses with imprisonment, fines or both as penalties.

-----

0171 -|

# UNITED NATIONS

## Security Council

**S**

Distr.
GENERAL

S/22784
11 July 1991

ORIGINAL: ENGLISH

NOTE VERBALE DATED 9 JULY 1991 FROM THE PERMANENT MISSION
OF ISRAEL TO THE UNITED NATIONS ADDRESSED TO THE
SECRETARY-GENERAL

The Permanent Representative of Israel to the United Nations presents his compliments to the Secretary-General of the United Nations and has the honour to refer to the Secretary-General's note SCPC/7/91(4-1) of 3 July 1991, concerning Security Council resolution 700 (1991).

The Permanent Representative has the honour to inform the Secretary-General that there are no relations whatsoever between Israel and Iraq, due to Iraq's longstanding hostility towards Israel.  Hence, Israel does not sell or supply any materials to Iraq, including the items listed in paragraph 24 of resolution 687 (1991), nor does it promote or facilitate such sales or supplies by its nationals or from its territory or using its flag vessels or aircraft.

-----

91-22572  2377c (E)

0172

## Security Council

Distr.
GENERAL

S/22800
16 July 1991
ENGLISH
ORIGINAL: FRENCH

LETTER DATED 16 JULY 1991 FROM THE PERMANENT REPRESENTATIVE OF
FRANCE TO THE UNITED NATIONS ADDRESSED TO THE SECRETARY-GENERAL

In accordance with paragraph 4 of resolution 700 (1991), I have the
honour to transmit to you the following information on the measures instituted
by my Government, in accordance with paragraph 8 of the Guidelines, for
meeting the obligations set out in paragraph 24 of resolution 687 (1991).

1.    The general embargo on arms for shipment to Iraq was imposed,
nationally, on 3 August 1990 by the French Government.  The decision in
question was implemented immediately, with retroactive effect.  In view of the
nature of the French arms-exports control system (which is itself based on the
general principle of prohibition, a principle which only government
authorities may waive, on a case-by-case basis), the decision has been
implemented at both levels of control exercised by the French authorities,
namely:

A.    Control of commercial operations of enterprises.

All operations involving canvassing for business (exploration of general
market conditions, excluding the submission of formal proposals), negotiations
(initiation of talks that may reach the point where a draft contract is
submitted) and sales (signature of a contract) are subject to the French
Government's prior consent.

In the case of Iraq, on the instructions of the Prime Minister, consent
has not been given in respect of the three stages in question in any instance
since 3 August 1990.  Authorizations already granted have been cancelled.  All
approaches made, all commercial negotiations and the signing of any contract
for materials with Iraq has been strictly prohibited since that date.  All
violations of these prohibitions are subject to prosecution.

B.    Control of the actual export of materials.

Once a contract has been signed, the military equipment ordered may not
leave French territory until the customs authorities have, with the consent of
the Ministry of Defence and the Ministry for Foreign Affairs, issued a special
export licence (authorization for the export of military equipment).

91-23003   2577d (E)                                                    /...

0173

Since 3 August 1990, on the instructions of the Prime Minister, the issuance of such authorizations has been prohibited. Authorizations previously granted in respect of contracts authorized earlier have been cancelled, in accordance with the relevant French provisions, and as a result all materials (both complete systems and spare parts) for shipment to Iraq have completely ceased to leave French territory. A prohibition similar to the prohibition on the departure of materials from French territory applies to materials admitted to French territory in the past under the legal system of temporary admission (in the case of materials returned to France for repairs).

Moreover, the introduction into French territory of any military equipment from Iraq or of Iraqi origin is now absolutely prohibited. This prohibition applies equally to imports proper and to transit, storage in a free zone and temporary admission.

This set of measures, which has to date permitted full implementation of the United Nations embargo, remains in effect.

(Signed) Jean-Bernard MERIMEE

-----

0173 ─l

**UNITED
NATIONS**

**S**

# Security Council

Distr.
GENERAL

S/22801
16 July 1991

ORIGINAL:  ENGLISH

NOTE VERBALE DATED 12 JULY 1991 FROM THE PERMANENT
REPRESENTATIVE OF HUNGARY TO THE UNITED NATIONS
ADDRESSED TO THE SECRETARY-GENERAL

The Permanent Representative of the Republic of Hungary to the United Nations presents his compliments to the Secretary-General of the United Nations and, with reference to his Note SCPC/7/91/4-1 of 3 July 1991, has the honour to inform that the Republic of Hungary, in full conformity with the spirit and letter of the relevant Security Council resolutions, strictly abides by the prohibitions against the sale or supply of arms to Iraq, and the pertinent organs of the State ensure the strict enforcement of such prohibitions.

-----

91-23009  2559j (E)

0174

# UNITED NATIONS

## Security Council

S

Distr.
GENERAL

S/22802
16 July 1991

ORIGINAL:  ENGLISH

---

NOTE BY THE SECRETARY-GENERAL


The attached note verbale, dated 9 July 1991, was addressed to the Secretary-General by the Permanent Observer of the Holy See to the United Nations.

91-23015  2470f (E)

0175  /...

<u>Annex</u>

<u>Note verbale dated 9 July 1991 from the Permanent
Observer of the Holy See to the United Nations
addressed to the Secretary-General</u>

The Permanent Observer of the Holy See to the United Nations presents his
compliments to the Secretary-General of the United Nations and has the honour
to refer to the Note SCPC/7/91(4-1) of 3 July 1991, requesting information
regarding the application of the provisions in paragraph 4 of Security Council
resolution 700 (1991).

The Holy See is pleased to restate what has been said in the Note 4856/90
of 26 November 1990, that in accordance with its particular character, it does
not have any type of commercial, financial or economic activities with Iraq
nor does it supply any goods to Iraq. The activities over which the Holy See
has some control in Iraq are purely of a spiritual, religious and educational
nature.

-----

0176

주 국 련 대 표 부

주국련  20313-**575**                    1991 . 7 . 18·

수신 장관

참조  국제기구조약국장, 중동아프리카국장

제목  이락 핵사찰


이락핵사찰 관련 안보리 문서를 별첨과 같이 송부합니다.

    첨 부 :  상기 안보리 문서.   끝.

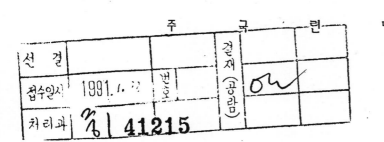

0177

# UNITED NATIONS

**Security Council**

S

Distr.
GENERAL

S/22761
5 July 1991
ENGLISH
ORIGINAL: SPANISH

LETTER DATED 4 JULY 1991 FROM THE SECRETARY-GENERAL
ADDRESSED TO THE PRESIDENT OF THE SECURITY COUNCIL

I have the honour to transmit to you herewith the report of the high-level mission, composed of Mr. Hans Blix, Director-General of the International Atomic Energy Agency, Mr. Rolf Ekéus, Executive Chairman of the Special Commission established under Security Council resolution 687 (1991), and Mr. Yasushi Akashi, Under-Secretary-General for Disarmament Affairs, which I sent to Iraq at the request of the members of the Security Council, as noted in the statement by the President of the Council of 28 June 1991 (S/22746).

(Signed)  Javier PEREZ DE CUELLAR

91-21936  2439g (E) /...

0178

<u>Annex</u>

[Original: English]

<u>Report of the high-level mission to Iraq</u>

### A.  Introduction

1.   The report of the high-level mission is submitted to the Security Council, through the Secretary-General, within the context and the framework of the statement by the President of the Council of 28 June 1991 (S/22746), pursuant to which the mission was constituted.  Furthermore, the mission has understood that it was to proceed against the background of the three incidents of 23, 25 and 28 June 1991 covered in the President's statement. The report, therefore, does not deal with the experience of three other teams dispatched to Iraq under the provisions of section C of Security Council resolution 687 (1991).  The cooperation extended by the Iraqi authorities to these inspection and disposal teams was found to be satisfactory and gave rise to no complaints in respect of the granting of immediate and unimpeded access or of other rights of the Special Commission established under Security Council resolution 687 (1991) and the International Atomic Energy Agency (IAEA) under the resolution.

### B.  Composition of the high-level mission

2.   The high-level mission was composed of Mr. Hans Blix, Director-General of IAEA, Mr. Rolf Ekéus, Executive Chairman of the Special Commission and Mr. Yasushi Akashi, United Nations Under-Secretary-General for Disarmament Affairs.  The Secretary-General requested Mr. Ekéus to lead the mission.

3.   The mission was assisted by a team of experts:  Mr. M. El Baradei (IAEA); and Mr. Johan Molander and Mr. John Scott (Office of the Special Commission).

### C.  Itinerary of the high-level mission

4.   The mission assembled in Bahrain on 29 June 1991.  On 30 June, the mission proceeded to Baghdad, where it remained until 3 July.  On 3 July, the mission travelled to Geneva, reported orally to the Secretary-General on 4 July on the outcome of its work and adopted its report.

0179      /...

### D.  Meetings in Baghdad with high-level members of the Iraqi Government

#### 1.  Schedule of meetings

5.    During its stay in Baghdad, the mission held six meetings with the following members of the Iraqi Government:

30 June 1991

    8 p.m. - 9.45 p.m.                     Mr. Ahmed Hussein,
                                            Minister for Foreign Affairs

1 July 1991

    11.15 a.m. - 1.30 p.m.               Mr. Tariq Aziz,
                                            Deputy Prime Minister

                                            The Minister for Foreign Affairs

    8.30 p.m. - 9.15 p.m.               The Minister for Foreign Affairs

2 July 1991

    10.30 a.m. - 1.30 p.m.               The Deputy Prime Minister

                                              The Minister for Foreign Affairs

                                            General Hussein Kamel Hassan,
                                            Minister of Defence

                                            Dr. Homan Abdul Khaliq,
                                            Chairman of the Atomic Energy
                                            Commission of Iraq

    7.35 p.m. - 8.30 p.m.               Mr. Saadoun Hammadi,
                                              Prime Minister

    10.35 p.m. - 11.30 p.m.            The Minister for Foreign Affairs

6.    At the final meeting with the Foreign Minister, the mission presented in broad outline the findings it intended to present to the Secretary-General and to the Security Council.  On the request of the Foreign Minister for another meeting the following day, the mission stated that at that point no new developments of significance to its tasks could be expected.  The mission recalled that it had already extended its visit by one day and that the Security Council had requested the mission to report to it at the earliest opportunity.  If, however, further developments from the Iraqi side were to be forthcoming, they could be communicated to and presented in New York or Vienna.

/...

0180

## 2. Presentation of the demands of the Security Council

7.    During its meetings, the mission emphasized that it had been sent to Iraq in order to convey the urgent demand of the Security Council for unequivocal assurances that the Government of Iraq would take all the necessary measures to ensure that no hindrances were placed in the way of the discharge by the Special Commission of its mandate under Security Council resolution 687 (1991) and would accord, in compliance with Iraq's obligations and commitments vis-à-vis the United Nations and IAEA, full cooperation, including immediate and unimpeded access to sites declared or designated under paragraphs 9 and 13 of Security Council resolution 687 (1991), to the inspection teams sent to Iraq by the Special Commission and IAEA.  The mission further emphasized that it was under instructions from the Council to obtain unconditional guarantees for the safety and security of all personnel engaged in the performance of functions in connection with Security Council resolution 687 (1991).  It was also under instructions to seek detailed information on undertakings and measures by the Government to ensure compliance at all levels, including local military and civilian authorities, with Iraq's obligations under Security Council resolution 687 (1991).

8.    In transmitting the Security Council's demands, the mission stressed the Council's grave concern over the incident of 28 June, in particular the use of firearms by Iraqi personnel, and drew attention to the fact that the members of the Council had strongly deplored the incidents of 23, 25 and 28 June 1991 and had condemned the conduct of the Iraqi authorities in this connection.  It also underlined that the President's statement recorded the unanimous view of the members of the Council.

9.    The mission drew attention to the fact that the Security Council remained seized of the matter.  The mission underlined the importance of full compliance by Iraq so as to enable the United Nations to continue to carry out resolution 687 (1991) and that any non-compliance by Iraq would have serious consequences.  The mission reiterated the view of the Security Council on the threat that weapons of mass destruction pose to peace and security in the Middle East and on the need to work towards the establishment in the Middle East of a zone free of such weapons.

## 3. Assurances given by the Government of Iraq

10.  The mission received from the Ministers with whom it met the various assurances indicated below:

(a)  A decision by the President of Iraq, which had been conveyed to the Security Council in New York by the Permanent Representative of Iraq to the United Nations (S/22749), to the effect that the President had ordered all the Iraqi authorities concerned to extend full cooperation to the United Nations representatives and to facilitate their tasks in line with the obligations undertaken by Iraq.  The President had also instructed that all bureaucratic problems arising in the cooperation process should be overcome and had

/...

0181

authorized the Minister for Foreign Affairs to issue immediate instructions to all authorities and departments which the United Nations representatives desired to visit and inspect to give access without hesitation;

(b)  A further statement by the President of Iraq which, inter alia, contained the assurance that Iraq had abandoned all activities that might be in contravention of Security Council resolution 687 (1991);

(c)  An assurance that Iraq would take all necessary measures to ensure that no hindrances were placed in the way of the inspection activities of the Special Commission and IAEA and that it would accord full cooperation to the inspection teams, including immediate and unimpeded access, and the right to stop and inspect vehicles in movement;

(d)  The information that, in order to implement the assurances of cooperation at all levels, orders had been issued to all Iraqi military and civilian personnel to that effect "and so as to ensure the safety and security of all personnel engaged in the performance of functions in connection with Security Council resolution 687 (1991);"

(e)  The information that full authority had been given to the Minister for Foreign Affairs to issue directives relating to compliance with Special Commission and IAEA requests under resolution 687 (1991), and that a high-level military liaison officer was, as of that point, placed in the Ministry of Foreign Affairs with authority to grant immediate access to any military site or installation.

4.  Access to the objects observed by the nuclear inspection team

11.  The mission insisted throughout on the call by the members of the Security Council that Iraq grant the nuclear inspection team, present in Iraq, immediate and unimpeded access to the objects which the team had endeavoured to inspect on 23, 25 and 28 June 1991.  The mission reiterated this call when it was reported to it that materials which the team was invited to inspect at Fallujah on 1 July and on 2 July 1991 did not comprise objects which the team had observed on 28 June.

12.  The Iraqi side explained that some equipment and material belonging to the Atomic Energy Commission of Iraq had been transferred to the Ministry of Defence for purposes of destruction of items that might be in contravention of Security Council resolution 687 (1991) and of redistribution of other items which could be used for the civilian reconstruction programme in Iraq.  It was further stated that some of this equipment and material had been present at the Fallujah site.  No specification of these items was given, but the Chairman of the Atomic Energy Commission of Iraq promised to provide, in the near future, a list of all items that had been destroyed.  Following these explanations, in the afternoon of 2 July the inspection team, accompanied by the Director-General of IAEA, was taken to a destruction site and was shown

/...

0182

certain destroyed equipment. The large pieces of equipment which were thus inspected were related to nuclear research and could not have had relevance for the production of weapons-usable material. No meaningful explanation was given why they had been destroyed.

13. The mission stated that if Iraq had interpreted Security Council resolution 687 (1991) in such a way as not to cover research or other facilities, or equipment for the enrichment of uranium or the separation of plutonium, an additional declaration would be needed to include such items as centrifuges, calutrons, facilities for production of uranium tetrachloride or uranium hexafluoride. The Chairman of the Atomic Energy Commission of Iraq stated categorically that there had not been and there was currently no programme under the Commission for the enrichment of uranium in Iraq. The Deputy Prime Mnister added that there was only one nuclear programme in Iraq.

### 5. Observations by the Government of Iraq

14. The Iraqi side, while reiterating the Government's acceptance of the Security Council's resolutions, none the less considered the resolutions to be harsh and unjust. In this connection, reference was made in particular to Security Council resolution 699 (1991), regarding the liability of Iraq for the costs incurred under section C of Security Council resolution 687 (1991) and their offer to undertake the destruction of chemical weapons. The mission stated that this offer was under serious consideration in the Special Commission.

15. The Iraqi side, when referring to the incidents of 23, 25 and 28 June 1991, complained that insufficient notice of inspection had been given. Furthermore, insistence on undertaking the inspections during the Muslim religious holiday of Eid, when the civilian or military officers concerned could not be easily contacted, was inappropriate. Iraq's industrial base had been badly damaged during the conflict and serious communications and logistical problems existed. All these factors had contributed to the incidents. The mission stated that appropriate notice would always be given, but that the Special Commission and IAEA had the right to inspect mobile objects with short or no notice. The inspection teams had no intention to disregard the religious feelings of the people of Iraq. However, it was now a common feature of verification under modern arms control agreements that inspections might take place at any time when there were reasons for believing that otherwise the purposes of the inspection might be frustrated. Furthermore, on 23 June, it was noticed that considerable Iraqi activity was under way at the inspection site, despite the religious holiday.

16. The Iraqi side referred to its reservations concerning the composition of certain inspection teams and expressed the hope that in the future they would be more widely drawn. The mission stated that, in composing the teams, primary emphasis had to be put on technical competence. Most teams were composed of personnel of many nationalities. A restricting factor existed in the nuclear weapons and related fields, where the available expertise was

/...

0183

largely limited to the five nuclear-weapons States.  It was agreed that the selection of the members of the inspection teams was the sole prerogative of the Special Commission and of IAEA.

### E.  Findings of the high-level mission

17.  In spite of their unambiguous character, the general assurances given and the specific measures promised can only be evaluated in the light of present and future implementation by the Iraqi authorities.  As described in the present report, the Iraqi response to the request for access to the objects which the inspection team had endeavoured to inspect on 28 June falls short of what has been called for by the Security Council.

Geneva, 4 July 1991

(Signed)  Rolf EKEUS        (Signed)  Hans BLIX        (Signed)  Yasushi AKASHI

-----

0184

# UNITED NATIONS

**S**

## Security Council

Distr.
GENERAL

S/22762
5 July 1991

ORIGINAL: ENGLISH

### LETTER DATED 5 JULY 1991 FROM THE SECRETARY-GENERAL ADDRESSED TO THE PRESIDENT OF THE SECURITY COUNCIL

Further to my letter of yesterday's date (S/22761), I wish to inform you that, while in Geneva on 4 July 1991 and having received the report of the high-level mission which I had earlier dispatched to Iraq at the request of the members of the Security Council, I asked the Permanent Representative of Iraq to the United Nations Office at Geneva to see me.

In our meeting, at which I was accompanied by the members of the high-level mission, I asked the Permanent Representative to convey an informal paper to H.E. Mr. Saddam Hussein, President of the Republic of Iraq. The Permanent Representative undertook to do so immediately. The text of the paper is attached as annex I to the present letter.

I have today received in response a communication from His Excellency the President of Iraq, under cover of a transmittal note signed by the Permanent Representative of Iraq to the United Nations in New York. The texts of both the transmittal note and the President's communication are attached hereto as annexes II and III.

(Signed) Javier PEREZ DE CUELLAR

91-21954  2490e (E)

/...

0185

<u>Annex I</u>

[Original: English]

<u>Paper handed by the Secretary-General to the Permanent
Representative of Iraq to the United Nations Office at
Geneva on 4 July 1991</u>

The high-level mission was given unambiguous assurances as regards full cooperation and specific measures to ensure compliance by Iraq with its obligations under Security Council resolution 687 (1991).

However, the response by Iraq to the request for access to the objects, which the nuclear inspection team had observed on a long convoy of trucks and had endeavoured to inspect on 28 June, was deemed not satisfactory by the mission. Only a full demonstration of what all these objects were and inspection of them by a nuclear inspection team would be satisfactory.

The high-level mission noted information given to it that a decision had been taken by Iraq not to retain any items that might be in contravention with Security Council resolution 687 (1991), nuclear or other, and that equipment of the Atomic Energy Commission of Iraq had been transferred to the army, some for destruction and the other for use in the reconstruction work. Explanations were not given on what nuclear items Iraq had considered to be in contravention with Security Council resolution 687 (1991).

Full explanations about nuclear activities and equipment that had been deemed by Iraq to be in contravention of the resolution and inspection of this equipment and facilities related to them – destroyed or not – are imperative.

0186

/...

## Annex II

[Original: English]

## Letter from the Permanent Representative of Iraq to the United
## Nations addressed to the Secretary-General

On instruction from my Government, I have the pleasure of enclosing
herewith a facsimile message in Arabic from H.E. President Saddam Hussein
dated 5 July 1991 (Baghdad time) in reply to Your Excellency's message handed
to the Permanent Representative of Iraq to the United Nations Office at
Geneva, Ambassador Barzan Al-Tikriti.

(Signed)  Abdul-Amir AL-ANBARI
Iraq's Permanent Representative

0187        /...

## Annex III

[Original: Arabic]

### Letter dated 5 July 1991 (Baghdad time) from President Saddam Hussein addressed to the Secretary-General

We highly appreciate the initiative of the Secretary-General of the United Nations and affirm the guarantees, given to the high-level mission during its visit to Baghdad, whereby prompt and unimpeded access will be ensured to the locations and items designated for inspection in accordance with Security Council resolution 687 (1991), in addition to guaranteeing the security and safety of members of the inspection team. We also affirm that Iraq is committed to the fulfilment of its obligations under the aforesaid resolution.

With respect to the concerns of the mission, it has been arranged that the mission should be provided with a list of the items about which it sought information. This list will be ready on the evening of Sunday, 7 July, or the morning of Monday, 8 July 1991, at which time it may be studied by the inspection team.

-----

0188

## Security Council

Distr.
GENERAL

S/22786
13 July 1991
ENGLISH
ORIGINAL: ARABIC

IDENTICAL LETTERS DATED 13 JULY 1991 FROM THE PERMANENT
REPRESENTATIVE OF IRAQ TO THE UNITED NATIONS ADDRESSED
RESPECTIVELY TO THE SECRETARY-GENERAL AND THE PRESIDENT
OF THE SECURITY COUNCIL

On instructions from my Government, I have the honour to transmit
herewith a letter dated 13 July 1991 from Mr. Ahmad Hussein, Minister for
Foreign Affairs of the Republic of Iraq, concerning Iraq's compliance with
Security Council resolution 687 (1991).  I also transmit two letters, dated
10 and 12 July 1991, from the Minister to Mr. Hans Blix, Director-General of
the International Atomic Energy Agency, concerning Iraq's accounts of nuclear
materials.

I should be grateful if you would have this letter and its annexes
circulated as a document of the Security Council.

(Signed)  Abdul Amir A. AL-ANBARI
Ambassador
Permanent Representative

0189

91-22745  2464f  (E)                                                    /...

Annex I

Identical letters dated 12 July 1991 from the Minister for
Foreign Affairs of Iraq addressed to the Secretary-General
and the President of the Security Council

Iraq has accepted all the resolutions adopted by the Security Council and expressed its willingness to cooperate with the Council, the Secretary-General and his representatives in ensuring the serious and good-faith implementation of those resolutions, despite Iraq's deep feeling that they are biased and unjust.

During the past months, Iraq has actively and painstakingly fulfilled its obligations despite continued attempts to cast doubts as to its intentions ... attempts which have been accompanied by various forms of threat and distortion.

When confusion arose as to the work of the inspection teams, Iraq expressed its willingness to receive the mission appointed by the Secretary-General with Mr. Ekéus at its head. The mission was received at the highest levels in Iraq, and a serious and practical dialogue was conducted with a view to facilitating its task and overcoming whatever obstacles might arise in its work, particularly in the extremely difficult circumstances confronting Iraq with respect to communications, transport and services as a result of the military action against it from 17 January to 28 February 1991, which inflicted widespread destruction on the country's civilian infrastructure.

The high-level mission led by Mr. Ekéus was given categorical assurances in connection with all the requests it made, whether with regard to the security and safety of the inspection teams - which had not in fact been exposed to any form of danger - or to the facilitation of its task of inspection under the terms of Security Council resolutions. During the mission's stay in Baghdad, all practical measures considered appropriate by the mission were taken to facilitate its task of inspection, and these measures were indicated in its report to the Security Council.

In response to the proposal made by Mr. Blix, Director-General of the International Atomic Energy Agency (IAEA), during discussions in Baghdad, the Iraqi Government submitted a long list of all the devices, equipment and locations of interest to the mission and explained the history and nature of the Iraqi peaceful nuclear programme, which was also explained in the letter of the Minister for Foreign Affairs. This could have been included among the results and achievements of Mr. Ekéus' mission to Baghdad if he had accepted the proposal of the Minister for Foreign Affairs that he extend his stay in Baghdad for one further day. The letter detailed the reasons which, in the opinion of the Iraqi Government, justified the non-submission of this information at an earlier date. In the course of his response, the Minister went on to resolve and explain all the queries directed to him by the Director-General of IAEA with respect to the details of his letter

0190

/...

incorporating the lists and the programme. You may wish to study the letters dated 10 and 12 July 1991 from the Minister for Foreign Affairs to Mr. Blix. In addition, our Ambassador in Vienna, the Permanent Representative of Iraq to the International Atomic Energy Agency, provided an official explanation to the Director-General concerning the comments raised at the unofficial meeting of the Board of Governors held last week, as well as of the comments made by Mr. Blix.

Nevertheless, despite the serious and active cooperation displayed by Iraq in connection with this and other issues relating to the implementation of the Security Council resolutions, the United States - before, during and after the mission's visit - has launched and continues to conduct a large-scale frenzied campaign of threats to carry out further military aggression against Iraq. American officials have begun to speak openly of their intention to attack, of the preparations under way for this purpose and of the means available for such action. American officials have used this issue as an additional excuse to maintain the economic sanctions against Iraq, to interfere in its internal affairs and to impose their wishes on the noble people of Iraq in a manner which is flagrantly incompatible with international laws and conventions and with the text of the Security Council resolutions themselves.

The United States is currently preparing for a further massive military attack on Iraq. As a pretext for such an attack, it is declaring that it intends to strike at the locations and equipment which aroused the concerns of the high-level mission. Iraq has already declared - and today reaffirms - its absolute willingness to enable the United Nations inspection teams to visit and view all such locations and equipment and to interact with them in accordance with the Security Council resolutions.

Why, then, does the United States resort to military means to strike against Iraq if its true objective is to implement the Security Council resolutions?

The correct conclusion, which becomes apparent from all the statements made by American officials, is that the United States wishes, by launching this new attack, to achieve political aims which have no connection with the Security Council resolutions and the concerns expressed therein. By doing so, it is continuing the process which it began on 17 January, when it made use of Security Council resolution 687 (1991) not to evict Iraq's armed forces from Kuwait, as specified in the resolution, but to destroy Iraq's economic capacities, infrastructure and achievements in terms of science and civilization, in order to promote its own objectives, and those of zionism, of achieving complete hegemony over the Middle East region. It is now preparing to carry out the second stage of this plan, having failed to achieve all the objectives of the first stage between 17 January and 28 February 1991 and in the course of the subsequent events, in which the United States played a major role.

/...

0191

Iraq is once again subject to the threat of massive military aggression by the United States, which is once again using the Security Council resolutions and the concerns expressed therein as a pretext and cover to launch this attack.

Iraq has accepted the Security Council resolutions, despite its legitimate feelings with respect to them. It has declared and confirmed its willingness to implement them and is entirely willing to cooperate with the Council and the Secretary-General in order to ensure their implementation.

The Security Council is not supposed to allow any one of its members to act in the name of the Council in order to promote its own aggressive and expansionist aims in a manner inconsistent with international laws, values and conventions.

We hope that the Security Council will put an end to this aggressive behaviour on the part of America against a noble and independent State Member of both the United Nations and the international community which has suffered as a result of aggression and whose people is continuing to suffer from the unjust and biased economic sanctions. We hope that those States members of the Council which recognize their responsibility in matters of peace and security and the rights of peoples to freedom, dignity and independence will take a stand commensurate with their legal responsibilities as members of the Security Council, and with their consciences, to forestall this new stage of the American aggression against Iraq.

(Signed)   Ahmad HUSSEIN
Minister for Foreign Affairs of the
Republic of Iraq

0192   /...

### Annex II

### Letter dated 10 July 1991 from the Minister for Foreign Affairs
### of Iraq addressed to the Director-General of the International
### Atomic Energy Agency

We have received, by way of Iraq's representative to the International Atomic Energy Agency (IAEA), your letter to us of 9 July 1991.

In response to your request for comments on the contents of your letter, we should like to provide you with the following observations and explanations:

You mentioned in your letter that Iraq had a uranium enrichment programme which it had not subjected to IAEA safeguards in accordance with the agreement concluded between the Government of the Republic of Iraq and the International Atomic Energy Agency (INFCIRC/172). We should like to make the point in this context that the safeguards agreement, which is based on the Treaty on the Non-Proliferation of Nuclear Weapons, does not prevent any State Party to the Treaty from conducting research and development in the field of uranium enrichment without informing the Agency, provided that such research does not reach the stage which requires notification and subjection to the safeguards system. This fact is illustrated in table 3, transmitted together with my two letters of 7 July 1991: the three methods are still at the stage of research and development, and there is no isotope enrichment unit under the terms of article 98 of the safeguards agreement. We understand article 28 of the safeguards agreement as referring to meaningful (significant) quantities of nuclear materials. In this regard, we wish to refer to the definition of a meaningful (significant) quantity of nuclear material, as contained in article 89 of document IAEA/SG/INF/1, which defines the term as corresponding to 75 kilograms of uranium enriched at a rate of less than 20 per cent of uranium-235. One half kilogram is thus well below that threshold.

We should also like to refer to the findings of the Zancker Commission, which adopted criteria for the monitoring and export of sensitive technologies. The work of that Commission was of major importance in determining much of the contents of the safeguards system. The Commission stated that the smallest quantity of enriched uranium which could be subjected to monitoring was one active kilogram. In this connection, we should also like to refer you to paragraph 300 of document IAEA/SG/INF/1(Rev.1), issued in 1987.

All the above remarks confirm that the quantity under discussion is not covered by the safeguards system.

/...

0193

     With regard to your remarks concerning the uranium enriched by a
centrifuge system, we have checked the English translation, as provided by
IAEA, of our letter and the tables transmitted therewith against your comments
in your letter.  We note a discrepancy between that translation and, on the
one hand, the contents of your letter and, on the other, the Arabic text of
our letter.  For this reason, we consider it most important to provide an
accurate technical explanation of the matter.

     One model of a centrifuge was tested rather than a series of
centrifuges.  The object of testing the one model was to determine the
centrifuge's separation performance.  Accordingly, the material was rotated in
the centrifuge, the enriched product was mixed with the spent product and both
were used to feed the centrifuge once again.  Due to the use of the rotation
principle in the experiment, no enriched material was accumulated.  This
constitutes an accurate scientific explanation of the statement in the table
to the effect that no appreciable quantities were enriched in the course of
the tests, because the level of enrichment achieved was nullified by the
aforementioned mixing process.

     It will be clear to you from the above remarks that the centrifuge
enrichment method is still at an early stage of scientific research.

     You established some sort of link between the production of one half
kilogram of uranium enriched at a rate of 4 per cent of uranium-235 and
article 34 (c) of the agreement.  We understand all three paragraphs of
article 34 to deal with the subject of the import and export of nuclear
materials from and to Iraq, and Iraq's consequent obligations to notify the
Agency of any nuclear material.  Article 34, paragraph (c), refers to the
importation by Iraq of nuclear material in any form, at any level of
refinement, and at any stage of the nuclear fuel cycle.  However, the half
kilogram of uranium under discussion, enriched at a rate of 4 per cent, was
not imported by Iraq but produced locally in the course of experiments for
research and development purposes.  Our interpretation of article 34 is that
it does not cover this case.  Even if we suppose that the provisions of
article 34, paragraph (c), go beyond the context of importation, we believe
that our comments below on article 42, and particularly on the definitions of
technical terms contained therein, justify our affirmation that article 34,
paragraph (c), does not apply in the case of one half kilogram of uranium
enriched at a rate of 4 per cent.

     With respect to the references in your letter to article 42, the
information contained in table 3 relating to the three enrichment methods does
not in any way indicate the existence of a "facility", but only of
technological components which are still at the development stage and whose
production and engineering specifications have not yet been completely
finalized:  certain physical and engineering aspects are not yet fully
understood and require further research and development before it is possible
to adopt industrial, engineering and planning specifications for the purpose
of constructing an integrated facility, with a determined capacity,
operational procedure and other technical details which would make it possible
to provide the Agency with final design data.

0194                                                          /...

These specifications cannot be determined before actual tests are carried out using uranium. For this reason, it is our interpretation that article 42 does not apply to the current state of enrichment activities as described in table 3, transmitted together with my two letters of 7 July 1991.

As you notice, we have endeavoured in this letter to provide a precise account of the scientific and technical facts as well as to explain our position of commitment to the various articles and paragraphs of the safeguards agreement. Nevertheless, we are prepared to dispatch a specialized technical mission, if you so wish, to answer questions and offer clarifications if you should have any further queries.

(<u>Signed</u>)  Ahmad HUSSEIN
Minister for Foreign Affairs
of the Republic of Iraq

0195                    /...

## Annex III

### Letter dated 12 July 1991 from the Minister for Foreign Affairs of Iraq addressed to the Director-General of the International Atomic Energy Agency

Further to our letter dated 10 July 1991, and with reference to your letter of 11 July 1991, which stated that there were large quantities of nuclear materials which have not previously been reported under the terms of paragraphs 34 (c) and 34 (b) of the safeguards agreement, we wish to provide the following comment and explanation:

1.  With regard to the quantities of yellow-cake and uranium dioxide: the Ministry of Defence requested the Atomic Energy Commission to carry out research and tests into the use of ceramic and metallic uranium for non-nuclear purposes, one of its concerns being to strengthen the anti-armour missile warhead.

This research has made considerable progress but has not yet been completed, particularly from the points of view of technology and fabrication.  The programme requires large quantities of uranium and, because these quantities were not needed for nuclear purposes, the Agency was not informed under the terms of paragraph 34 (b) of the safeguards agreement.

We should also like to point out that the Atomic Energy Commission always, on its own initiative, offered to show stocks of nuclear materials not covered by the inspection to the Agency's inspectors during their visits for that purpose.  This measure was designed to illustrate our good faith, given that those materials were in the stores together with the other nuclear materials being investigated by the inspectors:  the inspectors indicated that the yellow-cake was not subject to inspection and did not at any time ask to investigate or to check whether notification was or was not required.

2.  With regard to the uranium hexafluoride:  the quantity of this substance (465 grams of natural uranium) is minimal.  No nuclear laboratory working with such materials would do so unless it had to:  this quantity, in our opinion, does not require notification or control.

3.  With regard to the quantities of uranium tetrachloride:  these are used to feed the test systems for electromagnetic enrichment.

As you know, the rate of the flow of the material produced in the enrichment cell to the cell's feed material is usually very low:  this is true of all enrichment methods.  In electromagnetic enrichment in particular, the material is not rotated automatically in the separator:  the required quantity of feed material depends on a number of factors, including the rate of evaporation of the material in the oven, its ionization capacity, the proportion of positive uranium ions extracted from the source to other ions, the rate of flow to the collector from the extractor, the collection capacity

/...

0196

and thus the weight of uranium-235 in the collector and the rate of enrichment achieved.

One half kilogram of uranium enriched at a rate of 4 per cent requires approximately one half ton of uranium tetrachloride for its production.  It will be clear from the above remarks that the quantity of 2.5 tons mentioned in the table constitutes a normal quantity for the feeding of experimental separators:  we do not believe that it requires notification.

In conclusion, despite our clarifications above, we believe that our notification of these materials (as transmitted in our letter of 7 July 1991), although provided under the terms of Security Council resolution 687 (1991), in any event constitutes a corrective measure which we believe to be sufficient under the terms of paragraph 19 of the safeguards agreement.

(Signed)  Ahmad HUSSEIN
Minister for Foreign Affairs of Iraq

-----

0197

# UNITED NATIONS

**S**

## Security Council

Distr.
GENERAL

S/22788
15 July 1991

ORIGINAL:  ENGLISH

### NOTE BY THE SECRETARY-GENERAL

The Secretary-General has the honour to transmit to the members of the Security Council the attached communication which he has received from the Director-General of the International Atomic Energy Agency (IAEA).

91-22864  2499e (E)

0198

/...

<u>Annex</u>

<u>Letter dated 12 July 1991 from the Director-General of the
International Atomic Energy Agency addressed to the
Secretary-General</u>

Attached herewith is a consolidated report on the first two IAEA
inspections under Security Council resolution 687 (1991).  You may deem it
appropriate to transmit this report to the Security Council members.

(<u>Signed</u>)  Hans BLIX

0190 /...

Enclosure

# CONSOLIDATED REPORT ON THE FIRST TWO IAEA INSPECTIONS UNDER SECURITY COUNCIL RESOLUTION 687 (1991) OF IRAQI NUCLEAR CAPABILITIES

## INTERNATIONAL ATOMIC ENERGY AGENCY

### 11 July 1991

0200

/...

## CONSOLIDATED REPORT ON THE FIRST TWO IAEA INSPECTIONS UNDER SECURITY COUNCIL RESOLUTION 687 (1991) OF IRAQI NUCLEAR CAPABILITIES

1.  This report summarizes the principal findings of the first two inspections under Security Council resolution 687 (1991) conducted by the IAEA of Iraqi nuclear capabilities. These inspections were carried out between 15 - 21 May 1991 and 22 June - 3 July 1991 with the assistance and co-operation of the Special Commission of the United Nations. The first inspection was carried out by a team of 34 drawn from 20 Member States and was headed by Mr. D. Perricos of the IAEA as Chief Inspector. The second inspection consisted of a team of 18 personnel from 8 Member States and was headed by Mr. M. Zifferero (22 June - 26 June) and Mr. D. Kay (26 June - 3 July), both from the IAEA.

2.  These two initial inspections had three principal inspection objectives:
     •first, the verification of the accuracy and completeness of the Iraqi declarations submitted under the requirements of Security Council resolution 687,
     •second, to conduct inspections of sites designated by the Special Commission established under resolution 687 where there were ground to believe that undeclared nuclear activities had been conducted or that undeclared equipment might be stored, and
     •third, to develop an over-all picture of the nature, direction and capabilities of the Iraqi nuclear programme.

*Verification of the accuracy and completeness of the the Iraqi declarations*

3.  The declaration by the Government of Iraq of 27 April 1991 principally concerned facilities, material and activities at Al-Tuwaitha Nuclear Research Centre.[1] Inspection of Al-Tuwaitha found the

---

[1] Al-Tuwaitha Site Map in Annex I

0201

/...

following:

### a. Facilities

i.    The inspection found that many building where significant activities may have taken place were thoroughly destroyed -- in many cases by military activities during the conflict, but in some significant cases by extensive clearing operations carried out by Iraqi authorities during and after the conflict. In almost all cases documentation and records had disappeared and were not available. Smear tests and samples of intact or only partially damaged equipment and of the surrounding areas were taken and their analysis continues. However, much of the site was damaged or cleared to such an extent that this analysis process is very difficult, and in some cases is incapable of definitive results. The overall impression is of a site where most significant buildings have been thoroughly destroyed or cleared and, with only a few exceptions noted below, provide only limited concern for future verification unless substantial rebuilding takes place.[2] However, it is clear that much of the equipment which once existed at Al-Tuwaitha has been removed to other locations, most of which were not disclosed to the first two inspections.

ii.    Research reactors. (B24 and B13)[3] Both the Tamuz 1 & 2 reactors were heavily damaged. They would be difficult to restore and, in any event, the weapons significance of the facilities is now dependent on the HEU fuel only. In the case of Tamuz 1, there had been no attempt to rebuild the reactor since the 1981 attack, and the heat exchangers and pumps were found in a separate store and had not been used elsewhere. The building housing the IRT-5000 reactor was very heavily damaged, but the pool with reactor fuel and storage racks was still intact, albeit covered with substantial amounts of debris and rubble. The fuel was still inside the core, the pool and the external storage bay. The fuel is highly enriched uranium (80% and 36%) and, therefore, requires future action to remove it as required by resolution 687. After the fuel is removed the remains of the reactor building will be unusable.

iii.    Hot cells. The hot cells in the reactor building (B24) are mechanically badly damaged with the master-slave manipulators

---

[2] Annexes II and III summarize the status as of the first inspection.

[3] Numbers refer to Al-Tuwaitha Site Map in Annex I

0202                              /...

destroyed on the outside but with the concrete structure intact. Because of the surrounding debris it was impossible during the first mission to confirm the situation inside the cell and monitoring is required until the status is determined. Hot cells with damaged manipulators, but with their basic structure sound, remain in the Radioisotope Production Laboratory (B15). Additional hot cells remain in the "LAMA" Hot Metallurgy Testing Laboratory and in the radioactive waste treatment station. Future monitoring will be required of all these cells.

iii. **Laboratory and Workshop Building (B23).** The Iraqi authorities declared this building to have been used mainly for laser and optics work. However, due to the total destruction of this building and the removal by Iraq of all accessible equipment it was not possible to verify its use.

iv. **"LAMA" Hot Metallurgy Testing Laboratory (B22).** This building had been heavily bombed and there was no independent evidence of the use that had been made of this building. There had been salvage of some of the equipment from the two hot cells.

v. **Radioactive Waste Treatment Station (B35).** This building was partially damaged, but had two hot cells in good condition and with the machinery inside the station undamaged. The cells were not equipped with manipulators and were equipped for the specialized waste treatment process consistent with the declared use of the building.

vi. **Radiochemistry Laboratories (B9).** All three compartments of the hot cells with 150 mm of lead shielding were intact. The first part was used for dissolution, the second for equipment maintenance and the third for mixer settlers. The equipment had been used for separation of fission products from spent fuel. A separate room had 10 free-standing alpha glove-boxes for actinide separation. The process was on a small scale (2.26 g of plutonium was declared as separated) but has a larger significance in establishing the capability for plutonium separation.

vii. **Radioisotope Production Laboratory (B15).** This building contained two hot cells, one with 900 mm of shielding, the other with 1200 mm barytic shielding. The building was extensively damaged with all services destroyed. There were also originally 23 lead cells which are now scattered as a result of the bombing. the applications for which this building was declared to be used would be allowed under the terms of

0203 /...

resolution 687, but future monitoring would be required to ensure that its use was limited to these purposes.

viii. **The "Italian" Area (B73).** This area was heavily bombed and the fuel fabrication plant and chemical engineering research were almost completely destroyed. The material testing building sustained some damage but the essential equipment survived.

ix. **Materials Testing laboratory (Ceramics and Metals) (B63).** The building was rendered unusable by the bombing, and all of its equipment had been removed. Equipment said by the Iraqis to be from this building was later shown to the first inspection team. This equipment, if indeed from this building, would be consistent with its stated use.

x. **Nuclear Physics Laboratories (B80).** The Iraqi authorities declared that these building had been devoted to plasma physics, ion source physics, magnet development and for future operation of a cyclotron. The building had been heavily damaged during the bombing and had been subjected to an unusually heavy site clearance operation by the Iraqis -- which included even removing the substantial, concrete reinforced floor and -- by the time of the second mission -- regrading the site to a level field. All equipment had been removed from the building before the first mission -- except for two magnets left on the top of the rubble. The building had been serviced by unusually large electrical (7.4 megawatts) and cooling services which appeared to exceed its declared needs.

xi. **Complex Chemistry and Chemical Engineering Research and Development (B85).** The declared purposes of this building were chemical and chemical engineering-related R&D, including a pilot-scale extraction process to recover uranium from ore with a high organic content. The building had been very extensively damaged, first from bombing, then from a vigorous removal operation of the Iraqi authorities. At the time of the first inspection, Iraq had completely removed the two process halls of this building, and by the second inspection very little remained of this complex. The building had an unusually large ventilation system, but the lack of any residual equipment together with the extensive site levelling has made it difficult to determine with certainty the actual uses of this building. Environmental samples were taken and are now being analyzed.

/...

0204

### b. Nuclear Materials

i. With respect to the nuclear material declared by Iraq, the Agency inspection teams had to locate, identify, characterize, verify, "freeze" the material so it could only be moved with Agency approval and assess the accessibility for removal of the nuclear-weapons-usable material. The Iraqi declaration of 27 April 1991 had covered all the nuclear material that had been subject to safeguards.[4] The Iraqi authorities had relocated a substantial amount of the nuclear materials to both areas adjacent to and further removed from Tuwaitha.[5]

ii. Extensive verification efforts were carried out during the first inspection on all declared nuclear material. For the nuclear weapons-usable material this involved the following: The presence of all fresh high enriched uranium was confirmed by measurements (17664 g U/12633 g U-235). The presence of irradiated high enriched uranium was confirmed -- [61 items = 16.8 kg U =52% verified by fuel type identified and non-destructive assay (NDA) carried out] [41 items = 8.3 kg U =26% verified by item counting and NDA] [35 items = 7.0 kg U =22% presence indirectly confirmed by radiation dose mapping]. Presence of recovered plutonium [2.26 g] was confirmed.

iii. For non-nuclear weapons-usable material the measurements involved: The presence of low-enriched uranium was confirmed by measurement [irradiated fuel, 10% enrichment = 69 items = 87.8 kg U] [fresh bulk = 2.6% enrichment = 75 items =1762 kg U]. The presence of depleted and natural uranium was confirmed by measurement [3% of inventory =327 kg uranium was reported to be under rubble]. The presence of yellow cake was confirmed by measurements[752 items = 204 tons of natural uranium]. The presence of previously exempted material was confirmed.

iv. The nuclear material outside of the damaged reactor was brought under Agency custody by means of the extensive applications of Agency seals and a regime was established for frequent inspection until this material can be removed from Iraq. Studies were begun for the

---

[4] Annex IV provides an overview of the nuclear materials and there locations.

[5] Annex V indicates the distribution of this material.

0205

/...

removal from the damaged reactor of the material still there and for applying seals as an interim control measure.

## Inspection of Sites Designated by the Special Commission

4.    Beginning with the first IAEA inspection, short-notice inspections were carried out of sites designated by the Special Commission. These have included sites at Tarmiya (20 May and 24 June), Abu Ghraib 23, 25, and 26 June), Al Hamath ( 24 June), Zaafaraniya (26 June), Al Musayyib (27 June) and Falluja (28 June). At two of these site, the Iraqi authorities denied the right of access for the purposes of inspection and removed materials even after the Chief Inspector had ordered that no material or equipment be moved for the sites under the inspections had been completed. Photographic evidence substantiated a strong case that the material which was moved was related to undeclared uranium enrichment activities.

## Over-all Development of the Iraqi Nuclear Programme

5. At the end of the second inspection, the team concluded that based on the evidence it had found the Iraqis had been pursuing an undeclared uranium enrichment programme using the electromagnetic isotope separation technique (EMIS).[6]

6. The technologies that must be mastered for a successful EMIS programme include high current ion source development, high voltage DC power supply design and manufacture, high current power supply

---

[6] EMIS is accomplished by creating a high current beam(10's to 1000's of milliamps) of low energy (10's of KeV) ions and allowing them to pass through a magnetic field (typically 3000-7000 Gauss. or .3-.7 Tesla). The heavier ions bend in a larger radius than the lighter ions and suitable placed collector pockets capture the different isotopes. EMIS is the process originally used by most of the nuclear weapons states to prepare their first highly enriched uranium for nuclear explosives. Its advantages are a well understood design, with much detail available in the open literature, and the ready availability of much of the hardware. The disadvantages of EMIS are the large energy cost per unit of HEU produced and high labor costs associated with operation. This latter disadvantage can now be reduced, however, with the use of readily available computer control software.

0206

/...

design and manufacture, large vacuum system design and operation, collector design and fabrication, and insulator design and fabrication. In addition specific chemical process technologies are required for operation of a uranium EMIS facility: acid washers to clean the vacuum chambers, combustors to burn the graphite collectors, dissolvers to dissolve the ash, solvent extraction systems to purify the uranium solutions, and chemical reactors to prepare uranium tetrachloride feed material. Mechanical engineering capabilities are required for fabrication of massive steel magnet pole pieces, support fixtures, and equipment transport. By the end of the second inspection the following dedicated facilities for each of these required technologies had been located and inspected by the first two IAEA inspection teams. These facilities included:

i.     **Buildings Within the Berm at Tuwaitha.** When the first IAEA team visited Tuwaitha it was noted that building 80 had installed power of 7.4 megawatts. This is an inordinately large amount of power for a building of its size and declared function. Building 85 was declared to be a chemical engineering building and therefore should have had equipment in it that would have allowed lab/pilot scale EMIS process chemistry to be demonstrated. These buildings were heavily damaged during the war, as were many other buildings at Tuwaitha. However, these two buildings were singled out for unusually thorough demolition after the first team's visit. The sites where these buildings stood have been graded and cleared to an inexplicable extent. This action, in combination with the extraneous rubble which the first team noted covered the site, suggests an attempt to render difficult the identification of the activities and purposes of these buildings. Environmental samples were taken from nearby objects during this inspection.

ii.     **The Al Hamath Workshop.** A significant new site was inspected outside the berm just south of the water purification complex in the northwest portion of the Tuwaitha facility. This site was called Al Hamath by the Iraqis. Our Iraqi military representative stated that the site was used for truck maintenance. This declaration was later amended when the Iraqis said that the facility was a machine shop. Neither declared usage of these buildings is credible. The site had two high bay buildings sharing over 1 megawatt of electrical service and a suitably sized water purification and chiller system. Neither building had been damaged during the war, yet both buildings had been stripped of their contents and the concrete floors had sections removed. If the

0207     /...

facilities had been used for either of the declared purposes there would be no need for either this much power or this much cooling capacity, and there certainly would be no need to gut the buildings. These high bay buildings each had multiple utility drops consisting of high capacity, 380 volt, three phase receptacles, and 220 volt single phase receptacles cooling water facilities spaced along the walls. Each building had large traveling cranes of the same type installed at Tarmiyah, one of which was labeled, "Iraqi Atomic Energy Commission". One of the two cranes was very strongly magnetized. It is the consensus of the team that this site was used as a magnet test facility. Because there was not a nearby suitable chemical processing facility, and because the installed power is relatively low, it is surmised that this facility did not do actual uranium isotope separation (though environmental samples were taken at this site). It is surmised that buildings 80 and 85 did do lab/pilot scale uranium isotope separation with approximately five units for some unknown period of time. The Al Hamath buildings are believed to have been used for magnet tests (possibly including coil winding) and for engineering integration tests of separator systems.

iii. **Tarmiyah.** The Tarmiyah site[7] when inspected by the first team was noted as being unusual because of the mix of buildings with unusually large installed electrical power co-allocated with buildings with large chemical processing capabilities. When the second team reinvestigated the facilities it was clear that the site was a multi-billion dollar EMIS facility. Building 33 was stated by the Iraqis to be used for transformer fabrication. In the technical view of the inspection team this is simply not credible. A transformer plant required metal forming, coil winding, and other capabilities that were clearly absent from this building. The building had two ten ton bridge cranes and two twenty-five ton bridge cranes, an enormous installed electrical supply (over 100 megawatts), and a supply of purified and chilled water. These features are consistent with building 33 housing EMIS machines. The interior of the building was configured as a large bay with two large (5m by 60m) parallel piers for electromechanical equipment with utility outlets and space suitable for approximately 100 EMIS units. The EMIS units would sit approximately three meters above the floor of the central bay, with the power supplies in the adjacent bay and the vacuum pumps on the floor. It is surmised that this building was the site for the first stage of enrichment. The consensus of the team is that this building was never operational, with initial operation six to eighteen months away.

[7]Tarmiyah Site Map in Annex VI

0208

/...

Building 245 is in important ways a smaller version of building 33. The building has approximately 40 megawatts of power, uninterruptable power systems, for control computer power and a large unfinished control room.

It is hypothesized to be the building for the second stage of enrichment. The building could have held 20 EMIS units. The facility utilities were incomplete and it is believed that this facility was twelve to eighteen months from operation.

Building 46 was a process chemistry building that was suitable for high quality batch chemistry work. The building had little process equipment installed and was probably six to twelve months from first operation. This building may have been designed for uranium tetrachloride processing.

Building 57 was stated as being for parts cleaning. The washing facilities in the building were designed for washing heavy objects of the size postulated for the EMIS vacuum chamber. A rail system two meters above the floor was installed for conveniently loading a heavy object into the pressure washers. This building was incomplete with first operation estimated to be in six to twelve months. The team emphasizes that this building was built to conveniently wash parts of a particular configuration and it is the team's opinion that these parts were to be vacuum boxes used in EMIS separators.

Building 225 was stated by the Iraqis to be a heavy metal recovery facility. This is assessed to be a true statement. The building appears to be designed for recovering uranium for recycle into the process. The air handling and filtration equipment in this building was enormous. It is surmised that the extensive filtration was both to conserve valuable enriched material and to prevent isotopic signatures from escaping the plant.

The configuration of buildings 33 and 245 with their unusual electrical and cooling utilities led the team to conclude that Tarmiyah was an EMIS site. The co-located buildings containing all of the necessary ancillary functions completes the case. The only purpose of a multi-billion dollar facility of this type apparent to the team is EMIS of uranium. It is the opinion of the team that Tarmiyah was never operational. Initial startup of the facilities was six to eighteen months away. It has effectively been rendered non-operational and may be adequately monitored by periodic inspections.

0209

/...

iv.    **Zaafarniyah.** The IAEA had reason to believe that the Al Dijjla and Al-Rabee sites located in Zaafarniyah were used to fabricate EMIS components. Al Dijjla is a Ministry of Industry site with electrical engineering design and fabrication facilities. The manufacturing plants inspected were observed to have the following capabilities: coil winding, chassis assembly, computer aided design, printed circuit board fabrication, and control system design and assembly. Some of the equipment at Tarmiya appeared to originate from this site. It is the team's belief that the required electrical components for an EMIS program could be designed and fabricated at Al Dijjla but that this facility is not dedicated to EMIS work.

The Al-Rabeeh metal working shops were excellently equipped for precision work as well as very large metal piece work on steel, stainless steel, and aluminium. There was no evidence that facilities for working with pyrophoric (e.g. uranium) or toxic (e.g. beryllium) are present. Al-Rabeeh clearly has the capacity to fabricate the major EMIS metal components but was not being used for EMIS fabrication at the time of the inspection.

v.    **Possible EMIS Components and Equipment.** As detailed elsewhere in the full inspection report many storage facilities and trucks were inspected by the team. A substantial amount of dual-use equipment suitable for use in EMIS power supplies was noted. None of this equipment is conclusive by itself, but taken as a whole, enough equipment was documented to state that there seemed to be an unusual amount of electrical equipment that would be appropriate for an EMIS program. Equipment that appeared to be real EMIS equipment (coils, magnet pole pieces, and vacuum chambers) was seen and photographed by several team members as the Iraqis attempted to move it from Fallujah.

*Conclusions*

There is Iraqi declared evidence of the research and development required for EMIS work (ion source, magnet development, and insulator research at Tuwaitha). There is documented evidence of the ability to manufacture all required components for an EMIS separator. There is evidence that lab or pilot scale EMIS development was done at Tuwaitha. There is further evidence that this research was successful and that a large EMIS process plant was under construction at Tarmiyah. Conclusive evidence that uranium isotope separation was accomplished must await the results from the environmental samples. Uranium unusually depleted in U-235 would be prima facie evidence that EMIS

0210                    /...

(large scale laser isotope separation is not credible for Iraq) has been done in Iraq. Accurate assessments of actual production are impossible at this point. It is the opinion of this team that Tarmiyah has never operated and that Tuwaitha had facilities to operate at most five to ten separators. If each separator can produce 1 gram of highly enriched uranium per day (as estimated in a technical-note prepared by the second inspection team) then the maximum amount of HEU produced can be estimated if the initial commissioning dates and operating time can be determined. Our best estimate is that Tuwaitha could have had five machines operating for no more than two years and could not have produced more than three kilograms of highly enriched uranium.

Annex I

The Tuwaitha site map

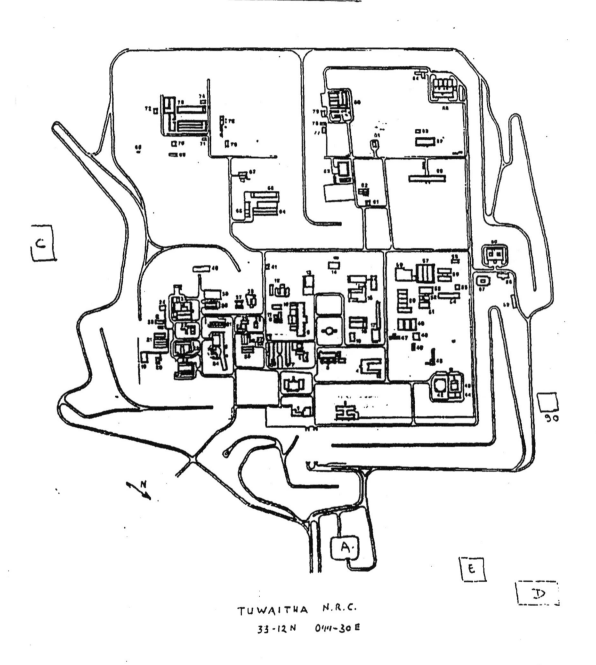

TUWAITHA  N.R.C.
33-12 N   0444-30 E

/...

0212

ACTION TEAM CONFIDENTIAL

UNSC 687 ACTION TEAM
FIRST ON-SITE INSPECTION

### Annex II

### List of buildings at Al-Tuwaitha

| Bldg. No. | Iraqi Declaration 1991-05-15 | Inspector's specification (if different) |
|---|---|---|
| 1 | Personal Control Office | |
| 2 | Restaurant | |
| 3 | Administrative Building | |
| 4 | Biology and Agricultural Labs | |
| 5 | Head Administration | |
| 6 | Administration | |
| 7 | Administration | Training Office |
| 8 | Training Offices | External Relations Department |
| 9 | Chemical Analyses Labs and Radiochemical Labs | |
| 10 | Chemical Analyses Labs | |
| 11 | Telephone Communication | |
| 12 | Engineering Services Workshop | Engineering & Neutron Generator |
| 13 | Research Reactor IRT-5000 | |
| 14 | Sub-Station | |
| 15 | Isotope Production Laboratory | |
| 16 | Mechanical Production Workshop | Workshop for IRT |
| 17 | Mechanical Production Workshop | |
| 18 | Medical Analyses Lab | |
| 19 | Offices and Stores | Open Air Pool |
| 20 | Offices and Stores | |
| 21 | Offices and Stores | |
| 22 | Hot Laboratories LAMA | |
| 23 | Laboratory Workship Building | |
| 24 | Tamuz-2 Zero Power Reactor | |
| 25 | Store | |
| 26 | Chemical Cleaning Workshop | |
| 27 | Caravan | |
| 28 | Caravans | |
| 29 | Chemical Cleaning Workshop | Caravan |

0213

/...

| Bldg No. | Iraqi Declaration Hypothesis | Inspectors specification (if different) |
|---|---|---|
| 30 | Chemical Cleaning Workshop | |
| 31 | Cooling Tower | Cooling Tower for Tamuz |
| 32 | Cooling Tower | Warehouse |
| 33 | Offices | |
| 34 | Offices and Stores | |
| 35 * | Radioactive Waste Treatment Station (RWTS) | |
| 36 | Store | Solid Waste Store |
| 37 | Training Offices | Storage |
| 38 | Training Offices Labs | |
| 39 | Store | Permanent Solid Waste Storage |
| 40 | Solid Waste Storage | Waste Storage for IRT |
| 41 | Control Room for No. 40 | Nuclear Instrument Calibration and Waste Storage |
| 42 | Technical Library and Conference Rooms | |
| 43 * | Technical Library and Conference Rooms | |
| 44 | Technical Library and Conference Rooms | |
| 45 | Water Treatment Station | |
| 46 | Biology and Agricultural Labs | |
| 47 | Biology and Agricultural Labs | |
| 48 | Biology and Agricultural Labs | |
| 49 | Biology and Agricultural Labs | |
| 50 | Mechanical Workshops and Stores | (Includes also IQZ-) |
| 51 | Mechanical Workshops and Stores | |
| 52 | Mechanical Workshops and Stores | |
| 53 | Mechanical Workshops and Stores | |
| 54 | Mechanical Workshops and Stores | Graphite Workshop |
| 55 | Mechanical Workshops and Stores | |
| 56 | Mechanical Workshops and Stores | |
| 57 | Mechanical Workshops and Stores | |
| 58 | Cafeteria | |
| 59 * | Health Physics Building | |
| 60 | Offices | |

0214...

| Bldg No. | Iraqi Declaration 1991-05-18 | Inspector's specification (if different) |
|---|---|---|
| 61 | Incinerator | |
| 62 | Sewage Station | |
| 63 | Cold Material Testing Laboratories | |
| 64 | Chemical Waste Treatment (liquids) | Rad Waste Process Building |
| 65 | Chemical Waste Treatment (liquids) | |
| 66 | Chemical Waste Treatment (liquids) | Offices/Training Building |
| 67 | Deionized Water Production Units | |
| 68 | Utilities | Storage |
| 69 | Utilities | Oil Storage |
| 70 | Utilities | Electrolytical/Production of Hydrogen |
| 71 | Utilities | |
| 72 | Utilities | |
| 73 | Workshops | Workshop for Fuel Fabrication Laboratory and Hall for Material Testing |
| 74 | Power Sub-Station | |
| 75 | Caravans | |
| 76 | Power Sub-Station | Canteen |
| 77 | Utilities Workshop | |
| 78 | Utilities Workshop | |
| 79 | Caravans | |
| 80 | Nuclear Physics Laboratories | |
| 81 | Cafeteria | |
| 82 | Electronic Research Laboratories | Electronics Department & Computer Center |
| 83 | Utilities | |
| 84 | Utilities | Chemistry & Chemical Engineering R&D |
| 85 | Chemical Research Laboratories | |
| 86 | Mechanical Design Laboratories | |
| 87 | Medical Centre | |
| 88 | Health Center | |
| 89 | Caravans | |
| 90 | Polymer Chemistry Laboratory | |

bldgrev/hb/91 06-04

0215

## Annex III

### Summary of follow-up actions

| | Building | Status of Building | Recommended further Action |
|---|---|---|---|
| 1 | B24 TAMUZ 1,2 | heavily damaged | Future monitoring of recovered equipment from Tamuz 1 (e.g., heat exchangers and pumps) required |
| 2 | B24 Hot Cells | badly damaged (but concrete structure intact) | Monitoring until positive confirmation of status |
| 3 | B23 Laboratories and workshop | totally damaged | Future monitoring of recovered equipment (e.g., lasers and optics work) required |
| 4 | B22 "LAMA" | damaged | - Monitoring of the status of hot cells<br>- Future monitoring of recovered equipment (e.g., some parts of 2 hot cells — one concrete and one lead) required |
| 5 | B35 Radioactive waste treatment | partially damaged but 2 hot cells in good condition | Future monitoring of hot cells |
| 6 | B13 IRT-5000 | heavily damaged | Removal of 80% and 36% enriched fuel |
| 7 | B13 Hot Cells | concrete structure undamaged | - clearance of debris<br>- monitoring until positive confirmation of status and removal of fuel from IRT-5000 |
| 8 | B9 Radiochemistry Laboratories | equipment within B9 largely escaped damage | Future monitoring |

/...

0216

| | Building | Status of Building | Recommended further Action |
|---|---|---|---|
| 9 | B15 Radioisotopes Production Laboratory | damaged but 2 hot cells structure intact | Future monitoring if the building is restored |
| 10 | B73 The "Italian" area | heavily bombed | - Future monitoring of the material testing laboratory<br>- Future monitoring of recovered equipment (e.g., equipment relevant to reprocessing) required |
| 11 | B64, 56, 66, 67 | buildings damaged | Future monitoring |
| 12 | B63, B80, B85 (new R&D area) | heavily damaged | Future monitoring of recovered equipment (e.g., related to material testing, plasma physics and uranium extraction) required |
| 13 | B45 to B58 Workshop area | many buildings, one still usable | - Future monitoring<br>- Future monitoring of recovered equipment (e.g., graphite machine shop tools) required |
| 14 | Remaining areas | many buildings are still usable | - Monitoring of any future reuse of buildings<br>- Check of removed equipment |

(0185B)

0217

/...

Annex IV

UNSC687

Summary-description of locations

| NO. | LOCATION | | STATUS | |
|---|---|---|---|---|
| 1 | IQA- IRT Research Reactor | | 1. | Facility destroyed; however no $H_2O$ leackage for core pool and spent fuel detected yet. |
| | | | 2. | Nuclear Material: |
| | | | (a) | Apparently no damage of fuel since contamination of pool water not above normal level. |
| | | | (b) | In both pools significant amounts of soil and rubble were discovered. |
| | | | (c) | It was not possible to confirm the presence of all fuel items. |
| | | | (d) | Fresh fuel removed, verified at new site. |
| 2 | IQB- Tamuz 2 Research Reactor | (empty = no nuclear material present) | 1. | Facility destroyed. |
| | | | 2. | Nuclear material: all material (fresh and spent fuel) was removed from the facility. (Fresh fuel to Site A, spent fuel to Site B). |
| 3 | IQC- Fuel Fabrication Laboratory | | 1. | Facility destroyed, area contamination. |
| | | | 2. | Nuclear Material:<br>- Fuel assemblies damaged, under rubble<br>- 53 out of 55 fuel rods recovered.<br>- 74% of bulk material recovered, rest suspected under rubble. |
| 4 | IQZ- Storage Facility | (empty = no nuclear material present) | 1. | Facility destroyed. |
| | | | 2. | Nuclear material: all nuclear material removed to a new storage. |
| 5 | New Storage Facility | | | Nuclear Material: |
| | | | (a) | Previously "exempted" material |
| | | | (b) | IQZ- material = DU, NU, LEU (2.6%) |
| | | | (c) | rods, pellets recovered from IQC-. |
| 6 | Location A | | | Nuclear Material: |
| | | | (a) | Fresh fuel, HEU; from IQA- |
| | | | (b) | Fresh fuel, HEU; from IQB- |
| 7 | Location B | | | Nuclear Material: Spent fuel from IQB-. |
| 8 | Location C | | | Nuclear Material: |
| | | | (a) | Yellow Cake in drums |
| | | | (b) | Bulk material recovered from IQC. |

**ACTION TEAM CONFIDENTIAL**

0218 /...

June 13, 1991                                      Annex V

## Location, types and quantities of nuclear fuel assemblies

I. Fresh Fuel Assemblies at Location A Adjacent to Nuclear Site

- 68 items of IRT-5000, tubular type, total U-235 content 10,973 g (enrichment: 80%) 1/
- 10 items EK-36 type (rod cluster) total U-235 content 1,272 g (enrichment: 36%)
- 1 item Osirak type (French MTR) total U-235 content 388 g (enrichment: 93%)

II. Spent Fuel Assemblies Stored at Location B Near Nuclear Site

- 38 items Osirak type (French MTR) total U-235 content 11,050 g (enrichment: 93%)
- 20 items IRT-5000 tubular type initial U-235 content 3,165 g (enrichment: 80%) 2/
- 3 items EK-36 type (rod cluster) initial U-235 content 360 g (enrichment: 36%) 3/
- 69 items EK-10 type (rod cluster) initial U-235 content 8,776 g (enrichment: 10%) 4/

III. Spent Fuel Assemblies Remaining in the IRT 5000 Core, Pool and Storage Bay 5/

- 22 items in core, IRT-5000 tubular type, total U-235 content 3,510 g (enrichment: 80%)
- 42 items in adjacent storage bay, IRT-5000 tubular type, total U-235 content 6,832 g (enrichment: 80%)
- 12 items in core pool storage rack, IRT-5000 tubular type, total U-235 content 1,890 g. (enrichment: 80%)

1/ Detailed drawings available. Two items damaged but nuclear material not affected.

2/ Estimated burn-up is 40%.

3/ Burn-up unknown, but probably very low.

4/ Removal of these items still to be decided.

5/ Detailed drawing of fuel assembly available. Estimated average burn-up of 42 items and the 12 items is 40%; burn-up of remaining 22 items in core unknown.

0219

/...

## Annex VI

### Tarmiya
### Possible Nuclear Facility
### 33-36N 044-23E

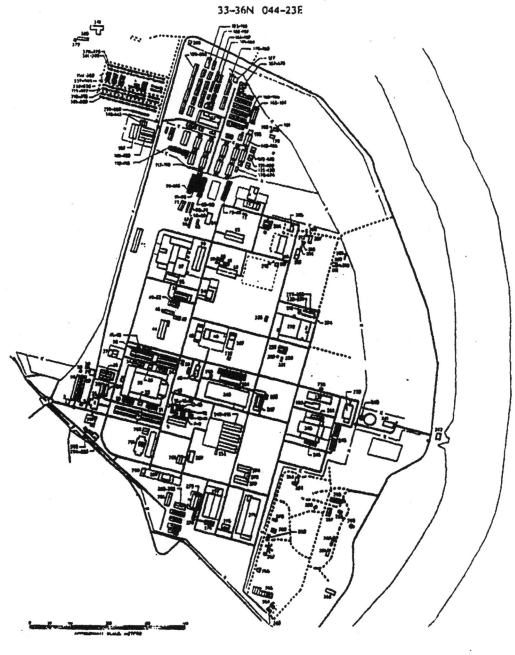

0220

## Security Council

Distr.
GENERAL

S/22803
16 July 1991
ENGLISH
ORIGINAL:  ARABIC/ENGLISH

---

LETTER DATED 15 JULY 1991 FROM THE PERMANENT REPRESENTATIVE OF
IRAQ TO THE UNITED NATIONS ADDRESSED TO THE SECRETARY-GENERAL


On instructions from my Government, I have the honour to inform you that
on 14 July 1991 in certain circles it was once again asserted that under
pressure and threats Iraq had submitted further lists, and it was claimed in
those circles that Iraq was thus continuing to reveal what it had previously
attempted to conceal.  Nothing could be further from the truth.  What actually
occurred is as follows:

On 8 July 1991 - just a few hours after the Iraqi Minister for
Foreign Affairs had sent a letter, dated 7 July 1991, to the
Secretary-General of the United Nations and to the President of the
Security Council - Iraq submitted lists of materials to the chief
inspector of the international inspection team that was and still is
present in Iraq, even before the chief inspector had received the lists
in question from Vienna.  After the chief inspector had examined the
above-mentioned information set out in lists annexed to the letter from
the Iraqi Minister for Foreign Affairs, the international inspection team
and the Iraqi side agreed that the facilities and laboratories where the
equipment in question was installed and the facilities in which the
equipment had been manufactured should be named.  This is the information
set out in the lists that the Iraqi side submitted on Sunday,
14 July 1991.  It is thus entirely clear that these lists do not contain
any new elements, but rather form an integral part of the information
that Iraq submitted on 7 July 1991.

Annexed hereto is a letter from the chief inspector of the
international inspection team, dated 11 July 1991, in which the chief
inspector refers to the agreement reached between the two sides, as well
as two letters from the Iraqi side, dated 13 and 14 July 1991,
respectively, in reply to the chief inspector's letter.


91-90002   2386c (E)                                                    /...

0221

I should be grateful if you would have this letter circulated as a
document of the Security Council.

(Signed)  Abdul Amir AL-ANBARI
Ambassador
Permanent Representative

02⬚⬚

/...

## Annex I

## Letter dated 11 July 1991 from the Chief Inspector of the IAEA Inspection Team addressed to the Chief of the Iraqi Inspection Team

I refer to our meeting of 9 July 1991 and the actions we discussed as required for the implementation of this phase of the IAEA inspection mission.

A key action that I requested was the preparation of a complete list of facilities related to the third stage of the nuclear programme declared in the letter of 7 July 1991 from the Iraqi Minister of Foreign Affairs to the United Nations Secretary-General. This programme covered the acquirement of the nuclear know-how for critical and important stages of the fuel cycle. I wish by this letter to repeat my request for this list, which should include the following information:

1.    Facilities where the relevant research was conducted;

2.    Facilities where the declared equipment were installed and/or used;

3.    Facilities in which these equipment were manufactured;

4.    Facilities where the nuclear material listed in table 9, annexed to the letter of 7 July 1991 was produced.

I would appreciate if this list is given to me as soon as possible and in any case before the end of the day of Saturday 13 July 1991.

(Signed)  D. PERRICOS
Chief Inspector
IAEA Inspection Team

0223 /...

<u>Annex II</u>

<u>Letter dated 13 July 1991 from the Chief of the Iraqi
Inspection Team addressed to the Chief Inspector of
the IAEA Inspection Team</u>

With reference to the letter from the Iraqi Minister for Foreign Affairs
dated 7 July 1991, and the tables annexed thereto, in connection with which
you requested clarifications in your letter of 11 July 1991, I have the honour
to transmit to you herewith the following documents:

1.    Table No. 1, listing the places where the activities referred to in
tables 1 to 14 in annex I to the above-mentioned letter from the Iraqi
Minister for Foreign Affairs were conducted;

2.    Table No. 2, indicating the sites where the nuclear materials listed in
table 9 in annex II to the above-mentioned letter from the Iraqi Minister
for Foreign Affairs were produced;

3.    With regard to the facilities in which the installation of equipment had
not been completed, which are listed in tables 1 to 8, annexed to the
letter from the Iraqi Minister for Foreign Affairs dated 7 July 1991, I
wish to state the following:

     (a)  The equipment listed in tables 1 to 5 was located at the
At-Tarmiyah site and in building No. 80 at At-Tuwaythah;

     (b)  The equipment referred to in tables 6 and 7 was located at a
site at Mosul;

     (c)  The equipment referred to in table 8 was installed in building
No. 63 at At-Tuwaythah.

                                        (<u>Signed</u>)  A. I. AL-HIJAJ
                                           Chief, Iraqi Inspection Team

0224

/...

## Annex III

## Letter dated 14 July 1991 from the Chief of the Iraqi Inspection Team addressed to the Chief Inspector of the IAEA Inspection Team

With reference to the letter from the Iraqi Minister for Foreign Affairs dated 7 July 1991 and to the tables annexed thereto, in connection with which you requested clarifications in your letter of 11 July 1991, and further to our letter dated 13 July 1991, I have the honour to transmit to you herewith the list of the facilities where the materials listed in tables 1 to 8 in annex II to the above-mentioned letter from the Iraqi Minister for Foreign Affairs were produced.

(Signed)   A. I. AL-HIJAJ
Chief, Iraqi Inspection Team

-----

0225

## 1. UN에 의한 이라크 核査察의 根據

o 核非擴散條約(NPT)과 國際原子力機構(IAEA)

- 이라크는 核武器의 水平的 擴散을 防止하기 위한 核非擴散條約(NPT)의 당사국인 동시에 國際原子力機構(IAEA)의 核安全協定(Safeguard Accord)에도 署名한 國家로서 自國內 核施設을 利用한 核武器 製造與否를 確認하기 위한 IAEA의 現場査察要求에 응할 義務가 있음.

o 安保理 決議 687號

- 유엔 安全保障理事會는 決議 687號를 통해 休戰을 決意하면서 對이라크 經濟制裁措置의 解除以前에 이라크로 하여금 保有한 非通商武器體系, 즉 大量破壞武器(핵무기, 화학무기, 생물학무기)를 完全 廢棄하도록 함.
- 따라서 이라크는 保有한 大量 破壞武器를 廢棄해야 하는 同時에 核武器의 새로운 開發도 禁止됨.

o 中東軍縮과의 連繫

- 軍備增强의 惡循環은 中東地域을 항상 不安定狀態에 빠뜨린다는 認識과 安保를 理由로 過多한 大量破壞武器를 保有하여 隣接國 侵略에 惡用하는 事例를 막아야 한다는 共同認識에서 美·蘇·英·佛·中 5대 武器輸出國은 對中東 武器輸出 抑制를 推進中임.
- 이라크의 核武器 開發意圖는 이러한 中東軍縮을 통한 平和維持 構想과는 相値되는 것임.

## 2. 이라크 核査察 現況과 問題點

o 安保理決議 687號에 의해 構成된 유엔 特別委員會에서 3次에 걸쳐 이라크 核査察

- 濃縮 우라늄의 他地域 移動與否 確認을 위해 接近하는 核査察團에게 이라크 병사 空砲 發射
- 核査察團의 査察要求 拒否는 IAEA 規定에 違背

0226

o 이라크측은 2次에 걸쳐 UN에 核技術, 裝備 및 核物質 明細書 提出

- IAEA에 未通報한 우라늄 濃縮計劃 是認

- 우라늄 濃縮用 同位元素分離裝置(Calutron) 30기 保有

- 獨自的으로 開發한 電氣磁場分離法(Electroric Separation Process)
  使用 (제2차 세계대전 당시 미국이 사용하던 원시적인 방식)

- IAEA에 보고한 80파운드 이외에 1-9 파운드 追加保有
  (망명 이라크 과학자는 90파운드 정도 추가보유 주장)

o 美國은 이라크가 繼續 核査察을 拒否할 경우 核施設 攻擊을 公言

- 攻擊할 수 있는 根據는 安保理가 이라크로 하여금 決議 內容을 遵守
  하도록 保障하는 措置를 취할수 있다는 決議 687號의 內容임.

- 부쉬 大統領, 20여개의 爆擊對象 이라크 指揮統制本部 選定 承認 報道

- 英國, 프랑스도 軍事的 制裁 方式에 同意

## 3. 北韓 核査察과의 關係

o 北韓은 核非擴散條約 當事國이면서도 義務事項인 國際原子力機構의 核
  安全協定에는 署名하지 않고 있다가 最近에야 國際的 壓力에 屈伏하여
  一旦 國際原子力機構와 協定에 관한 協商을 마친 狀態임.

o 그렇지만 이라크의 例에서도 볼수 있듯이 重要한 것은, 協定에의 署名
  與否가 아니라 核을 平和的인 目的으로만 利用한다는 基本 姿勢임.

o 我國은 中東의 軍縮과 平和維持를 위해 이라크가 지체없이 유엔 核査察團
  에게 보유 核施設 일체를 숨김없이 完全 公開하여 또다른 中東危機를 막을
  수 있기를 希望하며 아울러 北韓도 核安全協定의 誠實한 履行者가 되기를
  促求함.

0227

# 외 무 부

종 별 :

번 호 : UNW-1869                    일 시 : 91 0719 1900

수 신 : 장 관(국연,중동일,기정) 사본:노창희대사

발 신 : 주 유엔 대사대리

제 목 : 걸프사태(유엔동향)

　　1. 현재 이락 체류중인 유엔 핵사찰반 (3차)은 7.20이락을 출발하며 새로운 시찰반(4차)이 다음주 이락 도착예정이라고 하는바, 이락의 농축 우라늄 생산량에 관한 7.18 유엔 이락군비 통제 특위측의 언론 발표문을 별첨송부함.

　　2. 이락의 인도적 수요실태 조사를 위해 6.29-7.13 간 동국을 방문한 유엔대표단 (단장: SADRUDDIN AGAKHAN 대표)보고서가 금일 안보리문서로 배포된바, 동보고서 주요부분을 별첨송부함.

　　3. 한편 안보리 대이락 제재위원회가 7.22회의소집 예정인바, 동회의 동향은 추보위계임.

　　첨부:1. 상기특위발표문( IK/36)

　　2. 유엔대표단보고서( S/22799)

　　3. 관련 NYT,WP 기사:UNW(F)-338

　　끝

　　(대사대리 신기복-국장)

---

국기국　　1차보　　　중아국　　　국기국　　　외정실　　　분석관　　　안기부

91.07.20　　08:58 WG

외신 1과 통제관

0228

# United Nations

충 14 매

## Press Release

**Department of Public Information • News Coverage Service • New York**

IK/36
19 July 1991

### SPECIAL COMMISSION SAYS QUESTION OF HOW MUCH ENRICHED MATERIAL MAY HAVE BEEN ACCUMULATED BY IRAQ MUST REMAIN OPEN

#### 'Nothing Offered by Iraq' So Far 'To Give Confidence in a Conclusion' That Significant Quantities of Enriched Uranium Have Not Been Produced

The following press statement was issued last night by the Special Commission set up under Security Council resolution 687 (1991) on a cease-fire in the Gulf conflict:

In the view of the United Nations Special Commission, a thorough analysis of data and equipment, as well as continued inspections of designated sites, are essential to establish the facts in Iraq with regard to the full scope of the Iraqi nuclear programme.

The reporting received from the team presently in the field and earlier reports from inspection teams make clear that there is much work to be done before any conclusions can be reached about whether or not more equipment or material remain to be turned over to the International Atomic Energy Agency (IAEA)/Special Commission. Furthermore, preliminary findings apply to only few facilities, some of which Iraq originally failed to declare.

The new information offered by the Government of Iraq was made available after an IAEA/Special Commission inspection team discovered activities aimed at hiding the equipment and keep the Iraqi EMIS (electromagnetic isotope separation) enrichment programme secret. It would thus be inappropriate for the Special Commission to take the Government of Iraq's statements at face value. Iraq has now revealed work in three enrichment technologies. Only further inspections can establish the extent of the activities with regard to enrichment, and whether Iraq has not been active in other technologies in this field as well.

The question of how much enriched material may have been accumulated by Iraq must remain open, that is to say, there is nothing offered by Iraq to date to give confidence in a conclusion that significant quantities of highly enriched uranium have not been produced.

\* \*\*\* \*    14 — 1

## INTRODUCTION

1.    The decision to undertake the present mission was made by the Secretary-General, his Executive Delegate Sadruddin Aga Khan, and the executive heads of United Nations specialized agencies and programmes responsible for the humanitarian programmes in Iraq, Kuwait and the Iraq/Turkey and Iraq/Islamic Republic of Iran borders at a meeting held at Geneva on 13 June 1991.  Extensive first-hand reports had been received in previous weeks indicating that the conditions of the civilian population in many parts of Iraq were steadily deteriorating.  The onset of summer was likely to exacerbate the situation further, while the return of large numbers of those displaced was also having a considerable impact on severely strained food, medical, water and infrastructural resources.

2.    Given the indications of the worsening plight of the majority of Iraq's population, the meeting decided that a high-level mission should proceed to Iraq to assess the current humanitarian needs and recommend measures to address them.  The mission was to be action- and field-oriented, should be carried out rapidly and should focus in particular on the emergency needs of vulnerable groups.  Within its overall framework, the mission would concentrate on four main sectors:  food supply; water and sanitation; health; and energy (with special reference to power generation).

3.    The mission was led by the Secretary-General's Executive Delegate, Sadruddin Aga Khan, and was composed of experts from the relevant United Nations programmes and agencies, namely, UNICEF, WHO, FAO, WFP, UNHCR and UNDP, as well as consultants, specialists and eminent personalities from outside the United Nations system.  The latter comprised participants from Canada, France, the Netherlands, Norway, Sweden, the United Kingdom of Great Britain and Northern Ireland, the United States of America and the Commission of the European Communities.  While not part of this mission, a separate team from the International Telecommunication Union (ITU) was in Iraq at the same time.  Several of their findings are noted in the present report and a summary of their own mission report is included as appendix X.

4.    Mission members received briefings at Geneva from the Executive Delegate before flying to Baghdad on 29 June to join with staff from United Nations agencies already in the country.  The first part of the mission was devoted to information collection and analysis in Iraq.  At Baghdad mission members were briefed by United Nations staff, non-governmental organizations (NGOs), and the International Committee of the Red Cross (ICRC) and were welcomed by the Minister of State for Foreign Affairs and members of the National Committee for the Coordination of Relief and Assistance.  After meetings and discussions with staff of the relevant technical ministries on 1 July, mission members visited various sites, mainly outside Baghdad, from 2 to 7 July.  The mission divided into four teams, which visited sites in 16 of the 18 governorates (including Baghdad).

/...

14-2

5.     The Executive Delegate and additional mission members arrived in Baghdad on 8 July.   Together with certain members of his team, he met with various government officials, including the Deputy Prime Minister, the Foreign Minister, ministers of relevant technical Ministries and other senior officials.   The Executive Delegate also visited the southern region in order to further the provision of relief assistance to vulnerable groups and displaced persons in the area of the marshes.   The mission team departed for Geneva on 13 July.

6.     The Executive Delegate and members of the mission greatly appreciated the support and cooperation extended to them by the Iraqi authorities throughout the course of their stay in the country.

## I.   BACKGROUND TO THE SITUATION IN IRAQ

7.     As of mid-1990, Iraq was in certain respects fast approaching a standard comparable to that of some highly industrialized countries in the sector areas of concern to the present mission.   A wide-reaching and sophisticated health system had been put in place, capable of routinely providing services such as kidney dialysis treatment in regional hospitals.   The provision of clean drinking water was the norm, with over 1,500 treatment units nationwide providing a very high quantity of water (e.g., over 450 litres per person per day in Baghdad).   Sewage treatment, including a number of very large and technically sophisticated plants, kept the quality of the water in the Tigris and Euphrates rivers at a reasonable level.   While poverty and moderate malnutrition remained a problem in some areas, severe malnutrition, and related syndromes such as marasmus and kwashiorkor, were not major public health problems.   A key component of the country's infrastructure and services was the generation of power through a system of 20 main stations.   These stations provided power not only for the 70 per cent of the population living in urban areas, but also for many of those in outlying regions, as well as for the large amount of irrigated farm land.   The country had a modern telecommunications network in both the urban and the rural areas, serving millions of Iraqis through 900,000 telephone lines.

8.     An essential basis for this complex and extensive infrastructure was trade.   For example, most of the machinery, as well as the spare parts to keep it running, was obtained from outside the country.   Approximately 70 per cent of the food needs of the country were met through imports from abroad.   What primarily paid for this level of imports was revenue from the sale of oil.

9.     After the invasion of Kuwait by Iraqi forces on 2 August 1990, the situation started to change abruptly.   From 6 August, by its resolution 661 (1990), the Security Council imposed on all States a comprehensive package of financial and economic sanctions.   The war in January and February 1991 brought about massive destruction in many elements of the physical and service infrastructure.   This was followed by further major damage created by the civil conflicts that ensued.   These internal conflicts also led to the displacement in March and April 1991 of an estimated 400,000 persons to the

/...

Turkish border and approximately 1.2 million to the border with the Islamic
Republic of Iran or into that country itself.

10.  In February 1991, a joint WHO/UNICEF team assessed the impact of the war
on the women and children of Baghdad.  From 10 to 17 March, a United Nations
mission assessed the urgent humanitarian needs in Iraq and presented its
findings in the Secretary-General's report of 20 March 1991.  This led to an
initial appeal by the Secretary-General on 8 April for $US 178 million for aid
to vulnerable groups in Iraq.  On 9 April, the Secretary-General appointed
Sadruddin Aga Khan as his Executive Delegate for United Nations humanitarian
programmes for Iraq, Kuwait and the Iraq/Turkey and Iraq/Islamic Republic of
Iran border areas.  A small core Office of the Executive Delegate was
subsequently established with the help and support of UNDP.  A second appeal
was then made on 12 April for $US 400.2 million for refugees and displaced
persons on the borders of Iraq and Turkey and in the Islamic Republic of Iran.

11.  These two appeals were consolidated on 15 May, together with additional
needs not previously covered.  On 12 June 1991, an updated and revised appeal
was issued for $US 448.9 million.  This included $US 34.9 million for the
deployment of a United Nations guards contingent inside Iraq.  Of the funds
requested, approximately half had been pledged to date.  The majority of the
funds received are designated for aid to refugees and returnees.

12.  United Nations assistance in Iraq is currently provided under the terms
of the Memorandum of Understanding signed by the Foreign Minister of Iraq and
the Executive Delegate on 18 April 1991 and an annex to it dated 25 May 1991.
Eight United Nations agencies operate in the country with approximately
400 international staff (as of 30 June), of which 197 are United Nations
guards and 140 UNHCR staff.  Further deployment will bring the contingent to
its full complement of 500 guards.  Other agencies providing assistance
include an estimated 20 international NGOs, ICRC, and the International
Organization for Migration.

## II.  SUMMARY OF MAIN FINDINGS AND RECOMMENDATIONS

13.  The mission members concluded that the scale of damage and decline in
Iraq in the past year had indeed been dramatic.  Eight years of war with the
Islamic Republic of Iran had taken their toll even before the destruction of
the Persian Gulf war.  In significant parts of the country, the destruction
caused by the internal civil conflicts that followed the war was comparable or
even greater.  A final factor had been the consequence of economic and
financial sanctions imposed on Iraq, including the freezing of its foreign
assets and a ban on the international sale of its oil.  It was clear to the
mission that the impact of the sanctions had been, and remains, very
substantial on the economy and living conditions of its civilian population.
The mission was informed that the last reserves of food commodities that are
included in the ration basket are in the process of being exhausted.

/...

14-4

14.  During the past several months major efforts have been made by the Government of Iraq to restore the country to some semblance of its pre-war situation.  These efforts have been only partially successful.  For example, a number of bridges have been repaired, and with the limited pumping of oil for local consumption, internal transport capabilities have in large part been restored.

15.  However, the mission found that in the sectors of concern to it, the process of restoration had in many crucial respects reached its limit.  Indeed, there are a number of problem areas that are likely to worsen in the foreseeable future.  A review of several of the main findings within each of the sectors, which are discussed in more detail in the later sections of this report, gives reason for alarm.

16.  As far as water is concerned, damage to water-treatment plants and the inability to obtain needed spare parts have cut off an estimated 2.5 million Iraqis from the government system they relied upon before the war.  The perhaps 14.5 million Iraqis who continue to receive their water through this system are now provided on average with one quarter the pre-war amount per day.  Much of this water is of doubtful quality, owing to such problems as defective treatment and lack of sufficient hours of electric power.  Major damage was also suffered by the national sewerage system owing to the loss of electric power during the war.  Most of this damage has not been repaired, with raw sewage now flowing in some city streets and into the rivers.  Diarrhoeal diseases, thought to be mainly caused by water and sewage problems, are now at four times the level of a year ago.  The country is already experiencing outbreaks of typhoid and cholera.

17.  The health of the population in Iraq is now challenged by growing environmental hazards, insufficient access to quality medical care and inadequate nutrition.  Public health programmes have reduced their activities for lack of supplies.  Hospitals and public health centres are severely affected by lack of electricity, water and medicines.  Medical, surgical, dental and laboratory equipment suffer from the lack of spare parts, reagents and maintenance.  The fleet of vehicles that once assured the effectiveness of the health services has been reduced to a few units.  Iraq used to import annually approximately $US 360 million worth of drugs and medical appliances alone.  It is highly improbable that international humanitarian aid will be able to meet this demand.  Mechanisms need to be established urgently for the country to procure its own medical supplies and to maintain its equipment in operation.  Failing this, the health situation will further worsen.  Vulnerable groups, each day more numerous, will be the first victims.

18.  As for the food supply, the position is deteriorating rapidly in virtually all parts of the country.  Preliminary forecasts for the current main harvest indicate that this year's aggregate cereal production will be around one third of last year's.  This will further increase the country's dependence on imports, which even in good years has meant that approximately 70 per cent of its food needs must be imported.  Data collected on prices throughout the country show tremendous levels of inflation.  For example,

/...

14-5

current retail prices for wheat and rice - the two normal staple food items - remain 45 and 22 times their corresponding price levels of last year, while average incomes have shown only moderate gains. The government rationing system, even if basically equitable in its distribution, can provide only about one third of the typical family's food needs, resulting in a strikingly low level of dietary intake. The situation is particularly alarming with respect to the nutritional status of children, pregnant and lactating mothers as well as households headed by widows. Several independent studies and direct observation by the mission confirmed the high prevalence of malnutrition among children. There are numerous, reliable reports of families resorting to sales of personal and household items to meet their immediate needs. Taken collectively, this information clearly demonstrates a widespread and acute food supply crisis which, if not averted through timely intervention, will gradually but inexorably cause massive starvation throughout the country.

19. The current emergency feeding programmes, such as those being implemented by WFP for vulnerable groups, refugees, returnees and internally displaced persons accordingly acquire special significance and need to be maintained for at least the next few months. The process of repatriation must be encouraged by the continued provision of timely and adequate amounts of relief aid, not least to ensure that the situation in the areas to which the refugees are returning reverts to normal as quickly as possible. It should be noted that the economic sanctions also lessen the ability of the returning refugees to resume their ordinary lives and traditional economic activities. Indeed, the mission was informed by the Kurdish leadership that the sanctions were taking an unfortunately harmful toll upon the living conditions of the Kurdish population.

20. In terms of power generation, Iraq's capacity had been reduced to a negligible level by the end of February 1991. At present, the power generating capacity has been restored to 25 per cent of the pre-war level. As it is operating continuously, electricity production is about 40 per cent of the 1990 level. However, this restoration process has been accomplished through such methods as cannibalizing parts from damaged units, making risky makeshift repairs and operating the remaining plants without the normal breaks for maintenance and repairs. At this point, little more can be done to increase power generation further unless major imports of new parts are allowed. Barring this, power output can be expected to decline from now on. The mission has also assessed the situation of the oil sector. The requirements of the internal market can essentially be met with the current production and refining capacity, although with repairs needed soon for some refineries that are in precarious condition. The main concern is the oil export capacity, which is now only one third of the pre-war level.

21. As for telecommunications, the ITU team noted that at least 400,000 of the original 900,000 telephone lines were damaged beyond repair, while additional ones were partly damaged. The main microwave links connecting most of the cities were also damaged. This has had an obvious negative impact on the operation of health and social services as well as on humanitarian

/...

14-6

assistance programmes.  All international telecommunications were put out of
service.  Even after restoration work, the system can still handle only
30 per cent of its pre-war internal service, while international
telecommunications remain out of service.

22.  Clearly, the situation described above is one that deserves urgent
attention and immediate response.  In considering what actions to recommend,
the mission came to a series of additional conclusions.

23.  As spelled out in the specific sector reports, the primary action that is
needed to address these needs is the import of material goods.  This includes
such items as drugs, vaccines, medical equipment, ambulances, spare parts and
replacements for water and sewerage equipment, food and agricultural inputs
and equipment and parts for power generation plants and the oil sector, as
well as for the telecommunications network.

24.  A review of the relevant Security Council resolutions and decisions by
the Security Council Committee established by resolution 661 (1990) concerning
the situation between Iraq and Kuwait indicates that the sale or supply to
Iraq of most of these items is not restricted, although for most items
notification to or prior approval by the Sanctions Committee would be
required.  Many fall under the clauses exempting "medicine and health
supplies" and "foodstuffs" from the sanctions (see resolutions 661 (1990),
666 (1990) and 687 (1991)).  Others fall under the category of materials and
supplies for "essential civilian needs" as exempted in resolution 687 (1991),
as well as the clause contained in the 20 March 1991 Sanctions Committee
decision.  The latter provides that civilian and humanitarian imports to Iraq,
as identified in the report of that date to the Secretary-General, are
integrally related to the supply of foodstuffs and supplies intended strictly
for medical purposes ... and that such imports should also be allowed ...,
subject to approval by the Sanctions Committee under its no-objection
procedure.  So far, the relevance to the humanitarian programme of the import
of spare parts and equipment for the restoration of electric power plants and
for the telecommunications network has not been recognized.

25.  In this context, the mission observed that, in most of the cases that
came to its attention, problems to date with importing the above items had
more to do with the financing of such imports than actual prohibitions.  The
question of financing becomes even more crucial in relation to future
importations that need to be made.

26.  The mission members utilized the best information available to them to
estimate the costs of returning the systems in each of the four sector areas
to their pre-war condition.  This proved possible for most sectors, with the
estimates being $US 12 billion for the power-generating capacity,
$US 6 billion for the oil sector, $US 450 million for the water and sanitation
systems, $US 2.64 billion for food imports and $US 500 million for
agricultural imports.  While these calculations were not possible for health,
an indicative figure would be the typical level of international imports for
the health sector for one year, which has been approximately $US 500 million.

/...

14-7

27. The principal criterion adopted by the mission in evaluating these needs has been that it is concerned not only with addressing immediate requirements of humanitarian scope and nature, but also with averting a crisis in the next 6 to 12 months. To illustrate this point, urgent measures must be taken now to ensure that the next agricultural planting season can be completed under reasonably normal conditions.

28. Consequently, the mission attempted to determine the costs for some lower level of actions, over a one-year time-frame. Figures were calculated for providing approximately two fifths of the pre-war per capita levels of clean drinking water and putting a corresponding proportion of the damaged sewage-treatment capacity back in operation. Expenditures for imports for health services were calculated at the pre-war level. Food import calculations were based on the ration level that WFP provides to sustain disaster-stricken populations. Special supplemental feeding programmes to support the nutritional needs of malnourished children and pregnant and lactating mothers for one year were calculated. Power generation estimates were based on restoring approximately one half of the pre-war capacity of the country. For the oil sector, the mission worked out a cost based on the consolidation of existing refineries, the restoration of lubrication units, the repair of the Iraq-Turkey pipelines, and of the oil facilities in the Kirkuk areas. This would not include repair of the southern oil fields.

29. The total estimated costs for this greatly reduced level of services came to approximately $US 6.8 billion over a one-year period. This includes $US 180 million for water and sanitation, $US 500 million for health services, $US 53 million for supplemental feeding, $US 1.62 billion for general food imports, $US 300 million for essential agricultural needs, $US 2 billion for the oil sector and $US 2.2 billion for power generation. If this analysis is applied to a four-month time-frame, the requirements would come to $US 60 million for water and sanitation, $US 167 million for health services, $US 18 million for supplemental feeding, $US 540 million for food imports, $US 100 million for essential agricultural imports, $US 667 million for the oil sector, and $US 1.1 billion for power generation. The power and oil sectors include allowances for the front-end costs occurring in these sectors. Thus, the total for an initial four-month period would be $US 2.63 billion.

30. The massive financial requirements to establish even this reduced level of service are of a scale far beyond what is, or is likely to be, available under any United Nations-sponsored programme. The current United Nations appeal for humanitarian assistance for Iraq, Kuwait and the border areas with the Islamic Republic of Iran and Turkey has received only some $US 210 million to date. Most of these funds are pledged for the needs of refugees and returnees. Further, any additional requests for aid to Iraq must compete with a continually lengthening list of other emergency situations around the world with very compelling needs.

/...

31.  It is evident that the Iraqi Government itself will have to revise its priorities and mobilize all internal resources.  It will also have to finance the import of the type of materials under discussion, for which it has already requested approval from the Security Council Committee established by resolution 661 (1990).  It certainly appeared that the Iraqi Government has the potential itself to generate the funds required to cover the needs identified by the team.  This could be done either by the unfreezing of substantial amounts of Iraqi assets now held abroad or through the pumping and subsequent international sale of oil.  The mission was informed that foreign exchange reserves of only $US 14.75 million were on hand in the central bank and that the Government's holding of gold bullion in support of the national currency had remained constant for the last 20 years.

32.  With respect to the possible sale of oil by the Iraqi Government to finance such imports, paragraph 23 of Security Council resolution 687 (1991) empowers the Security Council Committee established by resolution 661 (1990) to approve exceptions to the prohibition against the import of commodities and products originating in Iraq, with the explicit purpose of assuring "adequate financial resources" on the part of the Iraqi Government to procure medicine and health supplies, foodstuffs and materials and supplies for "essential civilian needs".

33.  According to the Government, the current oil-production capacity of the country is 1,455 million barrels per day.  Taking into account internal consumption requirements, the production available for export could be about 1 million barrels per day.  This would mean a potential net revenue of $US 5.5 billion over one year.  Furthermore, in order to increase the production to the pre-war level, extensive repairs and rebuilding would have to take place, particularly in the Basra area.  The mission therefore recommends that Iraq be allowed to import over a four-month period $US 1 billion worth of equipment, spare parts and consumable materials to start restoration of the oil sector.

34.  If the Security Council Committee were to decide that Iraq should be allowed to use funds from oil sales or facilitate the use of blocked accounts in order to meet urgent humanitarian needs, the Government indicated that it would cooperate in making available documentation relating to sales of crude oil as well as purchases of the authorized imports.  It noted that all revenues accruing from oil sales were normally held in United States banks and that a suitable device for monitoring such credit balances could be established.  This procedure could include information on the use of unfrozen accounts.  In addition, the staff of the United Nations and other humanitarian agencies present in Iraq, as well as special missions designated by the Secretary-General as required, might for instance submit periodic assessments and in particular report on the changes in the composition of the rations of foodstuffs and the provision of health and social services brought about by increased imports.  The staff concerned would also obtain up-to-date information on the repair and improvement of power-generating capacity, the operation of water and sewerage plants and the like.  The envisaged procedure would thus help to ensure the actual receipt of the civilian and humanitarian goods in Iraq and their utilization by the intended beneficiaries.

/...

14-9

35.  In summary, the mission recommends that:

(a)  Immediate steps be taken to alleviate the priority needs identified by the mission in the areas of food supply, health services, water and sanitation, power generation, the oil sector and telecommunications;

(b)  To meet these needs, essential goods and materials should be imported, including:

(i)  Food to meet the minimum consumption requirements, in part to reduce and shorten the emergency relief operation now in operation at donors' expense;

(ii)  Agricultural inputs, including fertilizers, pesticides, animal feed and drugs, machinery and spare parts needed to repair the damaged irrigation and drainage system;

(iii)  Drugs, including raw materials needed for local pharmaceutical production, vaccines, medical supplies and medical, surgical, dental and diagnostic equipment for the health system;

(iv)  Vehicles (and spare parts for them) needed by the health system, including ambulances;

(v)  Spare parts, supplies and equipment and replacement pumps and other heavy equipment needed by water-treatment and pumping facilities and by the sewage treatment system;

(vi)  Equipment, materials and spare parts for the electric power system, the oil sector and for the telecommunication sector;

(c)  A monitoring system should be instituted for this purpose.  The relevant commercial transactions relating to the export of oil and the import of the above-mentioned goods and services could be made sufficiently transparent at the international level to allow adequate controls with respect to their shipment and entry into Iraq.  The monitoring arrangements in the context of the United Nations humanitarian presence in Iraq, as outlined in paragraph 13 of the Memorandum of Understanding of 18 April 1991, could be further developed and strengthened so as to provide adequate information on the destination and use of the goods in question.

14-10

# Iraq Says All Arms Have Been Disclosed

### By PAUL LEWIS
Special to The New York Times

BAGHDAD, Iraq, July 18 — Iraq gave the United Nations a formal pledge today that it has no more clandestine nuclear plants and that it has revealed all its nuclear secrets.

The pledge was given to the chief United Nations nuclear inspector, Demitri Perricos, by Jaafar Dhia Jaafar, the deputy chairman of Iraq's Atomic Energy Commission and deputy minister for industry.

"They have made a declaration that they have declared everything they must declare," Mr. Perricos said afterwards.

Nevertheless Mr. Perricos and other inspectors made clear today that they remained suspicious, pointing out that they have been misled continually by Baghdad over the last four months.

### More Inspections to Come

Another team will return to Baghdad later this summer to continue inspections. In particular, it will look at conventional high-explosive plants to see whether Iraq was trying to build a trigger for an atomic bomb.

Mr. Perricos said the United Nations inspectors would make a new report to the Security Council at the end of next week. The inspectors are preparing Iraq's "weapons-usable" nuclear equipment for destruction or removal under the terms of the Security Council's Persian Gulf war cease-fire resolution.

Today's declaration and the new Security Council report that will be based on it are likely to persuade President Bush to suspend his recent threat to take military action if Iraq does not cooperate with United Nations plans for removing its dangerous nuclear equipment. United Nations officials here said.

Mr. Perricos said Iraq has not declared any new stocks of highly enriched uranium suitable for weapons beyond the roughly 90 pounds already declared to the International Atomic Energy Agency in Vienna and placed under safeguards to insure it is not used for military ends.

Iraq has said it managed secretly to produce about a pound of uranium that was not highly enriched and would not work in a bomb. An inspector said that on the basis of the machinery the team has seen, Iraq could not have produced any more highly enriched material than this.

Last week the United States rejected an earlier Iraqi declaration, in which Baghdad confessed to having a secret uranium enrichment program that might produce nuclear explosives, saying it was still inadequate and incomplete.

At that point, United Nations officials say, Dr. Jaafar met personally with the inspectors for the first time since they arrived and started providing them

## Suspicions still linger, despite a formal pledge.

with what one inspector described as "a deluge of information."

In earlier replies to the inspector's demand for an explanation of the secret enrichment program, United Nations officials say Iraq was evasive.

The Foreign Ministry argued at one point that Iraq was not required to report its enrichment activities to the international atomic energy group, although the inspectors said that as a signer of the Nuclear Nonproliferation Treaty it had such an obligation.

Iraq also maintained it need not report certain sensitive materials because it had only small quantities of them.

The United Nations inspectors asked for today's pledge on Wednesday, after deciding that Iraq finally appeared to be telling the truth about its secret nuclear activities.

The United Nations inspectors were informed of Iraq's clandestine enrichment program by the Special Commission in New York charged with removing Iraq's weapons of mass destruction, which gets its information from American and other Western intelligence agencies.

The inspectors' task therefore has been to force Iraq to declare this subterfuge by mounting challenge inspections of suspect plants and to persuade Baghdad to provide information that might lead inspectors to other secret plants.

Last April, Iraq said it had already declared all its nuclear activities and placed them under safeguards.

Then on July 7 it filed a second declaration at the urging of the United States, revealing the clandestine enrichment plants.

The main enrichment center, at Tarmia near Baghdad, contained about 30 machines called calutrons, which enrich uranium by the electromagnetic method. Inspectors say only 6 to 12 of these were operational when the allies bombed the plant during the gulf war. The plant was about six months from becoming operational.

Iraq then tried to hide the evidence by trucking the remains of the calutrons to various military camps and burying them. But the convoy was spotted by the inspectors, and the Security Council demanded an explanation from Baghdad which eventually produced the July 7 declaration.

In fact, United Nations officials say that when they bombed the Tarmia plant the allies thought it was a factory for building centrifuges, which are also used for enriching uranium.

But the inspectors discovered the truth after the war when they visited the site. The Iraqis then said they had abandoned centrifugal enrichment because it required many imported parts. They found they could manufacture calutrons themselves without arousing international suspicion.

Iraq had a second enrichment plant at Sharqat near the northern city of Mosul, which also used the electromagnetic method.

The inspectors were told that this was a backup for Tarmia and that Iraq did not intend to use it. The plant was about 18 months from becoming operational when it was destroyed by allied bombing.

14-11

# U.N. Says Iraq 'Tricked' Aid Mission

### By Trevor Rowe
Special to The Washington Post

UNITED NATIONS, July 18—Baghdad appears to have "tricked" a U.N.-led delegation looking into reports that the Iraqi army was harassing Shiite Muslims trapped in the marshes of southern Iraq, a U.N. official said here today..

The delegation, which was led by Prince Sadruddin Aga Khan, the U.N. secretary general's special representative for humanitarian affairs in the region, visited the Hammar region last week following reports that 40,000 to 100,000 Shiites, who had fled there after a failed uprising against Baghdad in March, had been surrounded by Iraqi forces.

But when the U.N. delegation arrived, the soldiers had apparently withdrawn, and press reports suggested they had been ordered to do so in an attempt to persuade the U.N. Security Council to ease trade sanctions. When the delegation departed, some U.N. personnel were left behind to distribute food to the Shiites. On July 16, Iraq told them to leave the area.

In a letter to Iraqi Foreign Minister Ahmed Hussein Khudayer dated July 15, a copy of which was obtained by The Washington Post, Sadruddin suggests that the Iraqis attempted to dupe the delegation.

"It was accordingly with a sense of deep concern and dismay that I learned from unimpeachable sources that as soon as our mission had left the area, and in particular on the 12th and 13th of July, a heavy military presence was redeployed to take up the same positions which had obviously been vacated mainly for the duration of our visit," the prince wrote.

"Furthermore, my United Nations staff, which had remained in Hammar together with United Nations Guards to assist the local authorities in distributing the contents of our convoy to those in need, were summarily requested to leave the area. They complied with these instructions but not before noting carefully that military checkpoints and gun emplacements had been reinstalled every 50 meters [54 yards] along the lakeside and that checkpoints had also been reinstated every 500 meters [546 yards] along the main road to Hammmar," the prince said.

In his letter, Sadruddin warns that the Iraqi actions "will constitute a further negative element" when the Security Council considers lifting sanctions.

The letter was dated the same day that the U.N. delegation headed by Sadruddin formally recommended to the United Nations that it ease its sanctions against Iraq because they were harming Iraqi civilians. It is unclear when Sadruddin learned that Iraq had apparently misled him about the deployment of troops.

"Your government's untimely action will certainly complicate our task and seriously hinder our efforts to help Iraq in resolving the difficulties addressed by my mission," the letter said.

At the moment, Sadruddin is pressing Baghdad for permission to open two humanitarian centers in southern Iraq to help the Shiite population. The prince is scheduled to address the U.N. sanctions committee on Monday in New York.

14-12

# U.N. Nuclear Body Cites Baghdad for Violations

By R. Jeffrey Smith
Washington Post Staff Writer

The International Atomic Energy Agency yesterday formally condemned Iraq for violating its agreement with the agency to declare and submit for inspection all of its nuclear research, in a move that supported the Bush administration's contentions about Iraq's efforts to build a nuclear weapon.

IAEA officials in Vienna, noting it was the first time that a state party to the Non-Proliferation Treaty has been cited for concealing efforts to develop nuclear weapons, said Iraq's behavior had raised new questions about the adequacy of existing international safeguards against weapons proliferation.

Baghdad, which recently amplified on its July 7 admission of the covert effort, has insisted that its program was for purely peaceful purposes and that it is now fully cooperating with the IAEA, a United Nations organization.

But senior U.S. officials said yesterday that, contrary to statements attributed to United Nations experts in Iraq, the government of Iraqi President Saddam Hussein was not fully cooperating in the disclosure of its nuclear activities and had not surrendered all of its stockpile of highly enriched uranium.

In Athens, President Bush told a news conference that the United States is "still turning up evidence that the Iraqi dictator is still trying to perfect some nuclear capability." Asked if U.N. inspectors quoted Wednesday in Western news reports from Baghdad were missing

See IRAQ, A16, Col. 3

something, he replied, "I'm sure they must have."

Officials at the State Department and the Pentagon also reiterated statements that Iraq is continuing to withhold information about its nuclear capabilities and equipment, taking a different view from U.N. inspectors quoted as saying Baghdad had recently "come clean."

The statements were made in response to a Reuter news agency report of statements by sources "close to" the U.N. inspection team.

Secretary of Defense Richard B. Cheney told the Associated Press in an interview yesterday that "there shouldn't be any doubt in . . . [Saddam's] mind that we're deadly serious about his coming into compliance" with U.N. Security Council resolutions demanding the elimination of Iraq's bomb-building capability.

"We obviously always have the ultimate sanction of military capability if we're called upon to use it," Cheney said, noting that the United States still has "significant capabilities" in the region, including Marine amphibious units, two aircraft carriers and an allied strike force in Turkey.

IAEA director general Hans Blix, speaking after the agency's board of governors adopted the Iraqi censure, said he believed Baghdad no longer had the capacity to produce enriched uranium for an atomic bomb, but reserved judgment as to whether Iraq had now declared all of its nuclear facilities, special correspondent Michael Z. Wise reported from Vienna.

"Iraq has not fully disclosed its uranium enrichment and nuclear weapons capabilities," U.S. Ambassador to the United Nations Thomas Pickering told a hearing of the House Foreign Affairs subcommittee on the Middle East. He said Iraq still falsely insists that a key uranium enrichment facility "is a plant with a peaceful purpose."

Pickering also criticized Iraq for failing to allow U.N. inspectors to use air transport for rapid inspections outside the Baghdad area.

14-13

Several U.S. officials also challenged the quoted assertion of U.N. team members in Iraq that allied bombing raids had destroyed Iraqi key uranium enrichment equipment before it had produced a significant quantity of the bomb ingredient. The claim was published in yesterday's editions of the New York Times.

U.N. officials in New York responded to the controversy with a statement that the team's official reporting made clear that "there is much work to be done before any conclusions can be reached about whether or not more equipment or material remain to be turned over" to the agency. "Only further inspections can establish the extent of the activities with regard to enrichment," because of a lack of confidence in Iraq's claims, the statement said.

One U.S. government analyst said the U.N. team had put an "optimistic blush" on Iraq's activity and was "treating Saddam like he's innocent until being proven guilty." The analyst said Washington still believes that a significant uranium stockpile was probably made and hidden by the Iraqis, and that it would need much more information to become convinced otherwise.

Pickering said that "the technical judgments . . . are not fully in yet" about how sizable the Iraqi stockpile is. Other officials have cited a preliminary intelligence community estimate that the stockpile is large enough for at least one nuclear weapon, or roughly 15 to 25 pounds, while Iraq has admitted making only one pound.

Pentagon spokesman Rick Oborn said that "we know of other sites" involved in uranium enrichment activities besides those at the Tuwaitha and Tarmaiya facilities, which were partially bombed by allied forces during the Persian Gulf War, but he declined to provide details. U.S. and diplomatic sources have said further U.N. inspection of nuclear sites in Iraq is expected next week.

The Iraqi violations highlighted the need to improve the existing system to thwart the proliferation of atomic weapons, IAEA director general Blix said. He called for member states to grant the IAEA the right to inspect suspected nuclear sites not openly declared by member states and suggested that intelligence agencies of these states might provide information on their whereabouts directly to the agency.

Blix said that "we did not find the replies made by the [Iraqi] foreign minister persuasive" after the evidence of covert activities first surfaced. Iraq told the agency that there was no legal need to divulge all of its nuclear installations and that Baghdad had "sound reasons related to its national security" for keeping some information secret.

According to Blix, Iraq maintained a huge facility at Tarmaiya, designed to house 90 electromagnetic isotope separators. Eight of these began operation in September 1990. Iraq originally described this facility as a factory for the production of transformers, but Blix said scientists there were able to produce a pound of uranium enriched to the rate of four percent.

This is a relatively low level of enrichment since a rate exceeding 90 percent is required to make a bomb. Blix said the agency had not turned up evidence that Iraq produced more than this amount and dismissed as speculation reports, based on statements by an Iraqi defector, that Iraq had enriched about 88 pounds of uranium up to weapons-grade levels.

He said that "on the basis of what we have seen and inspected . . . there is no longer any capacity to produce enriched uranium."

Under a safeguards agreement between Iraq and the IAEA that took effect in 1972, Baghdad agreed to open its declared nuclear facilities to twice yearly inspections. The agency is preparing a long-term plan for intensive monitoring of Iraqi nuclear capacity. The IAEA hopes to begin removing nuclear material from Iraq in September and send it to reprocessing firms in Britain and France.

*Staff writer John Yang in Athens and special correspondent Trevor Rowe at the United Nations contributed to this report.*

14-14

0242

# 외 무 부

종 별 :

번 호 : UNW-1872

일 시 : 91 0719 1900

수 신 : 장 관(중동일,국연) 사본:노창희대사

발 신 : 주 유엔 대사대리

제 목 : 대이락 무기류 공급금지

연: UNW-1470,1566

1. 유엔사무총장은 연호 안보리 결의 (700 호) 에 의거 아국의 표제관련 조치내용을 유엔측에 봉보하여 줄것을 별첨 서한으로 요청하여왔음. (봉보기한:8.1.)

2. 유엔측에 봉보할 문안 (영문)을 주국련 20313-574 (91.7.18)을 참고, 회시바람.

첨부:상기 사무총장 서한: UNW(F)-341

끝

(대사대리 신기복-국장)

중아국      1차보      국기국      국기국      외정실      분석관      안기부

PAGE 1

91.07.20      09:01 WG

외신 1과 통제관

0243

·UNITED NATIONS·  NATIONS UNIES

POSTAL ADDRESS—ADRESSE POSTALE: UNITED NATIONS. N.Y. 10017
·CABLE ADDRESS—ADRESSE TELEGRAPHIQUE: UNATIONS NEWYORK

REFERENCE: SCPC/7/91(4-1)

*UNW(F)-341  10719  1900*
*( 중동부. 국연 )*
*총 2 매*

The Secretary-General of the United Nations presents his
compliments to the Permanent Observer of the Republic of Korea to
the United Nations and has the honour to refer to resolution
700 (1991), adopted by the Security Council at its 2994th meeting,
on 17 June 1991, in connection with its consideration of the item
entitled "The situation between Iraq and Kuwait", a copy of which is
attached.

The Secretary-General wishes, in particular, to draw attention
to paragraphs 2, 3, 4 and 5 of resolution 700 (1991), which read as
follows:

"The Security Council,

...

"Acting under Chapter VII of the Charter of the United
Nations,

...

"2. Approves the Guidelines to Facilitate Full
International Implementation of paragraphs 24, 25 and 27 of
Security Council resolution 687 (1991), annexed to the report
of the Secretary-General (S/22660);

"3. Reiterates its call upon all States and international
organizations to act in a manner consistent with the Guidelines;

"4. Requests all States, in accordance with paragraph 8
of the Guidelines, to report to the Secretary-General within
45 days on the measures they have instituted for meeting the
obligations set out in paragraph 24 of resolution 687 (1991);

"5. Entrusts the Committee established under resolution
661 (1990) concerning the situation between Iraq and Kuwait
with the responsibility, under the Guidelines, for monitoring
the prohibitions against the sale or supply of arms to Iraq
and related sanctions established in paragraph 24 of resolution
687 (1991)".

*# UNW-1872*
*첨부함*

Annexes enclosed

*2 -1*

0244

# UNITED NATIONS  NATIONS UNIES

-2-

In pursuance of paragraph 4 of resolution 700 (1991), the Secretary-General would appreciate receiving as early as possible, but no later than 1 August 1991, information on the measures instituted by His/Her Excellency's Government, in accordance with paragraph 8 of the Guidelines, the text of which is annexed to the enclosed report of the Secretary-General pursuant to paragraph 26 of Security Council resolution 687 (1991) (S/22660), for meeting the obligations set out in paragraph 24 of resolution 687 (1991).

3 July 1991

S. B.

2 - 2

0245

**General Assembly · Security Council**

Distr.
GENERAL

A/45/1037
S/22812
19 July 1991

ORIGINAL: ENGLISH

GENERAL ASSEMBLY
Forty-fifth session
Agenda item 153
IRAQI AGGRESSION AND THE CONTINUED OCCUPATION
  OF KUWAIT IN FLAGRANT VIOLATION OF THE
  CHARTER OF THE UNITED NATIONS

SECURITY COUNCIL
Forty-sixth year

### Note by the Secretary-General

The Secretary-General has the honour to transmit to the members of the General Assembly and of the Security Council a letter dated 19 July 1991 addressed to him by the Director-General of the International Atomic Energy Agency concerning the resolution adopted on 18 July 1991 by the Board of Governors of the Agency entitled "Iraq's non-compliance with its safeguards obligations" (see annex).

91-23434   2515e (E)

/...

0246

ANNEX

### Letter dated 19 July 1991 from the Director-General of the International Atomic Energy Agency addressed to the Secretary-General

At its meeting on 18 July 1991 the Board of Governors of the International Atomic Energy Agency found that the Government of Iraq had not complied with its obligations under its safeguards agreement with the Agency. The resolution of the Board, adopted by 29 votes to 1, with 3 abstentions, is attached (see appendix).

Article XII.C of the Agency's Statute and Article III.2 of the Agreement Governing the Relationship Agreement between the United Nations and the International Atomic Energy Agency require the Board to report non-compliance with safeguards obligations to the Security Council and General Assembly of the United Nations. I would, therefore, appreciate it if you could bring the Board's finding to the urgent attention of the Security Council and of the General Assembly. A copy of the records of the Board's meeting will be sent to you as soon as they are available.

In accordance with Article VII of the Relationship Agreement, I am at the disposal of the Security Council should the Council so desire.

(Signed)  Hans BLIX
Director-General

0247

/...

APPENDIX

Iraq's non-compliance with its safeguards obligations

Resolution adopted by the Board of Governors of the
International Atomic Energy Agency on 18 July 1991

The Board of Governors,

(a) Stressing the importance of non-proliferation of nuclear weapons to international and regional peace and security,

(b) Expressing grave concern about the conclusion of the report of the Director-General (GOV/2530) that the Government of Iraq has failed to comply with its obligations under its safeguards agreement with the International Atomic Energy Agency (INFCIRC/172),

(c) Recalling United Nations Security Council resolution 687 (1991), which, inter alia, called upon Iraq to declare all its nuclear activities to the International Atomic Energy Agency,

(d) Noting with appreciation the efforts of the Director-General and his staff to implement the tasks assigned to the Agency by that resolution, and the diligent and effective conduct of the Agency's inspections of Iraqi nuclear activities,

(e) Expressing grave concern about the evident deception and obstruction of the International Atomic Energy Agency inspectors in their efforts to carry out the Security Council's mandate in resolution 687 (1991) in violation of that resolution and the undertakings by Iraq governing the status, privileges and immunities of the Agency and the inspection teams mandated under Security Council resolution 687 (1991),

1.   Finds, on the basis of the report of the Director-General in GOV/2530, that the Government of Iraq has not complied with its obligations under its safeguards agreement with the Agency (INFCIRC/172);

2.   Condemns this non-compliance by the Government of Iraq with its safeguards agreement;

3.   Calls upon the Government of Iraq to remedy this non-compliance forthwith, including placing any and all additional source and special fissionable material within Iraq's territory, under its jurisdiction or its control, regardless of quantity or location, under Agency safeguards in accordance with the relevant provisions of INFCIRC/172 and in accordance with relevant technical determinations of the Agency;

0248

/...

4. _Decides_, in accordance with Article XII.C of the Statute, to report this non-compliance to all members of the Agency and to the Security Council and General Assembly of the United Nations;

5. _Calls upon_ Iraq to cease all obstruction or interference with the International Atomic Energy Agency inspection teams in their efforts to implement Security Council resolution 687 (1991);

6. _Requests_ the Director-General to keep the Board and the General Conference informed of progress in the implementation of this resolution so that they may consider appropriate action in accordance with Article XII.C and XIX.B of the Statute in the event of the Government of Iraq's failing to take fully corrective action;

7. _Decides_ to inscribe an item entitled "Iraq's non-compliance with its safeguards obligations" on the agenda of the September Board of Governors and requests the Director-General to include such an item in the provisional agenda for the thirty-fifth regular session of the General Conference.

-----

0249

외 무 부

종 별 :

번 호 : UNW-1876          일 시 : 91 0722 1800

수 신 : 장관(국연,중동일,기정)

발 신 : 주유엔대사

제 목 : 걸프사태(유엔동향)

연: UNW-1835,1869

1. 안보리 제재위 동향

가.동 제재위는 금 7.22 회의를 갖고 SADRUDDIN AGAKHAN 대표로 부터 연호 이락의 인도적 수요실태 보고를 청취하였음.(동 보고요지는 당관에서 입수한 별첨자료참조바람.)

나.동 대표가 이락민의 긴급수요품목 수입을 위한 재원조달 방법으로서 이락산 석유 수출허용 또는 이락해외자산 동결해제 문제를 제기한것과 관련, 금일회의시미, 영국등은 본건의 실제적 시행에 따르는 제반통제 및 감시방안에 관심을 보인것으로 알려짐.

다.본건토의를 위해 제재위는 7.24 다시 회의소집 예정이며, 동회의에 앞서 제재위 의장(오지리)이 이사국들과 개별협의를 가질것 이라고함.

2.이락 핵사찰

가. IAEA 측은 지난주 핵사찰반 제3진이 임무를 종료하고 귀환함에 따라 금주중제4진을 이락에 파견 예정이라고함.(제3진 임무종료에 즈음한 IAEA측 발표내용 별첨)

나. IAEA 이사회는 이락의 핵안전협정 불이행을 규탄하는 결의를 ⑦.18채택한바, 동 내용이 7.19 자 총회및 안보리 문서로 배포됨.( A/45/1037,S/22812)

3.북부 이락사태

가.지난주 북이락 SULAYMANIYAH 에서 발생한 이락군 및 쿠르드족간 유혈충돌사태와 관련 SADRUDDIN AGA KHAN 대표는 양측의 자제를 촉구한것으로 알려짐.

나.한편,금일 안보리 제재위에서 동 대표는 여사한 사태가 신뢰분위기를 저해할것을 우려하였으며,남부지역에 이락군이 재투입되고 있는데 대해서도 유감을

국기국    차관    1차보    중아국    외정실    분석관    정와대    안기부

PAGE 1                                   91.07.23    08:01 ED

외신 1과 통제관

0250

표시하였음.

    첨부:1. KHAN 대표 보고요지,

    2. 핵사찰관련, IAEA측 안보리문서및 발표내용,

    ). NYT 지 W.SAFIRE칼럼기사: UNW(F)-345

    끝

    (대사 노창희-국장)

UNW(F)-345  10722  6
(국연 중동원. 기정)  총 9 대

UNW-1876

# Talking points for presentation to Sanctions Committee of report of mission to assess humanitarian needs in Iraq led by the Executive Delegate of the Secretary General

New York, 22 July 1991

Excellencies, distinguished members of the Sanctions Committee,

The decision to undertake a "high-level mission to assess Iraq's humanitarian needs" was taken at the meeting of Executive Heads of UN Specialized Agencies and Programmes responsible for the humanitarian programme in the region, held in Geneva on 13 July under the chairmanship of the Secretary-General. The mission's mandate was - I quote -- "to conduct an updated and more precise assessment of the current humanitarian needs and recommend measures to address them". The mission had, as such, no precise remit to deal with the issue of sanctions nor to report specifically to the Security Council: I am, however, most grateful for this opportunity to speak to the distinguished members of this Committee today and to review with you some of our findings and conclusions.

In the opening pages of the report, I have had occasion to express my thanks to the members of the mission and my particular appreciation to those expert participants from outside the United Nations - whom I might term the "Friends of the Executive Delegate". I am very happy, in this context, that Sir John Moberly has been able to join us today. I am also very pleased that the United Nations experts designated as "team leaders" for the four key sectors - Water and Sanitation, Health, Food Supply and Energy - are with us here: they are, respectively, Charles Lamuniere of UNICEF, Daniel Tarantola of WHO, Rodolphe Joseph of FAO and Edwin Moore formerly of the World Bank. In addition, Thierry Brun, who worked with us as a consultant for UNICEF, will be able to discuss with you any questions you might have on nutrition issues.

This was a "field-based" mission. The various teams looking into the four main sectors under consideration visited the length and breadth of the country during the course of their evaluation:

-   The food sector team conducted market surveys in 16 out of the 18 Governorates, covering most provincial capitals and accounting for some 95% of the national food crop production;

-   The water and sanitation team undertook extensive visits to the Governorates of Kut, Amarah, Basrah, Erbil and Dohuk, reviewing the situation with local authorities, plant operators and the local population. They inspected treatment plants and met with Ministry of Health, and Water authorities, in Baghdad;

#UNW-1876#
청우맞

9-1

- The health team visited paediatric wards and heath centres in 5 Governorates in the south and 6 in the north. They had extensive discussions with medical, surgical, and nursing staff;

- The energy sector team carried out assessments from Basrah in the south to Mosul in the north, visiting 15 power generating plants and many transmission sub-stations.

Mission members met with Iraqi officials at all levels, as well as reviewing current conditions with the local population in all regions. They met with the Ministers from all the areas under consideration - as well as with the Minister of Defense - and with their technical aides. The discussions culminated in a high level inter-ministerial meeting, chaired by the Minister of State for Foreign Affairs and attended by all the relevant Ministers, including the Ministers of Health, Trade, Food and Oil. Various members of the mission also had extensive talks with the Deputy Prime Minister, Mr. Tariq Aziz.

The outcome of these activities is contained in the report which the Secretary-General has submitted to you. And as I indicated above, my colleagues will be very glad to discuss with you their various findings in the different sectors. Whatever the details of the assessment however, the basic facts of the situation we have to deal with are the following:

- There is a clear and undeniable humanitarian need in Iraq;

- It is absurd and indefensible for the United Nations to pay for these needs when numerous other urgent crises and disasters, from Bangladesh to the Horn of Africa, cry out for our attention;

- Iraq has considerable oil reserves and should pay to meet these needs itself;

- If this committee were to decide that Iraq should be allowed to use funds from oil sales or facilitate the use of blocked accounts to meet "Essential civilian needs", a suitable control mechanism and monitoring system should be identified and put in place.

In the report, the mission members have put forward certain ideas and suggestions for an approach to this problem which - if the Sanctions Committee were to decide that if Iraq's funds might be used to meet the needs identified - would help (and I quote) "to assure the actual receipt of the civilian goods in Iraq and their utilisation by the intended beneficiaries".

9-2

It is evident that this central paradox - namely that it is completely unacceptable for the United Nations humanitarian agencies and the donor community to fund Iraq's needs in competition for finite resources with cases of destitution and desperation elsewhere - must be resolved. As I have already intimated, and as we stated clearly in the report, it was not our mandate to specify the details of the mechanisms required. Moreover, the timing of our mission coincided with many other developments affecting Iraq and its relations with the international community.

Our visit, however, was unrelated to the concerns of other ongoing special United Nations missions to Iraq. We did not intend to make determinations within the purview of the Security Council and more particularly of this Committee. At this stage, I would not wish to propose more precise formulae concerning such matters as the possible sale of oil, and the unfreezing of blocked assets, the purchasing system comprising commodities to be imported, the procurement process and monitoring and control, as well as monitoring within Iraq.

We might exchange ideas on such matters should that be the wish of the Sanctions Committee. On the last point, my colleagues from the United Nations specialised agencies and programmes might have views on their organizations' capabilities in reviewing the ongoing situation in Iraq in their specific areas of confidence. They may have suggestions in such fields as nutritional surveillance, public health assessments, checks of market prices and the like. A significant United Nations presence in Iraq may be able to make a contribution in this regard. But I would not wish to preempt the discussion nor predict the distinguished Committee members' reaction to the report's finding and conclusions. These matters are of course primarily for you to decide. I might add here, however, my conviction that it was not the Secretary-General's intention to create an Office of the Executive Delegate on a permanent basis: our role, as I see it, is to serve as "trouble shooters" and as a catalyst, certainly not to build institutions.

Given the solid and thorough work done by our teams, I do not believe we are crying wolf. It is entirely true, however, that vigilance remains our watchword in this operation. The situation in the North and the South continues to be critical. Recent events concerning the Kurdish population in the North have threatened to undermine that climate of confidence so necessary at this delicate juncture.

9-3

As for the South, during my stay in Baghdad, in order to assure the provision of humanitarian assistance to displaced people in the area of the southern marshlands where we had identified a particularly urgent need, mission members and I travelled on 11 July to Nasariya and to villages along the edge of the marshes in that region. We arranged for a United Nations convoy carrying supplies from WFP, UNICEF and UNHCR to meet up with us in the village of Hammar, where we established that the difficult situation in which those displaced found themselves could be eased by UN humanitarian assistance. We noted the apparent suspension of military activities and that this had provided an opportunity which had apparently been seized by a number of those displaced to return to their homes. Unfortunately, in subsequent days we have received reliable reports indicating a renewed increase in the military presence in the area. Furthermore, we have not yet received the authorization urgently requested to establish an UNHUC (United Nations Humanitarian Centre), with a complement of United Nations Guards, from where we can be assured of access to the displaced population in the marshes.

The guards have assumed numerous duties as agreed with the Iraqi government in the MOU, including the protection of UN personnel and premises. They have further provided escorts for convoys of food, medicine, general relief supplies, as well as for UN repatriation convoys. They have patrolled routes of returnees, towns, and generally all areas of UN humanitarian assistance operations. We have received numerous reports describing exemplary conduct of the guards under the most difficult conditions.

I hardly need to remind the members of this Committee that we are not facing an easy situation. There are numerous issues over which members will no doubt wish to express their misgivings and many questions must indeed be answered to the satisfaction of the international community. But since I have been assigned responsibility for the humanitarian programme in Iraq and the region, it is my duty to caution that because there is an element – however justifiable – of distrust, the Iraqi civilian population and particularly the vulnerable groups, will be the first to suffer.

9-4

## ANNEX

### Letter dated 19 July 1991 from the Director-General of the International Atomic Energy Agency addressed to the Secretary-General

At its meeting on 18 July 1991 the Board of Governors of the International Atomic Energy Agency found that the Government of Iraq had not complied with its obligations under its safeguards agreement with the Agency. The resolution of the Board, adopted by 29 votes to 1, with 3 abstentions, is attached (see appendix).

Article XII.C of the Agency's Statute and Article III.2 of the Agreement Governing the Relationship Agreement between the United Nations and the International Atomic Energy Agency require the Board to report non-compliance with safeguards obligations to the Security Council and General Assembly of the United Nations.  I would, therefore, appreciate it if you could bring the Board's finding to the urgent attention of the Security Council and of the General Assembly.  A copy of the records of the Board's meeting will be sent to you as soon as they are available.

In accordance with Article VII of the Relationship Agreement, I am at the disposal of the Security Council should the Council so desire.

(Signed)  Hans BLIX
Director-General

9-5

/...

APPENDIX

Iraq's non-compliance with its safeguards obligations

Resolution adopted by the Board of Governors of the
International Atomic Energy Agency on 18 July 1991

The Board of Governors,

(a)  Stressing the importance of non-proliferation of nuclear weapons to international and regional peace and security,

(b)  Expressing grave concern about the conclusion of the report of the Director-General (GOV/2530) that the Government of Iraq has failed to comply with its obligations under its safeguards agreement with the International Atomic Energy Agency (INFCIRC/172),

(c)  Recalling United Nations Security Council resolution 687 (1991), which, inter alia, called upon Iraq to declare all its nuclear activities to the International Atomic Energy Agency,

(d)  Noting with appreciation the efforts of the Director-General and his staff to implement the tasks assigned to the Agency by that resolution, and the diligent and effective conduct of the Agency's inspections of Iraqi nuclear activities,

(e)  Expressing grave concern about the evident deception and obstruction of the International Atomic Energy Agency inspectors in their efforts to carry out the Security Council's mandate in resolution 687 (1991) in violation of that resolution and the undertakings by Iraq governing the status, privileges and immunities of the Agency and the inspection teams mandated under Security Council resolution 687 (1991),

1.  Finds, on the basis of the report of the Director-General in GOV/2530, that the Government of Iraq has not complied with its obligations under its safeguards agreement with the Agency (INFCIRC/172);

2.  Condemns this non-compliance by the Government of Iraq with its safeguards agreement;

3.  Calls upon the Government of Iraq to remedy this non-compliance forthwith, including placing any and all additional source and special fissionable material within Iraq's territory, under its jurisdiction or its control, regardless of quantity or location, under Agency safeguards in accordance with the relevant provisions of INFCIRC/172 and in accordance with relevant technical determinations of the Agency;

9—6

/...

4.  **Decides**, in accordance with Article XII.C of the Statute, to report this non-compliance to all members of the Agency and to the Security Council and General Assembly of the United Nations;

5.  **Calls upon** Iraq to cease all obstruction or interference with the International Atomic Energy Agency inspection teams in their efforts to implement Security Council resolution 687 (1991);

6.  **Requests** the Director-General to keep the Board and the General Conference informed of progress in the implementation of this resolution so that they may consider appropriate action in accordance with Article XII.C and XIX.B of the Statute in the event of the Government of Iraq's failing to take fully corrective action;

7.  **Decides** to inscribe an item entitled "Iraq's non-compliance with its safeguards obligations" on the agenda of the September Board of Governors and requests the Director-General to include such an item in the provisional agenda for the thirty-fifth regular session of the General Conference.

-----

9-7

# IAEA

**INTERNATIONAL ATOMIC ENERGY AGENCY**
WAGRAMERSTRASSE 5, P.O. BOX 100, A-1400 VIENNA, AUSTRIA.
TELEPHONE: 1 2360, TELEX: 1-12645, CABLE: INATOM VIENNA.
TELEFAX: 431 234564

2 July 1991
PR 91/25
FOR IMMEDIATE RELEASE

1991-07-22   765287

**PRESS RELEASE** FOR USE OF INFORMATION MEDIA · NOT AN OFFICIAL RECORD

## COMPLETION OF THIRD IAEA INSPECTION

## UNDER UN SECURITY COUNCIL RESOLUTION 687

A team of experts from the International Atomic Energy Agency (IAEA) supported and assisted by experts provided by the Special Commission established by UN Security Council Resolution 687 has now returned from Iraq and is preparing its report for submission to the Security Council, through the Secretary-General of the United Nations. This mission – the third IAEA inspection mission under resolution 687 to Iraq – contained the inspection of Iraq's nuclear capabilities begun in May.

The mission was able to inspect and place under Agency seals a considerable amount of nuclear material and a number of equipment items related to the newly disclosed Iraqi uranium enrichment programme. While the team was able to obtain substantial information regarding this extensive programme, much work and analysis nevertheless remains before any conclusion can be made as to the full extent, scope and capabilities of the Iraqi programme and as to the completeness of the Iraqi declarations to date. New material was made available by Iraq to the inspection team as late as its last inspection day in Iraq on 18 July.

A considerable inspection effort thus remains ahead of the IAEA before the full picture of the Iraqi nuclear efforts can be drawn with confidence.

A fourth inspection team is ready to leave Vienna soon.

* * * * *

9-8

WILLIAM SAFIRE

# Saddam's Deadline

WASHINGTON

George Bush has given Saddam Hussein until Thursday of this week to "come clean" on his possession of, and capacity to produce, weapons of mass destruction, as agreed in the premature suspension of hostilities that preserved his army.

As we approach July 25, two possibilities exist, as Jacobovsky told the Colonel: Either Iraq will make public every device for the production of nuclear material, poison gas, germ weapons and rockets for their delivery — or Iraq will release just enough data to discourage the U.S., Britain and France from carrying out their U.N.-sanctioned option to use force.

If Mr. Hussein startles the world by revealing all, thereby ending his threat, fine; but if he does not — if he retains just enough secret nuclear material to level Tel Aviv or enough bacteria to be able one day to threaten a Saddam Plague in New York or Paris — there are again two possibilities:

Either President Bush will profess to see a good start in the partial disclosure and will vitiate his credibility by pushing the deadline back — or he will do what he has done with his past air-war and land-war deadlines to the Iraqi dictator: strike hard at Baghdad's potential for mass destruction.

If he flinches, or temporizes by explaining he doesn't yet know where

## Will Bush strike again?

to bomb, Mr. Bush will lose the war of nerviness and a Democratic opponent may emerge at last pledging to "finish the job"; but if the President remains consistent and carries out his threat to bomb, there are two possibilities:

Either he tries "surgical strikes" at a few targets, which would make a punishing point but not remove Saddam Hussein's potential for massive vengeance — or he could resume the systematic aerial destruction of the Republican Guard, source of the dictator's power, with its 700 gunships and 3,000 tanks and 50,000 civilian-killers.

Enough of the Jacobovsky logic. Ever since the wrong turning of March 26, when Mr. Bush decided a Sunni minority's military dictator-

ship would be better than a Sunni-Kurdish-Shiite sharing of power — and was assured that such a transition to Saddam II was in the works — U.S. policy has been rolling down the wrong track.

With absolute candor, Mr. Bush has made it known that he wants a military junta to oust Mr. Hussein and continue "stable" Sunni domination of the other three-fourths of Iraqis. Publicly, repeatedly, he has promised an end to sanctions only if the Iraqi Army replaced Saddam I with another member of its brutal leadership clique.

To that too-personalized end, he has spent three months trying to get another Sunni strongman to stage a coup. The C.I.A. has labored mightily to bring this about, to no avail. The pressure of economic sanctions did not induce Saddam Hussein to leave Kuwait and it will not induce his generals to overthrow him, because the hardship is inflicted only on the Iraqi people, not on them.

Now Mr. Bush is at last awake to the reality in Baghdad. If he dithers with a year of sanctions, letting U.N. inspectors dicker with Iraqis about inspections, Saddam Hussein will create a weapon capable of being smuggled into two or three major cities and can then blackmail the world.

Alarmist? The man who set fire to Kuwait and poison-gassed the Kurds and insanely called destruction down on half his army would not hesitate to imperil millions of Westerners, even if his moment of vengeance triggered the obliteration of his own country.

That is why the coalition's hard core (Bush, Major, Mitterrand) must consider the use of major force soon. Targeting suspected nuclear and germ sites misses both the weaponry and the point: only the targeting of the Republican Guard and its bases and equipment for extended pounding will induce the directly threatened elite to conspire to kill their Caesar.

Eyes have at last been opened to Saddam Hussein's superpower equalizer; last year's "5 to 10 years away" complacency has been stripped from our confounded analysts.

Mr. Bush's eyes remain to be opened, however, to the folly of replacing Saddam I with Saddam II. The U.S. should be encouraging power-sharing leading to democracy, not a new face at the helm of the same dictatorship. If we put in "our" strongman, he will soon seek to surpass his predecessor.

That will bring up two possibilities . . .   ◻

9-9

美, "이라크, 유엔의 최종시한 불응"

(워싱턴 로이터=聯合) 이라크는 25일까지 자국 핵능력을 완전 개방할 것을 요구한 유엔의 최종시한에 불응했다고 美백악관이 밝혔다.

로먼 포파뒤크 백악관 대변인은 이날 기자들에게 사담 후세인 이라크 대통령이 "필요한 정보를 제출하지 않았다"고 말하면서 이같이 밝혔다.

그는 이 최종시한이 군사적 보복 위협을 수반한 것은 아니었다고 강조하고 "25일로 정한 이 최종시한은 사담 후세인 이라크 대통령 정부가 앞서 유엔이 결의한 요구조건들을 충실히 이행하고 있느냐를 유엔이 판단할 수 있는 기준이 된다는 측면에서 중요한 것"이라고 말했다.

그러나 그는 美國이 후세인으로 하여금 이같은 최종시한을 무시하게 하도록 하려는 의도는 결코 없었다고 강조하면서 美國이 그동안 후세인에게 유엔 결의를 완전히 준수해야 할 것임을 분명히 해왔기 때문에 후세인의 이번 유엔 결의 무시는 불행한 일이라고 덧붙였다.

그는 이어 군사적 공격이 뒤따를 가능성이 있느냐는 기자들의 질문에 "나는 그 가능성을 결코 배제하지 않는다"고 전제하면서도 "7월 25일 오늘은 군사적 행동을 취하는 최종시한이 아니라는 점을 여러분들에게 지적하고 싶다"며 "그러나 나는 미래의 어떤 계획이나 행동들을 가정하지 않겠다"고 답변했다.

그는 이와함께 후세인 대통령이 핵관련 장비들을 은폐하는 "포탄 게임"을 벌이고 있다고 비난하면서 후세인에게 유엔 조사단의 요청에 응해줄 것을 강력히 촉구했다.(끝)

(YONHAP) 910726 0119 KST

8

0261

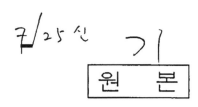

# 외 무 부

종 별 :

번 호 : UNW-1924        일 시 : 91 0725 2015

수 신 : 장 관(국연,국기,중동일)

발 신 : 주 유엔 대사

제 목 : 이락 핵사찰

연: UNW-1876

1. IAEA 이사회가 지난 7.18. 이락핵안전 협정불 이행을 규탄하는 연호 결의를 채택한것과 관련 A.HUSSEIN 이락외상은 7.23자 유엔사무총장앞 서한에서 동 결의가 불공평하고 균형을 잃은 조치이며, 이락에 대한 군사행동 재개를 전문기구 (IAEA) 를 통해 합법화해 보려는 저의에서 나온것이라고 주장하였음.

2. 상기 서한에서 이락츠이 제기한 IAEA 결의 관련 항의 요지는 다음과같음

가. 핵안전협정 34조 B.C 항 (사찰범위) 및 19조 (시정조치) 에 대한 해석상의 이견, 유사한 사례와의 균형문제

나. 핵사찰반 최종보고서가 제출되기도 전에 IAEA이사회에서 본건 처리

다. 핵사찰관련 이락측의 협조 사실 및 현지사찰반 평가 왜곡

3. 동 서한은 안보리문서로 곧 배포예정인바, 당관에서 입수한 동서한 내용을 별첨 송부함.

첨부:상기 이락측 서한: UNW(F)-356

끝

(대사노창희-국장)

---

국기국    1차보    중아국    국기국    외정실    분석관    안기부

외신 1과 통제관

0262

Sir,

We have examined the resolution of the Board of Governors of the
International Atomic Energy Agency, adopted on 18 July 1991 on the basis of
the report of the Director-General of the Agency (document GOV/2530).

We should like to set out our official position on the aforementioned
resolution, as follows:

1.   We have carefully studied the contents of this document and find that it
takes as its fundamental premise article 34, paragraphs (b) and (c), of the
safeguards agreement concluded between Iraq and the Agency (INFCIRC/172).

We have already expressed our views with respect to these two paragraphs
of article 34 in our two letters to the Director-General of the International
Atomic Energy Agency dated 10 and 12 July 1991.  Whereas the Agency could have
considered our point of view and taken some time to reach a joint
understanding with us of the sense of this article, the Director-General
instead hastened to pronounce judgements against Iraq on the grounds that it
had not provided the Agency with information on certain nuclear materials.
The Director-General did not, however, bear in mind the following points:

(a)  Iraq did in fact officially provide information on the nuclear
materials to the Agency, as set out in our letter of 7 July 1991.

(b)  The said materials were subjected to inspection by the third
international team, which left Iraq on 19 July 1991:  that information is now
in the Agency's possession.

Accordingly, it was entirely possible for the Director-General of the
Agency to treat those developments as constituting a corrective measure in
accordance with article 19 of the agreement, to be dealt with in the same way
as previous similar cases addressed by the Agency.  We should like to draw
attention to a similar case, as mentioned in the 1984 report on safeguards
implementation (document GOV/2201), which referred to the export by Luxembourg

of 41 tons of enriched uranium to Israel.  Or are we not entitled to inquire
why the 11,000 tons of enriched uranium produced each year at power stations
which are not subject to the Agency's safeguard system do not attract the same
attention as do the tiny quantities of yellow cake and uranium compounds
present in Iraq?

3 - 1

It is our belief that the submission to the Board of Governors of the International Atomic Energy Agency did not conform to the criteria applied by the Agency in previous cases, nor did it have adequate legal justification.

2.    We were not expecting such a meeting to be convened before the Agency's inspection teams had finished their last round of inspections and submitted their final report and conclusions, in accordance with the provisions of article XII.C of the Agency's Statute.  We believe that the results of the teams' work are of direct relevance to the discussion of an item of this nature, and we also believe that it is improper to take results of the teams' work in isolation, without awaiting the amalgamation of all such results and the drawing of overall conclusions.

3.    In adopting its resolution, including preambular paragraph (d) and operative paragraph 5, the Board of Governors chose entirely to ignore the following truths and facts:

(a)  Iraq has so far been visited by three nuclear inspection teams and three teams with responsibilities in other fields.  They all received full cooperation from Iraq, except for one team which encountered some confusion. This we have already explained to the President of the Security Council and to the high-level mission which visited Iraq and of which the Director-General of the International Atomic Energy Agency was a member.  Iraqi officials at the highest levels gave firm assurances of Iraq's absolute willingness to provide every facility to all teams and to cooperate with them in the performance of their duties.

(b)  The high-level mission submitted its report to the Security Council and clearly mentioned the assurances provided by Iraqi officials.  It noted that the teams' future visits would demonstrate the extent of Iraq's cooperation.

It would have been more appropriate if the Director-General of the International Atomic Energy Agency - as a member of the high-level mission - had explained this to the Board of Governors and if the Board had postponed the inclusion in its resolution of preambular paragraph (d) and operative paragraph 5 until such time as at least one of the inspection teams had completed its work subsequent to Iraq's explanation of the reasons for the confusion which had occurred with the second inspection team and to the expression of Iraq's clear and confirmed commitments.

3 - 2

(c)  The Board of Governors of the International Atomic Energy Agency
held its meeting concerning the resolution on 18 July 19__ i.e. the last day
of the third inspection team's stay in Iraq.  The leader of the team and all
its members expressed their great satisfaction with the full cooperation shown
by Iraq, yet the Board of Governors did not take this into account and adopted
its resolution before examining the team's report.  Does this not give rise to
some questions?

We are confronted with an incomprehensible situation.  While Iraqi
technicians and the technicians of the inspection teams are cooperating and
working together on a scientific level, we find the Board of Governors
insisting on condemnation of Iraq for its lack of cooperation.

We are consequently alarmed and dissatisfied and conclude that the
resolution was adopted on the basis of predetermined political concepts and
motives, the intention being to bestow technical legitimacy through a
specialized agency in preparation for a fresh act of military aggression
against Iraq, following the full revelation by Iraq of its nuclear programme.
Neither is it a secret to anyone that the same parties which induced the Board
of Governors to adopt this resolution are endeavouring to maintain the embargo
and sanctions imposed on Iraq, without any legal or moral grounds, in the hope
of starving the Iraqi people and thus creating a pretext for intervention in
Iraq's internal affairs and an attempt to subject it to the will of foreign
Powers.

In affirming Iraq's official position with respect to the unjust and
unbalanced resolution adopted by the Board of Governors of the International
Atomic Energy Agency, we wish to emphasize our profound concern at the absence
of a spirit of fairness and justice in the dealings of certain parties in this

regard, despite Iraq's undertaking to fulfil its obligations under Security
Council resolution 687 (1991).  We also request that you have this letter
circulated as a document of the Security Council.

Accept, Sir, the assurances of my highest consideration.

(Signed)  Ahmad HUSSEIN
Minister for Foreign Affairs
of the Republic of Iraq
Baghdad, 12 Muharram A.H. 1412
(23 July A.D. 1991)

H.E. Mr. Javier Pérez de Cuéllar         3-3
Secretary-General of the United Nations

## 1. UN에 의한 이라크 核査察의 根據

o 核非擴散條約(NPT)과 國際原子力機構(IAEA)

- 이라크는 核武器의 水平的 擴散을 防止하기 위한 核非擴散條約(NPT)의
  당사국인 동시에 國際原子力機構(IAEA)의 核安全協定(Safeguard Accord)
  에도 署名한 國家로서 自國內 核施設을 利用한 核武器 製造與否를 確認
  하기 위한 IAEA의 現場査察要求에 응할 義務가 있음.

o 安保理 決議 687號

- 유엔 安全保障理事會는 決議 687號를 통해 休戰을 決意하면서 對이라크
  經濟制裁措置의 解除以前에 이라크로 하여금 保有한 非通商武器體系,
  즉 大量破壞武器(핵무기, 화학무기, 생물학무기)를 完全 廢棄하도록 함.

- 따라서 이라크는 保有한 大量 破壞武器를 廢棄해야 하는 同時에 核武器의
  새로운 開發도 禁止됨.

o 中東軍縮과의 連繫

- 軍備增强의 惡循環은 中東地域을 항상 不安定狀態에 빠뜨린다는 認識과
  安保를 理由로 過多한 大量破壞武器를 保有하여 隣接國 侵略에 惡用하는
  事例를 막아야 한다는 共同認識에서 美·蘇·英·佛·中 5대 武器輸出國은
  對中東 武器輸出 抑制를 推進中임.

- 이라크의 核武器 開發意圖는 이러한 中東軍縮을 통한 平和維持 構想과는
  相値되는 것임.

## 2. 이라크 核査察 現況과 問題點

o 安保理決議 687號에 의해 構成된 유엔 特別委員會에서 3次에 걸쳐 이라크
  核査察

- 濃縮 우라늄의 他地域 移動與否 確認을 위해 接近하는 核査察團에게
  이라크 병사 空砲 發射

- 核査察團의 査察要求 拒否는 IAEA 規定에 違背

0266

o 이라크측은 2次에 걸쳐 UN에 核技術, 裝備 및 核物質 明細書 提出

   - IAEA에 未通報한 우라늄 濃縮計劃 是認

   - 우라늄 濃縮用 同位元素分離裝置(Calutron) 30기 保有

   - 獨自的으로 開發한 電氣磁場分離法(Electronic Separation Process)
     使用 (제2차 세계대전 당시 미국이 사용하던 원시적인 방식)

   - IAEA에 보고한 80파운드 이외에 1-9 파운드 追加保有
     (망명 이라크 과학자는 90파운드 정도 추가보유 주장)

o 美國은 이라크가 繼續 核査察을 拒否할 경우 核施設 攻擊을 公言

   - 攻擊할 수 있는 根據는 安保理가 이라크로 하여금 決議 內容을 遵守
     하도록 保障하는 措置를 취할수 있다는 決議 687號의 內容임.

   - 부쉬 大統領, 20여개의 爆擊對象 이라크 指揮統制本部 選定 承認 報道

   - 英國, 프랑스도 軍事的 制裁 方式에 同意

## 3. 北韓 核査察과의 關係

o 北韓은 核非擴散條約 當事國이면서도 義務事項인 國際原子力機構의 核
安全協定에는 署名하지 않고 있다가 最近에야 國際的 壓力에 屈伏하여
一旦 國際原子力機構와 協定에 관한 協商을 마친 狀態임.

o 그렇지만 이라크의 例에서도 볼수 있듯이 重要한 것은, 協定에의 署名
與否가 아니라 核을 平和的인 目的으로만 利用한다는 基本 姿勢임.

o 我國은 中東의 軍縮과 平和維持를 위해 이라크가 지체없이 유엔 核査察團
에게 보유 核施設 일체를 숨김없이 完全 公開하여 또다른 中東危機를 막을
수 있기를 希望하며 아울러 北韓도 核安全協定의 誠實한 履行者가 되기를
促求함.

0267

APPENDIX

Iraq's non-compliance with its safeguards obligations

Resolution adopted by the Board of Governors of the
International Atomic Energy Agency on 18 July 1991

The Board of Governors,

(a) Stressing the importance of non-proliferation of nuclear weapons to
international and regional peace and security,

(b) Expressing grave concern about the conclusion of the report of the
Director-General (GOV/2530) that the Government of Iraq has failed to comply
with its obligations under its safeguards agreement with the International
Atomic Energy Agency (INFCIRC/172),

(c) Recalling United Nations Security Council resolution 687 (1991),
which, inter alia, called upon Iraq to declare all its nuclear activities to
the International Atomic Energy Agency,

(d) Noting with appreciation the efforts of the Director-General and his
staff to implement the tasks assigned to the Agency by that resolution, and
the diligent and effective conduct of the Agency's inspections of Iraqi
nuclear activities,

(e) Expressing grave concern about the evident deception and obstruction
of the International Atomic Energy Agency inspectors in their efforts to carry
out the Security Council's mandate in resolution 687 (1991) in violation of
that resolution and the undertakings by Iraq governing the status, privileges
and immunities of the Agency and the inspection teams mandated under Security
Council resolution 687 (1991),

1.     Finds, on the basis of the report of the Director-General in
GOV/2530, that the Government of Iraq has not complied with its obligations
under its safeguards agreement with the Agency (INFCIRC/172);

2.     Condemns this non-compliance by the Government of Iraq with its
safeguards agreement;

3.     Calls upon the Government of Iraq to remedy this non-compliance
forthwith, including placing any and all additional source and special
fissionable material within Iraq's territory, under its jurisdiction or its
control, regardless of quantity or location, under Agency safeguards in
accordance with the relevant provisions of INFCIRC/172 and in accordance with
relevant technical determinations of the Agency;

9-6

/...

# 이라크에 대한 IAEA 특별 핵사찰(Special Inspection) 실시 경위

91.7.27.
국제기구과

## 1. 제1차 핵사찰

### 가. 배 경

o 91.4.17. 유엔 안보리 휴전결의(687호, 91.4.3)에 의거 이라크 군비통제
특별위원회(Special Commission)설치, 이라크에 핵무기 및 생화학무기
정보제공 요청

- 안보리 결의 687호는 대이라크 경제제재조치해제 이전에 이라크 보유
대량파괴 무기(핵무기, 생.화학무기)를 완전히 폐기토록 규정

o 91.4.27. 이라크, 동 결의에 따라 이라크내 핵물질 및 시설관련 정보를
안보리에 제출

- 핵시설 24군데 가운데 18군데가 다국적군 공습으로 파괴되었고, 농축
우라늄도 IAEA 정기사찰을 받고 있는 20kg뿐이라고 밝힘

o 91.5.14-22. IAEA 사찰관과 안보리 특별위원으로 구성된 핵사찰반(34명)
이 이라크에 대한 제1차 핵사찰 실시

- 4.27. 이라크가 보고한 Al Tuwaitha 핵연구 시설내 핵물질의 양과
상태를 검증

- 기타 특별위원회가 IAEA에 제시한 Tarmiya 지역내 핵시설 건설 확인

### 나. 사찰결과

o 79개의 고농축 우라늄(HEU), 천연우라늄들의 핵물질 존재확인

- 1 -

0269

o Al-Tuwaitha 의 핵 시설건물이 폭격으로 파괴되어 동 시설내의 핵활동
  여부 확인 불가

  - 각종 문서와 기록의 분실로 과거 활동의 추적 불가

o 또한 많은 핵시설 장비등이 타지역으로 이전되었음이 확인

  - 사찰단은 이라크측에 이전된 핵 시설장비의 완전한 list 요청


2.  제2차 핵사찰

가.  경위

  o 이라크가 핵무기 원료및 생화학 무기의 보유량을 실제보다 줄여서 허위
    신고했다는 망명 이라크 핵과학자의 증언을 기초로 제2차 핵사찰 실시
    결정

    - 6.15자 뉴욕타임즈는 이라크는 91.4. 유엔 안보리에 신고한 양보다
      40kg의 고농축 우라늄을 더 갖고있고 핵개발 센타 8개소중 3개소만
      걸프전시 파괴되고 나머지는 지하 비밀장소에 남아있다고 보도

  o 사찰반은 6.23-28간 유엔특별위원회(Special Commission)가 지명한 지역
    (바그다드 Abu Gharaib 육군병영등)을 제2차 사찰하려 하였으나, 이라크
    당국이 동 사찰반의 접근을 금지, 제한 또는 사찰반 접근에 앞서 사찰
    대상 물체를 사전 제거함으로써 실질적으로 사찰을 행하지 못함

    - 6.28에는 이라크 육군 병영 보초의 소총발사 위협으로 접근 제지

    - 당시 유엔 사찰반은 농축우라늄의 타지역 이동여부 확인과 농축우라늄을
      제조할수 있는 동위 원소 분리장치(calutrons)을 찾아볼 계획이었음.

  o 6.28. 유엔 안보리는 의장성명을 통해 이라크의 사찰불응을 규탄하고,
    H. Blix IAEA 사무국장, R.Ekeus 유엔특위 위원장등으로 구성된 고위급
    대표단(high-level mission)을 이라크에 추가 파견하여 이라크에 대한
    제2차 핵사찰을 재개함(6.30-7.3)


- 2 -

0270

나. 사찰결과

　　o 2차 사찰결과 사찰반은 이라크가 유엔 특별위에 보고치 않은 핵관련
　　　장비(3kg 정도의 고농축 우라늄을 생산가능한 5개정도의 동위 원소 분리
　　　장치)를 갖고 있음을 밝혀냄
　　　- 사찰반의 요청에 따라 이라크는 핵시설 및 물질관련 추가 리스트를
　　　　안보리에 제출키로 함


3.　제3차 핵사찰

　o 91.7.7. 이라크 외무장관은 유엔사무총장앞 서한을 통해 이라크내 핵시설과
　　물질에 관한 추가 리스트를 제출함
　o 동 서한에서 이라크측은 ①IAEA에 밝히지 않은 우라늄 농축계획이 일부 있었
　　음을 시인(농축계획의 평화적 목적 및 국가 안보상 이유로 보유유지 불가피
　　성 주장)하고, ②우라늄 농축용 calutron 30기(대부분 파괴되었다고 주장)
　　등의 장비와 ③IAEA에 공개해온 농축 우라늄(HEU) 80파운드외에 1-9 파운드의
　　추가 농축우라늄 보유 인정(이라크 자체 기술로 농축시킨 우라늄 0.5kg포함)
　o 이라크가 제출한 새로운 핵관계 정보에 따라 이라크에 이미 파견되어 있던
　　사찰반은 7.7 부터 제3차 핵사찰을 실시함(7.7-20)
　o 7.12. 유엔 안보리 5개 상임이사국은 주유엔 이라크 대사를 소환, 7.25까지
　　이라크가 모든 핵개발 계획과 핵시설 및 물질을 공개할것 통보, 이에 응하지
　　않으면 이라크가 중대한 결과에 직면할것이라고 경고.
　o 7.13. 미국은 이라크가 핵무기 개발을 완전공개하지 않을 경우 대이라크
　　군사력 사용을 재개하겠다고 경고
　　- 7.14. 영국, 프랑스도 군사적 제재 방식에 동의
　　- 7.12자 뉴욕타임즈지는 이라크가 핵폐기 의무를 이행하지 않은 경우 공격할
　　　20여개의 이라크내 핵목표를 부쉬대통령이 승인했다고 보도


- 3 -

0271

o 제3차 사찰 실시기간중 이라크는 기 제출한 2차 보고서에 추가하여 7.14.
새로운 핵시설 명세(내용미상)를 안보리에 통보하였으며, 7.12자 외상 명의
유엔 사무총장 및 안보리 의장 앞 서한(안보리문서 S/22786으로 배포)을 통해
"미국이 중동지역에서의 패권 장악을 위해 이라크에 대한 대규모 군사공격을
준비중이라고 주장, 안보리가 이라크에 대한 미국의 재공격을 저지시켜줄것을
요청"하였음.

4. 제4차 핵사찰

o 또한, 7.18. IAEA는 특별이사회를 소집하여, 이라크가 IAEA와 체결한 핵
안전협정상의 의무를 불이행한것을 규탄하고 그양이나 소재에 관계없이 그
영토내에 있는 모든 핵물질을 IAEA의 감시하에 둘것을 촉구하는 결의(별첨)를
채택
   - 핵안전협정 34조 (B).(C)항 (사찰범위)관련 이라크측은 자국의 핵시설 및
   물질이 평화적 목적에 사용한것이라고 주장
   - 따라서 동 결의가 사찰반의 왜곡된 평가에 근거, 이라크에 대한 군사행동
   재개를 합법화해 보려는 저의에서 나온것이라고 비난
o 유엔과 IAEA는 이라크에 핵시설 공개 최후통첩 시한으로 제시한 7.25일에
제4차 핵사찰반을 파견함(7.27부터 약2주일 정도 사찰실시예정)
   - 4차 핵사찰 목적은 이라크의 원심분리기를 사용한 우라늄 농축양의 정밀
   파악에 있음
o 미국은 이라크가 유엔이 정한 시한인 25일까지 필요한 핵관련 정보를 제출
하지 않은 점을 감안, 4차 핵사찰결과를 주시하여 이라크측이 계속 핵시설을
은폐하고 사찰에 비협조적일 경우 다국적군(영,불)과 함께 군사보복 재개
가능성 시사.                     끝.


첨 부 : IAEA 이사회 결의 (91.7.18자)


- 4 -

0272

※ 참고사항

 o 이라크는 그간 고농축 우라늄(HEU) 생산을 위해 전기자장분리법(electromagnetic), 원심분리법(centrifugal)및 화학적 분리법(chemical-seperation
  processes)를 병행하여 추진해온것으로 밝혀짐

 o 상기 방법은 지극히 원시적인 방법으로 히로시마 투하 원폭 1개(HEU 약 1kg
  상당)를 제조하기 위해 1,000 여개의 동위원소 분리장치(calutron)를 사용
  5,--6,000명의 인력을 수년간 투입하여야 함

  - 분리장치 기계는 크기가 매우 크므로 인공위성등에 의해 쉽게 탐지가 가능
   하며, 경제적 실효성이 거의 없는 장치임.

 o 북한의 경우는 상기 방법을 통한 우라늄 농축시도 보다는 풀루토늄 생산을
  위한 핵 재처리 시설(reprocessing facility)의 건설에 중점적 노력을 기울
  이고 있는것으로 추측됨. (이라크보다는 발전된 핵기술 보유)

APPENDIX

Iraq's non-compliance with its safeguards obligations

Resolution adopted by the Board of Governors of the
International Atomic Energy Agency on 18 July 1991

The Board of Governors,

(a) Stressing the importance of non-proliferation of nuclear weapons to
international and regional peace and security,

(b) Expressing grave concern about the conclusion of the report of the
Director-General (GOV/2530) that the Government of Iraq has failed to comply
with its obligations under its safeguards agreement with the International
Atomic Energy Agency (INFCIRC/172),

(c) Recalling United Nations Security Council resolution 687 (1991),
which, inter alia, called upon Iraq to declare all its nuclear activities to
the International Atomic Energy Agency,

(d) Noting with appreciation the efforts of the Director-General and his
staff to implement the tasks assigned to the Agency by that resolution, and
the diligent and effective conduct of the Agency's inspections of Iraqi
nuclear activities,

(e) Expressing grave concern about the evident deception and obstruction
of the International Atomic Energy Agency inspectors in their efforts to carry
out the Security Council's mandate in resolution 687 (1991) in violation of
that resolution and the undertakings by Iraq governing the status, privileges
and immunities of the Agency and the inspection teams mandated under Security
Council resolution 687 (1991),

1.    Finds, on the basis of the report of the Director-General in
GOV/2530, that the Government of Iraq has not complied with its obligations
under its safeguards agreement with the Agency (INFCIRC/172);

2.    Condemns this non-compliance by the Government of Iraq with its
safeguards agreement;

3.    Calls upon the Government of Iraq to remedy this non-compliance
forthwith, including placing any and all additional source and special
fissionable material within Iraq's territory, under its jurisdiction or its
control, regardless of quantity or location, under Agency safeguards in
accordance with the relevant provisions of INFCIRC/172 and in accordance with
relevant technical determinations of the Agency;

9-6

/...

# 외 무 부

종 별 :

번 호 : UNW-1953         일 시 : 91 0729 1930

수 신 : 장 관(국연,국기,중동일,국연)

발 신 : 주 유엔 대사

제 목 : 안보리(비공식 협의)

   1. 안보리는 명 7.30 비공식 협의를 갖고 H.BLIX IAEA사무총장으로 부터 <u>핵사찰 관련 보고를 청취예정인바,</u> 명일 비공식협의시에는 이락핵사찰 문제외에 유엔 레바논 평화 유지군 (UNIFIL) 임무기간 연장, 안보리 운영개선 (TRANSPARENCY 문제)를 토의할 것으로 알려짐.

   2. IAEA 이락 핵사찰반 제3진 (7.7-18) 보고서가 금 7.29 안보리문서로 배포된바, 동보고서 내용을 별첨송부함.

   첨부:상기 보고서: UNW(F)-365 끝

   (대사 노창희-국장)

---

국기국     1차보     중아국     국기국     국기국     외정실     분석관     안기부

PAGE 1                         91.07.30    09:14 WG

외신 1과 통제관

0275

UNW(FI)-365  10729  1930
( 국민 . 국가 . 중동원 . 국연 )          총 11 대

## Enclosure

### REPORT ON THE THIRD IAEA ON-SITE INSPECTION IN IRAQ UNDER SECURITY COUNCIL RESOLUTION 687 (1991)

### 7-18 July 1991

## Salient points

The IAEA team, which arrived on the eve of the day when the Government of Iraq disclosed its enrichment programme, devoted most of its time to performing inspections in order to verify the Government's declaration and fill gaps in it and to seeking explanations.

Although the Iraqi side was cooperative in facilitating the team's efforts and provided many clarifications about the declared enrichment programme, the team considers it likely that the full extent of the centrifuge enrichment work has not yet been disclosed; the possibility also exists that there are still undeclared locations with sensitive equipment and material.

The leader of Iraq's enrichment programme, Dr. J. Jaffar, Deputy Chairman of the Iraqi Atomic Energy Commission and Deputy Minister for Industry and Minerals, denied that any political decision had been taken to use the enrichment programme to develop nuclear weapons. The primary aims were stated to be development of the country's technological and industrial infrastructure and the production of fuel for research reactors and a future nuclear power programme. The team noted that the possibility of combining separators with high capacity/modest separation factor and separators with low capacity/high separation factor suggests a specific intention to produce highly enriched uranium.

Through imports and indigenous production, Iraq had accumulated a large inventory of natural uranium.

Uranium tetrachloride - feed material for the electromagnetic isotope separation (EMIS) enrichment method - was produced in a factory outside Mosul and at Tuwaitha. The buildings were severely damaged.

The Iraqi side confirmed earlier inspectors' suspicions that Tarmiya was the main production site for the enrichment of uranium by the EMIS method. A layer of concrete which had been poured over a key component of the separators in order to conceal it was removed at the request of the team, which was then able to confirm that the installation in question had indeed been constructed for enrichment purposes.

The Iraqi side gave the team videotapes showing the inauguration of the Tarmiya plant (in February 1990) and what the plant looked like after the bombing; it had been extensively damaged. The team made a tape of what it looks like now.

# UNW-1953
첨부목                    11-1                           /...

0276

On the basis of the design data provided by the Iraqi side, the team considers that Tarmiya, if fully operational, with 90 separators running at design capacity, could have produced up to 15 kilograms of highly enriched (93 per cent) uranium a year, or proportionally more uranium at a lower enrichment.

It was confirmed that, as surmised, the facility at Ash Sharqat had been built as a replica of Tarmiya and was not, as alleged during the inspection, a factory for the plastic coating of equipment. Most of the facility was destroyed by bombing, at which time it was about 85 per cent completed; no separators had yet been installed.

Milligram quantities of uranium enriched to a level of 40-45 per cent and other quantities enriched to lower levels at Tuwaitha were declared. At Tarmiya, batches of uranium with enrichment levels ranging up to 10 per cent were declared, giving together 0.6 kilograms with an average enrichment level of 4 per cent.

It was confirmed that the Research Centre at Tuwaitha was the site of all the research and development work on uranium enrichment, including EMIS, centrifuge enrichment and chemical enrichment. The relevant facilities at Tuwaitha were completely destroyed.

/...

11-2

0277

## INTRODUCTION

1.    The present report summarizes findings of the third inspection carried out by IAEA under the terms of Security Council resolution 687 (1991) with the assistance and cooperation of the Special Commission of the United Nations. The team consisted of 26 inspectors and 11 supporting staff, comprising 22 nationalities.  It was headed by Mr. Demetrius Perricos of IAEA as Chief Inspector.  The team arrived in Iraq on 6 July 1991 and started the inspection on 7 July.  The original schedule was for the inspection to end on 12 July but, owing to a new declaration of the Iraqi authorities dated 7 July which provided additional information on Iraq's nuclear programme, it was necessary to extend the inspection to 19 July.  The team was reduced to 20 inspectors as from 13 July.

2.    The inspection team verified, to a large extent, the information contained in the Iraqi declaration of 7 July regarding Iraq's enrichment programme, which was supplemented by information presented to the team at its request on 14 July.  A number of follow-up actions have been identified and will have to be performed during subsequent inspection missions.  It was not possible for the inspection team to verify the extent of the centrifuge enrichment programme, nor could the team exclude the possibility that there are still undeclared locations with sensitive equipment or material installed, in use or stored.  In addition, the industrial and technological infrastructure which has been built in connection with this programme has to be assessed, and the information provided to the team regarding the industrial establishments involved in this effort has to be verified.

3.    The process of additional clarification by Iraq and subsequent verification and further questioning by the inspection team went on throughout the two-week inspection period, and it will continue during subsequent inspections.  A large number of samples were collected, but they have not yet been analysed; also, many documents, some provided by Iraq and others collected at various sites by the inspection team, have still to be fully evaluated.  No access problems were encountered and the attitude of the Iraqi authorities to the team was one of cooperation throughout the period of the inspection.

## I.   THE IRAQI ENRICHMENT PROGRAMME

4.    According to a statement by Dr. J. Jaffar, leader of the enrichment programme, Vice-Chairman of the Iraqi Atomic Energy Commission and Deputy Minister for Industry and Minerals, the primary motive for proceeding with a uranium enrichment programme was the expected contribution to the technological and industrial infrastructure of the country regardless of whether the programme was successful.  The need for uranium enrichment was ascribed to the need to fuel research reactors and possibly, at some point in the future, power reactors.  Dr. Jaffar noted that a capability to produce highly enriched uranium may create, in his words, a "political option" for the

/...

11-3

0278

S/22837
English
Page 6

development of nuclear weapons.  However, he steadfastly denied that a
decision to develop nuclear weapons had been taken or that any weapons
development work had been done.

5.    At one time or another, gaseous diffusion, electromagnetic isotope
separation (EMIS), gas centrifuge and chemical exchange technologies were
examined by Iraq.  The commitment to EMIS for production-scale development and
deployment followed early successes with the method and, more importantly, the
demonstration that the separator units and magnets could be made in Iraq.

6.    According to the disclosures made to date, efforts comparable to that
devoted to EMIS were not made as regards other separation technologies.  Iraqi
declarations indicate that research on gas centrifuge technology was second in
priority and that some promising results were recently achieved, including
successful single-machine trials with $UF_6$ gas.  Operating data from some of
these trials were presented to the inspection team on the last day of the
inspection period, but it seems likely that the full extent of the centrifuge
work has not been disclosed.  There is no doubt that Iraq has developed the
technological and industrial infrastructure necessary for EMIS.  As far as
centrifuge enrichment is concerned, Iraq was developing an indigenous
technology even if they were dependent on foreign suppliers for key components
and materials.


A.    Uranium enrichment research and development at Tuwaitha

7.    Research, development and testing of EMIS components were carried out in
the Nuclear Physics Building (80).*  Reviews of an Iraqi-provided videotape
showing the EMIS facilities in the building, together with examinations of
components of the 1,000-millimetre separators (this number refers to the
radius of the ion beam in the separator tank) and the model 106 ion source
test stand are consistent with Iraq's declaration.  In the opinion of the
inspection team, the facility was not designed for - nor was it capable of -
producing enriched uranium in quantity.  The Iraqi statement that the only
real obstacle remaining in the development of an efficient EMIS system was an
improved ion source is consistent with experience elsewhere in the world.
Work on graphite collectors and on the configuration of ion sources and
collectors was also carried out in this building.  Research on EMIS chemistry
was carried out in the nearby Chemical Research Building (85).  A small pilot
line for the production of $UCl_4$ was also contained in this building.  Both
buildings, 80 and 85, have been levelled and the rubble removed.  Experiments
with gas centrifuge enrichment were declared by Iraq to have occurred in the
Cold Material Testing Building (63).

_____

     *    The numbers in parentheses refer to the locations indicated on the
Tuwaitha site map in annex I to the present report.

                                                                       /...

                              11-4

                                                                    0279

S/22837
English
Page 7

### B. Acquisition of natural uranium (Al Qaim and Akashat)

8.    Iraq has accumulated, through imports and indigenous production, a large inventory of natural uranium. The indigenous material is largely from an uranium extraction facility (producing yellow cake) associated with a superphosphate plant at Al Qaim. The facility was extensively damaged during the bombing. There is no evidence that the facility served any purpose beyond that declared. The operator stated that a total of 168 metric tons have been produced since the facility was commissioned in 1984. This amount is considerably below the production capacity of 103 metric tons a year. The operator's explanation was that the uranium content of the phosphate ore was far lower than expected. Samples of the ore were taken to investigate this issue.

9.    Akashat is an open-cast mine which feeds Al Qaim. No other activities were detected during the inspection.

### C. $UO_2$ conversion and $UCl_4$ production (Mosul Production Facility)

10.    The team founded that $UCl_4$ production had been carried out at a facility outside Mosul. A standard production process with $UO_2$ feed and $CCl_4$ as the chlorination reagent was used. The facility included a $UO_2$ conversion capability. It was stated that the $UCl_4$ plant had gone into production in August 1990 and operated for about six months. The plant manager indicated that production had been limited for most of that time because of corrosion problems. The inspection team found no evidence contradicting those statements. The $UCl_4$ production building had suffered substantial damage, and the $UO_2$ building had completely collapsed and was covered with debris. There was also an Iraqi statement that the $UCl_4$ used for EMIS development and testing at Tuwaitha and Tarmiya had been produced in Building 85 at Tuwaitha.

### D. EMIS: the facilities at Tarmiya and Ash Sharqat

11.    The Tarmiya site has been described in previous inspection reports (see S/22788). The third inspection team visited the site again following Iraqi confirmation that the site had been used for EMIS and further declarations regarding the extent of the EMIS installations and operations. The team found evidence confirming statements about the number and type (1,200 mm) of EMIS units installed in Building 33. The process building contained two areas (A and B) for EMIS installations. An eight-separator system (nine magnets) had been installed in area A during January and February 1990. A 17-separator system was in the process of being installed (three magnets were in place) in area B at the time operations ceased.

12.    In an attempt to conceal the EMIS equipment from the inspection teams, the return irons and rails for the separators had been covered with concrete. This was removed at the team's request. The length of the installed return

/...

11-5

0280

S/22837
English
Page 8

iron in both area A and area B conformed to system specifications provided by
Iraq and to independent separator component measurements made by the
inspection team.

13.   An Iraqi video film made at the time when the installation of magnets,
vacuum chambers and end pieces for the eight-separator system was completed
(February 1990) and one made in February 1991, after the bombing, were
provided to the inspection team.  The latter video film appeared to confirm
that only three magnets had been installed, without vacuum chambers, and that
area B had therefore not yet been operational.  A computer printout showing
the performance of one of the separators during a run late in December 1990
was provided.  The data have not been examined in detail, but it appears that
the ion beam current was not up to the design value.  The number of separators
ultimately intended for Building 33 has not been determined.  The facility
design provides for a maximum of 70 separators, but Iraqi authorities
indicated that no decision had been taken beyond those concerning the 25
separators installed or being installed.  Facility specifications indicate
that Building 245 was designed to accommodate 20 of the smaller (600 mm)
units, which have a higher separation factor.  Uranium recovery, the
construction and configuration of ion sources and collectors and the
construction of separator tank liners were all done at the Tarmiya site.

14.   A second facility, a replica of Tarmiya, was being constructed at
Ash Sharqat.  According to information provided during the inspection,
construction at Ash Sharqat started shortly after that at Tarmiya but none of
the major buildings had been commissioned.  The overall state of completeness
was about 85 per cent at the time when most of the facility was destroyed.
There was no sign that installed equipment had been removed, as had happened
at other sites.  The electric power supply to the site is very substantial
and, while installation was not complete, the substation serving the site
would certainly provide power at a level equivalent to that at Tarmiya.  At
the time when this site was inspected, the Iraqi authorities had not declared
it as a nuclear facility; they stated the purposes of the installations at
Ash Sharqat to be the protective coating of large pipes and containers and the
production of machine tools.  The Iraqi authorities have since stated that the
Ash Sharqat facility was constructed from the plans used at Tarmiya.  Further,
they have indicated that the replication of important buildings had become a
policy of the Iraqi Government.  It is not clear whether Iraq intended to
utilize the Ash Sharqat facility for uranium enrichment as long as the Tarmiya
facility continued to function.

/...

11-6

0281

### E.  Material and equipment declarations*

15.  Declarations of material directly associated with the operation of EMIS development units in Building 80 at Tuwaitha were provided to the team on the last day of the inspection period.  Milligram quantities of uranium enriched up to a level of 40-45 per cent and a few kilograms of uranium depleted down to a level of .02 per cent were included.  Material in five enrichment ranges (up to 10 wt. per cent U-235) resulting from the testing of EMIS production units at Tarmiya was declared, and samples were taken.  Again, only small amounts of material were involved.  This material was declared on 7 July as about 0.5 kg with an average enrichment of 4 per cent.

16.  All tell-tale equipment at Tuwaitha, Tarmiya and the Mosul Production Facility had been removed and turned over to the Iraqi Army for destruction and concealment.  The Army proceeded to transport the equipment to remote locations where much of it was destroyed and buried.  Equipment from Tuwaitha and Tarmiya was distributed among locations 1-5 and 8, and equipment from the Mosul Production Facility was taken to locations 6 and 7 (near Mosul).  Much of the equipment was destroyed to the point where it was no longer recognizable.  The inspection team tried to concentrate on major EMIS components identified as end pieces, double-pole magnets with coils, vacuum chambers, liners, ion sources and collectors.  The end pieces, magnets and vacuum chambers could not be destroyed completely and, given the circumstances, the inventory was reasonably consistent with Iraqi declarations.  However, no collectors and only one ion source were found. Several pieces of a collector were eventually provided, but the locating of ion sources and collectors will have to be a major follow-up activity.  Iraq's clarification dated 18 July included components (but no ion sources or collectors) for six 600-mm separators intended for installation at Tarmiya. With the exception of one dipole and several coils, this equipment has not been found by the inspection team.  The equipment inventories at locations 6 and 7 are consistent with the declared purpose of the Mosul Production Facility.  Facilities where EMIS components were fabricated were identified by Iraq.  Some of these facilities had been inspected before the declaration, during the second IAEA on-site inspection, as a result of designation by the Special Commission.

17.  In the opinion of the inspection team, the broad goals cited by the Vice-Chairman of the Iraqi Atomic Energy Commission neither require nor justify the construction of a facility the size of Tarmiya, much less two such facilities.  Design drawings of Building 33 and Building 245 show a combination of high-capacity/modest separation factor units and low-capacity/high separation factor units.  This is the type of arrangement that would be configured if the goal was to produce highly enriched uranium. Design data provided by Iraq indicate that if Tarmiya had become fully

---

        *  For the area of Tuwaitha and Tarmiya and equipment locations 1-8, see the map contained in annex II to the present report.

/...

11-7

0282

S/22837
English
Page 10

operational, with 90 separators running at design capacity, up to 15 kilograms a year of highly enriched uranium or proportionally more uranium at lower enrichments could have been produced using natural uranium as the feed.

### F.  Gas centrifuge enrichment

18.  In the 7 July declaration, Iraq listed certain gas centrifuge activities, equipment and components.  Additional data were also made available, including information about a planned project to build a 100-machine gas centrifuge cascade.  Iraq claimed that it had not progressed beyond the point of conducting single-machine trials with $UF_6$ gas and that the technical specifications for its gas centrifuge had not yet been fully determined.  It was also claimed that it had had only very limited capabilities for centrifuge component manufacturing and no significant stockpiles of special materials (e.g., 350-grade maraging steel).  In addition, it was claimed that there had been only very limited, laboratory-scale activities with $UF_6$.

19.  On the basis of the evidence available to date, the inspection team cannot draw conclusions as to whether Iraq's gas centrifuge declarations are complete.  A statement made regarding the technical status of machine operations and performance which had been achieved appears plausible, though its accuracy cannot be verified.  The precise status of the "planned" project to build a 100-machine gas centrifuge cascade remains a question mark. Furthermore, it appears probable to the team that the full extent (material, equipment and locations) of Iraq's gas centrifuge component manufacturing infrastructure has yet to be revealed.

### II.  NUCLEAR MATERIAL VERIFICATION

20.  In addition to the reverification activities performed on the nuclear material presented to the first inspection team, the following quantities of nuclear material stated in the declaration of 7 July were verified:

|  | (kilograms) |
|---|---|
| Yellow cake | 331 368 (corrected value) |
| $UO_2$ | 116 173 |
| $UCl_4$ | 2 577 |
| $UF_6$ | 0.465 |
| ADU | 1 850 |
| $UO_3$ | 2 050 |
| $UF_4$ | 310 (corrected value) |
| $UO_4$ | 2 255 |

11-8

/...

S/22837
English
Page 11

Also, one drum of scrap material and two drums of $UO_4$ sample bottles which
had not been included in the 7 July declaration were brought to the Tuwaitha
site and verified.  The weights of this material were not provided and, owing
to its late arrival, it was not possible to determine them.  Furthermore,
235 kg of natural uranium in $U_3O_8$ form and four natural uranium fuel
elements, which had previously been under safeguards and which were recovered
from the rubble after the first inspection, were brought to the storage area
at Tuwaitha and verified.  The irradiated heavily enriched uranium (HEU) fuel
elements in the IRT 5000 reactor were fully verified during the inspection.

21.  Hot cells and glove boxes.  The hot cells and glove boxes present at
Tuwaitha were all inspected, and all the manipulators of the hot cells which
had not been severely damaged were sealed for unique identification purposes.

22.  Removal of fuel items.  The conditions for removal and transportation of
both fresh and irradiated highly enriched fuel elements were examined and
discussed with the Iraqi authorities.  In order to minimize the costs, the
Iraqi authorities expressed the wish to perform as many of the activities as
possible involved in the removal of fresh fuel and the loading of irradiated
fuel into transport containers.  Further discussions on this matter will take
place in the near future.

### III.  OTHER INSPECTIONS

23.  Facility near Tuwaitha.  The third inspection team examined a facility
which the Iraqi side had identified as the Engineering Research Centre under
the Ministry of Higher Education.  The facility was surrounded by a low berm
and a fence and had guard towers at each fence corner.  Most of the equipment
had been removed but some evidence found in the buildings suggested that the
facility was a forensic laboratory of the Ministry of the Interior.  The team
is confident that no nuclear activities were conducted at the facility.

24.  Al Qa Qaa Facility.  At the invitation of the Iraqi authorities,
inspectors visited this facility, which was declared to be a high-explosive
testing facility.  It did not appear to the inspectors that the facility
possessed the diagnostic capability to support other than conventional
explosive and ordnance production.

/...

11-9

0284

S/22837
English
Page 12

Annex I

TUWAITHA SITE MAP

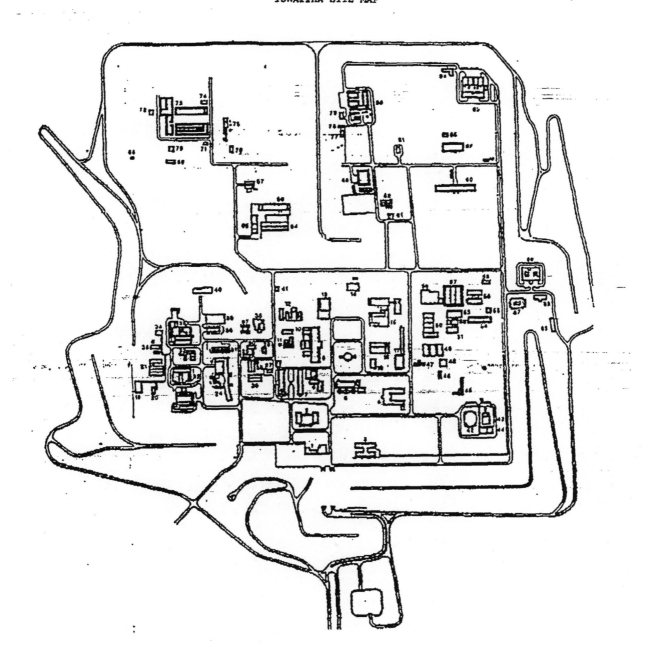

/...

0285

# 외 무 부

종 별 :

번 호 : UNW-1970 　　　　　　　　　일 시 : 91 0730 2000

수 신 : 장 관 (국연,중동일,국기,기정)

발 신 : 주 유엔 대사

제 목 : 안보리동향(비공식협의)

　　연: UNW-1953

　　1. 안보리는 금 7.30 오후 비공식협의를 개최한바, 당관에서 탐문한 금일협의 주요결과를 아래보고함.

　　가. 이락 핵사찰

　　1) H.BLIX IAEA 사무총장, R.EKEUS 이락 군비통제특위의장으로 부터 핵사찰 (제3진 사찰결과) 및 여타 대량 파괴무기 폐기 현황을 청취함.

　　2)화학무기는 당초 이락이 제출한 현황보다 다량보유한 것으로 나타나고 있으며, 생물무기 조사반을 8월초 이락파견 예정이라고함. 탄도미사일 관련재확인을 위한 조사반은 9월 파견계획중임.

　　3) BLIX 총장은 이락 핵개발이 평화적 목적을 위한 것으로 보기 어렵다는 강한 의구를 표시한 것으로 알려짐.

　　나. 유엔 안보리 평화유지군 (UNIFIL) 임무기간연장

　　1)7.31 안보리 공식회의에서 동 임무기간 연장을 위한 안보리 결의 채택예정 (동결의와 별도로 레바논 당국의 남부지역 관할권 회복노력을 지지하는 안보리의장 명의 성명도 발표계획)

　　2)단, UNIFIL 군요원 10 프로 감축문제에 대해서는 여전히 이사국들간에 합의가 이루어지고있지 않은바, 상기 결의안중 관련문안 표현을 놓고 현재 교섭이 진행중인 것으로 알려짐.

　　다. 안보리 운영개선 (TRANSPARECNY 문제)

　　1)일단 유엔일보 (JOURNAL) 및 구내 방송활용문제를 시행키로 하고 이문제를 사무국에 제기 예정임.

　　2)총회앞 활동보고 문제등에 관해서는 의견이 일치되고 있지 않은것으로 알려짐

| 국기국 | 1차보 | 중아국 | 국기국 | 외정실 | 분석관 | 안기부 |
|---|---|---|---|---|---|---|

91.07.31　10:23 WG

외신 1과 통제관

0286

2. 한편 안보리상임이사국 (PERM-5) 들은 이락석유수출 일부 허용을 위한 안보리결의안을 교섭중이라고 하는바, 당관에서 입수한 동결의안초안 (불란서 초안)주요골자는 다음과 같음.

　　가.6개월간 이락산 석유일정량 (정확한 수량은추후결정)수출허용

　　1)이락산 석유구매시 동구매자가 안보리 대이락제재위 승인요청

　　2)동 구매대금은 유엔구좌 (ESCROW ACCOUNT)에 입금되며, 식량등 민수용필수품목 수입대금은 동구좌에서 지불

　　3)동 필수품의 이락내 공평한 배급을 위한 유엔감시 절차마련

　　나.유엔사무총장은 본건 구좌로 부터 이락배상, 대량파괴무기 폐기, 쿠웨이트 재산반환, 이락-쿠웨이트 국경획정에 따른 제반경비 지불

　　다.사무총장은 상기 사항이행과 관련된 보고서를 안보리에 제출

　　라.이락은 자국의 금,외화보유고 현황을 매월제출

　　첨부:상기 안보리결의안 초안: UNW(F)-371

　　끝

　　(대사 노창희-국장)

ZW(FI)-371 10730 2=
( 국면. 중동일. 국기. 기정)   총4매

"The Security Council,

A. <u>Recalling</u> its resolutions 660 (1990), 661 (1990), 665 ( 1990), 666 (1990), 670 (1990), 674 (1990), 687 (1991), 688 (1991), 692 (1991) et 699 (1991),

B. <u>Taking note</u> of the report (S/.....) dated 15 July 1991 of the inter-agency mission headed by the executive delegate of the Secretary Géneral for the United Nations inter-agency humanitarian programme for Iraq, Kuwait and the Iraq/Turkey and Iraq/Iran border areas,

C. <u>Gravely concerned</u> by the nutritional and health situation of the Iraqi civilian population as described in this report, and by the risk of a rapid deterioration of this situation,

D. <u>Taking note</u> of the conclusions of the abovementionned report, and in particular of the proposal for oil sales by Iraq to finance immediate humanitarian relief,

E. <u>Conscious</u> of the need to achieve effective monitoring and transparency in the equitable distribution of humanitarian relief to all segments of the Iraqi civilian population,

F. <u>Recalling and reaffirming</u> in this regard its resolution 688 (1991) and in particular the importance which the Council attaches to Iraq allowing unhindered access by international humanitarian organisations to all those in

÷ UNW-197 ⓪
첨부믹                         4 -1

need of assistance in all parts of Iraq and making available
all necessary facilities for their operation, and in this
connection stressing the important and continuing role
played by the Memorandum of Understanding between the United
Nations and the Government of Iraq of 18 April 1991
(S/22663),

G. Recalling that, pursuant to resolutions 687
(1991), 692 (1991) and 699 (1991), Iraq is required to pay
the full costs of the Special Commission and the IAEA in
carrying out the tasks authorised by section C of resolution
687 (1991), and that the Secretary général ⬛⬛⬛ in his
report to the Security Council of 15 July 1991 (S/22792),
submitted pursuant to paragraph 4 of resolution 699 (1991),
expressed the view that the most obvious way of obtaining
financial resources from Iraq to meet the costs of the
Special Commission and the IAEA would be to authorise the
sale of some Iraqi petroleum and petroleum products, and
recalling further that Iraq is required to pay the expenses
of the United Nations Compensation Commission, as well as
its contributions to the Compensation Fund and half the
costs of the Iraq-Kuwait Boundary Demarcation Commission,
and recalling further that in its resolutions 686 (1991) and
687 (1991) the Security Council demanded that Iraq return in
the shortest possible time all Kuwaiti property seized by it
and requested the Secretary-General to take steps to
facilitate this,

H. Acting under chapter VII of the Charter,

1. Authorizes the import during a period of six
months from the date of passage of this resolution of a
specified quantity of petroleum and petroleum products
originating in Iraq for the purposes set out in this
resolution and subject to the following conditions :

*to be specified in accordance with the as part of the decisions to .. taken under para 3*

*P.4*

4-2

.../...

*( petroleum and )*

(a) Notification by the purchaser to and approval of each purchase of Iraqi petroleum products by the Security Council Committee established by resolution 661 (1990),

(b) Payment of the full amount of each of these purchases of Iraqi petroleum and petroleum products directly by the purchaser into a escrow account established by the Secretary General for this purpose,

(c) Payments from this account for the purchase of foodstuffs, medecines and essential civilian needs, as provided in paragraph 20 of resolution 687, to be subject to the joint authorisation of both Iraq and the Committee established by resolution 661 (1990),

(d) Establishment of control procedures within Iraq under United Nations monitoring and supervison to ensure equitable distribution to meet humanitarian needs of these supplies in all regions of Iraq and to all categories of the Iraqi population,

(e) Implementation of the authorisation in 3 tranches by the Security Council Committee established under Security Council resolution 661, only when the Council has taken the decision provided for in paragraph 2. below ~~decision~~ on the implementation of this resolution.

2. Decides in addition, that the Secretary-General is authorized to make payments from this escrow account to finance the obligations of Iraq, including the cost to the United Nations and other humanitarian organizations of monitoring and surveillance and of any other humanitarian expenditures in Iraq, appropriate

4-3

.../...

payments to the United Nations Compensation Fund, the costs of carrying out the tasks authorised by section C of resolution 687 (1991), the costs incurred by the United Nations in facilitating the return of all Kuwaiti property seized by Iraq and half the costs of the Boundary Commission.

3. Requests the Secretary General, within 30 days of the date of adoption of this resolution, to submit a report to the Security Council for decision on measures to be taken in order to implement paragraphs 1(a), 1(b), 1(c), and 1(d), estimates of the humanitarian requirements of Iraq and the amount of Iraq's financial obligations set out in the para 2 above, for the period of the authorization in para 1 above.

4. Requires the Government of Iraq to provide to the Secretary-General and appropriate international organizations on the first day of the month immediately following the adoption of the present resolution and on the first day of each month thereafter until further notice, a statement of the gold and foreign currency reserves it holds within Iraq.

5. Calls upon all States to cooperate fully in the implementation of this resolution.

6. Decides to remain seized of the matter.

4-4

외      무      부

원 본

종    별 :

번    호 : UNW-1983 　　　　　　　　　일    시 : 91 0731 1930

수    신 : 장 관(국연,국기,중동일,기정)

발    신 : 주 유엔대사

제    목 : 걸프사태(유엔동향)

　　1.유엔이락 군비통제 특위측으로 부터 탐문한 바에 의하면, 안보리 휴전결의에 의거한 이락 대량파괴무기 폐기관련 주요추진 현황 및 향후 계획을 아래보고함.

　　가.특위 조사반활동

　　1)금 7.31 현재까지 총 6개 조사반 기파견 사찰실시, 앞으로 10개 조사반 파견

　　2)핵분야 : 제4진이 7.27 부터 사찰활동중(2주간체류)

　　3)화학무기 : 제1진 활동 (6.9-15)에 이어 2,3 진이 8월중 사찰예정, 9월에 1진 기사찰지역( SAMARRA부근)재사찰

　　4)생물무기 : 8.2 제1진 사찰개시

　　5)탄도미사일 : 1차 사찰 및 폐기작업 (6.30-7.7)에 이어7.18-30 추가 폐기실시, 8월 생산시설 사찰계획

　　나.이락군비통제 검증시행

　　안보리 휴전결의(687 호) 10조에 의거유엔사무총장은 특위와 협의하여 향후 검증시행안을 마련 8.2 한 안보리에 제출토록 되어있음.

　　2.한편 유엔측 발표에 의하면 이락은 8.5이락-사우디 접경에서 유엔측 입회하에쿠웨이트 에금괴 3,216 개 (개당 12.5 키로)를 반환예정이며, 은행권, 주화는 따라추 후 반환하겠다고 함.(이외에 주요반환 예정 품목으로는 민항기, 박물관, 도서관소장품이 있으나 소장품류는 차후에 반환절차협의 예정으로 알려짐)

　　첨부 : 1. NYT 기사, 2. WSJ 지 KAREN HOUSE 기고문 : UNW(F)-374 끝

　　(대사 노창희-국장)

---

국기국　　1차보　　　중아국　　　국기국　　　외정실　　　안기부

PAGE 1 　　　　　　　　　　　　　　　　　　　　　91.08.01　　09:55 WH

　　　　　　　　　　　　　　　　　　　　　　　　외신 1과 통제관

　　　　　　　　　　　　　　　　　　　　　　　　　0292

*UNW(㈱)-374 /0731 19㠰*
*(국연·국기 중동분 기저)*

*총 2아*

# U.N. Team Finds Chemical Arms 4 Times Greater Than Iraq Claims

### By FRANK J. PRIAL
Special to The New York Times

UNITED NATIONS, July 30 — The head of a special United Nations commission overseeing the elimination of Iraq's chemical and nuclear arsenals told the Security Council today that his inspectors had found Iraqi chemical weapons in quantities more than four times greater than Baghdad had acknowledged.

The official, Rolf Ekeus, said that where Iraq had reported having from 10,000 to 11,000 chemical shells and warheads, the inspectors had found 46,000. Instead of the 650 tons of raw material for such weapons Iraq had reported, he said the inspectors found 3,000 tons.

Mr. Ekeus said a large number of the chemical weapons declared by the Iraqis or discovered by the inspection team had turned out to contain "relatively harmless" tear gas. But he emphasized that they were military weapons, to be used in combat, rather than riot-control weapons normally used by the police.

### Search for Biological Arms

He said some of the chemical warheads were armed with Sarin, a powerful nerve gas, and that some of the warheads were fitted on Scud missiles. Scuds armed with conventional explosives were fired at Saudi Arabia and Israel during the war.

The new disclosures led Mr. Ekeus to re-emphasize his complaint that Iraq continues to obstruct efforts to find and destroy all its weapons of mass destruction.

"We still lack sufficient cooperation from the Iraqis," Mr. Ekeus said. "And we hope it will be forthcoming."

He said a special team of inspectors would be going into Iraq on Saturday exclusively to look for biological weapons, even though Iraq has stated unequivocally that it has none.

"They will be looking at non-declared sites," he said.

The fourth agency inspection team began work in Iraq Saturday and will remain for two weeks, Mr. Ekeus said. He said that beginning in September, some 70 weapons and munitions experts would spend six to eight weeks at a declared chemical-weapons site near the city of Samarra, which was first visited by United Nations teams in June.

### 6 Inspection Missions

The 25-square-mile site, which contains 70 buildings, "is heavily contaminated and has unexploded ordnance," he said. Two other teams are to visit other chemical-warfare sites in August, at times and place to be announced later.

In all, 6 inspection missions have been carried out in Iraq by the special commission and 10 more are "in the active planning stage," Mr. Ekeus said.

Speaking to reporters after the Security Council meeting, the British representative, Sir David Hannay, agreed that "there is real doubt whether disclosures are the full and complete disclosures we are looking for."

He also noted that the effort to force Iraq to adhere to the Security Council resolutions was "rolling forward" and was "yielding fruit, slowly but surely." He said he expected inspections to continue into October.

Mr. Ekeus announced that 62 Iraqi ballistic missiles had been destroyed along with an unspecified number of launchers and missile decoys. A search is under way, he said, to make sure no more ballistic missiles exist in Iraq.

### Concealing a Major Program

Hans Blix, head of the International Atomic Energy Agency and the official in charge of eliminating Iraq's nuclear weapons program, took part in today's consultations and said afterward that despite the efforts of three teams of inspectors, "important components" of Iraq's uranium-enrichment program were still missing.

"Some information has been given," he said. "But there is still much to be wished for."

In his remarks to the Council, Mr. Blix defended the International Atomic Energy Agency's condemnation of Iraq's attempts to hide the size and nature of its nuclear materials production program. Iraq had responded to the condemnation by saying the amount of undeclared material was insignificant and argued that now that the amount was known, it was no longer in noncompliance.

"The failure of Iraq to report had regard not just to a technical matter involving small quantities of nuclear material," Mr. Blix said, "but amounted to an attempt to conceal a major program for the enrichment of uranium."

Part of the nuclear agency's mandate under Security Council Resolution 687, which set conditions for a cease-fire in the Persian Gulf war, is to set up a program for longterm monitoring and verifying Iraq's adherence to the resolution's provisions for Iraqi disarmament.

### Inspections to Continue

An interim program continuing the present program of onsite inspections will continue.

But, Mr. Blix said, "Regrettably, we do not yet have an inventory of all nuclear material in Iraq." He continued, "It would be premature to submit any final proposal for future ongoing monitoring and verification."

Mr. Blix said that while it was too early to draw lessons from the current inspections, the fact that from the early 1980's until now Iraq was able to conduct its uranium enrichment program undetected cast doubts on the agency's verification program.

"We need more teeth in it," he said.

Mr. Blix noted that the Iraqi nuclear program was particularly difficult to uncover because it was "indigenous." He said the usual way to verify nuclear program is through declarations from the country involved and from its suppliers.

"In this case, it wasn't enough," he said. "Fortunately, we had intelligence from outside."

In the future, he said, inspectors must have access to all information, including satellite data, they must have the right to go everywhere and they must have the backing of the Security Council if that right is denied.

UNW-1983
첨부물

ㅗ-ㅣ

0293

## Ask Moscow To Help Take Out Saddam's Nukes

By KAREN ELLIOTT HOUSE

If the Bush-Gorbachev summit in Moscow produces a bumper sticker, it ought to be "Make Love and War."

Indeed, if the two leaders genuinely want to use the Middle East as a test tube for developing the new great-power formula of the '90s, there is a little unfinished business to deal with before they get on with convening Mideast peace conferences, redrawing maps of the region, twisting allies' arms, creating Palestinian entities, and proclaiming peace in a part of the world that's rarely had it. That little bit of business is Saddam Hussein.

In what almost seems a rerun of last August's theatrics, the Iraqi dictator is again thumbing his nose at the international community and George Bush, with a series of half-truths and taunts in defiance of Iraq's commitment to disclose fully its nuclear facilities and capabilities.

While the Iraqi people suffer both postwar deprivation and, more significantly, Saddam's continuing tyranny, Saddam continues alternately to strut and slither with no apparent acknowledgment that he lost one of the most decisive military engagements in modern history. Lessons, military or otherwise, are not taught until they are learned. And Saddam clearly remains the recalcitrant student.

So, what are we to do now? Do we move on to hold a graduate seminar on peace for the rest of the Middle East's unruly students while Saddam is still kicking the teacher in the shins? Shouldn't we quiet the class bully before preaching concord to the rest of the room?

*George Bush*

It's George Bush embraces Mikhail Gorbachev in Moscow, he has the chance to demand a token of genuine Soviet commitment to great-power cooperation in return for the many favors the Soviets will be asking of him. What the U.S. should request: a U.S.-Soviet air attack on Saddam's nuclear sites.

It's a small favor compared, for example, to the U.S. going along with the pretense that the Soviet Union is still a super-power at all by any measurement other than missile throwweights. It's in Mr. Gorbachev's own interest, since his fraying empire includes more than 50 million unhappy Muslims and since Saddam's nuclear weapons, once developed, will be closer to the Soviet Union than to America. It's a modest means of making amends for the Soviets' very half-hearted support of Operation Desert Storm. And, it's a modest price of admission to the Mideast peace-making process for a nation that has spent the past several decades single-mindedly seeking to stick it to America throughout the Mideast by supporting every dictator, terrorist, ideology and cause inimical to U.S. interests and to peace.

It also might have some impact. Imagine the scene: Messrs. Bush and Gorbachev standing together in front of television cameras at the Kremlin to announce jointly that as of five minutes ago U.S. carrier-based bombers and Soviet land-based MiGs have taken off in a coordinated assault to destroy once and for all Saddam's nuclear sites.

That announcement out of the way, the leaders could go on to outline, with considerably more credibility than they currently have, their plans for a Middle East peace conference this fall. Who knows, the rest of the Middle East might then actually pay attention to the second announcement and take a peace conference seriously rather than merely play along for temporary tactical and publicity advantages.

A demonstration of U.S.-Soviet political and military purpose against Saddam certainly doesn't guarantee that Syria's Hafez Assad or Israel's Yitzhak Shamir will lie together as lambs in the cozy setting of a peace conference. But the absence of such a demonstration—with Saddam flagrantly flouting U.S. and international will—virtually guarantees a peace conference will lack lasting substance and results.

The players at such a conference inevitably see more

*Mikhail Gorbachev*

risks than rewards in peace-making. While the status quo may be less than ideal, the alternatives can surely be worse. For an Assad, whose rule rests more on Saddam-style brutality and external "threats" (Israel and the U.S.) than on diplomatic cleverness, genuine peace might well end the raison d'être of his rule.

For the Palestine Liberation Organization and assorted Palestinian factions, a Mideast settlement would mean having to get serious about governance—perhaps even governance representative of the Palestinian people—rather than relying on the attention-getting theatrics that have been the PLO's primary purpose for decades.

For Jordan's King Hussein, peace always holds the dread potential of eventually turning his kingdom into a Palestinian state. For the Saudis, the peace process requires that worst of all prospects—decisions. And for the Israelis, who for decades have advanced the concept that peace is worth the yielding of land, there would now be the grim prospect of conceivably having to do so. In consequence, Israeli Prime Minister Shamir already is loudly announcing that the parameters for any peace conference are "peace for peace" and no longer land for peace.

With all this going against peace prospects, the one slim chance of success rests on the credibility of those convening the peace conference. And in the Middle East, credibility stems from power and the demonstrable willingness to use it. Saddam still offers that target of opportunity.

*Ms. House is vice president, international, of Dow Jones & Co.*

2—2

0294

외교문서 비밀해제: 걸프 사태 22
걸프 사태 유엔안전보장이사회 동향 5

초판인쇄 2024년 03월 15일
초판발행 2024년 03월 15일

지은이  한국학술정보(주)
펴낸이  채종준
펴낸곳  한국학술정보(주)
주 소  경기도 파주시 회동길 230(문발동)
전 화  031-908-3181(대표)
팩 스  031-908-3189
홈페이지  http://ebook.kstudy.com
E-mail  출판사업부 publish@kstudy.com
등 록  제일산-115호(2000. 6. 19)

ISBN  979-11-6983-982-2  94340
       979-11-6983-960-0  94340 (set)